NEW BUSINESS VENTURES
AND THE
ENTREPRENEUR

NEW BUSINESS VENTURES AND THE ENTREPRENEUR

Second Edition

Howard H. Stevenson
Sarofim - Rock Professor of Business Administration
Michael J. Roberts
Associates Fellow
H. Irving Grousbeck
Lecturer in Business Administration
All of the Harvard University
Graduate School of Business Administration

 1985

Homewood, Illinois 60430

Case material of the Harvard Graduate School of Business
Administration is made possible by the cooperation of business
firms and other organizations which may wish to remain
anonymous by having names, quantities, and other
identifying details disguised while maintaining basic
relationships. Cases are prepared as the basis for
class discussion rather than to illustrate either effective
or ineffective handling of an administrative situation.

ISBN 0-256-02166-X

Library of Congress Catalog Card No. 84–81414

Printed in the United States of America

4 5 6 7 8 9 0 K 2 1 0 9 8 7

To
Patrick Rooney Liles   (1937–1983)
teacher
scholar of entrepreneurship
business leader
athlete
friend

FOREWORD

Entrepreneuring has come of age in the United States. In growing numbers, men and women of all ages are taking up careers in younger businesses, both startups and going concerns. On college campuses, it is now socially acceptable, even laudatory, to join an unknown company. Employment levels in larger companies have plateaued, even dipped. The tide is changing. This book is written to help those who want to participate directly in that change.

One element of the folklore of the times is that 9 out of 10 new businesses fail. While the statistic may have some historical validity, and may even be true today if every airport pretzel stand is included in the calculation, the folklore is misleading. The success rate for new businesses is much, much higher—over 50 percent—for companies that systematically take advantage of what is known today about making new ventures fly. This book pulls together and adds to the best of that knowledge. Building on the earlier work and format of the late Pat Liles, Howard Stevenson has developed a powerful teaching and learning device. The combination of truly interesting cases and concise, pertinent readings provides the necessary ingredients for a rich course on entrepreneuring at a time when the demand for such courses is increasing.

The team of Stevenson, Roberts, and Grousbeck is uniquely qualified to create this important work. They combine an exciting blend of successful, new venture operating experience and pedagogical prowess. They know whereof they write and teach. In addition, I sense in the fabric of the material a pervasive desire to be of real service to those who will guide our next generation of companies.

> **Steven C. Brandt**
> Stanford University
> *Graduate School of Business*

INTRODUCTION

We have several objectives in writing this book. We believe that the topic of entrepreneurship is an exciting and important one. For those students of management who have decided to pursue a career as an entrepreneur, we think this book will provide some of the knowledge and skills required. For those who may be undecided, or perhaps committed to a more "traditional" career, many of the ideas in this book have value for those in more structured business settings. Executives are often called upon to deal with, and even to manage, entrepreneurs. Friends and acquaintances may contemplate starting new ventures and want the advice and financial support of acquaintances in management positions.

Most importantly, we believe that all students of management have a great deal to learn from the study of entrepreneurship. The process of identifying and pursuing opportunity, the hallmark of the entrepreneur, has become increasingly important in restoring the competitive position of many U.S. industries in the international marketplace.

Organization and Contents

This book is organized into four parts:

—**Part One:** Introduction. This part forms the core of the text's organizing framework. Its two chapters provide both a working definition of entrepreneurship and a framework for understanding the entrepreneurial process. The cases provide an opportunity to test these frameworks.

—**Part Two:** Evaluating Opportunity and Developing the Business Concept. This part looks at the first two steps in the process of starting a new venture. The chapters look at methods of valuing and purchasing business opportunities as well as some of the legal aspects of the organization. The cases require evaluating business opportunities and formulating strategies to exploit these opportunities.

—**Part Three:** Assessing and Acquiring Resources. This part looks at two of the entrepreneur's critical steps—assessing required resources and acquiring those resources. The chapters focus on understanding and techniques for acquiring both financial and nonfinancial resources. The cases cover a variety of issues, including deal structure, securities law, and venture capital.

—**Part Four:** Managing and Harvesting the Venture. Here we look at some of the unique challenges of managing an entrepreneurial firm. Included are some approaches to harvesting the economic value that the entrepreneur has created. Chapters cover the problem of bankruptcy and the process involved in a public offering. Cases focus on the operating problems of new ventures and the issue of managing growth in a rapidly expanding business.

Together, these parts trace the entrepreneurial process from the initial idea through business operations to the harvest.

Throughout the book, we have exhibited some of our own biases. One of which we are aware has to do with the material that has been included as exhibits. Whenever possible, we have included *actual* documents: business plans, prospectuses, leases, laws, and legal opinions. While some of this material is detailed and highly specific, it is well worth the effort. This is the stuff of which real business is made; better to discover some of the subtleties of the tax code or lease provisions now than when you're sitting down to form a real venture.

Although the detail is included, please do *not* consider the technical notes, the exhibits, and the appendices as substitutes for detailed current investigation of law, regulation, markets, and practices. This is a rapidly evolving field. Although every effort has been made to be clear, current, and complete, you must consult good attorneys, accountants, and investment advisers before proceeding.

Acknowledgements

Patrick R. Liles taught the New Ventures course at Harvard from 1969 to 1977. Pat was to have been a co-author of this book. His untimely death in the fall of 1983 prevented us from enjoying his collaboration. Yet, in a very real sense, his early work in the field, his previous edition of this book, and his vision of the entrepreneur provided a strong foundation on which to build. We dedicate this book to Pat, both in recognition of his accomplishments and our respect for them, and out of our own sense of loss.

In addition to Pat's involvement with the course, many others participated in its teaching and development over the past 40 years. We are indebted to Myles Mace, Frank L. Tucker, Malcom Salter, Thomas Raymond, Philip Thurston, Jim Morgan, Richard Reese, Richard Von Werssowetz, Robert Kent, Associate in Communication, and John Van Slyke for building the New Ventures course at Harvard and providing a solid foundation for our own work. Many other students and scholars of entrepreneurship not at Harvard have contributed helpful comments: Jeffry Timmons, Barry Unger, Steve Brandt, Zenas Block, ·Karl Vesper, and Neil Churchill.

Thanks are also due:

—James H. Snider and Peter Tolnai for their help with First Place (A).

—Peter Lombard and Ricardo Rodriguez for their help with ICEDELIGHTS.

—Richard Von Werssowetz for his help with Commercial Fixtures, Inc., Duncan Field, Steven B. Belkin, Ruth M. Owades, Stratus Computer, and Michael Bregman.

—Paul Brountas, of the law firm of Hale & Dorr, Boston, for his work on Universal Robotics Corporation.

—Richard E. Floor, of the law firm of Goodwin, Procter & Hoar, Boston, for his help with Viscotech, Inc., and the chapters on Securities Law and Private Financing and Securities Law and Public Offerings.

—Martha Gershun for Dragonfly and the chapter on bankruptcy.

—Liz Hovey for the chapter Techniques of Purchasing a Business.

—Philip Thurston and Richard Reese for Steve Cox.

—Kenneth R. Davis, formerly of the Amos Tuck School, for his help with the history of Atlas Lighting Co. through 1975.

The case writing and research was sponsored by the Division of Research; we are grateful to Raymond Corey and Kathryn May of the Division as well as to the Associates of the Harvard Business School, who provided much of the funding. Dean John McArthur has been a supporter of our efforts in the entrepreneurship area. Without his encouragement, and the support of many alumni, including Arthur Rock and Fayez Sarofim who gave the chair in entrepreneurship, this book would not have been written.

The task of compiling this text was an arduous one. We wish to express our appreciation to Joanne Goodreau who cheerfully organized this material and to the word processing staff, under the direction of Rose Giacobbe, which expertly typed and revised the manuscript. Audrey Barrett was extremely helpful in securing the permissions needed to complete the book.

Paula Duffy made a major contribution to the clarity of presentation through her marvelous editorial assistance.

We are indebted to the entrepreneurs who gave so willingly of their time, energy, and ideas so that we could collect this case material. They provide one of the most critical elements of entrepreneurial success: role models. Steve Belkin, Ruth Owades, Heather Evans, Bill Foster, Michael Bregmann, and Vincent Lamb are all real people who have shared their experiences with us; others have chosen to remain anonymous. To all we owe thanks for their cooperation. Ultimately it is through the sharing of their experience that we can learn.

Finally, each of us would like to make a more personal statement of thanks to our families:

—To Sarah and the boys: Willie, Charley, and Andy. Thanks for the patience in helping me to pursue this passion. And to my parents, Ralph and Dorothy Stevenson, and aunt and uncle, Boyd and Zola Martin, thanks for helping me get a running start into this field.

H. H. S.

—To my parents, Herb and Joan Roberts, for all their love, support, and encouragement.

M. J. R.

—To my wife Sukey for her love, laughter, adaptability, and constant encouragement, and to my mother Emily for the loving lessons of the value of integrity and hard work.

H. I. G.

CONTENTS

Part 1 Overview   1

    Chapter 1 A Perspective on Entrepreneurship   2
            2 A Framework for Understanding the
               Entrepreneurial Process   16

    Case 1-1 First Place (A)   24
         1-2 ICEDELIGHTS   51

Part 2 Evaluating Opportunity and Developing the
        Business Concept   83

    Chapter 3 Valuation Techniques   86
            4 Techniques of Purchasing a Company   96
            5 The Legal Forms of Organization   122

    Case 2-1 Tru-Paint, Inc.   136
         2-2 Commercial Fixtures, Inc.   143
         2-3 Duncan Field   163
         2-4 Wilson Cabinet Co.   181
         2-5 Electrodec   187

Part 3   Assessing and Acquiring Resources   219

    Chapter 6   Alternative Sources of Financing   222
          7   Deal Structure   232
          8   Securities Law and Private Financing   239
          9   Intellectual Property   251

    Case 3–1   Steven B. Belkin   260
        3–2   Ruth M. Owades   286
        3–3   Heather Evans   308
        3–4   Allen Lane   353
        3–5   Steve Cox   381
        3–6   Clarion Optical Co.   402
        3–7   Viscotech, Inc.   413
        3–8   Universal Robotics Corporation   443
        3–9   Computervision vs. Automatix (A)   457
     3–10   Stratus Computer   484

Part 4   Managing and Harvesting the Venture   511

    Chapter 10   Bankruptcy: A Debtor's Perspective   513
        11   Securities Law and Public Offerings   529

    Case 4–1   American Imports   545
        4–2   Dragonfly Corporation   579
        4–3   Eric Weston   608
        4–4   Michael Bregman   631
        4–5   SSS   658
        4–6   Atlas Lighting Company   698

Case Index   729
Subject Index   731

Part One

OVERVIEW

This first section of *New Business Ventures and The Entrepreneur* attempts to introduce you to the topic of entrepreneurship. As you will see, we have a specific idea of what entrepreneurship is and a framework for understanding the issues which entrepreneurs face as they try to establish and run a business.

Chapters 1 and 2 really form the core of the conceptual framework we will be using throughout the text. It is well worth spending some extra time on the ideas presented in these chapters; it will aid you considerably in understanding and analyzing the cases that follow.

The two cases in this section illustrate the wide range of decisions and problems with which entrepreneurs must deal in their attempts to start new business ventures. Before jumping in and analyzing any particular issue, try to understand fully all of the issues in the case.

Chapter 1

A PERSPECTIVE ON ENTREPRENEURSHIP

This chapter represents an attempt to define the term *entrepreneurship.* Let us begin by establishing a number of premises that are basic to our thinking. First, the search for a single psychological profile of the entrepreneur—the conventional approach to the subject—is bound to fail. For each of the traditional definitions of the entrepreneurial type, there are numerous counterexamples that disprove the theory. We are simply not dealing with one kind of individual or behavior pattern, as even a cursory review of well-known entrepreneurs will demonstrate. Nor has the search for a psychological model proven useful in teaching or encouraging entrepreneurship. Whatever the psychological roots of the entrepreneurial spirit may be, it is our belief that it is primarily a situational phenomenon. Companies are capable of creating or destroying entrepreneurship by the nature of the culture and climate they establish.

A second basic premise is that the strengthening of entrepreneurship has become a critically important goal of American society. Because the rate of change in the environment has increased dramatically at the same time that existing opportunity streams have been largely played out, creative approaches to managing are required. The first 30 years of the postwar period in the United States were characterized by an abundance of opportunity, brought about by expanding markets, high investment in the national infrastructure, mushrooming debt. In this environment, it was possible to succeed in business with the sloppiest of practices, but this is no longer true. Access to international resources is no longer guaranteed; government regulation has brought a recognition of the full costs of doing business, many of which had been hidden previously; competition from overseas has put an end to American dominance in numerous industries; technological change has reduced product life in other industries; and so forth. In short, it is less possible to control the business environment; a successful firm is now one that is either capable of rapid response to changes that are beyond its control or is so innovative that it contributes to change in the environment.

A final basic premise is that many of the practices of what we usually consider well-managed companies tend to inhibit entrepreneurial behavior. These practices developed in the context of abundant opportunity and were adequate in that context, but they are no longer effective. Individuals are primarily motivated by self-interest and they understand their self-interest extremely well. We have unfortunately built organizations in which individuals will pursue their personal self-interest without focusing on the goals of the organization. It is this tendency that has created the short-term focus and narrow, bureaucratic thinking that is the subject of so much attention in the popular press. Formal organizational practices such as planning systems, budgeting cycles, and incentive programs do not adequately encourage the pursuit of opportunity. It is essential that we develop new systems and organizational cultures if we are to improve entrepreneurial practice in our firms.

Given these fundamental assumptions, we have attempted to draw a rough paradigm of entrepreneurship. We are not trying to identify a single model of the human being who is the entrepreneur. Rather, we are examining a *range* of individual or corporate behavior on a spectrum that runs from what we call the "promoter"—the type who says, "I can make it happen"—to the "trustee," who says, "I must guard what I have." In the following discussion, we will use these two extreme types to locate the end points of the spectrum. The entrepreneur, however, is not identical to the promoter, but rather occupies a range on the promoter end of the spectrum. Likewise, what we will call the administrator, for lack of a better term, occupies a range on the trustee end of the spectrum. As we shall see, there is some overlap between entrepreneurial and administrative behavior. In addition, we can observe an individual or corporation taking an entrepreneurial approach to some issues and an administrative approach to others. Our concern throughout will be to distinguish between the two types of behavior and to identify those practices that encourage or inhibit entrepreneurship in organizations as they grow beyond being simply an extension of a dominant individual. Our primary concern here will be with the practices of growing organizations, or fostering of corporate entrepreneurship.

As we look at business practices that either encourage or discourage entrepreneurial behavior, we should note that, throughout our discussion, pressures for greater entrepreneurship are primarily external to the firm, while those factors that inhibit entrepreneurial behavior are internal. Thus, there is a clear need to develop managerial practices that foster flexibility and responsiveness.

We will examine five key dimensions of business that are traditionally elements of general management. They represent stages in the decision-making process, and each dimension builds on the previous dimension. Attention to each stage of the paradigm is essential to the task of establishing the dynamic of entrepreneurship.

STRATEGIC ORIENTATION

A promoter is truly opportunity driven. His or her orientation is to say, "As I choose my strategy, I am only going to be driven by my perception of the opportunities that exist in my environment, and I am not constrained by the resources at hand." A trustee, on the other hand, is resource driven and tends to say, "What do I do with my resources? My responsibility is to manage effectively the resources that I control within my organization."

The administrator's approach recognizes the need to examine the environment for opportunities, but is still constrained by a trustee-like focus on resources: "I will prune my opportunity tree based on the resources I control. I will not try to leap very far beyond my current situation." An entrepreneurial orientation places the emphasis on opportunity: "I will search for opportunity, and my fundamental administrative task is to acquire the resources to pursue that opportunity." These perspectives are represented on Exhibit 1.

EXHIBIT 1

Promoter	*Strategic Orientation*		*Trustee*
Driven by perception of opportunity	⟵——— Entrepreneurial Domain ———⟶ ⟵——— Administrative Domain ———⟶		Driven by resources currently controlled
Pressures toward *This Side*		*Pressures toward* *This Side*	

Diminishing opportunity
  streams
 Rapidly changing:
  Technology
  Consumer economics
  Social values
  Political rules
		Social contracts
		 Performance measurement
		  criteria
		 Planning systems and
		  cycles	

It is this inclination that has led to one of the traditional definitions of the entrepreneur as opportunistic or, more favorably, creative and innovative. But the entrepreneur is not necessarily concerned with breaking new ground; opportunity can also be found in a new mix of old ideas or in the creative application of traditional approaches.

We do observe, however, that firms tend to look for opportunities where their resources are. Even those firms that start as entrepreneurial by recognizing opportunities often become resource-driven as resources accrete to the organization.

The pressures which push a firm towards the entrepreneurial range of behavior include the following:

— Diminishing opportunity streams: old opportunity streams have been largely played out. It is no longer possible to succeed merely by adding new options to old products.
— Rapid changes in:
  • Technology: creates new opportunities at the same time it obsoletes old ones.
  • Consumer economics: changes both ability and willingness to pay for new products and services.
  • Social values: defines new styles and standards and standards of living.
  • Political roles: affects competition through deregulation, product safety, and new standards.

Pressures which push a firm to become more "administrative" than entrepreneurial include the following:

— The "social contract": the responsibility of managers to use and employ people, plant, technology, and financial resources once they have been acquired.
— Performance criteria: how many executives are fired for not pursuing an opportunity, compared with the number that are punished for not meeting return on investment targets? Capacity utilization and sales growth are the typical measures of business success.
— Planning systems and cycles: opportunities do not arrive at the start of a planning cycle and last for the duration of a three- or five-year plan.

COMMITMENT TO OPPORTUNITY

As we move on to the second dimension, it becomes clear that the definition of the entrepreneur as creative or innovative is not sufficient. There are innovative thinkers who never get anything done; it is necessary to move beyond the identification of opportunity to its pursuit.

The promoter is a person willing to act in a very short time frame and to chase an opportunity quickly. Promoters may be more or less effective, but they are able to engage in commitment in a rather revolutionary fash-

EXHIBIT 2

Promoter	Commitment to Opportunity		Trustee
Revolu- tionary with short duration	←————————→ Entrepreneurial Domain ←————————→ Administrative Domain		Evolu- tionary of long duration
Pressures toward *This Side*		*Pressures toward* *This Side*	

Action orientation
Short decision windows
Risk management
Limited decision
   constituencies
		Acknowledgment of
		   multiple constituencies
		Negotiation of strategy
		Risk reduction
		Management of fit	

ion. The duration of their commitment, not the ability to act, is all that is in doubt. Commitment for the trustee is time-consuming, and once made, of long duration. Trustees move so slowly that it sometimes appears they are stationary; once there, they seem frozen. This spectrum of behavior is shown on Exhibit 2.

It is the willingness to get in and out quickly that has led to the entrepreneur's reputation as a gambler. However, the simple act of taking a risk does not lead to success. More critical to the success of the entrepreneurs is knowledge of the territory they operate in. Because of familiarity with their chosen field, they have the ability to recognize patterns as they develop, and the confidence to assume the missing elements of the pattern will take shape as they foresee. This early recognition enables them to get a jump on others in commitment to action.

Pressures which push a business towards this entrepreneurial end of the spectrum include:

— Action orientation: enables a firm to make first claim to customers, employees, and financial resources.
— Short decision windows: due to the high costs of late entry, including lack of competitive costs and technology.
— Risk management: involves managing the firm's revenues in such a way that they can be rapidly committed to or withdrawn from new projects. As George Bernard Shaw put it, "any fool can start a love affair, but it takes a genius to end one successfully."
— Limited decision constituencies: requires a smaller number of responsibilities and permits greater flexibility.

In contrast, administrative behavior is a function of other pressures:

— Multiple decision constituencies: a great number of responsibilities, necessitating a more complex, lengthier decision process.
— Negotiation of strategy: compromise in order to reach consensus and resultant evolutionary rather than revolutionary commitment.
— Risk reduction: study and analysis to reduce risk slows the decision-making process.
— Management of fit: to assure the continuity and participation of existing players, only those projects which "fit" existing corporate resources are acceptable.

COMMITMENT OF RESOURCES

Another characteristic we observe in good entrepreneurs is a multistage commitment of resources with a minimum commitment at each stage or decision point—in other words, a lack of resource intensity. The promoters, those wonderful people with blue suede shoes and diamond pinky rings on their left hands, say, "I don't need any resources to commence the pursuit of a given opportunity. I will bootstrap it." The trustee says, "Since my object is to use my resources, once I finally commit I will go in very heavy at the front end."

The issue is: What resources do you need to pursue a given opportunity? There is a constant tension between the adequacy of commitment and the potential for return. Managing this tension is part of the challenge and excitement of entrepreneurship. Many entrepreneurs, when looking back on their careers, say that the high point comes when they place their last chip on the table, still knowing it may not be enough. These are the times when optimism, experience, and courage are required elements of success. On the other hand, the trustee side of the spectrum deals with this challenge by careful analysis before the act and heavy commitment of resources after the decision to act.

At one extreme are the corporate dinosaurs of the world where, to get a single letter into the mail, a full-time secretary and a word processing unit are needed. As a good entrepreneur, however, I would write the letter myself or ask to use someone's office typewriter. Somehow the letter would get out. Good entrepreneurial management requires that you learn to do a little more with a little less. Exhibit 3 addresses this concept.

People need to do more with less and also to understand that most of the risk in entrepreneurial management lies not in misperception of opportunity, but in trying to pursue opportunity without adequate resources. One of the fundamental errors of large corporations, on the other hand, is overcommitment of resources. In studying real estate, I never

EXHIBIT 3

Promoter	Commitment of Resources	Trustee
Multistaged with minimal exposure at each stage	Entrepreneurial Domain ← → ← Administrative Domain →	Single staged with complete commitment upon decision
Pressures toward This Side		*Pressures toward This Side*
Lack of predictable resource needs Lack of long-term control Social need for more opportunity per resource unit International pressure for more efficient resource use		Personal risk reduction Incentive compensation Managerial turnover Capital allocation systems Formal planning systems

saw anyone fail who went in with all equity. Failures came when people pursued an opportunity that was too great for their own resources and thus used extensive leverage. Time and costs killed them when they could not come up with additional resources at critical decision points. You rarely see failure on the part of large companies as long as management is willing to throw resources at a problem, although you may wonder whether they will ever get any return on their investment. Overinvesting lowers return and thus diminishes future opportunities.

On this dimension we have the traditional stereotype of the entrepreneur as tentative, uncommitted, or temporarily dedicated—an image of unreliability. In times of rapid change, however, this characteristic of stepped, multistage commitment of resources is a definite advantage in responding to changes in competition, the market, and technology. The entrepreneur will leave something in reserve, and is thus able to see the game as one in which multiple plays are possible.

The process of committing resources is pushed towards the entrepreneurial domain by several factors:

— Lack of predictable resource needs: forces the entrepreneurs to commit less up front so that more will be available later on, if required.
— Lack of long-term control: requires that commitment match exposure. If control over resources can be removed by environmental, political, or technological forces, resource exposure should also be reduced.

— Social needs: multistaged commitment of resources brings us closer to the "small is beautiful" formulation of E. F. Shumacher, by allowing for the appropriate level of resource intensity for the task.

— International demands: pressures that we use no more than our "fair share" of the world's resources, e.g., not the 35 percent of the world's energy that the United States was using in the early 1970s.

The pressures within the large corporation, however, are in the other direction—toward resource intensity. This is due to:

— Personal risk reduction: any individual's risk is reduced by having excess resources available.

— Incentive compensation: excess resources increase short-term returns and minimize the period of cash and profit drains—typically the objects of incentive compensation systems.

— Managerial turnover: creates pressures for steady cash and profit gains, which encourages short-term, visible success.

— Capital allocation systems: generally designed for one-time decision making, these techniques assume that a single decision point is appropriate.

— Formal planning systems: once a project has begun, a request for additional resources returns the managers to the morass of analysis and bureaucratic delays; managers are inclined to avoid this by committing the maximum amount of resources up front.

CONTROL OF RESOURCES

When it comes to the control of resources, the promoter mentality says, "All I need from a resource is the ability to use it." These are the people who describe the ideal business as the post office box to which people send money. For them, all additional overhead is a compromise of a basic value. On the other hand, we all know companies that believe they do not adequately control a resource unless they own it or have it on their permanent payroll.

Entrepreneurs learn to use other people's resources well; they learn to decide, over time, what resources they need to bring in-house. They view this as a time-phased sequence of decisions. Good managers also learn that there are certain resources you should never own or employ. To return to the real estate example, very few good real estate firms employ an architect. They may need the best, but they do not want to employ him or her, because the need for that resource, although critical to the success of the business, is temporary. The same is true of good lawyers. They are useful to have when you need them, but most firms cannot possibly afford to have the necessary depth of specialization of legal professionals constantly at their beck and call.

EXHIBIT 4

Promoter	*Control of Resources*		*Trustee*
Episodic use or rent of required resources	←——— Entrepreneurial Domain ———→ ←——— Administrative Domain ———→		Ownership or employment of required resources
Pressures toward This Side		*Pressures toward This Side*	
Increased resource specialization Long resource life compared to need Risk of obsolescence Risk inherent in any new venture Inflexibility of permanent commitment to resources		Power, status, and financial rewards Coordination Efficiency measures Inertia and cost of change Industry structures	

Exhibit 4 illustrates this dimension.

The stereotype of the entrepreneur as exploitative or even parasitic derives from this dimension: the entrepreneur is adept at using the skills, talents, and ideas of others. Viewed positively, this ability has become increasingly valuable in the changed business environment; it need not be parasitic in the context of a mutually satisfying relationship. Pressures towards this entrepreneurial side come from:

— Increased resource specialization: an organization may have a need for a specialized resource like a VLSI design engineer, hi-tech patent attorney, or state-of-the-art circuit test equipment, but only for a short time. By using, rather than owning, a firm reduces its risk and its fixed costs.
— Risk of obsolescence: reduced by merely using, rather than owning, an expensive resource.
— Increased flexibility: the cost of exercising the option to quit is reduced by using, not owning, a resource.

Administrative practices are the product of pressures in the other direction, such as:

— Power, status, and financial rewards: determined by the extent of resources ownership and control in many corporations.

— Coordination: the speed of execution is increased because the executive has the right to request certain action without negotiation.
— Efficiency: enables the firm to capture, at least in the short run, all of the profits associated with an operation.
— Inertia and cost of change: it is commonly believed that it is good management to isolate the technical core of production from external shocks. This requires buffer inventories, control of raw materials, and control of distribution channels. Ownership also creates familiarity and an identifiable chain of command, which become stabilized with time.
— Industry structures: encourage ownership to prevent being preempted by the competition.

MANAGEMENT STRUCTURE

The promoter wants to feel the way events are unfolding through direct contact with all of the principal actors. The trustee views relationships more formally, with specific rights, responsibilities, and delegation of authority. The decision to use and rent resources and not to own or employ them will require the development of an informal information network. Only in systems where the relationship with resources is based on ownership or employment can resources be organized in a hierarchy. In large businesses we see an increasing need to develop networking, because hierarchy breaks down when all elements of success cannot be contained within the sub-elements of the structure. Informal networking that arises in response to this need is often formalized in matrix management and other committee structures. Exhibit 5 illustrates this range of behavior.

EXHIBIT 5

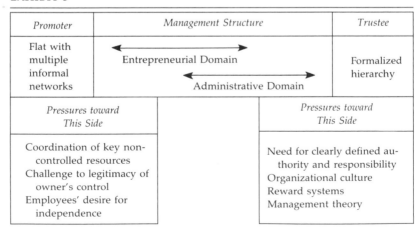

Promoter	Management Structure	Trustee
Flat with multiple informal networks	Entrepreneurial Domain ◄────────► Administrative Domain ◄────────►	Formalized hierarchy
Pressures toward This Side		*Pressures toward This Side*
Coordination of key non-controlled resources Challenge to legitimacy of owner's control Employees' desire for independence		Need for clearly defined authority and responsibility Organizational culture Reward systems Management theory

Many people have attempted to distinguish between the entrepreneur and the administrator by suggesting that being a good entrepreneur precludes being a good manager. The entrepreneur is stereotyped as egocentric and idiosyncratic and thus unable to manage. However, though the managerial task is substantially different for the entrepreneur, management skill is nonetheless essential. The variation lies in the choice of appropriate tools.

More entrepreneurial management is a function of several pressures:

— Need for coordination of key noncontrolled resources: results in need to communicate with, motivate, control, and plan for resources *outside* the firm.
— Flexibility: maximized with a flat and informal organization.
— Challenge to owner's control: classic questions about the rights of ownership as well as governmental environmental, health and safety restrictions, undermine the legitimacy of control.
— Employees' desire for independence: creates an environment where employees are unwilling to accept hierarchical authority in place of authority based on competence and persuasion.

On the other side of the spectrum, pressures push the firm toward more administrative behavior. These include:

— Need for clearly defined authority and responsibility: to perform the increasingly complex planning, organizing, coordinating, communicating, and controlling required in a business.
— Organizational culture: which often demands that events be routinized.
— Reward systems: which encourage and reward breadth and span of control.

SUMMARY

To summarize, we have gathered all of the key dimensions onto one chart (see Exhibit 6).

Throughout, we have emphasized that tensions exist between the best of current management practices and current needs. There is no one right way, no good or bad. There are often equally strong reasons to be on the entrepreneurial side of the chart as to be on the administrative side. The crying need is for management to know there are choices and to act intelligently in making those choices.

One major point of this discussion has been to describe the pressures toward trustee-like behavior that come just from the acquisition of resources. The best administrative practices lead to immobility and lack of ability to respond to new opportunity. The best of administrative science has contributed to closed organizations.

Why is this relevant today? Society needs corporations to focus on opportunity because the changing environment requires new commitments and new flexibility. Strengths have become weaknesses, and weaknesses, strengths. There is an equal need for new ideas and new conceptions of structure, measurement systems, and concepts of management legitimacy.

Why, we should ask, are the entrepreneurial practices that appear on the left side of the chart not considered legitimate management for implementation? What would foster entrepreneurial management? Our task is to study the concepts, skills, attitudes, management systems, and cultures that allow managers to resist the pressures toward trustee behavior. Through this process, it should be possible to discover what needs to be done to nurture entrepreneurship within our society.

EXHIBIT 6
Entrepreneurial Management Summary

Pressures toward This Side	Promoter	Key Business Dimension	Trustee	Pressure toward This Side
Diminishing opportunity streams Rapidly changing: Technology Consumer economics Social values Political rules	Driven by perception of opportunity	**Strategic Orientation** Entrepreneurial ↕ Administrative	Driven by resources currently controlled	Social contracts Performance measurement criteria Planning systems and cycles
Action orientation Short decision windows Risk management Limited decision constituencies	Revolutionary with short duration	**Commitment to Opportunity** Entrepreneurial ↕ Administrative	Evolutionary of long duration	Acknowledgement of multiple constituencies Negotiation of strategy Risk reduction Management of fit
Lack of predictable resource needs Lack of long-term control Social needs for more opportunity per resource unit International pressure for more efficient resource use	Multistaged with minimal exposure at each stage	**Commitment of Resources** Entrepreneurial ↕ Administrative	Single-staged with complete commitment upon decision	Personal risk reduction Incentive compensation Managerial turnover Capital allocation systems Formal planning systems

Pressures toward entrepreneurial	Entrepreneurial	**Control of Resources** Entrepreneurial ↕ Administrative	Administrative	Pressures toward administrative
Increased resource specialization Long resource life compared to need Risk of obsolescence Risk inherent in any new venture Inflexibility of permanent commitment to resources	Episodic use or rent of required resources		Ownership or employment of required resources	Power, status and financial rewards Coordination Efficiency measures Inertia and cost of change Industry structures
Coordination of key noncontrolled resources Challenge to legitimacy of owner's control Employees' desire for independence	Flat with multiple informal networks	**Management Structure** Entrepreneurial ↕ Administrative	Formalized hierarchy	Need for clearly defined authority and responsibility Organizational culture Reward systems Management theory

Chapter 2

A FRAMEWORK FOR UNDERSTANDING THE ENTREPRENEURIAL PROCESS

"A Perspective on Entrepreneurship," presents a paradigm for understanding entrepreneurial behavior. The paradigm breaks general management down into a number of key dimensions: strategic orientation, commitment to opportunity, commitment of resources, control of resources, and management structure. It describes the range of managerial behavior along each of these dimensions, and discusses the specific spectrum of behavior which can be characterized as entrepreneurial.

This chapter attempts to serve as a conceptual bridge between this view of where entrepreneurial behavior fits within the broad spectrum of management behavior and an in-depth understanding of the *actual process* of entrepreneurship.

Entrepreneurship is the process of creating value by pulling together a unique package of resources to exploit an opportunity. Because the entrepreneur never controls all of the necessary resources, pursuing the opportunity requires "bridging the resource gap." Such a process requires a series of choices which must be made in a manner which is both internally consistent and externally appropriate to the market.

The remainder of this chapter will:

— Describe the elements of the entrepreneurial process.
— Discuss:

- The issues the entrepreneur must resolve as he/she moves through each step of the entrepreneurial process.
- The analytical techniques which can be used to help resolve these issues.

ELEMENTS OF THE ENTREPRENEURIAL PROCESS

For each of the key business dimensions there exists an "entrepreneurial process element" which describes the basic decisions and actions the entrepreneur must take. These elements are arranged below:

Key Business Dimension	*Entrepreneurial Process Element*
Strategic orientation	Evaluating the opportunity
Commitment to opportunity	Developing the business concept
Commitment of resources	Assessing required resources
Control of resources	Acquiring needed resources
Management structure	Managing and harvesting the venture

It is important to understand that, while these process steps are arranged in their natural order, they cannot be dealt with in isolation. For instance, in order to evaluate an opportunity, the entrepreneur needs to have some idea of the concept of the business, the resources the execution of that concept will require, and the cost of those resources. Only then can the entrepreneur properly judge the attractiveness of the opportunity. Nonetheless, this order is an accurate approximation of the sequence in which one should "loop through" those steps.

Evaluating the Opportunity

The first step in the entrepreneurial process is evaluating the opportunity.

Issues. The entrepreneur must address a number of issues including:

— What are the forces which are creating the opportunity?
  - Technological change.
  - Government regulation.
  - Shifts in market demand.
— What are the dimensions of the "window of opportunity"?
  - Market size.
  - Time horizon.
  - Growth.
— Does the product/service meet a real need?
— What are the key risks?
  - Market.
  - Competition.
  - Management.

- Technology.
— What is the value of the opportunity?
  - What is the financial return?
    - Capital.
    - Risk.
    - Time.
  - What personal nonfinancial rewards does the opportunity offer?
  - Does the opportunity offer access to follow-on opportunities/additional options?
    - Expansion.
    - Diversification.
— What is the opportunity cost of pursuing the opportunity?
— What are my personal requirements?
  - Goals.
  - Skills and interests.
  - Risk profile.

Analytical techniques. In order to address these issues, the entrepreneur has a number of analytical techniques at his disposal. These include:

— Valuation techniques.
  - Cash flow/NPV.
  - Market multiples.
  - Liquidation value.
— Risk versus reward analysis.
— Self-assessment.
  - Risk profile.
  - Skills, values inventory.

Developing the Business Concept

A good business concept must simultaneously exploit the opportunity and fit with the entrepreneur's own goals and abilities.

Issues. The entrepreneur must address the following issues in determining an appropriate strategy for exploiting the opportunity:

— What is the appropriate time horizon for viewing the opportunity?
— What exit routes should be contemplated from the very beginning?
— How can barriers to entry be erected?
  - Cost.
  - Technology.
  - Product differentiation.
— What strategy should the business follow?
  - How can customers be identified, reached, and persuaded to innovate?

- What risks will the organization elect to accept? How will the business position itself between suppliers and customers to guarantee maximum economic profit?
- What form should the organization take?

Analytical techniques. To resolve these issues, the entrepreneur can avail him/herself of a number of tools:

— Economic analysis.
  - Cost structure.
  - Critical size/economies of scale.
— Industry analysis.
  - Trends.
  - Demand pattern.
  - Strategic group analysis.
— Competitive analysis.
  - Key competitors.
  - Strengths and weaknesses.

Assessing Required Resources

In assessing required resources, the entrepreneur must balance his/her own limited resources with the need for sufficient resources to exploit the opportunity.

Issues. To make intelligent choices and "do more with less" the entrepreneur must address the following issues:

— Given both the risks which the concept entails and the unique approach to capitalizing on the opportunity:
  - What resources are absolutely critical?
  - What resources can we live without?
— What are the downside risks associated with insufficient resources?
— What resources does the entrepreneur (group) currently possess?
— What gaps remain?
— Who are the likely suppliers of the remaining resources?
— What are the alternative mechanisms of control for these resources?
— For each resource
  - What is the minimum level required?
  - What is the optimum level?
  - How much is required to ensure a "safety margin?"
— What is an appropriate time horizon for assembling this package?
— What are the other organizational dependencies?
  - Real estate.
  - Technology.
  - Government/regulatory.

Analytical techniques. Several analytical techniques can be brought to bear on these issues, including:

— Cash flow/gap analysis.
— Critical path analysis.
— Assessment of leverage.
— Financial forecasting.
— Sensitivity analysis.

Acquiring Needed Resources

Here the entrepreneur attempts to gain control over the needed resources while giving up as little as possible.

Issues. The entrepreneur must address the following issues:

— What are the alternative sources of needed resources?
  • Financial.
  • Nonfinancial.
— What are the critical needs of the suppliers of resources?
— What "deal" can be structured to achieve our desired ends?
  • What "value" does the venture create and control?
  • What must be given up to get these resources?
— What incentives are required to give others a stake in the venture's success?
— What action plan will result in successful acquisition of these resources?
  • How should resource commitment be staged?
  • What checkpoints will mark significant reduction of risk or uncertainty?
  • What outside advice, expertise, will be necessary?

Analytical techniques. The analytical techniques which can help the entrepreneur resolve these issues include:

— Valuation methodologies.
— Residual pricing techniques.
— Deal analysis.
  • Sources of return.
  • Risk/reward trade offs.

Managing and Harvesting the Venture

Now the entrepreneur must translate careful choices into economic performance, deal with the problems that arise as the business (hopefully) progresses, and decide when to harvest the venture.

Issues. To manage and harvest the venture effectively, the entrepreneur must deal with a variety of issues including:

— What key internal and external elements must be managed?
— What is the appropriate organizational structure for managing?
— What control systems are needed to monitor performance?
— How should I deal with problems?
  • Legal.
  • Operating.
  • Bankruptcy.
— What harvest strategy is appropriate?
  • When should I harvest?
    – Personal costs and benefits.
    – Financial costs and benefits.
  • What conditions will trigger a harvest?
  • What conditions could preclude a harvest?
  • How should I harvest?
    – Go public.
    – Sale of business.

Analytical techniques. The entrepreneur's ability to deal with these issues will be enhanced by use of:

— Operating statement analysis.
— Valuation.

SUMMARY

The issues and techniques we've discussed have been summarized in Exhibit 1. In addition to developing the concepts and skills outlined above, this book seeks to develop a certain attitude, or point of view, on general management.

This attitude stems from the unique role and responsibility of the entrepreneur. Unlike other managers, who may have responsibility for a certain aspect or a specific function, the entrepreneur is ultimately accountable for the entire venture. It is this extremely close identity with the business that makes success so very rewarding, and failure so difficult. This unique role breeds a certain set of attitudes, including:

— An action orientation: the entrepreneur cannot afford to merely elucidate the dimensions of the problem; he or she *must act.*
— An attention to detail: because the entrepreneur is ultimately accountable for the venture, he cannot afford to delegate final responsibility for "details" to others, including trained professionals. The entrepreneur *must* be familiar with legal, financial, and tax "details" which can impact the business significantly.

Indeed, the whole process of entrepreneurship involves far more than the problem solving often associated with management. The entrepreneur is a finder and exploiter of opportunities. Consequently, successful students of entrepreneurship must develop a similar attitude toward case situations: going beyond analysis of the case problems to an elucidation of the range of alternatives and the selection of a particular plan of action designed to seize the opportunity.

EXHIBIT 1
Summary

	Entrepreneurial Process Element				
	Evaluate the Opportunity	*Develop the Business Concept*	*Assess Required Resources*	*Acquire Needed Resources*	*Manage and Harvest the Venture*
Issues	Understand forces creating opportunity Assess window of opportunity Determine real value of product/service Assess risks Assess returns, value Determine fit with personal goals, skills	Determine appropriate time horizon Develop exit routes Design barriers to entry Develop strategy Determine form of organization	Determine critical/non critical resources Assess risks of different resource strategies Evaluate entrepreneur/group's existing resources Identify gaps Identify suppliers of remaining resources Develop alternative approaches to resource control Assess other organizational dependencies	Identify alternative sources Assess critical needs of likely suppliers Develop deal structure Develop an action plan	Assess key variables Develop management structure Implement control systems Deal with potential problems Develop a harvest strategy
Analytical techniques	Valuation Risk/reward Self-assessment	Economic Industry Competitive	Cash flow Critical path Assessment of leverage Financial forecasting Sensitivity analysis	Valuation Pricing Deal structure	Valuation Financial Analysis

FIRST PLACE (A)

"My life plan when I left the Pacific Business School was to found a company and become a multimillionaire by the age of 30, take a Doctorate and pursue an academic career, and finally retire to the Bordeaux region of France to write. Given my experience, objectives, and time frame, I considered myself to be restricted to industries with a certain set of characteristics.

"I have long been fascinated with restaurants; however, my industry experience has been only a short period as a manager and several summers in hourly positions. I have never held a line marketing position with a restaurant organization, and my opinions and theories on restaurant marketing have developed through readings and personal observation. Having therefore not been indoctrinated with restaurant marketing techniques, I have had the opportunity to critique the traditional concepts as an industry spectator. I am convinced that the industry has misapplied traditional consumer marketing techniques.

"Despite my confidence in the First Place concept, I have spent considerable time considering the business risks caused by my relative lack of restaurant operations experience. In my opinion, the restaurant industry is one where the adage applies that 20 years of experience is only 1 year of experience repeated 20 times. I feel that I have had sufficient experience; I feel that I have surpassed the critical level of knowledge, following which my learning could only proceed in diminishing returns. I feel I am ready.

"I have spent the last four months researching the restaurant industry, especially the competitive structure and key operating parameters of restaurants in the 'casual social and convenience middle market.' To find this information, I combed trade publications and traveled extensively to witness first-hand the most successful operations of my prospective competitors. Given my lack of industry experience, I have been guided by the belief that this comprehensive research is the best way for me to establish my credibility."

BACKGROUND

In June of 1978, Jack Paston graduated from the Pacific Business School and took a job as vice president of marketing for a computer software company. While working at this job he developed a business plan to start his own restaurant. The following is an abridged version of this plan. The full table of contents is shown below.

Business Plan for First Place
Table of Contents

Section	Page
Introduction	2
Evolution of the Middle Market	2
Consumer Behavior	3
A New Approach to Concept Development	4
The First-Place Concept—A Summary	6
Key Financial Characteristics	7
Corporate Objectives	7
Direct Competition	7
First Place Unique Success Factors	8
Management of Risks	9
Customer-Visible Operations	
Menu	Omitted
Portions	Omitted
Presentation	Omitted
The Physical Menu	Omitted
Theme	Omitted
Merchandising	Omitted
Pricing	Omitted
Promotion	Omitted
Site Selection	10

Customer-Invisible Operations
  Kitchen Operations   11
  Dining Room Operations   Omitted
  Bar Operations   Omitted
  Control and Measurement Systems   Omitted
  Period Control Systems   Omitted
  Physical Facilities   Omitted
  Dining Room Design and Decor   Omitted
  Kitchen Design and Layout   Omitted
  Human Resources Management   Omitted

Introduction

The restaurant industry has undergone dramatic changes over the past 20 years. What used to be a cottage industry composed of "mom and pop" operators is now a sophisticated, chain-dominated business. This transformation has been most evident in the fast-food segment of the industry where operators have introduced total standardization to all aspects of food service. During the 1960s and 1970s, the fast-food segment dominated the restaurant industry, and the operators who best served this market achieved spectacular growth.

The restaurant industry continues to evolve, however. There is considerable evidence that the fast-food segment of the industry has reached the maturity stage in its overall life cycle and that other segments of the industry will outperform the fast-food operators during the decades ahead. In particular, my research indicates that a "middle market" is developing as consumers' tastes and preferences shift away from the traditional fast-food eating experience. In this business plan I have outlined the marketing basis for this middle market opportunity and briefly presented the concept which I feel can be implemented to exploit this situation.

Evolution of the Middle Market

Growth Potential

The vast majority of concepts introduced during the 1960s and 1970s were in the fast-food segment of the industry. Restaurants opened featuring a wide array of food products, from soup to nuts and from muffins to baked potatoes. The fast-food segment was highly attractive to restaurant operators. This situation has now changed. The growth of the fast-food operators has leveled off. At the same time, consumer demand in the middle market has greatly increased. (See Exhibit 1 for 1978 growth rates of representative restaurants.) Since these shifts in consumer demand were not anticipated by the food service industry, the middle market is currently very underdeveloped. A clear opportunity exists for the introduction of new restaurant concepts which appeal to the middle market.

Concentration of the Industry

The increasing dominance of chain operators is a major trend within the industry. In 1975, chains accounted for 30.7 percent of industry sales; during 1980, their aggregate market share is forecasted to reach 50 percent. However, this statistic disguises the fact that chain market share varies greatly within each price segment of the industry. The table below demonstrates that as guest check averages increase, the aggregate market share maintained by chain operators decreases dramatically.

Segment Name	Price Range	Aggregate Chain Market Share within Each Segment
Fast food	$2.49 and under	86%
Upscale fast food	2.50 – $4.99	26
Middle	5.00 – $7.49	12
Gourmet	7.50 and up	8

Quite clearly, the fast-food segment is dominated by the sophisticated chains while the higher priced market segments continue to be controlled by "mom and pop" operators.

Research indicates that the consumer acceptance of chain concepts will continue to increase. It is predictable that the upscale fast-food and middle-market segments will follow the example of the fast-food segment and become dominated by a few chain operators. Accordingly, this trend toward increased industry concentration will benefit those operators who have developed superior concepts and have the management ability to expand their operations without any loss of control. It therefore becomes important to quickly define, introduce, and expand a new concept in order to take advantage of this trend.

Consumer Behavior

Customers' Eating Out Frequency

Consumers' aggregate frequency of eating out has increased dramatically over the past two decades. This is clearly demonstrated by the fact that the ratio of grocery store sales to restaurant sales has decreased from 85:15 in 1963 to 75:25 in 1978.

This consumer behavior pattern is largely explained by two sociological phenomena. First, during the period 1950–1976, married female participation in the work force increased from 20 percent to 46 percent. Accordingly, the majority of wives now have considerably less time to plan and prepare meals at home and would prefer to eat out with their families instead. The extra income of these households with working female members also contributes to this increased eating out frequency. Second, eating out is no longer a "special event"; it is a generally accepted part of contemporary urban life. Consumers are willing to trade off the higher absolute cost of a restaurant meal for the factors of convenience, variety and speed.

Since both of these phenomena are expected to continue, it appears that the overall rate of growth experienced by the restaurant industry will remain strong. The industry is forecasted to grow 3.4 percent per annum in real terms over the next five years.

Customers' Menu Preferences

Institutions Magazine annually conducts a "Menu Census" in which they survey restaurant operators to determine trends in consumer tastes and preferences for menu items. The scores for freshness and nutrition indicate that consumers are increasingly preferring fresh products which require less extensive cooking and preparation. The data also indicate that consumers are increasingly demanding portion size options in order to gain flexibility in their ordering patterns; this trend favors restaurants with a la carte menus with different portion sizes over those offering an entire "traditional dinner." Finally, the score for price/value indicates that although consumers maintain a definite price/value relationship, consumers' price sensitivity appears to be declining.

Six other editorial statements included in the 1979 Menu Census are as follows:

> "Salads of all kinds continue to sell well."
> "Soups sell. New entries and old favorites score well."
> "Price increases have led some operators to cut back the number of entrees offered, but patrons are discovering new tastes."
> "Fish and seafood prices have turned away some operators and patrons. The alternatives are innovative new offerings or the addition of 'healthy' foods."
> "Hamburgers and cheeseburgers show signs of slipping."
> "America's sweet tooth cannot be ignored, but patrons appear to be eating fewer desserts." (Note, however, ice cream obtained the highest score of all dessert products.)

A New Approach to Concept Development

The traditional approach to restaurant concept development has been quite simplistic. Operators would choose the most promising demographic segment as their target market, develop a menu traditionally favored by this group, and select a location where the concentration of these individuals was high. The operator might also implement a "gimmick" to distinguish his restaurant from others serving that market.

You will notice that this concept development process ignores the consumer behavior of the individuals making up the target demographic group. In my opinion, this concentration on overall demographic variables has led to an oversimplified approach to restaurant marketing. As an example, consider the weekly eating out habits of Mr. Smith, an average consumer.

> On Monday, Mr. Smith has a business luncheon with a client at a fashionable downtown restaurant. On Tuesday, he and his family have a quick dinner at a restaurant close to their home before attending the movies. While shopping on Wednesday evening, Mr. Smith and his wife stop for hamburgers at a local fast-food restaurant. On Thursday, Mr. Smith's birthday, the couple dine at their favorite romantic restaurant. Friday, Mr. Smith has pizza and beer with old school friends while his wife shops. On Saturday, bringing the kids home from the baseball game, he stops at a fast-food outlet for take-home chicken.

An analysis of Mr. Smith's eating out habits during that week indicates that, according to the traditional marketing approach, he entered virtually every market segment.

> Monday: formal tablecloth
> Tuesday: family
> Wednesday: fast food (hamburgers)
> Thursday: atmosphere
> Friday: specialty (pizza)
> Saturday: fast food (chicken)

- 4 -

However, during the week Mr. Smith obviously maintained a constant demographic profile—age, sex, marital status, family size, income level, etc. Therefore, although operators attempt to target their concepts towards specific demographic groups, the Mr. Smith example illustrates that any given demographic group may patronize any type of restaurant, depending upon the individual customer's requirements at any given moment. Based upon this observation, it is clear that demographics may be of limited use in selecting and attracting a target market.

I have developed an alternative approach for concept development which focuses upon the two real problems in restaurant marketing:

(A) Why do people eat out? (The Eating-Out Decision)
(B) How do they select specific restaurants? (The Restaurant Selection Process)

Instead of considering overall demographic variables, my approach considers the individual consumer's reason(s) for eating out and examines his/her expectations for the eating out experience.

(A) The Eating-Out Decision. It is my contention that people eat out for 10 basic reasons and that all restaurant visits can be assigned 1 of these 10 categories. THESE 10 CATEGORIES THEN REPRESENT THE SEGMENTS OF THE RESTAURANT INDUSTRY BASED UPON THE CUSTOMER'S ACTUAL MOTIVATION FOR EATING OUT. I have termed these 10 segments the "Motivation Groups."

Of the 10 Motivation Groups, the two which are of particular interest are the Convenience and Casual Social segments, since they constitute the majority of the middle market.

Convenience. The convenience market segment describes restaurant occasions where consumers consider the extra cost of a restaurant meal to be less than the time and trouble of preparing food at home. The customer's "make-or-buy" decision is either impulse or a planned purchase.

Casual Social. The casual social market segment describes restaurant occasions where a group of people, who are quite familiar with each other on a social basis, meet for a meal.

It should be clear that the individuals who are motivated to eat out for convenience and casual social reasons may be drawn from virtually all demographic segments. Restaurant concepts should therefore be targeted to attract a specific Motivation Group, not a selected demographic segment. (See Exhibit 2 for descriptions of the other eight motivation groups.)

(B) The Restaurant Selection Process. How does a customer belonging to a specific Motivation Group select a restaurant? Consider the following argument.

The overall eating-out experience consists of four major components: food, service, atmosphere, and price. These four major components can be further broken down into their basic elements; these individual elements are called the "PRODUCT ATTRIBUTES." It should be noted that all Product Attributes are relevant for all restaurant experiences, and that the Product Attributes are variable factors which are determined by the restaurant operator.

Furthermore, when a customer is a member of any given Motivation Group, the customer maintains a set of expectations which describes all aspects of his/her upcoming eating experience. Accordingly, CUSTOM-

ERS WILL CHOOSE THE RESTAURANT WHICH BEST FULFILLS THEIR
NEEDS AND EXPECTATIONS AT THAT PARTICULAR TIME. Stated another
way, customers will select the restaurant where the Product Attributes most
closely correspond with the expectations of their Motivation Group.

A Summary of Expectations can be developed which describes the
optimal condition for each of the Product Attributes for a given Motivation
Group. If correctly developed, this Summary of Expectations then defines the
Product Attributes which the restaurant operator must fulfill in order to attract
a given Motivation Group.

I have prepared a Summary of Expectations for the Convenience and
Casual Social Motivation Groups (see Exhibit 3). When these summaries
are compared with each other, it becomes evident that they share very similar
sets of Motivation Group expectations. Accordingly, it should be possible to
attract both Motivation Group segments by "managing" the Product Attributes
to appeal to one Motivation Group without offending the other. Furthermore,
the customer-expected Product Attributes of these 2 Motivation Groups appear to coincide directly with the characteristics of the successful middle market restaurants. The specific characteristics of the First Place concept have
therefore been developed to be consistent with the expectations of the Convenience and Casual Social Motivation Groups.

The First-Place Concept

The key characteristics of the first-place concept are briefly summarized below. Further details on these aspects may be found in the Customer-
Visible Operations section of the Business Plan.

Name. The name of the restaurant would be First Place. The accompanying promotional phrase to be included in the logo would be "Where Win-
ners Can Be Choosers."

Theme. A sports theme would be developed with particular attention
to individual sports such as skiing, swimming, cycling, track and field, in addition to the traditional team sports. Equal emphasis would be placed upon men's
and women's athletics. The theme would be implemented through authentic
artifacts, photographs, menu descriptions, food server uniforms, etc.

Menu. Approximately 80 sandwiches would be available, of which 30
would be served hot. These would range from a simple "ham and swiss" to
relatively exotic and complicated sandwiches with unusual ingredients. The
menu would also offer 10 hamburgers which would differ only in the toppings
available. First Place would also offer approximately 25 salad products; of
these, 5 would be pre-prepared specialty salads (e.g., Caesar), and 20 would
be green garden salads assembled to order in the kitchen using different combinations of ingredients. About 15 hot and cold soup recipes would be developed and, of these, 6 would be available daily on a rotating basis. The principal dessert would be ice cream and related products, including banana splits,
parfaits, and sundaes. The restaurant would be fully licensed for alcoholic
beverages.

Site Selection. The concept is intended to be implemented in suburban
and neighborhood areas with a high population density and a high mean
household income level. An optimal location would be within a major suburban shopping mall. Approximately 5,000 square feet are required.

Service and Atmosphere. Full table service would be provided. The atmosphere would be casual and relaxed.

Pricing. The menu, portions and prices have been structured so that guest check averages will be between $6.50 and $6.75.

Turnover. The customer service and food production operations are designed to ensure that customers can complete a typical meal within 45 minutes without rushing.

Capacity. Approximately 180 seats.

Key Financial Characteristics

The projected annual sales volume is $2 million with a profit after tax of $312,000. The break-even sales volume would be slightly over $800,000. The total expected capital requirement is $296,000, which assumes that the building and primary kitchen equipment are fully leased. Exhibit 4 indicates the various pro forma operating results and capital requirements for various possible sales volumes.

Corporate Objectives

It is my intention to develop First Place into a major chain which can achieve a prominent position within the new generation of middle market restaurants. Accordingly, I would seek to verify the validity of the concept with the first unit, refine operations to a highly structured level, and subsequently expand by the addition of new units both in Canada and the United States.

All units would be company owned and operated, and growth would proceed as financial resources and management capabilities permitted. There would be no franchising. It would be my intention to locate four or five units within each selected market to achieve synergistic effects in marketing and management. I also feel that it is very important to have an on-site regional manager responsible for no more than six units.

Direct Competition

During the past few years, various operators have recognized the existence of the middle-market opportunity and have developed new concepts. The success of these operators was noted in the 1978 Tableservice Operations Report published by Laventhol & Horwath, an accounting firm which is heavily engaged in consulting to the restaurant industry. The following statements were made by members of their consulting staff:

> A middle-market segment is developing in Kansas City as a result of the escalating prices of the specialty restaurants. This segment, characterized by heavy decor, full-service menus, youthful service personnel and $3–$6 check averages is capitalizing on both young families and singles who demand specialty restaurant atmosphere and service but are value conscious.
> Especially noteworthy are those moderately priced restaurants which have responded to clearly identified segments of demand by being innovative in service, menu, and decor.
> They (the customers) don't mind paying the price for food of good quality and quantity.

Moreover, it appears that success in the middle market is not restricted to any specific food type(s). Most important, a few restaurants whose menus revolve around "exotic" sandwiches and salads have opened quite successfully in various markets. In Exhibit 5, I have compared First Place with several of its most successful competitors along certain key operating parameters.

This analysis demonstrates that the First Place concept is viable, and can be expected to achieve the financial projections indicated. It is quite clear that the market will support a superior sandwich, soup and salad concept targeted towards the middle market.

First Place Unique Success Factors

For a new venture to be successful, it must possess definite conceptual, strategic, technological, or management advantages in order to effectively compete. The First Place concept possesses the following four Unique Success Factors.

High Menu Variety: Limited Food Inventory

Although the menu offers a great variety within each product line, (soups, salads, sandwiches and desserts), it requires a very limited number of raw materials to execute. Through the various combinations and permutations of ingredients, the 80 sandwiches, 25 salads and large number of desserts would require approximately 24 meats and cheeses, 19 produce products, 6 breads, 8 ice cream types, and sundry nonperishable seasonings and condiments to produce.

Product Assembly and Delivery Time

The entire menu has relatively high advance preparation requirements; the soups must be cooked beforehand and all the ingredients for salads and sandwiches must be prepared prior to peak meal periods. When any given menu item is ordered by a customer, the product can be produced by the kitchen and available for customer delivery within five minutes of ordering.

Diversification of Ingredient Requirements

Many restaurant concepts suffer from very high exposure to volatile commodity prices of their primary raw materials. The raw material requirements for First Place are fully diversified across meats, dairy, produce and baked goods. Furthermore, even within an ingredient line such as meat, the raw material requirements are diversified into beef, fowl, pork, etc. The First Place concept will therefore suffer very little cost pressure due to fluctuating *individual* commodity prices, and ingredient diversification assures that food costs will vary directly with the overall food price index.

Coincidence of High Volumes and Increased Gross Margin

Restaurant operations are typically very seasonal, with summer volumes being traditionally higher as demonstrated in Exhibit 6. This situation is aggravated in Canada by the severity of the winter season. Although the raw material ingredients are fully diversified overall, produce will clearly form a major component of the aggregate food cost. Since produce costs decline substantially during the summer months, overall food costs will be lowest when volumes are highest.

Weekly Sales Patterns

Restaurants are typically busiest on Fridays and Saturdays, with significantly lower business volumes throughout the rest of the week. Exhibit 6 illustrates the typical distribution of meals by day of the week for the 3 principal types of restaurants described in the literature. Obviously, the key to success within the industry depends upon increasing sales Sunday through Thursday. If the Motivation Group approach to restaurant marketing is valid, it appears that the problem of highly variable daily sales volumes can be effectively managed within the First Place concept. It is evident that the weekend sales increases experienced by most operators are generated by the Sexual, Formal Social, Personal Event, and Entertainment Motivation Groups. First Place does not compete for these groups. Instead, First Place competes for the Convenience and Casual Social Motivation Groups whose restaurant occasions occur throughout the week as a result of the "fast-paced" contemporary North American lifestyle. First Place would therefore attract early week business at a significantly greater rate than the industry average, thereby establishing a much smoother weekly sales pattern.

Management of Risks

The restaurant industry has developed a reputation as a high-risk business. Many potential investors have felt that the apparent risks were unmanageable and that the food service industry should therefore be avoided as an investment possibility.

In my opinion, many of these risks can be minimized if the concept is fundamentally sound and the operations managed according to generally accepted management principles. This section lists five often mentioned risks and describes how they would be managed under the First Place concept.

1. "Labor costs are going up and up. Besides that, it's impossible to find the good people that you need to work in restaurants."

   Contrary to the popular view, it has been my experience that restaurant employees can be effectively managed if the proper policies are developed and implemented, and if sufficient management attention is paid to potential employee problem areas. In First Place, programs would be introduced for employee training and development, merit compensation, internal promotion and tip pooling to provide employees with a well-structured working environment and incentives for superior performance.

2. "Restaurants don't do very well during recessions."

   During times of generally poor economic conditions, restaurants in the lower and middle price ranges do very well while expensive restaurants do quite poorly. Because of the trading down phenomenon and the increased disposable income spent on restaurant meals, middle and lower priced restaurants actually benefit from recessions.

3. "Employees will steal anything that's not chained down in a restaurant."

   Employee theft of both food and equipment is a major problem within the industry. But certain control and measurement systems have proven to be extremely effective in limiting employee theft in similar restaurants. Therefore, although the problem exists, it can be managed and minimized to an acceptable level.

4. "It will be very difficult to compete with the established fast food chains if they decide to enter the middle market."

   The development of the middle market has not gone unnoticed by the major fast-food chains and they are attempting to diversify their menus and upgrade their decors. However, the efforts of the fast-food chains to reposition themselves in the marketplace will be unsuccessful for several reasons. First, their existing consumer images are already very well established; the changes in consumer tastes and preferences for the overall eating out experience far exceed their ability to upgrade their physical facilities from counter service and the production of a very limited menu, both of which are inconsistent with consumer preferences in the middle market. Finally, their sites were selected based upon consumer traffic patterns which fa-

vored fast food purchases (e.g., highway interchanges). Many of their locations are therefore appropriate only as fast food outlets and it is doubtful that
a chain would risk diluting its customer image by modifying some units to
appeal to the middle market while not changing others.
5. "I don't think that a sandwich-oriented menu will attract customers for dinner on a consistent basis."
    Studies clearly demonstrate that the ratio of lunch to dinner business
is remarkably constant between the fast food and middle market segments
and that middle market restaurant occasions are relatively evenly split between lunch and dinner, regardless of food type.

Customer Visible Operations

Obviously, the most important factor which determines the lunch/dinner
mix is site selection. As mentioned previously, the First Place concept is designed to be implemented in major suburban shopping malls. Lunch business
would consist of shoppers, the staff of the shopping center, and retailers and
workers from nearby office buildings. Dinner business would be derived from
shoppers, people returning home from the city, and area residents who wish to
eat out for convenience and/or casual social reasons.

Site Selection

    As explained previously, there are only two important considerations
in restaurant site selection: traffic and personal disposable income. Due to the
shopping and residency patterns which have evolved in most North American
cities, exposure to these variables is maximized by locating in, or near, major
suburban shopping malls.
    The advantages of mall locations are well documented. First, the
data indicates that the greatest absolute expenditure on food away from home
is made by families residing in the neighborhood/suburban areas of the major
metropolitan markets. Second, other research demonstrates that, over the past
five years, restaurants located in these neighborhood/suburban areas have
had a sales growth rate which exceeds that of the industry by 29.5 percent.
Finally, in 1975, the National Restaurant Association conducted a study in
which they examined the eating-out habits of customers during shopping trips.
Interestingly, 65 percent of the respondents indicated that they ate out either
always, frequently, or fairly often during shopping trips. Their average evening expenditure on eating-out was $4.22, or $6.07 in inflation-adjusted 1979
dollars.
    Furthermore, as growth proceeds, it may prove worthwhile to develop
free-standing units adjacent to major malls for three reasons. First, the
comparative traffic and visibility characteristics for "in-mall" and "shopping
center peripheral" locations are quite similar. However, free-standing sites
have a significantly greater opportunity for attracting late evening business
than do in-mall locations which suffer when the rest of the mall closes at 9 or 10
P.M. Second, in-mall locations may attract too many weary shoppers who order
minimal amounts; these shoppers are too lazy to make the effort to cross the
parking lot. Finally, the previously mentioned National Restaurant Association
study found that 41 percent of respondents preferred visiting restaurants within walking distance of their shopping location, instead of eating within the
mall. This figure rose to 48 percent for families with incomes greater than
$25,000.

Customer Invisible Operations

Kitchen Operations
1. Forecasting: Following the first month of operation, daily meal counts and the sales mix should become quite stable. Forecasting systems can then be implemented to ensure that raw material purchases and daily food preparation are adequate to meet daily requirements without overprocuring and sacrificing freshness.
2. Purchasing: All purchased food products would be specified by weight, size, quality, and brand name (if applicable). Only authorized products would be purchased. All purveyors would have to be approved by myself and checks would only be issued to vendors on the approved listing.
3. Receiving: The quality of the incoming raw materials must obviously be maintained in order to serve a high quality product. Accordingly, all goods would be inspected for quality and freshness when received, and products which do not meet specifications would be returned. It has been my experience that purveyors will deliver only the best products to an account if they know that substandard products will be consistently returned.
4. Food preparation and assembly: All preparation procedures, specifications, recipes and assembly instructions would be tightly specified. For example, based upon the daily forecast, food preparation employees would know exactly how much of each ingredient to prepare (e.g., 15 pounds of ham to be sliced into 4-ounce portions at slicer setting 22). For the assembly of sandwiches, salads, and desserts, menu boards would be fixed on the wall in front of the respective work areas listing the contents of each product as well as assembly instructions. For example, Salad #16 (Large) might read as follows:

Endive/Iceberg lettuce mixture	2/3 bowl
15 carrot slices	sprinkled
15 mushroom slices	sprinkled
8 cherry tomatos	outside
8 cucumber slices	outside
3 tablespoons chopped scallions	sprinkled
4 cauliflower wedges	inside
1 broccoli stem	lay on top

5. Other kitchen policies and procedures
   a. Quality control testing.
   b. Clean-up procedures.
   c. Portion control checks.
   d. Movement of inventory from primary storage to secondary storage to current use.
   e. Production and rotation policies for soups.

EXHIBITS
1. Chain restaurant growth analysis
2. Remaining eight motivation groups
3. Product attributes for the convenience and social motivation groups
4. Pro Forma Income Statements
5. Direct competition comparisons
6. Patterns of restaurant sales
7. Ingredients

8. Calculation of food costs and guest check average
9. Kitchen equipment cost
10. Leasehold improvement costs, furniture and fixture costs
11. Pre-opening expenses
12. Occupancy and equipment leasing costs
13. Pro Forma Cash Flows

Note: Unless otherwise stated, all exhibits and figures have been computed based upon the following assumptions.

(1) The turnover cycle is 45 minutes.
(2) The Guest Check Average is $6.68.
(3) The restaurant contains 180 seats.
(4) The restaurant utilizes 5,000 square feet.
(5) Total annual sales are $2,000,000.
(6) During the first two months of operations sales volumes will reach forecasted levels due to the well documented "honeymoon" effect.
(7) During the first two months food and labor costs will exceed normal levels by 20 percent due to start-up inefficiencies.

EXHIBIT 1
Chain Restaurant Growth Analysis *(Fiscal 1978)*

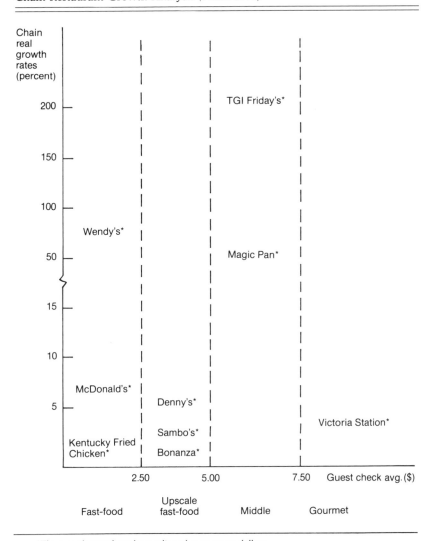

*The growth rates have been adjusted to constant dollars.

EXHIBIT 2
Remaining Eight Motivation Groups

1. Expediency
   The consumer's single reason for eating out is immediate hunger satisfaction.
2. Available at Restaurants Only
   In this market segment, the primary reason for eating out is to consume a food item which cannot be prepared at home.
3. Business
   The primary purpose for business meals is to provide the participants with a quiet and uninterrupted setting for private conversation.
4. Personal Events
   Dinners are typically used to celebrate memorable events such as birthdays, anniversaries, and promotions.
5. Institutional Events
   These are meals held by a group of coworkers (e.g., office parties), bowling leagues, civic organizations, etc.
6. Sexual
   Dinner dates provide a socially acceptable setting for couples to get further acquainted.
7. Formal Social
   The primary purpose for formal social restaurant visits is to entertain a person or group where circumstances dictate that proper decorum be observed.
8. Entertainment
   Within this segment, some form of entertainment forms a major component of the overall eating out experience.

EXHIBIT 3
Product Attributes for the Convenience and Social Motivation Groups

Product Attributes	Expectations of Convenience Motivation Group	Expectations of Casual Social Motivation Group
Food	Food	Food
Food quality	Primary importance	Equal in importance to
Portion size	Quality	social aspects
Taste	Nutrition	Acceptable to all in
Nutrition level	Portion sizes	party
Menu variety	Limited menu may be	Portion size high
Freshness	inhibitor; standard	Quality must be
Liquor availability	menu should appear	moderate to high
Presentation	Interesting taste, not too	Exotic menu substantial
Caloric content	bland	marketing
		Nutrition very important

EXHIBIT 3 (*concluded*)

Product Attributes	Expectations of Convenience Motivation Group	Expectations of Casual Social Motivation Group
Service	Service	Service
Turnover time Reservations or not Seating hostess or not Friendliness of staff Customer/staff interaction Payment method Entertainment Pacing of meal Flexibility in service style Attention to detail	High service level Pacing of meal highly structured Turnover cycle: 40–50 minutes Moderate seat comfort required Knowledge of menu by foodserver high Most group sizes: 2's and 4's Reservations not required Hostess required to organize seating Licensed lounge not required	Friendly and easygoing Hostess to organize seating Reservations not required Licensed lounge if customers have to wait Turnover cycle: 50–60 minutes Payment: postmeal, foodserver, credit cards must be accepted Medium-size groups (6–8 people) Flexibility in meal pacing Seating comfort is moderate Knowledge of menu by foodserver high
Atmosphere	Atmosphere	Atmosphere
Noise level Lighting Intensity of theme Degree of privacy Decor Seating comfort Music (type, volume)	Moderate noise level Music with moderate volume, relatively contemporary Some distractions, but able to be ignored Privacy can be varied by choice Casual and relaxed	Informal and relaxed Privacy varied but not too high Decor, noise level: moderate Ambient entertainment but customer should be able to ignore it Music: contemporary, medium volume
Price	Price	Price
Food Beverage Tipping Patterns	Guest check less than $7.50 Tipping pattern: 10–12%	Moderate prices ($5–$7.50 guest check averages) Liquor prices not excessive Tipping pattern: approximately 12%

EXHIBIT 4
Pro Forma Income Statements

	Worst Case	Planned Volume	Best Case
Food	$ 883,000	$1,766,000	$2,649,000
Liquor/Wine/Beer	117,000	234,000	351,000
Total sales	1,000,000	2,000,000	3,000,000
Cost of goods	320,000	640,000	960,000
Gross margin	680,000	1,360,000	2,040,000
Direct labor	224,000	338,000	455,000
Management payroll	79,000	79,000	96,000
Payroll related expense	31,000	44,000	57,000
Employee bonus plan	0	20,000	30,000
Total labor	334,000	481,000	638,000
Maintenance and repairs	24,000	36,000	48,000
Laundry	9,000	18,000	27,000
Serviceware	15,000	22,000	29,000
Guest supplies	7,000	14,000	21,000
Utilities	25,000	35,000	45,000
Credit card commissions	15,000	30,000	45,000
Licenses	1,000	1,000	1,000
Miscellaneous (telephone, office, etc.)	4,000	5,000	6,000
Total other variable	100,000	161,000	222,000
Total operating costs	754,000	1,282,000	1,820,000
Equipment leasing	32,000	32,000	32,000
Occupancy costs	100,000	160,000	240,000
Taxes	8,000	8,000	8,000
Advertising and Promotion	5,000	10,000	10,000
Insurance	10,000	10,000	10,000
Depreciation and Amortization	18,000	18,000	18,000
Total overhead	173,000	238,000	318,000
Profit before tax	73,000	480,000	862,000
Income tax (assumes 35% effective tax rate)	25,000	168,000	302,000
Net earnings	$ 47,000	$ 312,000	$ 560,000

Note: During the first year of operation, pretax earnings would be decreased by $41,000, representing the write-off of pre-opening expenses.

EXHIBIT 5
Direct Competition Comparisions

Restaurant Name	Total Sales ($)	Annual Meals Served	Number of Seats	Guest Check Average ($)	Required Seat Turnover per Day
FIRST PLACE (at break-even sales volume)	$ 800,000	120,000	180	$6.67	1.85
FIRST PLACE (at expected sales volume)	2,000,000	300,000	180	6.67	4.63
MR. GREENJEANS (Toronto, Ontario)	2,000,000	312,000	160	6.41	5.41
D. B. KAPLAN'S (Chicago, Illinois)	3,000,000	650,000	300	4.61	6.05

EXHIBIT 6
Patterns of Restaurant Sales

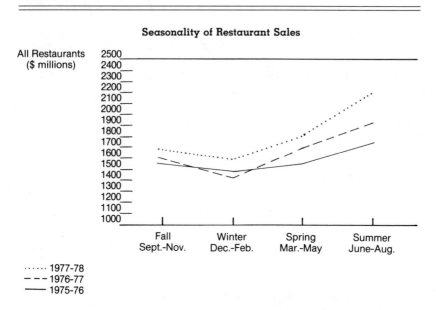

Seasonality of Restaurant Sales

All Restaurants ($ millions)

...... 1977-78
- - - 1976-77
——— 1975-76

Meal Distribution by Week Day and Restaurant Type

	Noon Meal			Evening Meal		
Day of Week	Family	Fast-Food	Atmosphere	Family	Fast-Food	Atmosphere
Monday	13	10	11	7	9	8
Tuesday	12	14	15	12	17	10
Wednesday	16	15	20	11	15	14
Thursday	13	18	18	11	15	13
Friday	22	19	23	23	22	21
Saturday	13	17	8	20	13	22
Sunday	11	7	5	16	9	12
Totals	100	100	100	100	100	100

EXHIBIT 7
Ingredients

Meats	Cheeses	Salads	Miscellaneous	Ice Creams	Ice Cream Sauces/Toppings
Turkey	Swiss	Iceberg lettuce	Tomato slices	Chocolate	Blueberry
Bacon	Provolone	Romaine lettuce	Lettuce	Vanilla	Chocolate-fudge
Hamburgers	American cheddar	Chickory (endive)	Onions (sauteed)	Strawberry	Pineapple
Ham	Sharp cheddar	Asparagus	Beer mustard	Butterscotch	Strawberry
Crab meat salad	American colby	Beets	Cole Slaw	Banana	Cherry
Roast beef		Broccoli	Carbur's "Special" sauce	Black cherry	Marshmallow
Corned beef		Cabbage	Garlic mayonnaise	Pistachio nut	Peanuts
Shrimp salad		Carrots	Raw white onions	Coffee	Jimmies
Steak (broiled)		Cauliflower	Avocado spread		Walnuts
Pastrami		Celery	Green peppers		Raisins
Knockwurst		Cucumbers	Russian dressing		Marshmallows (mini)
(grilled)		Mushrooms	Taragon mayonnaise		Smarties
Chicken livers		Onions (Bermuda)	Mushrooms (sauteed)		Chocolate chips
(grilled)		Onions (scallions)	Horseradish mayonnaise		Whipped cream
Tuna salad		Radishes	Mushrooms (raw)		Banana slices
Oysters (fried)		Spinach	Peanut butter		Strawberries

EXHIBIT 7 (*concluded*)

Meats	Cheeses	Salads	Miscellaneous	Ice Creams	Ice Cream Sauces/Toppings
		Tomatoes	Blue cheese dressing		
		Tomatoes (cherry)	Mayonnaise (plain)		
		Oranges	Bermuda onions (slices)		
			Chili mayonnaise		
			Sauerkraut		
			Jelly		
			Tomato (broiled)		
			Tartar sauce		
			Avocado slices		
			Sour cream		
			Honey		
			Marshmallow		
			Banana		
			Cottage cheese		
			Kidney beans		
			Cucumbers		
			Hot crushed peppers		
			Hot cherry peppers		

EXHIBIT 8
Calculation of Food Costs and Guest Check Average

	(1)	(2)	(3)	(4)	Guest Check	
	Average Product Price ($)	Average Product Cost ($)	Average Food Cost (%) (2) ÷ (1)	Probability of Being Ordered by a Customer	Average Excluding Liquor ($) (1) x (4)	Weighted Product Food Cost ($) (2) x (3)
Product						
Sandwiches	3.75	1.30	35	.75	2.8125	.984
Salad—Large	3.95	1.30	33	.20	.7900	2.610
—Small	2.55	.65	25	.50	1.2750	.319
Soup	1.55	.45	26	.25	.3875	.101
Beverage	.45	.20	44	.90	.4050	.178
Dessert	1.50	.55	33	.15	.2250	.074
Total					$5.895	$1.917

Sales Mix Weighted Food Cost: $\frac{\$1.917}{\$5.895} = 32.5\%$

Projected Food Revenue per person: $5.895
Projected Liquor/Wine/Beer Revenue per person: $.78
Projected Total Guest Check Average: $6.675

- 21 -

EXHIBIT 9
Kitchen Equipment Cost

Equipment	Cost
Dishwasher	$ 12,000
Walk-in cooler (18' by 6')	11,000
Garbage compactor (2,000 pounds per day)	10,000
Microwave ovens (2)	8,000
Slicers (2) (automatic, with portion control)	7,200
Shelving	5,500
Exhaust hood	5,000
Soup kettles (2) (1–50 gallons, 1–40 gallons)	5,000
Broiler	5,000
Ice machines (2) (1–200 pounds per day) (1–200 pounds per day)	4,000
Range (8 burners, with oven)	3,000
Undercounter freezer/work table (6-door, 120 cubic feet)	3,000
Shredder/dicer	3,000
Refrigerators (2) (72 cubic feet)	3,000
Beer cooler (4-door, self-contained compressor)	2,500
Fryolator	2,000
Ice cream freezer	2,000
Draft beer dispenser (including chiller)	2,000
Dishwashing sinks	1,500
Coffee machines (2) (5-pot)	1,500
Glass chiller	1,300
Plate chiller	1,300
Soda fountain system	1,000
Refrigerators (2) (14-cubic feet)	1,000
Spring-loaded ice bins (2)	1,000
Scales (3) (1–receiving) (2–portion control)	1,000
Kitchen smallware	15,000
Serviceware (adjusted to projected sales mix and sufficient for three complete turnovers)	11,000
Miscellaneous equipment	5,000
Total kitchen equipment cost	$133,800

EXHIBIT 10
Leasehold Improvement, Furniture, and Fixture Costs

Leasehold Improvements Cost

Item	Cost
Architect's professional fees	$ 20,000
Wall finishings	20,000
Partitions, other specialized interior finishings	15,000
Artifacts, photographs	15,000
Bar structure	10,000
Project manager	9,000
Carpets	7,000
Merchandising displays	6,000
Exterior signage	2,000
Miscellaneous	5,000
Total leasehold improvements cost	$109,000

Furniture and Fixture Costs

Item	Cost
Chairs	$ 9,000
Lighting (including emergency)	8,000
Tables	5,000
Music system	3,000
Safe, office furnishings and equipment	3,000
Washroom accessories	1,000
Burglary system	1,000
Miscellaneous	3,000
Total furniture and fixtures cost	$33,000

EXHIBIT 11
Pre-Opening Expenses

Item	Cost
Capitalized, leasehold improvements	
Architect's professional fees	$ 20,000
Construction—Project manager	9,000
Subtotal	29,000
Capitalized, organization costs	
Professional fees, legal and accounting	15,000
Professional fees, restaurant design	15,000
Menu design	2,000
Subtotal	32,000
Expensed from earnings	
Salary (3 managers for 2 months)	10,000
Salary (1 secretary for 6 months)	7,000
Pre-opening hourly training	5,000
Manager recruiting (placement fees)	4,000
Menu printing	3,000
Menu development and testing	2,000
Hourly employee training materials	2,000
Licenses and applications	1,000
Miscellaneous pre-opening expenses	
(telephone, postage, office supplies,	
storage, printing, etc.)	7,000
Subtotal	41,000
Total pre-opening expenses	$102,000

EXHIBIT 12
Occupancy and Equipment Leasing Costs

It has been assumed that the occupancy cost for 5,000 square feet of space in a prime location would be the greater of either $20 per square foot ($100,000 per annum) or 8 percent of gross revenues. Under this assumption, the gross revenue leasing arrangement would come into effect at a sales volume of $1,250,000 which is well above breakeven. It has been further assumed that the landlord would be responsible for providing adequate heat, air conditioning, electrical, gas, and plumbing systems.

It has also been assumed that $108,000 of primary kitchen equipment would be obtained through some sort of leasing arrangement. The assumed terms were a closed five-year lease with an internal rate of return to the lessor of approximately 18 percent.

EXHIBIT 13
Pro Forma Cash Flows

Expense Item	Preopening Cash Flow		Operating Cash Flows—First Fiscal Year			
	Q$_1$-1980	Q$_2$-1980	Q$_3$-1980	Q$_4$-1980	Q$_1$-1981	Q$_2$-1981
Professional fees						
Architects	$6,000	$6,000	$8,000	—	—	—
Tax and accounting	5,000	5,000	5,000	—	—	—
Restaurant design	5,000	5,000	5,000	—	—	—
Salaries						
Managers	—	10,000	—	—	—	—
Secretary	3,500	3,500	—	—	—	—
Construction—Project manager	4,500	4,500	—	—	—	—
Management recruiting (placement fees)	—	4,000	—	—	—	—
Licenses and applications	500	500	—	—	—	—
Menu testing and development	2,000	—	—	—	—	—
Menu design and printing	1,000	4,000	—	—	—	—
Hourly training materials	—	2,000	—	—	—	—
Preopening hourly training	—	5,000	—	—	—	—
Miscellaneous preopening expenses	3,500	3,500	—	—	—	—

EXHIBIT 13 (*concluded*)

Expense Item	Preopening Cash Flow		Operating Cash Flows—First Fiscal Year			
	Q₁-1980	Q₂-1980	Q₃-1980	Q₄-1980	Q₁-1981	Q₂-1981
Serviceware	—	—	11,000	—	—	—
Smallware	—	—	15,000	—	—	—
Furniture and Fixtures	—	—	33,000	—	—	—
Leasehold improvements	—	—	80,000	—	—	—
Working capital	—	—	122,000	—	—	—
Add: Funds provided by operations	—	—	51,000	$69,000	$62,000	84,000
Add: Depreciation and amortization	—	—	4,500	4,500	4,500	4,500
Total cash flow	($31,000)	($53,000)	($223,500)	$73,500	$66,500	$88,500
Total cumulative cash flow:	($31,000)	($84,000)	($307,500)	($234,000)	($167,500)	($79,000)

Case 1–2

ICEDELIGHTS

On March 10, 1983, Paul Rogers, Mark Daniels, and Eric Garfield walked out of their final negotiating session with ICEDELIGHTS. The three were negotiating for the Florida franchise rights to ICEDELIGHTS, a European-style cafe/ice cream shop selling a variety of beverages and frozen desserts.

The session had gone fairly well, and they felt as though they had gotten most of the concessions that they wanted. Yet, mixed with this air of excitement was a sense of trepidation. There was a great deal of work that remained to be done on the deal, not the least of which was the securing of additional financing. In addition, other issues remained: Did the Florida market offer good potential for an ice cream business? Did the deal make good business sense? Was it right for them personally at this point in their careers? Did they have the skills and resources to make the business work, assuming that the deal came off? Did the same factors that made them good friends make them good business partners?

BACKGROUND

Paul Rogers, Mark Daniels, and Eric Garfield were three second-year students at the New York School of Business (NYSB) who had all been classmates in their first year. (See resumes, Exhibit 1.) The idea of starting, or buying, their business arose during the week just prior to the start of second-year classes. The three had rented a house on Cape Cod for a week. Fresh from their summer jobs, they naturally shared their views of what their summer experiences had been like, and what impact these experiences would have on their career choices.

— Paul, 26, had spent two-and-a-half years with State Street Bank in Boston. He had worked for the summer as an associate with the New York investment bank of Warburg Paribas Becker, and had enjoyed the experience. Paul, however, was excited by the challenge and rewards of creating and managing an enterprise of his own at an early stage in his career.
— Mark, 25, had spent two years with McKinsey & Co., and had also turned to investment banking for the summer. While he had enjoyed this experience, Mark felt a genuine desire for the independence and satisfaction of owning and managing his own business. He was unsure how additional work in either consulting or investment banking would bring him closer to this goal.
— Eric, 30, had spent five years with Celanese in the international finance area. After pursuing positions with investment banks and consulting firms, Eric accepted a position with McKinsey's Atlanta office. Although he enjoyed the experience a great deal, Eric also felt drawn towards owning his own business. The independence, financial rewards, and opportunity to manage and truly create an organization seemed unequaled in any other career.

During that week on Cape Cod they spent a great deal of time on the beach and in the local bars discussing their experiences, and speculating on what lay ahead. They talked about what they were looking for in a career: each of them wanted a job he would truly enjoy, independence, and great financial rewards. In addition, there was something incredibly appealing about building and managing an organization—really creating a business—being an entrepreneur. Moreover, it was clear that none of the "traditional" opportunities offered this. The idea of "having our own business" took hold.

Each of them had, at different times, thought that running his own business might be fun. During that week, they realized that this opportunity was the only option that would truly satisfy their objectives. Slowly, the focus of their thoughts turned to "How do we get there?"

Their discussions surfaced two fundamentally different approaches:

— The first approach, the "conservative" one, had two possibilities:
  • They could pick an industry, really try to learn a business, develop their management skills, and keep an eye out for opportunities; they

were bound to learn a great deal, and they would be making their mistakes on someone else's money. In four or five years, they were bound to spot an opportunity and could then obtain the financing. Everyone says, "the money's there if you have a good idea."

- Or, they could get into the deal flow; go to work for a venture capital firm or the M&A area of an investment bank. They would learn how to evaluate deals and make contacts with people that could provide financing. Then they would buy something for themselves and run it!

— The second approach was, "Why wait?" They argued that they had the skills and abilities to run a business. Not a high-tech or sophisticated manufacturing firm, but surely there were some businesses that they had the collective talent to manage—all they had to do was find one. Further, in four or five years, it would be much harder to do. One would be used to the financial security and life style of corporate life; it wouldn't be easy to go back to $25,000 or $30,000 and 80-hour weeks. Finally, with a wife, family, car payments, a mortgage, and a summer home or ski house on the way, the risks associated with failure would be far greater down the road.

As school began, they decided that it was certainly worth trying to find a business.

THE SEARCH

The three began talking with professors at the Business School, lawyers, and business contacts. They asked for advice and mentioned that they were in the market to buy a company. It soon became clear that they needed some concrete specifications regarding the businesses they were interested in, both as a guide to potential sources of information and to show a minimum level of commitment to the project. A brief specifications sheet was pulled together (Exhibit 2) which described the businesses they would be interested in, and included their resumes.

The process proceeded through October and November with little in the way of results. People were generally helpful and encouraging, but it was very tough to get specific leads.

In late November, Paul's father, Mr. Rogers, mentioned that some friends of the family had recently purchased the ICEDELIGHTS franchise for Oregon and California; he had heard that Florida might be available. The three were excited about the possibility even though retailing had not been one of the industries targeted in their specifications sheet. The skills required to run a food franchise seemed within their range of abilities. It sounded like a fun business, and the potential financial rewards seemed to be great.

ICEDELIGHTS

ICEDELIGHTS was a Boston-based chain of food outlets selling a variety of beverages, pastries, and frozen desserts. There were currently nine stores in the New England area (primarily Boston), with several more scheduled to be opened during 1983. ICEDELIGHTS had sold its first franchise rights (Oregon and California) in June 1982, and the first of these stores was scheduled to open in the summer of 1983.

The four of them met with ICEDELIGHTS on December 10. Bob Andrews, the chairman, revealed that they had received dozens of franchise requests for Florida. He mentioned seven individuals in particular, each with extensive experience in either the fast-food industry or Florida real estate and who clearly had the financial resources required. Yet he felt that, at this time, ICEDELIGHTS was stretched to its capacity. They had grown slowly and carefully, and were committed to maintaining a quality operation. Managing their existing locations and their own expansion, as well as providing a high level of assistance to the California franchise, would consume their available resources for the near future.

ICEDELIGHTS' conservative approach was due in large part to problems the company had had in its early years. Bob Andrews purchased ICE-DELIGHTS when it had two locations. Early expansion resulted in financial problems when the company did not have the necessary organization and control systems in place.

Following this meeting, they met with the president of ICEDELIGHTS— Herb Gross. As the chief operating officer, he provided the group with a more detailed description of the ICEDELIGHTS operation. He, too, stressed ICEDELIGHTS commitment to slow, *quality* growth. He felt, however, that there was some possibility that a deal could be worked out. Paul, Mark and Eric expressed their enthusiasm for the business, and their desire to really get involved in the day-to-day, hands-on operations of ICEDELIGHTS. They left impressed with the quality of ICEDELIGHTS management and its potential for growth.

During this conversation, Paul, Mark, and Eric gained a better understanding of how ICEDELIGHTS worked. The heart of the concept revolved around several factors: first, ICEDELIGHTS sold an Italian "gelati" type ice cream which was extremely rich and "homemade" looking and tasting. Yet, through a great deal of effort, ICEDELIGHTS had been able to perfect the process of freezing this "homemade" ice cream. This enabled ICEDELIGHTS to manufacture each of the products centrally, freeze them, and then sell on the premises of each store location. Most shops with a high-quality ice cream made the product on the premises. Moreover, ICEDELIGHTS had built and developed a very impressive organization. Their ongoing standardization of production, training, accounting, and control systems, store management, and store design and construction convinced Paul, Mark, and Eric that they would receive a great deal of support as a franchise. Finally, by marketing the concept as a café, this chain was able to derive sales throughout the day from coffee, pastry, and light snacks as well as ice cream in the afternoon and evening.

At this point, Paul, Mark, and Eric felt that a real opportunity was finally within their grasp. They realized that a great deal of work lay ahead if they were to have any chance of pulling the deal off. The opportunity to do a field study in the New Ventures area seemed to be an excellent vehicle to both accomplish this effort and get some advice from a knowledgeable advisor. They put together a proposal (Exhibit 3) which was accepted.

The group met briefly with ICEDELIGHTS again in early January. Bob Andrews and Herb Gross indicated that they were interested in pursuing the Florida franchise further. They were very impressed with Paul's, Mark's and Eric's abilities and willingness to get involved in the day-to-day operations of the franchise. The other groups had all been interested in purchasing the franchise as an investment. They viewed the desire to be involved in the operations as crucial to maintaining the quality of the operation. A dinner was scheduled for January 11 to discuss how to proceed.

THE DEAL

On January 11, Paul, Mark, Eric, and Mr. Rogers met Bob and Herb at a restaurant in Boston. ICEDELIGHTS indicated that they did want to go ahead with the Florida franchise, but because they were so stretched, they did not want to be legally bound to proceed. Nonetheless, they recognized that, because of their job search situation, Paul, Mark, and Eric did need some security that the deal would come off. So ICEDELIGHTS proposed the following terms:

The franchisee (Paul, Mark, Eric, and Mr. Rogers) would:

— Pay $200,000 up front.
  • $100,000 development fee for the State of Florida.
  • $100,000 in five prepaid franchise fees of $20,000 each. This was prepayment for the first five stores.
— Pay $20,000 per store opened (after the first five, which were prepaid as above).
— Pay a 5 percent royalty on sales.

In exchange, ICEDELIGHTS would allow them to use the ICEDELIGHTS name, sell them products for roughly 32 percent of suggested retail price, train them, train one manager per store opened, and provide them with assistance in finding real estate, selecting locations, and constructing stores. In effect, ICEDELIGHTS would provide them with the first few locations as "turnkey" operations.

Because ICEDELIGHTS did not wish to be legally obligated to proceed if they felt that their operation was still stretched to capacity, these terms would be subject to an option.

The parties would sign an option which specified the terms of the franchise agreement (as above):

— The franchisee (Paul, Mark, Eric, and Mr. Rogers) would make a deposit of $75,000. If ICEDELIGHTS did not agree to proceed within nine months, the group would get back its $75,000 plus interest.
— If ICEDELIGHTS did agree to proceed, the franchisee would pay the remainder of the up-front fee ($125,000) and proceed.
— If the franchisee did not agree to pay the remaining fee and proceed, they would forfeit the $75,000 deposit.

ICEDELIGHTS stressed that they were personally committed to going ahead with the Florida franchise as soon as California was running smoothly. They said that it was in everyone's best interest that they not be obligated to proceed if they did not feel that they could provide the franchisee with the level of support required. They further felt that by locking in the terms of the franchise, they were bringing something to the deal.

Another dinner was scheduled for January 25, two weeks hence, when Paul, Mark, Eric, and Mr. Rogers would deliver their decision to ICEDELIGHTS.

Paul, Mark, and Eric had two weeks to make a decision. The main issue now seemed to be financing. As the former president of a Boston-area bank, Mr. Rogers had a great many friends and associates who were potential sources of financing. Mr. Rogers began approaching them in hopes of finding one or two individuals to back the entire deal.

In the meantime, Paul, Mark, and Eric tried to pull together some financial data which would allow them to generate pro forma financials and estimate both the financing required and the attractiveness of the operation.

First, they compared the terms of the ICEDELIGHTS franchise with those of other leading franchises (Exhibit 4). On one hand, ICEDELIGHTS seemed expensive for a new and unproven franchise. Yet, it appeared to offer excellent profit potential, and they were obtaining the rights to the entire state of Florida.

They did try to get some idea of the market potential which Florida offered, and pulled together the data shown in Exhibit 5.

Next, they looked at the store-level income statement (Exhibit 6). The operation appeared to be incredibly profitable, particularly in light of the investment required. At $160,000 investment per store, they estimated that they would require $750,000 in financing, as follows:

Up-front fee	$200,000
First three stores	480,000
Working capital	70,000
	$750,000

Next, they had to think about how to structure the deal and how much equity to keep: Could they keep enough to make it financially rewarding to them and attractive enough for investors? Would the operation require continued infusions of cash for growth?

They knew that the more debt they could put in the capital structure the better, due to the deductibility of interest payments, and the nondeductibility of dividends. They also knew that there were certain IRS regulations which limited the amount of debt they could have. They looked up the applicable section of the Tax Code, Sec. 385, and its explanation (see Exhibit 7). Further, debt and fixed interest payments would both restrict their growth and increase the riskiness of the venture.

After running some preliminary pro formas (Exhibit 8), they decided on a first cut at the deal capital structure. It seemed as though they could give 25 percent of their company away and still give investors an attractive return.

Mr. Rogers' contacts had said they were enthusiastic about the concept, but in the two-week period, they were unable to get any firm commitments. Mr. Rogers himself, however, had agreed to invest $75,000 in the venture.

On further reflection, Paul, Mark, and Eric decided that the deal was attractive to them even if they had to give up a good deal more than the 25 percent which they had projected. The enthusiasm which Mr. Rogers' contacts had expressed convinced them they would be able to raise the money. They decided to proceed.

On January 25, they met with ICEDELIGHTS and indicated that the terms were acceptable, and that they wanted to go ahead with the deal. They agreed that their lawyers would be in touch to draw up the papers.

FINANCING

The following weekend, Paul, Mark, and Eric raced to produce a prospectus. They spent all day Saturday writing the document and hosted a previously planned dinner party Saturday evening for eight friends. At 1 A.M. Sunday morning, after a great dinner, a lot of wine, and a cut-throat game of charades, one guest suggested that they charge over to his office to type the document. A normally staid law firm was transformed as 11 typists pounded out the prospectus until 4:30 in the morning. The document, excerpted in Exhibit 9, presented the concept for the business, and the proposed financing and capital structure.

ment, excerpted in Exhibit 9, presented the concept for the business, and the proposed financing and capital structure.

During the next three weeks, they spoke to friends and associates of Mr. Rogers, presenting their business plan. At the end of three weeks, they had informal "commitments" for 15 units, or $405,000. With Mr. Rogers' $75,000, they had $450,000, and were only $300,000 shy.

During this time, it became clear that they would have to give up more than the original 25 percent they had planned. Not surprisingly perhaps, potential investors were somewhat put off by the 75/25 split in the deal. Paul, Mark, and Eric decided that as long as they were giving up more of the company they could raise a bit more money, and they revised the deal as shown in Exhibit 10.

In the process of determining the original deal, the three thought that investors would primarily be concerned with their overall return—ROI, IRR, NPV, or whatever. But, in fact, their requirements were more complex:

— Short-term repayment of original investment, with significant control during this phase.
— Long-term capital gain with reduction in investor control once original investment repaid.

There were also significant differences in the level of sophistication of potential investors. Some liked the concept, and that was sufficient. For others, a detailed analysis of investors' versus founders' risk and reward was required.

In addition, there were several other issues which remained to be settled, including:

— Form of organization. They had made a preliminary decision to use a straight corporation, but it was possible that a Sub-S or Limited Partnership made more sense.
— Legal counsel. They had decided to use Ernest Brooke, an acquaintance of Mr. Rogers who had indicated an interest in investing. Yet, a few weeks had gone by and he now seemed more hesitant. Further, he did not have any particular expertise in securities or corporate law and had not been particularly helpful.
— The market. Was Florida really a good spot for this business? Throughout, they had attempted to obtain market information on Florida without spending the time and expense on a lengthy trip. The data they had obtained seemed inconclusive.

Throughout this period, the second-year recruiting season was in full swing. Because they were emotionally committed to the ICEDELIGHTS deal, and because it was consuming so much of their time, none of the three was actively pursuing other opportunities. Each of them had the opportunity to return to the firm where they had worked for the summer, as well as one or two other possibilities.

THE DECISION

It was now February 22, and they had gotten a preliminary set of documents to review. The time when they would actually have to sign papers and put down their $75,000 seemed to be drawing near. A meeting was set for March 10 to put the finishing touches on the agreement.

At this point, Mark began having some strong doubts about the advisability of proceeding. He expressed them this way:

> I started getting these funny feelings in the pit of my stomach. I guess it was fear. It seemed to me that we had all gotten very caught up in the enthusiasm of the project, and had not been as hard-nosed about the business decisions as we should have been.
>
> First, we had not even been to Florida. Eric lived there, and was home at Christmas, but we never thoroughly investigated the market. We didn't know if there was competition there, and if there *were* other ice cream shops/cafés, how were they doing? Who knew if old people would be attracted to the rich and different style of ice cream we offered?
>
> Second, I began to question the nature of our agreement and relationship with ICEDELIGHTS. It seemed to me that we were absolutely, critically dependent on them for real estate and product. We didn't have the credibility, contacts, or track record to get the prime real estate that we needed. We were dependent on Bob Andrews for that. Similarly, one of our real competitive advantages was the cost and quality of our product. They were under no legal obligation to supply us, and we had no right to build our own production facility. What happened if they decided to expand their own operation, and couldn't supply us? This gelati is not like hamburger buns—you can't just pick it up anywhere. I thought that our agreements should recognize this dependency and that ICEDELIGHTS should take 25 percent of our company instead of the $200,000 up front. This would give them a real financial incentive to act in our best interests.
>
> Finally, there was my relationship with Paul and Eric. There had been some tension lately. It was obvious that I was more conservative, more risk-averse then they. I was worried about how this might affect our working relationship. I was uncomfortable with the notion that I could be outvoted on a decision and committed to a course of action that I wasn't comfortable with.

At this same time, Mr. Rogers was in Florida and reported that there were a small number of ice cream shop/cafés serving gelati. Further, one of these shops was not doing too well. Obviously, there were a great many of the typical ice cream shops, including Haagen-Dazs, Baskin-Robbins, and several local chains. Still, he felt that there were ample locations to provide for a fast growing business. They also learned that there were two other operations with a similar focus on gelati—Gelateria Italia and Gelato Classico—which were centered in California, but had recently started to franchise.

In preparation for their March 10 meeting, they decided that they would:

1. Go to Florida over spring break to thoroughly investigate the market.
2. Press ICEDELIGHTS to provide further assurances that they would be able to deliver the real estate support and product that they needed.

The issue relative to their attorney was still dragging on. Mark had mentioned his concerns about Ernest Brooke to a friend, John Stors, who was an attorney with a prominent local law firm. John had offered to check with other lawyers in his firm to see if anyone had ever dealt with Brooke. Sure enough, a half-dozen or so lawyers in the office knew Brooke and had dealt with him on tax, real estate, divorce, and estate issues. One mentioned that he had won a case in court over Brooke, a case that Brooke should not have lost. And most damaging of all was the revelation that Brooke was known to be a very close, personal friend of Bob Andrews, ICEDELIGHTS chairman.

Based on this, they decided to use Evan Post and risk alienating Brooke, who seemed willing to invest $30,000 maximum. Post had a reputation as an excellent counsel for small start-ups, as well as good contacts with potential investors. They spoke with Brooke who was quite accommodating, and who agreed that the lure of potential investors was attractive, and a legitimate reason for including Evan Post.

Finally, they had exhausted all of Mr. Rogers' contacts and were still about $400,000 short (some investors' "commitments" had evaporated over the past month). They had a meeting with a newly formed venture capital partnership just prior to their March 10 meeting. The venture capital firm indicated that they were extremely interested, but they would require more ownership in the company for their investment. This firm was a particularly attractive partner because its principals had extensive experience running a Kentucky Fried Chicken franchise.

At the March 10 meeting, ICEDELIGHTS responded to their concerns. First, they agreed that the franchisee would not have to pay the remaining $125,000 until ICEDELIGHTS had furnished them with one suitable location and the lease had been signed. Further, ICEDELIGHTS agreed that the franchisee would have the right to build a production facility if ICEDELIGHTS became unable to supply them with product.

The closing date for the deal was set for March 25; in two weeks they would have to put up their $75,000 and sign the franchise and option agreements.

During this time, they had to decide whether to proceed or not. Three major questions remained:

— Was there real potential for this business in the Florida market?
— Did the option and franchise agreement make good business sense?

— Did the returns justify the risks?

If they did decide to proceed, they had to resolve the remaining financial issues:

— How much of the company could they give up and still have the deal be attractive to them? They had revised the deal as shown in Exhibit 10, but knew that they might have to give up even more of the company.
— Should they go ahead and commit $75,000 under the option agreement before they had the full $825,000 of financing secured, hoping to obtain the remainder before the option was exercised?
— Should they go with less than $825,000 and plan a second offering after the first store was up and running?

Finally, they each had their own personal feelings about the deal.

Mark:

ICEDELIGHTS' concessions did reassure me to a certain extent, but I still have some very uncomfortable feelings.

First, the prospects for the business in Florida are still unclear to me; we haven't been to Florida yet, but I have the sense that we will find *some* attractive locations. But in order to meet our projections and investors expectations, we have to grow extraordinarily quickly.

Second, even if the business does well, we are still critically dependent on ICEDELIGHTS. I think that real estate and product are our two key factors for success, and we really can't control them—they are in ICEDELIGHTS' hands. And if they don't perform, our only remedy is to sue. It really scares me to think that we will have the responsibility for $825,000 of other people's money, but can't control the two most important elements of the business.

Finally, I do question whether we have the skills to really make this work. I think that we have been pretty naive so far, and very much caught up in the excitement of actually doing a deal. Fortunately, it hasn't cost any money and we've learned a lot.

Paul:

The concessions that we won from ICEDELIGHTS reassured me of their continuing commitment to the Florida franchise. We would have preferred giving ICEDELIGHTS a small equity stake in the company, but they were not interested in this proposition.

Like Mark, I am concerned about the market; I do want more than just a "gut feel" that the market is there. This issue is particularly pressing because the closing date of March 25 will come before we have a chance to get to Florida over spring break. We need some concrete research before that.

Money is also still a problem. We have "informal commitments" for about $300,000 of the $825,000 needed; experience has taught us that these are often more "informal" than they are commitments. A venture capital firm has expressed very strong interest in a $400,000 to $500,000 investment, but we've grown skeptical of verbal commitments, and are still looking for other investors.

Both Eric and I have picked up on Mark's concerns and feel that we are dealing with them. I've started to get the impression, though, that Mark is veiling a lot of his more personal concerns about the venture in terms of business risk.

As far as I'm concerned, we've been lucky so far—things have gone very smoothly. Now it is time to start running fast, tying up all the loose ends. I'm exhilarated by the prospect of this, and the thought that we are really right on the verge of finally having our own company.

Eric:

I feel that we really have a great opportunity here. I'm really excited by the idea of creating and managing our own organization. It is a fairly simple business and ICEDELIGHTS has done a great deal to build and standardize the organization. With their systems and support, I am very confident that we can be successful.

I spent Christmas break in Florida, and I believe that the market prospects are very good. The population base is an Eastern, upscale, sophisticated one. The economies of the business are such that we can be profitable even with a small volume. Finally, all of our investors believe that Florida is an attractive market.

I think that ICEDELIGHTS' concessions assured us of the product supply and real estate support that we needed. After we get a few stores up and running, we will have developed a name for ourselves, and won't need their real estate assistance anyway.

I understand Mark's concerns, but there are always going to be risks. In this case, they are manageable, and the return justifies them. There is little to be gained by waiting to start our own business; in a few years the risks will seem even greater. Now we have very little to lose.

I really don't feel that any additional assurances will satisfy Mark's doubts. In fact, I think that Mark would be uncomfortable with *any* deal. His lack of commitment is a real problem at this point, and needs to be cleared up before it becomes a personal business problem for all of us.

EXHIBIT 1
Resumes

PAUL ROGERS

Education

1981–1983
NEW YORK SCHOOL OF BUSINESS
ADMINISTRATION   NEW YORK, NY
Candidate for the degree of Master in Business Administration in June 1983.

1974–1978
HARVARD COLLEGE   CAMBRIDGE, MA
Bachelor of Arts degree in June 1978. Majored in modern European history. Vice president of the Delphic Club; presently serve as graduate treasurer.

Work Experience

Summer 1982
WARBURG PARIBAS BECKER   NEW YORK, NY
Corporate Finance. Summer associate. Worked on the initial public offering of a manufacturer of computer memory devices. Assisted in the preparation of the prospectus, due diligence investigations, and marketing of this successful offering. In addition, performed preliminary debt rating analysis and lease-versus-buy analysis for prospective clients.

Summer 1981
NEWBURY, ROSEN & CO., INC.   BOSTON, MA
Corporate Finance. Wrote the prospectus for a $600,000 private placement for a start-up venture in the electronic test equipment rental industry. Performed industry, competitive, and market analyses.

STATE STREET BANK
AND TRUST COMPANY, INC.   BOSTON, MA
1981
Corporate Finance Department. Senior analyst. Worked with three-person team in structuring private placements and assembling prospectuses. Co-authored prospectus for $10 million private placement to regional retailing chain. Participated in presentations of services to a large high-technology firm.

1980–1981
Corporate Services Department. Senior analyst. Assisted vice president of department in establishing a Eurodollar loan syndication portfolio, in which State Street acted as lead manager and agent. Marketed this service to prospective clients. Made both individual and joint presentations to foreign banks interested in joining syndicates. Managed negotiations among the client, legal counsel, and the banking syndicate for a $10 million revolving loan syndication to a major toy manufacturer. Helped bring to a closing two additional term loan syndications totalling $14 million.

1978–1980
Commercial Credit Training Program. Trainee. Completed the training program in eighteen instead of the stipulated 24 months.

EXHIBIT 1 (*continued*)

1975–1978
HASTY PUDDING THEATRICALS   CAMBRIDGE,MA
Producer of this broadway-like musical comedy show. Selected script, hired
professional director, set designer, music arranger, and costume designer, and
coordinated an 80-person company. Budget for 1978: $110,000. Improved financial
controls and initiated a fund drive.

Personal Background

Raised in Boston. Have lived and traveled extensively abroad. Flexible on relocation.
Fluent in French.

References

Personal references available upon request.

November 1982

MARK DANIELS

Education

1981–1983
NEW YORK SCHOOL OF BUSINESS
ADMINISTRATION   NEW YORK, NEW YORK
Candidate for the degree of Master in Business Administration in June 1983. General
management curriculum. Awarded First-Year Honors. Representative to Admissions
and Financial Aid Advisory Committee.

1975–1979
HARVARD COLLEGE   CAMBRIDGE, MASSACHUSETTS
Awarded Bachelor of Arts, *cum laude*, in Economics, June 1979. Wrote Senior
Honors Thesis on strategic implications of cost and market structure in the
publishing industry. Served as Editor-in-Chief, Harvard Yearbook Publications;
Treasurer, D.U. Club; Class Representative, 1979 Class Committee; Executive
Committee member, Harvard Fund. Elected Trustee of Yearbook.

Business Experience

Summer 1982
MORGAN STANLEY & CO.   NEW YORK, NEW YORK
Worked as a summer associate in corporate finance and mergers and acquisitions
areas. Assisted in the development and implementation of a strategy for divesting a
client's shipping subsidiary. Assisted in the defense of an oil services client engaged in
a hostile takeover.

1979–1981
McKINSEY & COMPANY   NEW YORK, NEW YORK
                                       TOKYO, JAPAN
Functioned as a consultant to top management of McKinsey's clients in the
telecommunications, computer, and office products industries. Assessed the
competitive cost position of a major international manufacturer of
telecommunications products. Managed internal research project on Japanese

EXHIBIT 1 (*continued*)

competition in high technology industries. Transferred to McKinsey's Tokyo office to develop a strategy for a British client seeking to enter the Japanese office products market. Wrote and presented report to Board of Directors in London.

Current Activities

Currently teaching two courses at New York College, serving as business tutor at Kirk House (an undergraduate residence), and working as an admissions counselor at the New York Business School. Specific responsibilities include:

Tutor, New York College Economics Department, teaching "Managerial Economics and Decision Theory."

Teaching Assistant, New York College General Education Department, teaching "Business in American Life."

Nonresident Business Tutor, Kirk House, advising undergraduates on careers and graduate education.

Counsellor, New York Business School Admissions Office, interviewing prospective students.

Personal Background

Enjoy sailing, racquet sports, travel, and photography.

References

Personal references available upon request.

September 1982

ERIC GARFIELD

Education

1981–1983
NEW YORK SCHOOL OF BUSINESS
ADMINISTRATION   NEW YORK, NEW YORK
Candidate for the degree of Master in Business Administration in June 1983.
Pursuing a general management curriculum with emphasis on finance. Awarded COGME Fellowship.

1970–1974
UNIVERSITY OF FLORIDA   GAINESVILLE, FLORIDA
Earned a Bachelor of Science degree in Accounting with additional concentration in Economics. Awarded membership in Beta Alpha Psi and Phi Eta Sigma, two honorary scholastic fraternities.

Business Experience

Summer 1982
McKINSEY & COMPANY, INC.   ATLANTA, GEORGIA
Associate. Analyzed financial performance and product-line profitability, as part of a strategy study, for a major pharmaceutical company. Recommended a new pricing and production strategy. Prepared and presented report to client.

EXHIBIT 1 (*concluded*)

CELANESE CORPORATION   NEW YORK, NEW YORK
1979–1981
International Finance Manager. Supervised the preparation and analysis of strategic
plans and operating budgets. Prepared financial analysis for potential foreign
acquisitions and divestitures. Collaborated in cost reduction project resulting in
annual savings of $5 million.

1978–1979
Financial Analyst. Prepared financial analysis for capital expenditure projects and
for actual monthly results versus budget.

1976–1978
International Auditor. Supervised audit team in performing operational audits.
Developed audit programs for foreign installations.

1975–1976
MINNESOTA MINING AND MANUFACTURING (3M) CARACAS, VENEZUELA
Senior Cost Analyst. Prepared product analysis required by the Venezuelan
government for the introduction of new products. Analysis included marketing,
production and financial data.

1974–1975
PRICE WATERHOUSE & CO.   MIAMI, FLORIDA
Staff Auditor. Performed financial audits of manufacturing and service
organizations.

Personal Background

Fluent in English and Spanish. Enjoy participative sports, reading historical novels
and international travel.

References

Personal references available upon request.

September 1982

EXHIBIT 2
Specifications Sheet

Dear:

We are currently second-year students at the New York School of Business and are
interested in acquiring a company. We have the skills and abilities necessary to successfully
manage a going concern and to create value for our backers and ourselves.

As explained in the attached specification sheet, we seek to acquire a medium-size
firm. We feel our skills are applicable to a broad range of industries—from general industrial
to consumer goods.

As the accompanying resumes indicate, the three of us have varied and
complementary skills. We have backgrounds in planning, finance, control, operations, and
general management. We believe that our abilities, combined with hard work and intense
commitment, will enable us to succeed in such a venture.

We would greatly appreciate the opportunity to discuss our ideas with you and would
be grateful for any suggestions you might have.

Sincerely,

EXHIBIT 2 (*concluded*)

SPECIFICATIONS

GENERAL: Established manufacturing firms engaged in the production of Industrial and/or Consumer Goods.

SALES VOLUME: $5,000,000 – $10,000,000.

LOCATION: Preferably, but not exclusively, Northeast.

PRODUCT: Basic product with established market.

EXAMPLES: Include, but are not limited to the following:
Industrial equipment
Food packaging and processing
Control systems and equipment
Electronic equipment
Plastic molding
Construction equipment
Oil field machinery
Sporting and athletic goods
Precision instruments

EXHIBIT 3
Field Study Proposal

Outline of Proposed Field Study

STEP I. Understand Existing Operations in New England, including: products, manufacturing, distribution, retail location strategy, advertising/merchandising strategy, cost structure, customer profile, management structure and systems, and personnel requirements.

STEP II. Evaluate Implications for Franchise, including: potential profitability and growth, competition, cost impact, tailoring of concept, relations with franchisor, key risks, and financial requirements.

STEP III. Evaluate and Structure Deal, including: management structure and responsibilities, form of organization, and legal/tax aspects.

STEP IV. Prepare Business Plan, including: introduction, company description, risk factors, products, market, competition, marketing program, management, manufacturing, facilities, capital required and use of proceeds, and financial data and financial forecasts.

EXHIBIT 4
Food Franchises—Terms

	Franchise Fee per Location ($000)	Royalty (% Sales)
ICEDELIGHTS	20	5
Gelateria Italia	15	0
Gelato Classico	30	0
Baskin-Robbins	0	0
Carvel	20	Varies
Swensen's	20	5.5
Haagen-Dazs	20	$0.60/gallon
Long John Silver Seafood	10	4
H. Salt Fish & Chips	10	Varies
Kentucky Fried Chicken	10	4
Church's Fried Chicken	15	4
McDonald's	12.5	11.5
Wendy's	15	4
Burger King	40	3.5
Burger Chef	10	4
Taco Bell	45	5
Domino's Pizza	10	5.5
Pizza Inn	15	4
Shakey's Pizza	15	4.5
Orange Julius	18	6

EXHIBIT 5
Population Growth and Income Levels in Florida

City	1980 Population (000)	1970–1980 Growth (percent)	1979 Median Family Income
Boston*	563	(12.0%)	$14,3l8
Jacksonville	540	7.1	17,646
Miami	346	3.6	13,384
Tampa	271	7.2	15,412
St. Petersburg	238	10.2	15,476
Ft. Lauderdale	153	l0.1	19,275
Hialeah	145	42.2	17,070
Orlando	128	29.3	16,312
Hollywood	121	l4.2	19,890
Clearwater	85	63.5	18,528
Gainesville	81	26.6	17,425
Largo	58	141.7	16,252
Pompano	52	36.6	20,447
Boca Raton	49	75.0	26,910
Sarasota	49	20.0	16,661

*For reference only.

EXHIBIT 6
Financials

Pro Forma Income Statement: Store Level

Sales		$550,000
Fixed costs:		
Rent (1,000 to 12,000 square feet)	$ 25,000	
Management salaries	30,000	
Variable costs:		
Cost of product	192,500	
Payroll	52,500	
Royalty to parent (5%)	27,500	
Shipping	16,500	
Advertising	5,500	
Other	11,000	
Rent override*	13,500	
Total costs		374,000
Pretax store contribution		$176,000

Capital Requirements per Store

Construction, leasehold improvements	$ 60,000
Equipment costs	85,000
Fees and miscellaneous expenses, capitalized	15,000
Total	$160,000

*A "percent-of-sales" bonus to the landlord after a base sales level is reached.

EXHIBIT 7
Section 385 of Tax Code and Accompanying Explanation

Law

Treatment of Certain Interests in Corporations as Stock or Indebtedness.

(a) *Authority to Prescribe Regulations.* The Secretary is authorized to prescribe such regulations as may be necessary or appropriate to determine whether an interest in a corporation is to be treated for purposes of this title as stock or indebtedness.

(b) *Factors.* The regulations prescribed under this section shall set forth factors which are to be taken into account in determining with respect to a particular factual situation whether a debtor-creditor relationship exists or a corporation-shareholder relationship exists. The factors set forth in the regulations may include among other factors:

(1) Whether there is a written unconditional promise to pay on demand or on a specified date a sum certain in money in return for an adequate consideration in money or money's worth, and to pay a fixed rate of interest.

(2) Whether there is subordination to, or preference over, any indebtedness of the corporation.

EXHIBIT 7 *(concluded)*

(3) The ratio of debt to equity of the corporation.
(4) Whether there is conversibility into the stock of the corporation.
(5) The relationship between holdings of stock in the corporation and holdings of interest in question.

Explanation

The distinction between debt and equity is an important one, because of the different tax treatment accorded to each. Interest paid on debt is deductible, while dividends distributed on stock are not. Similarly, the repayment of principal is tax free.

In brief, in order to be classified as debt, a security must meet certain tests.

Essentially, the two key factors are:

— Proportionality: If debt is *not* held in proportion to equity, then the security will usually be treated as debt. If, however, the debt securities *are* held in proportion to equity, then the debt may be classified as equity if "debt is excessive."

— Excessive debt: debt is typically *not* excessive if:
 • The outside debt/equity ratio is less than 10:1. The outside ratio includes *all* creditors.
 • The inside debt/equity ratio is less than 3:1. The inside ratio excludes debts to independent creditors.

However, even if debt is excessive by these tests, it still may not be excessive if the corporation pays a reasonable rate of interest on the debt, and the financial structure would be acceptable to a bank or similar lender.

Source: Reproduced with permission of the publisher from P-H *Federal Taxes.* Copyright 1983 by Prentice-Hall, Inc., Englewood Cliffs, N.J. 07632.

EXHIBIT 8
Preliminary Pro Forma Cash Flow Statement (in thousands of dollars)

	Year 1	Year 2	Year 3	Year 4	Year 5	Year 6	Year 7	Year 8	Year 9	Year 10
Number stores, total	2	6	10	15	20	20	20	20	20	20
New stores	2	4	4	5	5	—	—	—	—	—
Existing stores	0	2	6	10	15	20	20	20	20	20
Sales	800	2,600	4,600	7,000	9,500	10,000	10,000	10,000	10,000	10,000
Operating income	130	470	390	1,375	1,900	2,100	2,100	2,100	2,100	2,100
Store opening expenses	100	200	200	250	250	—	—	—	—	—
Franchise fees	40	80	80	95	75	—	—	—	—	—
Corporation overhead	115	205	425	575	725	800	800	800	800	800
Income	(125)	(15)	185	455	850	1,300	1,300	1,300	1,300	1,300
Tax	(60)	(7)	35	200	380	580	580	580	580	580
AT income	(65)	(8)	150	255	470	720	720	720	720	720
– Store investment	250	500	500	625	625	—	—	—	—	—
– Corporation investment	10	20	50	50	50	—	—	—	—	—
+ Depreciation	40	120	200	300	400	400	400	400	400	400
+ Franchise fees (prepaid)	40	80	80	—	—	—	—	—	—	—
Cash + or –	(180)	(320)	(270)	(375)	(175)	400	400	400	400	400
Total cash + or –	(305)	(335)	(120)	(120)	295	1,120	1,120	1,120	1,120	1,120
Cumulative cash + or –	(305)	(640)	(760)	(880)	(585)	535	1,655	2,775	3,895	5,015

EXHIBIT 9
Excerpts from Prospectus

THE OFFERING
Terms of the Offering

The Company is offering 25 Investment Units. Each Unit consists of 100 shares of its Class A Common Stock (zero par value), offered for $2,000 and $25,000 of the Company's Debentures.

	Per Unit	Total
Equity	$ 2,000	$ 50,000
Debentures	25,000	625,000
Total	$27,000	$675,000

All subscriptions shall be for at least one full unit. The Company currently plans to call for each subscription according to the following schedule:

Approximate Timing	Amount per Unit	Description
Immediately	$ 2,000	Equity
July 1 - September 1, 1983	$15,000	Debentures
January 1 - March 1, 1984	$10,000	Debentures

The Company reserves the right to accelerate or delay the timing of these contributions as its business requires, and will give investors thirty (30) days written notice of such requirements. Investors who are unable to meet subsequent contribution requirements will forfeit their contributions to date unless a suitable substitute can be found by the investor.
THE SECURITIES OFFERED HEREBY ARE NOT REGISTERED UNDER THE SECURITIES ACT OF 1933, AS AMENDED AND MAY NOT BE SOLD, TRANSFERRED, HYPOTHECATED OR OTHERWISE DISPOSED OF BY AN INVESTOR UNLESS SO REGISTERED OR, IN THE OPINION OF COUNSEL FOR THE COMPANY, REGISTRATION IS NOT REQUIRED UNDER SAID ACT.

Capitalization

The capitalization of the Company as of the conclusion of the Offering, assuming all units are sold, will be as follows:

Debt	$675,000
Equity	$ 75,000

EXHIBIT 9 (*continued*)

This capital consists of the $675,000 raised from the Offering *plus* $75,000 contributed by the Founders.

The Founders will purchase 7,500 shares of the Company's Class B Common Stock for $25,000, and will also contribute $50,000 in debt.

The resulting capitalization is detailed below:

Debt		
Investors	$625,000	
Founders	50,000	
		$675,000
Equity		
Investors	$ 50,000	
Founders	25,000	
		$ 75,000
Total capital		$750,000

Description of Shares and Debentures

The investment units each consist of 100 shares of the Company's Class A Common Stock (zero par value) representing 1 percent of the total outstanding Common Shares of the Company. In total, the Class A stockholders will have representation on the Board of Directors equal to 50 percent of the total number of directors. When the Debentures have been repaid in full, the Class A board representation will be reduced to a pro rata share.

The Founders' Class B stock will be restricted as to dividends until the Debentures have been repaid in full.

The Debentures will be issued with a face value of $5,000 each, and will pay interest at 15 percent per annum, cumulative with the first payment deferred until the end of Year 2. Interest payments will be made annually. The Debentures will have a maturity of five (5) years, and will be callable.

Use of Proceeds

The amount to be received by the Company from the sale of the Investment Units offered herein is $675,000. The Company intends to use these funds, in addition to the $75,000 contributed by the Founders, for the following purposes:

Development rights for the state of Florida	$100,000
Prepaid franchise rights for the first five stores	$100,000
Capital for three ICEDELIGHTS stores	$480,000
Working capital	$ 70,000
	$750,000

EXHIBIT 9 (*continued*)

Dividends

The Company plans to pay no dividends for a period of five (5) years, and until such time as the Debentures have been paid in full. Following this five-year period, the Company does have the intention of distributing dividends to its investors. No assurance can be made, however, that the Company will, in fact, be able to pay such dividends. Such payment is a matter to be determined from time to time by the Board of Directors and, of necessity, will be based upon the then existing earnings and cash position of the Company, as well as other related matters.

Reports to Stockholders

The Company will furnish its shareholders audited financial statements on an annual basis as well as unaudited quarterly reports of operations and financial condition.

Financial Projections

Following a period of identifying suitable real estate, negotiating loans, and equipping locations, the Company anticipates commencing retail operations no later than early 1984. Ten-year financial projections (attached) are based on the following assumptions.

Store Openings

The Company anticipates opening stores according to the following schedule:*

	Year									
	1	2	3	4	5	6	7	8	9	10
Number of stores opened	3	4	5	5	5	2	2	2	1	1
Cumulative number of stores in operation	3	7	12	17	22	24	26	28	29	30

Sales Level and Growth

Based on its knowledge of sales volumes in existing ICEDELIGHTS locations, and its knowledge of the Florida market, the Company estimates $550,000 in base-level sales. This base level for new stores inflates at the rate of 5 percent per year. Store-level sales grow as follows:

---

*The decline in the rate of openings after Year 5 reflects the Company's desire to show 10-year financial projections, and does not serve to indicate the Company's estimate of the total potential of the Florida market.

EXHIBIT 9 (*continued*)

Year	Total Rate of Growth	Real Growth	Inflation
1	15%	10%	5%
2-10	13%	8%	5%

Capital Requirements

Based on its knowledge of existing ICEDELIGHTS locations, the Company estimates a cost per store of $160,000. This breaks down as follows:

Construction costs	$60,000
Equipment costs	85,000
Fees and miscellaneous expenses	15,000
Total capital costs	$160,000

The capital costs are depreciated or expensed as follows:

a. Construction costs over 10 years, the assumed life of a lease.
b. Equipment costs over five years.
c. Architectural fees and other expenses are expensed in the year incurred.

Store Expenses

The Company estimates store level operating expenses as follows (as a percentage of sales):

Cost of product (including packaging)	35%
Payroll	15
Rent (1,000 to 1,200 square feet required)	7
Royalty	5
Shipping	3
Advertising	1
Other (telephone, cleaning, etc.)	2
Total expenses...	68%

Amortization

The $100,000 development rights are amortized over the 20-year life of the agreement.
THE ATTACHED PROJECTIONS REPRESENT OUR ASSESSMENT OF THE POTENTIAL FOR THE FLORIDA MARKET. THESE ESTIMATES ARE BASED ON DISCUSSIONS WITH MANAGEMENT AND OUR OWN INVESTIGATION OF THE EXISTING OPERATION. WE BELIEVE TRHAT THESE FIGURES ARE REPRESENTATIVE OF CURRENT OPERATIONS AND DO FAIRLY REFLECT THE LEVEL OF OPERATIONS ANTICIPATED IN FLORIDA. NONETHELESS, THEY ARE ONLY PROJECTIONS, AND MUST BE VIEWED AS SUCH.

EXHIBIT 9 (continued)
Projected Income Statement (in thousands of dollars)

					Year					
	1	2	3	4	5	6	7	8	9	10
Net Sales	$962	$3,340	$6,617	$10,815	$15,719	$20,392	$24,580	$29,386	$34,482	$39,839
Store level expenses:										
Variables	654	2,271	4,500	7,354	10,689	13,867	16,714	19,982	23,448	27,091
Fixed	53	174	330	521	730	900	1,025	1,160	1,784	1,398
Depreciation	69	165	295	430	575	585	574	545	480	415
Operating income	186	730	1,492	2,510	3,725	5,040	6,267	7,699	8,770	10,935
Start-up expenses	103	140	180	173	162	67	69	71	36	37
Corporate overhead	105	215	415	580	680	810	906	1,017	1,110	1,203
Amortization	5	5	5	5	5	5	5	5	5	5
Earnings before interest and taxes	(27)	370	892	1,752	2,878	4,158	5,287	6,606	7,619	9,690
Interest expense:										
Investor	0	216	101	101	75	0	0	0	0	0
Bank		15	15	15	0	0	0	0	0	0
Profit before taxes	(27)	139	776	1,636	2,803	4,158	5,287	6,606	7,619	9,690
Taxes	0	52	357	753	1,289	1,913	2,432	3,039	3,505	4,457
Net income	(27)	87	419	883	1,514	2,245	2,855	3,567	4,114	5,233

EXHIBIT 9 (*continued*)
Projected Balance Sheet (*in thousands of dollars*)

					Year					
	1	2	3	4	5	6	7	8	9	10
Assets										
Cash	$320	$105	$ 24	$ 225	$ 936	$3,400	$6,445	$10,153	$14,537	$19,964
Prepaid fee	40	0	0	0	0	0	0	0	0	0
Development agreement	95	90	85	80	75	70	65	60	55	50
Net fixed assets	268	715	1,220	1,632	1,940	1,726	1,541	1,405	1,140	951
Total assets	$723	$910	$1,329	$1,937	$2,951	$5,196	$8,051	$11,618	$15,732	$20,965
Liabilities										
Bank debt	0	100	100	0	0	0	0	0	0	0
Investor debt	675	675	675	500	0	0	0	0	0	0
Total liabilities	675	775	775	500	0	0	0	0	0	0
Equity										
Paid-in capital	75	75	75	75	75	75	75	75	75	75
Retained earnings	(27)	60	479	1,362	2,876	5,121	7,976	11,543	15,657	20,890
Total equity	48	135	554	1,437	2,951	5,196	8,051	11,618	15,732	20,965
Total liabilities & equity	$723	$910	$1,329	$1,937	$2,951	$5,196	$8,051	$11,618	$15,732	$20,965

EXHIBIT 9 (*continued*)
Projected Cash Flow (*in thousands of dollars*)

					Year					
	1	2	3	4	5	6	7	8	9	10
Net income	($27)	$ 87	$419	$ 883	$1,514	$2,245	$2,855	$ 3,567	$ 4,114	$ 5,233
Depreciation	69	165	295	430	575	585	575	545	480	415
Amortization	5	5	5	5	5	5	5	5	5	5
Prepaid expense	60	40	0	0	0	0	0	0	0	0
Cash from operations	107	297	719	1,318	2,094	2,835	3,434	4,117	4,599	5,653
Capital expenditures:										
Development agreement	100	—	—	—	—	—	—	—	—	—
Prepaid Fees	100	—	—	—	—	—	—	—	—	—
Store construction and equipment	337	612	800	842	883	371	389	409	215	226
Cash generated: surplus/(deficit)	(430)	(315)	(81)	476	1,211	2,464	3,045	3,708	4,384	5,427
Financing:										
Equity	75	0	0	0	0	0	0	0	0	0
Debentures	675	0	0	(175)	(500)	0	0	0	0	0
Bank debt	0	100	0	(100)	0	0	0	0	0	0
Net cash flow	320	(215)	(81)	201	711	2,464	3,045	3,708	4,384	5,427
Beginning cash	0	320	105	24	225	936	3,400	6,445	10,153	14,537
Ending cash	$320	$105	$ 24	$ 225	$ 936	$3,400	$6,445	$10,153	$14,537	$19,964

EXHIBIT 9 (*concluded*)

Cash Flow and Internal Rate of Return to One Unit Shareholder (*in thousands of dollars*)

						Year					
	0	1	2	3	4	5	6	7	8	9	10
Investment	$27	—	—	—	—	—	—	—	—	—	—
Interest	—	—	$8	$4	$4	$ 3	—	—	—	—	—
Return of principal	—	—	—	—	$4	$21	—	—	—	—	—
Share of cash flow (1%)	—	—	—	—	—	—	$25	$30	$37	$44	$ 54
Share of estimated market value at 10 times earnings*	—	—	—	—	—	—	—	—	—	—	$523
Net cash flow to investor	($27)	—	$8	$4	$8	$24	$25	$30	$37	$44	$577

Annualized internal rate of return = 49%

*For illustrative purposes only.

EXHIBIT 10
Summary of Changes to the Offering

The Offering

The Company is offering 25 investment units. Each unit consists of 150 shares of its Class A Common Stock (no par value), offered for $5,000 and $25,000 of the Company's debentures.

	Per Unit	Total
Equity	$ 5,000	$125,000
Debentures	25,000	625,000
Total	$30,000	$750,000

All subscriptions shall be for at least one full unit. The Company currently plans to call for each subscription according to the following schedule:

Approximate Timing	Amount Per Unit	Description
Immediately	$ 2,500	Equity
July 1-September 1, 1983	17,500	Equity and 3 debentures
January 1-March 1, 1984	10,000	2 debentures

The Company reserves the right to accelerate or delay the timing of these contributions as its business requires, and will give investors thirty (30) days written notice of such requirements. Investors who are unable to meet subsequent contribution requirements will forfeit their contributions to date, unless a suitable substitute can be found by the investor.

The securities offered herein are not registered under the Securities Act of 1933, as amended and may not be sold, transferred, hypothecated or otherwise disposed of by an investor unless so registered or, in the opinion of counsel for the Company, registration is not required under said Act.

Capitalization

The capitalization of the Company, as of the conclusion of the offering, assuming all units are sold, will be as follows:

Debt	$675,000
Equity	$150,000
Total	$825,000

The capital consists of $750,000 raised by the offering plus $75,000 contributed by the founders.

The founders will purchase 6,250 shares of the Company's Class B Common Stock for $25,000 and will also contribute $50,000 in debt.

EXHIBIT 10 (*concluded*)
Revised Cash Flow and Internal Rate of Return to One Unit Shareholder (*in thousands of dollars*)

	Year										
	0	1	2	3	4	5	6	7	8	9	10
Investment	$30	—	—	—	—	—	—	—	—	—	—
Interest	—	—	$5	$3	$3	$ 3	—	—	—	—	—
Return of principal	—	—	—	—	$5	$20	—	—	—	—	—
Share of cash flow (1½%)	—	—	—	—	—	—	$37	$46	$56	$66	$ 82
Share of estimated market value at 10 times earnings*	—	—	—	—	—	—	—	—	—	—	$785
Net cash flow to investor	($30)	—	$5	$3	$8	$23	$37	$46	$56	$66	$867

Annualized internal rate of return = 52%

*For illustrative purposes only.

Part Two

EVALUATING OPPORTUNITY AND DEVELOPING THE BUSINESS CONCEPT

In this part of the book, we look at the first two fundamental issues which the entrepreneur must address:

— Is this a good opportunity?
— What business strategy will most fully exploit the opportunity?

WHAT IS AN OPPORTUNITY?

One of the entrepreneur's most important tasks is to identify opportunities. The capacity creatively to seek out opportunity is the starting point of entrepreneurship for both the individual and the firm.

In order to qualify as a good opportunity, the situation must meet two conditions:

1. It must represent a future state which is desirable.
2. It must be achievable.

Obviously, this issue cannot be addressed in isolation. It is difficult to understand how attractive an opportunity is until one has developed an idea of what the business strategy will be, what resources will be required to pursue the opportunity, how much those resources will cost, and finally, how much value will be left over for the entrepreneur. Nonetheless, the step of evaluating the opportunity is the starting point for this thought process.

Chapter 3, "Valuation Techniques," looks at some of the quantitative techniques for assessing the financial value of a business opportunity. It is important to remember, though, that there may be significant nonfinancial value in an opportunity which these techniques cannot measure. Some opportunities, for example, may not be worth much but may open doors to other opportunities which may have considerable value. For some entrepreneurs, the opportunity to work on an interesting idea, with good people, and to be one's own boss compensates for what may be only a mediocre opportunity in a financial sense.

Chapter 4, "Techniques of Purchasing a Company," explores some important factors the entrepreneur must consider when purchasing a business; these include legal and tax issues, as well as various methods of structuring the transaction.

DEVELOPING THE BUSINESS CONCEPT

Once an opportunity is identified, the entrepreneur must develop a business concept and strategy to exploit that opportunity. Often, this strategy will proximately determine the success or failure of a business, even if the entrepreneur has identified a wonderful opportunity.

Federal Express, for instance, decided to serve the same market that Emery Air Freight was serving. But Federal chose a much different strategy: a high fixed-cost hub system which was critically dependent upon volume. Federal Express' strategy has allowed it to operate at lower costs, and thus to surpass Emery in the express delivery market.

To maximize the odds of its success, a new venture should offer products or services which can profitably meet the needs of the markets it attempts to serve. But a new venture has an important advantage over an existing business. It can be created specifically to respond to market needs. Too often existing firms spend enormous resources searching for a market for the products or services produced by their operating assets.

Chapter 5, "The Legal Forms of Organization," should help the entrepreneur to configure his or her venture in the manner most conducive to the accomplishment of stated objectives. This chapter describes the tax, control, liability, and other aspects of various legal forms of organization.

THE CASES

Tru-Paint and Commercial Fixtures both deal with the issue of assessing and valuing an opportunity. These cases point out the difficulty of trying to evaluate an opportunity in a vacuum; clearly, these businesses are attractive at *some* price. But, what exactly is that price? On what does it depend? And how does one ensure that the price to be paid is less than the *value* of the business? If the entrepreneur pays exactly what the business is worth, s/he has not created any value.

Duncan Field looks at the more complex situation in which an entrepreneur must make a decision as to a bid on a business, while having very little information in hand. How should he arrive at a value if he decides to proceed?

Wilson Cabinet Co. addresses the issue of the most appropriate legal form of organization, and explores the circumstances under which one form is preferable to another.

Electrodec is a case which centers around students who have done an exhaustive evaluation of a market opportunity. They must now develop a business strategy for exploiting the opportunity. What is the target market segment? How should the product be priced? Sold? Where should the business be located? How much financing will be required to exploit the opportunity?

Chapter 3

VALUATION TECHNIQUES

One of the entrepreneur's critical tasks is determining value. This is important not only for the individual about to purchase a company, but also for the entrepreneur who is starting a firm and is attempting to estimate the value the business may have in the future. Finally, understanding value is a key step for the entrepreneur about to harvest a venture, either through sale or taking the business public.

Financial theorists have developed many techniques which can be used to evaluate a going concern. Of course, for a large public company, one could simply take the market value of the equity. For a going concern with a long history of audited financials, earnings and cash flow projections are possible. But the valuation of a small, privately held business is difficult and uncertain at best.

This note will briefly outline some of the more widely used valuation approaches, including:

— Asset valuations.
— Earnings valuations.
— Cash flow valuations.

ASSET VALUATIONS

One approach to valuation is to look at the underlying worth of the assets of the business. Asset valuation is one measure of the investor's exposure to risk. If within the company there are assets whose market value approximates the price of the company plus its liabilities, the immediate downside risk is low. In some instances an increase in the value of the assets of a company may represent a major portion of the investor's anticipated return. The various approaches to asset valuation are discussed below.

Book Value

The most obvious asset value that a prospective purchaser can examine is the book value. In a situation with many variables and unknowns it provides a tangible starting point. However, it must be remembered that it is only a starting point. The accounting practices of the company as well as other things can have a significant effect on the firm's book value. For example, if the reserve for losses on accounts receivable is too low for the business it will inflate book value and vice versa. Similarly, treatment of asset accounts such as research and development costs, patents, and organization expense can vary widely. Nevertheless, the book value of a firm provides a point of departure when considering asset valuation.

Adjusted Book Value

An obvious refinement of stated book value is to adjust for large discrepancies between the stated book and actual market value of tangible assets, such as buildings and equipment which have been depreciated far below their market value, or land which has substantially appreciated above its book value which stands at the original cost. An adjustment would probably also reduce the book value of intangible assets to zero unless they, like the tangible assets, also have a market value. The figure resulting from these adjustments should more accurately represent the value of the company's assets.

Liquidation Value

One step beyond adjusted book value is to consider the net cash amount which could be realized if the assets of the company were disposed of in a "quick sale" and all liabilities of the company were paid off or otherwise settled. This value would take into account that many assets, especially inventory and real estate, would not realize as much as they would were the company to continue as a going concern or were the sale made more deliberately. Also, calculation of a liquidation value would make allowances for the various costs of carrying out a liquidation sale.

The liquidation value, it should be noted, is only an indication of what might be realized if the firm were liquidated immediately. Should the company continue its operations and encounter difficulties, most likely a subsequent liquidation would yield significantly less than the liquidation value calculated for the company in its current condition.

The liquidation value of a company is not usually of importance to a buyer who is interested in the maintenance of a going concern. One would assume, however, that the liquidation value would represent some kind of a floor below which the seller would be unwilling to sell because he should be able to liquidate the company himself.

Replacement Value

The current cost of reproducing the tangible assets of a business can at times be significant in that starting a new company may be an alternative means of getting into the business. It sometimes happens that the market value for existing facilities is considerably less than the cost of building a plant and purchasing equivalent equipment from other sources. In most instances, however, this calculation is used more as a reference point than as a seriously considered possibility.

EARNINGS VALUATIONS

A second common approach to an investor's valuation of a company is to capitalize earnings. This involves multiplying an earnings figure by a capitalization factor or price earnings ratio. Of course, this raises two questions: (1) Which earnings? and (2) What factor?

Earnings Figure

One can use three basic kinds of earnings:

— Historical Earnings: The logic behind looking at historical earnings is that they can be used to reflect the company's future performance; there is no logic in evaluating a company on the basis of what it has earned in the past. As will be discussed below, however, historical earnings should be given careful consideration in their use as a guide to the future. They should provide concrete realism to what otherwise would be just a best guess.

Historical earnings per se can rarely be used directly, and an extrapolation of these figures to obtain a picture of the future must be considered a rough, and frequently a poor, approximation. To gain the benefit from the information in a company's financial history of past operations, it is necessary to study each of the cost and income elements, their interrelationships, and their trends.

In pursuit of this study it is essential that random and nonrecurring items be factored out. Expenses should be reviewed to determine that they are normal and do not contain extraordinary expenses or omit some of the unusual expenses of operations. For example, inordinately low maintenance and repair charges over a period of years may mean that extraordinary expenses will be incurred in the future for deferred maintenance. Similarly, nonrecurring "windfall" sales will distort the normal picture.

In a small, closely held company, particular attention should be given to the salaries of owner-managers and members of their families. If these salaries have been unreasonably high or low in light of the nature and size of the business and the duties performed, adjustment of the earnings is required. An assessment should also be made of the depreciation rates to determine their validity and to estimate the need for any earnings adjustments for the future. The amount of federal and state income taxes paid in the past may influence future earnings because of carryover and carryback provisions in the tax laws.

— Future Earnings under Present Ownership: How much and in what ways income and costs are calculated for future operations depends to a large degree upon the operating policies and strategies of management. The existing or future owners' approach will be influenced by a host of factors: management ability, economic and noneconomic objectives, and so on. In calculating future earnings for a company these kinds of things must be considered and weighed.

A calculation of value based upon the future earnings of the company should provide an indication of the current economic value of the company to the current owner. To an investor, including the present owner as an investor, this figure should provide an economic basis for that individual's continued activity and investment in the company. (As we shall discuss later, there is usually more to a potential seller's position than just an economic analysis of his/her own future as an investor.) To an investor who anticipates a change in management with his investment, a calculation of value based upon earnings from the current owner's continuing with the company is *not* a meaningful assessment of the value of the company to the investor.

— Future Earnings under New Ownership: These are the earnings figures which are relevant to the investor who is investing in the turnaround of a dying company or in the reinvigoration of a stagnant one. The basis for the figures—the assumptions, relationships between costs and income, and so on—will probably show significant variance from the company's past performance. Plans may be to change substantially the nature of the business. The evaluation and investment decision may also involve large capital investments in addition to the purchase price of the company.

It is the future earnings of the new operation of the business which are helpful in determining the value of the company to the entrepreneur as these are the earnings which will influence the economic return. Most likely these kinds of projections will have large elements of uncertainty, and one may find it helpful to consider the high, low, and most likely outcomes for financial performance.

In addition to deciding on an earnings period upon which to focus, there is also the issue of "what earnings?" That is, profit before tax, profit after tax, operating income, or earnings before interest and taxes (EBIT). Most valuations look at earnings after tax (but before extraordinary items). Of course, the most important rule is to be consistent: don't base a multiple on earnings after tax, and then apply that multiple to EBIT. Beyond this, the most important factor to consider is precisely what you are trying to measure in your valuation. A strong argument can be made for using EBIT. This measures the earning power and value of the basic, underlying business, *without the effects of financing.* This is a particularly valuable approach if the entrepreneur is contemplating using a different financial structure for the business in the future.

Price-Earnings Multiple

Next, we have the issue of what multiple to use. Assuming that the investor's primary return is anticipated to result from sale of the stock at some future date, the investor should then ask the question: Given the anticipated pattern of earnings of this company, the nature of the industry, the likely state of the stock market, and so on, what will the public or some acquisitive conglomerate be willing to pay me for my holdings? In terms of some multiple of earnings, what prices are paid for stock with similar records and histories? To estimate with any degree of confidence the future multiple of a small company is indeed a difficult task. In many instances working with a range of values might be more helpful. This great uncertainty for a potential investor in estimating both a small company's future earnings *and* future market conditions for the stock of that company in part explains why his return on investment requirements for a new venture investment are so high.

Again, it is important to remember to be consistent: Always derive the multiple as a function of the same base you wish to apply it to; profit after tax, EBIT, or whatever.

Up until this point, we have been discussing methods of arriving at a value for the business as a whole. While the entrepreneur is naturally concerned with this issue, s/he is also concerned with the valuation of his/her piece of the business.

Residual pricing is a technique which addresses this issue. Essentially, residual pricing involves:

— Determining the future value of a company in Year *n* through one of the methods described above.
— Applying a target rate of return to the amount of money raised via the initial sale of equity.
— Using this information to develop a point of view on how much equity the entrepreneur must give up in order to get the equity financing required.
— The "residual," or remaining equity, can be retained by the entrepreneur as his return.

For example, if a company is projected to have earnings of $100,000 in Year 5, and if (after some analysis) it seems that the appropriate P/E for the company is 10, then we can assume that the company will be worth $1,000,000 in Year 5. Now if we know that the entrepreneur needs to raise $50,000 from a venture capital firm (in equity) to start the business, and if the venture firm requires a 50 percent annual return on that money then that $50,000 needs to be worth $50,000 × (1 + 50 percent)^5 = $380,000. So in theory at least, the entrepreneur would have to give 38 percent of the equity to the venture firm in order to raise this money.

CASH FLOW VALUATIONS

Traditional approaches to evaluating a company have placed the principal emphasis upon *earnings*. Assuming that the company will continue in operation, the earnings method posits that a company is worth what it can be expected to earn.

But this approach is only partially useful for the individual entrepreneur who is trying to decide whether or not to invest in a business. Again, the entrepreneur must distinguish between the value of the business as a whole and the portion of that value which can be appropriated for himself or herself. The entrepreneur must address the need to acquire resources from others, and must understand that he or she will have to give up a portion of the value of the business in order to attract these resources. In addition to personal or subjective reasons for buying a business, the entrepreneur's chief criterion for appraisal will be return on investment. Because an entrepreneur's dollar investment is sometimes very small, it may be useful to think of return more as a return on his or her *time*, than a return on his or her dollar investment. To calculate the latter return, the entrepreneur must calculate his or her *individual* prospective cash flow from the business. It is the entrepreneur's return *from* the business, rather than the return inherent in the business itself, which is important. As we shall see, there are several different types of cash flow which can accrue to the entrepreneur.

Operating Cash Flows

Cash or value which flows out of the business during its operations include:

— Perquisites: Perquisites are not literally cash at all, but can be considered cash equivalents in terms of their direct benefits. Business-related expenses charged to the company (e.g., company car and country club memberships) are received by the individual and are *not taxed* at either the corporate or personal level. Their disadvantage is that they are limited in absolute dollar terms.
— Return of Capital via Debt Repayment: This class of cash flow is a *tax-free* event at both the corporate and personal level. An additional advantage to this type of flow is that it can occur while enabling the entrepreneur still to maintain a continuous equity interest in the company. Its disadvantage is, of course, that it requires him/her to make the original investment.
— Interest and Salary: Both of these items constitute personal income and are taxed as such at the personal level. However, no tax is imposed at the corporate level.
— Dividends: As a means of getting cash from a venture, dividends are the least desirable as the resulting cash flow has undergone the greatest net shrinkage. Dividends incur taxes first at the corporate level (at the 22 percent or 48 percent rate as income accrues to the corporation) and then again at the personal level (at the personal income tax rate as the dividend payment accrues to the individual). At the maximum corporate income tax rate of 48 percent and the maximum personal income tax rate of 50 percent, we can see that this devastating double taxation can reduce $1 of pretax corporate profit to $.24 aftertax cash flow to the individual.

Terminal Value

Another source of cash is the money the entrepreneur pulls out of the business when the venture is harvested. Again, there are several elements to this aspect of return.

— Return of Capital via Sale: If the owner/manager sells all or part of the business, the amount he receives up to the amount of his cost basis is a *tax-free* event at both the corporate and personal level. Since a sale of his or her interest is involved, however, it is evident that unlike a return of capital via debt repayment, the owner/manager does not maintain his or her continuous equity interest in the concern. Also, like a

cash flow based on debt retirement, an original investment is necessary.
— Capital Gain via Sale: When capital gains are realized in addition to the return of capital, no tax is imposed at the corporate level, and the tax rate at the personal level is less than for regular income.

Tax Benefits

While not precisely cash flow, tax benefits can enhance cash flow from other sources. For example, if a start-up has operating losses for several years, and if these losses can be passed through to the individual, then they create value by sheltering other income. Because entrepreneurs are often in a low-income phase when starting a business, these tax benefits may be of limited value to them. However, if properly structured, these tax benefits can provide substantial value to investors. In a situation where the structure and form of the organization (i.e., a corporation), does not permit the losses to flow through to the individual, these losses can be used to offset income of the corporation in prior or future years.

The entrepreneur must also take into account his negative cash flows. Three types of negative cash flows are particularly important:

— Cash portion of the purchase price.
— Deficient salary.
— Additional equity capital.

Frequently the most critical aspect of the cash portion of the purchase price is that it must be small enough for the entrepreneur to be able to pay in the first place. In this kind of situation the seller finances the purchase of his company by taking part of the purchase price in the form of a note. The seller then receives cash later on from future earnings of the company or from its assets. Of course, the less cash s/he is required to put up, the more cash the entrepreneur has available for other uses and the greater the opportunity he or she has to produce a high ROI. On the other hand, too much initial debt may hamstring a company from the start, thereby hurting the venture's subsequent financial performance and the entrepreneur's principal source of return—be it the cash withdrawn from the company or the funds received from eventual sale of the company.

The significance to the entrepreneur of a negative cash flow based on a deficient salary is clear—a lower income for personal use than could be obtained elsewhere. In addition, there is the effect that these early negative flows may have on the entrepreneur: faced with an immediate equity requirement for working capital or fixed assets, the owner/manager may be forced to seek outside investors, thereby diluting his or her future value in the business and also introducing the possibility of divergent goals in the financial and other aspects of the company's operations.

At this point in our analysis it will appear obvious to some that the next step for the entrepreneur is to find the present value of the cash flow he predicts for the venture. In other words, discounting the value of future cash flows to arrive at a value of the venture in terms of cash today. We shall see, however, that in many respects this approach raises more questions than it answers, and therefore its usefulness to the analysis is questionable at best.

The essence of the problem is that present value is basically an investment concept utilizing ROI to determine the allocation of a limited supply of funds among alternatives, whereas the entrepreneur is faced basically with a personal situation where return on both investment and *time* are key. In addition, the entrepreneur may have made a considerable investment in generating the particular option, and it is difficult to weigh this tangible opportunity against unknown options. Because the entrepreneur does not have a portfolio of well-defined opportunities to choose from, he needs to define some standard of comparison. This is typically the salary that could be obtained by working.

In an investment analysis utilizing present value, the discount rate is selected to reflect uncertainty associated with cash flows; the higher the uncertainty, the higher the discount rate and, consequently, the lower the present value of the cash flows. In the corporate context there is usually a minimal ROI criterion for noncritical investments to keep the ROI greater than the firm's cost of capital.

For the individual entrepreneur, however, the decision to buy or to start a company is fundamentally a subjective one. Return on investment and time for this kind of decision is measured not only in terms of dollars, but also in terms of what s/he will be doing, who his or her associates will be, how much time and energy will have to be expended, and what lifestyle will result. Different kinds of ventures present *different kinds of return* on time. As cash to the entrepreneur is an important enabling factor for *some* of the things the entrepreneur is seeking, it is important that he or she calculate what these cash flows might be and when they can be expected. However, because decisions affecting cash flow also affect the other returns to the entrepreneur and because these other returns may be at least as important as the financial returns, a present value calculation often is not the most important measure.

In thinking about the attractiveness of a particular opportunity an entrepreneur rarely has easily comparable alternatives. More than likely the decision is either to go ahead with a venture or to stay where he or she is until something else comes along. Perhaps the most useful way to think of this position is to imagine an individual looking down a corridor which will provide a range of opportunities—opportunities to achieve different levels of financial and other rewards with their accompanying risks and sacrifices. Financial theorists, for instance, have recently begun to study investments in terms of their ability to generate a future stream of growth opportunities.

SUMMARY

The previous discussion has outlined a variety of different approaches to the valuation of a firm. It is important to remember that no single approach will ever give the "right" answer. To a large extent, the appropriateness of any method of evaluation depends upon the perspective of the evaluator. However, both in this course and in "real life" one must come to some point of view on the worth of a firm, no matter how scant the data. This is very important, even if the value is only a preliminary one, because it permits the individual to delve further into the issues at hand.

Nonetheless, the true purpose of the analysis is not to arrive at "the answer" but to:

— Identify critical assumptions.
— Evaluate the interrelationships among elements of the situation to determine which aspects are crucial.
— Develop *realistic* scenarios, not a best case, worst case analysis.
— Surface and understand potential outcomes and consequences, both good and bad.
— Examine the manner in which the value of the business is being carved up to satisfy the needs of prospective suppliers of resources.

No single valuation captures the true value of any firm. Rather, its value is a function of the individual's perception of opportunity, risk, the nature of financial resources available to the purchaser, the prospective strategy for operation, the time horizon for analysis, alternatives available given the time and money invested, and prospective methods of harvesting. Price and value are not equivalent. If the entrepreneur pays what the business is worth, he has not appropriated any value for himself. The difference is determined by information, market behavior, pressures forcing either purchase or sale, and negotiating skills.

Chapter 4

TECHNIQUES OF PURCHASING A COMPANY

One approach which an entrepreneur can use to get into business is to purchase, rather than start, a company. An acquisition can take many forms, and the form chosen is likely to have significant impact, not only on the remaining enterprise and its structure but also on all parties involved in, and affected by, the transaction. The appropriate form for a given transaction will depend upon a number of factors: federal income tax considerations (Will the proceeds be characterized ordinary income or capital gain? Can the bilevel corporate tax be avoided? Will there be recapture?); accounting considerations (Do we want to structure the transaction as a purchase? Would we meet the eligibility requirement for pooling?); applicable state corporate law (What percentage of shareholders must approve the transaction? Are appraisal rights the only remedy available to dissenting shareholders?); timing; the preferences and configuration of major shareholders; issues of control; and other important considerations.

Two things are critical to the success of an acquisition. First, the entrepreneur should establish and keep his or her business objectives clearly in mind. Current and projected earnings, depreciation methods, cash flow, and other financial considerations should affect the entrepreneur's analysis and ultimate choice of form. Second, the entrepreneur should ensure that he or she is well advised. There is absolutely no substitute for the advice of a tax lawyer who is thoroughly familiar with this complex and evolving area of the law, one who has both a broad understanding of the field and a firm grasp of the current technical requirements. The IRS subjects such transactions to detailed scrutiny, and noncompliance with a minor technicality or violation of an underlying purpose of the reorganization provisions of the Internal Revenue Code (IRC) will transform what appeared to be a tax-free reorganization into a taxable transaction.

The following is a brief description of various ways to structure acquisitive transactions, and of other types of reorganization of which the entrepreneur should be aware, accompanied by a brief outline of the advantages and drawbacks of each. Throughout the diagrams which follow, B will indicate the buyer, S the seller or selling shareholders, A the acquiring corporation, T the target corporation, SC a subsidiary corporation and SH the shareholder(s).

FEDERAL INCOME TAX CONSIDERATIONS

Taxable Transactions: Purchases for Cash and/or Notes

In these the buyer purchases the stock or assets of an enterprise for cash or for cash and long-term notes (which would not be considered cash equivalents).

Forms of stock purchase transactions. There are several forms of transactions including:

— Purchase of Stock (or Assets) by an Individual.

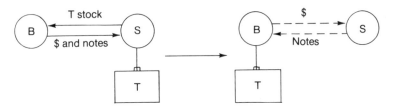

Here B (the buyer) obtains, from a lender or the seller, the financing with which to purchase the stock or assets of T (the target corporation). B gains control of T, and over time pays off the notes out of his salary or other distributions made to B by T. This is a relatively simple and clean transfer from S (the selling shareholders) to B. However, there are potential problems. In most circumstances the proceeds of the sale will be taxed to S as capital gain, probably long-term capital gain. If, however, the purchase price is contingent upon, or represents a percentage of, future earnings, the IRS may consider the seller to be a joint-venturer. The future receipts would be deemed distributions and taxed at ordinary income rates. In addition, interest on the notes, whether actual or imputed, will be taxed to S as ordinary income (see the discussion of imputed interest below).

Another problem lies in the fact that the funds used by B to pay off the notes (i.e., T's earnings) are taxed twice: once as ordinary income to T when earned, and once as ordinary income to B upon receipt (as dividend). This double taxation can be avoided by using one of the methods which follow.

— "Seed Purchase" by B (a "Bootstrap Acquisition").

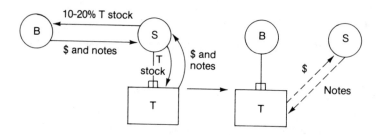

Here the buyer purchases a small amount, say 10–20 percent, of T's outstanding stock, from S for cash. T then repurchases the remainder from S in exchange for cash and/or long-term notes. B now has control of T and T will pay off the notes out of its earnings. Like an outright purchase, this transaction is also clean and easy from the seller's point of view, but avoids the problem of bilevel taxation. Here, as above, the IRS may recharacterize the "sale" as a joint venture unless the seller will receive a fixed consideration approximating fair market value.

— Purchase of T's Stock by A.

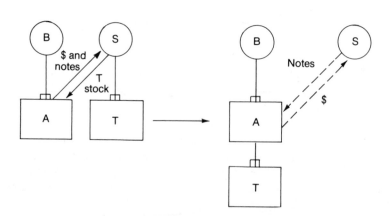

Here B creates a new (or uses an existing) controlled corporation, A. A buys all the outstanding stock of T for cash and/or its notes, and T becomes a wholly owned subsidiary of A. One of two options is then available to A: (1) A may proceed to pay off the notes to S out of T earnings which are distributed to A as dividends (Internal Revenue Code Section 243 (a) (3) exempts dividends paid to a corporation by an affiliate from tax) or (2) A may liquidate T into itself and use both T's earnings and/or assets to pay off its notes to S (IRC 332 exempts A from tax upon the liquidation of a controlled subsidiary).

Structuring the transaction in this way not only avoids the bilevel corporate tax, but also, by using a corporate entity, insulates B from being a party to the exchange. As an IRC 332 liquidation will trigger the recapture[1] provisions of the Internal Revenue Code, B should be sure to ascertain the extent to which, if at all, T will be subject to recapture tax upon liquidation.

Problems with stock purchases in general. There are several potential problems with acquiring stock as opposed to assets:

— Tax Basis in Acquired Assets.
As a rule, A will receive a "carryover" basis (i.e., A will carry T's book valuation of T's assets over onto A's balance sheet) in T's assets when T becomes a subsidiary. Where the fair market value of an asset exceeds its adjusted basis in T's hands, however, A may want to take depreciation deductions from the higher value. Upon acquiring T, A will have three options: (1) A may allow T to continue operating as a subsidiary, maintaining its existing asset basis and tax history. (2) A may liquidate T under IRC 332 in which case it will receive a carryover basis in T's assets. (3) A may, within 75 days of acquiring at least 80 percent of T's outstanding stock, elect, under IRC 338, to "step-up" the basis of T's assets without liquidating T. An IRC 338 election allows A to write up the basis of T's assets to a value equal to A's basis in the T stock, giving A a higher depreciable basis. However, the buyer should be aware that because the code treaties and IRC 338 election as a "deemed IRC 337 sale" of T's assets by T, the election will trigger any recapture of T.

In situations involving 338 elections, it should be noted that if A does not get 100 percent of T's stock, some T shareholders will not be taxed and there will be no theoretical "justification" for excusing A from corporate-level tax. In order for A to get a 100 percent step-up in

---

[1]*Recapture* is a technical term which refers to the IRS's ability to "recapture" taxes which were previously not paid due to the use of accelerated depreciation. For instance, if T had assets which were depreciated using the use of accelerated depreciation, but purchased by B before the end of their depreciable lives, the IRS would claim that T had "unfairly" obtained the tax benefit of accelerated depreciation. T would then have to pay a recapture tax which would allow the IRS to recapture the tax which had initially been lost.

the basis of T's assets, A must pay a tax on an amount equal to the value of the remaining unacquired percentage of T stock.

— Unforeseen Liabilities of T.

When A (or B) acquires the stock of T, it also acquires all the tax, litigation-related, and other outstanding liabilities of T. In order to protect itself against existing or potential liabilities of which it is unaware, A may seek to withold a portion of the purchase price for a specific period following the sale. Alternatively, the parties may agree to place a certain percentage of the purchase price in escrow, pending a reallocation and/or adjustment of the price to compensate for any liabilities which may come to light after the closing. In many cases the parties will formally agree on who will assume the risk of certain liabilities for a certain period following the sale. A may avoid the issue entirely by purchasing T's assets and leaving T's stock in the hands of its shareholders. (See the discussion of asset purchases below).

— Minority Shareholders.

In situations where most, but not all, of T's shareholders sell their stock to A (or B), A will control T but will have to cope with minority shareholders. B can choose to live with them or, if they prove to be a problem, to isolate them from further involvement in T's affairs. If A creates a new corporation, X, it can either (1) vote to merge T into X under terms which give the minority shareholders cash in exchange for their T stock or (2) vote to have T sell substantially all of its assets to X (or A) and then liquidate, distributing the cash proceeds of the sale to T's shareholders. Either course of action will give the minority shareholders cash and leave A in control of T's operations.

Purchase by A of T's assets. A can avoid these potential problems by purchasing T's assets.

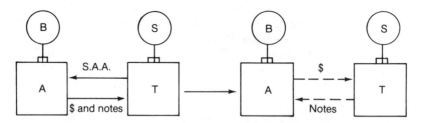

In an assets purchase A (or B) purchases "substantially all" of T's assets for cash and/or notes and the assets come to rest in A. The IRS considers "substantially all" of T's assets to be at least 90 percent of T's net assets or at least 70 percent of T's gross assets, although case law suggests that less may be required depending upon context and circumstances.

By structuring the acquisition in this way the entrepreneur may purchase only the assets desired and may worry less about unforeseen liabilities. A will get a step-up in basis in T's assets as the purchase price is allocated among them. Although there will be no problem of minority shareholders after the acquisition, it should be noted that state laws may require that 51 percent to two thirds of T's shareholders approve such an asset sale when it is not done in the ordinary course of T's business.

Several problems may arise in the context of an assets purchase:

— Buyer and seller may disagree as to the allocation of the purchase price among the assets transferred. The buyer will want to allocate as much as possible to wasting assets in order to depreciate, the seller to capital assets in order to receive capital gain treatment. In most cases the parties agree upon a negotiated allocation. Where no agreement can be reached or where the IRS finds the allocation unreasonable, the IRS may make its own determination based on what it considers to be fair market value. The parties should also bear in mind that T, upon sale, must pay tax on any assets which fall within the recapture provisions of the Code.

— T will usually pay capital gains taxes upon sale of its assets, but the distribution of proceeds following sale may be taxed as ordinary income to T's shareholders. This problem may be avoided if S liquidates T under IRC 337. Under IRC 337, if T's assets are sold pursuant to a plan of liquidation, T will recognize no gain upon sale. [Note: there are certain statutory exceptions to this rule, which include recapture, LIFO inventory and other items. In addition, gain will be recognized if the liquidation is actually an assignment of income to be received in the future or is effected solely for the purpose of tax avoidance.] The liquidation proceeds will usually be taxed to T shareholders as capital gain.

— If T retains the proceeds of the sale and invests them it may be deemed a "personal holding company" by the IRS and subject to tax under IRC 551; it may also become subject to an accumulated earnings tax under IRC 531. Meticulous attention to detail and the advice of astute tax specialists will ensure that these pitfalls are avoided.

Use of installment sale treatment. Installment sale treatment (under IRC 453) may be critical to the success of an entrepreneur who is interested in acquiring resources with little capital, and may be used by the parties in connection with the transactions described above. An installment sale allows the buyer to defer payments, and the seller to defer recognition of gain (and thus, tax), until actual receipt of the deferred payment. An installment sale is defined as a sale in which at least one payment will occur after the close of the taxable year of sale. Notes issued to S by the purchaser will not be considered a "payment" unless they are basically cash equivalents.

A word of caution: If no interest is stated on the notes, or if the stated interest is less than 9 percent simple interest, pursuant to the IRC 483 the IRS will impute to them interest of 10 percent compounded semiannually.

This will affect the calculation of total purchase price and how much of each payment will be considered principal (capital gain) or interest (ordinary income) to the seller. These rates are changed from time to time by regulation.

Appraisal rights. The availability and requirements for exercise of appraisal rights by minority shareholders vary with state law and are applicable to both taxable acquisitions and tax-free reorganizations. (Tax-free reorganizations are discussed below.) In the context of certain transactions, the corporate law of a given state may allow dissenting shareholders, provided they follow certain specified and complicated procedures, to receive the "fair value" of their shares in lieu of the cash or securities offered to them in the transaction. Valuation methods are hotly litigated, are of uncertain reliability, and do not consider any potential synergistic gains generated by the reorganization. The acquirer should consider (1) the potential costs of litigating the issue of valuation and paying off dissenters and (2) whether the exercise of appraisal rights is the exclusive remedy available to dissenters. Where it is not the exclusive remedy available, dissenting shareholders may be able to enjoin, and thus delay or actually halt, a transaction.

Nontaxable Reorganizations

Certain corporate transactions are granted tax-free status under the Internal Revenue Code. The theory underlying the reorganization provisions is "that the new property is substantially a continuation of the old investment still unliquidated; and, in the case of reorganizations, that the new enterprise, the new corporate structure and the new property are substantially continuations of the old still unliquidated." [Treasury Regulation 1.1002-1(c)]

If a transaction is a reorganization which proceeds "pursuant to a plan" of reorganization, no gain or loss is recognized by a corporation which exchanges property for stock of securities of another "party" to the reorganization; no gain or loss is recognized by shareholders upon the exchange of their securities; gain or loss will be recognized by any party receiving "boot" in the transaction; and many of the tax attributes of the target corporation may be inherited by the acquiring corporation. *Boot* is cash, short-term notes, or forms of property *other than stock*.

The reorganization provisions, as will be seen, allow the acquirer a good deal of flexibility. For instance, if the purchase price, payable in A shares, is made contingent upon certain factors, a transaction may still qualify as a reorganization if (1) all the shares will be distributed within five years, (2) at least half of the maximum number of shares are transferred at the closing, and (3) the right to receive the A shares in the future is nonassignable. A comparison of reorganization and other acquisition techniques is included in Exhibit 1.

EXHIBIT 1

Comparison of Reorganization with Other Acquisition Techniques

	Reorganization	*Purchase*
1. Recognition of gain or loss	Generally no current recognition	Generally taxable currently
2. Basis and holding periods of assets and stock or securities	Substituted or derivative basis and holding periods	"Cost" or new basis and holding periods
3. Character or recognized gain or loss	Dividend possibility	Generally capital gain or loss
4. Survival of corporate tax attributes	Generally carryover to transferee per §381	Generally extinguished (if seller liquidates)
5. Other aspects:		
a. Deductibility of payments on securities issues	Dividends on stock not deductible	Interest on debt securities generally deductible
b. Effect of acquisition on equity, control, and earnings of buyer corporation	Equity and control diluted (but can use "pooling" accounting)	No "dilution" (but "purchase accounting")
c. Risk and growth potential	Continuing proprietary stake in affairs of buyer (risk of gain and loss continued)	Low (or no) risk, and no growth potential (sellers have "cashed-in")

Source:Boris I. Bittker and James S. Eustice, *Federal Income Taxation of Corporations and Shareholders,* 4th ed. (Boston: Warren, Gorham and Lamont, 1979), pp. 13–14.

The choice of the right form of reorganization will depend on careful analysis of many factors. The entrepreneur contemplating a reorganization should consider, as a preliminary matter, the following questions: What are the tax and accounting implications of the form proposed? What approvals, by shareholders or directors or both, are required by state law or relevant securities exchanges? What type of consideration will be used? What percentage of T is to be acquired? What liabilities are to be assumed? Will the consent of affected lenders be required? Which of T's patents, licenses, and contracts are assignable? What remedies are available to dissenting T shareholders? Are there potential antitrust problems? What regulatory approvals may be required? What other state, sales, and real estate taxes may be involved? How will a given form of reorganization affect employee contracts and other labor-related items? Will the transaction trigger "golden parachute" provisions in the employment contracts of T's management? Does T have foreign affiliates? What are the relative time, expense, and transaction costs involved? How will reorganization costs be accounted for? What records and information must be filed with the SEC? What notifications must be filed under the Hart-Scott-Rodino Act? What is required in order to comply with relevant SEC and state securities laws?

A word of caution to the entrepreneur considering a reorganization: Find a specialist in the reorganization field who is familiar with, and can interpret, the most recent rulings of the IRS and the courts. The reorganization provisions of the IRC interact in complicated ways with other sections of the statute and the advice of an expert is essential. In addition, the IRS uses various judicially-constructed doctrines to attack tax-free transactions and recharacterize them as taxable exchanges [see below, Section II.B(8)]. To qualify, the transaction must comply not only with the letter of the reorganization provisions but also with their underlying purpose.

Section 351 Incorporations. Under IRC 351, no gain or loss is recognized by the parties if property is transferred to a corporation solely in exchange for its stock and securities and if the transferors are in control of the corporation immediately following the exchange. The theory behind this nonrecognition provision is that such an exchange represents only a change in the *form* of the transferor's ownership of the property exchanged.

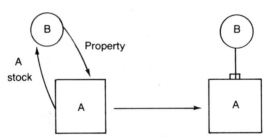

In a 351 exchange, B (or B and others) transfers property (which may include cash, but not services) to A (a new or existing corporation) and receives only A stock in exchange. If B (or B and others) controls A immediately following the exchange, no gain or loss will be recognized by B or A. The IRC defines *control* in the reorganization context to be at least 80 percent of the combined voting power of all classes of voting stock plus at least 80 percent of all nonvoting classes of stock. [IRC 36 (c).] A will receive B's adjusted basis in the contributed property, increased by any gain A recognizes in the transaction.

351 exchanges are commonly used to set up corporations and to allow B to defer recognition of realized gain. In some instances, however, if B intends to contribute property which has declined in value, an outright sale by B may be more beneficial to the parties, as it would allow B to take a tax loss and would give A a lower basis in the asset.

Several aspects of a 351 exchange may prove problematic. As mentioned above, services are not "property." In addition, any boot received by B is considered taxable gain. No taxable losses may be taken by B and no carryovers of tax attributes are allowed. (For a more detailed discussion of tax attribute carryovers see below, Section II.C.) Any assumption (by A) of B's liabilities will not be considered boot unless the liabilities assumed exceed B's adjusted basis in the contributed property.

Mergers: "A" reorganizations. Generally speaking, in a statutory merger T's enterprise is automatically absorbed into A by operation of law, and A automatically inherits all the assets and liabilities of the disappearing corporation. Shareholders and creditors of T become shareholders and creditors for A. A consolidation, also considered an "A" reorganization, is a merger of both A and T into a third corporation, X.

— Regular "A" Reorganization: Statutory Merger.

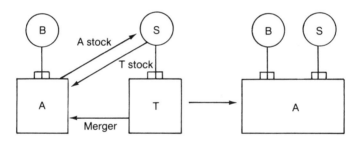

In a regular "A" organization [IRC 368(a)(1)(A)], T shareholders surrender their T stock in exchange for consideration received from A. This consideration may be stock, notes, cash, or some combination of such property. T, with all its assets and liabilities, merges into A by operation of applicable state law, and B and S both become shareholders of A. T shareholders will recognize taxable gain to the extent of any boot received in the exchange.

In order to qualify as an "A" reorganization the "continuity of interest" requirement must be met. This means that unless the proportion of proprietary consideration received by T shareholders is such that the original owners maintain a specified level of interest in the reorganized enterprise, the transaction will be deemed a sale and will be taxed as such. (The continuity of interest doctrine is discussed in more detail below.)

Mergers are used for many reasons. Most important, the code is relatively flexible as to the type of consideration which T shareholders can receive. Nonvoting stock, securities, and boot may be received by T shareholders without disqualifying the transaction's tax-free status.

In addition, differential treatment of shareholders is possible, allowing, for example, some T common shareholders to receive cash in exchange for their shares while other T common shareholders receive voting stock of A. Because the combination is affected by operation of law, a merger may be simpler and generate fewer transaction costs than, for example, a sale of assets.

Several aspects of a merger may, however, prove problematic. In most instances T shareholders must approve the transaction, and A must be able to persuade from 51 percent to two thirds of them to approve, depending on the jurisdiction. In addition, the T shareholders become shareholders of A, which may interfere with B's plans for the ongoing enterprise. Because A accedes to all of T's liabilities, known and unknown, upon merger, it may inherit more problems and less value than it had previously supposed. In some circumstances an "A" reorganization involving affiliated corporations may mean that the consideration received by T shareholders is taxed as a dividend or redemption. And finally a "creeping merger" (e.g., A purchases 100% of T stock and then merges T out of existence) may be considered by the IRS to be in reality a purchase followed by a liquidation, because in looking at the transaction as a whole it appears that T shareholders have "cashed out" of their investment and there is no continuity of interest.

— "A" Reorganization Followed by A's Drop- Down of T's Assets.

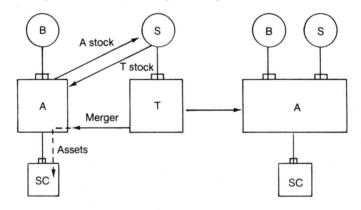

In this case the merger proceeds as above. A then creates (or uses an existing) subsidiary (SC), and following the merger drops all or a part of T's assets down into SC. This drop-down of assets will not disqualify the transaction as an "A" reorganization. The requirements and potential problems involved are identical to those discussed above in relation to regular "A" reorganizations. The advantage here is that the transfer ensures that T's assets and operations do not come to rest in the acquiring corporation.

— Forward Triangular Merger [IRC 368 (a)(2)(D)].

Triangular mergers (also known as subsidiary mergers) are used in instances where it is undesirable to have T merge directly into A. A may be a holding company, T may be suspected of having unknown liabilities, or there may be other reasons why A shareholders seek a less intimate combination. The code provides that although A is not technically the acquiring corporation, its stock may be used in the merger without disqualifying it as a tax-free organization.

The configuration of a forward triangular merger is as follows:

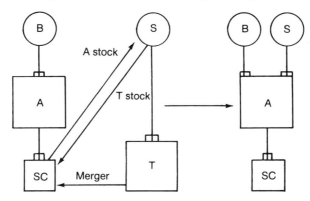

A creates SC, whereupon T merges into SC and T shareholders receive A stock in exchange for their T shares, becoming shareholders of A. In this way T's assets and liabilities never come to rest in A. To qualify as a tax-free reorganization the transaction must meet the qualifications outlined above for "A" reorganizations, with the additional requirement that SC receive substantially all of T's assets. While A stock may be used (or SC stock), use of both A and SC stock is prohibited. Many of the potential problems outlined above in relation to regular "A" reorganizations may be present here.

— Reverse Triangular Merger.

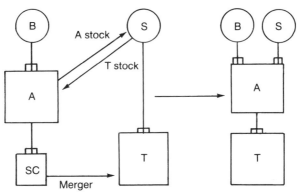

In a reverse triangular merger SC merges into T. T becomes a subsidiary of A, and T shareholders become shareholders of A.

The requirements of a reverse triangular merger are more stringent than those of a forward triangular merger. Here T must get substantially all the properties of S, T shareholders must receive voting stock of A, and A must be in "control" of T after the smoke clears.

A reverse triangular merger may be more advantageous in that T remains in existence, and thus leases, government-issued licenses, non-transferable contracts, and the like will remain unimpaired. The disadvantages, aside from the more stringent requirements, are similar to those outlined above for other forms of merger.

"B" reorganizations: Stock-for-Stock Exchanges. In a "B" reorganization [IRC 368(a)(1)(B)], A acquires the stock of T from T shareholders in exchange for part or all of the voting stock of A (or its subsidiary), and has control of T immediately after the acquisition. Whether or not it had control of T immediately prior to the acquisition is irrelevant.

— Regular "B" Reorganization.

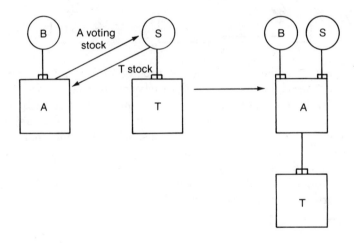

Here, T shareholders exchange their T stock for solely voting stock of A, with the result that T becomes a subsidiary of A. A's basis in the T stock is considered to be equal to the T shareholders' basis in their T stock, because A has no basis in its newly issued shares to carry over into its newly acquired T stock. This will make it difficult for A to calculate its basis in the T stock where the T stock was widely held before the acquisition.

The code's requirements for a "B" reorganization are quite strict. Only voting stock of A (or SC, in the case of a subsidiary "B" reorganization, discussed below) may be used. Use of both A and SC voting stock will disqualify the transaction. Likewise, the presence of any boot at all will disqualify the transaction. As mentioned above, A must have control (as defined in IRC 368 (c)) immediately following the acquisition.

The "B" reorganization is useful because A need only use its own shares as currency in the exchange. T remains intact and does not become lodged in A. This type of acquisition may not require the approval of T shareholders and is less likely to trigger appraisal rights under applicable state corporation law.

However, there can be problems with "B" reorganizations. A major consideration, of course, is that T shareholders do not have the option of cashing out, and therefore must be convinced to become joint-ventures in the reorganized entity. Compliance with the code's "solely voting stock" requirements for "B" reorganizations may also lead to difficulties.

Because the presence of boot destroys the transaction's tax-free status, where some T shareholders want cash, A may want to consider an initial purchase of some B stock for cash. Then a stock-for-stock exchange may be effected involving the remaining T shareholders. (This is called a "creeping B" reorganization.) As long as the two transactions appear sufficiently unrelated, cash paid for the first block of shares should not disqualify the tax-free status of the second exchange. The IRS, however, may "bust" or "collapse" the stock-for-stock exchange and view the two steps as a single transaction. Alternatively, where some T shareholders want cash, it may be possible to avoid the presence of boot by having T repurchase the dissenters' shares prior to or following the stock-for-stock exchange. In "B" reorganizations, any assumption of a shareholder's liabilities by A may be considered boot by the IRS, but it should be noted that fractional shares, or small amounts of cash issued in lieu of fractional shares, will not be considered such.

Problems may also arise where section 368(a)(1)(B) overlaps other sections of the code. For example, the IRS may view a "B" reorganization followed closely by a liquidation as a "C" reorganization (discussed below), on the grounds that A was actually seeking T's assets. Likewise, if A transfers its stock to T in exchange for T stock, the transaction may fall within either IRC 351 or IRC 368, with different implications. It should again be evident that the advice of a specialist in the field is critical.

— Subsidiary "B" Reorganization.

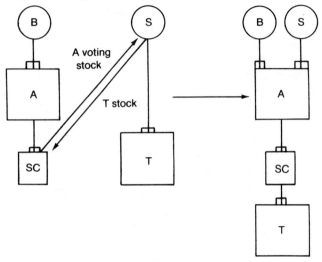

Here, A creates (or uses existing) subsidiary corporation SC. T share-holders surrender their stock to SC and receive solely voting stock of the parent corporation, A. T then becomes a subsidiary of SC.

As with subsidiary mergers (see above), the utility of this form lies in the fact that A is not technically a party to the reorganization, al-though use of its stock does not disqualify the transaction's tax-free sta-tus. The requirements and problems involved are similar to those dis-cussed above for regular "B" reorganizations.

— Regular "B" Reorganization and Drop-Down of Stock into a Subsidiary.

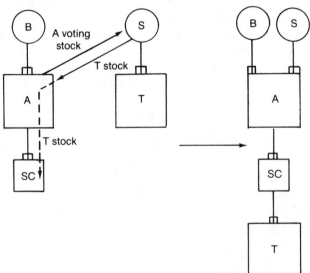

Here, T shareholders surrender their stock to A in exchange for solely voting shares of A. A may then drop the T shares down into subsidiary SC without disqualifying the transaction's tax-free status. T becomes a subsidiary of SC. This structure is useful when it is desirable for SC, and not A, to hold the T stock. The requirements and problems involved are similar to those of a regular "B" reorganization.

— "Forced" or "Collapsed" "B" Reorganization.

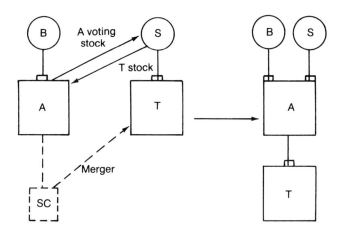

Here, A creates SC, T and SC vote to merge, and SC merges into T. T shareholders get A stock and T becomes a subsidiary of A. The legal form is that of a Reverse Triangular Merger (see above), but for tax purposes the IRS may ignore the existence of the transient subsidiary and treat the transaction as a "B" reorganization. This may be useful because while the process and resulting corporate configuration is that of a reverse triangular merger, the "B" reorganization requirements are less exacting than those of such a merger. Furthermore, under the merger voting statutes, dissenting T shareholders must either take A stock or exercise appraisal rights, but may not remain as shareholders of T.

"C" reorganizations: Stock-for-assets exchanges. This form is often called a "practical merger." In a "C" reorganization [IRC 368 (a)(1)(C)], A acquires substantially all of the properties of T in exchange for solely voting stock of A (or its parent). Unlike a "B" reorganization, up to 20 percent of the consideration paid by A may be boot without destroying the transaction's tax-free status.

— Regular "C" Reorganization.

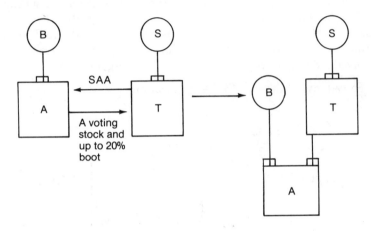

In a regular "C" reorganization T shareholders vote to sell substantially all of T's properties to A. T then sells those properties to A in exchange for solely voting stock of A, or for solely voting stock and boot. T's assets come to rest in A, and T becomes an A shareholder. T may then liquidate and distribute the A shares to its shareholders, or continue its existence.

To qualify as a "C" reorganization, A must get "substantially all of the properties" of T at the time of transfer. Although the IRS asserts that this means at least 90 percent of net assets or at least 70 percent of T's gross assets, case law indicates that a smaller percentage may suffice. The entrepreneur should be aware that any threshold asset distributions made by T prior to transfer may be counted by the IRS in determining whether the "substantially all" requirement has been met. The exchange must be solely for voting stock, for the presence of any nonvoting stock will destroy its tax-free status. However, up to 20 percent of the consideration received may be boot. Any of T's liabilities assumed by A will be disregarded in determining whether the "solely voting stock" requirement has been complied with, but may be considered boot."

By structuring the transaction as a "C" reorganization A can ensure that it gets only T's assets, free of any unknown liabilities which it might inherit in a statutory merger. A "C" may also be easier than a "B' where T's stock is widely held, and may in some instances not requir the approval of T's shareholders.

Some aspects of a "C" reorganization may prove to be problematic. In crafting a "C" reorganization the amount of boot must be calculated carefully, especially if T retains any assets. Any assumption of liability may be considered the equivalent of cash. Although the results of a "C" resemble those of a merger, the negotiation and preparation of conveyance documents for all items to be transferred may prove complicated and costly when compared with the transaction costs involved in a more simple merger. Where an essentially divisive transaction may be characterized as either a "C" or a "D" reorganization (discussed below) it will be treated as a "D" reorganization.

— "C" Reorganization with Drop-Down of Assets.

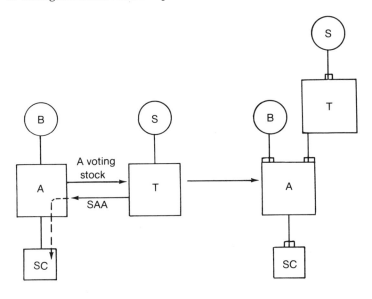

Here, T transfers substantially all of its properties to A in exchange for solely voting stock of A. T then becomes a shareholder of A. If A drops down the acquired T assets into SC (which existed prior to, or was created especially for, the transfer), the tax-free status of the transaction will remain undisturbed. This ensures that T's assets will not lodge in A. The requirements and potential problems are similar to those of a regular "C" reorganization.

— Subsidiary "C" Reorganization.

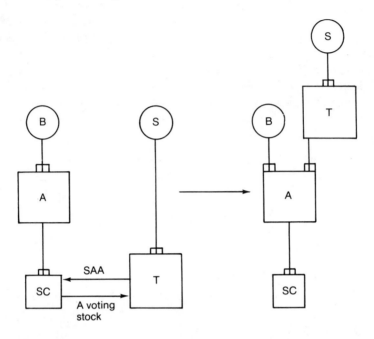

Here, T transfers substantially all of its properties to SC in exchange for solely voting stock of A. The assets remain in SC and T becomes an A shareholder. This structure keeps A from being technically a party to the transaction. The requirements and potential problems are similar to those of a regular "C" reorganization.

"D" reorganizations: Spin-offs, split-ups and split-offs. A "D" reorganization [IRC 368(a)(1)(D)] is one in which A transfers all or a portion of its assets to SC, where SC is controlled by A (or A shareholders) immediately following the transaction. To qualify, the stock or securities must be distributed by A pursuant to a plan of reorganization and the transaction must meet the requirements of IRC sections 354–356.

— Transfer and Liquidation.

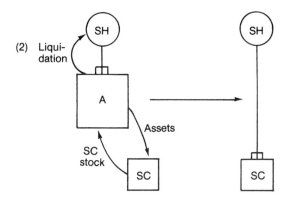

IRC 354 describes the situation in which A (the parent corporation) transfers substantially all of its assets to SC and then liquidates itself, usually distributing the SC shares to its shareholders. The Code requires that substantially all of A's assets be transferred to the subsidiary and that A distribute all its holdings in liquidation.

— Divisive Reorganizations.

A divisive reorganization [IRC 355] is often used to separate a business segment or a principal from an ongoing enterprise. It is also a mechanism by which a corporation can be persuaded to transfer some of its assets to the entrepreneur in a tax-free transaction. There are a host of other situations in which a divisive reorganization may prove useful. It may be used to comply with local law that demands that two businesses be separated; to comply with an antitrust decree; to segregate hazardous activities from others; to separate a portion of the business in order to allow its employees to share in the profits of its operations; to settle a dispute between, or to break a deadlock among, shareholders; to expand the amount of credit available to both businesses; or to accomplish other similar ends. In transactions defined by IRC 355, stock of SC (a newly created or existing subsidiary) is transferred to A shareholders (as a dividend or in exchange for A stock) in pursuance of a plan of reorganization. A discussion of the requirements of an IRC 355 transaction follows a brief description of the forms such transactions may take.

- Spin-Off

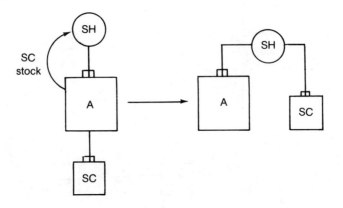

Here, A distributes the stock of its subsidiary, SC, to its shareholders who then become shareholders of both A and SC.

- Split-Off.

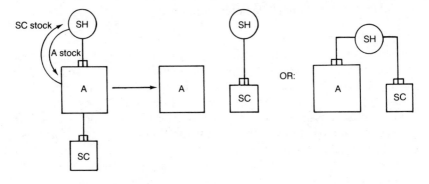

Here, A shareholders exchange all or a part of their A stock for stock of SC. The A shareholders become shareholders of SC and may or may not remain shareholders of A.

- Split-Up.

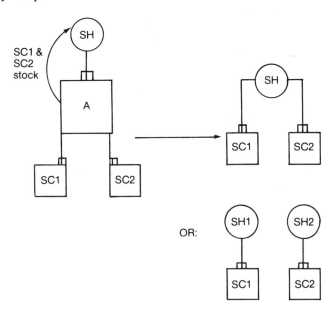

Here, A distributes all of its stock in two subsidiaries, SC1 and SC2, to its shareholders pursuant to a plan of complete liquidation. A disappears and A's shareholders become shareholders in one or both subsidiaries.

In order to qualify as an IRC 355 "D" reorganization a transaction must meet a number of criteria. A must be in control of SC prior to the distribution. Both SC and A must continue in the "active conduct of trade or business" after the transaction is completed. A must either (1) distribute all of its SC stock or (2) distribute control of SC and convince the IRS that no tax-avoidance purpose infected the transaction. It is imperative that the taxpayer be able to prove that the transaction had a legitimate business purpose. In addition, the transaction must not be a "device" to distribute A's earnings to its shareholders as capital gain rather than as a dividend. For example, a prearranged or immediate sale of stock by A's shareholders following the distribution may be evidence that the distribution was intended primarily as a device to transfer cash to shareholders at capital gain rates.

Problems arise from the complexity of the "D" reorganization provisions and the precision required in compliance. Even though the reorganizations are divisive in nature, the continuity of interest requirement is still present. Where Code provisions overlap, the provisions of IRC 355 will usually "trump" others.

Pervasive judicial doctrines which may "trump" all forms of reorganization. Prior to the 1954 revision of the Internal Revenue Code, courts developed a number of judicial doctrines which attempted to enforce the spirit, as well as the letter, of the statutory provisions governing reorganizations. Courts often disregarded the technical form of a transaction to look carefully at its substance. Where the substance of a "reorganization" seemed to fall outside the scope of the legislative purpose of the reorganization provisions, i.e., where a change in structure seemed not to be simply a change in the form of ownership, courts did not hesitate to find a taxable transaction.

These doctrines still pervade the field of reorganization law, despite the fact that the 1954 code, its subsequent amendments, and the accompanying Treasury Regulations clarified many areas of confusion and contain more technical and explicit requirements than earlier statutes. The IRS continues to use these doctrines as weapons to puncture, unwind, and tax those party to what are asserted to be tax-free reorganizations.

— The Business Purpose Requirement.

Every reorganization must be driven by a legitimate business purpose. Needless to say, tax-avoidance alone is not considered to be a legitimate business purpose. Even if all the statutory requirements are met, the transaction

> may be disregarded as a "sham," or its form may be recast so as to reflect its economic "substance," or interdependent steps in a "single transaction" may be collapsed in order to prevent overreaching taxpayers from doing indirectly what they cannot do directly.[2]

Be wary of the transaction that looks too good to be true.

— The Step Transaction Doctrine.

The step doctrine requires that "all integrated steps in a single transaction . . . be amalgamated in determining the true nature of a transaction."[3] The courts have not, however, developed a clear test for when the *steps*, single transactions in themselves, will be collapsed and viewed as a whole. For example, where, in a "creeping B" reorganization, A's initial step of purchasing T shares for cash is not "old and cold" at the time of the stock-for-stock exchange, the courts and IRS may

---

[2]Boris I. Bittker and James S. Eustice, Federal Income Taxation of Corporations and Shareholders, 4th ed. (Boston: Warren, Gorham and Lamont, 1979), pp. 14–128.

[3]Ibid., pp. 14–128.

collapse the two transactions into one and find that the presence of cash boot disqualifies the exchange from being characterized as a "B" reorganization.

— The Continuity of Interest Requirement.

The continuity of interest doctrine demands that original owners maintain a continuing interest in the reorganized entity. To distinguish a "reorganization" from a "sale" (in which property owners have essentially "cashed out" of their investment) the courts have focused on the nature and extent of the shareholders' continued interest, and also on the relation of shareholders to one another following the transaction. Factors which the courts have considered to be important include (1) the nature of the consideration received; (2) the percentage of continuity preserved; (3) the number of owners remaining in the enterprise; and (4) the length of time during which shareholders remain in control following the transaction.

— The Continuity of Business Enterprise Requirement.

To qualify as a reorganization the Treasury Regulations require "continuity of business enterprise under modified corporate forms." [Regs. 1.368–1(b).] The type of activity carried on need not be identical, as long as some business activity continues. For instance, where a reorganization is merely a step in the winding-up of a business, the transaction may be viewed by the IRS as part of a liquidation and taxed as such. Likewise, where a spin-off is followed by a cessation of business activity the IRS may also find a liquidaiton.

The Carryover of Tax Attributes of T Corporation

The entire area of tax law governing when and to what extent A may inherit and use the tax attributes of T is extremely complicated and in the process of change. The advice of a specialist in this area is critical to any entrepreneur considering an acquisition and anything other than a brief sketch would fall outside the scope of this note.

Generally speaking, the Internal Revenue Code [IRC 81] allows A, in the context of certain liquidations and reorganizations, to carryover and use, with certain limitations, the tax attributes of T. These tax attributes include net operating loss carryforwards, earnings and profits, capital loss carryovers, methods of accounting, inventory methods, methods of depreciation computation, installment methods, amortization of bond discounts and premiums, excess contributions to qualified deferred compensation plans, recovery of prior deductions to T, involuntary conversions, investment tax credits, and many others. Transactions in which carryovers may be possible include "A," "C," and "F" reorganizations, nondivisive "D" reorganizations and 332 liquidations. Factors which are usually considered in ascertaining the survivability of a given attribute include (1) the form of the readjustment (is there "continuity of entity?"); (2) continuity of business activity; (3) continuity of shareholder ownership; and (4) the presence of tax windfall or tax-avoidance motives.

ACCOUNTING CONSIDERATIONS: PURCHASE OR POOLING

Once a form has been chosen, one must consider whether the purchase or pooling methods of accounting will be used to reflect the transaction. Under the purchase method the purchase price is allocated among T's assets and these are reflected on A's books at their cost to A. Where the price paid by A exceeds fair market value, the excess must be considered goodwill and must be amortized over not more than 40 years. Under the pooling method all of the assets and liabilities of T are carried forward onto A's books on the same aggregate basis as they were reflected on T's books. Thus, the acquisition generates no goodwill which must be amortized over time. The general rule is that acquisitions must be accounted for using the purchase method unless *all* of the requirements for pooling treatment are met.

The requirements for pooling are outlined by the Accounting Principles Board (APB 16 and its amendments, if any). Briefly, in order to qualify for pooling treatment:

1. A must issue only voting common stock for at least 90 percent of either the assets or voting common stock of T.
2. A and T must have been autonomous, i.e., unrelated corporations, for at least two years prior to the date of the acquisition agreement.
3. Neither A nor T can own more than 10 percent of the other's voting common stock prior to the transaction.
4. The combination of the two corporations must be effected in a single transaction or within one year of initiating the plan of combination.
5. Neither A nor T may have altered the equity interest of its voting common stock in anticipation of the combination.
6. Any reacquisition by A or T of its own voting common stock in the two years prior to the transaction must not have been for the purpose of meeting the pooling requirements.
7. The relative interests of the T shareholders must not be realigned due to their exchange of T stock for securities of A.
8. Voting rights in A must be exercisable only by shareholders, not by voting trusts or other such voting agreements.
9. The acquisition must not be a contingent transaction in which additional stock may be issued over time.

10. A must not agree to reacquire, either directly or indirectly, all or part of the stock issued by it in the transaction.
11. A must not enter into any other arrangements beneficial to T shareholders.
12. A must not plan to dispose of a significant portion of T's assets in the two years following the transaction, unless such disposition takes place in the ordinary course of business or is effected to eliminate excess or duplicative capacity.

SUMMARY

The start-up venture requires resources of many kinds in order to expand. The decision to grow by combination or acquisition is a major one. When the right opportunity presents itself, the entrepreneur must consider the needs of his or her own venture, the facts and posture of the specific situation, and the desires of the parties who will be affected by the transaction. It should be clear by now that *how* the acquisition or combination is done is also a major, and very complex, decision. Devising the best structure requires the consideration of many factors, the advice of experts who are perhaps not so intimately familiar with the enterprise, and a clear sense of purpose. The entrepreneur considering an acquisition or combination should clarify his or her business objectives and then keep them clearly in mind throughout the process. Aside from that, he or she should seek out the best advice available and proceed.

Chapter 5

THE LEGAL FORMS OF ORGANIZATION

One of the key issues an entrepreneur must resolve when considering a new venture is what legal form of organization the enterprise should adopt. The most prevalent forms are:

— The individual proprietorship.
— The partnership.
  • General partnership.
  • Limited partnership.
— The corporation.
  • The S corporation (formerly Subchapter S).
  • The "regular" corporation.

Each of these forms of organization differs from the others along several dimensions. The characteristics of the business entity will determine its tax status. It is important to note that merely claiming partnership or corporate status *will not* result in the tax treatment accorded that form of organization. The IRS [see Internal Revenue Code Sec. 7701 (a) (3)] has elaborated four factors which determine the classification and resulting tax status of an organization:

1. Continuity of Life—An organization possesses continuity of life when the death, insanity, or retirement of an owner will not cause the organization's dissolution.

2. Centralization of Management—Management is centralized when continuing, exclusive authority to make managerial decisions is constituted in some subgroup of the organization's ownership.
3. Limited Liability—The liability of an organization is limited when no member of the organization is personally liable for debts or claims against the business.
4. Free Transferability of Interest—Interest can be freely transferred only when each member of the organization can transfer all attributes and benefits of ownership without the consent of other members.

As the table below indicates, the proprietorship and partnership occupy one end of the spectrum with regard to each of these criteria while the corporation occupies the other; the limited partnership form falls in the middle.

	Corporation, including S Corporation	Limited Partnership	Proprietorship/ Partnership
Continuity of life	Yes	No	No
Centralized management	Yes	Yes	No
Limited liability	Yes	Yes/No	No
Free transferability of Interest	Yes	No	No

It is also important to note that *any* business, which seeks tax treatment under any of the legal forms of organization *must* have as its objective the carrying on of a trade or business *for profit*. An individual cannot engage in a hobby, such as travel or purchasing books or stamps, and then claim tax deductions for expenses involved in pursuing these activities.

In most cases, the IRS has an incentive to tax as corporations entities which have claimed *not* to be corporations, but which, in fact, possess the characteristics of corporations.

In general, tax courts have found that:

— If the organization claims to be a corporation, and it possesses at least two of the four characteristics, it will be taxed as a corporation.
— If an organization claims to be a partnership, but in fact possesses three of the four characteristics of a corporation, it will be taxed as a corporation.

The remainder of this chapter will discuss each of the forms of organization mentioned above. Exhibit 1 lists several important aspects of the various legal forms of organization.

INDIVIDUAL PROPRIETORSHIP

The individual or sole proprietorship is the oldest form of organization: a person who undertakes a business without any of the formalities associated with other forms of organization. The individual and the business are one and the same.

Classification

A proprietorship is legally defined as follows:

— Continuity of life: The proprietorship ceases to exist upon the death, insanity, or retirement of the proprietor.
— Centralized management: A proprietorship is deemed not to have centralized management because the proprietor is viewed as the legal decision-making authority. Therefore, management is not centralized in any subgroup of the ownership.
— Limited liability: The individual proprietor is personally liable for all liabilities of the business.
— Free transferability of interest: The proprietor cannot freely transfer his interest; once s/he does, the proprietorship is dissolved.

Tax Status

The proprietorship does not pay taxes as a separate entity. The individual reports all salary and profit from both the business and any other sources on the personal income tax return. Note that the earnings (as reported on the company's income statement) of the business are taxed at the individual level whether or not they are actually distributed in cash. There is no vehicle for sheltering income. Moreover, the sole proprietor cannot deduct as a business expense the costs of medical or life insurance.

THE PARTNERSHIP

The General Partnership

A partnership is defined as "a voluntary association of two or more persons to carry on as co-owners of a business for profit." A partnership is more complicated than merely a collection of individuals. The partners must resolve and should set down in writing their agreement on a number of issues:

— The amount and nature of their respective capital contributions. One partner might contribute cash, another a patent, and a third property and cash.
— The allocation of the business' profits and losses.
— Salaries and drawings against profits.
— Management responsibilities.

— Consequences of withdrawal, retirement, disability, or death of a partner.
— Means of dissolution and liquidation of the partnership.

The Limited Partnership

A limited partnership is a partnership which has both limited *and* general partners.

— The general partner assumes the management responsibility *and* unlimited liability for the business.
— The limited partner has no voice in management and is legally liable only for the amount of the capital contribution plus any other debt specifically accepted.

In a limited partnership, the general partner may be a corporation (a corporate general partner). In situations where a corporation is the sole general partner, in order to ensure that there are sufficient assets to cover the unlimited liability which the general partner must assume, the corporate general partner must have a net worth equal to at least 10 percent of the total capitalization of the partnership.

Classification

A partnership is treated much like a proprietorship.

— Continuity of life: The partnership will cease to exist upon the death, insanity, or retirement of any of the partners, unless specifically reconstituted according to the governing law and documents of the partnership.
— Centralized management:
  • In a general partnership, management is not centralized because *all* of the partners have decision-making authority.
  • In a limited partnership, a subgroup of the owners—the general partners—has decision-making authority, and therefore, management is centralized.
— Limited liability: The nature of a partnership is such that someone, or some group, must accept unlimited liability.
  • In a general partnership, all of the partners have full, unlimited liability.
  • In a limited partnership, the limited partners' liability is limited to the capital contributed plus any other liability the limited partner agrees to accept. The general partners in a limited partnership *still* have full, unlimited liability.
— Free transferability of interest: Partnership interests are not freely transferable.

Tax Status

For tax purposes neither a general nor a limited partnership is considered a separate tax entity (although the partnership does file a return) but is merely a conduit through which income (or losses) is passed to the partners.

— Profit and losses are allocated to individuals in accordance with the partnership agreement, as long as that distribution has some basis in economic reality.
— Cash distributions are allocated in a manner which may or may not parallel profits and losses.

Generally, the following tax rules apply:

— The apportionment of profits and losses must have some economic substance; it may not be designed solely to avoid taxes.
— Generally, the amount of losses which a partner may deduct is limited to the amount of capital at risk, i.e., equity contributed plus debt assumed. (Note: Real estate partnerships are an exception to this "at risk" rule.)
— The income of the partnership is taxed at the personal level of the individual whether or not any cash is actually distributed.
— The distribution of cash out of income or retained earnings is not itself a taxable event. The only time when cash distributions are a taxable event is when the cash distribution exceeds the partners' basis in the partnership.
— The basis is equal to the amount of capital originally contributed, plus the amount of income on which tax is paid, less any cash distributions. (Example: An individual invests $100 in a partnership, and his share of income in Year 1 equals $30. He must pay tax on this $30 at the personal rate. His basis is now $130. If he receives a $20 cash distribution, his basis drops to $110.)

THE CORPORATION

Both the "regular" corporation and the S corporation are creatures of the law. The S corporation technically refers to an election which corporate shareholders may make to receive "Subchapter S tax treatment."

Classification

A corporation is defined according to the following criteria:

— Continuity of life: The death or divestiture of interest by any shareholder, or group, will not cause a dissolution of the corporation.

— Centralization of management: The decision-making authority of a corporation is legally constituted in the corporation's board of directors, rather than in the shareholders.
— Limited liability: The "corporate veil" protects the shareholder from personal liability (exception: owners of a corporation who are also managers of the firm are personally liable for certain liabilities which result from fraud or violations of the tax code).
— Free transferability of interest: Shareholders are usually free to sell their interest in the corporation without the consent of other shareholders. They may bargain this right away in the original shareholders' agreement. In the case of an S corporation, however, the sale of shares to any entity *except* an individual will automatically trigger the dissolution of S corporation status.

Legally, the organization of a corporation requires a charter, bylaws, a board of directors, and corporate officers (president, treasurer, clerk). The precise legal requirements are a function of the specific state law where the firm is incorporated.

Tax Status: S Corporation

The S corporation is a vehicle of Congress specifically targeted to give certain advantages to the small business. Essentially, an S corporation is treated like a partnership for tax purposes, i.e., it functions as a conduit through which income is allocated. However, the S corporation owners are afforded the same protection from unlimited liability as the owners of a corporation.

In order to qualify for S corporation status, the organization must meet a number of rather restrictive conditions. It must:

— Have only one class of stock, although differences in voting rights are allowed.
— Be a domestic corporation, owned wholly by U.S. citizens, and derive no more than 80 percent of its revenues from non-U.S. sources.
— Have 35 or fewer stockholders.
— Derive no more than 25 percent of revenues from passive sources, i.e., interest, dividends, and royalties.
— Have only individuals, estates, and certain trusts as shareholders, i.e., no corporations.

The election of S corporation tax status requires the unanimous consent of all shareholders. This status may be terminated by unanimous election, or if one of the above-mentioned conditions is broken.

Tax Status: Regular Corporation

Corporations do not receive a deduction for dividends paid to shareholders. Further, shareholders are taxed on the receipt of dividend income. Hence, shareholders are taxed twice on the same earnings. This "double taxation" is the main disadvantage of a corporation. (The exceptions to this rule are qualified investment companies and real estate investment trusts which qualify under Section 856–858 of the tax code.)

In order to avoid this double taxation, the principals of closely held corporations (especially wholly owned companies) often resort to the tactic of attempting to structure the return of earnings in a form that is deductible to the corporation, i.e., interest or salary. The IRS has a number of rules which deal explicitly with these issues.

— Salary: By raising his salary to a very high level, the owner of a corporation could effectively reduce earnings to zero, and pay tax only once, at a personal level, on salary received.
  • Federal Tax Code Section 162, paragraph (A) states that the IRS will permit ". . . a reasonable allowance for salaries or other compensation for personal services actually rendered."
  • The IRS can, upon audit, reclassify a portion of salary as dividends, and thus create both a corporate and a personal tax liability.
— Interest: By initially capitalizing the business with debt (rather than equity) the owners can receive some of their cash distributions in the form of interest rather than dividends. Interest expense is deductible by the corporation and is therefore a "cheaper" way to get money out of the business.
  • Federal Tax Code Section 385 deals with the issue of "thinly capitalized" corporations, i.e., where the IRS believes that the capital structure of the business is too heavily weighted in favor of debt.
  • In essence, the IRS can, upon audit, reclassify debt as equity and reclassify interest as dividends when:
    –The debt does not have the characteristics of debt, i.e., is held in proportion to stock, payment of interest is contingent upon certain conditions or interest is unreasonable.
    –The corporation has "excessive" debt, i.e., a debt to equity ratio of greater than 10:1.

Another disadvantage of the corporate form of organization is the inability to flow through losses. In a proprietorship, partnership, or Sub S corporation, losses will flow through to the owners of the firm for deduction that year on their personal tax return. A corporation accumulates tax losses for its own use in later years.

One exception in this area involves "Section 1244 stock." This is a special creature of the tax code. If a new business is formed using 1244 stock rather than regular common shares, and if the business goes bankrupt, owners of the stock can claim an ordinary income loss up to the amount of their investment. Had the company been formed with regular shares, the loss would have been a capital loss.

There are, however, several tax advantages to the corporate form of organization. These include:

— Deductibility of certain personal fringe benefits, such as medical and health insurance.

— The ability to shelter earnings, i.e., keep earnings within the company and transfer them out, as dividends, at a later date when the recipients may be in a more tax advantageous situation.

SUMMARY

Each of the various legal forms of organization is distinguished from the others in a variety of ways. Often the decision about which legal form to elect is made solely in an attempt to minimize taxes. While this is a legitimate economic aim, the forms of organization differ along many other important dimensions. It is important to have a full understanding of *all* of these differences before electing the legal form. The counsel of a competent attorney is usually called for.

130

EXHIBIT 1
Comparison of Various Legal Forms of Organization

	Proprietorship	Partnership	Regular Corporation	Subchapter S Corporation
Taxable year	Usually calendar year	Usually calendar year; however, September, October, or November can be elected	Any year-end is permissible	Optional original choice; changes of fiscal year-end generally limited to September, October, November, or December
Expensing of depreciable business assets	Limited to $5,000 in 1982, increasing to $10,000 in 1986	Limited to $5,000 in 1982, increasing to $10,000 in 1986		Limited to $5,000 in 1982, increasing to $10,000 in 1986
Ordinary distributions to owners	Drawings from the business are not taxable; the net profits are taxable; and the proprietor is subject to the tax on self-employment income	Generally not taxable	Payments of salaries are deductible by corporation and taxable to recipient; payments of dividends are not deductible by corporation and generally are taxable to recipient shareholders	Same as regular corporation
Limitations on losses deductible by owners	Amount "at risk," except with respect to real estate activities	Partner's investment plus his or her share of the partnership recourse liabilities except for real estate partnerships	No losses allowed to individual except upon sale of stock or liquidation of corporation	The shareholder's investment plus his or her loans to the corporation; basis of loans reduced by losses and distributions

Dividends received	$100 dividend exclusion ($200 on joint tax return)	Conduit	85% to 100% dividend-received deduction	Treated as ordinary income; no exclusion or deduction
Formal election required	No	No	Must incorporate under state law	Yes
Capital gain	Taxed at individual level; 60% deduction for long term	Conduit	Taxed at corporate level; alternative tax rate, 28%	Amounts flow through to extent of shareholder's portion of corporation's taxable income, but (unlike partnership) ordinary losses and capital gains are netted at corporate level
Capital losses	Carried forward indefinitely	Conduit	Carry back three years and carry over five years as short-term capital loss offsetting only capital gains	Carry over five years as short-term capital loss, offsetting only capital gains
Section 1231 gains and losses	Taxed at individual level, combined with other Section 1231 gains or losses of individual; net gains are capital gains for individual; net losses are ordinary losses for individual	Conduit	Taxable, or deductible at the corporate level	Net gain is a capital gain to the shareholder; net loss is an ordinary loss to the shareholder; however, corporation's 1231 losses are not netted with shareholder's 1231 gains
Basis of allocating income to owners	All income picked up on owner's return	Profit and loss agreement (may have "special allocations" of income and deductions if they reflect economic reality)	No income allocated to stockholders	Number of shares owned on the last day of the corporation's tax year

EXHIBIT 1 (*continued*)

	Proprietorship	Partnership	Regular Corporation	Subchapter S Corporation
Basis for allocating a net operating loss	All losses flow through to owner's return	Profit and loss agreement (may have "special allocations" of income and deductions if they reflect economic reality)	No losses allocated to stockholders	Prorated among shareholders on a daily basis
Group hospitalization and life insurance premiums and medical reimbursement plans	Itemized deductions: for medical expenses, half of insurance premiums up to $150, medicine and drugs in excess of 1% of adjusted gross income, other bills over 3% of AGI; no deduction for life insurance premiums	Cost of partners' benefits are not deductible as a business expense; may be treated as distribution to individual partners, eligible for some possible deduction as if paid by individual	Cost of shareholder-employee's coverage is generally deductible as a business expense if plan is "for the benefit of employees."	Same as regular corporation
Retirement benefits	Limited to H.R.-10 plan benefits, normally 15% of income up to $15,000; however, some defined-benefit H.R.-10 plans may provide more. For years beginning after 1983, limitation increases to essentially same as regular corporation	Same as individual	Normal corporate employee benefits subject to maximum pension to retired employees of $10,000 plus inflation	Corporation can deduct normal corporate employee contribution; however, owner-employee must add income contribution in excess of $15,000 to taxable income. For years beginning after 1983, limitation increases to essentially same as regular corporation

Organization costs	Not amortizable	Amortizable over 60 months	Amortizable over 60 months	Same as regular corporation
Partner's or shareholder's "reasonable" salary	Not applicable	Treated as an allocation of partnership profits and a conduit		Expense to the corporation, taxable to the shareholder-employee subject to FICA
Charitable contribution	Subject to limits for individual; gifts for the use of private foundation, 20% of AGI; gifts to public charity, cash 50% of AGI; appreciated property, 30% of AGI. Other limitations for specific items contributed	Conduit		Limited to 10% of taxable income before special deductions
Liability	Individually liable on all liabilities of business	General partners individually liable on partnership's liabilities; limited partner liable only up to amount of his or her capital contribution	Capital contribution is limit of liability of shareholder	Same as regular corporation
Qualified owners	Individual ownership	No limitation	No limitation	Only individuals, estates, and certain trusts may be shareholders
Type of ownership interests	Individual ownership	More than one class of partner permitted	More than one class of stock permitted	Only one class of stock permitted
Transfer of ownership	Assets of business transferable rather than business itself	New partnership usually created; consent of other partners normally required if partnership interest is to be transferred	Ready transfer of ownership through the use of stock certificates; restrictions may be imposed by shareholders' agreement	Shares can be transferred only to individuals, certain types of trusts, or estates; no consent by new shareholders to Subchapter S election is needed

EXHIBIT 1 (*concluded*)

	Proprietorship	Partnership	Regular Corporation	Subchapter S Corporation
Capital requirements	Capital raised only by loan or increased contribution by proprietor	Loans or contributions from partners (original, or newly created by remaking partnership)	Met by sale of stock or bonds or other corporate debt	Met by sale of stock or bonds, but corporation has only one class of stock and is limited to 35 shareholders
Business action	Sole proprietor makes decisions and can act immediately	Action usually dependent upon the unanimous agreement of partners or general partners	Unity of action based on authority of board of directors	Same as regular corporation except unanimous consent is required to elect or revoke Subchapter S status
Management	Proprietor responsible and receives all profits or losses	Except for limited or silent partners, investment in partnership involves responsibility for management decisions	Shareholder can receive income without sharing in responsibility for management	Same as regular corporation
Flexibility	No restrictions	Partnership is contractual arrangement, within which members can do in business what individuals can, subject to the partnership agreement and applicable state laws	Corporation is a creature of the state functioning within powers granted explicitly or necessarily implied and subject to judicial construction and decision	Same as regular corporation

Investment credit	Limited by tax liability up to $25,000 plus 90% of liability in excess of $25,000 (85% for tax years beginning after 1982)	Conduit	Conduit	Offset to taxes at corporate level; subject to $25,000 plus 90% of liability in excess of $25,000 (85% for tax years beginning after 1982)
Tax preferences (minimum tax)	Through 1982, 15% of tax on preferences in excess of either $10,000 or one-half of taxes paid (but capital gains preference and adjusted itemized deductions preference subject to alternative minimum tax). After 1982, add-on minimum tax is eliminated, and all preference items are subject to an expanded alternative minimum tax	Conduit	Conduit	Taxed at corporate level; 15% on preferences in excess of either $10,000 or tax liability, whichever is greater. In addition, for years beginning after 1982, benefits of certain preferences are "cut back" by 15% in computing taxable income. Amount of "cut back" preference is reduced for purposes of computing add-on minimum tax
Character of income and deductions	Taxed at individual level; long-term capital gains deduction; limitation on investment interest deductions	Conduit	Taxed at corporate level	Except as to long-term capital gains, income and profits are computed at corporate level, so that characteristics are determined at corporate level and do not flow to shareholder

Source: S. Jones and M.B. Cohen, *The Emerging Business* (New York: Coopers & Lybrand, 1983).

Case 2–1

TRU-PAINT, INC.

On April 19, 1961, Warren G. Hamer received a telephone call from
John M. Dublois, a finder, about a company which was for sale. After being reassured that he would receive a finder's fee of 5 percent of the purchase price, Dublois indicated that he would bring the information over
to him in the morning. Dublois apologized for not thinking of Mr. Hamer
earlier but only five days were left to submit a bid.

Mr. Dublois appeared early the next morning at Hamer's office with
the three pages of information contained in Exhibit 1.

A quick check of the competitive situation with the Tru-Paint president disclosed that in the specific field of liquid paint dispensed in tubes
for use in home decoration, Tru-Paint's sales were larger than any of its six
competitors. Of the six competitors, only three distributed their products
through the house-party plan.[1] In the more general home hobbycraft and
industrial markets, Tru-Paint had to meet intense competition with firms
of significantly greater sales and resources.

There were certain aspects of the purchase which made Mr. Hamer
apprehensive about the deal. First, the manner in which the company was
being sold was very unusual and the time period to evaluate the situation
was very short. Second, no assurance could be given that the present
management would stay on and Mr. Hamer did not want to become ac-

tively involved in the management of a small company such as Tru-Paint. Finally Mr. Hamer was worried about the restriction on contacting the company's distributors and the effects of the company's sale upon their continued loyalty.

Not wanting to commit a significant amount of his assets to the venture if he decided to undertake it, Mr. Hamer contacted a former associate, Mr. Blake. Edmund J. Blake, Jr., was a vice president of P. W. Brooks & Co., a medium-sized Wall Street investment banking firm which had specialized in unit financing programs, primarily in the utility and chemical industries, during the past 55 years.

On Friday, April 21, Mssrs. Hamer and Blake met with Mr. Henry L. Aaron, president of the E-I Mutual Association, and with Mr. Joseph Reimann, president of Tru-Paint, Inc. The company's office was in one corner of a large, basement room in an old commercial section of the city. The entire production facility consisted of vats and tanks for mixing and filling the ball-point tubes and a shipping area for packaging the tubes after they were filled. The history of the company, presented by Aaron and Reimann, is summarized in Exhibit 2.

APPENDIX: PARTY PLAN SELLING

There are three basic methods of house-to-house direct selling in which a salesman demonstrates and sells his products in a prospective customer's home: cold canvassing, coupon advertising, and party plan selling. The differentiating characteristic between these forms of direct selling is the method of generating prospects.

In cold canvassing a salesman, without first having made appointments, systematically knocks on every home or apartment door of a street until he encounters an interest in his product. If invited into the home, he demonstrates his product and attempts to make a sale.

Coupon advertising generates potential customers by means of reader service coupons attached to advertisements and promotional materials. When a reader of an advertisement or promotional handout sends in a reader service coupon requesting more information about a product, a salesman is sent to the reader's home to demonstrate and sell the product.

The party plan generates prospects by encouraging housewives to hostess a coffee and doughnut party for her friends; the stated purpose of the party to the guests being the opportunity for the company salesman to demonstrate and sell the company's products. The incentive for the housewife to hostess a party is the prospect of receiving a gift certificate from the company's hostess gift catalogue which usually includes both company and noncompany home products. The value of the hostess's gift is a function of the dollar sales resulting from her party, the number of people who attend, and the number of additional hostesses recruited from the party.

For example, a Tru-Paint dealer (salesman/woman) might start developing a prospect-customer list by persuading a friend or relative to hostess a Tru-Paint Embroidery Party for a hostess gift. At this party the dealer would exhibit the range of materials to which Tru-Paint could be applied, available predesigned patterns, and all the necessary accessories needed to accomplish Tru-Paint embroidery. The dealer would receive from this party (1) a commission from the sales that were made and (2) leads on additional hostesses for future parties. Thus the party process frequently tends to snowball because of the "friends have different friends" phenomenon which can generate a constant supply of new prospects for the distributor as well as produce a customer list for potential repeat sales.

The major advantage of home selling is that it focuses the attention of potential buyers only on the company product being sold. This elimination of competing products tends to make closing a sale easier than is possible in the more competitive environment of a retail outlet where similar and substitute products are displayed. Some advantages of the party plan over cold canvassing and coupon advertising as a means of home selling are (1) less sales resistance is met in the home because the hostess is sponsoring the product to her friends and the guests know in advance the selling purpose of the party; (2) customer and prospect lists grow faster and each sales call generates a larger sales volume since more than one family attends each party and hears each sales presentation; and (3) its respectability is generally greater in the eyes of the public because of its nonabrasive prospecting and straightforward selling approach.

Companies and products that employ the party plan selling method exclusively or in addition to cold canvassing and coupon advertising are:

Cosmetics	*Apparel*
Studio Girl Inc.	Beeline Fashions Inc.
Mary Kay Inc.	Queensway to Fashion Inc.
Fashion Two Twenty Inc.	Dutchmaid Inc.
Vanda-Beauty Counselor Inc.	Joya Fashions
a subsidiary of Dart Industries	a subsidiary of Jewel Fashions
Vivian Woodward Inc.	
a subsidiary of General Foods	

Lingerie	*Household Products*
Claire James Inc.	Tupperware Home Parties
Penny Rich Inc.	Stanley Home Products

EXHIBIT 1
Information and Terms and Conditions Relative to Proposed Sale by E–I Mutual Association of Its Wholly-Owned Subsidiary, Tru-Paint, Inc.

Tru-Paint, Inc., is located at 82 Main Street, West Orange, New Jersey. It manufactures and distributes on a nationwide basis, liquid paint dispensed in ball-point tubes. The product is sold under the registered trademarks "Tru-Paint" and "Liquid Embroidery"; and is used primarily for hobby work of a decorative nature. It bears the Good Housekeeping seal of approval. In addition, Tru-Paint, Inc. manufactures or has manufactured a line of products accessory to its paints.

The product is distributed chiefly on the so-called party plan basis, with distributors located at various points throughout most of the United States.

The company has operated under its present ownership for the last five years, during which the volume and profit have steadily increased.

Terms and Conditions of Sale
1. Cash bids will be received up to and including April 24, 1961.
2. Bids shall be accompanied by a 5 percent deposit.
3. Bids shall be firm until 5 P.M., May 24, 1961. Acceptance may be made by a telegram filed before that date and hour or by letter postmarked prior to that date and hour.
4. Seller reserves the right to reject any or all bids.
5. Closing shall be at Seller's option between June 19 and June 23, 1961, inclusive.
6. Inspection of plant facilities is invited.
7. Bids shall be submitted subject to the understanding that Seller's distributors may not be contacted by, or on behalf of, Bidder and that any violation of this restriction shall result in automatic forfeiture of deposit.
8. Audited financial statements for 1957, 1958, 1959, and 1960 are annexed.
9. All bids shall be submitted to:
> Henry L. Aaron, President
> E–I Mutual Association
> 670 Q Street
> West Orange, New Jersey

Please mark the envelope "Confidential." All inquiries shall also be directed to Mr. Aaron, who may be reached by telephone at REdwood 5-1234.

EXHIBIT 1 (*concluded*)
Copy of Audited Statements

Balance Sheets

Assets	1960	1959	1958	1957
Current assets:				
Cash	$ 90,094	$ 89,790	$ 81,844	$ 70,639
Note receivable	23,902	—	—	—
Accounts receivable (Less allowance for doubtful collections)	63,107	45,505	35,746	28,091
Inventories	91,079	75,704	59,050	59,261
Prepaid expenses	9,090	6,130	4,700	2,239
Total current assets	277,272	217,129	181,340	160,230
Furniture, fixtures, machinery and equipment, motor vehicles	22,669	17,604	15,328	15,148
Less accumulated depreciation	13,944	10,323	9,645	6,437
	8,725	7,281	5,683	8,711
Covenant not to compete, foreign license agreement, patents, etc.	82,180	122,180	192,180	193,180
Less accumulated amortization	24,566	52,264	51,915	35,963
	57,614	69,916	140,265	157,217
Goodwill	70,000	70,000	—	—
Total assets	$413,611	$364,326	$327,288	$326,158
Liabilities				
Current liabilities:				
Note payable		27,500	100,000	175,000
Accounts payable and accrued liabilities	22,397	19,683	11,781	9,993
Federal income tax payable	71,249	60,966	46,889	32,589
Total current liabilities	93,646	108,149	158,670	217,582
Capital stock and surplus:				
Authorized 1,000 shares of common, no par value—issued and outstanding	2,000	2,000	2,000	2,000
Earned surplus	317,965	254,177	166,618	106,576
Total capital stock and surplus	319,965	256,177	168,618	108,576
Total liabilities	$413,611	$364,326	$327,288	$326,158

Statement of Income and Surplus

	1960	1959	1958	1957
Net sales	$688,327	$597,603	$481,350	$466,580
Cost of goods sold	431,975	359,956	288,188	289,519
Gross profit	256,352	237,647	193,162	177,061
Selling, shipping, general and administrative expenses	87,362	78,893	67,692	64,788
Operating profit	168,990	158,754	125,470	112,273
Other income	1,972	1,614	4,706	6,453
Net income	$170,962	$160,368	$130,176	$118,726
Other charges:				
Provision for amortization	12,301	12,801	16,952	17,452
Interest	624	4,121	6,293	9,185
	12,925	16,922	23,245	26,637
	158,037	143,446	106,931	92,089
Provision for federal income tax	71,249	60,966	46,889	32,589
Net profit for the year	$ 86,788	$ 82,480	$ 60,042	$ 59,500
Surplus January 1	$254,177	$166,618	$106,576	$ 47,076
Add: Partial disallowance by Treasury Department of amortization of foreign license agreement, patents, etc.		12,452		
		$179,070		
Deduct: Additional federal income taxes		7,375		
		$171,697		
Dividends $23.00 per share	23,000		—	—
Earned surplus December 31	$317,965	$254,177	166,618	$106,576

EXHIBIT 2
Background of the Company (summarized) as Described by Messrs. Aaron and Reimann

Tru Paint was organized in 1948 to exploit the possibilities of the ball-point paint dispenser. The company was the original manufacturer of ball-point paint dispensers and paint compounds suited to this use. The company originally utilized both manufacturer's agents and direct contacts to sell their products through large retail outlets. By 1954 Tru-Paint sales through the retail outlets had grown to over $1 million.

By 1953, however, the large paint manufacturers were introducing competitive products with by-product pricing. The company foresaw that additional competition would create a substantial decline in the company's profit margins. This factor coupled with disagreements within the management group placed Tru-Paint on the sales block. Thus, in early 1954, the original owners were approached by E–I Mutual with a purchase offer.

E–I Mutual Association was founded in 1949 by the son of Thomas A. Edison, Mr. Theodore Edison, then president of Edison Electric, as an experiment in labor management relations. It was his thesis that if employees became stockholders in other companies, they would be more sympathetic to the needs of the stockholders and the management of their own company. He set up the association with about $1 million worth of stock in Edison. The original intent was that E–I Mutual should invest these funds in small companies, but by 1954 it had sizable investments in American Telephone and Telegraph, General Motors, General Electric and other blue chip stocks. An employee of Edison could purchase one share of E–I Mutual $3 dividend stock at $10 a share for each year that he worked for the company up to a limit of 15 shares. If, for any reason, his employment was terminated, the employee had to sell back to the association one share of his holdings each year following separation at the same $10 per share price.

In 1954, Joseph Reimann, as president of E–I Mutual Association, learned of the availability of Tru-Paint and recommended that E–I Mutual purchase 100 percent ownership for some $300,000. The membership voted and approved this recommendation. Subsequently, Mr. Reimann became president of Tru-Paint.

Mr. Reimann realized that the Tru-Paint distribution system needed to be revamped and it was his idea to market the company's products under the home party plan. By 1957, the company distributed its products to the consumer market primarily through independent distributors under the home party plan. In developing its distributor organization throughout the United States, Tru-Paint entered into exclusive territorial franchise agreements with its distributors.

Tru-Paint supplied kits consisting of its line of paint-filled ball-point tubes, various accessories such as embroidery hoops to hold the stamped materials taut, and sample pieces of fabric printed with a design on which the novice could practice. The distributor was free to make his own arrangements with other suppliers to sell at the same parties, products such as stamped textiles, glass, and leather to which the Tru-Paint line of color tubes could be applied. The distributors were also free to create and manage their own organizations of demonstrators. The growth and selection of the independent distributors for Tru-Paint could be characterized as somewhat haphazard. Vast differences in population, size of territory, and normal trading areas were noticeable between distributors. By 1960, the company had 17 exclusive distributors.

Prior to the end of 1960, several of the company's distributors had indicated an interest in purchasing Tru-Paint if E–I Mutual decided to sell its interest.

In 1959, the Company's products were awarded the Good Housekeeping Seal of Approval by *Good Housekeeping* magazine.

Case 2-2

COMMERCIAL FIXTURES, INC.

It would take only a few quick strokes of his pen to fill out the bid form and but an instant to seal the envelope. Gordon Whitlock caught himself in momentary wonder that this simple form would have such a dramatic effect on the next few years of his life. Tomorrow, February 23, 1979, at 12 o'clock noon, the envelopes from Gordon and his partner, Albert Evans, would be opened to determine which of them would buy out the other and own Commercial Fixtures Inc., the company built by their fathers. After working together for over 25 years, the two partners had decided that this was the best way to resolve differences of opinion that had arisen over how to manage the company.

COMPANY DESCRIPTION

Commercial Fixtures Inc. (CFI) manufactured custom-engineered fluorescent lighting fixtures used for commercial and institutional applications. Sales in 1978 were $4 million with profits of $115,000.

Most sales were standard items within the nine major lines of products designed and offered by the company. Ten percent of sales were completely custom-designed or custom-built fixtures, and 15 percent of orders were for slightly modified versions of a standard product. In 1978, CFI shipped 66,000 fixtures. Although individual orders ranged from one unit to over 2,000 units, the average order size had been fairly consistently 15–20 fixtures. Modified and custom designed fixtures averaged about 25 per order. Gordon Whitlock, CFI president, described their market position:

> Our product marketing strategy is to try to solve lighting problems for architects and engineers. We design products which are architecturally styled for specific types of building constructions. If an architect has an unusual lighting problem, we design a special fixture to fit his needs. Or if he designs a lighting fixture, we build it to his specifications. We try to find products that satisfy particular lighting needs that are not filled by the giant fixture manufacturers. We look for niches in the marketplace.
>
> Having the right product to fit the architect's particular needs is the most important thing to our customer. Second is the relationship that the architect, the consulting engineer, or the lighting designer has with the people who are representing us. The construction business is such that the architect, engineer, contractor, distributor, and manufacturer all have to work as a team together on a specific project to ensure its successful completion. The architect makes a lot of mistakes in every building he designs, unless he just designs the same one over and over. Consequently, there's a lot of trading that goes on during the construction of a building, and everybody's got to give and take a little to get the job done. Then the owner usually gets a satisfactory job and the contractors and manufacturers make a fair profit. It requires a cooperative effort.
>
> Most of our bids for orders are probably compared with bids from half a dozen other firms across the country. Since a higher percentage of our orders are for premium-priced products, we are not as price sensitive as producers of more commonplace lighting fixtures. It is difficult for a small firm to compete in that market. As many as 30 companies might bid on one standard fixture job.

CFI owned its own modern manufacturing facility located outside Denver, Colorado. Production consisted of stamping, cutting, and forming sheet metal, painting, and assembly of the fixture with the electrical components which were purchased from outside suppliers. The company employed a total of 104 workers, with 34 in sales, engineering, and administration and another 70 in production and assembly.

The company sold nationwide through regional distributors to contractors and architects for new buildings and renovations. Prior to 1976, CFI sold primarily to a regional market. At that time, marketing activities were broadened geographically. This was the primary reason that sales had been increasing over the last few years even during a weak construction market. (See Exhibit 1 for historical sales, earnings, unit sales, and employment.)

BACKGROUND

Commercial Fixtures, Inc. was formed in Golden, Colorado, in 1936 by Jonathan Whitlock and Julius Lacy. Each owned one half of the company.

Whitlock was responsible for finance and engineering and Lacy for sales and design. They subcontracted all manufacturing for the lighting systems they sold.

After several years, differences in personal work habits led Whitlock to buy out Lacy's interest. Jonathan Whitlock then brought in Paul Evans as his new partner. Evans had been one of his sheet metal subcontractors. Paul Evans became president and Whitlock, treasurer. Ownership was split so that Whitlock retained a few shares more than half because of his experience with Lacy.

In 1940, CFI began manufacturing and moved its operations to a multifloor 50,000 sq. ft. plant also located in Golden. The company grew and was quite profitable during the war years and during the following boom in construction of the early 1950s. Whitlock and Evans were quite satisfied with the earnings they had amassed during this period and were content to let the company remain at a steady level of about $1 million in sales and about $15,000 in profit after taxes.

Jonathan Whitlock's son, Gordon, joined CFI as a salesman in 1956 after graduating from MIT and then Colorado Business School. Paul Evans' son Albert, who was a graduate of Trinity College, also became a CFI salesman in 1957 when he was discharged from the service. The two sons were acquaintances from occasional gatherings as they were growing up, but had not been close friends.

In 1959, Jonathan Whitlock had a heart attack and withdrew from the management of the business. Although he remained an interested observer and sometime advisor to his son, Jonathan was inactive in company affairs after this time. Paul Evans assumed complete management overview of the company.

Gordon Whitlock moved inside to learn about other parts of the company in 1960. His first work assignments were in manufacturing and sales service. Albert Evans joined his father in the manufacturing area a year later. Gordon became sales manager, Albert became manufacturing manager, and at Paul Evans' suggestion, another person was added as financial manager. These three formed a middle management triumvirate that worked well together, but major decisions were still reserved for Paul Evans, who spent less and less time in the office.

As the new group began revitalizing the company, a number of employees who had not been productive and were not responding to change were retired early or asked to leave. When the man who had been Paul Evans' chief aide could not work with the three younger managers, they ultimately decided he had to be discharged. Paul Evans became so angry that he rarely entered the plant again.

For several years the three managers guided the company as a team. However, there were some spirited discussions over the basic strategic view of the company. As sales manager, Gordon Whitlock pressed for responding to special customer needs. This, he felt, would be their strongest market niche. Albert Evans argued for smooth production flows and less disruption. He felt they could compete well in the "semistandard" market.

In 1962, the fathers moved to restructure the company's ownership to reflect the de facto changes in management. The fathers converted their ownership to nonvoting class A stock. Each transferred 44 percent of his nonvoting stock to his son. Jonathan Whitlock decided to relinquish his voting control at this time in an effort to help things work as the new generation took over. Accordingly, Gordon and Albert were each issued 50 percent of the class B voting shares.

In 1961, Gordon Whitlock began to work with an individual in forming a company in the computer field which rented extra space from CFI. CFI provided management and administrative support, helping the new company with bidding and keeping track of contracts. Although Albert Evans was not active in this company, Gordon split his partial ownership in this new company with Albert because they were partners and because Gordon was spending time away from CFI with the computer company.

With the heavy demands of the start-up over the next three years, this new effort began to weaken the relationship between Gordon and Albert. At the same time, Albert and the financial manager began to have strong disagreements. These seemed to arise primarily from forays in cost analysis which led the financial manager to question some of Albert's decisions. There were also differences of opinion over relations with the work force and consistency of policy. Albert preferred to control the manufacturing operation in his own way. Gordon felt Albert could be more consistent, less arbitrary, and more supportive of the work force. When the computer company was sold in 1968, the financial manager joined it as treasurer and resigned from CFI.

GROWING CONFLICT

The departure of the financial manager led to a worsening of the relationship between Gordon and Albert. Gordon had been made company president in 1963. Gordon recalled the decision:

> Paul Evans had resigned as president and the three of us were sitting around talking about who should be president. Albert Evans finally said, "I think you should be it." And I said, "O. K."

Yet even with this change, the three managers had really operated together as a team for major decisions. Now, Gordon was upset that they had lost an excellent financial manager, someone critical to the operation (due, in his opinion, partially to the disagreements with Albert). There was also no longer a third opinion to help resolve conflicts. Although the financial manager was replaced with an old classmate of Albert's, the new manager became one of several middle level managers who had been hired as the company grew.

The pressures of growth created more strains between Gordon and Albert. Sales had reached $1 million and had begun to tax CFI's manufacturing capacity. Gordon felt that some of the problems could be alleviated if Albert would change methods that had been acceptable during slacker periods but hindered intense production efforts. Albert had different views. Both agreed to look for additional space.

The transition to a new factory outside Denver, Colorado, in 1970 eased the stresses between the partners. A major corporation had purchased an indirect competitor to obtain its product lines and sold CFI the 135,000 sq. ft. plant. CFI also entered into an agreement to manufacture some of the other company's light fixtures as a subcontractor. The plant was in poor condition and Albert Evans took over the project of renovating it and continuing production of the other company's lines. Gordon Whitlock remained in Golden running the CFI operation alone until it became possible to consolidate the entire operation in Denver. Gordon described this interlude:

> The next year was a sort of cooling off period. Albert was immersed in his operation and I was geared into the continuing operation. Albert had always enjoyed projects of this sort and was quite satisfied with this arrangement.
>
> Then in 1972 we hired a plant manager to run the Denver plant and Albert came back to work in Golden. By that time, of course, a lot of things had changed. All of Golden had been reporting to me. I had somewhat reshaped the operation and the people had gotten used to my management style which was different than Albert's.
>
> Albert's reaction was to work with the design and engineering people, but he really wasn't involved very much with the daily manufacturing any more. He developed a lot of outside interests, business and recreation, that took up much of his time.
>
> I was very happy with that arrangement because it lessened the conflict. But when he did come back, the disagreements would be worse. I guess I resented his attempts to change things when he only spent a small amount of time in the company.
>
> Then in 1973 we made the decision to sell the Golden plant and put the whole company in Denver. We were both involved in that. Most of our key people went with us. Albert and I were very active in pulling together the two groups, in integrating the operation.
>
> That began a fairly good time. I was spending my time with the sales manager trying to change the company from a regional company to a national one and was helping to find new representatives all over the country. Evans spent his time in the engineering, design, and manufacturing areas. There was plenty of extra capacity in the new plant, so things went quite smoothly. In particular, Albert did an excellent job in upgrading the quality standards of the production force we acquired with the plant. This was critical for our line of products and our quality reputation.

This move really absorbed us for almost two years. It just took us a long time to get people working together, to produce at the quality level and rate we wanted. We had purchased the plant for an excellent price with a lot of new equipment and had started deleting marginal product lines as we expanded nationally. The company became much more profitable.

As the company expanded, a group of six people formed the operating team. Albert Evans concentrated on applications engineering for custom fixtures and new product design. In addition, there were a sales manager, financial manager, engineering manager, the plant manufacturing manager, and Gordon. Disagreements began again. Gordon recounted the problems:

Our operating group would meet on a weekly or biweekly basis, whatever was necessary. Then we would have monthly executive committee meetings for broader planning issues. These became a disaster. Albert had reached the point where he didn't like much of anything that was going on in the company and was becoming very critical. I disagreed with him as did the other managers on most occasions. Tempers often flared and Albert became more and more isolated.

He and I also began to disagree over which topics we should discuss with the group. I felt that some areas were best discussed between the two of us, particularly matters concerning personnel, and that other matters should be held for stockholders meetings. The committee meetings were becoming real battles.

In 1977, Paul Evans died. Although he had remained chairman of the board, he had been generally inactive since 1961. Jonathan and Gordon Whitlock and Albert Evans became the only directors.

SEARCH FOR A SOLUTION

Gordon Whitlock was discouraged by the continuing conflicts with his partner and had sought advice on how to remedy the situation from friends and associates as early as 1969. In 1977, Gordon was beginning to believe that he and Albert had just grown too far apart to continue together. However, Gordon had to find a mutually agreeable way to accomplish a separation. One partner could buy the other out, but they would have to agree on this and find an acceptable method. Albert seemed to have no interest in such an arrangement.

During 1977, the differences between the partners grew. The vacillations in leadership were disruptive to the operation and made other employees very uncomfortable.

By early 1978, the situation was growing unbearable. Gordon recalled the executive committee's annual planning meeting in January:

It was a total disaster. There were loud arguments and violent disagreements. It was so bad that no one wanted ever to participate in another meeting. We were all miserable.

What was so difficult was that each of us truly thought he was right. On various occasions other people in the company would support each of our positions. These were normally honest differences of opinion, but politics also started to enter in.

When Gordon returned from a summer vacation in August, he was greeted by a string of complaints from several of CFI's sales agents and also from some managers. Gordon decided that the problems had to be resolved. Gordon sought an intermediary:

I knew that Albert and I weren't communicating and that I had to find a mediator Albert trusted. I had discussed this before with Peter Dowling, our attorney. Peter was a boyhood friend who had grown up with Albert. I felt he had very high integrity and was very smart. Albert trusted him totally and Peter was probably one of Albert's major advisers about things.

When I first talked to Dowling in March, he basically said, "Well, you have problems in a marriage and you make it work. Go make it work, Gordon." He wasn't going to listen much.

Then in early September I went back to say that it wasn't going to work any more. I asked him for his help. Peter said that Albert had also seen him to complain about the problems, so Peter knew that the situation had become intolerable.

Dowling prepared a memorandum describing the various options of changing management and/or ownership that were available to partners who were having disagreements. Gordon decided to encourage one of Dowling's options which called for each partner to name a price for the business. Previously, some of Gordon's own advisers had suggested this same outlet.

Both directly and through Dowling, Gordon pressed Albert to agree to such an arrangement. Although Albert, too, was unhappy with their conflicts, he was hesitant to accede.

Gordon felt that there were several principal reasons for Albert's reluctance. One was the fact that Albert's only work experience was with CFI. This was limited primarily to managing manufacturing operations he had known for years. Second, Gordon thought Albert was very uncertain as to how to value the company since he had little formal training in financial analysis and had not been directly involved in the financial operations. Gordon felt that this made Albert's task of setting a bid price more difficult than his own. Finally, there was the emotional tie to the company and the avoidance of such a momentous decision.

As discussions began to result in the formulation of a buy-sell agreement, Albert's reluctance waxed and waned. Just before Christmas, Evans called Whitlock who was sick at home and said he had decided to fire the financial manager and become the treasurer of the company. He could look at the figures for a year or so and then make a better decision. Gordon felt the financial manager was essential and could not be discharged. He thought this was really more of an attempt to buy time.

After two more months of give and take in developing a formula and bid conditions, Whitlock and Evans finally signed a mutual buyout agreement on February 16, 1979. It called for sealed bids in a specific format with the partner offering the higher price buying out the other (Exhibit 2). The bids would be submitted in one week. Gordon credited Peter Dowling with convincing Albert to sign:

> I think Peter got him to sign it by sheer force of personality. By saying this situation is just not right, it's screwing up the company, you're not happy. You won't be happy until it's solved. This is a reasonable way to solve it and you damn well ought to take the chance. Because later, if you pass this up, it's just going to get worse.

VALUING THE COMPANY

Before preparing his bid, Gordon reviewed the thinking he had done since first considering the idea of buying or selling the company. He began with the company's current position. With the serious discussions going on about the buyout agreement, preparation of the financial statements for 1978 had been accelerated and they were already completed. (These are shown together with the results for 1977 and 1976 as Exhibit 3.)

Gordon had also begun developing the bank support he might need to fund a buyout. The company's banker indicated that he would loan Gordon funds secured by his other personal assets if Gordon was the buyer, but that since he had not worked with Albert, the bank would decline to finance an acquisition with Albert as the buyer. In addition, the bank would continue the company's existing line of credit which was secured by CFI's cash and accounts receivable. The maximum which could be borrowed with this line was an amount equal to 100 percent of cash plus 75 percent of receivables. Both types of borrowing would be at 1 percent over the prime rate (then about 9 percent).

Gordon had worked with the banker to begin financial projections he could use in establishing his bid. These projections set out pro forma operating results *before* taking the bid conditions into consideration. By structuring the financial projections in this manner, the results of *operating* assumptions could be separated from *bid* structures. Various combinations of bid conditions could be easily tested based on this set of business operating results. Long-term debts that would be assumed with the business were included within the operating projections. Other bank financing requirements would be influenced by the bid terms and were left separate. The banker completed one sample projection using the minimum $500,000 bid and token $10,000 per year noncompete payments (Exhibit 4).

To be conservative, Gordon had made the sales projections about 10 percent lower each year than he really thought they would achieve. Because fixed costs would not rise appreciably with modest increases in sales, any improvements in sales volume would be particularly advantageous to profits. The asset and liability assumptions were based on company experience, but there could be fluctuations in items such as lengths of receivables and inventory turns. He felt he should consider how these various changes would impact his financing requirements and his price assessment.

Gordon also had sought out common evaluation techniques. By looking through business periodicals and talking to friends, he found these methods were not necessarily precise. Private manufacturing companies were then most often valued at between 5 and 10 times after tax earnings. Book net asset value also helped establish business worth, but was often adjusted to reflect differences between the market values of assets and the depreciated values shown on balance sheets. For CFI, this was true because they had obtained their new plant at an excellent price. Gordon felt it alone was probably worth $200,000 more than stated book.

To Gordon, the variations in worth suggested by these different methods not only reflected the uncertainty of financial valuation techniques, but also showed that a business had different values to different people. His bid would have to incorporate other more personal and subjective elements.

One important consideration was what amount of personal resources he could and should put at risk. Both he and Albert were financially very conservative. Neither of them had ever had any personal long-term debt—even for a house. Gordon could gather a maximum of $650,000 of assets outside of CFI that could be pledged to secure borrowing. His bank had already confirmed that he could borrow against those assets. However, for him to put his entire worth at risk, he would want to be very comfortable that the price was a reasonable one. Gordon described his feelings:

> You get very protective about what you have outside the company. The problem you always have with a small company is that most of your worth is tied up in it and you may have very little to fall back on if something goes sour. We both have never been big leverage buyers or anything like that.

Besides the element of increased financial risk, there were several other considerations that tempered Gordon's willingness to pay a very high price. Since they had moved to the plant in Denver, the one hour commute to work had been a bit burdensome. It would be nice not to have that drive. Gordon also felt he had good experience in the complete general management of a business and his engineering undergraduate degree and MBA gave him a certain flexibility in the job market. This was important, because for both financial and personal reasons, he felt he would still have to work should he lose the bid.

On the other hand, some factors encouraged Gordon to be aggressive. His father cautioned him to be reasonable, but Gordon knew his father would be very disappointed if Gordon lost the company. And Gordon himself had strong emotional ties to CFI. Gordon also developed a point of view that in some ways he was buying the entire company rather than half:

> I'm sitting here with a company that I have no control over because of our disagreements. If I buy the other half share, I'm buying the whole company—I'm buying peace of mind, I could do what I want, I wouldn't have to argue. So I'd buy a "whole peace of mind" if I bought the other half of the company.

Gordon felt that differences in personal values had been the major reasons two friends had suggested two very different bids. Both had been business school friends and had been very successful entrepreneurs. However, one suggested a bid value for the other half of the company of $850,000 and the other suggested $1,100,000. Gordon commented:

> Philip, who suggested the lower bid, was much more similar to me in lifestyle. He was involved with his family and a number of other activities. Mark, who suggested the higher bid, was unmarried and intensely involved in his company. The company was his life. However, all of the many friends I consulted cautioned me that I would be better off financially if I bought the company and urged me not to "get cute" and undervalue it.

Finally, Gordon considered his competitive position versus Albert. Although Albert had not accumulated the personal resources that Gordon had, he did have a relative with a private company that Gordon knew had an accumulated earnings problem and had the ability to match Gordon's resources. This relative would also be giving Albert financial advice in setting a value for the company. Albert also probably had fewer job prospects if he sold out. His undergraduate study was in liberal arts and his entire experience was within CFI. Gordon also thought Albert might have some doubts about his ability to manage the company on his own.

THE BID

The bid structure was a very simple one. The minimum bid was $500,000 in cash. Additional amounts could be added either to the cash portion and/or to a five year noncompetition agreement. The bids would be evaluated on a present-value basis using an 8 percent discount rate. That rate was selected as equivalent to cash invested at the current return of AAA-rated bonds. Both Gordon Whitlock and Albert Evans were satisfied that was fair. The minimum cash payment had been established to protect the interests of the seller and to reduce possible future uncertainty and upleasantness if the company's position should change substantially. The noncompetition payments would be obligations of CFI but also would be personally guaranteed by the buyer.

Now it was time to decide on a price and then try to get some sleep. Gordon put the form down and walked around the room. He sat down once again, uncapped his pen and began to enter his bid.

EXHIBIT 1
Historical Performance

Year	Net Sales	Profit after Tax	Number of Fixtures Shipped	Total Employees	Hourly Employees
1978	$4,412,191	$115,209	66,000	104	70
1977	$3,573,579	$101,013	58,000	94	58
1976	$2,973,780	$106,528	52,000	82	52
1975	$2,935,721	$ 63,416	54,000	82	50

EXHIBIT 2
Buy/Sell Agreement

AGREEMENT made on this 17th day of February 1979, between Albert W. Evans of Denver, Colorado (hereinafter called "Evans") and Gordon M. Whitlock of Denver, Colorado (hereinafter called "Whitlock").

WHEREAS, Evans and Whitlock each own shares of the voting and nonvoting capital stock of Commercial Fixtures Inc. (CFI) and desire to arrange for the purchase by one (or the purchase of CFI) of all shares of capital stock of CFI owned by the other;

NOW, THEREFORE, in consideration of the foregoing and of the mutual agreements contained herein, Evans and Whitlock agree as follows:

1. Evans and Whitlock will each submit to David Austin, the named senior partner of CFI's accounting firm, by noon on February 23, 1979 (the "Bid Date") a proposal to purchase (or to have CFI purchase some or all of) the other's shares of capital stock of CFI (such proposal to be on the Bid Form attached hereto as Attachment A):

   a. Such proposal shall include all of the stock owned by the other and shall specify the number of shares to be purchased by him, and by CFI and the purchase price, which price shall be not less than $500,000 in the aggregate and shall be paid in full at the Closing hereinafter specified, except as the parties shall otherwise agree.

   b. Such proposal shall specify the amount of the equal annual payments to be made by CFI over the five-year period from 1979 through 1983 in consideration of a noncompetition agreement for such period covering the United States to be executed by the seller in the form attached hereto as Attachment B, such annual payments made in equal installments at the end of each calendar quarter commencing March 31, 1979.

2. If either Evans or Whitlock fails to submit such a proposal by the Bid Date (except for causes beyond his reasonable control in which event a new Bid Date will be established by Austin) the party so failing shall sell his capital stock to CFI upon the terms specified in the other's proposal. If neither party submits such a proposal by the Bid Date this agreement shall terminate.

3. With respect to each proposal, Austin shall add the amount of the purchase price submitted under Section 1(a) and the amount of the annual payment to be made under Section 1(b) above (discounted to present value as at January 1, 1979 as to all payments to be made on or after January 1, 1979 at the rate of 8 percent per annum), and thereby determine which of the submitted proposals is the highest price (the determination to be made as set forth in the Bid Form Computation attached hereto as Attachment C). The party submitting the highest proposal shall be the buyer (which term shall include CFI to the extent such proposal provides that it shall purchase shares). If both offers

EXHIBIT 2 (*continued*)

are determined by Austin to be equal, the buyer shall be determined by an auction as follows:

  a. The parties with such others as they choose to bring shall meet at Austin's offices at a time and a date specified by Austin.
  b. Commencing with Evans (unless he declines to raise his bid in which case commencing with Whitlock) the parties shall submit successive bids of not less than $5,000 in excess of the last bid submitted by the other party.
  c. A party shall have 15 minutes after the bid of the other party in which to submit his own bid and if he fails to submit a bid at least $5,000 higher than other party's last bid, then the last highest bid will be the buyer, except that if neither party raises his original bid then Austin shall determine the buyer by a flip of the coin.
  d. If a party fails to attend such meeting, the other party shall be the buyer, unless such failure was for causes beyond the reasonable control of the party in which case Austin shall set a time and date for another meeting.

All determinations of Austin under this and the preceding Section, which shall include the question of whether causes beyond the reasonable control of a party prevented the party from acting, shall be final and binding on the parties. Compliance with this agreement shall be determined by Austin and his determination thereof shall also be final and binding on the parties.

4. If Whitlock is the seller, Evans shall cause CFI at the Closing either (*a*) to redeem for $75,107.50 all shares of capital stock of CFI owned of record or beneficially by Jonathan Whitlock upon tender of certificates for the same endorsed to CFI or (*b*) to continue to pay a $10,000 annual pension to Jonathan Whitlock and to pay the premiums on the $75,000 life insurance policy held by CFI on Jonathan Whitlock's life and to place such insurance policy in a separate trust which trust shall be the beneficiary under such policy, all in such a manner as to place such policy and proceeds beyond the reach of CFI's creditors, and promptly upon receipt the proceeds of such policy shall be paid by the trust to Jonathan Whitlock's estate in consideration of the endorsement to CFI or the certificate for the shares of capital stock to CFI held by the estate. The bills of Peter Dowling to CFI, including those for arrangements leading to this agreement, shall be the responsibility of CFI regardless of which party is the buyer.

5. Austin shall notify the parties in writing promptly upon any determination that a party has failed to satisfy Section 2 hereof and promptly upon any determination made under Section 3 above. The closing date on which the buyer shall make his payment under Section 1(a) and the seller shall endorse his shares of capital stock to CFI to the buyer, shall be April 15, 1979 or such earlier date as the buyer shall designate. If the buyer shall fail to make the Section 1(a) payment at the Closing, the other party will become the seller upon the lower terms of the original seller's proposal and Austin shall reschedule the Closing on a date within 90 days. If at the new Closing the new buyer fails to make the Section payment, this agreement shall terminate. Payment of amounts owed by CFI under Section 1(b) above (and under Section 4 if Whitlock is the seller) shall be personally guaranteed by Evans or Whitlock, as the case may be, in the form attached hereto as Attachment D, and overdue payments of such amounts shall bear interest at the rate of 15 percent from the date due. There shall be credited against payment to be made under Section 1(b) with respect to 1979 commencing March 31, 1979, the amount of salary received by the seller for 1979. At the Closing the seller shall execute an agreement not to compete with CFI for five years in the United States. The seller's employment, salary, blue cross/blue shield, group insurance, all other payments and benefits, except those

EXHIBIT 2 (*concluded*)

provided herein, shall terminate at the Closing. The seller may retain the CFI automobile now used by him and ownership thereof will be transferred to the seller by CFI.

WITNESS our hands and seals on the date first set forth above.

_____

Albert W. Evans

_____

Gordon M. Whitlock

Attachment A—Bid Form
PURCHASE PRICE (SECTION 1–a) $_____

NONCOMPETITION AGREEMENT
(SECTION 1–b) $_____

    AMOUNT PER YEAR $_____

    TOTAL AMOUNT (5 YEARS)
    (TO BE PAID IN EQUAL
    QUARTERLY PAYMENTS) $_____

_____   _____

Date   Signature

Attachment C—Bid Computation Form

	Evans	Whitlock
Purchase price (1a):	$	$
Noncompetition agreement (1b):		

	Evans	Whitlock
Yearly amount for five years	$	$
Discounted value (DV)	_____	_____
Adjusted purchase price	$_____	$_____

The discounted value shall be the present value of the yearly amount paid quarterly for 20 quarters discounted at an interest rate of 2 percent per quarter.

This shall be computed as follows:

$$DV = \frac{\text{Yearly amount}}{4} \times 16.3514 = \text{Yearly amount} \times 4.08786.$$

EXHIBIT 3
Financial Statements

COMMERCIAL FIXTURES INC.

Balance Sheets

Years Ended December 31

Assets	1978	1977	1976
Current assets:			
Cash	$ 51,248	$ 3,778	$ 70,520
Accounts receivable			
Customers	600,361	430,750	318,356
Refundable income taxes ..	23,001	—	—
Other	—	2,276	5,289
	623,362	433,026	323,645
Less allowance for doubtful			
receivables	3,500	3,500	3,500
	619,862	429,526	320,145
Inventories			
Raw materials	291,790	259,550	277,072
Work in process	534,438	483,357	316,113
	826,228	742,907	593,185
Prepaid insurance and other .	14,028	20,134	26,070
Total current assets	1,511,366	1,196,345	1,009,920
Property, plant, and equipment:			
Buildings and improvements .	341,426	325,686	295,130
Machinery and equipment ..	210,493	173,073	135,419
Motor vehicles	32,578	32,578	29,421
Office equipment	42,866	43,905	36,949
	627,363	575,242	496,919
Less accumulated depreciation	273,284	233,444	185,215
	354,079	341,798	311,704
Land	11,101	11,101	11,101
Total property, plant, and equipment	365,180	352,899	322,805
Other assets:			
Cash surrender value of life insurance policies (less loans of $19,748 in 1978, $19,590 in 1977 and $19,432 in 1976)	81,978	77,215	72,569
Total assets	$1,958,524	$1,626,459	$1,405,294

EXHIBIT 3 *(continued)*

Liabilities	1978	1977	1976
Current liabilities:			
Current maturities of long-term debt	$ 12,184	$ 10,558	$ 9,000
Note payable—bank	325,000	200,000	—
Note payable—officer	—	30,000	39,000
Accounts payable			
Trade	389,582	295,208	313,203
Employees' withholdings	4,875	3,197	3,070
	394,457	298,405	316,273
Amount due for purchase of treasury stock	—	—	75,000
Accrued liabilities			
Salaries and wages	93,713	57,534	48,413
Commissions	41,474	26,010	12,878
Sundry	14,528	11,357	4,796
Income taxes	—	18,036	19,800
	149,715	112,937	85,887
Total current liabilities	881,356	651,900	525,160
Long-term debt	176,522	189,122	195,710
Stockholders' equity:			
Contributed capital			
6% Cumulative preferred stock—authorized 10,000 shares of $10 par value; issued 2,000 shares	20,000	20,000	20,000
Common stock			
Class A (nonvoting) Authorized 15,000 shares of $10 par value issued 8,305 shares	83,050	83,050	83,050
Class B (voting) Authorized 5,000 shares of $10 par value; issued and outstanding 20 shares	200	200	200
	103,250	103,250	103,250
Retained earnings	892,396	777,187	676,174
	995,646	880,437	779,424
Less shares reacquired and held in treasury—at cost			
2,000 shares 6% cumulative preferred stock	20,000	20,000	20,000
2,308 shares Class A common stock	75,000	75,000	75,000
	95,000	95,000	95,000
Total stockholders' equity	900,646	785,437	684,424
Total liabilities	$1,958,524	$1,626,459	$1,405,294

EXHIBIT 3 (*continued*)

Statement of Earnings

Year Ended December 31

	1978	1977	1976
Net sales	$4,412,191	$3,573,579	$2,973,780
Cost of goods sold			
Inventories at beginning of year	742,907	593,185	416,512
Purchases	1,599,426	1,275,665	1,109,781
Freight in	19,520	26,595	20,966
Direct labor	430,154	360,568	328,487
Manufacturing expenses	977,299	802,172	673.643
	3,769,236	3,058,185	2,549,389
Inventories at end of year	826,228	742,907	593,185
	2,943,008	2,315,278	1,956,204
Gross profit	1,469,183	1,258,301	1,017,576
Product development expenses	131,746	128,809	102,299
Selling and administrative expenses	1,112,542	915,140	740,801
	1,244,288	1,043,949	843,100
Operating income	224,895	214,352	174,476
Other deductions or (income)			
Interest expense	56,259	37,790	32,416
Payments to retired employee	10,000	10,000	20,000
Miscellaneous	(923)	(1,551)	(6,193)
	65,336	46,239	46,223
Earnings before income taxes	159,559	168,113	128,253
Provision for income taxes	44,350	67,100	49,000
Earnings before extraordinary income	115,209	101,013	79,253
Extraordinary income—life insurance proceeds in excess of cash surrender value	—	—	27,275
Net Earnings	$ 115,209	$ 101,013	$ 106,528
Earnings per share of common stock	$19.15	$16.79	$13.10

EXHIBIT 3 *(concluded)*

Statement of Changes in Financial Position
Year ended December 31

	1978	1977	1976
Working capital provided from operations:			
Earnings before extraordinary income................	$115,209	$101,013	$ 79,253
Add item not requiring outlay of working capital			
Depreciation....................................	55,978	50,658	44,267
Working capital provided from operations	171,187	151,671	123,520
Extraordinary income from life insurance proceeds......................................	—	—	27,275
Capitalized equipment lease obligation..................	—	5,295	—
Proceeds from cash surrender value of life insurance policies	—	—	51,877
Total working capital provided.....................	171,187	156,966	202,672
Working capital applied:			
Additions to property, plant, and equipment.......	68,259	80,752	47,107
Increase in cash surrender value of life insurance policies—net of loans.....................	4,763	4,646	5,954
Reduction of long-term debt	12,600	11,883	8,996
Purchase of 2,308 shares of nonvoting Class A stock...	—	—	75,000
Total working capital applied...................	85,622	97,281	137,057
Increase in working capital..............................	$ 85,565	$ 59,685	$ 65,615
Net change in working capital consists of:			
Increase (decrease) in current assets:			
Cash..	$ 47,470	$(66,742)	$ 64,854
Accounts receivable—net	190,336	109,381	(3,548)
Inventories...	83,321	149,722	176,673
Prepaid expenses	(6,106)	(5,936)	(4,980)
	315,021	186,425	232,999
Increase (decrease) in current liabilities:			
Current portion of long-term debt...................	1,626	1,558	500
Notes payable to bank...............................	125,000	200,000	—
Note payable officer	(30,000)	(9,000)	—
Accounts payable	96,052	(17,868)	107,153
Amount due for purchase of treasury stock......	—	(75,000)	75,000
Contribution to profit-sharing trust	—	—	(20,000)
Accrued liabilities.....................................	54,814	28,814	(7,619)
Income taxes	(18,036)	(1,764)	12,350
	229,456	126,740	167,384
Increase in working capital..............................	$ 85,565	$ 59,685	$ 65,615
Working capital at beginning of year...................	544,445	484,760	419,145
Working capital at end of year..........................	$630,010	$544,445	$484,760

EXHIBIT 4
Pro Forma Financial Statements

Income Statement for Projections

	Historical Percentages			Projected Percentages			(Thousands of Dollars)		
	1976	1977	1978	1979	1980	1981	1979	1980	1981
Net sales	100.0	100.0	100.0	100.0	100.0	100.0	4,800	5,100	5,400
Cost of goods sold	65.78	64.79	66.70	67.0	67.0	67.0	3,216	3,417	3,618
Gross income	34.22	35.21	33.30	33.0	33.0	33.0	1,584	1,683	1,782
Operating general & admin.†	28.61*	29.28	28.25	28.0	28.0	28.0	1,344	1,428	1,512
Profit before taxes and purchase financing	5.61†	5.93	5.05	5.0	5.0	5.0	240	255	270
Noncompete payments							10	10	10
Interest for "other bank debt"‡							74	70	63
Profit before taxes							156	175	197
Taxes	38.2§	39.9	27.8	39.0	39.0	39.0	61	68	77
Net earnings							95	107	120

*Historical and projected percentages include interest for long-term debt *only* as well as a $25,000 cost redution for the reduced salary requirements of a replacement for Evans.
†Profit after adjustments to operating G&A.
‡Interest for "other bank debt" is assumed to be 10 percent times "other bank debt" outstanding at the end of the prior year.
§Effective tax rate.

Projected Beginning Equity Position

Total equity, December 31, 1978:	$900,646
Less cash payment of purchase price:	500,000
Beginning equity, January 1, 1979:	400,646

EXHIBIT 4 (continued)

Balance Sheet Accounts for Projections

(thousands of dollars)

	Historical			Projected				At Closing			
	1976	1977	1978	1979	1980	1981		1978	1979	1980	1981
Assets:											
Cash								50	50	50	50
Accounts receivable (Days)	39.3	43.9	51.3	52.0	52.0	52.0		620	684	727	769
Inventories (Turns)	3.3	3.1	3.6	3.8	4.0	4.1		826	846	854	882
Prepaids								14	15	15	15
Total current assets								1,510	1,595	1,646	1,716
Net fixed assets								365	370	370	370
(Assume policies cashed in)								0	0	0	0
Total assets								1,875	1,965	2,016	2,086
Liabilities and Equity:											
Operating accounts payable (Days)	59.0	47.0	48.9	50.0	50.0	50.0		394	441	468	496
Accrued expenses and taxes								150*	150	150	150
Total existing long-term debt ($000)	205	200	189					189	176	163	148
Liabilities from ongoing operations								733	767	781	794
Other bank debt								741	702	632	569
Total liabilities								1,474	1,469	1,413	1,363
Equity at beginning of year†								401	401	496	603
Net earnings for year								NA	95	107	120
Total equity								401	496	603	723
Total liabilities and equity								1,875	1,965	2,016	2,086

*In a purchase by an *outside* buyer, this is often zero at closing. These liabilities are paid off rather than transferred and new accruals are gradually rebuilt in the normal course of business.

†See calculations of beginning equity elsewhere in exhibit.

EXHIBIT 4 (*concluded*)

Sources and Uses of Funds
(thousands of dollars)

	1979	1980	1981
Sources:			
Net earnings	95	107	120
Plus depreciation	56	56	56
Funds provided by operations	151	163	176
Increase in accounts payable	47	27	28
Increase in accrual expenses and taxes	0	0	0
Increase in other bank debt	—	—	—
Total Sources	198	190	204
Uses:			
Increase in accounts receivables	64	43	42
Increase in inventories	20	8	28
Increase in prepaids	1	0	0
Increase in fixed assets*	61	56	56
Decrease in long-term debt	13	13	15
Decrease in other bank debt	39	70	63
Total uses	198	190	204

Note: Total sources must equal total uses.
*Reinvestment in plant and equipment is assumed to equal depreciation after the first year.

Case 2-3

DUNCAN FIELD

On Monday morning, September 11, 1978, Duncan Field was continuing his negotiations with Bob Baer, senior vice president of Galaxy Industries. Bob stated:

> Duncan, we're not willing to give you any further information at this time. We still have to be convinced that you and your investors will not have any difficulty handling an acquisition of this size.

Duncan shuddered as Bob continued:

> *You* are the one who came to us and badgered us into considering the sale of our East Valley CATV systems, remember? This is as far as we go—$9 million for the sale of the systems. We are prepared to execute this three-page letter agreement we developed together and accept your $50,000 good faith money. Or, we will simply keep the systems and continue operating them as we had always planned. Which will it be?

Duncan Field knew that he had only a few moments to evaluate his alternatives and respond to Mr. Baer.

BACKGROUND

Duncan Field, 34, had grown up in the suburbs of Pittsburgh where his father was employed by a large national company. His family moved to southern Ohio during Duncan's high school years, then he attended Duke University in North Carolina where he received a Bachelor's degree in mechanical engineering. Engineering had been a struggle and, while Duncan valued the training, he decided he wouldn't be happy as a professional engineer. Duncan had married during his junior year and his wife agreed to support them while he attended Wharton to study business. [All quoted comments are Duncan's unless otherwise noted.]

> I had taken a lot of business courses at Duke because I wasn't sure if our finances would allow graduate school. Compared to engineering school, business school was a whole lot easier for me, so I used the opportunity to round out my education. I read widely, took some social psychology and communications courses.
>
> My specialty area was investment finance, but my courses were not particularly concentrated.

After receiving an MBA degree in 1968, Duncan and his wife moved to St. Paul where Duncan began work for Paul Russell, vice president of a large commercial bank.

> I was an assistant loan officer, and was authorized to make loans, but I really chased Paul's. He had probably 200 accounts which were primarily newer high-tech companies and CATV ("community antenna television," usually known as "cable TV"). Paul was quite a character who didn't delegate well, but was very active, exciting, and stimulating. He had a real interest in the entrepeneur and in start-up ventures.
>
> One of Paul's responsibilities was the bank's venture capital subsidiary. With Paul's style, I ended up acting as the chief operating officer of that subsidiary, without the title, but clearly with those responsibilities. I followed a portfolio of about 50 investments and analyzed new proposals as they came in. I must have looked at over 200 a year, of which we did maybe 5. We made both direct equity investments and also used debt instruments through an SBIC.
>
> Start-ups were flying high then, and there were so many opportunities mixed with so many harebrained schemes that you found yourself looking for reasons not to do the investment. If you couldn't find any reasons not to invest, you did it.
>
> Every person who comes to you *believes* his or her scheme is going to succeed. They've written out why it's going to succeed and are committing their future to it. If you took that at face value, you'd make every investment that came in. Yet clearly, the majority of them don't succeed. So you checked out everything they said. When you found one whose story checked out completely, you did it. Then it became just a question of pricing.

THE MOVE TO CABLE TELEVISION

Once I had a little money in my pocket, I made several investments in the stock market. I based my choices on stock that was undervalued based on operating results and current position. The results were nearly disastrous, but I finally salvaged about what I would have made in a savings account. I then recalled some advice a friend's father had passed along: "Don't invest in anything you can't control."

I'd modify that to "something on which you don't have a significant impact or which depends on someone else's opinion for value rather than simply the results of the enterprise." The stock market is two or three iterations removed from how successful a business is. I decided that wasn't the way for me to make my fortune.

After four years with the bank, Duncan attempted to convince the bank to sponsor a separate investment vehicle to raise outside funds to invest in the cable TV industry. Some of the bank's best customers were so successful that they had requirements above the bank's legal loan limit. This was threatening the bank's leadership position on those accounts. The new fund Duncan suggested would provide the bank the means to service those accounts and also the means for bank officers, including himself, to build equity by partial ownership.

It was approved all the way up to the president of the bank, but the chairman thought better of it. My feeling was they just didn't like the idea of doing something that "ritzy."

I then decided that I wanted to pursue the cable TV industry. I had become knowledgeable in it. It was a fun industry and was really a numbers game. There were good rules of thumb to predict value and performance—investors and bankers love that. So I started feeling out people I knew in the industry, looking for a company I could join.

Duncan joined Cosmopolitan Cable Corp. in 1972. Their understanding was that Duncan would go into the field as a general manager as soon as a suitable opportunity arose. Until then, he became director of corporate development and worked as an assistant to Glen Ryan and David Brett, the company's founders.

I did some secondary work on a loan agreement from the other side of the table, chased some franchise opportunities, some possible acquisitions. I analyzed our existing operations to help us predict more closely what we could expect from new systems. It gave me a chance to learn more about the business and I think they enjoyed having someone to do a lot of the dog work.

It took longer than we expected to find a suitable opportunity for me to get to the field. One early start-up was given to a more experienced person and then we just didn't start anything up for a while. After a year and a half, we won a big franchise in Texas, our largest project to date. It was clearly more than I could have handled and they put the head of their largest group of systems in charge of it. I said, "Look, I'm getting nowhere fast, so send me out as a number two man. Let me learn from the ground up. I just want to get out to the field." So I went out as an assistant general manager.

It was a fantastic learning experience, being in on the ground floor. We didn't have our permanent office, we had very few employees, we had made no major decisions on billing systems or electronics or the major suppliers. No marketing had been done. It was a chance to be there right from the beginning and ask at least 10,000 stupid questions. For nine months I acted as the controller and we also hadn't yet hired a customer service manager or office manager, so I played those roles as well.

The general manager was really good and our engineer was also excellent. In the cable TV industry, the engineer reports to the general manager, but really runs a separate little empire on the side. Everything in the field—doing installations, repairing things, constructing things—all came under the system engineer. Inside things such as billings, sales, marketing, were under the customer service manager.

After a year and a half in Texas, Cosmopolitan was awarded franchises in several communities in Indiana. Duncan was made regional vice president and was given responsibility for building the systems.

They put me together with an experienced and very capable system engineer. In the four years we were there, we went from a motel room to a system almost 600 miles long with 30,000 customers.

GOING OUT ON HIS OWN

While Duncan had worked at the bank, he had gotten to know another Wharton graduate, Frank Gilmour. Frank had taken over responsibilties for the bank's venture activities when Duncan left and had later joined one of the leading independent venture capital companies which also had several cable TV investments. For some time, Frank had urged Duncan to start his own cable TV business.

He mentioned it when I went to Texas and mentioned it when I went to Indiana. He brought it up again about a year later, just sort of bugging me to do something. "When are you going to leave and do your own thing? When are you going to learn to make some money off the deal?"

I said I just didn't know. I didn't feel comfortable that I knew enough about the business to go out and be sure I'd succeed. At the bank and at Cosmopolitan I learned the great strength of never missing a projection. I wanted to feel I would do the same.

I also felt that I had accepted a big obligation to Cosmopolitan in Indiana. When I finished that, I'd have earned my spurs and then we'd talk again.

At Cosmopolitan, Duncan had participated in one of the better stock option plans in the industry. However, he also had seen the value of a larger part of ownership in cable systems. He discussed several plans for managers at Cosmopolitan to gain more personal tax benefits and a better equity ride. One plan would have been for managers to purchase and lease back various real estate properties used by their systems. Cosmopolitan now did this with third parties. Another plan would be for managers to be allowed to purchase other cable systems that were not large enough to be interesting to Cosmopolitan.

Glen Ryan and David Brett decided that these plans would result in too many potential conflicts. They were particularly concerned about what might happen should one of the managers' ventures encounter difficulties.

> So, I decided that if I ever wanted to make any serious money, I'd have to leave and try it on my own.

Duncan reoper. ed his discussions with Frank Gilmour. Gilmour had the right to make investments separately from his venture capital firm. He said his family owned a small firm with an unused $300,000 line of credit which the family was willing to use to fund a cable venture. Frank would use his contacts and experience to help raise the additional financing that would be required. At first, Duncan tried to find an opportunity as a "cast off" from Cosmopolitan. He was spending part of his time trying to find new systems for Cosmopolitan. Duncan felt that this would lead to an opportunity that would be suitable for his own first system, but which would be too small, in a less desirable area (especially one at a distance from their current geographical concentrations) or otherwise unattractive to Cosmopolitan.

> I think it is unusual for someone starting a venture or leaving to take a new job to not have a new job or new venture lined up before they leave the old one. Certainly with the risk involved in starting a new venture, you don't want to get hung up in "no man's land" halfway between two ventures.
>
> It was difficult to reconcile looking for my own system while I was working for Cosmopolitan. I had agreed with Frank Gilmour that Cosmopolitan would get first choice on anything I came up with. I was working there, using their telephones and their time chasing acquisitions which I wanted to make for them. I wasn't going to take the best one and do it on my own. I also had an agreement attached to my stock options not to compete with Cosmopolitan for one year, although I felt I was unlikely to buy any systems they would be interested in.

After several months, Duncan found he wasn't making much progress. He had maintained a very small staff for the Indiana systems and found he simply had very little time to seek any acquisitions.

> We had a very tight operation. As a matter of fact, we were already making money—actual profits after depreciation and interest, not only cash flow—which was unheard of. Cable systems usually report losses for some time after they're built. I seemed to be doing 16 different jobs and if I had any brains, I would have gotten more help.
>
> Then our regional operating manager was moved to help start another franchise. I knew I was on the verge of leaving and felt my successor should

have the right to choose the replacement. So it became even more difficult to seek acquisitions for either of us.

Frank Gilmour and his family offered to support Duncan for one year of an independent search for a cable acquisition. Duncan would be paid the same salary and insurance benefits he had at Cosmopolitan. Gilmour would also pay search expenses and hold a $250,000 pool of equity ready for an investment. In return, Duncan and Gilmour's family would split 50/50 the equity they wouldn't have to give away to raise other financing. These resources eliminated most of the risk of the search for Duncan and he felt the career risks of leaving were also low:

> Our industry has such fast growth. I'd done what people thought was a good job. If at the end of that year I had fallen on my nose, I really expected to go back to work for another cable company. It might not be as good as Cosmopolitan or have as good an option plan, but I wasn't going to starve. I could clearly end up with a comfortable position in another operation.
>
> If we managed to buy a system and failed, I still felt the career risk was not too high. I think people forget that if you try to start a new venture, you can fail with grace. But be sure you don't take any bankers down with you—they're not compensated for taking high risks. And it would be nice not to take any venture capitalists down either.
>
> If you're a good manager, you can always go back and get another good job in another firm, probably just as good as you had before. And you can try it again later if you want to *and* if you've gotten the bankers out whole. Venture capitalists understand that some ventures don't make it—that's why they get a bigger rate of return.

After giving 90 days notice to "pass the baton," Duncan exercised his vested stock options and left Cosmopolitan in February 1978.

BEGINNING THE SEARCH FOR AN ACQUISITION

Duncan and Frank quickly decided they would pursue the purchase of an existing system rather than attempt to win a franchise and build one. Cable systems were sold fairly often and trying to win a franchise normally required a lot of time and effort, at least $10,000–$20,000 in expenses, and involved competing with often 5 to 10 applicants with no certainty of winning. Instead, they would rather acquire a system and try to improve its operations.

They incorporated as Federated Cablevision, Inc. to establish a name and an image of professionalism. To limit overhead expense, Duncan set up an office in his home.

> My wife and I moved into what had been a small study and I took over our large bedroom downstairs. I bought a used desk and typewriter and some old files. There was no point in moving because I had no idea where we'd end up.

Duncan used a number of means to try to locate cable systems for sale. Through trade magazines, Duncan had been able to identify 10 business brokers who dealt with broadcasting properties. There were two or three that specialized more in cable and did most of the volume of sales. Glen Ryan and David Brett also referred possible properties to Duncan from time to time as did other Cosmopolitan regional managers.

> I asked the other regional managers to keep their eyes open for me. "Obviously, do what's right for you, but if you're not interested and think I might be, I'd sure appreciate it if you'd steer it in my direction."

Duncan had felt they might easily find a system to buy in three to six months and that it would take about three months to close the purchase. His first real opportunity came during the first month. A local group in a community in California had won rights to a new franchise and was offering to sell the rights rather than build the system. Although this was not quite the established company they had planned to buy, Duncan felt it was a real opportunity.

> The toughest thing to do in the cable business is to build a system from scratch and market it successfully. And that's what I had been doing for the past six years.
>
> But this area was not without risk. The market only needed cable so-so. This would take all our resources, but we could probably make it. You feel that these are the risks of a new venture, so why not get on with it? I wanted to do it.
>
> I went down to look at it on a Wednesday and left at the end of the day Thursday. I was very excited, but wanted to project costs and analyze it. The broker who dropped me off had another meeting scheduled two hours later with some representatives of a large broadcasting group. They came in with their checkbook and bought it. I was back in Indiana sharpening my pencils and they just bought it! I hadn't made an offer! I wanted to make sure it was something we wanted to do.
>
> Looking back, it would have been a great deal. But nonetheless, I wouldn't have done it differently. There are people out there who will buy things without thinking twice, but I'm just not going to compete with that. That particular group had a lot of cash and simply wanted growth.
>
> You just have to realize there's going to be fallout at every stage of the game. You have to look at a lot of deals to see one you want. You're going to see several you want to buy that will be sold before you can reach an agreement. You're going to sign agreements on some that will fall apart before they get closed. You just have to keep banging away. I knew that and so did Frank Gilmour.

Over the next several months, Duncan was disappointed about the quality of deals he was seeing from brokers. He felt this was because of his low financial credibility and because of his insistence on investigating the deals and offering what he considered fair value. Duncan used every device he could think of to build credibility. He sold his background in the industry and pointed to his financial partner who was with a respected venture company which had, in fact, done several cable deals. He had business cards and stationery printed and installed a separate business telephone with an answering service.

> The people I called didn't know I was working out of my house. I typed all my own letters and used "ms" for my secretary's initials for "myself." My friends kidded me about the lousy typewriter, but at least my letters were typed and I didn't make mistakes. I used printed note paper whenever I could so that I could write those out. No one ever had occasion to visit me at my office.
>
> When people asked for our credit references, I'd tell them we'd just gotten started and were looking to acquire our first operation. I resold my background and partners. I didn't try to make them think I had a big operation, but I'm sure many pictured me in a nice office building with a secretary and people helping me analyze the deals.

Duncan realized his insistence on evaluating deals was at odds with most brokers' desires.

> I'm hampered by the fact that I'm so cheap. Brokers just want to move the property. They want someone who'll come in and ask two or three dumb questions and say, "I'll buy." In this business, brokers receive about a 1.5 percent commission on the sales price. They don't care if you buy something for $9 million or $8.2 million—it's not much difference to *them*.
>
> If you want to take time to negotiate and settle on a price and ask every question under the sun; if you then want to go out and line up at least a tentative financing package, and are willing to put up some good faith money— say $10,000—and are willing to sign a letter of intent; if you want to take all that time, they don't want to deal with you. They *will* deal with you, but they'll spend their time with those who will buy right away.
>
> As a result, I didn't see anything first. I was always down the list. They always profess that they show everyone the deals at the same time, but they don't. I probably never saw some of the better opportunities. At that time, cable systems didn't sell particularly fast, so I still had time to look at some. But I was going to analyze my deals because I didn't want to fail. We could not *afford* to make a mistake our first shot out of the box. That had to be a success.

CONTINUING THE SEARCH

As the weeks went by, Duncan settled into an active search pattern. Although he had an office at home, he would dress respectably and kept standard office hours. Besides pursuing leads from brokers, he searched through the trade magazines for interesting prospects. He would call systems of interest to see if he could open up the possibility of a sale.

Industry fact books provided other leads. These gave statistical summaries of every cable system in the country, with ownership, numbers of subscribers, how many homes they passed, and sizes of the communities they covered.

> The fact books were always outdated, but the information was enough to start with. For example, I would plot all the stations owned by large multiple systems operators on a map. If I could find one location remote from the others, I thought that might be an opportunity, so I'd try to find a contact that I could approach or would just "cold call." If I could keep them from hanging up, I'd try to get the chance to talk further.
>
> There were about 2,500 systems in the country, and I read about and considered practically every one during my first six months out.

Duncan visited a number of systems and made offers on several without success.

> It's just hard to close a deal. On one system I really wanted, I made an offer and then there were a series of counter-offers, but we got stuck someplace, maybe 10 percent off. We had doubts as to how seriously he wanted to sell it.
>
> The brokers sometimes have conflicting interests, too. You figure in our business that *they'll* end up buying the best ones. They'll let you be the stalking horse for them, then they'll buy it on their own.

Duncan spent a lot of time trying to close one system in Maryland.

> I hit one system in Maryland that we agreed on right away. I had gotten enough information from the broker and from talking to the people at the system by telephone that this should be a *good* deal.
>
> So I went down there to confirm that what I was told was true. This time I took *my* checkbook! I made sure from that broker that they wanted a $5,000 deposit and made sure we had that much in our account.
>
> I still liked what I saw, so we negotiated out a price and drafted a three-page agreement. The next day, we took it to his attorney who made a few changes. We signed it and I gave the broker my $5,000 check. This was the end of April 1978.

The Maryland system was a very small one, serving a population of about 15,000. It had substantial construction left to be done, but Duncan and Frank felt they could build it up and make a good capital gain. They were prepared to do a number of smaller deals to build up a group and this could be the start.

As Duncan tried to close the deal, problems continued to crop up.

> There were a half-dozen stockholders and while I was negotiating with the president, the others kept changing their minds. First, one shareholder in Delaware decided he didn't want to sell. Then he decided he might but began objecting to the deal. We couldn't get him on the phone and we couldn't tell *what* he was objecting to, but he wouldn't agree.
>
> Another shareholder then appeared and said he didn't want to sell, in fact, he wanted to buy it. So he didn't want to go through with this deal and the

president wasn't authorized to act, etc., etc. We put forth that the president was authorized and that we felt they had an obligation.

All this time—it's now July—we're trying to put together a complete purchase agreement that's now running 40–50 pages. We had a big discussion about the form of purchase. It was supposed to be the purchase of assets. This meant the current owner would be liable for ordinary income taxes on part of the depreciated value of assets due to recapture. The first guy finally got us to agree to a stock purchase. In effect *we* ended up paying a higher price.

The second shareholder wanted us to pick up a few other things, then they told us that instead of serving a population of 15,000 they could only serve 13,000.

Figuring the size of the system and the service area had been a continuing problem. Their maps and records were very sketchy, so I had even tried to physically count potential subscribers on a couple of occasions—going out in a car, driving up and down the streets. Now it's hard to follow a cable in the air and count houses at the same time. Besides I would think I saw a single family home and they would say, no, there's another door to a basement apartment in the back and it's really a two-family house. So I just gave up.

After a lot of soul-searching, I finally said, "O. K. We'll accept the 13,000 people and still buy it at the same price." Finally we got the full agreement signed up in August.

I decided one last time to check their notes. We had demanded they warrant the number of people in their service area as part of the contract. They didn't want to since they hadn't done a count. We had insisted that they do a count which is where the 13,000 number came from. Now, after it's all signed up, I get their notes and the notes themselves said only 10,000! Essentially an out-and-out lie!

I said forget it. That's too low. We're backing out. Give us our deposit and expense money back. They said, "Well, it's a nice day, isn't it?"

I don't know how many trips I'd made down there. I'd paid an engineer to check out the system for us. I'd hired an FCC attorney who instructed them on how to clear up *their* FCC legal problems so the system could be transferred. Our corporate attorney had invested I don't know how much time in it, and the bankers were all lined up. We had at least $15,000 cash out plus the $5,000 deposit plus an equal amount of my time. The facts were in our favor, but to get a legal judgment takes so much time and is so futile, most people just chalk it up to experience.

EAST VALLEY CATV

Although the Maryland deal had been Duncan's highest priority during the spring and summer, he had continued to seek other opportunities. In May, he had begun to pursue several cable systems owned by a subsidiary of Galaxy Industries.

Galaxy owned several cable TV systems, but I had heard rumors that they might be unhappy with systems in three towns in East Valley. They had acquired them with some other properties, and several suppliers to the industry and lawyers I knew thought they might be bought.

I called Robert Baer, Galaxy's vice president of finance, who wouldn't give me *any* information. He said they had no interest in selling. I vacationed in the same region, so I just drove to the towns to see what I could find out. I visited each system as a possible customer to pick up their rates and programming, to talk to their employees, and just to crane my neck around to see what I could see. Their receptionists described the parts of town where their service was and was not available, which helped me gauge undeveloped potential.

Duncan sought other sources of information about the East Valley systems:

The state cable commission had some general financial reports. I also collected all the census data I could find and determined how many occupied year-round housing units there were in each town. I obtained copies of the franchises from the town halls. In no case did I say who I was or why I was interested. I checked reception at TV dealers around town. They don't like cable because it reduces the number of antennas they sell. So you always hear the worst about the systems from them. I could flip channels in their stores to see how well we'd be able to market in each area.

In July, I called Robert Baer again and said I'd like to make an offer. He said, "Well, it's not for sale, but I suppose if you make me an offer I have to listen. Let me think about it and call me back." When I called several days later, Bob said, "No, don't even make me an offer. I don't even want to hear about it."

I said I was going to make an offer anyway. Bob said, "If you call and make an offer, I'd have to pass it along, but it's a waste of time." I said, "Fine."

Duncan felt the East Valley systems were solid opportunities. He was determined to open negotiations even without Galaxy's cooperation.

I spent all my extra time in August trying to come up with an offer without having a single, solitary piece of information from them. I thought about what I knew. Bob had mentioned one reason they couldn't sell the systems was that they were operated together with two other systems. When they later said not to bother to make an offer, I decided that I would have a chance only if I made an offer for the whole group. So I did my research on the two other systems.

I knew I had to make a *serious* offer. Yet I didn't know how good the properties might really be. If they were really good and my offer was too low, I would be left out and would never get another phone call answered.

I also didn't know how bad the properties might be. If I really went in high, I could be badly taken, because the game Baer was playing was not to give me *any* information. But I had to make a real offer or I wouldn't get to first base.

So I went in with an offer I thought he couldn't refuse. I had arranged a meeting, saying I was going to be in their headquarters city on other business.

I said I would offer $7 million. He said, "I don't see how we could possibly do something for that, but let me think about it."

Bob called me back on the phone in a few days and said $7 million was not enough, but how about $9 million? I finally knew he was serious. What a great day that was!

THE NEGOTIATIONS

Many phone calls, letters, and discussions followed during the end of August and early days of September as Duncan and Bob Baer tried to establish an agreement on price.

Cable TV systems are normally priced based on multiples of net operating income. Profits don't mean anything in our industry because the capital investment in the system results in high depreciation. Also, most systems are highly leveraged and have interest payments.

For a system that was solid and had some growth potential we expected to pay about seven times net operating income—profits before interest, depreciation, and taxes. However, there can be quite a bit of latitude, depending on the situation. For more mature situations where you expected less growth, you'd expect to pay maybe five times cash flow. In an early situation or for a franchise, you'd then pay about $10 to $20 a home. Down in Maryland we had been talking almost $30 per home in a situation with negative cash flow! You just have to assess what you can build, how long it will take to gain your market, and what you can carry.

Another rule of thumb is that you could expect that 50 percent of the homes you pass by with your cable would subscribe. Yet that varied from 30 percent or less in some sections with good reception to up to 80 precent in others. Those figures are for ultimate market saturation. Of course you also had to forecast the level of saturation each year as you built up to that level.

Other pricing factors included projections of the percentages of customers who would subscribe to additional services such as Home Box Office. You also had to consider the costs of turnover—a lost customer decreased revenues much more than the marginal reduction in expenses.

Because Bob Baer still refused to give me any detailed information about the East Valley systems, our pricing negotiations really involved developing a price backed by a set of formulas of minimum values of various operating factors. Actually, it was more Bob standing fast and me arguing that this town might be worth seven times cash flow but that one was more mature and definitely worth less! It was really a lot of fun arguing back and forth, but no matter what arguments I used, it became apparent that the price was going to be $9 million.

CONSIDERING FINANCING

Duncan was also discussing the price and possible financing with Frank Gilmour. Duncan prepared an operating projection based on his assumptions about the systems. Then he and Frank reviewed the type of financing that might be available and added a target structure of debt and equity. Frank would invest up to $500,000 in equity. All other financing would have to be obtained from other sources.

Duncan's and Frank's projections (Exhibit 1) incorporated a number of assumptions. Some of these follow:

— A purchase price of $9 million cash.
— The requirement to recognize certain recapture income arising from the necessary technical structure of buying the systems.
— The expectation that banks would reliably lend five times current net operating income for cable TV systems. The net operating income for 1978 was estimated to be $1,200,000.
— The current prime rate was 9½ percent.
— An expectation of 6 percent annual inflation consistent with current expectations and built into projected costs and revenues.
— Subordinated debt and equity investors would demand return rates of 15 percent to 30 percent compounded annually, depending on relative position, total leverage, their evaluation of the management and of the system, and skill at negotiation.
— Real population growth of three systems was limited to 1 percent per year and was held at zero for two of the operations.

They expected to raise a total of $9,650,000 to pay the purchase price, closing costs, and provide working capital. The assumed sources of funds were:

$6,500,000	Senior debt from banks at 11 percent.
$1,700,000	Senior subordinated debt with a 14 percent current return and callable warrants. The warrants had a price schedule calculated to give a total compounded return of 18 percent when called.
$1,000,000	Junior subordinated debt with a 10 percent current return and warrants for 20 percent of the equity. If the systems were sold in five years for 7.5 times net operating income plus net current assets, this would provide an additional 17 percent return or "a total return of 27 percent."
$ 450,000	Equity to be put up mainly by the Gilmours, split 50/50 with Duncan.
$9,650,000	Total financed.

All of these assumptions were made by Duncan and Frank as experienced estimates. They felt they were unlikely to get better ranges of current rates by talking to financing sources unless they were actually negotiating a deal they already controlled. In addition, Galaxy was adamant that all discussions be kept extremely confidential. If Galaxy felt the contemplated sale was the subject of open discussion or even speculation, Duncan and Frank agreed that the deal would probably fall apart.

In addition to maintaining the uncertainty over whether or not financing could be obtained in the amounts needed and for acceptable rates, this lack of financial backing weakened Duncan's negotiating position. Federated Cablevision was hardly a giant in the industry and Galaxy had expressed concern that they might strike a deal, word would get out, then Federated would not be able to finance the purchase. Nonetheless, Duncan had been able to keep negotiations moving including preparation of a three-page purchase agreement.

The agreement included a $50,000 good faith deposit which Federated would pay to Galaxy. If Federated could not close the deal, Frank's $50,000 would be forfeited. However, Duncan knew that Bob Baer and Galaxy Industries had a long-held reputation for the highest business standards and integrity. Therefore, Duncan did feel comfortable that the $50,000 would be returned if Galaxy should back out of the sale. (His Maryland experience had taught him that such sketchy purchase agreements could not guarantee a sale, and their $5,000 deposit there was still tied up.) Yet even with that uncertainty, he and Frank would have to commit a great deal of time and effort to arrange financing once the agreement was made. With interest rates beginning to move upward, financing wouldn't be easy.

A QUESTION OF COMMITMENT

Duncan wanted to buy the East Valley systems but realized that a whole range of risks still remained. He still had been unsuccessful in obtaining actual operating information from Galaxy. Working from limited confirmations by Bob Baer of Duncan's stated assumptions and by considering key operating indicators, Duncan had included important minimums of current operating profit, residential dwellings passed by cable, numbers of current customers, and price rates in the proposed contract. The contract also allowed an engineering inspection of the systems. The price would be $9 million plus net current assets with an adjustment for changes from assumed depreciation. Still every contingency certainly was not covered. Duncan decided to make one more attempt to convince Bob to give him East Valley's operating results.

EXHIBIT 1
East Valley Financial Projections (*in thousands of dollars*)

	1979	1980	1981	1982	1983	1984	1985	1986
Net operating income	$1,240	$1,360	$1,570	$1,590	$1,800	$1,780	$1,950	$1,910
Interest: Senior 11%	720	710	690	630	530	430	310	190
Senior sub 14%	240	240	240	240	240	240	240	240
Junior sub 10%	100	100	100	100	100	100	100	100
Total interest	1,060	1,050	1,030	970	870	770	650	530
Depreciation	510	1,170	1,600	1,360	1,170	810	680	580
Subtotal	(330)	(860)	(1,060)	(740)	(240)	200	620	800
Recapture income*	—	1,650	1,380	—	—	—	—	—
Profit before taxes	(330)	790	320	(740)	(240)	200	620	800
Taxes	—	150	130	(300)	(240)	—	200	360
Profit after taxes	(330)	640	190	(440)	(240)	200	420	440
Beginning Cash	—	170	160	200	260	220	170	110
Cash from operations	180	160	410	920	930	1,010	1,100	1,020
Closing costs	(200)	—	—	—	—	—	—	—
Senior debt	6,500	(100)	(300)	(800)	(900)	(1,000)	(1,100)	(2,300)
Senior subordinated debt	1,700	—	—	—	—	—	—	—
Junior subordinated debt	1,000	—	—	—	—	—	—	—
Equity	450	—	—	—	—	—	—	—
Long-term assets	(9,460)	(70)	(70)	(60)	(70)	(60)	(60)	(60)
Ending cash	170	160	200	260	220	170	110	(1,230)

EXHIBIT 1 (*concluded*)

	1979	1980	1981	1982	1983	1984	1985	1986
Amortization and depreciation								
10-year straight-line (S.L.) closing costs $200k	20	20	20	20	20	20	20	20
8-year 150% Alpha Plant write-up to $4,360k	350	817	664	539	438	356	289	235
8-year 150% South Plant write-up 1980 to $3,000k	100	75	563	457	371	302	245	199
8-year 150% new additions to plant	43	85	82	79	76	74	71	69
4-year S.L. Alpha noncompete $500k	—	125	125	125	125	—	—	—
3-year South noncompete $250k	—	—	83	83	83	—	—	—
15-year S.L. Alpha franchises $640k	—	43	43	43	43	43	43	43
16-year S.L. South franchises $250k	—	—	16	16	16	16	16	16
Total	$ 513	$1,165	$1,596	$1,362	$1,172	$ 810	$ 684	$ 582

*Duncan Field is buying stock, liquidating the company (which makes him show recapture income and thus pay taxes) and then writing up the assets. The recapture income is shown only to compute taxes due; recapture income is not included in the calculation of cash flow.

APPENDIX: BACKGROUND MATERIAL ON THE CATV INDUSTRY IN 1978

Cable television originated in the United States in the early 1950s as a means of importing network (CBS, NBC, and ABC) television by microwave and/or coaxial cable transmission to areas which, for geographical and topographical reasons, could not receive off-air broadcasts. A typical system generally receives broadcast TV signals with an antenna mounted on a tall tower. These signals are then improved through a variety of amplifiers, signal processors, and electronic filters at the head end and then sent through the systems along a network of coaxial cable (trunk line) which is carried on exisitng telephone poles. A subscriber is then connected to the network with an inexpensive coaxial wire from his TV set (house drops).

The industry has grown enormously since its origins. By the end of 1977, over 3,911 systems served over 12.6 million subscribers with up to 32 channels of program variety, with expectations that as many as 20 million subscribers would be served by 1980. The industry has enjoyed a compounded annual growth rate of over 20 percent during the past 20 years.

FCC regulations, until quite recently, confined the construction of most CATV systems to areas or markets outside the so-called top 100 markets (essentially the areas within a 35-mile radius of the main post office of the 100 largest metropolitan areas in the United States). These systems that lie outside the top 100 markets are generally referred to as *classical systems*, that is, customers are willing to pay to be connected to the cable TV system because they will receive substantially more and better quality TV signals than are obtainable with ordinary household TV antennas. The ratio of paying subscribers to homes passed by cable is called "saturation" or "penetration" and is frequently used as a measure of a system's success as it will determine the revenue used per mile of plant that is generated. Generally, a system with about $200 of revenue per mile per month is barely able to pay its operating expenses, and thus its *operating cash flow* (revenues less direct operating expenses), is said to be zero. Since the incremental cost of serving additional customers is quite nominal, cash flow increases rapidly once saturation exceeds the system's break-even, and frequently systems which are generating $400 of revenue per mile per month are capable of converting half this amount into cash flow which is largely available for debt service. A typical classical system achieves customer saturation of at least 50 percent within three years of operation and is thought to have the potential of 75 percent or greater saturation after about 7 to 10 years of operation. Because such a great portion of a mature cable system's operating financial inputs are fixed and determinable (subscriber rates, capital plant and financing costs), classical systems represent credit risks which are probably more quantifiable than in any other industry except, perhaps, utilities.

The financial demands of the rapidly-growing CATV industry have traditionally exceeded the industry's ability to fund internally. By 1976, the nation's 3,350 CATV systems supported $1.3 billion in debt, and capital expenditures for new and rebuilt plants are estimated to be $250 million annually. Traditional sources of industry debt financing have been equipment suppliers, commercial banks, and life insurance companies. It is estimated that the life insurance industry has committed approximately $500 million of debt funds to the CATV industry and that commercial banks have committed in excess of $550 million.

A significant recent development in the CATV industry has been the introduction of pay cable. There are two major types of pay cable packages which are in use today. A number of companies including Home Box Office, a subsidiary of Time, Inc., have contracted with film makers for the showing of various movies including many popular first-run movies. "Live" events such as sports are also made available to these companies. The movies and live events are conveyed to satellites from which they may be received by cable systems whose operators have purchased the right to show such premium programming to their subscribers. Once a basic CATV system is in place, the incremental capital equipment required to receive and distribute pay cable consists mainly of a large receiving dish or "earth station" and devices located at each viewer's home which can be programmed to block or allow passage of the pay cable signal *(traps or converters)*. Earth stations cost roughly $20,00 to $50,000 (if not shared with other systems) and traps cost approximately $5 to $10 per subscriber.

As an alternative to this, many companies distribute Pay TV to their customers on a "stand-alone" basis. In a stand-alone situation, the cable company contracts for films and events through a booking agent. Films are delivered to the company and transmitted to customers directly from the company. Thus, no earth station is needed, and the capital expenditure involved is reduced to approximately $15,000.

HBO, or similar Pay packages, are generally offered to subscribers for a fee of approximately $7 to $9. Fifty percent of these Pay revenues generally flow to the Pay company, with 50 percent flowing to the cable company to cover overhead and profits.

Stand-alone packages are generally less expensive, costing the subscriber anywhere from $3 to $5, although some stand-alone packages offering extensive movies and events do cost more. Generally, 35 percent of Pay revenues flow to the film distributor, leaving the cable operator with 65 percent. There is, however, a monthly fixed cost associated with the mailing of films and the operation of the film transmitter which must be covered in a stand-alone situation.

Case 2–4

WILSON CABINET CO.

It was mid-December of 1983, and though Sarah Wilson was anxious to be in the "holiday spirit," she couldn't help but be in a somber mood. It had been a tough year. Her husband, Edmund Wilson, had died a few months earlier after a debilitating fight with cancer. Nor had it been a good year for their company, Wilson Cabinet. Now, as year-end approached, Sarah faced a puzzling array of issues relative to the form of organization under which Wilson's operations should continue.

HISTORY

Edmund Wilson had founded Wilson Cabinet in 1948. The business sold custom-designed and manufactured cabinetry to hotels, offices, educational facilities, and other large institutions in the Tampa, Florida, area. Wilson would bid on plans specified by the architect, and then perform the wood work, the final assembly, and the installation. Edmund was an excellent marketer and did a good job of working with the architect to develop the cabinetry design. His wife Sarah did most of the bookkeeping and administrative work. The business required the skills of trained carpenters, who were difficult to find. The firm employed 35 workers, and would typically do between $2 and $3 million in business a year, with the average order size being near $300,000. (See Exhibit 1 for financials.)

The business had begun as a partnership with Sarah and Edmund as equal partners. In 1970, Edmund had given the firm's production manager, Sid Stevens, a 12 percent limited partnership interest; Edmund and Sarah had assumed the position of general partners.

RECENT EVENTS

In 1982, Sid Stevens had suffered a minor heart attack and had decided to begin his gradual retirement from the business. Then, in early 1983, Edmund Wilson discovered that he had a rapidly advancing cancer and was told that he had nine months to live. By October, he was dead.

The Wilsons' only child, a son Roy, had architectural training and was a creative designer. In 1980, he had borrowed most of the Wilsons' liquid capital to invest in a housing development in Sarasota, Florida. Roy had built a model home and invested a considerable amount in the infrastructure of the development (roads, water, sewers, etc.). Unfortunately, interest rates skyrocketed and the actual building of homes was an uneconomic proposition. Roy had sold the land, but the Wilsons retained an investment in the two model homes which had been built.

Following his father's illness and his own unsuccessful development efforts, Roy had come back to work for the family business. He proved to be an adept designer and salesman, but was a poor manager of the manufacturing process. A consultant had recommended that the Wilsons hire a professional controller.

CURRENT SITUATION

Fortunately, the partnership maintained a $150,000 life insurance policy on each of the Wilsons. The partnership also had a buyout agreement with Stevens which permitted the firm to purchase his interest for $150,000.

These recent events had forced Sarah into making what she knew would be some difficult and important decisions. To help her think these through, she, Roy, and her accountant had prepared the pro forma financials which appear in Exhibit 1. Unfortunately, these were not very certain for a number of reasons:

— Sarah did not know how much she would have to pay a professional manager/comptroller, particularly if she did, in fact, give the individual a stake in the business. Her pro formas assumed a $45,000 per year salary for a controller, and $45,000 for Stevens (or his replacement).
— One large job, which would be completed in the next three to four months, was for a company that was having financial difficulties. If the customer went bankrupt, it could wipe out all of 1984's earnings.

Sarah had spoken with several individuals about the decisions she needed to make, and had received a great deal of advice, some of it conflicting. (See Exhibit 2 for personal balance sheet.)

— Roy, her son, said that he was committed to running the business and that ownership of the business should be transferred to him.

— Stevens, 58, felt that the business was in a period of transition and that he should be bought out now that the business had $150,000 of cash on hand (as a result of the insurance policy), and given his own precarious health.

— On the advice of a consultant, the Wilsons had begun looking for a controller. The several qualified candidates they had spoken with had all indicated a desire for a "piece of equity" should they join the business.

— Sarah Wilson's brother, a lawyer, had recommended that she give up the least possible amount of control in the firm in order to protect her own interests. He also recommended that she maintain the partnership form of organization in order to minimize taxes. (See Exhibit 3 for corporate tax rates, and Exhibit 4 for personal tax rates.) Sarah would finish the 1983 tax year as a "qualifying widow" according to the tax code, and would file as a "single taxpayer" in future years.

For the sake of her analysis, she decided to assume that Wilson would be her only source of income, and that any dividends from Wilson would be taxed at ordinary income rates, as detailed in Exhibit 4.

As she sat down to analyze the situation, Sarah realized she would have a difficult time reconciling these different points. She needed to find a plan which would minimize taxes, while allowing her to both maintain control and give some incentive to her son.

EXHIBIT 1
Financials

WILSON CABINET CO.
Balance Sheet
December 31, 1983 (Estimated)
Assets

Cash		$ 23,284
Cash receivable (insurance policy)		150,000
Accounts receivable		248,314
Construction and estimated earnings in excess of billings uncompleted contracts*		303,943
Furniture and fixtures		497,695
		$1,223,508

Liabilities and Stockholders' Equity

Accounts payable		$ 166,448
Loans payable		210,668
Paid-in capital	40,000	
Earnings in excess of distribution†	806,392	
Partners' equity		846,392
		$1,223,508

Income Statements *(in thousands of dollars)*

	Historical			Pro Forma			
	1981	*1982*	*1983E*	*1984*	*1985*	*1986*	*1987*
Revenue	2,919	2,808	1,789	2,900	3,100	3,400	3,600
Cost of goods sold	2,339	2,203	1,489	2,305	2,450	2,690	2,835
Gross margin	580	605	300	595	650	710	765
Selling	170	190	180	180	180	180	180
General and administrative	200	215	215	200	200	210	215
Management	45	45	45	90	90	90	90
Profit before tax	165	155	(140)	125	180	230	280
Distributions to partners	100	100	100				

*This item essentially includes work-in-process inventory, i.e., the material and labor content as well as a portion of the profit of cabinets which have been built but not yet delivered and billed.
†This is the equivalent of retained earnings in a partnership.

EXHIBIT 2
Sarah Wilson's Personal Balance Sheet—December 31, 1983 *(exclusive of investment in Wilson Cabinet)*

Assets		Liabilities and Surplus	
Cash	$ 8,112	Personal Loans	$ 20,246
Securities	92,327	Mortgage own home	50,100
Market value of home	120,648	Mortgage–investment homes	100,640
Market value investment homes (2)	350,200	Net worth	400,301
Total	$571,287	Total	$571,287

EXHIBIT 3
Corporate Tax Rates

Total Income		Tax
Over	*But Not Over*	
$ 0	$ 25,000	15%
25,000	100,000	3,750 + 18% of amount over $ 25,000
50,000	75,000	8,250 + 30% of amount over $ 50,000
75,000	100,000	15,750 + 40% of amount over $ 75,000
100,000	–	25,750 + 46% of amount over $100,000

EXHIBIT 4
Personal Tax Rates

1983 Tax Rate Schedules   Your zero bracket amount has been built into these Tax Rate Schedules.

Caution: You must use the Tax Table instead of these Tax Rate Schedules if your taxable income is less than $50,000 unless you use **Schedule G** (income averaging), to figure your tax. In that case, even if your taxable income is less than $50,000, use the rate schedules on this page to figure your tax.

Schedule X
Single Taxpayers
Use this Schedule if you checked **Filing Status Box 1** on Form 1040—

If the amount on Form 1040, line 37 is: Over—	But not over—	Enter on Form 1040, line 38	of the amount over—
$0	$2,300	—0—	
2,300	3,400	......11%	$2,300
3,400	4,400	$121 + 13%	3,400
4,400	8,500	251 + 15%	4,400
8,500	10,800	866 + 17%	8,500
10,800	12,900	1,257 + 19%	10,800
12,900	15,000	1,656 + 21%	12,900
15,000	18,200	2,097 + 24%	15,000
18,200	23,500	2,865 + 28%	18,200
23,500	28,800	4,349 + 32%	23,500
28,800	34,100	6,045 + 36%	28,800
34,100	41,500	7,953 + 40%	34,100
41,500	55,300	10,913 + 45%	41,500
55,300	....	17,123 + 50%	55,300

Schedule Z
Unmarried Heads of Household
(including certain married persons who live apart—see page 6 of the instructions)

Use this schedule if you checked **Filing Status Box 4** on Form 1040—

If the amount on Form 1040, line 37 is: Over—	But not over—	Enter on Form 1040, line 38	of the amount over—
$0	$2,300	—0—	
2,300	4,400	......11%	$2,300
4,400	6,500	$231 + 13%	4,400
6,500	8,700	504 + 15%	6,500
8,700	11,800	834 + 18%	8,700
11,800	15,000	1,392 + 19%	11,800
15,000	18,200	2,000 + 21%	15,000
18,200	23,500	2,672 + 25%	18,200
23,500	28,800	3,997 + 29%	23,500
28,800	34,100	5,534 + 34%	28,800
34,100	44,700	7,336 + 37%	34,100
44,700	60,600	11,258 + 44%	44,700
60,600	81,800	18,254 + 48%	60,600
81,800	....	28,430 + 50%	81,800

Schedule Y
Married Taxpayers and Qualifying Widows and Widowers

Married Filing Joint Returns and Qualifying Widows and Widowers

Use this schedule if you checked **Filing Status Box 2 or 5** on Form 1040—

If the amount on Form 1040, line 37 is: Over—	But not over—	Enter on Form 1040, line 38	of the amount over—
$0	$3,400	—0—	
3,400	5,500	......11%	$3,400
5,500	7,600	$231 + 13%	5,500
7,600	11,900	504 + 15%	7,600
11,900	16,000	1,149 + 17%	11,900
16,000	20,200	1,846 + 19%	16,000
20,200	24,600	2,644 + 23%	20,200
24,600	29,900	3,656 + 26%	24,600
29,900	35,200	5,034 + 30%	29,900
35,200	45,800	6,624 + 35%	35,200
45,800	60,000	10,334 + 40%	45,800
60,000	85,600	16,014 + 44%	60,000
85,600	109,400	27,278 + 48%	85,600
109,400	....	38,702 + 50%	109,400

Married Filing Separate Returns

Use this schedule if you checked **Filing Status Box 3** on Form 1040—

If the amount on Form 1040, line 37 is: Over—	But not over—	Enter on Form 1040, line 38	of the amount over—
$0	$1,700	—0—	
1,700	2,750	......11%	$1,700
2,750	3,800	$115.50 + 13%	2,750
3,800	5,950	252.00 + 15%	3,800
5,950	8,000	574.50 + 17%	5,950
8,000	10,100	923.00 + 19%	8,000
10,100	12,300	1,322.00 + 23%	10,100
12,300	14,950	1,828.00 + 26%	12,300
14,950	17,600	2,517.00 + 30%	14,950
17,600	22,900	3,312.00 + 35%	17,600
22,900	30,000	5,167.00 + 40%	22,900
30,000	42,800	8,007.00 + 44%	30,000
42,800	54,700	13,639.00 + 48%	42,800
54,700	....	19,351.00 + 50%	54,700

Case 2-5

ELECTRODEC

In April 1983, Andy, Tom, and Pete began spring break of their second year at The Northern Business School with a great deal of work ahead of them. The three had spent that winter and spring working on a field study for Electrodec, a small electronics firm. Now their efforts indicated that there was a promising market for one of Electrodec's new products, and each of the men had an offer to join the firm as both an employee *and* equity owner.

Each young man had to decide whether or not this business represented an attractive opportunity for himself, and if so, what share of equity ownership was appropriate.

ELECTRODEC

Electrodec was a small firm located in Charlotte, North Carolina, with 1982 sales of approximately $300,000 (see Exhibit 1 for recent income statement and balance sheet). The company designed and manufactured several sophisticated electronic instruments which recorded and analyzed data, and there were eight employees (see Exhibit 2).

The president/founder and sole owner of Electrodec, Kirk Nolan, had been responsible for establishing his firm as a true "state-of-the-art" engi-

Copyright © 1983 by the President and Fellows of Harvard College.
Harvard Business School case 9-384-078.

neering and product development center. Clients included NASA, the Department of Defense, General Electric, and other firms with sophisticated engineering needs. The firm operated in a very informal and open manner and, as Exhibit 3 indicates, Kirk Nolan was intimately involved with virtually every aspect of the firm's work.

Historically, Electrodec had derived a majority of its income from custom R&D projects which had subsidized product development efforts. For example, the firm had done a great deal of work for the Electric Power Research Institute, winning these contracts over competition from GE, Hughes Aircraft, and others.

Electrodec had two specific products lines:

1. Laser Doppler Velocimeters (LDV) which provided an accurate means of measuring flow speed without actual contact with the material, e.g., air in a wind tunnel, molten metals in production.
2. An electronic recording and data acquisition (ERDAC) product line, which measured, recorded, and analyzed electric signals. Some of these ERDAC products were geared specifically towards the electric utility environment.

A new ERDAC product, the 1620, was currently in development and was targeted toward the electric utility market. It was the market potential of the ERDAC 1620 which was the object of their field study and subsequent enthusiasm. The ERDAC 1620 was in the last phase of design, and work on a prototype had begun.

BACKGROUND

Andy Barnes, Tom Templeton, and Pete Rhodes had all been first-year section mates at the Northern Business School (NBS). (See Exhibit 4 for resumes.) They worked with one another on a variety of group projects during the first year, and were enthusiastic about the prospect of working together on a field study. They each brought varied experience to the team.

Andy Barnes

Andy, 27, had worked for Electrodec the previous summer. He had met Kirk Nolan, Electrodec's president, during his years at Westinghouse's Advanced Systems Technology division, where Electrodec had been a subcontractor to Andy on various projects. Andy had extensive experience in the design and development of power systems. He had left Westinghouse to get his MBA because of a long-standing interest in management and the realization that "I didn't have enough gray hair to get the job I wanted at Westinghouse."

Andy left his summer job at Electrodec convinced that the ERDAC 1620 was a promising product, and relatively certain that he would return to the firm. The field study's purpose was to evaluate the market potential of the ERDAC 1620, and recommend a plan for capitalizing on its potential.

Tom Templeton

Tom Templeton, 24, had received his master's degree in Mechanical Engineering from MIT just prior to starting business school. He had received his B.S. degree in three years and worked for Hughes aircraft before returning to MIT for his master's degree. His experience with Hughes had been focused on prototype design and the start-up of manufacturing operations. Tom had always been interested in business, had owned a luncheonette during college, and was a licensed real estate broker. His summer job with J. Makowski Associates had added to his experience in project management and consulting.

Pete Rhodes

Pete Rhodes, 27, had graduated from the Naval Academy in 1976 and had served for five years in various capacities in the Navy's nuclear submarine program. This experience had given Pete a significant exposure to both engineering and managing people. He chose to concentrate on the latter, and left the Navy to attend NBS. His first-year exposure to marketing had led him to accept a summer job with Procter & Gamble's sales program. He returned from the summer with a strong interest in a career in sales and marketing.

Kirk Nolan

Kirk Nolan, Electrodec's president, age 38, had been oriented toward engineering since his high school days, and had even published some technical work prior to attending college.

Kirk attended Rensselaer Polytechnic Institute from 1963–1971, when he was awarded his Ph.D. in Electrical Engineering. Kirk and a partner founded Electrodec as an engineering consulting firm. When his partner suddenly died, Kirk assumed ownership and control.

Kirk was clearly the driving force behind Electrodec and vital to its operations. Kirk was motivated far more by the engineering challenge of an assignment than by the profit potential. He would frequently fly off on a moment's notice to solve a difficult engineering problem on projects in response to customer requests.

THE MARKET

The ERDAC 1620 was designed specifically for the utility customer. Kirk and Andy felt sophisticated electronic equipment could meet these customers' needs better than existing electromechanical products.

Utility Customer Needs

In order to understand why such equipment was useful, it was necessary to understand how a typical utility's power network was configured.

Power systems consisted of generation stations and load centers. A generation station, such as a nuclear power plant, produced power for several load centers (Figure 1). This power was carried via transmission lines, which were the familiar steel towers with multiple wires that cross the United States.

Where lines met, or branched out, there existed "mini-hubs" which packaged and monitored the flow of electricity so that it was sent most efficiently. These were called substations.

In order to deliver electricity safely, and with minimum wear and tear on the transmisison equipment, the power must be carried in a stable manner—i.e., at a constant frequency and voltage. When there was a significant disturbance on a power line—which could be caused by a falling tree, lightning, or equipment failure—relay equipment automatically shut down the line to prevent damage to the system.

At this point, other power sources would be automatically brought on line. On occasion, when the utility could not fill the gap with power of its own, it would purchase electricity from another utility company. In the case of a severe fault in the Florida power system, for instance, the Florida Power & Light Company would purchase electricity from Georgia at a rate which varied from $10,000 to $50,000 per hour. They would then determine the location of the fault, and repair it. Only a very low percentage of faults, however, necessitated the purchase of power from other utilities.

FIGURE 1
Typical Power Transmission System

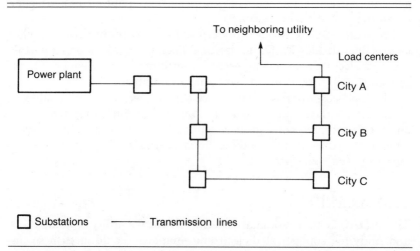

The Utility Market

Historically, utilities have been permitted to earn a target rate of return on capital (ROC). Utilities could expand their investment base, and then request rate increases to obtain their target ROC. The utilities' costs skyrocketed in the 1970s, due principally to the rise in the price of oil. At the same time, public interest research groups (PIRGs) became more active.

This led to frequent refusals of utility rate increases, a fall in utilities' ROC, decreased profitability, a consequent rise in the utilities' cost of capital and ultimately, a decrease in the utilities' ability to spend money on capital equipment.

In response to a shortage of funds, the utilities cut back on installing generating facilities (i.e., power plants) and added additional transmission and distribution facilities to existing generation capacity rather than build expensive new generation stations. See Exhibit 5 for data on utility company capital spending.

Electric Power Recording Equipment

Electric power recording equipment (EPRE) consisted of several types of equipment which were attached to transmission lines and serve varying functions:

— Fault recorders: sensed and recorded variations in current, voltage, and frequency. Typically called oscillographs, these machines would record data for a few seconds after a fault (and in some cases, for a few milliseconds prior to a fault). Permanent records of surges on the power line would then be available for analysis by the utility engineer. These data would not, however, help the power company determine the cause and location of the fault. Further, these data were not remotely accessible and the engineer had to travel to the transmission substation to obtain them.

Essentially, this equipment told the utility that the system protection scheme was operating properly. This equipment typically cost $70,000 to $80,000.
— Event recorders: monitored and logged the operation of transmission and relay equipment during routine operation and system disturbances. This equipment told the utility precisely which pieces of equipment operated, and when. This permitted the utility to monitor the performance of the different components of the transmission and protection system. This equipment typically cost $20,000 to $45,000.
— Fault monitor: a combination of an event recorder and a fault recorder in one cabinet. This provided both the wave form data from the oscillograph and the data on the operation of specific pieces of transmission and relay equipment. This equipment typically cost slightly more than

the sum of the individual event and fault recorders, i.e., $80,000 to $100,000.

The Market for EPRE

The market for EPRE was driven by the growth in transmission and distribution substations. These substations exist at the beginning and end of power lines, as well as at other points where lines meet or branch out.

Growth in substations was, in turn, driven by the demand for electric power. When a new area required power service, new lines were laid and substations added. Or, if an existing area demands greater amounts of power, new lines with new substations could be added.

When a new substation was added, there also existed an opportunity to add a piece of EPRE, such as a fault recorder. If the substation was a major one—carrying power into New York City or Boston, for example—the utility would certainly want to monitor the equipment there. If, on the other hand, the substation was only carrying a small amount of electricity to a remote area, monitoring this equipment would be less important.

Utilities classify substations by the amount of electricity that passes through them. There are standard categories that run from the largest— 765 kilovolts (kv)—to the smallest (69 kv and less). Generally, most substations of 500 kv and up would have EPRE, and some proportion of the smaller substations would also have EPRE. See Exhibit 6 for a forecast of substation growth.

THE ERDAC

Electrodec's ERDAC 1620 was a sophisticated microcomputer-based system which performed the functions of both fault recorders and event recorders and provided the following additional features:

- Greater number of inputs—permitted the monitoring of a greater number of lines and pieces of equipment.
- Remote access to data—information was available on-line; travel to actual transmission line and recording equipment was not required.
- System integration—provided features of fault recorder and event recorder in one instrument.
- Lower maintenance—no mechanical parts to break down.
- Software availability—ERDAC 1620 could be used as a personal computer with commonly available software.
- Fault locating utility—system could pinpoint location of fault.
- Sophistication—better bandwidth, range, resolution, and accuracy in data recording.Self-diagnostic ability—identified recording device malfunctions before actual fault.
- Prefault data availability—system recorded data prior to fault occurrence.

The ERDAC system consisted of two units:

1. The ERDAC 1620—the monitoring and recording device.
2. The ERDAC 1625—the computer which would analyze the data which the 1620 would collect. Each 1625 could monitor and analyze up to 15 1620s.

Electrodec planned to design and build the electronic "guts" of the product, but would subcontract the fabrication of printed circuit boards and metal cabinetry. Electrodec would provide a turnkey system which integrated the 1620 with a playback unit which would analyze and print out the data captured by the ERDAC 1620.

THE FIELD STUDY

The field study's major goal was to assess and quantify the market opportunity the ERDAC 1620 represented, and to identify the critical path for capitalizing on it. The team sent out a questionnaire (see Exhibit 7) to the largest 150 independently owned utilities. They received an extremely high response, giving them data on utilities which represented over 50 percent of the operating capacity in the United States. (See Exhibit 8 for results.) Between January and April 1983, the team identified and addressed several issues with the help of these data.

The Utility Customer

The utility market consisted of a very diverse customer base. Numerous aspects of a utility's operating environment affected the purchase decision for this equipment. Among these were the network's complexity, service area size, growth, cost of downtime, frequency of faults, its power generation source (e.g., nuclear), and the sophistication of its engineering staff.

Equipment was purchased on the basis of a bidding system where the engineering staff would specify a list of acceptable suppliers who would then bid to obtain the business. (See Exhibit 9.)

Utilities were notoriously conservative and would not use a product that did not have a proven track record. Most design engineers wanted several references before they would consider buying unfamiliar equipment. Risk reduction was a major concern for utility engineering personnel. For this reason performance was seldom compromised for price. Price sensitivity was also reduced because equipment of this nature became part of the utility's rate base (i.e., utilities were permitted to earn a certain percentage rate of return on capital; when their capital base increased, so did their allowable dollar profit.)

Value-Added of ERDAC

The ERDAC 1620 had several advantages over competitors' equipment based on its sophisticated array of features. These advantages provided value to the utility by both lowering costs and improving operations, as shown below:

Value-Added of ERDAC versus Conventional Equipment

Lower Costs	*Improved Operations*
Lower Labor Costs	Easier storage of records
—Fewer man-hours repairing equipment	More timely fault analysis
—Fewer man-hours retrieving data	More accurate understanding of network
Fault locating reduces cost of downtime	operation
—Purchase of electricity at premium from	Faster fault resolution reduces system risk
neighboring utility	More inputs can be monitored
—Community impact	

The study team attempted, based on discussion with the utilities, to derive a "theoretical value-added premium," i.e., how much more a utility customer would be likely to pay for each of the ERDAC's unique features. This premium is expressed as a percentage of the base price for a standard fault recorder.

They identified the following features and their "theoretical premiums":

Feature	*Premium*
Remote access to data	5%
Lower maintenance costs	10
Self-diagnostic ability	10
Greater number of inputs for analysis*	20
Selectivity, resolution, accuracy	20
Fault locating ability*	25
Integration of event and fault recorder*	5
Use as personal computer availability of software*	5
Availability of prefault data*	5
Total	105%
Without special case	45%

*These premiums are "special case," i.e., will be valued by only some utilities with certain equipment configurations. Other premiums should be valued by all utilities.

Market Size and Potential

In order to estimate market size, the team divided potential demand into three segments, and then attempted to estimate each one. These segments were:

— Growth: equipment needed because new transmission lines were built. The size of this segment was estimated based on a forecast for substation growth given in Exhibit 6. The team made a series of assumptions both about the percentage of substations of each size which would re-

Potential Market Size—ERDAC 1620

	Segment	*Pessimistic*	*Best Guess*	*Optimistic*
Size of total	Growth	80	91	105
segment (units)	R/failure	117	194	291
	R/value-added	28	82	262
	Total	225	367	658
Electrodec	Growth	15	33	45
market share of	R/failure	15	33	45
each segment (%)	R/value-added	100	100	100
(percent)	Total	130	166	190
Resultant Electrodec				
sales (units)	Growth	12	30	47
	R/failure	18	64	131
	R/value-added	28	82	262
	Total	58	176	440

quire EPRE, and about what Electrodec's market share of each segment would be. These assumptions varied between the pessimistic and optimisic scenarios.

— Replacement on failure (R/failure): equipment which was replaced when it failed. The team estimated an installed base of roughly 2,900 units. Based on its survey, the team then assumed an economic life of 25 (pessimistic) to 10 years (optimistic assumption).

— Replacement on value-added (R/value-added): equipment which was replaced due to new equipment with better features. The team assumed that from 1 percent (pessimistic) to 10 percent (opmistic assumption) of the installed base could be replaced.

The team attempted to size the market (in units) for 1984 in three different scenarios: pessimistic, best guess, and optimistic (see above).

Cost

The team also performed a detailed analysis of the cost for the ERDAC unit:

	Material	*Total Direct Labor Cost*	*Material and Labor*
ERDAC 1620:			
Totals	$32,028	$9,420	$41,448
ERDAC 1625			
Playback analysis and central controller	$18,160	$ 500	$18,660

Competition

The industry, following the utilities' historic conservatism, had been very slow to change technically. The industry was dominated by Powerpath, Inc., although other firms also competed.

Powerpath had been the dominant supplier of recording instrumentation to the utilities for over 40 years. Although they had the dominant market share, Powerpath was generally disliked by utilities because of their:

— Exorbitant prices for spare parts.
— Frequent breakdown of equipment.
— Extremely long wait for spare parts.

In addition, Powerpath had recently been involved in an extended price war with Serol, a company founded by an ousted ex-president of Powerpath. Powerpath cut prices drastically, which damaged Serol's profitability severely; after two years of this price war, Powerpath bought Serol, and *doubled* prices the next day.

UNRESOLVED ISSUES

The field study raised several issues which would have to be dealt with if Electrodec were to attempt to enter the market. These included the issues described here.

Price

The unit (without computer and printer) could be built for roughly $42,000; a standard Powerpath fault recorder sold for $65,000. Yet, the ERDAC unit also filled the role of a fault monitor, which sold for closer to $100,000. And there were 10 times as many fault recorders as fault monitors. If the ERDAC sold for $70,000 to $80,000, they should be able to compete very effectively in the fault recorder market (they had used a price of $76,000 in their market survey). But they would be charging far too little for the unit if it were a fault monitor. If the unit were priced near the $100,000 mark, they would capture this full value, but would be less effective in competing for fault recorder business.

Sales Force

Because the ERDAC is technologically sophisticated and the selling cycle is a long one, a direct sales force seemed appropriate. Yet, as the team's own analysis showed, this option raised fixed costs tremendously. The alternative would be to use manufacturers' reps who would work solely on a commission basis.

Cost of Sales Force Alternatives

Assumptions: Average unit price is $76,000.
Base salary $25,000.
Commissions: $600/unit for first 10 units.
            $2500/unit for all others.
Five salesmen are hired.

Direct Sales Force Costs:

Fixed costs

Salary	(5 × $25,000)	$125,000
Benefits	(.5 × 5 × $25,000)	62,500

Travel
  50% on road @ $100/day
    (this covers gas, food and lodging
    125 days × $100 × 5)   62,500
Office expenses
  50% in office @ $20/day
    (this covers phone and supplies
    125 days × $20 × 5)   30,000
                                 $262,500

Variable costs
  Assume 50 units sold:
    50 units × $600 commission   30,000

Total Costs of Direct Sales Force $292,500

Manufacturer's Rep Costs:
Variable cost = 10% commission = $7,600/unit

$$\text{Break-even} = \frac{\$292,500}{\$7,600} = 39 \text{ units}$$

Location

While Charlotte had been a fine place for Kirk himself to run Electrodec as essentially a "consulting engineer's shop," manufacturing would be a different story altogether. Charlotte lacked:

— A major airport, required for quick selling trips to out-of-state locations.
— A stable base of skilled labor.
— An attractive climate and social amenities for attracting and keeping skilled professionals.

These would all be important factors in getting Electrodec's ERDAC off the ground, and would be even more important as the company grew.

The study team had identified Atlanta as a location which met all the above criteria and was personally preferable. Any move would have to occur quickly—Electrodec's current facilities were not large enough to support the building of even one finished unit (the metal cabinetry which houses the unit is very large). But, with the product in the delicate proto-type phase, did it make sense to move *away* from the only trained workers that Electrodec had?

Long-Term Strategy

In the short term, Electrodec's strategy was to build a technologically su-perior product, charge a premium price, and compete against Powerpath based on its poor reputation for reliability and spare parts availability. Electrodec's other product—the LDV—is in a completely different line of business altogether. Was Electrodec a "one-trick pony" or did it have the potential to establish itself over the long term with a succession of prod-ucts?

Keeping All the Balls in the Air

Work on the prototype had begun several months ago, and was proceed-ing slowly for a number of reasons:

— It was difficult to get Kirk to focus on the project. He was often running off to work on various consulting projects, which provided the cash that the company needed to operate in the short term.
— The final design had yet to be "frozen" so design changes occurred fre-quently.
— There was a long lead time for parts; a resistor or capacitor which cost a few pennies could delay completion of a $50,000 unit for up to two months.
— The magnitude of the development work was enormous for such a small company, and hence, cash flow was strained. This forced Elec-trodec to divert its resources toward projects which would generate short-term revenues.

  Still, Electrodec had accepted a few orders for the ERDAC and there were prospects for several more. This made them more confident and they knew it would help them raise the financing they needed. One of Power-path's really weak points, however (and a key element of Electrodec's strategy), was a reputation for reliability and on-time delivery. Should they accept orders before the product was perfected?

  They knew that capital might be difficult to raise, and they were sure that having a working prototype would make the process easier, improve their bargaining position, and enable them to drive a better deal. But, if they didn't get money soon, they would not be able to start making commitments for the upcoming move, wherever it might be. Their pro forma financials had been run under two different assumptions (see Exhibit 10):

1. A $1 million equity investment in September 1983 and an additional $1 million in June 1984.
2. No equity investment.

The Decision

Finally, each of the men had to make a decision about how well this opportunity fit his own personal abilities and career plans. They described their feelings.

Andy

I really believe that this is a terrific opportunity for all of us. Personally, I have a great deal of experience in the power systems area, and I am convinced that there is a market for the product. We do have a lot of work ahead of us— finding a new location, getting a prototype built, and hiring a sales force; but I'm very confident that we will be able to accomplish this. Kirk is a terrific guy and a real engineering talent.

Tom

I was very surprised when Andy called me and offered me a position with Electrodec. It's very tempting—with a piece of the equity, there could be a large financial upside, and I have enjoyed working with Kirk and everyone at Electrodec.

Still, there are plenty of risks. I have no electrical engineering background. Kirk and Andy say the product will work, but I don't have the technical competence to make that judgment on my own. It seems to me that we are really in a bind: We don't want to get venture money until we have a prototype, can't build units until we have a new location, but need money for a new location.

Finally, I'm getting married in a couple of months, and my fiancee has a full scholarship to a graduate school in Boston. What will we do in Charlotte or Atlanta? I'm already in over my eyeballs in debt—I'm borrowing money to pay for my honeymoon—and Electrodec won't be generating any cash for quite a while.

I also have some other very attractive offers, including:

— A one-third partnership in an area engineering consulting/development firm.
— A position as a general manager of one of the subsidiaries of the consulting firm I worked with last summer.
— A position with a New England conglomerate which is considering entering the robotics area. I would work with the CEO and strategic planning group for a year, and if we decided to proceed, I would be the general manager of the robotics division.

Each of these positions offers the ability to work in an area that I'm very interested in, live in New England, and start making some money right away.

Pete

My offer from Electrodec was a surprise, too. I've been recruiting pretty heavily in the sales and marketing area, and have some attractive offers from Procter & Gamble, General Foods, Bath Iron Works, and Gould. My wife and I are both from Boston and have some very close ties there.

Although this opportunity has gotten me pretty excited about working for a small company—my own company at that—I do have some concerns. Financially, the upside is attractive, but I'm heavily in debt, have a 3-year-old kid, and my wife is seven-months pregnant.

I also question whether Electrodec can really handle three MBAs.

Finally, I am less optimistic about the product than Kirk and Andy. I think it's going to be very tough to get a prototype up and working. Kirk just isn't focusing his energies on it. I wonder if he has the discipline to do the kind of work that's required.

Kirk summed up his views as well:

The field study has pointed out a market potential far in excess of that which I'd expected. There really is a strong demand from the utility customer for this product. It is an opportunity to use very sophisticated technology in an area that hasn't seen it yet, and the utilities are very excited about it.

For me, this is a very fundamental change in the business: to go from a consultant/tinkerer to a full-fledged manufacturer. There certainly are risks to bringing on the additional overhead, and I will be giving up a good-sized piece of the equity. But I have complete faith in Andy, and I would rather own a small percent of a bigger business.

I hope that Tom and Pete decide to join us. We really need their help in manufacturing and sales, and if they want to have their own business, they should do it now because it gets much more difficult to do it later on.

EXHIBIT 1
Financial Statements

ELECTRODEC
Income Statement
As of February 28, 1983

	6 Months 2/28/83	Percent	12 Months 2/28/83	Percent
Sales	$ 92,590	100.00	$302,380	100.00
Cost of sales	19,605	21.17	109,205	36.12
Gross profit	$ 72,985	78.83	$193,175	63.88
Operating expenses:				
Sales expenses	$ 15,158	16.37	$ 35,877	11.86
General and administrative expense	39,808	42.99	103,480	34.22
Research and development	18,010	19.45	32,383	56.80
Total expenses	$ 72,976	78.82	$171,740	56.80
Operating profit	9	0.01	21,435	7.09
Other income	20,099	21.71	22,287	7.37
Other expense	(12,018)	(12.98)	(18,595)	(6.15)
Net profit	8,090	8.74	25,127	8.31
Income taxes	(388)	(.42)	(2,388)	(.79)
Net income	$ 7,702	8.32	$ 22,739	7.52

Balance Sheet at February 28, 1983

Assets

Current assets:
Cash	$ 4,519	
Receivables	127,186	
Inventories	112,728	
Prepaid insurance	572	
Due from officers	17,918	
Total current assets		$262,923

Fixed assets:
Equipment	36,353	
Accumulated depreciation	(12,124)	
Net book value		24,229
Total assets		$287,152

Liabilities and Equity

Current liabilities:
Accounts payable	$ 12,395	
Commissions payable	19,959	
Accrued expenses	21,598	
Notes payable	110,000	
Payroll and sales taxes	19,622	
Income taxes	1,500	
Total current liabilities		$185,074

(continued)

EXHIBIT 1 (*concluded*)

Equity:	
Common stock	35,100
Retained earnings	44,238
Current income (Loss)	22,740
Total equity	102,078
Total liability and equity	$287,152

EXHIBIT 2
Organization Chart

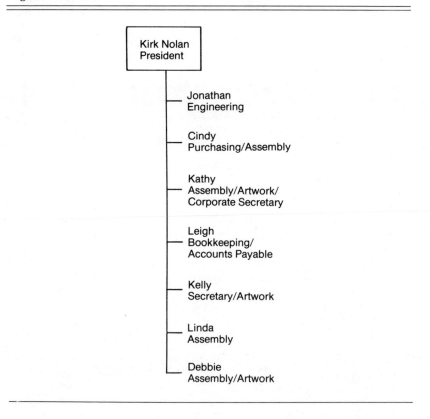

EXHIBIT 3
Typical Job Order Flow

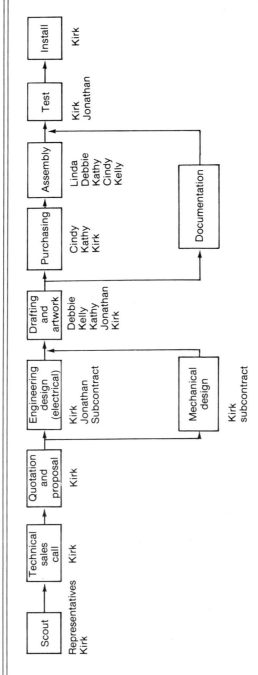

EXHIBIT 4
Resumes

PETER RHODES

Education
1981-1983
NORTHERN BUSINESS SCHOOL
Candidate for the degree of Master in Business Administration in June 1983. Followed general management curriculum in first year. Second-year emphasis directed toward marketing, production, and operations management. Member of the Finance and Marketing Clubs.

1972-1976
UNITED STATES NAVAL ACADEMY   ANNAPOLIS, MD
Awarded Bachelor of Science degree in History. Superintendent's List. Varsity track team letterman. Company Commander responsible for the military training of 100 men.

Business Experience
Summer 1982
THE PROCTER & GAMBLE DISTRIBUTING COMPANY   CHICAGO, IL
Summer Sales Management Intern. Responsible for 50 retail accounts. Made sales presentations and merchandising recommendations to these accounts. Attended one-week sales training course. Completed special projects for the District and Division managers.

Military Experience
1976-1981
11/79-8/81
UNITED STATES NAVY, Progressed from Ensign to Lieutenant
Weapons Officer on board the nuclear fast attack submarine USS Pargo (SSN 650). Department head, responsible for operation and maintenance of the ship's weapon, sonar, and fire control equipment. Supervised 30 men. Department awarded Antisubmarine Warfare (ASW) "A" during this period. Personally awarded two Navy Commendation Medals for superior performance.

11/78-11/79
Communicator on board USS Pargo (SSN 650). Organized and trained 10 electronic technicians and radiomen. Molded an effective communications team that was able to meet all communications requirements during a Mediterranean deployment. Awarded Navy Achievement Medal.

3/78-11/78
Reactor Controls Assistant on board USS Pargo (SSN 650). Responsible for the preventive and corrective maintenance of the reactor control and protection equipment. Led and trained the reactor control electronic technicians. Successfully completed an Operational Reactor Safeguard Examination and qualified in submarines during this period.

9/76-3/78
Student in the Naval Nuclear Power Training Pipeline. Qualified to supervise the operation and maintenance of a naval nuclear power plant.

EXHIBIT 4 (*continued*)

Personal Background

Grew up in Massachusetts. Willing to travel. Interests include athletics, sailing, and literature. Married. Excellent health.

References

Personal references available on request.

TOM TEMPLETON

Education

1981–1983

NORTHERN BUSINESS SCHOOL
Candidate for the degree of Master in Business Administration in June 1983. Concentration in marketing and finance. Tutor for first-year finance. Member of Management Consulting, Small Business, and Marketing Clubs.

1976–1981

MASSACHUSETTS INSTITUTE
OF TECHNOLOGY   CAMBRIDGE, MASSACHUSETTS
Bachelor of Science and Master of Science degrees in Mechanical Engineering in January 1980 and June 1981 respectively. Concentration in design and dynamics. Master's thesis dealt with advanced manufacturing systems within the East Peoria Plant of Caterpillar Tractor Company and their impact on the "L" series crawler tractor design.

Graduate of Engineering Internship Program. President of Pi Tau Sigma, Mechanical Engineering Honor Society. Wunsch Foundation Award for Design Excellence. Hughes Masters Fellowship. Naval Reserve and NROTC Training. Freshman Advisor. Varsity Letterman in Lacrosse.

Business Experience

1982

J. MAKOWSKI ASSOCIATES, INC.   BOSTON, MASSACHUSETTS
Consultant, Energy Industry. Coauthor of MBTA Prospectus to solicit private investments in cogeneration projects. Project developer in coal conversion of paper company utilizing fluidized bed combustor and third party financing. Preliminary engineering, logistics and financial analyses presented to Haverhill Gas Board of Directors as a diversification opportunity. Structured and negotiated exclusive contract to sell submetering billing system to northeast utilities. Initiated current investigation to structure and secure third party financing of flash gas recovery and cogeneration project at the Everett LNG storage facility.

1978 –1981

HUGHES AIRCRAFT COMPANY   CULVER CITY, CALIFORNIA

1981

Assistant to Program Manager. Laser Augmented Airborn Tow (LAAT) Program. Extensive interdepartmental and vendor coordination to resolve system problems. Matrix organization structure implied dual operating responsibilities of Program Office and Departmental organization. Broader exposure to defense contract preparation and budgeting.

EXHIBIT 4 *(continued)*

1980

Member of Technical Staff, LAAT Program. Coordinated efforts of designers, draftsmen, and technicians to identify and implement system revisions facilitating mass production. Follow-up engineering support of manufacturing start-up at alternate plant site.

Summers
1978–1979

Engineering Analyst, Fighting Vehicle System. Analyzed boresight specifications of missile launcher, optical elements tolerance study, mirror head balancing, and computer methods in product design.

Other Experiences
1979–1981

PLOUGHMAN'S PUB   CAMBRIDGE, MASSACHUSETTS
Owner-manager, luncheonette. Duties included inventory control, bookkeeping, budgeting and hiring. Fifteen part-time employees. Up to 300 customers daily.

1980
Licensed Real Estate Salesperson in California.

Patent
Patent Pending, 1980, "Double-Sided Lockbar," designed for Julius Koch Company. New Bedford, Massachusetts.

Publication
"INDUSTRIAL INNOVATION: The Dynamics of Product and Production Process Change," Master's Thesis, Massachusetts Institute of Technology (Cambridge: MIT Press, 1981).

October 1982

ANDREW BARNES

Married, one child
Excellent health
Security Clearance: Secret

Experience
Summer 1982

ELECTRODEC   CHARLOTTE, NORTH CAROLINA
Self-employed consultant to a high technology venture. Performed duties of chief operating and financial executives including the successful negotiation and structuring of debt financing, establishment of accounting and control policies, and the implementation of a computer-based accounting system. Conducted market research and formulated pricing and distribution policies. Supported sales efforts through customer calls and contract negotiation. Supervised production scheduling and generated personnel plans.

1978–1981
WESTINGHOUSE ELECTRIC
CORPORATION   PITTSBURGH, PENNSYLVANIA

EXHIBIT 4 *(continued)*

1980–1981

Director of Product Integrity and Productivity, Advanced Systems Technology Division: Developed and implemented strategic programs to ensure continuing market leadership as a staff assistant to the division General Manager. Initiated the company's first engineering/professional Quality Circle program.

1978–1980

Senior Engineer and Project Manager, Advanced Systems Technology Divison: Promoted through four engineering levels while functioning as a Project Manager. Directed the technical and financial aspects of a development program for a major product line and large-scale contract research projects. Conducted several smaller consulting efforts oriented toward problem solving in a variety of industries.

1974–1977

VOUGHT CORPORATION OF LTV,
INCORPORATED   DALLAS, TEXAS
Engineer-in-Training/Co-op: Assigned as an Assistant Engineer to various programs to perform circuit and logic design, systems instrumentation, computer systems analysis and programming, and development of life-cycle cost models for logistics purposes.

Education
1981–1983

NORTHERN BUSINESS SCHOOL
Candidate for the degree of Master in Business Administration, June 1983. General management curriculum. Electives in marketing, finance, and technology management. Member of Marketing. Finance, Investment, and International Business Clubs. Intramural athletics.

1978–1980

CARNEGIE-MELLON UNIVERSITY   PITTSBURGH,
                                                                                         PENNSYLVANIA
Received Master of Science in Electrical Engineering degree from the Carnegie Institute of Technology, May 1980. Specialized in power and energy related topics.

1973–1977

GEORGIA INSTITUTE OF TECHNOLOGY   ATLANTA, GEORGIA
Received Bachelor of Electrical Engineering, Cooperative Plan degree, December

1977.

Emphasis on digital communications and instrumentation. Academic honors include Eta Kappa Nu, Secretary; Omicron Delta Kappa, and Dean's List. Elected President and Secretary of the Society of ANAK, Georgia Tech's highest honorary; named ODK Leader of the Year at Georgia Tech, 1977. Appointed Director and Chairman of the Board of a new $5.5 million student athletic complex; responsible for administrative, policy, and programming matters including a yearly operating budget of $450,000.

Personal Background

Author of three technical papers and five engineering reports. Hold two patent disclosures in power related areas. Lecturer at the Westinghouse Advanced School in Power Engineering, 1979. Member of Georgia Tech's Committee of 20 Advisory

EXHIBIT 4
(concluded)

Board. Have lived in various sections of the United States and Europe. Working knowledge of German and French. Licensed Engineer-in-Training.

References

Personal references available upon request.

November 1982

EXHIBIT 5
Total Industry Electric Power System Capital Expenditures (in millions of dollars)

	Generation	Transmission	Distribution	Miscellaneous	Totals
1972	9,737	2,148	3,989	777	16,651
1973	10,924	2,450	4,434	915	18,723
1974	12,504	2,451	4,577	1,024	20,556
1975	12,724	2,379	4,071	981	20,155
1976	16,612	2,945	4,548	1,084	25,189
1977	19,094	3,106	4,523	988	27,711
1978	21,951	2,736	4,347	1,216	30,250
1979	24,875	3,384	5,329	1,666	35,254
1980	25,688	3,280	5,307	1,650	35,925
1981	25,823	3,168	4,950	1,882	35,823
1982	29,836	3,497	5,228	1,654	40,216
1983*	28,189	4,182	5,496	1,988	39,855

*Prospective.
Source: Electrical World, March 1983, p. 62.

EXHIBIT 6
Utility Market Forecast for Transmission and Distribution Substations (Units)

Size (kv*)	1981 Actual	1982	1983	1984	1985	1986–88
765	3	1	0	4	1	5
500	15	18	10	6	19	36
345	59	45	41	40	27	78
230	70	84	70	74	67	162
161	38	42	37	34	28	76
138	226	193	227	157	186	376
115	251	239	198	189	175	406
69 and less	581	508	509	435	380	906

Source: Electrical World, August 1982, p. 66.
*Kilovolts

EXHIBIT 7
Questionnaire (*with Sample Responses*)

Dear Sir:

We are doing field research on the market for oscillographic, fault, and event recording devices used on utility tranmission lines. This research will be used to write a case study for the MBA curriculum. As a user of this equipment, your comments would be invaluable to us in formulating an accurate representation of this market. If you choose to pass this form on to someone with more specific knowledge, please write his or her name, position, and phone number on top of this page.

In light of your busy schedule, we hope that you can provide us with answers to the following questions at your convenience:

(1) How many oscillographic recorders do you presently own?
    13 oscillographs
(2) Who are the manufacturers and what percent does each represent?
    Powerpath Exclusive
(3) What is the age distribution for this equipment?
    1967 (10 of 13)   1972 (3 of 13)
(4) What percent of the time is fault/transient activity not recorded because of equipment failure?
    2%
(5) What percent of the time are electro-mechanical, oscillographic recorders not functioning because of maintenance or failure?
    5%
(6) Do you consider service good (i.e., spare parts costs and speed of delivery)?
    I would rate the service fair to poor.
(7) How many channels do you use per recorder?
    32 channels
(8) What would you expect to pay for a fault and event recording device with 32 analog channels?
    $60,000
(9) How many fault/event recorders do you expect to buy in the next five years?
    12
(10) How much of a premium (over the price you quoted in #8) would you be willing to pay for a "digital" device which offered the following features:

FEATURE	PREMIUM (percent)
A. Remote access, immediate recognition of fault activity, and network monitoring. One central computer located at engineering headquarters can monitor 12–20 substations simultaneously.	20%
B. Lower maintenance. Downtime reduced to less than 5 percent. No mechanical parts to break down and no ongoing calibration.	10%
C. Self diagnostics. Identifies equipment malfunction BEFORE fault activity, thereby eliminating the chance of transients not being recorded because of unidentified recorder failure.	0%
D. Much great number of digital and analog inputs which can be added modularly (up to 64 analog channels and 500–1,000 event channels).	5%

EXHIBIT 7 (*concluded*)

E. More selective data, improved resolution, accuracy, intelligence
and programmability (40kHz bandwidth to record switching
surges, and 72dB dynamic range to record 1 percent harmonics).   2%

F. Fault "locating" ability, Resolution 3 percent.   0%

G. Integration of sequence of events recording and fault recording
into one instrument.   15%

H. Availability of supplemental software packages to automatically
locate faults on network, perform a harmonic analysis, calculate
rise times, record inventory, etc.   0%

I. Availability of 1–2 hours of prefault data.   0%

Please feel free to include any additional thoughts you may have on this subject area.
Because of our academic requirements, we hope you will be able to respond to these
questions some time during the next week. We would be happy to provide you with a
summary of our findings.

Thank you for your assistance.

Sincerely,

EXHIBIT 8
Results of Survey

1. AGE DISTRIBUTION OF INSTALLED BASE

0–5 years	26%
5–10 years	15%
10–15 years	27%
15–20 years	18%
20–50 years	14%

2. SERVICE RESPONSE: Utility rating of service as. . .

Good	22.5%
Fair	29.0%
Poor	48.5%

3. FREQUENCY OF UNRECORDED FAULT ACTIVITY

Mean = 9.5%

4. DOWNTIME PERCENTAGE

Mean = 11%

5. COST

This survey question was clearly worded ambiguously and caused confusion. Major
sources of divergence originated if:

a. The customer had not purchased equipment for many years.
b. Had last purchased equipment during the 1980–81 price war.
c. Had unusual network requirements.

EXHIBIT 8 (*concluded*)

d. Did not understand what a fault monitor was versus a fault recorder. As best can be diciphered, the following mean expectations of cost were derived:

Event recorder	= $30,000
Fault recorder	= $60,000
Fault monitor	= $85,000

6. UTILITY VALUATION OF FEATURES

	Feature	Mean
		(% premium)
A.	Remote access	3.9%
B.	Maintenance	2.8
C.	Self-diagnostics	1.7
D.	More inputs	4.5
E.	Sophistication	2.2
F.	Fault locating	2.8
G.	Integration of S.E.R.	3.1
H.	Software availability	2.8
I.	Prefault data	0.5
	CUMULATIVE*	24.3%

7. ADJUSTED PREMIUMS

Because the utilities were asked to provide the above premiums as a percentage of cost, different cost estimates by different utilities make the comparison of premium values like comparing "apples and oranges." Consequently, to provide a uniform basis of comparison, the following adjustments were made to each premium:

Adjusted Premium = Features Premium (%) ÷ Largest Premium (%)

Each feature's premium was divided by the largest premium assigned by that utility. This procedure essentially ranks each premium from zero to one, with "0" representing a feature of no value to the utility and "1" representing the most important feature to the utility.

Features Ranked in Order of Importance

		Adjusted Premium
#1	Remote access	.50
#2	More inputs	.39
#3	Maintenance	.36
#4	Fault locating	.35
#5	Integration of S.E.R.	.32
#6	Software availability	.30
#7	Self-diagnostics	.26
#8	Sophistication	.23
#9	Prefault data	.05

*Features D and G are not entirely independent, therefore, a 22% cumulative premium is viewed as more accurate.

EXHIBIT 9
Buying Model for Fault Monitors

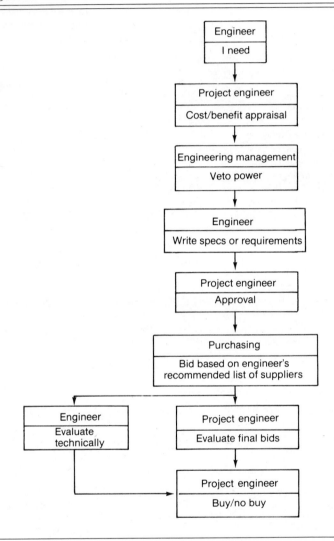

EXHIBIT 10
Financial Pro Formas

Assumptions

Sales: Beginning in August 1983, only ERDAC 1620 sales are projected since it is anticipated the product line will consume virtually all of Electrodec's available resources.

Cost of Goods Sold: 50 percent of sales with a 15 percent decline along experience curve.

Selling Costs: Salaries, overhead, and expenses of building a five-person sales force, plus 12 percent for commissions, advertising and promotion.

Interest: 12 percent interest rate. The model is not sensitive to 25 percent fluctuations in rate.

Taxes: 28 percent rate for $100K or less. 30 percent effective mid-range rate. 35 percent effective high-range rate.

Cash: 30 percent of sales base, minimum.

Receivables: 45 days.

Inventory: 6 turns per year (building to order).

Depreciation: 5 years ACRS.

Accounts Payable: 34 percent of sales base—effectively 30 days with material cost assumptions.

Full-Year Income Statements, Ending Fiscal Year February 28 *(Assuming $1,000,000 Equity Investments, September 1983 and July 1984)*

	1984	1985
Sales	$1,701,700	$11,612,700
Gross margin	793,287	5,768,335
Total selling, general and administrative	555,606	2,119,505
Earnings before interest and taxes	237,681	3,648,830
Interest	10,700	20,800
Taxes	69,199	1,263,932
PAT	$ 157,782	$ 2,364,098

EXHIBIT 10 (continued)
Pro Forma Financials Assuming No Equity Investment

Quarterly Income Statements (in thousands of dollars)

	June-Aug. 1983	Sept.-Nov. 1983	Dec. 1983-Feb. 1984	March-May 1984	June-Aug. 1984	Sept.-Nov. 1984	Dec. 1984-Feb. 1985	March-May 1985
Number of units	2	4	3	3	4	5	6	7
Sales	194.0	276.0	228.0	228.0	304.0	380.0	456.0	532.0
Gross margin	92.8	124.7	106.4	108.5	147.5	186.6	226.5	267.3
Selling costs	36.0	29.8	24.9	24.9	49.1	57.4	65.7	74.0
G&A	72.0	66.0	66.0	66.0	75.0	95.0	75.0	75.0
Total S, G&A	107.5	95.8	90.9	90.9	124.1	132.4	140.7	149.0
EBIT	(14.7)	28.9	15.5	17.6	23.4	54.2	85.8	118.3
Interest	6.2	6.7	5.5	5.4	7.7	9.0	9.0	9.0
Taxes	—	—	3.2	7.8	6.5	16.9	27.9	39.3
PAT	(20.9)	22.2	6.8	4.4	9.2	28.3	48.9	70.0

EXHIBIT 10 (*continued*)

Quarterly Balance Sheet

	June 1983	August 1983	November 1983	February 1984	May 1984	August 1984	November 1984	February 1985	May 1985
Current assets:									
Cash	$ 12,000	$ 30,000	$ 20,700	$20,700	$ 20,700	$ 27,600	$ 34,500	$ 41,400	$ 48,300
Receivables	60,000	150,000	103,500	103,500	103,500	138,000	172,500	207,000	241,500
Inventories	135,000	200,000	138,000	138,000	138,000	184,000	230,000	276,000	322,000
Prepaid expenses	20,000	20,000	20,000	20,000	20,000	20,000	20,000	20,000	20,000
Total current	227,000	400,000	282,200	282,200	282,200	369,600	457,000	544,400	631,800
Equipment	37,000	45,000	45,000	75,000	75,000	100,000	100,000	100,000	100,000
Depreciation	9,280	9,780	10,530	12,280	14,530	17,530	20,530	23,530	26,530
Net equipment	27,720	35,220	34,470	62,720	60,470	82,470	79,470	76,470	73,470
Total assets	254,720	435,220	316,670	344,920	342,670	452,070	536,470	620,870	705,270
Current liabilities:									
Accounts payable	13,600	34,000	23,460	23,460	23,460	31,280	39,100	46,920	54,740
Payroll	15,000	15,000	15,000	20,000	20,000	25,000	25,000	30,000	30,000
Taxes	2,000	2,000	2,710	4,088	4,630	9,220	20,006	31,087	42,454
Total current									
liabilities	30,600	51,000	41,170	47,548	48,090	65,500	84,106	108,007	127,194
Equity:									
Common stock	35,100	35,100	35,100	35,100	35,100	35,100	35,100	35,100	35,100
Retained earnings	56,836	45,208	68,987	80,865	88,312	100,430	131,735	183,618	256,611
Total equity	91,936	80,308	104,087	115,965	123,412	135,530	166,835	218,718	291,711
Short term debt*	132,184	303,912	171,413	181,408	171,168	251,040	285,529	294,145	286,365

*Note: Short-term debt is a "plug" figure.

EXHIBIT 10 (*continued*)

Pro Forma Financials Assuming $1,000,000 Equity Investment in September 1983 and $1,000,000 in June 1984

Quarterly Income Statements (in thousands of dollars)

	June–Aug. 1983	Sept.–Nov. 1983	Dec. 1983–Feb. 1984	March–May 1984	June–Aug. 1984	Sept.–Nov. 1984	Dec. 1984–Feb. 1985	March–May 1985
Number of units	2	7	8	16	26	44	52	60
Sales	194.0	504.0	608.0	1,216.0	1,976.0	3,444.0	3,952.0	4,560.0
Gross margin	92.8	229.5	283.8	579.1	958.5	1,641.7	1,963.0	2,290.8
Selling costs	36.1	54.5	97.3	174.1	283.0	442.5	508.7	574.9
G&A	71.3	89.3	106.9	121.4	135.7	136.4	154.0	163.6
Total S, G&A	107.4	143.8	204.2	295.5	418.7	578.9	662.7	738.5
Earnings before interest, taxes	(14.6)	85.7	79.6	283.6	539.8	1,062.8	1,300.3	1,552.3
Interest	6.2	1.5	0	2.5	1.5	2.0	0	0
Taxes	—	—	30.9	102.2	188.4	371.3	455.1	543.3
PAT	(8.4)	84.2	48.7	178.9	349.9	689.5	845.2	1,009.0

EXHIBIT 10 (*concluded*)

Quarterly Balance Sheet

	June 1983	August 1983	November 1983	February 1984	May 1984	August 1984	November 1984	February 1985	May 1985
Current assets:									
Cash	$ 12,000	$ 30,000	$ 489,609	$ 438,663	$ 124,200	$ 815,152	$ 303,600	$ 576,933	$1,109,311
Receivables	60,000	150,000	310,500	310,500	621,000	897,000	151,800	1,794,000	2,070,000
Inventories	135,000	200,000	414,000	414,000	828,000	1,196,001	2,024,001	2,392,001	2,760,001
Prepaid expenses	20,000	20,000	20,000	25,000	25,000	30,000	30,000	30,000	35,000
Total current	227,000	400,000	1,234,109	1,188,163	1,598,200	2,938,153	3,875,601	4,792,934	5,974,312
Equipment	37,000	45,000	45,000	40,000	200,000	250,000	400,000	450,000	450,000
Depreciation	9,280	9,780	10,530	13,780	20,280	29,980	51,980	75,580	97,180
Net equipment	27,720	35,220	34,470	126,220	179,720	220,020	348,020	374,420	352,820
Total assets	254,720	435,220	1,268,579	1,314,383	1,777,920	3,158,173	4,223,621	5,167,354	6,327,132
Current liabilities:									
Accounts payable	13,600	34,000	70,380	70,380	140,760	203,320	344,080	406,640	469,200
Payroll	15,000	15,000	15,000	20,000	20,000	25,000	25,000	30,000	30,000
Taxes	2,000	2,000	19,824	12,026	64,486	188,950	372,000	455,090	543,308
Total current liabilities	30,600	51,000	105,204	102,406	225,246	417,270	741,080	891,729	1,042,508
Equity:									
Common stock	35,100	35,100	1,035,100	1,035,100	1,035,100	2,035,100	2,035,100	2,035,100	2,035,100
Retained earnings	56,836	44,208	128,275	176,877	355,869	705,802	1,395,359	2,240,525	3,249,525
Total equity	91,936	79,308	1,163,375	1,211,977	1,390,969	2,740,902	3,430,459	4,275,625	5,284,625
Short term debt*	132,184	304,912	0	0	161,705	0	52,083	0	0

*Note: Short-term debt is a "plug" figure.

Part Three

ASSESSING AND ACQUIRING RESOURCES

This section addresses two of the most important issues faced by entrepreneurs as they start a new venture:

— What resources are needed?
— How are they to be acquired?

ASSESSING REQUIRED RESOURCES

In order to translate the business concept into a reality, the entrepreneur needs first to assess the resources which the venture will require. Entrepreneurs are often required to do more with less. By definition, they are attempting to achieve goals which will require considerably more resources than they currently control.

One of the key skills lies in distinguishing between those resources which are absolutely essential and those that would be nice to have but are not crucial.

Another technique is to distinguish between resources which must be "owned" and those which may be rented, contracted for, or even borrowed. Perhaps professional advice can be obtained based on friendship or the promise of future business. Doing more with less requires buying only what is needed and using the rest without actually owning it.

ACQUIRING NECESSARY RESOURCES

Having identified the required resources, it then becomes the entrepreneur's task to acquire them. This acquisition should be guided by a number of policies:

— First, the entrepreneur understands the need to commit quickly, and sometimes fully, in order to get to the next stage. This, perhaps, is why entrepreneurs are perceived as risk takers.
— Still, the entrepreneur must be flexible in these commitments, shifting resources once the desired end has been achieved.
— Finally, the individual must approach the acquisition process with the intention of giving up as little as possible in order to attract the needed resources. The rest of the value created thus accrues to the entrepreneur.

Financial Resources

Clearly, financial resources—dollars—are the most frequently needed. Chapter 6, "Alternative Sources of Financing," describes the spectrum of alternatives for obtaining financing. Chapter 7 looks at the technique of structuring a deal in order to obtain the required financial resources. Chapter 8 discusses the securities laws which impact the raising of funds and also describes the business plans and prospectuses which are typcially used.

Nonfinancial Resources

The entrepreneur must also secure the nonfinancial resources which the venture needs—a building, plant or office space, technology, management, and other employees.

Chapter 9, "Intellectual Property," describes the legal issues which surround ideas: patents, trademarks, trade secrets, confidentiality, and so forth. The entrepreneur must be aware of the serious repercussions which can result either from unfairly using someone else's idea or from failing to protect his/her own idea.

THE CASES

Steven B. Belkin, Ruth M. Owades, Heather Evans, and Steve Cox all describe individuals attempting to raise funds to finance a start-up venture. In addition to the issues surrounding financing, there are other questions as well: Is the venture a good opportunity? Has the entrepreneur adequately detailed the business concept and the resources needed to exploit the opportunity? What kind of investors should be targeted?

Allen Lane describes one man's search for a business. After many false starts, he is left with a business opportunity that looks attractive. Is it? If so, what kind of deal can be drafted to purchase the company?

Clarion Optical Co. describes an interesting opportunity for some employees to purchase their current employer's business. The case exposes the student to some of the quantitative techniques which lie behind the structuring of a deal.

Viscotech concerns a young company which may have violated the securities laws in its search for funds. The student is asked to address this issue and to recommend a plan for proceeding in light of the potential violation.

Universal Robotics provides for a discussion of many of the technical and legal terms which accompany the structuring of venture financing.

Computervision versus Automatix details a recent legal case concerning Automatix, founded by an ex-Computervision employee. Did he steal trade secrets or confidential information, or misappropriate a business opportunity, when he left to start Automatix?

Finally, Stratus Computer offers the student an opportunity to evaluate one entrepreneur's efforts to raise several million dollars of equity capital for a new high-technology venture.

Chapter 6

ALTERNATIVE SOURCES OF FINANCING

One of the most common issues confronted by the entrepreneur revolves around securing financing for the venture. Questions of how and when to raise money and from whom are frequent topics of concern. This chapter will describe some common sources of capital and the conditions under which money is typically lent or invested. Chapter 7, "Deal Structure," discusses the specific terms and pricing of capital.

AN OVERVIEW

As in most transactions, the owners of capital expect to get something in return for providing financing for the venture. In evaluating potential opportunities, the providers of funds will typically use some form of a risk/return model. That is, they will demand a higher return when they perceive a higher risk.

The entrepreneur's objective, of course, is to secure financing at the lowest possible cost. The art of successful financing, therefore, lies in obtaining funds in a manner which those providers of funds view as relatively less risky.

The entrepreneur can do several things to structure the financing so it will be perceived as "less risky":

— Pledge personal or corporate assets against a loan.

— Promise to pay the money back in a short period of time when the investors can judge the health of the business, rather than over the long term when its financial strength is less certain.
— Give investors some measure of control over the business, through either loan covenants or participation in management (i.e., a seat on the board).

Note that these are only a few of the possible mechanisms.

The liabilities side of the balance sheet itself provides a good overview of the potential sources of financing. Because this side of the balance sheet is arranged in order of increasing risk, it follows that the lowest cost forms of financing will usually be available from the higher balance sheet items.

START-UP FINANCING

Start-up financing provides the entrepreneur with a host of unique challenges. The highest risk capital (and therefore potentially highest return capital) is at the bottom of the balance sheet as equity. When a business is in the start-up phase, it is at its riskiest point. Therefore, equity capital is usually an appropriate source of financing during this period. That is not to say that debt capital is unattractive. It may even be available when secured by assets of the business, such as a building or equipment. However, some equity is usually required to get a business "off the ground." There is virtually no getting around the fact that the first investment in the business will be equity capital. This is required to demonstrate commitment on the part of the entrepreneur. Investors perceive, and rightly so, that the individual entrepreneur will be more committed to the venture if s/he has a substantial portion of personal assets invested in the venture. It is this fact which has led some to claim that: "You're better off trying to start a business with $5,000 than with $100,000 in personal resources. If you are relatively poor, you can demonstrate your commitment for a smaller sum." This statement presumes that you will be seeking capital from some *outside* source. If you were going to fund the venture all by yourself, you would naturally prefer to have $100,000 instead of $5,000.

There is another, more practical reason why this start-up phase will usually be financed with the entrepreneur's own funds. In order to raise money, you typically need more than an idea. The entrepreneur will have to invest some money in the idea, perhaps to build a prototype or do a market study, in order to convince potential providers of capital that the idea has potential.

This is not to say that these funds must be equity capital in the purest sense. That is, the money need only be equity from the point of view of potential investors in the business. The entrepreneur can obtain these "equity funds" by mortgaging personal assets like a house or car, borrowing from friends or relatives, even from a personal bank loan or credit card advances. The important fact is that when the money goes into the business, it does so as equity, not as debt to be repaid to the entrepreneur.

Some specialized firms provide "seed capital." Most venture capital firms require that a business move beyond the idea stage before they will consider financing it. Yet, some businesses require a good deal of work (and money) to get from the concept phase to the point where they can obtain venture capital financing. Seed funds can provide this kind of capital.

OUTSIDE EQUITY CAPITAL

Typically, the entrepreneur will exhaust his/her own funds before the business is a viable operation. At this point, it is usually still too early to obtain all of the required financing in the form of debt. The entrepreneur must approach outside sources for equity capital.

Private Investors

One popular source of equity capital is private investors, also known as *wealthy individuals*. These investors may range from family and friends with a few extra dollars to extremely wealthy individuals who manage their own money. Doctors frequently come to mind, and do, in fact, represent a significant source of private equity capital. Wealthy individuals may be advised by their accountants, lawyers, or other professionals, and the entrepreneur must deal with these people as well.

In order to approach wealthy individuals, you will usually need at least a business plan. A formal offering memorandum has the advantage of providing more legal protection for the entrepreneur in the form of disclaimers and legal language. However, it suffers from appearing overly negative, being more costly to prepare (it usually requires legal counsel), and also being limited by the SEC laws in terms of its distribution. That is, some of the SEC rules permit only 35 "offerees." Some legal advisers believe that you can show the business plan to more individuals, and then formally "offer" to only those individuals who have a real interest in investing.

One of the best ways to find wealthy investors is through a network of friends, acquaintances, and advisers. For instance, if you have used a local lawyer and accountant to help you prepare a business plan or offering document, these advisers may know of wealthy individuals who invest in ventures like yours.

At this point, it is worth reiterating the importance of following the securities laws and obtaining the advice of counsel. Because many of these wealthy individuals are "unsophisticated," they can (and often do, if the venture is unsuccessful) claim that they were misled by you, the conniving entrepreneur. A carefully drawn offering document is the key to legal protection in this instance.

Wealthy investors may be well-suited to participation in equity financings that are too small for a venture capital firm to consider (e.g., under $500,000). Wealthy investors are also typically thought of as being a less expensive source of equity than venture capital firms. This may be true. It is also true that:

— Wealthy individuals do not often possess the expertise or time to advise the entrepreneur on the operations of the business.
— Wealthy investors are far less likely to come up with additional funds if required.
— These investors are more likely to be a source of "problems" or frustration, particularly if there are a large number of them. Phoning frequently, or complaining when things are not going according to plan, they can create headaches for even the most well-intentioned of entrepreneurs.

Venture Capital

Venture capital refers to a pool of equity capital which is professionally managed. Wealthy individuals invest in this fund as limited partners, and the general partners manage the pool in exchange for a fee and a percentage of the gain on investments.

In order to compensate for the riskiness of their investments, give their own investors a handsome return, and make a profit for themselves, venture firms seek a high rate of return on their investments. Target returns of 50 percent or 60 percent are not uncommon hurdles for firms to apply to prospective venture capital investments.

In exchange for this high return, venture firms will often provide advice to their portfolio companies. These people have been through many times what the entrepreneur is usually experiencing for the first time. They can often provide useful counsel on the problems a company may experience in the start-up phase.

Venture firms can differ along several dimensions. Some prefer investing in certain kinds of companies. "Hi-tech" is popular with most, although perceptions of what precisely this is will vary widely. Some firms have a reputation for being very involved with the day-to-day operations of the business; others exhibit a more hands-off policy.

In approaching venture capitalists, the entrepreneur needs a business plan to capture the firm's interest. Here the document serves a far different purpose than it would in the case of wealthy individuals. A venture capital firm will expend a good deal of effort investigating potential investments. Not only is this sound business practice on their part, but they have legal obligations to their own investors.

Therefore, a business plan targeted to venture firms should be short, concise, and attempt to stimulate further interest, rather than present the business in exhaustive detail.

Most venture capitalists also report that it is only the naive entrepreneur who will propose the actual terms of the investment in the initial document. While the plan should certainly spell out how much financing the entrepreneur is seeking, to detail the terms (e.g., "for 28 percent of the stock. . .") is viewed as premature for an inititial presentation.

One topic which is frequently of concern to entrepreneurs is confidentiality. On the one hand, it seems wise to tell potential investors about your good ideas to get them interested in the company; on the other, what if someone else takes them? In general, venture capitalists are a professional group and will not disclose confidential information. It is more difficult, however, to make this statement about private sources of capital, like wealthy individuals.

Whatever the target investor audience, it is generally *not* a good idea to put truly proprietary material in a business plan. These plans are frequently copied, and could certainly be left accidentally on a plane or in an office. A business plan might, for example, describe the functions a new product would perform, but should probably not include circuit designs, engineering, drawings, etc.

Venture firms may not invest via a pure equity security. Some may invest a package of debt and equity, convertible debt or convertible preferred. Each of these has its advantages:

— A debt/equity package provides for the venture firm to get some of its funds back via interest, which is deductible to the company, and results in a tax savings. The investor can also recover tax free cash based upon repayment of loan principal.
— Convertible debt or preferred gives the venture firm a liquidation preference. If the venture should fail, the venture capitalist will have a priority claim on the assets of the business. Often too, the terms can force eventual repayment even if the firm never achieves "public" status.

Venture firms will usually "syndicate" a large investment. That is, they will attempt to interest other firms in taking a piece of the investment. This permits the firm to invest in a larger number of companies and thus spread its risk. This is particularly important on subsequent "rounds" or stages of financing. Other venture firms will want to see that the original firm(s) will continue their investment in the company. If the existing, more knowledgeable investors aren't interested in the company, why should a new venture firm be interested?

Public Equity Markets

Of course, the largest source of equity capital remains the public equity markets: The New York, American, and over-the-counter stock exchanges. Typically, however, a firm must have a history of successful operation before it can raise money in this way. In "hot" markets, some smaller, start-up companies have been able to raise public equity. The process is lengthy, detailed, and expensive. See "Securities Law and Going Public" for a discussion of the public equity markets.

Whether the investment is made by wealthy individuals or a venture capital firm, terms will have to be negotiated. In exchange for their investment, the investor will receive a "security" which represents the terms of his/her investment in the company. In the case of a public offering, the investment bank negotiates the terms on behalf of its clients. Venture capital firms and investment banks, of course, tend to be more sophisticated than the average wealthy investor.

DEBT CAPITAL

The other large category of capital is debt. Debt is presumed to be lower risk capital because it is repaid according to a set schedule of principal and interest.

In order to have a reasonable expectation of being paid according to this schedule, creditors lend against:

— Assets: Firms can obtain asset-based financing for most hard assets which have a market value. A building, equipment, or soluble inventory are all assets which a company could borrow against.
— Cash flow: Lenders will allow firms to borrow against their expected ability to generate the cash to repay the loan. Creditors attempt to check this ability through such measures as interest coverage (EBIT ÷ interest payments) or debt/equity ratio. Obviously, a healthy business with little debt and high cash flow will have an easier time borrowing money than a new venture.

Cash Flow Financing

Cash flow or unsecured financing is of several types, and can come from different sources.

— Short-term debt: Short-term unsecured financing is frequently available to cover seasonal working capital needs for periods of less than one year, usually 30 to 40 days.
— Line-of-credit financing: A company can arrange for a line of credit, to be drawn upon as needed. Interest is paid on the outstanding principal, and a "commitment fee" is paid up front. Generally, a line of credit must be "paid-down" to an agreed-upon level at some point during the year.
— Long-term debt: Generally available to solid "creditworthy" companies, long-term debt may be available for up to 10 years. Long-term debt is usually repaid according to a fixed schedule of interest and principal.

Cash flow financing is most commonly available from commercial banks, but can also be obtained from savings and loan institutions, finance companies, and other institutional lenders (e.g., insurance companies, pension funds). Because cash-flow financing is generally riskier than asset-based financing, banks will frequently attempt to reduce their risk through the use of covenants. These covenants place certain restrictions on a business if it wishes to maintain its credit with the bank. Typical loan covenants concern:

— Limits on the company's debt/equity ratio.
— Minimum standards on interest coverage.
— Lower limits on working capital.
— Minimum cash balance.
— Restrictions on the company's ability to issue senior debt.

These, and other covenants, attempt to protect the lender from actions which would increase the likelihood of the lender not getting its money back.

Asset-Based Financing

Most assets in a business can be financed. Because cash-flow financing usually requires an earnings history, far more new ventures are able to obtain asset-based financing. In an asset-based financing, the company pledges or gives the financier a first lien on the asset. In the event of a default on the financing payments, the lender can repossess the asset. The following types of financing are generally available:

— Accounts receivable: Up to 90 percent of the accounts receivable from creditworthy customers can usually be financed. The bank will conduct a thorough investigation to determine which accounts are eligible for this kind of financing. In some industries, such as the government business, accounts receivable are often "factored." A factor buys approved receivables for a discount from their face value, but collects from the accounts.
— Inventory: Inventory is often financed if it consists of merchandise which could be easily sold. Typically, 50 percent or so of finished goods inventory can be financed.
— Equipment: Equipment can usually be financed for a period of 3 to 10 years. One-half to 80 percent of the value of the equipment can be financed, depending on the salability or "liquidity" of the assets. Leasing is also a form of equipment financing where the company never takes ownership of the equipment, but rents it.
— Real estate: Mortgage financing is usually readily available to finance a company's plant or buildings; 75 to 85 percent of the value of the building is a typical figure.

— Personally secured loans: A business can obtain virtually any amount of financing if one of its principals (or someone else) is willing to pledge a sufficient amount of assets to guarantee the loan.
— Letter-of-credit financing: A letter of credit is a bank guarantee which a company can obtain to enable it to purchase goods. A letter of credit functions almost like a credit card, allowing businesses to make commitments and purchases in other parts of the world where the company does not have relationships with local banks.
— Government-secured loans: Certain government agencies will guarantee loans to allow businesses to obtain financing when they could not obtain it on their own. The Small Business Administration, the Farmers Home Administration, and other government agencies will guarantee bank loans.

Asset-based financing is available from commercial banks and other financial institutions. Insurance companies, pension funds, and commercial finance companies provide mortgages and other forms of asset-backed financing. Entrepreneurs themselves can also provide debt capital to a business once it has passed out of the risky start-up period.

INTERNALLY GENERATED FINANCING

A final category of financing is internally generated. This term describes:

— Credit from suppliers: Paying bills in a less timely fashion is one way to increase working capital. Sometimes, suppliers will charge you interest for this practice. In other instances, the costs may be more severe if a key supplier resource decides to stop serving you.
— Accounts receivable: Collecting bills more quickly will also generate financing.
— Reducing working capital: A business can generate internal financing by reducing other working capital items: inventory, cash, and so forth.
— Sale of assets: Perhaps a more drastic move, selling assets will also generate capital.

Each of these techniques represents an approach to generating funds internally, without the help of a financial partner. Although the purely financial costs are low, the entrepreneur must be wary of attempting to run the business "too lean."

SUMMARY

We've attempted to describe the spectrum of financial sources which an entrepreneur can tap both during the start-up phase and as a going concern. Exhibit 1 is an attempt to summarize these sources. Along the horizontal axis, we've tried to note whether the provider of capital tries to manage the risk/reward ratio by (1) increasing reward by raising the cost of funds or (2) decreasing risk by asserting some measure of control over the business. This is not an exhaustive list, but an overview of the most popular sources. In every case, there is a high premium on understanding both your own needs and the specific needs of the financier.

EXHIBIT 1
Alternative Sources of Financing

SOURCE	COST							CONTROL		
	Zero	Fixed Rate Short-term	Fixed Rate Long-term	Floating Rate Short-term	Floating Rate Long-term	Percent of Profits	Equity	Covenants	Voting Rights	Guarantee of Debt
Self			X		X		X		X	X
Family and friends		X	X	X	X		X		X	X
Suppliers and trade credit	X	X				X				
Commercial banks		X		X				X		X
Other commercial lenders		X	X		X			X		X
Asset-based lenders/lessors			X					X		
Specialized finance companies		X	X					X		
Institutions and insurance companies			X		X	X		X		
Pension funds			X			X	X	X		
Venture capital		X	X				X	X	X	X
Private equity placements							X	X	X	
Public equity offerings						X	X		X	
Government agencies (SBIC)			X		X	X				X
Other government programs			X					X		X

Chapter 7

DEAL STRUCTURE

A critical aspect of the entrepreneur's attempt to obtain resources is the development of an actual "deal" with the owner of the resources. Typically, the entrepreneur needs a variety of resources, including dollars, people, and outside expertise. As in any situation, the individual who desires to own, or use, these resources must give up something. Because the entrepreneur typically has so little to start with, s/he will usually give up a claim on some future value in exchange for the ability to use these resources now.

Entrepeneurs can obtain funds in the form of trade credit, short- and long-term debt, and equity or risk capital. This chapter will focus on the structure and terms of the deal which may be used to obtain the required financial resources from investors.

The note will center on financial resources because:

— Raising capital is a common problem which virtually all entrepreneurs face.
— Unlike people, technology, or outside expertise, which may have unique properties and are hard to discuss in general terms, money is typically a commodity.

WHAT IS A "DEAL"?

In general, a deal represents the terms of a transaction between two (or more) groups or individuals. Entrepreneurs want money to use in a (hopefully) productive venture, and individuals and institutions wish to earn a return on the cash that they have at risk.

The entrepreneur's key task is to make the whole equal to more than the sum of the parts. That is, to carve up the economic benefits of the venture into pieces which meet the needs of particular financial backers. The entrepreneur can maximize his/her own return by selling these pieces at the highest possible price, that is, to individuals who demand the lowest return. And the individuals who demand the lowest return will typically be those that perceive the lowest risk.

THE DEAL

In order to craft a deal which maximizes his/her own economic return, the entrepreneur must:

— Understand the fundamental economic nature of the business.
— Understand financiers' needs and perceptions of risk and reward.
— Understand his/her own needs and requirements.

Understanding the Business

The first thing the entrepreneur must do is assess the fundamental economic nature of the business itself. Most business plans project a set of economics which determine:

— The amount of the funds required.
  • The absolute amount.
  • The timing of these requirements.
— The riskiness of the venture.
  • The absolute level of risk.
  • The factors which determine risk.
— The timing and potential magnitude of returns.

It is important to remember that the venture itself does not necessarily have an inherent set of economics. The entrepreneur determines the fundamental economics when s/he makes critical decisions about the business. Still, there may be certain economic characteristics which are a function of the industry and environment, and which the entrepreneur will generally be guided by.

For instance, a venture such as a genetics engineering firm has characteristics that differ greatly from those of a real estate deal. The genetics firm may require large investments over the first several years, followed by years with zero cash flow, followed by a huge potential return many years out. The real estate project, on the other hand, may require a one-time investment, generate immediate cash flow, and provide a means of exit only several years down the road.

One technique for understanding a venture's economic nature is to analyze the potential source of return. Let's take this example—a paint business with the following projected cash flows:

	Year					
	0	1	2	3	4	5
Cash flow [$000 omitted]	(1,000)	400	400	400	400	5,600

Now, we can break this cash flow down into its components:

— Investment: money required to fund the venture.
— Tax consequences: not precisely a cash flow, but nonetheless a cash benefit which may accrue if an investment has operating losses in the early years.
— Free cash flow: cash which the business throws off as a result of its operations before financing and distributions to providers of capital.
— Terminal value: the after-tax cash which the business returns as a result of its sale. Here, this is assumed to occur at the end of Year 5.

Let's assume that these flows are as follows:

	Year					
Cash Flows ($000)	0	1	2	3	4	5
Original investment	(1,000)					
Tax consequences	—	300	300	0	(100)	(200)
Free cash flows	—	100	100	400	500	800
Terminal value (after tax)						5,000
Total	(1,000)	400	400	400	400	5,600

Now, we can calculate the IRR of the total investment: 64.5 percent.

Next, we calculate the present value of each of the individual elements of the return *at that IRR*, and then the percent which each element contributes to the total return. Of course, the present value of the total return will be equal to the original investment.

Element	Present Value @ 64.5% ($000)	Element's Percent of Total
Tax consequences	263	26.3
Free cash flows	322	32.2
+ Terminal value	415	41.5
Total	$1,000	100.0%

This analysis illuminates the potential sources of return inherent in the business, as projected.

The task of the entrepreneur is now to carve up the cash flows and returns and sell them to the individuals/institutions that are willing to accept the lowest return. This will leave the biggest piece of the economic pie for the entrepreneur. To do so requires an understanding of the financiers' needs and perceptions.

Understanding Financers

Providers of capital clearly desire a "good" return on their money, but their needs and priorities are far more complex. Exhibit 1 in Chapter 4 depicts some of the differences which exist among different financial sources. They vary along a number of dimensions, including:

— Magnitude of return desired.
— Magnitude and nature of risk which is acceptable.
— Perception of risk and reward.
— Magnitude of investment.
— Timing of return.
— Form of return.
— Degree of control.
— Mechanisms for control.

The priorities attached to the various elements may differ widely. For instance, institutions such as insurance companies and pension funds have legal standards which determine the type of investment which they can undertake. For others, the time horizon for their return may be influenced by organizational or legal constraints.

Certain investors may want a high rate of return and be willing to wait a long period and bear a large amount of risk to get it. Still other investors may consider any type of investment, as long as there exists some mechanism for them to exert their own control over the venture. To the extent that the entrepreneur is able to break down the basic value of the business into components which vary along each of these dimensions, and then find investors who want this specific package, the entrepreneurs will be able to structure a better transaction; a deal which creates more value for him/herself.

If we return to our example of the paint business which requires a $1 million investment, we can see how the entrepreneur can take advantage of these differences in investor characteristics.

— The tax benefits, for example, are well-suited for sale to a risk-averse wealthy individual in a high marginal tax bracket. Because the benefits accrue as a result of operating losses, if the business does poorly, the tax benefits may be even greater. But let's assume that the wealthy individual believes that these forecasts are realistic, and requires a 25 percent return. If we discount the tax benefits at this 25 percent required return, we arrive at a present value of $325,500. Therefore, this individual should be willing to invest $325,500 in order to purchase this portion of the cash flows. There must be economic substance to the transaction other than tax benefits. Care must be taken so that the investor can show prospect for economic gain. For this analysis, this tax-based requirement is ignored.

— The operating cash flows would, in total, be perceived as fairly risky. However, some portion of them should be viewed as a "safe bet" by a bank. Let's assume that the entrepreneur could convince a banker that no less than $60,000 would be available in any given year for interest expenses. Further, if the banker were willing to accept 12 percent interest and take all of the principal repayment at the end of Year 5 (when the business is sold), then s/he should be willing to provide $60,000 ÷ .12 = $500,000 in the form of a loan.

Now the entrepreneur has raised $825,500 and needs only $174,500 to get into business.

— The terminal value, and the riskier portion of the operating cash flows, remain to be sold. Let's assume that a venture investor would be willing to provide funds at a 50 percent rate of return.

First, we need to see precisely what cash flows remain:

	Year				
	1	2	3	4	5
Total	400	400	400	400	5,600
− Wealthy investor	300	300	0	(100)	(200)
− Bank	60	60	60	60	560
= Remaining	40	40	340	440	5,240

The remaining cash flows in Years 1 through 5 have a present value, at the venture firm's 50 percent discount rate, of $922,140. If we need $174,500, we need to give up $174,500 ÷ $922,140 = 18.9 percent of these flows in order to entice the venture investor to provide risk capital. These flows might well be sold to the tax-oriented investor in order to meet the requirements for economic substance. This leaves the entrepreneur with a significant portion of the above "remaining" flows. One can see how these differences in needs and perceived risk allow the entrepreneur to create value for him/herself.

Understanding the Entrepreneur's Own Needs

The example we have just worked through was based on the assumption that the entrepreneur wants to obtain funds at the lowest possible cost.

While this is generally true, there are often other factors which should affect the analysis.

The entrepreneur's needs and priorities do vary across a number of aspects including the time horizon for involvement in the venture, the nature of that involvement, degree of business risk, and so on. All of these variables will affect the entrepreneur's choice of a venture to pursue. However, once the entrepreneur has decided to embark on a particular business, his/her needs and priorities with respect the *financing* of the venture will vary with respect to:

— Degree of control desired.
— Mechanisms of control desired.
— Amount of financing required.
— Magnitude of financial return desired.
— Degree of risk which is acceptable.

For instance, in the above example, the entrepreneur could have decided to obtain an additional $100,000 or $200,000 as a cushion to make the venture less risky. This would certainly have lowered the economic return, but might have made the entrepreneur more comfortable with the venture.

Similarly, the bank which offered funds at 12 percent, or the venture investor, might have imposed a series of very restrictive covenants. Rather than accept this loss of control, the entrepreneur might rather have given up more of the economic potential.

In addition, the entrepreneur may need more than just money. There are times when some investors' money is better than others. This occurs in situations where once an individual is tied into a venture financially, s/he has an incentive to help the entrepreneur in nonfinancial ways. For instance, an entrepreneur starting a business which depends on securing good retail locations would prefer to obtain financing from an individual with good real estate contacts than from someone without those contacts. Venture capital firms are frequently cited for providing advice and support in addition to financing.

SUMMARY

Once the fundamental economics of a deal have been worked out, the entrepreneur must still structure the deal. This requires the use of a certain legal form of organization and a certain set of securities.

The vehicles through which the entrepreneur can raise capital include the general partnership, the limited partnership, the S corporation, and the corporation. While these forms of organization differ with respect to their tax consequences, they also differ substantially regarding the precision with which cash flows may be carved up and returned to various investors. In a limited partnership, for instance, virtually *any* distribution of profits and cash flow is feasible so long as it is spelled out clearly, and in advance in the limited partnership agreement. (Losses, however, are usually distributed in proportion to capital provided.) In an S corporation, on the other hand, where only one class of stock is permitted, investors can get a return in the form of tax losses which can be passed through, but founder's stock is equivalent to investors' stock and it is difficult to draw any distinctions in the returns which accrue to the two groups.

Securities can involve debt, warrants, straight or preferred equity, and a host of other legal arrangements. The structuring of securities requires the assistance of good legal counsel with expertise in securities and corporate law, as well as intimate knowledge of the tax code.

In the previous chapter, we looked at alternative sources of financing. Here, we've attempted to describe how the entrepreneur can structure a deal with these potential sources of capital. A well-structured deal will provide the financier with his/her desired return and still create substantial value for the entrepreneur.

Chapter 8

SECURITIES LAW AND PRIVATE FINANCING

Many business financing transactions are regulated by state and federal securities laws. The Securities and Exchange Commission (SEC) administers federal securities laws, and state securities laws (Blue Sky laws) are enforced by the respective states.

Securities laws apply to private business transactions as well as to public offerings in the stock markets. This chapter will focus on private financing; see "Securities Law and Public Offerings" for information on the public financing markets. Like tax laws, securities laws are complex and not always grounded in logic. The consequences of violation (even technical violation) can be vastly disproportionate to the harm inflicted and can include severe personal liabilities for management (including innocent management). In addition, a violation can preclude present and future business financings. Treatment and cure of violations, when possible, can be time-consuming and expensive. To complicate matters, securities regulation has changed dramatically over the past dozen years; first, in response to the speculative abuses of the late 60s and, more recently, in an attempt to modify regulations which would facilitate capital formation.

Statements contained in this chapter are of necessity general in nature and become outdated with the passage of time. Therefore, they should not be relied upon in formulating definitive business plans, but used rather as an indication of the nature and extent of securities regulation that may be ap-

Copyright © 1984 by the President and Fellows of Harvard College.
Harvard Business School note 9–384–164.

plicable in various circumstances. In this regard, it should be borne in mind that in addition to the federal securities laws, there are securities laws in each of the 50 states—many of which vary substantially from state to state.

WHAT IS A SECURITY?

The securities laws are applicable only if a *security* is involved in the transaction. The statutory definition of security includes common and preferred stock, notes, bonds, debentures, voting-trust certificates, certificates of deposit, warrants, options subscription rights, and undivided oil or gas interests. In fact, the definition is broad enough to encompass just about any financing transaction, whether or not a certificate evidencing the investor's participation is issued, so long as the investor's participation in the business is passive or nearly so. Generally, a security is involved whenever one person supplies money or some item of value with the expectation that it will be used to generate profits or other monetary return for the investor primarily from the efforts of others. Thus, a limited partnership interest is a security. So is a cow, if purchased together with a maintenance contract whereby someone else will raise, feed, and sell the cow without the participation of the investor. Similarly, an orange grove is a security if coupled with an agreement to maintain, harvest, and sell the orange crop; a condominium unit is a security if coupled with an agreement to rent the unit to others when not occupied by the owner; and parcels of oil property may be securities if sold with the understanding that the promoter will drill a test well on adjoining land. A franchise may or may not be a security, depending upon the extent of the participation of the investor. Generally, a transaction involves a security if there is an expectation of a "profit" or monetary return.

Despite the broadness of the above generalizations, there are some financing transactions that are deemed not to involve securities merely because they traditionally have not been considered to involve them. Thus, a note given in connection with a long-term bank loan is generally not considered a security although it falls squarely within the statutory definition. On the other hand, bank transactions only modestly removed from normal commercial practice may be deemed to involve securities. Active participation in the solicitation of a pledge of a third party's securities in connection with an outstanding loan to another party, for instance, would fit within the definition and thus be subject to the securities laws.

BUSINESS FINANCING DISCLOSURES

The financing of a business frequently involves the investment of money or some other item of value by a person who is not a part of management or otherwise familiar with all of the material aspects of the business. In order for an outside investor to make an informed investment decision, s/he must be made aware of the material factors that bear upon the present condition and future prospects of the business and of the pertinent details regarding participation in the business and its profits. The securities laws thus impose an obligation upon a business and its management to disclose such information to a potential investor together with the factors that adversely affect the business or which may reasonably be foreseen to do so in the future. In addition to financings by a company, these laws impose similar disclosure requirements whenever a member of management or a principal equity owner sells his personal security holdings to an outsider.

In financings involving outsiders, it is common practice (whether required or not) for management to prepare a prospectus, offering, circular, or memorandum describing the nature, condition, and prospects of the business and the nature and extent of the investor's participation in it. In this manner the pertinent disclosures are set forth in a permanent written record so that there can be no argument as to whether or not the disclosures have been made or what they were. Such a document traditionally discloses the terms of the offering, the use of the proceeds, the capitalization of the business (before and after the financing), contingent liabilities (if any), the operations of the business, its sources of supply, marketing techniques, competitors, and market position, its personnel, government regulation and litigation, its management and management's remuneration, transactions between the company and management, the principal equity owners of the business, and balance sheets and earnings statements of the business. Exhibit 1 provides an outline for such a document.

Historically, the SEC has discouraged the disclosure of forward-looking information such as projected earnings or dividends per share, and in fact has implied that disclosure of such information might be inherently misleading. In recent years, however, the commission has changed its view and has issued a series of rulings authorizing the disclosure of projections concerning revenues, income, earnings, dividends, and company objectives. In disclosing such information to prospective investors, management must act reasonably and in good faith, disclose any underlying assumptions, and correct information which becomes false or misleading over time.

Despite the fact that disclosure documents are often prepared and reviewed by attorneys and accountants, the law imposes the primary obligation for complete and accurate disclosure upon the company, its management, and principal equity owners.

It thus is essential that each member of management (including outside directors) and each principal equity owner be satisfied that the information in the disclosure document is accurate and complete based upon his or her own personal knowledge of the company and its records. The financial statements, for instance, are generally deemed to be the company's disclosures rather than the accountant's, and the company itself remains principally responsible for their accuracy, even when an audit has been performed. In fact, the company has no "due diligence" defense at all in a federally registered offering and is absolutely liable if any material misstatements or omissions occur anywhere in the prospectus.

A disclosure document which satisfies these disclosure standards often appears negative in its presentation. Such a document need not be unduly so in order to provide the necessary protection, and, in any event, what appears "negative" to management may not necessarily appear negative to the financial community, which is accustomed to reading disclosure documents of this type.

In order to alleviate this negative effect, some entrepreneurs will first prepare a "business plan" which is *not* an offering/disclosure document. The purpose of this document will be to stimulate investor interest. Having screened investors, the entrepreneur will then circulate a more formal offering/disclosure document. This technique is often effective, but still imposes a duty on the entrepreneur not to make any misleading claims in the business plan. In a public offering, such an approach, (called "gun-jumping") would clearly be illegal. See Exhibit 1 for an outline of a business plan and prospectus.

PRIVATE OFFERINGS

Private offerings are distinct from public offerings in a number of ways. Public offerings typically involve larger sums of money and may be sold through brokers. Public offerings require that the company go through an expensive and lengthy "registration" process to register the securities with the SEC. This process is discussed more fully in Chapter 11.

Federal securities laws and many state securities laws have long reflected the view that some potential investors are sufficiently sophisticated in business investment matters to be as able to investigate a business and assemble relevant data as are management and regulatory authorities. More recently, the Congress has recognized that small businesses wishing to attract capital may be unduly hampered by burdensome filing requirements. In such circumstances, preparation of an orderly and systematic discussion of the business in a formal prospectus and the review of this presentation by government agents is deemed unnecessary because the offerees are competent to assess the venture independently or because the issuer seeks to raise very limited amounts of capital. Thus, registration is unnecessary, and the company and its management and principal equity owners may rely upon one of the so-called private offering exemptions. (Local state securities laws in every state where a *purchaser* is residing should always be reviewed.)

Historically, the principal criteria of the availability of the private offering exemption have been business acumen or *sophistication* of the offerees, access to material information concerning the company, and the number of offerees (*not purchasers*). All of these items were highly subjective and the absence of guidelines often resulted in liability for issuers who mistakenly believed they came within the exemption. Beginning in the 1970s, however, the SEC attempted to bring more order to this area by releasing a series of rules which provide "safe harbors" within the general ocean of uncertainty embodied in these three traditional criteria. Regulation D represents the commission's most recent attempt to foster coherence and certainty.

Regulation D: The Various Rules

Six administrative rules, three of which set forth general definitions and three of which provide "safe harbors" for certain private offerings, comprise Regulation D. The operative rules—504, 505, and 506—broaden the scope of private offering exemption. Collectively, they are designed to simplify the existing rules and regulations, to eliminate unnecessary restrictions on small issuers' ability to raise capital, and to create regulatory uniformity at the federal and state levels. Each of the rules requires that a notice be filed with the SEC on Form D.

Rule 504. The first exemption, Rule 504, is especially useful to issuers seeking to raise relatively small amounts of capital from numerous investors. It permits an issuer to sell up to $500,000 of its securities during any 12-month period without limiting the number or sophistication of the investors and without prescribing any specific form of disclosure. The issuer may not, however, engage in general solicitation or advertising, and purchasers may not resell their shares without registration unless the offering is registered in states which require delivery of a disclosure document. The effect of the rule, then, is to delegate substantial responsibility regulating small issuers to the state agencies. Because Rule 504 is designed to assist small businesses, it is unavailable to investment companies or companies required to file periodic reports under the Securities Exchange Act.

Rule 506. In contrast to Rule 504, Rule 506 permits an issuer to sell an unlimited amount of its securities but only to certain investors. In this regard, the rule represents a continuation of the SEC's effort to codify some of the practices developed by lawyers and courts in applying the general private placement standards of sophistication, information, and numbers, and permits issuers to raise potentially substantial amounts of capital without registration. Rule 506 is available for transactions which do not involve more than 35 purchasers. Sales to accredited investors (defined below), relatives of issuers, or entities controlled by issuers are excluded from this total. The issuer must determine that each nonexempt investor meets the sophistication test, either individually or through a knowledgeable "purchaser representative;" but the issuer no longer need inquire as to the investor's ability to bear the financial risk of his investment. In determining sophistication, the issuer can insist that each purchaser or group of purchasers be represented by a person who would clearly meet any test of sophistication. The representative cannot be an affiliate, director, officer, employee or 10 percent beneficial owner of the company (although he can be paid by the company as long as this is disclosed) and must be accepted by the purchaser in writing as his representative.

Perhaps the most significant aspect of Rule 506 is the "accredited investor" concept. Such investors are presumed to be sophisticated and thus do not count against the 35 investor limitation. They include institutional investors such as banks, insurance companies, investment companies, ERISA employee benefit plans with over $5 million in assets, private business development companies, tax-exempt organizations such as colleges or universities with endowment funds of over $25 million, the issuer's directors, executive officers, and general partners, investors who purchase over $150,000 of the issuer's securities (provided that such investment does not represent more than 20 percent of any investor's net worth at the time of the sale), investors whose net worth is $1 million or more at the time of the sale, persons with incomes in excess of $200,000 in each of the last two years, and entities made up of certain accredited investors.

When an issuer sells securities under Rule 506 to accredited investors only, it is not compelled to make disclosures of any sort. If the sale involves both accredited and nonaccredited investors, by contrast, the disclosure requirements are more complex. Nonreporting companies must disclose the information contained in Part 1 of Form S–18 or available registration when offering less than $5 million of their securities (including two-year financials audited for the most recent year), and must disclose the information contained in Part 1 of an available form of registration when offering more than $5 million. If such disclosures would require "undue effort and expense," issuers other than limited partnerships may present a balance sheet as of 120 days prior to the offering. Reporting companies, on the other hand, must furnish Rule 14a–3 annual reports, definitive proxy statements, and Form 10–K if requested, *or* the information contained in their most recent Form S–1, Form 10, or Form 10–K (with appropriate updating) regardless of the size of the offering. All companies selling securities to accredited and nonaccredited investors must also furnish nonaccredited investors whatever exhibits and written material accredited purchasers receive, and must give all investors an opportunity to ask questions and receive answers prior to the sale. Finally, no issuer utilizing Rule 506 may engage in general solicitation or advertising.

Rule 505. Rule 505 adds some flexibility to Rule 506 for certain issuers. It permits the sale of $5 million of unregistered securities over any 12-month period to any 35 investors in addition to an unlimited number of accredited investors. The primary advantage of Rule 505, therefore, is the elimination of the sophistication test entirely and with it the elimination of the need for a purchaser representative.

The $5 million limit on sales during any year represents an increase from Rule 242's authorization of $2 million over six months. In addition, Rule 505 has expanded the class of eligible issuers by including non-North American issuers, oil and gas companies, and partnerships. Investment companies and issuers disqualified under Regulation A remain ineligible, however. Like Rule 506, Rule 505 prohibits general advertising or solicitation through public media of any kind, and imposes disclosure requirements identical to the Rule 506 requirements discussed above.

Section 4(6). Section 4(6) of the Securities Act, enacted as part of the Small Business Investment Incentive Act of 1980 and not technically a part of Regulation D, is the last of the new private placement exemptions. It permits companies to issue up to $5 million of their securities in any single offering without registration and restricts the class of purchasers in any such transaction to accredited investors. Issuers are not required to disclose any specific information and may not engage in any form of solicitation in connection with offers or sales. Given these requirements, any issuer who can meet the requirements of Section 4(6) can also qualify under Rules 505 or 506.

Regulation D: Other Information

In addition to these specific exemptions, Regulation D includes a number of broadly applicable provisions designed to streamline and simplify private offerings. For example, when calculating dollar limitations, issuers must integrate the proceeds from all other sales made six months before or after the offering which are exempt under Regulation D or in violation of registration requirements (other than offers to employee benefit plans). This precludes the argument that securities issued as part of a continuous offering fit within discrete exemptions. The regulation also provides that any securities issued pursuant to one of its exempting provisions (other than securities registered at the state level and issued under Rule 504) may not be resold without registration. In this regard the company must exercise reasonable care to prevent further distribution and should accordingly place restrictive legends on its certificates, enter "stop-transfer" orders, advise purchasers of the restrictions on resale, and secure representations that the securities are purchased for the individual's own account and not with any intention to redistribute. Finally, the regulation includes uniform rules permitting the payment of commissions on any exempt offering and governing notices of sales. For any type of offering, including offerings exempt under Section 4(6), the issuer must file five copies of Form D with the commission 15 days after the first sale, every 6 months thereafter, and 30 days after the final sale.

The burden of proving the availability of an exemption is upon the person asserting it. In order for the risk of nonavailability of the exemption to be reduced to an acceptable level, the issuer must complete positive and compelling documentary proof that each of the requirements for exemption has been met. This is particularly important if none of the "safe-harbor" rules applies. The sophistication of offerees should be thoroughly investigated *before* they are approached, and a memorandum setting forth their background and the reasons for the sophistication placed in the log. In making the initial presentation, use of a private placement memorandum should be made, each such memorandum being numbered and containing a legend that is not to be reproduced or disclosed to outsiders. The number of the memorandum and the date on which it is submitted to the offeree should be set forth in the log. If the offeree becomes an investor, the date on which he or she or a designated representative reviews the books and the records of the company, the books and records so reviewed, and the date on which s/he or the representative engaged in face-to-face negotiation with the issuer should be recorded in the log. At the end of the offering, a memo should be placed in the log stating that no persons other than those set forth in the log were contacted or offered any of the securities, such memo reciting that "offer" is understood to mean nothing more than creating a situation which can be construed as seeking a commitment (even informal) to acquire a security to be issued by a described company at a given price. The log should be placed in the company's permanent files as evidence of the availability of the private offering exemption for the financing.

Finally, and perhaps most important, an issuer must remember that all offerings, even if exempt from federal registration, remain subject to the antifraud and civil liability provisions of the federal securities laws and to the general requirements of state Blue Sky laws. Particular note should be taken of the fact that the safe-harbor exemptions provided under Regulation D are generally not available under state Blue Sky laws and that registration may be necessary in a given state for an offering which fully complies with Rules 504, 505, or 506.

RESALE OF RESTRICTED SECURITIES

Securities issued under one of the private offering exemptions or held by a member of management or a principal equity owner of the company (no matter how acquired, and whether registered or not) are deemed restricted securities. Resale of such securities is severely limited unless the securities are registered under the Securities Act of 1933. For this reason, it is common practice for venture capital firms, private placement investors, management, and such owners to obtain an agreement from the company to register the securities upon demand or to include them "piggyback" in any other SEC registration that the company might undertake.

If the securities are not registered or covered by Regulation A when they are resold, as a practial matter the resales must be made under SEC Rule 144, SEC Rule 237, or one of the private offering exemptions (not including the Regulation D exemptions for this purpose). Absent such an exemption, the resales will constitute unregistered offerings and subject the issuer and seller to potential liability. In addition, if the securities are transferred without consideration—by gift or upon death, for example—the restrictions generally bind the recipient.

Restrictions upon subsequent resale must be disclosed to potential investors in a private placement or the financing will be deemed by the SEC to violate the antifraud provisions of federal securities laws. This disclosure is often recited as part of the "investment letter" signed by the investor.

CONSEQUENCES OF VIOLATION

As a practical matter, in the past a vast majority of securities laws violations have not been investigated or litigated. However, the possibility of nonenforcement provides little comfort to potential defendants when commerical transactions of any size are involved. Moreover, transactions of today are potential lawsuits five years from now when investors may be more aware of their rights under the securities laws and more inclined to enforce them.

The consequences of violation of the securities laws in connection with a company's prior financings are rarely serious so long as its operations continue to be successful and this success is reflected in the price of its securities. If public estimates of a company's success have been too conservative, however, an investor who has sold his securities too cheaply may complain. Investors and regulators tend to scrutinize company disclosures in minute detail when a business turns sour, with the hopes of discovering some technical or other securities law violation to use in unwinding a financing, or holding management responsible.

The most serious consequence of violation of the securities laws is the potential civil liability that may be incurred by those persons deemed to have violated such laws or to have aided and abetted violations. When a corporation or other business entity is involved, management (i.e., officers and directors, general partners, etc.) and the company's principal equity owners may be held liable as controlling persons. In this regard, the corporate entity, which serves as an effective shield from liability in other situations, affords no protection from securities laws violations. The magnitude of the liabilities that may thus be incurred can be enormous. If a violation involves improper disclosure, the applicable statute of limitations does not begin until the person harmed discovers, or reasonably should discover, the improper disclosure. Furthermore, agreements to indemnify management and owners from liability for securities laws violations are of little use. Insurance from these liabilities is expensive and often difficult to obtain.

Suit under the securities laws by damaged investors or others is relatively easy to bring. Such suit may be brought in federal court in any jurisdiction in which any defendant is found or lives or transacts business, and service of process may be made anywhere it the world. A single plaintiff may bring a class action on behalf of all persons similarly situated, and courts award attorney's fees liberally to successful or settling plaintiff's attorneys as an inducement to bring such suits as private guardians of the public.

A company that makes an offer to an ineligible offeree in a nonregistered offering in which the private or intrastate offering exemption is relied upon is thus subject to a contingent liability to all investors in the offering for the aggregate amount of their investment. Under past practice, this contingent liability was deemed by the SEC staff to be cured by a subsequent registered or Regulation A offer to the investors to repurchase the shares sold in violation of the registration provisions. Subsequent financings without either the offer to repurchase or a disclosure of the contingent liability violate the antifraud provisions of the securities laws. Under recent SEC staff interpretations, even a registered offer to repurchase may not remove the contingent liability, and the contingent liablity must be disclosed in subsequent financings until the three-year statute of limitations has run, or else an antifraud violation will occur.

Uncorrected securities laws violations can preclude subsequent Regulation A or registered financings. The SEC may take administrative, civil, or criminal action, which can result in fine, imprisonment, court order requiring restoration of illegal gains, order suspending or barring activities with or as a broker-dealer, or other sanctions reflecting the nature and seriousness of the violation.

SUMMARY

Like many areas of the law, securities regulation is complex territory, fraught with countless opportunities for the entrepreneur to stumble. In the case of securities laws, an error can be particularly costly, making it difficult for the individual or the company to raise funds. For this reason, competent legal counsel is vitally important.

EXHIBIT 1
Business Plan and Prospectus Outline

Business Plan
1. Introduction (or Executive Summary)
   Short description of:
   — Business Objectives
   — Product
   — Technology and Development Program
   — Market and Customers
   — Management Team
   — Financing Requirements
2. Company Description
   — History and States
   — Background and Industry
   — Company's Objectives
   — Company's Strategies
3. Risk Factors
4. Products
   — Product Description and Comparisons
   — Innovative Features (Patent Coverage)
   — Applications
   — Technology
   — Product Development
   — Product Introduction Schedule and Major Milestones
5. Market
   — Market Summary and Industry Overview
   — Market Analysis and Forecasts
   — Industry Trends
   — Initial Product(s)
6. Competition
7. Marketing Program
   — Objectives
   — Marketing Strategy
   — Sales and Distribution Channels
   — Customers
   — Staffing
8. Management
   — Founders
   — Stock Ownership
   — Organization and Personnel
   — Future Key Employees and Staffing
   — Incentives (Employee Stock Purchase Plan)
9. Manufacturing
10. Service and Field Engineering
11. Future Products (Product Evolution)
    — Engineering Development Program
    — Future R&D
12. Facilities
13. Capital Requirements

EXHIBIT 1 (*concluded*)

14. Financial Data and Financial Forecasts
    — Assumptions Used
    — 3-Year Plan
    — 5-Year Plan
15. Appendixes
    — Detailed Management Profiles
    — References
    — Product Descriptions, Sketches, Photos
    — Recent Literature on Product, Market, etc.

Prospectus

When used as a legal prospectus, or offering memorandum, the following additions or changes should be made:
    — affix federal and state securities legends
    — affix "disclosures"
    — add a detailed "use of proceeds" section
    — add a section which describes the securities offered, in detail.
    — expand on the "Risk Factors" section to include dilution, nontransferability, and other risk factors which relate specifically to the securities being offered.

Remember—Obtain the counsel of a competent securities attorney.

Note: Use and dissemination should be restricted; document should be treated as confidential.

Chapter 9

INTELLECTUAL PROPERTY

In recent years, the world's major industrial economies have become considerably more knowledge-based. That is, high value-added, knowledge-intensive industries (such as electronics and service businesses) have grown at the expense of resource-based and commodity businesses. The rationale for this trend is clear: The major economic powers have focused their efforts on developing knowledge-intensive industries as a way to increase the income and standard of living of their populace, while decreasing their economy's dependence on diminishing natural resources.

As the U.S. economy has become more knowledge-intensive, legal minds have grappled with the issue of intellectual property. Who owns an idea? How can valuable knowledge and information be protected?

This note will address the various categories of protection afforded by the law, describe the nature of what can be protected, and discuss how that protection is achieved.

INTELLECTUAL PROPERTY

The area of intellectual property has challenged the legal system for hundreds of years and continues to do so. Common law has historically protected the property rights of individuals and corporations. But the area of intellectual property has presented new challenges to the legal system. If someone stole your wedding band, it would be fairly easy to prove—that individual would have the ring, and you would be without it.

Yet, how can you tell when someone has taken an idea or a concept? Intellectual property issues are particularly relevant in situations where an individual is working on some state-of-the-art process for his employer. During the course of developing the design, the employee has some "inspiration" which is outside the scope of the project's original bounds. Does this idea belong to the employer or the employee? Does it matter whether the inspiration occurred on the company's premises or while the employee was at home in the shower? Could the employee continue to work for the employer, but set up an independent business to exploit the idea?

A special patent law and patent court system was developed to deal specifically with these questions. Recently, however, intellectual property issues have arisen outside the bounds of traditional patent and trade secret law. The legal system is currently in the midst of grappling with these perplexing issues.

INTELLECTUAL PROPERTY AND THE LAW

Historically, it has been a specific goal of U.S. public policy to create the incentives required for the progress of technology. One of the means to this end has been through the system of patents and copyrights. These classes of intellectual property have arisen out of the statutes of the United States government, which are, quite literally, the laws of the United States as passed by Congress.

They include subjects such as:
— Title 11: Bankruptcy
— Title 23: Highways
— Title 39: Postal Service
— Title 50: War and National Defense

Each of the Titles lays down the law relating to the subject at hand, as well as the administrative systems the U.S. government will put in place to support each of the areas.

Specifically relating to intellectual property are two titles:
— Title 17: Copyrights
— Title 35: Patents

Patents and copyrights receive protection directly under this statutory framework, but the law in these areas is not governed exclusively by the language of the U.S. Code itself. Through their application and interpretation of the statutes in individual cases, judges define (and, indeed create) relevant legal standards. Such "common law," or judge-made law, adapts the patent and copyright laws to modern circumstances (short of constitutional amendments to the statutes themselves).

Out of common law principles have grown other areas of law which address intellectual property issues. These areas include trademarks, trade secrets, and confidential business information. Each of these topics will be explored in detail.

Patents

Patents are issued by the U.S. Patent and Trademark Office. There are three specific types of patents:

— Utility Patents: for new articles, processes, machines, etc.
— Design Patents: for new and original ornamental designs for articles of manufacture.
— Plant Patents: for new varieties of plant life.

It is important to understand the concept of a patent. A patent *does not* grant an individual exclusive rights to an invention. The inventor *already* has that exclusive right by dint of having invented the device in the first place; he/she can merely keep the invention a secret and enjoy its exclusive use.

Rather, the government grants the inventor the "negative right" to exclude others from making or using the invention. This right is granted in exchange for placing the information in the public domain.[1]

For instance, let's assume that the electronic calculator was a patentable invention, and that Mr. B was issued a patent on the device. Now, let us further assume that the idea of a checkbook holder with an electronic calculator was also patented, and that Mr. C was issued a patent on this invention. Mr. C would have the right to prevent others, including Mr. B, from manufacturing this device. However, Mr. C *could not* produce his article without the consent of Mr. B. In the event that patent infringement does occur, the patent holder can sue in civil court for damages. Should the patent holder become aware of potential infringement before the actual infringement occurs, he/she can sue for an injunction to prevent the infringement from actually occurring.

As mentioned, these kinds of legal battles occur in the civil courts. The purpose of the patent court system is to mediate patent claims. For example, when a patent claim is published in the *Patent Gazette*, others could come forward and challenge the patentability of the invention in the patent court system. One basis of challenge is for another inventor to claim that he/she was actually the first inventor. For this reason, it is recommended that inventors keep a daily record of their progress in a note-

---

[1]David A. Burge, *Patent and Trademark Tactics and Practice* (New York: John Wiley & Sons, 1980), p. 25.

book. These notes should record the inventor's progress and be signed and witnessed on a daily basis. In the event of a challenge, such a record will prove invaluable.

The three types of patents each cover different kinds of intellectual property and are governed by different regulations.

Utility Patents. A utility patent is issued to protect new, useful processes, devices, or inventions. First, what constitutes a patentable "invention?" The invention must meet several requirements:

— It must fall within one of the statutory categories of subject matter. There are four broad classes of subject matter: machines, manufacture, composition of matter, and processes.
— Only the actual, original inventor may apply for patent protection. In the case of corporations, for instance, the patent, when issued, is always granted to the individual and then *assigned* to the corporation.
— The invention must be new. That is, it will be considered novel if it is:
  • Not known or used by others in the United States.
  • Not patented or described by others in a printed publication in this or a foreign country.
  • Not patented in this country.
  • Not made in this country by another who had not abandoned, suppressed, or concealed it.
— The invention must be useful, even if only in some minimal way.
— The invention must be nonobvious. If the invention has been obvious to anyone skilled in the art, then it is not patentable.[2]

Finally, even if an invention meets all of these requirements, a patent can be denied if the application was not filed in a timely fashion. Specifically, if you used, sold, described in print, or attempted to secure a foreign patent application *more than one year prior* to your U.S. application, the patent will be denied.

Utility patents are issued for a term of 17 years.

The process of obtaining a patent is quite laborious. Patent attorneys, who specialize in the area, will draft the patent application which includes specific claims for the patentability of the invention. After several iterations of discussions with the patent office, some or all of the claims may be approved. This process frequently takes two years or longer.

Following acceptance of the patent by the Patent Office, a general description of the invention is published in the *Patent Gazette*. Interested parties may request a copy of the full patent from the Patent Office for a very nominal fee.

---

[2]Illinois Institute for Continuing Legal Education, *Intellectual Property Law for the General Business Counselor* (Chicago: Illinois Bar Center, 1973) pp. 1–16 through 1–24.

During the time between application for a patent and its issue, the invention has "patent pending" status. In some ways, this offers more protection than the actual patent. The invention will not be revealed by the government during this time, and others may be afraid to copy the invention for fear of infringing on the forthcoming patent.

Design Patents. A design patent protects the nonfunctional features of useful objects. In order to obtain a design patent, the following requirements must be met:

— Ornamentality—the design must be aesthetically appealing and must not be dictated solely by functional or utilitarian considerations.
— Novelty—the design must be new. The same criteria used for a utility patent will be applied here.
— Nonobvious—the design must not be obvious to anyone skilled in the art. This is a difficult standard to apply to a design and is quite subjective.
— Embodied in an article of manufacture—the design must be an inseparable part of a manufactured article.[3]

Design patents are issued for 3½, 7, or 14 years, depending upon the election of the applicant at the time of the application.

Plant Patents. A plant patent is obtainable on any new variety of plant which that individual is able to reproduce asexually. The new plant must be nonobvious. A plant patent is issued for a term of 17 years.

Copyrights

Copyright protection is afforded to artists and authors, giving them the sole right to print, copy, sell, and distribute the work. Books, musical and dramatic compositions, maps, paintings, sculptures, motion pictures, and sound recordings can all be copyrighted.

To obtain copyright protection, the work must simply bear a copyright notice which includes the symbol © or the word *copyright*, the date of first publication, and the name of the owner of the copyright.

Copyrighted works are protected for a term of 50 years beyond the death of the author.

Trademarks

A trademark is any name, symbol, or configuration which an individual or organization uses to distinguish its products from others.

---

[3]Burge, *Patent and Trademark*, pp. 137–38.

Trademark law is *not* derived from statutes of the Constitution, but is an outgrowth of the common law dealing with unfair competition.

Unfair competition is deemed to exist when the activities of a competitor result in confusion in the mind of the buying public.

Trademarks are typically brand names which apply to products, and servicemarks are names which apply to services.

There are several regulations which govern the proper use and protection of trademarks.[4] The scope of protection under the law is a function of the nature of the mark itself. Principal categories are:

— Coined marks—a newly coined, previously unknown mark is afforded the broadest protection, e.g., Xerox as a brand of copier, Charmin as a brand of toilet tissue.
— Arbitrary marks—a name already in use and applied to a certain product by a firm, but without suggesting any of the products' attributes, e.g., Apple Computer, Milky Way candy bars.
— Suggestive marks—a name in use, but suggesting some desirable attribute of the product, e.g., Sweet-n-Low as a low-calorie sweetener, White-Out correction fluid.
— Descriptive marks—a name which describes the purpose or function of the product. Descriptive marks cannot be registered until, over time, they have proven to be distinctive terms, e.g., "sticky" would probably not be approved as a trademarked brand name for glue.
— Unprotectable terms—generic names, which refer to the general class of product. Escalator, for instance, once a trade name, is now a generic term for moving staircases. One could not introduce a new brand of orange juice and call it "O.J."

In order to maintain a trademark, an owner must continue to use it and protect it. In this vein, some consumer product companies routinely produce and sell a few hundred items of several brand names which they have trademarked and wish to protect, but are not in normal production. Similarly, Coca-Cola has a crew of agents who routinely order "a coke" in establishments which do not serve Coca-Cola. If they are served a soda, they prosecute. In this way, they can maintain that they have attempted to keep their brand name from becoming a generic term. Aspirin, Cellophane, Zipper, and Escalator, are all names which have lost their trademark status.

Until a trademark is registered with the Patents and Trademark Office, it is desirable to use the ™ symbol after the name of a product, ℠ for services. After registration, the legend ® should be used.

4Burge, *Patent and Trademark*, p. 114.

Trade Secrets

A trade secret is typically defined as any formula, device, process, or information which gives a business an advantage over its competitors. To be classified as a trade secret, the information must not be generally known in the trade.

One cannot, by definition, patent a trade secret because the patent laws require that the invention be fully disclosed.

One advantage of a trade secret is that the protection will not expire after the 17-year term of the patent. Coke, for instance, maintains its recipe as a trade secret rather than patent it. Yet, should the information become public knowledge, their advantage could disappear quickly, and the inventor would have no claim on the process because it had not been patented.

Finally, should a firm decide to maintain a patentable advantage as a trade secret, and should another firm independently discover and patent that invention, this "second" inventor will have the right to collect royalties or force the "first" inventor to cease patent infringement. For this reason, many corporations routinely "defensively patent" and publish inventions so that others cannot.

In order for a company to maintain trade secret status for advantageous information, the company must keep the information secret and take precautions to keep it secret. These precautions include:

— Having certain policies relating to secret information.
— Making employees sign confidentiality and noncompete agreements.
— Marking documents "confidential" or "secret."

Confidential Business Information

The courts have also seen fit to protect a class of information less "secret" than a trade secret, but which is nonetheless confidential. The key here is that the information is disclosed in confidence, with the clear understanding that the information is confidential. Even if the information is in the public domain, if the recipient derives some value from the confidential disclosure he/she can be held liable for claims of unjust enrichment. There are several cases, for instance, where an inventor disclosed an idea to a second party, the second party searched out the idea in *existing* U.S. patents, found the idea was already the subject of a patent, and bought that patent from the holder. The courts held that the second party had to give the patent to the inventor because of the confidential nature of their relationship.[5]

---

[5]Illinois Institute for Continuing Legal Education, *Intellectual Property Law,* pp. 6–9, 10.

EMPLOYEE'S RIGHTS

Much of the law has evolved in an attempt to protect the rights of the enterprise. This has always been balanced, however, by the employee's right to earn a livelihood in the *best* potential source of livelihood. For instance, as an atomic engineer, the courts would protect my right to make a living as an atomic engineer, not merely earn a wage as a waiter or a bartender.

When a relationship between an employee and employer is severed, it is often the content of the written documents that will govern who has rights to what. Employment contracts, confidentiality, nondisclosure, and noncompete agreements all come into play. For this reason, prospective employees are well advised to read these documents carefully, and negotiate, rather than merely sign all of the papers which are typically associated with the first day on the job.

An employee can bargain away some of his/her rights in this area by signing inventions agreements, noncompete contracts, or employment agreements. However, the courts will not let an employee bargain away his/her fundamental right to earn a living from the best potential source.

If an employee signed an agreement which the courts found to be overly restrictive, the entire agreement would be thrown out. It is this fact which gives rise to the lawyer's advice that "It is better to sign an unreasonable employment agreement than a reasonable one."

There are three dimensions to the reasonableness test that the courts apply to employment agreements:

— Time horizon.
— Geographic scope.
— Nature of employment.

For instance, an employment contract which required an employee not to compete for six months, in the state of New York, as a designer of petroleum process facilities might be viewed as reasonable. While an agreement which specified a time horizon of one year and a geographic area of the United States would probably be viewed as unreasonable.

SUMMARY

It is clear that the body of legal knowledge in the intellectual property area is evolving rapidly. Yet, the processes which the law prescribes remain vitally important; in this area in particular, dotting the "i's" and crossing the "t's" is key. Whether it be keeping notebooks and records, filing patent claims, or reading the fine print on an employment contract, it is hard to overemphasize the importance of understanding the details.

In order to gain sufficient command of the relevant body of law, specialized legal counsel is called for. In an area which is changing so rapidly, one cannot rely on prior practices and "industry standard policies" for protection.

REFERENCES

American Bar Association. *Sorting out the Ownership Rights in Intellectual Property: A Guide to Practical Counseling and Legal Representation.* Chicago: American Bar Association, 1980.

Burge, David A. *Patent and Trademark Tactics and Practice.* New York: John Wiley & Sons, 1980.

Gallafent, R.J.; N.A. Eastway; and V.A.F. Dauppe. *Intellectual Property Law and Taxation.* Kensington, Calif.: Oyez, 1981.

Illinois Institute for Continuing Legal Education. *Intellectual Property Law for the General Business Counselor.* Illinois Bar Center, 1983.

Johnston, Donald F. *Copyright Handbook.* New York: R.R. Bowker Company, 1978.

Lietman, Alan. *Howell's Copyright Law.* BNA Incorporated, 1962.

White, Herbert S. *The Copyright Dilemma.* Chicago: American Library Association, 1977.

Case 3-1

STEVEN B. BELKIN

Wake up, Steven! It must be some mistake, but American Express is calling and says it's important. It's something about your credit rating.

His wife's voice roused Steven Belkin from a fitful sleep. A cascade of problems swept through his mind as Joan handed him the telephone:

This must be about my $15,000 overdue credit card bill. Joan hasn't realized I'm in quite so deep . . . she's going to be a bit shaken by this. I can see I'd better reassure her when I get off the phone . . . but to tell the truth, if I don't find investors soon, I'm really in trouble.

It was 11:30 the night of December 5, 1973. Steven Belkin had charged many of his expenses while trying to set up a new group travel business. Finding investors was proving much more difficult than he had anticipated and he had had to let his bill slip for a couple of months. Steven was going to have to find a new financing strategy fast to keep The Travel Group from being a one-way ticket to disaster.

BACKGROUND

Steven Belkin, age 26, had lived in Grand Rapids, Michigan, as a youth. There he had his earliest business experiences. When he was 12, his grandfather had given him some salvaged automatic letter openers. Steven decided to set up a raffle with $1 tickets and the letter openers as the prize. He enjoyed selling the tickets and felt wonderful telling the purchasers who had won. Another time he sold light bulbs door-to-door. Taking the idea from a school fund-raising project, he made it a summer job for his own profit. Steven's parents were of modest means and financial pressures were a source of family discord. Steven resolved that his own excellence and success would provide family happiness.

Several people advised Steven that the way to success was to couple engineering with business school. After graduating from high school where he had been captain of his basketball and tennis teams, Steven received an industrial engineering degree from Cornell. He concentrated on obtaining good grades at Cornell and also was active in student government and other school activities to improve his chances for admittance to graduate school. After graduation in 1969, Steven entered the MBA program at Harvard. Steven recalled an interview he had set up:

> I tried to figure out how best to improve my odds to get in. I came down and had an interview and talked to different people. I don't know if it helped— they say it doesn't, but I don't know. I always took the attitude to absolutely give everything you have. Then if you don't make it, at least you have given all you've got.

Steven saw life as a series of plateaus. At Cornell, grades had been important to reach the next level. Having reached business school, Steven now wanted to concentrate on learning about different kinds of business and on getting to know his classmates. Steven recalled:

> I felt I needed to get there faster than the usual course. It wasn't okay for me to get there in the regular process, riding someone else's wave. I needed to get ready to jump on my own wave. In order to do that, to speed up the process, I needed to have more experience and contacts than my years. You get that extra knowledge from the experiences of others. And the families and friends of your classmates are a wealth of contacts.

Steven and another student obtained the resume concession at Harvard Business School which not only helped with expenses, but also gave him a chance to meet all members of his class.

Innovative Management

During the summer between the first and second years of the MBA program, Steven decided he wanted to do consulting for small businesses. He asked friends and professors for leads, with little success. However, he did find that four graduating students were starting a new consulting company in that area which they would name Innovative Management (IM). Actually, one student had some possible business sources and had found a financial backer who would provide $50,000 for working capital. That student had asked the others to join for a salary and 5 percent portions of equity. Steven joined in the same fashion and the group quickly got underway. Steven described their start-up:

> We would go to bankers and individual venture capitalists who had made loans or investments in companies that weren't doing as well as they had hoped. We offered to go in and analyze the situation and either suggest that they write off the situation or propose a plan to improve the company. Then we would actually go in and implement our suggestions.
>
> The bankers and private investors we approached often didn't have the time or the ability to do this type of analysis. So they would go to the head of a company in trouble and point out that things weren't going very well, then suggest that the company employ us for the study as a condition of providing more funds. The companies would pay our fees which usually were $4,000 to $5,000.
>
> Initially, we would approach a new source of projects and offer to do the first job at no cost. After we showed what we could do, they would usually give us additional assignments.
>
> Our customers were companies with annual sales from $2 million to $10 million. Most were fairly new entities. Usually we could provide a needed control system, a marketing strategy—an entire business plan. Although the owners usually were under considerable pressure to let us in, they often were very stimulated by what we did. They knew they had problems and they didn't have the luxury of our education. After we gave our report to the financial backer, we also gave it to the company. Often we could provide our recommendation in only three or four days.
>
> By the end of the summer, we were so successful that we began hiring additional business school graduates. I continued to manage several others during my second year of school.

In addition to running the resume service and continuing his consulting business, Steven did a survey of interest in small business among students in the top 10 business schools as his second year project.

> My purpose was to show that there was a strong interest among these students in new ventures and starting your own company even though most schools were not teaching that. The survey confirmed this and I used the data to write some articles that we used to publicize our consulting firm. For example, we had stories in the *Boston Globe* and the SBANE [Small Business Association of New England] paper.
>
> People are always fascinated about people who do surveys and who have statistics. It makes you an instant expert to have a survey! It bought us new contacts and more credibility.

Looking back, Steven commented that he had done too much during the second year:

> I was incredibly busy. I cut a lot of classes. But the income was tempting and I was just ready to get the second year over with. But you are always going to

have work, yet you only have the second year of business school once. I missed an awful lot. I didn't realize then that the cases contained so much practical experience—I felt they were "text booky." I just didn't absorb that they really reflected day-to-day problems.

During the last half of the second year, Steven explored the job market, interviewing primarily with consulting firms. Although none of the firms caught his fancy, Steven thought the process was worthwhile:

It was a terrific educational experience to be able to talk to these high caliber people in the different companies where they were trying to sell you and tell you all about their companies. But I guess I was a bit spoiled after already having my teeth in it, giving suggestions to people and seeing them implement them the next week. The big companies seemed a little academic—nothing, really, compared to what I was doing.

Steven remained with Innovative Management when he graduated in June 1971. A year later, however, the company was sold and Steven decided to leave. Steven explained:

We grew from 5 people to 22 in that first two years. Then one of the individual venture capitalists who had given us some work wanted to buy the company. The other four founders wanted to sell, but I thought that we would lose our objectivity as an affiliated consultant. I wasn't very happy about it, so I left the firm.

Group Touring Associates

Having decided to leave Innovative Management, Steven Belkin reviewed his situation. Financially, he had limited resources. Steven had been earning almost twice the $12,000 typical starting salary of his class. Joan, whom he had married just after graduation, worked as a teacher for a smaller salary. Steven had received $15,000 for his interest in the consulting company but also still owed several school loans that were not yet due for payment. Their net worth was about $10,000. Steven had no special ideas for starting a different business and was not attracted to seeking a job with a larger company. It appeared to him that he should continue small business consulting on his own.

The sale of IM took place at the end of the summer of 1972. Before Steven embarked on an independent course, however, he was approached by Frank Rodgers, the original investor in Innovative Management. Rodgers had been squeezed out of that investment when the company was sold. Rodgers said he would like Steven to work for him helping other companies in which Rodgers had investments and Steven agreed.

Steven found he had a special attraction for a group travel company that was one of Rodgers' first assignments. This company, Group Touring Associates (GTA), developed tours which were sold to various groups by mail using their membership lists. GTA had been started by Robert Goode in 1966 with the backing of Rodgers and a few other private investors. Rodgers had invested $200,000 to date; the others, another $200,000.

Sales had grown to $1.8 million over the past year, but GTA had yet to make a profit. Losses had been increasing from $50,000 four years ago to over $250,000 last year. Robert Goode had convinced his investors to continue their backing by pointing to the rising sales. He contended that the front-end marketing costs of mailings and of setting up the trips would cause him to show losses as he grew. On the other hand, the unearned customer deposits made prior to the trips provided much of the cash needed for the growing operation. Rodgers agreed that some losses might have been necessary as the company got its start, but now was alarmed by the continuing deficits. Rodgers felt that the deposit cash flow was disguising more fundamental problems and wanted Steven to help the situation.

After a brief analysis of the business, Steven felt GTA had excellent potential and that it could be built profitably with better management. He accepted an offer to join the company and became GTA's executive vice president:

> Looking back at my other consulting clients, there wasn't one business that I wanted to do. I had done one project for another tour operator, but they marketed through travel agents and student groups. The combination of group travel with direct mail made this very fascinating to me—this was the business for me. Okay; I needed solid experience in this one. This was a good opportunity and I could earn a piece of the action.

A year later, Steven could point with pride to sales which had grown 50 percent and to a profit of over $150,000. Steven credited the turn-around to basic planning and well-managed execution:

> There was little organization when I came: no business plan, budgets, or anything like that. What I did was to clearly define our product and focus our operational and selling efforts. All within a budget and a plan. Before, the salespeople would try to find what trips various groups might be thinking about and come back and try to put one together. I introduced the strategy of defining the trips with the greatest general demand, then putting the trips together and having the salespeople fill them up.
>
> This strategy let us buy better, put together better promotional material, and better control our costs. I was very sensitive to the fact that we were in the direct mail business rather than just the group travel business. We had to provide better value for the travel dollar and promote it well by mail.

At the end of his first year as executive vice president, Steven reopened discussion about his future role in GTA with Robert Goode. He had initially accepted a salary of $22,000 with the understanding that they would renegotiate his position after Steven had proven himself. Now Steven felt he should receive a $30,000 salary and also be given 10 percent of the company. Robert would not agree. Steven recalled:

Robert and I went back and forth quite a bit. GTA was finally making money and I felt I deserved part ownership. Robert wouldn't go over $25,000 in salary and wanted to wait another year for the equity.

As we reached an impasse, Frank Rodgers arranged several more meetings between us. However, now that the company was profitable, Goode no longer needed more equity and Rodgers didn't have enough power to force Goode to agree to my demands. I think Robert also felt that he had run the company for six years and, now that I had gotten GTA over the hurdle, he wanted to be the boss again.

I tried very hard to reach an agreement; I wanted to stay. I felt that if I could be earning the $30,000 and have 10 percent of a profitable, growing company, I would be on my way to being successful. I was really running the show; I felt I was going to make money; I was fulfilling my entrepreneurial goals.

CONSIDERING AN INDEPENDENT COURSE

As Robert Goode's position hardened, Steven began to consider leaving GTA to start his own group travel packager. Looking at the industry structure made him feel this segment was a good opportunity. Potential air travelers could arrange pleasure trips directly on their own, choose ground packages offered by "tour wholesalers" such as American Express, or select complete air/ground packages such as those organized by GTA using chartered airlines. Traits of these choices are shown below:

TABLE 1
Comparison of Pleasure Travel Options

	Direct Selection by Traveler	Use of "Tour Wholesaler"	Charter Tours
Air travel	Via scheduled airline	Via scheduled airline	Charter
Land arrangements	Individual plans and arranges directly with provider or through retail travel agents	Provided by tour wholesaler	Provided by group travel wholesaler
Flexibility	Complete	Travel timing flexible Only selected destinations and accommodations	Fixed departure and return schedules Only selected destinations and accommodations
Usual cost	Highest price	Sold as service; cost often same as direct	30 percent to 40 percent lower
Sold by	Individual carriers, hotels, etc.; retail travel agents	Retail travel agents	Group-sponsored direct mail, some retail travel agents
Other limitations			Must be member of "affinity group"

Although the group air charter industry had only developed over the last 10 years after the introduction of jet air service, this mode of touring had already become a popular travel alternative. Steven felt the key attractions were lower cost, professional tour management, and the comfort and peace of mind of the sponsoring organizations' endorsements.

The lower costs were the direct result of the use of chartered aircraft—the group tour organizer guaranteed to pay for all seats and took the risk of filling the flight. Many travelers were willing to accept the fixed schedules of charters to take advantage of the lower prices. The offer of complete tour packages with professional tour guides was convenient, especially for travelers unfamiliar with the desired destination. Also, each traveler was a member of a group which sponsored the tour and could feel that his or her own representative would make sure the tour was a good trip and that the group would receive everything for which they had paid. This was particularly important in 1973 because there had been some recent publicity about tours which had been stranded or given inferior accommodations or service.

Steven saw these advantages as clear distinctions between group charter companies and tour wholesalers that used scheduled air carriers. The tour wholesalers also marketed primarily through retail travel agents whereas charter tours were normally sold using direct mail.

Looking at competition, Steven knew there were 10 major group tour operators in the United States. GTA ranked about seventh in that list. Where GTA provided tours for about 8,000 people per year, the largest U.S. operators moved about 50,000 customers yearly. As he viewed the market, he felt there was certainly room for one more:

> In the United States, there were regulations that you had to belong to an organization to go on a group trip. These had been eliminated about six years ago in Europe. With that, some of the group tour operators did more business than some of the scheduled carriers. The largest European companies running group charters were moving over a million people per year each. These regulations were relaxing in the United States, so I felt there would be great opportunities.

Steven received encouragement from Alan Lewis, GTA's most productive salesman. During Steven's negotiations with Robert Goode, Steven had described his growing frustration to Lewis. When Steven mentioned that he would be happy for Alan to join him if he left, Alan suggested that Steven should go out on his own whether or not Goode agreed to his demands. Alan would like to join him and was anxious to get an ownership position himself.

Steven's discussions with Goode made no further progress, so Steven resigned and left in early September 1973. Alan Lewis also resigned and the two of them began to develop The Travel Group, their own group travel business.

THE TRAVEL GROUP

Steven's idea for The Travel Group (TTG) was to duplicate the strategy that had been successful for Group Touring Associates. They would start with limited tour offerings to the most popular destinations, then expand as their reputation grew. They would use five sales representatives to call on groups across the United States to develop sponsors for direct mail promotions. They would carefully control their customer service and tour operations to minimize costs and gain customer satisfaction.

The tours they would offer were complex logistical tasks with large financial commitments. Running a tour meant chartering an entire plane which would accommodate up to 200 passengers. The company would also have to commit to blocks of hotel rooms and meals and provide ground transportation and other assorted support services. Once the package was planned, promotional material had to be written, printed, and distributed. Then inquiries had to be answered and reservations made.

To run the company, Steven would be president and major shareholder. He would be responsible for raising the capital they would need, for negotiating the trip arrangements, and for setting up the internal operations. Alan Lewis would be executive vice president. He would hire and manage the sales force, cover key clients personally, and work with sponsoring groups to fill the tours. Steven described their deal:

> I had planned to give five key salespeople 5 percent of the company each. Alan convinced me to give him the entire 25 percent and he would give away whatever was necessary to hire the others. Thus we became partners, but I would have a minimum of 51 percent ownership, Alan up to 25 percent, and the remainder would be for me or the investors. He ended up keeping all 25 percent after hiring four other excellent salespeople. Equity for our financial backers would come out of my share.

Steven and Alan immediately swung into action. Steven concentrated first on creating a business plan, while Alan began his search for salespeople and selling efforts for an initial tour he and Steven had outlined. By October 1, 1973, the business plan was finished and Steven prepared to raise $250,000:

> Developing the plan was fairly straightforward. We knew the basic charter travel destinations and seasons. We planned to run one airplane a week in season during the first year, two planes a week the second, and build each year. It was important to run "back to back" tours as much as possible so that the chartered plane could take one tour and return with the prior week's group. I added cost projections and made cash flow assumptions to give an overall financial plan.
>
> The plan showed an accumulated deficit of $155,000 for the five months before our first tour. Then I expected profits and tour deposits to provide cash

for growth. I felt I should raise $250,000 for a safe cushion to fund that deficit with room for unexpected costs, delays, or errors.

The business plan for The Travel Group is shown in Exhibit 1. Steven intended this document to be a simple, easy to follow business plan rather than a formal investment memorandum. He explained his reasoning:

> Most people make business plans so complicated that people understand nothing and get scared by them. If you repeat things two or three times, then they say, "Oh, yes. I understand that." They think they understand what they are investing in. If you keep giving them more and more inputs and ideas, they just can't absorb it.
>
> When people finish reading my verbal description, they understand what I have said. That does not mean they understand the business. But they have understood what I said, so therefore they think they understand the business.

Financing Strategy

Steven and Alan had direct experience in the operational tasks confronting them. Finding the needed financing was less familiar. However, several of Steven's earlier IM consulting assignments had involved raising money for smaller companies. Steven described IM's role:

> Some situations we investigated needed more equity along with the strategic and management changes we might suggest. If asked to implement our plan, we would agree to raise the money along with providing an executive vice president to bolster management and increase the company's credibility to investors. In return, we would receive part of the equity.
>
> We tried to keep this from being threatening to the president. Rather, we worked to convince the president that we'd be adding some new skills and helping to make the company valuable. Not like we were after the president's job.
>
> We'd approach individual venture capitalists for investments of $25,000 to $50,000 each. Our total needs were usually $100,000 to $200,000. The Rodgers family was very well connected and we had developed other contacts in the course of our projects.
>
> Pricing was rather arbitrary. The company probably didn't have earnings and we were selling the future. There was no scientific approach. We tried to show that the investors would double their money in a three-year period, then double it again to a value four times their original investment by the end of year five.
>
> Structurally, these investments sometimes ended up as a combination of debt and equity. This might be a loan with stock warrants. If all went well, they'd get most of their money back in a year or so and keep an equity ride with the warrants. The investors were very interested in not losing—not making mistakes, and less worried about how to get their equity out. That was less well structured—something down the road.

With this limited fund raising experience, Steven developed a financing strategy. First, he assessed the situation from an investor's point of view. TTG had a large upside. Few start-ups could show the rapid sales growth Steven had projected. There were good margins that gave an excellent profit potential and unusually attractive cash flows. The management team had strong credentials. Steven's education was a plus and both he and Alan had been successful running a similar company. They would also be using an experienced sales force. The group travel market in the United States had much less penetration than in Europe and should grow rapidly. Finally, there was little sophisticated competition in this industry so their management skills would give them an extra advantage.

To demonstrate long-term potential, Steven could also show evidence that a group tour operator could be attractive as a public stock offering. One large U.S. tour operator had gone public in 1967 at a price of $10 per share. Within two years, the price had risen as high as $93 per share. The shares were currently trading for about $8, but this was primarily the result of that company's poor results in diversifying into restaurants, cruise ships, and hotels.

Steven decided that this set of characteristics made TTG a good deal for institutional venture capital groups. He would attempt to raise the $250,000 in five units of $50,000. He hoped that two or three investors would subscribe to the entire total. Steven felt this was a better alternative than going to wealthy individual investors for smaller units:

> I thought the larger shots would be easier. I had the right background and credentials and a good business plan. I was sophisticated enough to present it to institutional investors. I felt this was a good package to offer, that they would buy me and would buy the business plan.

As insurance, Steven would also present the plan to a few individual investors, but his main thrust would be the institutional groups.

For leads, Steven turned to the "hit" list he had been developing since he had been in business school:

> I kept a notebook of people I met who might be good contacts. I'd put in notes on meetings and phone calls, addresses, correspondence. Some were filed in various institutional categories—others were just alphabetical.
>
> I put the people I would approach in priority by relationships. I wasn't going to ask people directly to invest. Rather, I would ask for their help: "What should I do to raise money?" I didn't want to put them on the defensive—once you ask them if they'd invest they have to protect themselves. This way, they could talk to me totally straight and really give me advice. If they *were* interested, then they would say they'd like to look at my plan further. Either way, they'd often recommend someone else to see.

Prospects 5: Investors 0

Steven had contacts with five well-known institutional venture capital companies. He approached each, describing his idea and asking advice. Out of these five, two were interested enough to ask to consider his plan.

After being initially encouraged by this interest, Steven soon began to feel that none of these firms was likely to invest. He described the problem areas he encountered:

> First, I was confronted with the developing fuel crisis. There were headlines in the newspapers saying airlines were cancelling charter flights. Only needed scheduled flights would be flying. There I was telling people I was starting a new charter company just as TWA was grounding all of its charters!
>
> I had to explain that I could buy space on regular flights if necessary, but that the *charter airlines* would continue to run. The charter airlines were separate airlines encouraged by the government so that additional aircraft would be available in a national emergency. They only flew charters and were not cancelling their flights. I also argued that if flights were rationed, my old relationships with the airlines and the professionalism we would be bringing in would give us preference in charter assignments.
>
> I felt I was making some of the venture capital companies comfortable about the fuel problem, but I also found them reluctant to invest because there were no hard assets to "lend" against. They'd say, "There's nothing there! You aren't buying any machinery, all the money's going for working capital. There's no product line, no proprietary technology."
>
> I believe they were thinking that if it didn't work, with hard assets they could still minimize their losses somehow and get something out of it. I got the feeling they were just more liberal bankers, which was different from my earlier concept of venture capitalists.

Approaching Wealthy Individuals

Scheduling appointments and follow-up visits with the venture capital companies took most of October with some discussions continuing into November. At the same time, Steven also was calling on wealthy acquaintances in a more casual way:

> I'd say, "You know I'm raising money on Wall Street, but this might be something you'd be interested in. I'd like to get your input. Do you have any suggestions?" I'd mostly ask for advice and references to other venture capitalists or investment bankers.

As it became evident that the venture capital companies were not showing great enthusiasm, Steven more seriously pursued wealthy individuals:

> I primarily approached other successful business executives who either still ran their own businesses or had sold their businesses in the last few years. I thought that a $50,000 investment would be easy for them. It was a lot tougher than I thought.
>
> By November, I was letting everyone know I was trying to start this company. I was using every contact I could to get referrals to wealthy investors.

Out of all of his contacts, Steven developed two serious leads. One investor who was also a friend indicated he might provide $20,000. The other wanted Steven to come back when he had raised most of the remainder of the offering. Steven had expected wealthy individuals to be excited by the opportunity he saw in TTG. Now he found that wealthy individuals were going to be more difficult to attract as investors than he had anticipated.

Offer of a Bank Loan

Steven's discussions with the wealthy individual who knew him did lead to an unexpected offer of debt financing. Steven explained:

> I didn't think any part of my deal was bankable at all. I clearly felt that all equity money would be required. Yet the one wealthy individual who was my friend said he did think the idea had merit and that he would introduce me to his bank. He gave me a very strong personal endorsement and to my surprise, his banker said he would match every dollar of equity I raised with one dollar of debt!
>
> Once this bank opened my eyes, I approached several downtown banks to see what they would do. They wouldn't have any part of a loan—there were no assets to lend against.
>
> The bank willing to give me a credit line was located outside of the main metropolitan area. They were more aggressive to compete, but they also saw TTG as a good cash flow generator and needed the deposits.

The loan offer opened welcome new possibilities to Steven. Now if he could raise as little as $125,000 in equity, the total of $250,000 would be available to him. However, the use of the debt line would greatly increase his own exposure because the bank would be lending against his personal guarantee. He was not anxious to do this himself and the idea was frightening to Joan:

> I was signing a $125,000 note, but my net worth was less than $10,000. Sure. I decided it didn't make any difference—if things went bad, I couldn't pay it anyway, so why worry about it? I would be more concerned about signing a $25,000 note because I conceivably could pay that.
>
> But they also required Joan to sign it and this was very, very stressful for her. It was overwhelming and very upsetting. We talked about it and I said it was the same way for me too. But if it's $125,000 or it's a million, it doesn't make any difference right now.

The note Steven and Joan Belkin signed was a contingent line of credit at 2 percent over the prime lending rate. The credit line would equal the amount of TTG's equity up to a maximum of $125,000. Steven could draw upon the line at his discretion. However, both he and Joan were very anxious not to use this credit so that they would not actually incur the personal liability of their guarantee.

Growing Pressures

Signing the credit line agreement and the slow progress in raising the needed equity were not the only sources of the pressures Steven felt building. There was also the hectic pace of beginning TTG operations.

If TTG was to run its first tour during the late winter season, the package must be put together and ready for sale by the beginning of January. To do this, Steven and Alan had been continually working to develop their first trip and get their sales effort underway since October. By October 15, they had hired a secretary who had worked with them at GTA and set up operations in Steven's apartment. By the end of October, they had added another secretary and the first additional salesman. Steven described what it was like:

> We just assumed we would get the money and that we had to make it work. So we had to get the sales.
>
> Joan was teaching, so she went off to work at 7 o'clock and came home about 3:30. She had been very, very helpful in putting together the business plan, but she's a very organized person and had her own work to do. When all the people were in the apartment, that started getting to her. Not only would there be no privacy and no quiet to plan her classes and grade papers, but sometimes we'd raid the refrigerator for lunch and she'd find that what she had planned for supper had disappeared. We would often work past seven o'clock talking to the West Coast. She could go into a bedroom by herself, but in that small two bedroom apartment, it was more of a prison than a refuge.
>
> On November 15, we rented a 10′ by 20′ office that had been the rental office in my apartment building so things were a bit better, but we still used my apartment. We were sharing desks and had no place to have meetings with potential backers or sales contacts. I always met people at the airport, said I was just leaving on a flight, then waited until they had gone before going back to our office.

Steve Belkin and Alan Lewis were funding the office expenses and salaries for the other employees from their own pockets. So far they had invested almost $10,000 in cash. In addition, each of them was charging every possible expense on their personal American Express credit cards. Since both of them were traveling around the United States and Europe to talk to group sales prospects, interview sales representative candidates, and set up the first tour, they had accumulated outstanding charges of about $15,000 each. They had both been heavy users of their credit cards before, which gave them high credit limits. They had made no payments since September and were starting to get overdue reminder letters which emphasized they were about to lose their hard-earned credit.

As business paused for the Thanksgiving holiday, Steven wasn't quite sure how much he should be thankful. There was little progress finding equity investors and Steven's bills and responsibilities grew.

He felt he had to provide others emotional support just when he was the least sure of what he might have done to his own position:

> I was having to play Mr. Completely-in-Control: "Everything is great. We're going to get our money." The only one who was really starting to worry was Alan. He was the only one I really talked to. He hadn't had much exposure to raising money. I was starting to let him know I was getting nervous and he didn't know how to read that. "What does it mean when Steve's nervous?"
>
> I'd also gone far enough that everyone knew I was doing this. It's not like I could have a quiet failure. I'd gone to close friends and family for contacts—the ones I'd worked so hard to impress. I'd always been Mr. Successful: "Here's Steve. He went to Harvard, was captain of his tennis team and basketball team, and always got good grades. He had his own consulting firm." Now Mr. Successful was starting his own company and Mr. Successful was in trouble.

WHAT NOW?

By the first week of December, Steven knew he had only a few weeks left before TTG would start to unravel. Finding money was the key:

> I felt I really had to switch gears here. I had to scrape it together. Initially I wanted to do it the business school way. Now, I had to become a street fighter. I might have to go out and beg, and it would be very difficult for me to go to people and say, "I need your help."
>
> I only had a little time. Should I put more emphasis on the venture capital route and really try to close one of those? Should I continue with the wealthy investors? Or should I go to friends and relatives and try to piece it together in fives and tens? Because I had so little time left, I really felt the main options I should consider were to find one venture capitalist for $250,000 or to go to friends for small amounts.

In deciding on his last ditch strategy, Steven also contemplated whether he should change his offering to be more attractive. Pricing had never been explicitly discussed with the institutional venture firms. When talking to wealthy individuals, Steven was offering to sell 250,000 shares at $1 per share. He and Alan would be issued 750,000. What ways of repricing or restructuring the deal would help him to raise his equity fast?

"This is not exactly how I thought it would be," Steven thought to himself as he struggled to find a creative solution that December evening. "This is a good opportunity. Why haven't I been successful raising the money yet? I wonder if it was a mistake to resign so quickly? Well, here I am. Maybe I'll think of something tomorrow." It seemed that he had just drifted away, when the phone rang.

EXHIBIT 1
TTG Business Plan—October 1, 1973

[The entire narrative of the business plan is reproduced below. Title pages have been removed and the layout has been condensed. Only selected financial exhibits are included.]

I. THE INTRODUCTION

The Travel Group is being formed to meet the tremendous need for low cost group travel. People now have more leisure time than ever before, and they are becoming aware that group vacations are available at prices almost everyone can afford. A week in Europe or the Caribbean for $199 per person is an affordable price for most people.

The group travel industry is less than 10 years old. The market penetration for this new industry has barely begun. There are unlimited groups available. Alumni organizations, professional associations, religious groups, fraternal organizations, employee associations, unions, corporations, women's clubs, etc. The Travel Group will be concentrating on "prime groups." These are organizations that are known to be extremely responsive to group travel (e.g., Shriners, medical associations, bar associations, teacher associations).

The Travel Group will provide "deluxe" group tours. The attitude of management is to send "prime groups" during "prime season." Hotel accommodations will be at deluxe hotels (e.g., Hilton, Sheraton, Hyatt), and air transportation will be via scheduled carriers (e.g., United, Braniff, American) when possible.

The Travel Group will be classified as a "back to back wholesaler" in the travel industry. The corporation will market its group tours to travel agents throughout the United States. This should comprise less than 10 percent of the sales during the first two years, but eventually should produce 25 percent of the sales volume.

The primary source of sales for The Travel Group will be through direct sales. The corporation will have their own sales force, and each salesman will be assigned a different territory.

During the first year of operations, The Travel Group projects the movement of only 6,861 passengers. The four salesmen that management will offer positions currently move more than 18,000 passengers per year. Thus, the first year projection of less than 7,000 passengers is quite conservative. Management has also allowed six months before the departure of the first flight. This will provide the sales force with more than sufficient time to sell the first back to back charters to Hawaii.

Sales of $2,766,397 are projected during this first year and a profit of $169,223.

The second year of operations, 1975, should produce sales of $8,059,589 with a profit before tax of $832,636. In five years, 1978, The Travel Group should achieve a sales volume of $18,241,542 and a before tax profit of $2,150,121.

EXHIBIT 1 (continued)

There is a tremendous positive cash flow in the group charter business. This allows for rapid expansion without additional financing. The potential of The Travel Group is open-ended, but management will expand cautiously.

II. THE INDUSTRY

The "back to back" group charter business is in the early stages of growth. The industry is less than 10 years old. The management in the industry is quite unsophisticated. Financial and management controls are lacking. The market penetration of group charters has barely begun. Few companies have creative and organized marketing programs.

The main regulatory organization in the industry is the Civil Aeronautics Board (CAB). The trend in the past two years has been for more and more "low cost group travel." The CAB is oriented toward making travel available at a cost affordable for the mass public. This is very favorable for firms like The Travel Group and, thus, governmental regulation should be beneficial to the company.

The United States is several years behind Europe in low cost vacations. In 1972 group vacation charters provided more revenue to the European airlines than the regularly scheduled flights.

In the United States, the same growth pattern is developing. In the past four years, charters on the North Atlantic have grown at the rate of 58 percent per year. In 1972 charter flights accounted for 30 percent of all passengers flown on the North Atlantic.

It is easy to understand this tremendous growth in the group charter business by simply looking at the money saved by a typical vacationer.

Assume an individual would like to travel to Hawaii for one week. He departs on a weekend, flies coach class, and all accommodations are deluxe:

	Regular Rate	Group Charter Rate	Savings
Air Fare	$510	$225	$285
Hotel	140	84	56
Dinners	56	40	16
Transfers	20	10	10
Tour Operator's Fee	0	113	−113
TOTAL COST	$726	$472	+$254
	****	****	*****

Thus, an individual can save 35 percent, or $254, during a one week visit to Hawaii.

III. THE COMPANY

The Travel Group will be selling deluxe "back to back" group charters. "Back to back" means that, for a set period of time, groups will be sent every week to a particular destination. The aircraft, which takes one group to the destination, will pick up the group that is ending their vacation. This allows substantial savings on air fare. There is also tremendous buying power at the hotels because rooms are utilized every week.

EXHIBIT 1 (*continued*)

These cost advantages will allow The Travel Group to sell vacations to destinations all over the world at savings of 35 percent or more (see Industry section).

The Travel Group will have salesmen assigned to different territories in certain sections of the country. These salesmen will call on prime traveling groups. They will be selling deluxe packages, principally during prime season. The "sell" is usually easy because the organization has nothing to lose and much to gain. The Travel Group will pay for the mailing of a brochure describing the vacation to all the members of the organization. For each reservation the group produces, the organization will be given about $15. Thus, if a group fills a 150-seat airplane, the organization will receive $2,250 (150 x $15) and will have provided vacations for its members at substantial savings.

Groups that will be approached by the sales force include Shriners, Masons, medical associations, bar associations, Elks, Moose, alumni associations, teacher associations, unions, employee groups, and Knights of Columbus. There is an unlimited number of groups. Management will develop a mailing list of all the prime groups in the country to provide additional direction for the sales force.

The cash flow in the business is very favorable. Deposits from passengers are often received more than 90 days in advance. Final payments from passengers are due 45 days before departure. Payments to the airlines occur 30 days before departure, and hotel bills are not paid until 30 days after departure. Thus, the majority of receipts are in-house 45 days in advance of departure while disbursements occur 15 to 45 days after the initial receipts are in.

IV. THE COMPETITION

The group travel industry is in its early stages of growth. The industry is less than 10 years old, and there is only a limited number of group tour operators. Sophisticated and experienced management is scarce in the industry. The few "back to back" group travel companies, which do exist, have had substantial sales growth in the past three years. In the last eighteen months, there have been several new companies started that have been running "back to back" charters. One of these companies had sales of close to $8 million during its first year and before tax profits of over $500,000.

Competition in the industry has not developed to the point of pricing of the same packages. Sales growth is achieved by contacting the proper groups and then appropriately following up these leads.

"Back to back" operators always concentrate on a few destinations. With the vast number of destinations, there is limited competition among tour operators in providing packages to the same place. For instance, one of the new tour operators is just specializing in running trips to Greece, while another has programs just to the Orient.

Currently the East Coast is the only section of the country that has become familiar, to some extent, with group charters. Amazingly, 60 percent of all charter flights are out of New York. The South, Midwest, and Central States have barely been touched.

Less than five "back to back" tour operators have a national sales force. The Travel Group's national sales force will be comprised of experi-

EXHIBIT 1 (*continued*)

enced travel salesmen who are currently working in different territories throughout the United States for other tour operators.

V. THE MANAGEMENT

There are two key departments in the group charter business. One is sales, and the other is operations. By providing a well-organized business plan and by making equity available, The Travel Group has attracted some of the most qualified people in the industry.

Mr. Steven B. Belkin will be president. He will be responsible for directing the operations of the company. Mr. Belkin is thoroughly familiar with the day-to-day operations as well as the overall business planning of a "back to back" tour operator.

He is a graduate of Cornell University and Harvard Business School. He was one of five founders of Innovative Management, a small business consulting firm in the Boston area. Some of his consulting projects included the development and implementation of a marketing program for a ski charter travel firm, running a chain of sport stores with sales of over $6 million, and serving as president of a film school and production company. When Mr. Belkin left and sold his interest in this consulting firm, it had grown to 22 full-time consultants.

For more than a year, Mr. Belkin has been devoting full time to a travel group charter firm which was in severe financial difficulties. With the development and implementation of a new business plan, creation of a national sales force, and tighter management and financial controls, this firm has now been turned around. The year before Mr. Belkin's involvement, the firm had sales of approximately $1 million with a loss of over $250,000. This year the company has already reported a respectable profit for the first six months and has more than doubled the previous year's sales.

The sales force that is available is comprised of some of the best salesmen in the industry. Each man has thorough familiarity and personal contacts with the prime groups in the different sections of the country.

The sales team will have a minimum of six months before the first back to back charter will start. This should provide more than sufficient time to sell the program. During the first year of operations, the sales force needs to move only 6,861 passengers. This year the four salesmen being considered moved more than 18,000 passengers. Thus, the first year programs should be sold fairly easily, and this will allow the sales team to start concentrating on the second year programs well in advance.

VI. THE FINANCIALS

[Some exhibits omitted.]

A. TRIP COST ANALYSIS

Exhibit	I	Hawaii
Exhibit	II	San Juan
Exhibit	III	Ad Hoc
Exhibit	IV	Acapulco
Exhibit	V	Spain

- 4 -

EXHIBIT 1 (*continued*)

B. PROFIT AND LOSS STATEMENTS 1974 and 1975

      Exhibit VI   Pro Forma Profit and Loss Statement (1974 and 1975)

      Exhibit VII   Plane and Passenger Projections (First Year 1974)

      Exhibit VIII   Monthly Pro Forma Profit and Loss Statement (First Year 1974)

      Exhibit IX   General and Administrative Expenses

      Exhibit X   Plane and Passenger Projections (Second Year 1975)

      Exhibit XI   Monthly Pro Forma Profit and Loss Statement (Second Year 1975)

C. CASH FLOW ANALYSIS

      Exhibit XII   Cash Flow Assumptions

      Exhibit XIII   Monthly Cash Flow Projections (First Year 1974)

      Exhibit XIV   Monthly Cash Flow Projections (Second Year 1975)

D. FIVE YEAR PROJECTIONS

      Exhibit XV   Pro Forma Profit and Loss Statements (1974–1978)

A great deal of time and effort has been devoted to the preparation of the following financial exhibits. Management will use them for budgeting as well as for projections.

The Trip Cost Analysis section clearly outlines the revenues and expenses associated with each trip on both a per passenger and per airplane basis. The air fare, hotel, meals, transfers, mailing, giveaways, and load factor are all expenses that have been determined by historical statistics and actual experience.

The Profit and Loss Statements for the first two years have been prepared on a month-to-month basis. Management has determined the number of planes and passengers that can be accommodated each month to a particular destination. During the first year of operation, no passengers are projected to be moved until June. There is a good possibility that ad hoc programs will be sold before this time, so sales and profit could be greater than projected.

The Cash Flows have been prepared for the first two years on a month-to-month basis. The cash flow assumptions are very important, and management feels the assumptions made are conservative.

The five year pro-forma profit and loss statement illustrates the potential of this new and growing business. The Travel Group hopes to have sales of over $18 million within five years and profits before tax of over $2 million.

EXHIBIT 1 *(continued)*

EXHIBIT I
COST ANALYSIS PER PASSENGER
HAWAII

Selling Price		$429 + 10% = $471.90
Direct Costs: Air	$225	
Hotel	84	
Meals	40	
Transfers	10	− 359.00
Gross Profit before Acquisition Costs		$112.90
Acquisition Costs:		
Mailing Costs 10¢ Brochure		
+ Non profit Mailer		
(.50% return rate)	$ 20.00	
Giveaways ($20/reservation + 1/20)	20.00	
Load Factor (90%)	20.00	− 60.00
Gross Profit		$ 52.90
		*******

****

Hawaii Trip Analysis per Plane

Total Sales	= $471.90 x 135 passengers	= $63,706
Cost of Sales	= $409.00 x 135 passengers	= $56,565
Total Profit	= $ 52.90 x 135 passengers	= $ 7,141

Options: $10 net/passenger = $1,350/plane

EXHIBIT VI
THE TRAVEL GROUP, INC.
PRO FORMA PROFIT AND LOSS STATEMENT (1974 AND 1975)

	1974	1975
SALES	$2,766,397	$8,059,589
Cost of Sales	2,345,594	6,870,953
Gross Profit	$ 420,803	$1,188,636
General and Administrative	251,580	356,000
Profit (before tax)	$ 169,223	$ 832,636
	*********	*********
Earnings per Share	$ .17	$ .83
Value/Share (10 multiple)	$1.70	$8.33
Number of Planes	44	128
Number of Passengers	6,861	22,183

EXHIBIT 1 (*continued*)

EXHIBIT VII
THE TRAVEL GROUP, INC.
PLANE AND PASSENGER PROJECTIONS
FIRST YEAR OF OPERATION (1974)

	January	February	March	April	May	June	July	August	September	October	November	December	Total
HAWAII													
Passengers						750	600	750	600	600	750	600	4,650
Planes						5	4	5	4	4	5	4	31
SAN JUAN													
Passengers											895	716	1,611
Planes											5	4	9
AD HOC													
Passengers						150	150	150	150				600
Planes						1	1	1	1				4
TOTAL PASSENGERS	0	0	0	0	0	900	750	900	750	600	1,645	1,316	6,861
TOTAL PLANES	0	0	0	0	0	6	5	6	5	4	10	8	44

EXHIBIT VIII
THE TRAVEL GROUP, INC.
PRO FORMA PROFIT AND LOSS STATEMENT
FIRST YEAR OF OPERATION (1974)

	January	February	March	April	May	June	July	August	September	October	November	December	Total
SALES													
Hawaii (150 Seat Plane) (31 planes) (4,650 passengers)						318,530	254,824	318,530	254,824	254,824	318,530	254,824	2,766,397
Hawaii Options (net)						7,500	6,000	7,500	6,000	6,000	7,500	6,000	
San Juan (179 Seat Plane) (9 planes) (1,611 passengers)											263,120	210,496	
San Juan Options (net)											4,475	3,580	
Ad Hoc Programs (4 planes) (600 passengers)						65,835	65,835	65,835	65,835				
TOTAL SALES 44 planes 6,861 passengers						391,865	326,659	391,865	326,659	260,824	593,625	474,900	2,766,397
COST OF SALES													
Hawaii						276,070	220,856	276,070	220,856	220,856	276,070	220,856	
San Juan											219,200	175,360	
Ad Hoc Programs						59,850	59,850	59,850	59,850				
TOTAL COST OF SALES						335,920	280,706	335,920	280,706	220,856	495,270	396,216	2,345,594
General and Administrative Costs	15,000	15,000	18,000	18,000	22,716	22,716	22,716	22,716	22,716	24,000	24,000	24,000	251,580
Net Profit (before tax)													$ 169,223

EXHIBIT 1 (*continued*)

EXHIBIT XII
CASH FLOW ASSUMPTIONS

A. Receipts
1. Deposits and final payments are only received 15 days before the date of the trip (very conservative since final payments are due 45 days before departure, and deposits are often received 90 days in advance).
2. Net Operational Tour Receipts are received the week of the trip.

B. Disbursements
1. Airlines are paid 30 days in advance.
2. Hotels are paid 30 days after the trip (requires letter of credit and cash deposits).
3. Meals and transfers are paid 30 days after the trip.
4. Acquisition costs are paid 30 days in advance.
5. Ad hoc program payments require $10,000 deposit 30 days before departure and the balance paid the week before departure.
6. General and Administrative Expenses are assumed to be paid/disbursements during the month they are expensed. (Conservative since telephone and travel and entertainment expenses are usually not disbursed until a minimum of 30 days after being expensed. These two expense categories are approximately 20% of G + A expenses.)

EXHIBIT XIII
THE TRAVEL GROUP, INC.
CASH FLOW PROJECTIONS
FIRST YEAR OF OPERATION (1974)

	January	February	March	April	May	June	July	August	September	October	November	December
RECEIPTS												
Hawaii					159,265	286,677	286,677	286,677	254,824	286,677	286,677	254,824
Hawaii Options (net)						7,500	6,000	7,500	6,000	6,000	7,500	6,000
San Juan										131,560	236,808	210,496
San Juan Options (net)											4,475	3,580
Ad Hoc Programs					32,918	65,835	65,835	65,835	32,918			118,504
TOTAL RECEIPTS				—	192,183	360,012	358,512	360,012	293,742	424,237	535,460	593,404
DISBURSEMENTS												
Hawaii					192,375	153,900	282,825	226,260	244,350	264,735	226,260	244,350
San Juan										100,000	80,000	199,200
Ad Hoc					10,000	59,850	59,850	59,850	49,850			92,880
General + Administrative	70,608	15,000	18,000	18,000	22,716	22,716	22,716	22,716	22,716	24,000	24,000	24,000
TOTAL DISBURSEMENTS	70,608	15,000	18,000	18,000	225,091	236,466	365,391	308,825	316,916	388,735	330,260	560,430
MONTHLY CASH SURPLUS (DEFICIT)	(70,608)	(15,000)	(18,000)	(18,000)	(32,908)	123,546	(6,879)	51,186	(23,174)	35,502	205,200	32,974
CASH BALANCE BEGINNING	—	(70,608)	(85,608)	(103,608)	(121,608)	(154,516)	(30,970)	(37,849)	13,337	(9,837)	25,665	230,865
CASH BALANCE ENDING	(70,608)	(85,608)	(103,608)	(121,608)	(154,516)	(30,970)	(37,849)	13,337	(9,837)	25,665	230,865	263,839

284

EXHIBIT 1 (*concluded*)

EXHIBIT XIV
THE TRAVEL GROUP, INC.
CASH FLOW PROJECTIONS
FIRST YEAR OF OPERATION (1975)

	January	February	March	April	May	June	July	August	September	October	November	December
RECEIPTS												
Hawaii	254,824	286,677	286,677	254,824	254,824	286,677	286,677	286,677	286,677	286,677	286,677	382,236
Hawaii Options (net)	6,000	6,000	7,500	6,000	6,000	6,000	7,500	6,000	7,500	6,000	7,500	6,000
San Juan	210,496	236,808	236,808	157,872	52,624					105,248	210,496	315,744
San Juan Options (net)	3,580	3,580	4,475	3,580	1,790						3,580	3,580
Acapulco	237,008	266,634	266,634	177,756	59,252					118,504	237,008	355,512
Acapulco Options (net)	5,400	5,400	6,750	5,400	2,700						5,400	5,400
Spain					148,006	333,014	333,014	333,014	333,014	148,006		
Spain Options (net)						4,500	5,625	4,500	5,625	4,500		
TOTAL RECEIPTS	717,308	805,099	808,844	605,432	525,196	630,191	632,816	630,191	632,816	668,935	750,661	1,068,472
DISBURSEMENTS												
Hawaii	226,260	264,735	226,260	244,350	226,260	264,735	226,260	282,825	226,260	282,825	226,260	398,250
San Juan	175,360	195,360	175,360	159,200	95,360	47,680				80,000	80,000	255,360
Acapulco	92,880	234,900	211,680	194,940	118,800	59,400				92,880	92,880	304,560
Spain					174,600	218,250	252,900	316,125	252,900	97,875	78,300	
General and Administrative	28,000	28,000	28,000	28,000	28,000	30,000	30,000	30,000	30,000	32,000	32,000	32,000
TOTAL DISBURSEMENTS	522,500	722,995	641,300	626,490	643,020	620,065	509,160	628,950	509,160	585,580	509,440	990,170

MONTHLY											
CASH SURPLUS/(DEFICIT)	194,808	82,104	167,544	(21,058)	(117,824)	10,126	123,656	1,241	123,656	83,355	241,221	78,302
CASH BALANCE BEGINNING	263,839	458,647	540,751	708,295	687,237	569,539	703,195	704,436	828,092	911,447	1,152,668	
CASH BALANCE ENDING	458,647	540,751	708,295	687,237	569,413	579,539	703,195	704,436	828,092	911,447	1,152,668	1,230,970

EXHIBIT XV
THE TRAVEL GROUP, INC.
PRO FORMA PROFIT AND LOSS (1974–1978)

	1974	1975	1976	1977	1978
SALES	$2,766,397	$8,059,589	$12,029,894	$15,124,878	$18,241,542
Cost of Sales	2,345,594	6,870,953	10,305,490	12,910,496	15,481,421
Gross Profit	420,803	1,188,636	1,724,404	2,214,382	2,760,121
General and Administrative	251,580	356,000	480,000	540,000	610,000
Profit (before tax)	$ 169,223	$ 832,636	$ 1,244,404	$ 1,674,382	$ 2,150,121
Earnings per Share	$ .17	$ .83	$ 1.24	$ 1.67	$ 2.15
Value/Share (10 price/earnings)	$1.70	$8.33	$12.44	$16.74	$21.50
Number of Planes	44	128	192	240	288
Number of Passengers	6,861	22,183	33,275	41,595	49,915

Case 3-2

RUTH M. OWADES

In late October 1978, Ruth Owades felt she must leave her job and fully commit to starting her own mail order company or else give up the idea. The company would be Gardener's Eden, which would offer unusual, practical, and hard-to-find tools by catalog to affluent home gardeners. She had developed the concept while working for Avion, a group of mail order companies. However, in a meeting September 2, the corporate management had turned down her proposal to start such a company within Avion. Ruth strongly believed in the potential of a gardening catalog and had been looking forward to running the new enterprise. Swallowing her disappointment, she asked for and received permission from Avion's chairman to use the idea and try to start the venture on her own if she could raise the money.

The days since had flown by as Ruth rushed to see if she could get a company underway in time to mail catalogs in January for the spring season. She felt that gardening would be a one season mail order segment and that further delay would mean waiting another year. Earlier, Ruth had developed a basic plan for starting this company using the resources of Avion's other divisions. Now, she had to adapt the idea to stand as an independent business, raise $250,000 in capital, and learn enough about the details of mail order operations to get started.

With Avion's agreement, Ruth had continued on their payroll to carry out certain specific projects. This gave her time to begin the process of raising funds. By the end of October, however, Ruth had to commit to merchandise orders, warehouse arrangements, office leases, and utility connections to make a January catalog possible. She couldn't even print catalogs without a company address and telephone number! To make these commitments, Ruth would have to leave her job at Avion and completely dedicate herself to getting Gardener's Eden going. Yet she was not entirely happy with the only financing group she had interested so far and was even less sure that she wanted to commit to the great Unknown—she really had no experience running a business. Time was running out for Ruth to decide what she should do.

BACKGROUND

Ruth M. Owades grew up in Los Angeles, where her father owned a small bookstore. She attended public schools and majored in French at Scripps College, graduating with a B.A. in 1966. After a year's study of French theater on a Fulbright grant in Strasbourg and Paris, she took a clerical job at the Economic Development Office for the City of Los Angeles, located in New York City. She married in 1969; her husband's job in the beer business took them abroad to Athens and, a year later, back to St. Louis. Analyzing her options, Ruth decided that she wanted a career in broadcasting. She took a few courses and started doing theater reviews on a local radio station. Then CBS Radio, St. Louis, hired her as Assistant Program Director.

When her husband took a new job in Boston in 1971, Ruth remained in St. Louis. But, as she put it, "my career came to a dead standstill; company culture would not allow for my not following my husband, and I moved to Boston." After a six months' job search, she found a position at WCVB-TV, Channel 5, as associate producer of a morning talk show. She continued:

> I spent a year there. The show had poor ratings and I grew frustrated. The show was canceled. I decided then and there: I'm going to be my own master. That was January 1973. I took out a map and drove over to the Harvard Business School.

As a student at HBS, Ruth started the Communication, Leisure (now Arts), & Entertainment Club. "At the time" she said, "there was no interest in broadcasting at HBS, nor was the broadcasting industry much interested in the school." As president of the CLE Club, Ruth was a sort of impresario: she encouraged the big networks—ABC, CBS, NBC—to interview on campus; she got major figures in the film and recording industries to speak as guests of the club. As for her own career, she was looking for a job in broadcasting:

> But the broadcasting offers weren't quite what I wanted. With an MBA I was going to be stuck in a finance job. Or in sales. I didn't want to sell *time*. I wanted something creative. And I was reluctant to move to New York. Besides, I'd made a deal with my husband: If he'd see me through the Business School, I'd take a local job that would support us, if necessary, while he quit his corporate job and set himself up as an independent technical consultant for the beer industry.

Graduating in the spring of 1975, at the bottom of an economic recession, Ruth took a job at United Brands, Boston, as Marketing Project Manager in a division of diversified groups. "At United Brands, which was formerly the United Fruit Company," she said, "my division included everything but bananas and meats." Six months later, she saw in the newspaper that the Avion Group, of Andover, Massachusetts, had reported good earnings. She knew the Chairman and CEO of Avion, Arthur Vinson: she had interviewed with him while seeking a summer job between her first and second years in the MBA program, and she had kept up occasional contact. She now wrote Vinson a letter of congratulations on Avion's profits. Shortly thereafter, Vinson called Ruth and invited her to lunch.

The Avion Group consisted of seven mail order companies which had all been acquired after achieving good individual success. These companies had flourished within Avion which had had spectacular growth. However, they were beginning to feel the effects of increased costs and competition in the mail order business. Each subsidiary company operated very independently, with a minimum of corporately-mandated financial controls. Now Vinson was examining better ways to coordinate and control the use of the company's resources. He and Edward Dowd, Avion's president and chief operating officer, were also particularly concerned that the group might be losing contact with their customers as they grew. He offered Ruth a new appointment: Director of Marketing.

AVION GROUP: MAIL ORDER COMPANIES

Ruth began work at Avion headquarters, a small office located north of Boston, with a variety of responsibilities. She wrote the annual report which covered the Group's seven mail order companies; she did market research and worked with the individual companies on special projects. She found she liked the mail order business:

> There was something about the whole mail order process that was fascinating to me. It was marketing—which I liked. It was communicating with your customer—which I liked. It was creative: nothing could be more creative than

putting together a catalog and writing the copy. And it was all very *measurable*. You mailed 250,000 catalogs. You knew exactly where each name came from. And you knew what the results were: which mailing list pulled, which didn't; which broke even, which made money. You advertised in certain magazines, and every ad was coded: you knew if it worked. I had heard the old advertising story: 50 percent of it works and 50 percent of it doesn't; the trouble is, we don't know which 50 percent. In mail order, you *do* know which 50 percent is working.

Mail order businesses particularly, and many small businesses in general, tend to be "mom-and-pop"—or just mom, or just pop—businesses. They start small, stay in the family, and some are very successful. Before costs got so high, you could place a mail order business almost anywhere in the country; you could take it with you to a retirement community. All of the mail order companies that Avion acquired had this profile. They had been started by a family or an individual, they were located in odd resort areas, and the ones now within Avion had done very well.

But the owners didn't care about customer profiles. They were making money, they were living where they wanted, they employed their relatives. When Avion came along to buy their companies, they got a fair amount of money or stock and usually stayed on for a time as president to run the operation. Avion would help them augment their management team, but Avion's strategy was not to meddle with a successful, ongoing company. (Arthur Vinson felt this "hands off" attitude was one of Avion's greatest strengths in acquiring the most desirable companies.) Even after control might be transferred to a "professional manager," the prior owners were very concerned with maintaining the characters of their old companies. The same management techniques and procedures were very often left in place. If they hadn't needed market research before, why did they need it now?

When I took the job with Avion, it was Arthur's point of view that the time had come—competition was increasing—to learn more about who our customers were: why they were buying and why they were not buying. And so I began to work with the individual companies on developing customer profiles—demographic and psychographic analyses. One of the things we discovered was that many people who buy by mail have a lot of hobbies, and one hobby that kept coming up in our analysis was gardening.

Another concern of mine at Avion was to see what I could do to make use of the assets of all these individual companies. Each company maintained its own mailing list, each maintained its own warehouse, each negotiated with a printer for the production of catalogs—all very expensive items. There were so many ways to gain efficiencies. To compare mailing lists, for example: Wouldn't it be useful to know who the really serious mail order customers were—people who might be buying from (say) three of Avion's seven companies? What about a coordinated effort in the mailing of all catalogs? And warehousing: What kind of savings could be had in a centralized warehouse and shipping operation, with a single computer to do it all? These were the sorts of questions I was exploring at headquarters. And my market research seemed to suggest an idea, to identify an opportunity for making something more out of our assets: to do a gardening catalog.

THE GARDENING CATALOG

In April 1978, some two years and four months after she had begun working at Avion, Ruth scheduled a meeting with Arthur Vinson and Ed Dowd. It was a relatively informal meeting in Vinson's office, but Ruth as usual came prepared. Her "pitch" was simple: *Given* a strong interest in gardening in the customer profiles of Avion companies, and *since* the assets were available (the mailing lists and off-season warehouse facilities), *therefore* it seemed obvious that Avion should try a gardening catalog. In particular, a catalog of "unusual, aesthetic accessories for the affluent gardener—*not* the necessities (they have those)—but exotica that would appeal to the well-to-do suburban housewife 'who has everything' and enjoys showing off her garden."

In her presentation, Ruth demonstrated some product samples, suggested some catalog names, pointed out the benefits to Avion of using existing resources to create something new, and addressed the question: Why Would We Succeed?

— We know our customers are interested in the products.
— We know our customers are mail order buyers.
— We know our customers have the money.
— We have the opportunity for a unique promotional effort, by using each Avion company to introduce the catalog to the customers on its mailing list.

Her research had shown "virtually nonexistent" competition, while considerable interest did exist in magazines on gardening. She then addressed the question: Why would Avion Company presidents cooperate?

— Because a successful Avion Group overall is best for each individual company. They see that more and more.
— Because we could set up a system where each company would get credited for some percent of profits or sales relative to the number of the company's mailing list of names used.
— Because eventually this operation would be a source of new names for all companies, too.

Ruth described the catalog, the sourcing of inventory, the use of an agency to produce the catalog, together with costs for photography, printing, and mailing at various levels. Then she described how resources available within Avion could be used for mailing lists, fulfillment, warehousing, and order processing. She emphasized the capacity of one Avion company to handle the effort during its slow season (January and following) and the fact that there should be no inventory obsolescence with such a nonfashion product line. Finally, she provided "likely" and "worst" case projections, with mailing schedules and time tables (see Second Presentation, below, and exhibits). And, of course, she proposed that she be the one to look into the idea, to see what the possibilities were.

Vinson and Dowd "loved it," she said:

> They loved the name ("Avant Gardener"), the idea, the samples. They saw advantages of the plan on Wall Street—for many years the whole point of Avion was to go public, and here was an opportunity to say, "Look! We've always been seven separate companies and see how we've created even more value out of existing resources." And they saw the sheer fun of it: life at headquarters was boring; there was nothing to touch, only reports.
>
> I saw a chance to get into line management, to get my hands dirty and to do something. They told me to go ahead and work on the idea, so I went back to my office and said to myself, "Great, but now what do I do? I don't know beans about starting a catalog!"

Without extra staff and without spending an inordinate amount of money (she had Vinson and Dowd's enthusiastic support of the idea, but no specific budget), Ruth worked for several months on a gardening catalog, in addition to her other duties. She registered catalog names, put together possible layouts, subscribed to industry magazines (*Nursery Business, Landscape News, Hardware Merchandising*, and the like), and researched merchandise sources in the catalog collection of the Massachusetts Horticultural Society and in visits to New England nurseries:

> It was a small office environment. I tend to get very enthusiastic about things, and when a new sample product for the catalog would come in, everyone would know about it.
>
> I think Arthur and Ed were perfectly pleased by the way things were going. And yet, when it really came to the point that I was actually going to do it, there was the feeling that since Avion had never started a company from scratch, it probably couldn't be done. So they kind of watched to see what I was doing. And, after a few months, when it looked, by God, like "she" was going to do it, everybody watched more carefully what was happening here. Is this what they wanted? They'd never started a company before; they'd always bought existing companies. What was the risk? The economy was soft. In other words, this was serious.
>
> Because it had a slow spring season, we were planning for Avion's Curtains/Curtains company to provide most of the operational support. James Blevins was the C/C president. In the middle of the summer I started to approach Arthur: "Don't you think it's time that we or you go to Worcester to set this up with James? There's a lot to be done." And Arthur would say, "Yes, I'll handle it. Let me handle it."
>
> As the weeks passed, Arthur didn't seem to be making much progress setting me up with C/C. When I'd ask, he'd say, "I'm working on it, thinking about it." He kept coming to me with a lot of negatives: "What about the fact that 90 percent of new companies fail? What about the difficulties of starting a new business, of getting mailing lists to work?" I heard through the grape-

vine that one of the other company presidents had told Arthur, "She cannot do it. It cannot be done."

I continued planning the first catalog. It would be small—60 or so items on 16 pages. I talked to a computer guy who was involved in maintaining existing company mailing lists. We were not going to spend any money on outside lists. We would take 50,000 names from each of several of the companies and print the catalog in different versions, each linked to the company from which we were getting the list. My plan was to have each company president introduce the catalog to his customers in a letter—like introducing a friend.

During the last months of the summer, Ruth sensed that at least some of the company presidents were quietly disparaging her plan. It appeared to her that the objections involved both her lack of operating skills and the encroachment into their operations that such a new venture implied.

In mid-August, things started to change. Arthur started asking, "Well, if we're really going to do it, maybe it should just be a division of Jane Gannon?" This was the shoe catalog subsidiary run by Arthur's cousin—the very president who had been most vocal in bringing up problems. On the one hand, his cousin didn't think it was a good idea. But if we were going to do it, it might as well be one of his companies. To that, I said NO.

Arthur asked Ruth to present her plan on September 2 to Avion's top management and a number of the key company presidents.

SECOND AND FINAL PRESENTATION TO AVION

I felt the deck was stacked and that the chances of my coming out of that meeting with a catalog were very very slim. Something had happened in the preceding two weeks, in the tone of discussions. I just knew that my back was up against the wall. When I left the house that morning I said to my husband, I feel I'm making a "Give me liberty or give me death!" speech.

Ruth knew all of the executives who attended her presentation. She had worked with them and their companies as corporate Director of Marketing developing customer profiles and helping with promotional literature. Those very profiles had identified their customers' high interest in gardening. But the idea of a gardening catalog—and a new and separate company that would use these companies' resources—would be a new direction for Avion. Ruth had her work cut out for her.

She began by pointing out the popularity of gardening in the United States and by showing various gardening magazines and recent big coverage of the subject in such weeklies as *People*: gardening had become a hobby in Hollywood's backyards and on Park Avenue's rooftops. She reviewed her market research: 62 percent of Avion's mail order customers showed an interest in gardening. And then she put the question:

How do we derive the best advantage of this information for the Avion Group?

And the answer:

By cross-utilizing this information—and the resources that we now have—to *create something new:* a gardening catalog; something that would be most beneficial to the Avion Group as a whole.

She introduced the name "Avant Gardener" and presented logos and catalog page-spreads designed by an advertising agency. She showed some sample products and identified the target audiences: the suburban indoor and outdoor gardener, and the urban indoor, patio, and rooftop gardener: primarily the 35–60 age group (and female). She discussed the lack of competition for this very special sort of tools and accessories catalog:

There are many seed and nursery catalogs, but nothing quite like what we're looking at—a catalog with attractive, useful, unusual products that gardeners could use immediately, inside and outside their homes. There is a real market niche that hasn't been filled and *we* can fill it.

Then she reviewed the reasons for probable success that she had given in her first presentation to Vinson and Dowd five months earlier. Since that time, she had worked hard on product sourcing and plans for catalog production, and now she presented her findings that:

1. Although there is no established "gardening accessories" trade show or showroom, I believe that we have successfully sourced the catalog, with many exclusive items, unique items, and useful items.
2. Catalog production is being worked out with Doane Associates, a Boston company, which has done very fine work for two of our companies. They have strong experience in direct mail (12 years) and we have confidence in their abilities. (They are optimistic about the results of this mailing.)

It was now time to discuss fulfillment and warehousing. From her staff position it was clear to Ruth that some of Avion's companies were carrying costly and nonproductive overhead in the mid-winter and early spring months. Their warehouses were, simply, idle in this period; and rising costs were a problem. She looked particularly at Curtains/Curtains, one of the companies with heavy fall and pre-Christmas business: it didn't stock its inventory until mid-summer; much of its inventory was new annually and subject to changing fashion and fresh appeal in the fall catalog; its February sales were a small fraction of November activity.

This is why we are looking to Curtains/Curtains for participation and discussion this afternoon. Because the gardening catalog would be dropped (i.e., mailed) in early January, we felt that the counterseasonality to the C/C business cycle would be a plus both to the gardening catalog and to C/C's bottom line.

Before the meeting, Ruth had made calculations for a number of situations (see Exhibit 1). She now presented a selected series of projections (see Exhibit 2) using a range of assumptions. These projections were based on the following facts and ranges:

— The average price per item in the catalog (from item selections): $20.
— Number of items ordered from C/C catalog per order (historical):   1.5 average/order.
— Sizes of mailings (thousands of catalogs):   200, 300, 400.
— Response levels (including pessimistic 2 percent):   2, 3, 4 percent.
— Average order sizes: $30, $35, $40.
— Gross margin (calculated by Ruth):   55 percent.
— Catalog expense for 16 pages + postage (estimated by Doane Associates):   according to mailing size.
— Fulfillment costs (maximum for any of Avion's companies):   20 percent of sales.
— Inventory write-down (Ruth felt unlikely because of nature of merchandise: little obsolescence):   10 percent of sales at 40 percent markdown.

Ruth found the going rough:

Everybody had their guns out. They had pages of questions. "What if this happened and what if that happened? What if the economy weakens? What if your average order is low? What if the spring weather is bad?" And of course I did not have solid answers for any of these hypothetical issues. I had no guarantee of what the results would be.

It was a very tough meeting. No conclusion was reached. I left the room. People divided up. A couple of people went into Arthur's office—it was like a political caucus. I came back into the meeting and everybody was sort of saying, "Well . . ." That was it: there were a bunch of "Wells . . ." And nobody said anything. Then Arthur said, "Let's break up this meeting now." It was extraordinarily uncomfortable.

Nothing was said, and I finally went into Arthur's office: "May I talk to you?" "Yes," I closed the door and said, "I don't understand what's happening. Do we have a catalog or do we not?" People don't like being put on the spot like that. But I didn't care. It was extremely important to me. He was sitting at his desk and would not look at me. I said, "Arthur, you don't have to say anything: I know." "Well, you know, I mean, it's just . . . the risk; the economy's looking bad; this is not a good time on Wall Street." I asked if there was any recourse; should I argue? He said no and that was it.

Arthur was very smart. He sensed the overall displeasure of the division presidents with the catalog. Even if he let me proceed with one division, he felt he still would not have diffused the overall unhappiness. More important to him was to have a happy team. This plan had started at corporate; you couldn't hide the fact that it was a corporate-engendered idea.

I remember that day well—Thursday, September 2, my birthday.

Friday, Ruth reported to work as usual and kept an appointment she had with Doane Associates, the advertising agency, to talk about the catalog. She told them what happened. Ruth had worked very closely with them while developing her concept and plan and they had been very supportive. They were of course disappointed, but remained very enthusiastic about the idea and suggested that Ruth call them next week to talk things over.

The Labor Day weekend that followed was a trying time for Ruth. She and her husband had planned a get-away to Montreal prior to his entering the hospital on Wednesday for life-threatening surgery. She was upset and angry about the cancellation of her project, but didn't want to upset her husband before surgery by discussing the results of the meeting with him, nor bring up the growing idea of possibly starting the gardening catalog on her own. Yet this was September. In order to catch not just the season but the year—a one-season year for gardening accessories—she would have to have a catalog in the mail in January. To do that, she would have to begin right away. That meant she would have to talk to Arthur first thing next week. Ruth described her thoughts that weekend:

> I thought about it at length and I knew that I wanted to try to do the catalog now. That was the first time I ever felt that I wanted to have my own company. I would have been perfectly content running it for Avion or someone else. But I wanted to do this—this particular idea. I had put so much effort into it, and I thought it had such a good niche in the market. Somebody should grab it! I had been rebuffed. I was angry and hurt, and my confidence was shaken. But I believed in the idea. I thought, "Just because a $50 million company says no, it doesn't have to be no. I'll prove to them that I can do it."
>
> One way or the other, I really made the decision to leave Avion that weekend. I don't think that there ever was a question in my mind of whether I should simply stay at Avion and do what I had been doing 10 months before. That was one advantage of not having people dependent on you for a salary. I didn't feel guilty about not being able to feed three children. Or myself, for that matter. I also knew that I was a marketable commodity: I could get another job. But I knew that, long term, it wasn't simply that the project was canceled. Rather, I was being told: "Ruth, you cannot do any more original work. We want people who will do the routine stuff and won't get in anyone's way."
>
> The project was canceled and that fired me up. I had lost creative opportunity at Avion.

On Tuesday, September 7, 1978, Ruth went to see Arthur Vinson and said, "You know I'm disappointed. And I know you're not happy about the decision. If I can raise the money, do you mind if I take the idea and do it on my own?" Arthur said, "Sure. Go ahead and try it." There was no thought at that time of Ruth's not performing her regular duties at Avion, including the annual report due out in October. But she and Arthur agreed that she would be on her own schedule, in the office or at home.

CAN SHE DO IT ON HER OWN?

One of the first things Ruth did after Arthur gave her the okay was to get in touch with Doane Associates to let them know that she was going to try to do the gardening catalog herself. They thought that it was a great idea and agreed to work with her. They even said they knew some people who might be interested in backing such a company, and said they would check and let her know. Ruth also called various vendors who had sent her product samples at Avion: she told them that Avion would not be doing the catalog, but that she might be calling them soon about new developments. Her husband's surgery had been successful, although his recuperation would require that he not speak above a whisper for a month or more. He was very supportive of the idea:

> He was a wonderful adviser. We worked together. I was fortunate to have him to *think* with me. But there was so much to do. The timing was incredible. I had to rethink and adapt my plan: I could no longer use Avion's resources. I had to find the money and put together the whole operation simultaneously. And the clock was ticking.

Ruth began thinking about the areas of her plan that would be different as a separate operation:

— The catalog. This could be prepared and mailed entirely by a professional mailer. The unit cost would be $0.25 if one group handled the whole job—design, photography, typesetting, printing and binding, sorting, mailing and prepaid postage. This could be done by Doane Associates, but other firms were available.

— Mailing lists. She would no longer have the use of Avion's mailing lists, but in doing market research she had learned a good deal about mail order customers and the mailing list industry. She could rent lists of recent mail order customers through brokers and would have to mix and merge these lists. Because of duplicates, she would have to rent 10 percent more names than catalogs she would send. The names alone cost $0.07 each, but she did not know the cost of computer time for merging and processing the list tapes. It was necessary to eliminate the duplicate names and to code and print all mailing labels in order by zip code and sector (required by the Postal Service for bulk mailing). She did have some contacts in computer firms she had developed at Avion.

— Fulfillment and overhead. These costs were the big question mark. At Avion she could count on the C/C warehouse and the office at head-quarters. The operation expenses were known, and more importantly, shared. Ruth did know that the cost to fill an order ranged from $2 to $5 for the Avion divisions. Now she had to find her own warehouse and shipping facilities and supplies, an office and its furnishings, and provide for all sorts of other overhead costs: telephone, credit and charge card margins, communications and customer services, staff.

Ruth decided that she should plan on a 400,000 catalog mailing. To do this, she estimated that she would need $250,000. But clearly, in addition to beginning to look for financing, she would have to get to work on the computer processing, fulfillment, and overhead questions. Investors might be willing to accept more speculative sales projections, but they would certainly want to know that the operational estimates were sound.

Ruth reported her initiatives as follows:

I started to investigate the various choices. I talked to a few friends from business school. "How could Avion have done that?" they asked. "It's yours now. You've got to go out and do it yourself. This is your opportunity. Go out and sell it to another company: let someone else hire you to do the idea." I tried that. I spoke to a fair-sized mail order company that I knew through my husband's business. They were located in Vermont. Their business was counter-seasonal to mine, and I thought we might have a fit. They were interested, but I think that they were frightened because Avion had not gone ahead with it. They never said no. But they never said yes. And time kept passing. I contacted several other big mail order houses where there were people I knew through industry contacts at Avion. But it was difficult.

Of course, I was always worried that "they might take the idea" and do it without me. Avion itself could start up six months later. My husband does a lot of inventing and we always used to worry when he'd take an idea to a company. But if you sit back and worry about it all the time, you're going to keep the idea but never see it come to fruition. You've got to take the risk.

I knew that you're supposed to have an elaborate plan and strategy. I didn't. I essentially took what I had used at that last meeting at Avion and made it a little nicer, adding a narrative. I talked to a couple of banks. They were utterly discouraging. I was looking for money and leads, but all I had was an idea. I was asking about anything and everything: I really wanted to get a feel for what was possible. I was asking for advice and was ready to talk with anyone who I thought would be helpful.

I had resolved that I would not approach anyone who had a financial connection with Avion—any of the venture capital people, any of their bankers. But I did keep in touch with Doane Associates and they introduced me to some people with private money to invest, in mid-September. They were three people acting as a group: a dentist, a lawyer, and the owner of a small business. They knew a little about mail order and knew that the Doane agency was very enthusiastic about what I had. I gave my "pitch" and provided some financial projections. They said they'd get back to me.

Meanwhile, I started to talk with some venture capital people in Boston. Greylock was the only big one: I knew somebody who knew somebody there. I also found a smaller venture capital group that was part of a stock brokerage firm that my husband and I used. These people were very nice, but in Boston high tech was the big thing. They weren't negative, but they were not encouraging. I didn't really have anything to show. What was there to invest in? Everybody's reaction was the same, voiced slightly differently: We can't invest in an idea, unless it's a patented high tech idea. It was too early. I only had an idea, some drawings, some numbers. The risk was too high, they thought.

So I tried New York, a friend of ours. Two people working out of a small office in Manhattan, managing other people's money. They just had too many projects.

To make matters worse, I was not only saying to all these people that I wanted $250,000, but I was also saying that I wanted it next week, please. I had my momentum to guard, but the economy was beginning to look weak and a number of people told me to wait until things got better.

I never asked any friends to invest, although a number did come to me with, "I have $30,000 to invest" or "I have $50,000." I thought about it and was very touched, but decided no. The possibility was that I would lose the money for them—and the friendship was too important. But I did start talking to individuals who were interested in mail order, some from the industry contacts that I had made and some from a corporation where I had tried to place the idea. I had asked, "Well, do you know anyone on a personal basis who might be interested in investing in this idea? I think it's terrific," although there were many days when I no longer thought it was so terrific—I was becoming discouraged, and I was becoming frightened, too. Could I really do it? I put up a bold front.

When my husband and I went to a dinner party, I would talk about what happened. I had been rebuffed by people in the industry. It was an interesting story. Someone would say, "Well, wait a minute. I know a guy who just liquidated his mother's stock portfolio. Why don't you talk to him?" I talked to my accountant, personal lawyer, dentist, doctor, everybody I knew in a professional capacity. I asked for leads—and came up with a couple. They almost invested. I thought of running an ad in *The Wall Street Journal*, but wasn't gutsy enough. Every way I wrote the ad, I couldn't imagine that I would respond to it. All of the negatives that people had posed to me came up in my mind.

I didn't find that many serious leads. I ended up talking to several individuals and groups who were interested in mail order. Mail order has a kind of cachet, a special excitement. Part of this interest is unfortunate; people think it's an easy business. Send out a catalog, and orders just pour in. You can mail it anywhere, from your corner mail box, and people everywhere will buy from you. There's a personal "thing" about mail order that people like, which allowed me to get as many people interested in it as I did.

While she pursued financing, Ruth had to face the question of a warehouse and office. She started by looking for space that was both warehouse and, potentially, office. The search was discouraging: space that she thought she could afford was dark, unheated, rat-infested, and without shelving. She also remembered that some of her merchandise would be heavy and shipped in on pallets: What would she do about forklift trucks—and the people to run them? She thought, "There must be a better way," and decided to pursue an office location separate from a warehouse.

I knew I couldn't subject myself to working in a dungeon. I'd get so depressed I wouldn't be able to work. One of the things I never liked about working at Avion was driving up to Andover every day. There are a few concessions you sort of allow yourself, and mine was to be in the city. I dislike the suburbs. So I started to look for office space in the city and found rents at all levels. I decided to try to get in one building in Copley Square, where I wanted to be. I managed to negotiate the rent down to practically nothing, but would have to sign a lease soon. Then I went to look for some sort of warehousing.

I called every single public warehouse in the greater Boston area to see whether they would simply let us use part of their space. They all thought I was crazy. It had never been done before. Finally, I was speaking to a friend who had graduated from HBS. She was doing warehousing for a company and said, "The warehouse that I use is hungry. They just lost a large account. And, by the way, they're smart. Why not give them a call?" I called the owner and explained what I wanted to do, something like this:

— I was a little mail order company, but there were a lot of mail order companies in New England. It made perfect sense for him to offer me a warehousing and shipping service and, once he did, the others were potential customers.
— He would receive merchandise from my vendors and store it.
— Daily, I would provide him with shipping orders for individual customers, together with typed shipping labels.
— Promptly he would make up the packages, using wrapping materials I would supply and which he would have stored with my merchandise.
— He would ship the packages out daily, via United Parcel Service (under contract to me), recording each package in the UPS log: order number, name and address, zip code, shipping zone, weight.
— I would pay him for each shipped package, at a flat rate.

The fellow was intelligent. He knew exactly what I wanted, and the timing was such that he responded positively. It would be a clean business for him, and he loved getting involved in a whole new thing. I wouldn't have to worry about storage costs, rent, staff, or utilities when my business was down; when my business was up, he would put on another person. I remembered that it cost the Avion divisions from $2 to $5 to fill an order, depending on the company. Before I sat down with him, face to face, I figured on starting at the $2 level and going from there. Actually, I started well under $2. You can sit across the table from someone and say, "I can't do it any other way. I can pay you $1.65 an order and no more. That's it." That really goes a long way, if they care; if they want the business and they care about helping you get started. I got a lot of mileage out of reminding people what it's like to get started, of making them *want* to help a struggling little company make it.

A week after her first meeting with the group of professional men that Doane Associates had introduced to her, Ruth got a phone call: "We would like you to meet with our accountant." It was late September, and by then Ruth had been in constant touch with her lawyer, trying to price the deal, to work out the percentages. Originally, she wanted to give up no equity—just to have loans. But people weren't excited: they wanted a "piece of the action." She hadn't yet talked price with the professional group, but with other parties she had found the range of equity expected to be 30–60 percent. She felt that since it was her idea and since she would be doing all the work, she had to hang on to at least 51 percent of the business plus a salary.

The accountant liked Ruth and said openly to the group, "She's a good investment." It wasn't a casual comment, and it confirmed for her what she had heard in talking with venture capital people: that they would really be betting on her since all she had was an idea. And this sense of her being "okay," a sort of "member of the group," led naturally to the notion that since there were four of "us," each would take 25 percent of the equity. Ruth let the discussion flow, without for the moment resisting the notion of 25 percent equity for her, for she wanted to see how they viewed the salary question. She decided to play a big card: "I want the salary I was making when I left Avion." "What?" said the accountant. "I never met a broad in my life worth that much money!" She listened quietly; she didn't react with anger—he had tried to make a clumsy joke. But she made it clear: she was willing to negotiate on what the salary would be, but 51 percent of the company would be hers. It was her idea and that was not negotiable. But she would put up 25 percent of the $200,000 they were actually discussing.

> As their demands became clear, I formulated my response to their demands. My husband and I had agreed that we would put up 25 percent. Neither I nor my husband thought that we could do it all by ourselves. We didn't know what the company would end up generating. The risk was too great. And there were two big questions: my self-confidence and my knowledge. There was the nagging question: Was Avion right? Did they just know something more than I did? We would never put in more than we could safely lose.

Over several meetings in a very short period of time, Ruth and the investors outlined basic terms of a possible agreement:

— Ruth would retain 51 percent of the equity, the group 49 percent.
— Ruth would accept considerably less salary than she had been making at Avion, and nothing initially.
— The investors would put up $150,000, Ruth $50,000.

— Ruth would hire Doane Associates to do the catalog.
— The investors would commit to a second round of financing of $20,000 each under the following conditions:
  • Unanimous judgment that the company needed it.
  • That it would be put to proper use.
  • That it would allow the continuance of operations.

> The meetings had come down to, "Well, now what?" I was raring to go; they were raring to wait. They had all the time in the world; I had no time. It was very frustrating.

SHOULD SHE DO IT?

Ruth now thought of her catalog as "Gardener's Eden." No matter what she called it, it was certainly no bed of roses. In the last weeks of October, Ruth felt she could put off some major decisions no longer. She reviewed what she had learned and what her situation now was.

She knew from her experience at Avion that superb service was fundamental to success: fast response to orders, having the merchandise in the warehouse, and having an excellent customer service department to handle problems and complaints. She had learned much about what it would take to create an operation that could establish her business and translate these precepts into action. She had to deal with an overwhelming number of questions:

— United Parcel Service: At first, when Ruth was considering the rental or purchase of a warehouse, UPS wanted to sell her some $4,000 worth of scales and other shipping equipment. Now that she had solved the warehouse problem, UPS still was asking for a $2,000 deposit for their service.
— New England Telephone and Boston Edison: Both wanted deposits of $500 for business service.
— Credit and charge card service: Master Card and Visa merchant service was offered through local banks and each was asking for 4 percent off the top; American Express was a single nationwide service and was asking for a 5.25 percent fee. Ruth asked around and found that the MC and Visa rates were variable, ranging from 3 percent up, dependent on sales volume and the bank. AMEX was less negotiable.
— Bad checks/bad credit cards: Ruth had heard about this problem at Avion. She asked some industry contacts for their experience and found that a 2–3 percent loss was common.
— Phone orders: Not knowing how many orders would come over the phone, she asked around: 5–10 percent without toll free service. She knew she couldn't afford an 800 number, but also found that free inward calling meant more complaints and information-seekers.

— Mail: If she leased the office in Copley Square, she would be facing 1:00 P.M. mail delivery—impossible for a mail order business. The Post Office asked a big fee for allowing patrons to make their own early pickup. A box would be out of the question: there would be too much mail.

— Office furniture: She would have to find all the furniture and equipment she had taken for granted at Avion on her own.

— Vendors and inventory: There were many growing mail order companies in 1978. Some of her potential suppliers were beginning to back away now that Ruth was no longer at Avion. She would have to aggressively go after shipping commitments and negotiate terms.

A company like Avion often ordered one third of the expected volume of an item initially, and reordered after two or three weeks of response to the catalog. Some vendors preferred orders for the entire expected quantity of an item, with partial deliveries staggered throughout a season. If the item didn't sell as well as expected, the later deliveries could be canceled without penalty. Some would deliver to an established company before a season (for example, December) and would allow payment well into the season (for example, April). Others wanted payment in 30 days. However, Avion's banker had warned Ruth that vendors would demand cash up front from a new company.

There did appear to be special attractions for a gardening catalog. While at Avion, Ruth had discovered that some gardening suppliers would welcome early shipments of their merchandise for a mail order catalog since normal retail shipments came four months later.

— Dun & Bradstreet: D&B wanted to interview her for a credit rating: they had had inquiries.

— Supplies: Ruth had to find and select cartons, packing material, tape, labels, etc.

— The catalog: Putting together the catalog would be a big task. Time was short. She could use Doane Associates, but could probably save a good deal of money by contracting the production of the catalog by herself—the photographer, designer, order form designer, and printer.

— Mailing lists: Ruth would have to contract soon for the use of mailing lists and for the computer time to merge them and to produce the labels. In the one-time use of a group of mailing lists, one must mail at a certain time so as not to conflict with other mailing contracts. That day had to be in early January. (Companies selling lists usually seed them with dummy names and addresses going to their own locations to help identify unauthorized use.)

Established companies received the names about 60 days before a mailing date and were expected to pay for use of the lists 30 days after mailing. However, Ruth had been told to expect a demand for cash up front here, too.

— Staff: How long could she continue alone?

Ruth was also still uncertain about how much money she really needed. At Avion, she could count on known historical response levels, using known customer mailing lists. Gardener's Eden would be an unknown company using a variety of rented mailing lists, mixed and merged for the first time. List brokers and Doane Associates felt a 1.4 percent response level might be more realistic. Ruth felt that she would therefore need a mailing of 400,000 to give her a secure customer base for future mailings. She calculated she could get by with such a 400,000 catalog mailing, a 1.4 percent response rate, and a $30 average order. These assumptions were less optimistic than those she had used in estimating a need for $250,000. However, it would not be unusual for a new mail order operation to run at a loss for the first few mailings. On the other hand, she no longer had to include direct warehouse expenses.

So far, her financing choice was limited: the three professional men said they would do the deal under the terms they had negotiated. Besides the fact that this would only result in $200,000 for the business, these three investors were not really professionals at dealing with fledgling companies. Ruth was not sure how well they would work together with her or among themselves.

Should Ruth leave her job, sink $50,000 into the venture, and do it? Should she stop and wait until she found a more perfect match? Some of her relatives were saying, "Wait a year. Go to other mail order companies. The ones you've talked to are stodgy New Englanders. Why not take the show on the road?" Her husband was steady and supportive. But in addition to enthusiasm for an idea, did she have enough knowledge and skill to make it happen?

EXHIBIT 1
Rough Profit Calculations for the Gardening Catalog—8/17/78

Mail 350,000 @ 2 percent response = 7,000 orders

× $30 average order =	$210,000	sales
	105,000	50% GM
−	95,000	catalog expense
$2 per order −	15,000	fulfillment
−	15,000	other
	$(20,000)	contribution
10% inventory write-down	(8,400)	
Adjusted contribution =	$(28,400)	

× $35 average order =	$245,000	sales
	122,500	50% GM
−	95,000	catalog expense
−	15,000	fulfillment
−	15,000	other
	$ (2,500)	contribution
10% inventory write-down	(9,800)	
Adjusted contribution =	$(12,300)	

Mail 350,000 @ 2.5 percent response = 8,750 orders

× $35 average order =	$306,250	sales
	153,125	50% GM
−	95,000	catalog expense
−	17,500	fulfillment
−	15,000	other
	$(25,625)	contribution
10% inventory write-down	(12,200)	
Adjusted contribution =	$ 13,425	

Mail 350,000 @ 3 percent response = 10,500 orders

× $30 average order =	$315,000	sales
	157,500	50% GM
−	95,000	catalog expense
−	21,000	fulfillment
−	15,000	other
	$ 26,000	contribution
10% inventory write-down	(12,600)	
Adjusted contribution =	$ 13,400	

× $40 average order =	$420,000	sales
	210,000	50% GM
−	95,000	catalog expense
−	21,000	fulfillment
−	15,000	other
	$ 79,000	contribution
10% inventory write-down	(16,800)	
Adjusted contribution =	$ 62,200	

EXHIBIT 1 (*concluded*)

Mail 400,000 @ 2 percent response = 8,000 orders

× $30 average order	=	$240,000	sales
		120,000	50% GM
	−	100,000	catalog expense
$2 order	−	16,000	fulfillment
	−	15,000	other
		$(11,000)	contribution
10% inventory write-down		(9,600)	
Adjusted contribution	=	$(20,600)	

× $35 average order	=	$280,000	sales
		140,000	50% GM
	−	100,000	catalog expense
	−	16,000	fulfillment
	−	15,000	other
		$ 9,000	contribution
10% inventory write-down		(11,200)	
Adjusted contribution	=	$ (2,200)	

Mail 400,000 @ 2.5 percent response = 10,000 orders

× $35 average order	=	$350,000	sales
		175,000	50% GM
	−	100,000	catalog expense
	−	20,000	fulfillment
	−	15,000	other
		$ 40,000	contribution
10% inventory write-down		(14,000)	
Adjusted contribution	=	$ 26,000	

Mail 400,000 @ 3 percent response = 12,000 orders

× $30 average order	=	$360,000	sales
		180,000	50% GM
	−	100,000	catalog expense
	−	24,000	fulfillment
	−	15,000	other
		$ 41,000	contribution
10% inventory write-down		(14,400)	
Adjusted contribution	=	$ 26,600	

× $40 average order	=	$480,000	sales
		240,000	50% GM
	−	100,000	catalog expense
	−	24,000	fulfillment
	−	15,000	other
		$101,000	contribution
10% inventory write-down		(19,200)	
Adjusted contribution	=	$ 81,800	

EXHIBIT 2
Projections Presented September 2, 1978

	200,000 Mailing			400,000 Mailing			600,000 Mailing		
Response: 2 percent									
Average order	$30	$35	$40	$30	$ 35	$ 40	$ 30	$ 35	$ 40
Contribution [$000]	(31)	(24)	(16)	(12)	1	15	1	22	44
Response: 3 percent									
Average order	$30	$35	$40	$30	$ 35	$ 40	$ 30	$ 35	$ 40
Contribution [$000]	(9)	2	13	30	51	73	66	98	130
Response: 4 percent									
Average order	$30	$35	$40	$30	$ 35	$ 40	$ 30	$ 35	$ 40
Contribution [$000]	13	27	41	73	102	131	130	174	216

	200,000 Mailing								
Response	2%			3%			4%		
Average order	$ 30	$ 35	$ 40	$ 30	$ 35	$ 40	$ 30	$ 35	$ 40
Sales [$000]	120	140	160	180	210	240	240	280	320
Gross margin @ 55%	66	77	88	99	116	132	132	154	176
Catalog expense including postage [$000]	74	74	74	74	74	74	74	74	74
Fulfillment and overhead @ 15% of sales [$000]	18	21	24	27	32	36	36	42	48
Write-down 10% of sales @ 40% markdown [$000]	5	5	6	7	8	9	9	11	13
Contribution [$000]	(31)	(24)	(16)	(9)	2	13	13	27	41

	400,000 Mailing								
Response	2%			3%			4%		
Average order	$ 30	$ 35	$ 40	$ 30	$ 35	$ 40	$ 30	$ 35	$ 40
Sales [$000]	240	280	320	360	420	480	480	560	640
Gross margin @ 55%	132	154	176	198	231	264	264	308	352
Catalog expense including postage [$000]	100	100	100	100	100	100	100	100	100
Fulfillment and overhead @ 15% of sales [$000]	36	42	48	54	63	72	72	84	96
Write-down 10% of sales @ 40% markdown [$000]	10	11	13	14	17	19	19	22	25
Contribution [$000]	(12)	1	15	30	51	73	73	102	131

EXHIBIT 2 (*concluded*)

				600,000 Mailing					
Response		2%			3%			4%	
Average order	$ 30	$ 35	$ 40	$ 30	$ 35	$ 40	$ 30	$ 35	$ 40
Sales [$000]	360	420	480	540	630	720	720	840	960
Gross margin @ 55%	198	231	264	297	347	396	396	462	528
Catalog expense including postage [$000]	129	129	129	129	129	129	129	129	129
Fulfillment and overhead @ 15% of sales [$000]	54	63	72	81	95	108	108	126	144
Write-down 10% of sales @ 40% markdown [$000]	14	17	19	21	25	29	29	33	38
Contribution [$000]	1	22	44	66	98	130	130	174	216

Case 3-3

HEATHER EVANS

It was May 10, 1983, and Heather Evans' graduation from Harvard Business School was less than a month away. Although she had just taken the last of her final exams that morning, Heather's thoughts could not have been further from school as she boarded the Eastern shuttle and headed back to New York. The trip was a familiar one, for Heather had been commuting between school and Manhattan in an attempt to get her dress company off the ground.

Many of the elements of the business were falling into place, but the securing of $250,000 in financing remained elusive. Her business plan had been in the hands of potential investors for over a month now, and her financing group was simply not coming together. Her contact at Arden & Co., a New York investment firm and hoped-for lead investor, was not even returning her phone calls. A number of small, private investors had been stringing along for some weeks, but whenever Heather tried to go that next step and negotiate specific financing terms with any one of them, the rest of the group seemed to move further away. Heather expressed her frustration:

> I was really counting on Arden & Co. to be my lead investor; this would lend both credibility to the deal and give me *one* party to negotiate terms with. Then I could go to these private investors, point to the deal I'd struck with Arden and say, "These are the terms—make a decision."

Now, if I give each of these investors what they want, I'll end up giving the company away. But I do need the money, and fast. In order to get out a holiday (winter) line, I need to start placing orders for fabric in the next month. All this, in addition to the rent and salaries I'm committed to.

I don't know whether I should stick with the private investors I have and somehow try to hammer out a deal; or really work on getting a venture firm as a lead investor—maybe there is still a chance of bringing Arden & Co. around. Maybe I should try to get less money, or move back my timetable and wait for spring to introduce a line.

HEATHER EVANS

Heather Evans graduated from Harvard College in 1979, having earned her philosophy degree in three years. A Phi Beta Kappa graduate, Heather had been a working model throughout her college career, appearing in such publications as *Mademoiselle*, *Seventeen*, and *GQ*. (See Exhibit 1.)

Heather applied to the Harvard Business School during her senior year, and was accepted with a two-year deferred admit to the class entering in 1981. She accepted a position with Morgan Stanley as a financial analyst. Heather explained the origin of her interest in a business career:

My father is an attorney with a Wall Street firm and many of my parents' friends were "deal-makers" who had gone to the Business School. I thought that I would like that kind of work and the lifestyle that went along with it. In addition, my career as a model gave me a taste of running my own business— the independence, the travel, the people—and I loved it. I knew, though, that I would need a good solid background to gain the skills and credibility necessary for success.

I thought that working for an investment bank like Morgan Stanley would give me the technical and financial training that I would need during my career.

Heather left Morgan Stanley and began her two years at HBS with her basic orientation unchanged:

I was still focused primarily on a deal-making, venture-capital type of career. I had always been interested in the fashion business, and thought that I might, at some point, financially back a designer. I decided to work on Seventh Avenue for the summer, and got a job as the assistant to Jackie Hayman, president of a woman's clothing company.

Heather saw the business and financial side of the business as well as the design and marketing aspects:

I was convinced and confident that I could run a business like this. That summer was actually the first time I believed that business school education had much value at all. I was able to understand the business very well, and my education and experience allowed me to grasp the fundamental issues quickly.

Heather returned to HBS in September, committed to starting her own venture in the garment industry.

THE EVOLUTION OF HEATHER EVANS INCORPORATED

Heather began by defining the concept of the company and its product line. Based on her experience in investment banking and at business school, Heather was convinced that the current mode of business dress for women—primarily suits—was, in fact, ill-suited to the demands and desires of businesswomen. Heather conceived a line of dresses in natural and wear-worthy fabrics which would better meet these women's needs (see business plan for full description).

In September, she began working with Robert Vin, an assistant designer in New York, in an attempt to transfer her concepts to finished design sketches and patterns. By November, it was clear to Heather that this arrangement was not going to work out; she decided that she would be both the chief designer and operating manager of her firm. Although it was an extremely untraditional approach to a start-up in the garment business, Heather reasoned that it would make more sense for her:

> First, I didn't get along that well with Robert on a personal level. More important, though, I found myself doubting both his design sense and my own ability to judge someone else's design sense. Fundamentally, I had more trust in myself and my abilities as a designer.

Thus was Heather Evans Incorporated born.

Heather spent November and December flying between Boston and New York, and developing, in further detail, her concept of the business. By December, Heather had put together a plan of action which she submitted for approval as a field study (see Exhibit 2). After her first-semester exams ended, Heather moved to New York. She scheduled all of her classes on Monday and Tuesday and planned to spend the rest of her time in New York getting the key elements of her business in place.

Staff

Heather decided that the first person she needed was an assistant designer. "I wanted someone who had the technical training and experience in design that I lacked. I needed someone who knew more about design than I did, but who didn't mind working for me as an assistant."

Heather interviewed several individuals, and in early February offered the position to Belinda Hughes, who had served as an assistant designer with two major firms. Heather began paying Belinda (out of her own pocket) to do free-lance work based on detailed discussions with

Heather about the content of the line, with the promise that full-time employment would begin in April or May.

Heather also began looking for a pattern-maker: someone who could transform a sample dress into specifications and a design for production.

Heather asked several industry acquaintances, and a vice president at Marjori (a major fashion manufacturer) recommended Barbara Tarpe. Heather called Barbara and the two hit it off. During their meeting, Barbara indicated that she would like an equity position in the company. Heather thought that Barbara could make a significant contribution, and that her request was reasonable. Heather genuinely liked Barbara and thought that she would make a good partner.

One week later, before proceeding further, Heather decided to call another friend in the industry who might know Barbara.

> Martin is an old friend, and I trust his judgment; he told me that Barbara was a terrible liar and had no real talent. I looked back at my original notes after our meeting: "Very good rapport with Barbara. She seems *HONEST*. Feel she can run entire inside of business." I didn't hire Barbara and was shocked at how wrong I could be about someone. I had always felt comfortable trusting my own judgment.

Office and Showroom Space

Heather spent countless afternoons scouring New York's garment district (around Seventh Avenue from 42nd to 34th Streets) for potential showroom, office and working space. Showroom space is very important, because store buyers visit here during the buying season to make their decisions.

> I decided that I needed about 1,500 square feet of space for an office, sample and pattern-making space, and a showroom. For $7 or $8 per square foot, I could get space in buildings which were somewhat off the main center of the district and which housed other relatively "unknown" designers. For $20–$25 per foot, I could be in a building which was more centrally located and which housed better-known firms.

By late February, Heather had decided to lease 1,500 square feet of space in a building at $10 per foot, for $1,500 per month.

Although the building was in a less desirable location, and would get less traffic from buyers than more expensive buildings, Heather reasoned that she should attempt to conserve as much cash as possible. Heather sent a deposit on this space, and would begin paying rent May 1.

A month later, an acquaintance in the garment business called and offered Heather space in 550 Seventh Avenue—the most prestigious building in the garment center, housing such designers as Ralph Lauren, Oscar de la Renta, and many other famous names. Heather would have her own office space, and would share the showroom space with another designer. Heather accepted his offer on the spot, even though she would have to start paying rent as of March 15, and the rent was $2,000, substantially more than the other building, and there was less space.

Financing

In the fall, Heather had begun talking informally with potential investors—friends at school and former colleagues in the investment banking and garment industry. She was hesitant, however, to do more than this until she had a business plan and a proposed deal.

Then in February, a friend and recent Business School graduate called to suggest that the two get together for a drink.

> Anne Snelling and I had both worked for Morgan Stanley and then gone on to the Business School. She had graduated one year earlier than I, and gone to work for Arden & Co. (a private investment bank). I assumed that our meeting would be social, but Anne was soon putting on the hard-sell for Arden, convincing me that they should do the whole deal. I was quite surprised, and pleased. Arden had an excellent reputation and their financing would be a "stamp of approval" on the deal.

Heather and Anne met once or twice during January and February, and Anne asked Heather to accompany her to Vail for a week of skiing over spring break the first week in March. Heather reasoned that it would be a wise move to go.

> I didn't really feel comfortable taking off for a week—I had an incredible amount to do. Yet, I was anxious for Arden's participation, so off to Vail I went. I was unsure whether Anne intended our week to be business or pleasure, but I brought along all of my papers, and was prepared to negotiate a deal.
>
> Once we got there, Anne said she wanted to talk about the deal, but was constantly on the phone pursuing other business. I came back to New York feeling pretty discouraged; we had never had a chance to really discuss my business.

Heather called Anne that next week and voiced her concern: time was running out, and Heather still had no clear idea where Arden or Anne stood on the issue.

> Anne suggested that we get together for dinner that evening and tie things up—I was relieved. But when I walked into the restaurant, Anne was sitting there with her sister, Susan, and Susan's fiancé. She apologized—they had just flown into the city and Anne had asked them to join us. I was livid.

At this point, Heather realized that the financing was not going to come as easily as she had hoped, and she began pushing some of her other potential investors to get a sense of their interest. She raced to finish the business plan (see Exhibit 3), and sent this out to Arden & Co. and 15 individual investors during the first week in April.

DOWN TO THE WIRE

During the month of April, the pace of Heather's efforts accelerated and the business began eating up more cash. Belinda's part-time salary was now running about $1,000 per month; rent was running $2,000 per month. Finally, Heather had begun shopping the fabric market and would soon have to order and pay for $3,000 worth of sample fabric.

Heather had already invested about $10,000 of her own funds in the business, and her remaining resources were dwindling quickly. Because of the timing of the cycles in the garment industry (see Exhibit 4) Heather would have a great many more expenses before any cash came back into the business; most significantly, she would have to pay for the fabric for the entire holiday line—about $40,000 worth.

Yet Heather was having a difficult time bringing the investor group together. Anne Snelling was not returning her phone calls, and the private investors were interested, but had made no firm commitments. Heather's major problem was trying to negotiate with all of these potential investors individually; without a lead investor, there was no one party to negotiate the terms of a deal with.

The process of raising funds was hampered by Heather's extremely busy schedule. Besides talking to retailers, working on designs, and getting settled in her new office space, Heather was still going to school during this time and exams were coming up. Heather commented on the strain:

> The spring semester was a rough one; trying to get my company started really took its toll. I had always considered myself a responsible student. I prepared about a half-dozen cases the entire semester, and only made it to half my classes. I felt badly about it, but I knew I had to do it to get my business going.

FINANCING OPTIONS

Heather had several options available, but knew that she did not have sufficient time to pursue them all.

Arden & Co.

Heather held out some hope that Arden was still interested in the deal. Perhaps if she really pushed for a commitment, Arden would come through.

Venture Capital Firms

Heather had spoken with one or two firms which had indicated some interest. She knew that starting fresh with people who were unfamiliar with the company, as well as dealing with the bureaucratic decision-making process, would take a great deal of time. In addition, Heather suspected that they might drive a harder bargain than private investors, but at this point she welcomed the opportunity to negotiate with anyone just to get an idea of what valuation to put on the company.

Helen Neil Fashions, Inc.

Heather had approached another small venture capital firm which had Helen Neil Fashions, Inc. in its portfolio of companies. Helen Neil herself was a proven designer, and the company had established a base of relationships with manufacturers and retailers. The company, however, lacked any real operating management. This venture firm had indicated an interest in financing Heather if she would ally herself with Helen Neil and essentially embark on a joint venture. This idea had not yet been broached with Helen Neil, however, and Heather knew that any deal was dependent on the approval of Helen and her company's management.

Private Investors

Heather had a pool of 20 or so private individuals who seemed interested in investing in the company. The problem here was the amount of time it took to negotiate with each of these people individually, and their diverse desires for the terms of the investment. Heather was unsure how to structure the deal to satisfy the divergent interests of these individuals whom she was fairly sure would invest under any reasonable set of terms. She had spoken to a small sample of these investors (see Exhibit 5) to get their point of view, but was hesitant to speak to any more investors before she could present them with a deal.

HEATHER'S REQUIREMENTS

Heather had given some thought to the different aspects of the deal and had decided that the following terms were important to her:

— Control of the company: Heather felt that she should be able to control over 50 percent of the equity, as well as have a majority of the voting control of the company.
— License of the name "Heather Evans": Heather felt that she had already expended considerable effort in building up her own name, and that if she left the company, she should have the right to use it.

— Ability to remain private: Heather did not want to be in a position where her investors could force her to become a public company. Liz Claiborne, a successful women's clothing company, had recently gone public, and potential investors were naturally excited by the returns inherent in a public offering. (See Exhibit 6 for excerpts from the Liz Claiborne prospectus.) Heather knew that she had to offer her investors some means of exit and getting a return on their investment.

With exams finally over, Heather could concentrate her full energies on pulling together her financial backing and getting the business off the ground.

EXHIBIT 1
Heather Evans Modeling One of Her Designs

EXHIBIT 2
Field Study Plan

The purpose of this project is to develop a business plan and a strategy for approaching investors for a women's designer clothing manufacturing company which I will form upon graduation from HBS. This company will offer high price, high quality dress and jacket combinations to executive women, ages 27 to 45.

The business plan will include:

I. A marketing plan, including an analysis of the relevant market, how I will position my product (in terms of price and image), and a retailing and promotion strategy.

II. A description of the organization, including people and physical plant.

III. Pro forma financial statements, based on sales projections from I, and operating costs from II.

IV. A financing proposal.

The attached time schedule outlines the process of putting together this plan. You will note that I have allotted substantial time to drafting and redrafting the plan, relative to research. This is because I have already spent a lot of time gathering information and find that I now need to organize that information in order to see what is missing. I will, however, spend the first half of January meeting with department store buyers to refine my retailing strategy, which I recognize is weak.

The final product for my Independent Research Report (IRR) will be the business plan actually presented to investors and a broader strategic document describing how the plan fits into my investor strategy.

Field Study Project Schedule Week of:

December 13, 1982	— Settle issue of adviser for IRR.
	— Gather examples of business plans.
December 20	— Complete survey of existing market research and financial information on comparable companies. (Sources: Fairchild Publications' library; 10-Ks ordered from companies.)
December 27,	— Vacation.
January 3, 1983	— Prepare preliminary outline of plan.
	— Review outline with adviser.
	— Set up meetings with buyers from Filene's, Nieman's, Macy's, Bergdorf, Saks, Bloomingdales, Nordstrom, and others.
January 10 and 17	— Prepare first draft of plan Parts I and II.
	— Meet with buyers.
January 24 and 31	— Talk with various industry contacts to fill information "holes," especially regarding Part II of plan. E.g., salary levels for various employees, equipment needs and costs, and optimal showroom and design studio locations.
February 7	— Prepare second draft of plan, including detailed pro formas (Part III).
	— Begin interviewing candidates for design assistant, sales/PR director, and business manager positions. (These individuals should be named in the plan.)
February 14	— Review second draft with adviser.
	— Present plan to CPA for review.
	— Prepare list of potential investors and consider order of approach.
	— Select law firm.

EXHIBIT 2 (*concluded*)

February 21 and 28	— Select and recruit key employees.
	— Revise plan, Parts I–III.
	— Present revised plan to lawyer.
	— Explore financial structure alternatives with lawyer, adviser and others.
March 7	— Draft Part IV of plan.
	— Determine preferred investor group profile and strategy for approaching investors.
	— Select factor and discuss terms, to the extent appropriate at that point.
March 14, 21, 28	— Vacation.
April 4 and 11	— Meet informally with key investors.
	— Finalize plan.
April 18	— Distribute plan to potential investors.

EXHIBIT 3
Heather Evans Incorporated Business Plan, April 7, 1983 (*Confidential*)

TABLE OF CONTENTS

	Page
I. SUMMARY	1
II. CONCEPT	2
III. MARKET	4
IV. MANAGEMENT AND OPERATIONS	7
V. FINANCIALS	9
APPENDIXES	26

HEATHER EVANS INCORPORATED BUSINESS PLAN
I. SUMMARY

COMPANY HEATHER EVANS INCORPORATED, incorporated in New York on March 9, 1983, and located in New York City.

BUSINESS The Company will design, contract for the manufacture of, and market a line of clothing for professional women.

MANAGEMENT *Heather H. Evans, President and Designer*

Ms. Evans will graduate from Harvard Business School in June 1983. She has worked as assistant to the president of Catherine Hipp, a designer clothing firm; as a financial analyst at Morgan Stanley, an investment bank; and as a photographic model, with Ford Models.

– 1 –

EXHIBIT 3 (*continued*)

	Belinda Hughes, Assistant Designer Most recently, Ms. Hughes was head designer at Creations by Aria. For two years before that, after her graduation from Parsons School of Design, she worked as Mr. Kasper's assistant at Kasper for J.L. Sports.
CONCEPT	The Company will offer a " designer" line to fit the lifestyle of professional women. Based on her experience in investment banking and at business school, Ms. Evans has conceived a style of clothing, based primarily on dresses, which better fits the lifestyle and demands of businesswomen than the suits and other looks currently offered to them by existing clothing manufacturers.
STATUS	The Company has already begun designing its Holiday line, obtained showroom and studio space in a prestigious designer building, reserved production capacity in a high-quality factory, and arranged for credit with an apparel industry factor.
	In order to present its first line for the Holiday 1983 season, the Company must be assured financing prior to May 1983. The Company is seeking $250,000, to cover start-up expenses, to fund development of its first line, and to provide initial working capital. Thereafter, the Company anticipates that it will generate sufficient cash from operations which, together with normal industry factoring, will fund growth internally.
Legal Counsel: Accountants: Bank:	Kaye, Scholer, Fierman, Hays & Handler Rashba & Pokart Citibank

II. CONCEPT

HEATHER EVANS INCORPORATED aims to become a substantial apparel company. Its success formula is a combination of powerful elements:

—a new look,
—for an unmet and quickly growing market,
—promoted and sold by a unique individual, Heather H. Evans,
—within a professionally managed and controlled organization.

Ms. Evans recognized the need for a *new look* for professional women when she shopped for clothes to wear to her job at an investment bank. She found few clothes that fit the functional demands of her work, while having some "style." Since then, she has spoken with hundreds of professional women who voice the same complaint. They work in an environment that strictly defines what is considered appropriate; "Seventh Avenue" does not understand these women.

The HEATHER EVANS "look" will be based on dresses, worn with untailored or softly tailored jackets, with —

—a clean and elegant silhouette;
—distinctiveness through cut and line, without frills, excessive detail, or sexual suggestiveness;

- 2 -

EXHIBIT 3 (*continued*)

—undistracting colors, in solids or subtle patterns (e.g., Glen plaid or pin-stripe);
—comfortable fit;
—travel-worthy fabrics in all-natural fibers, such as silk-wool blends; and
—quality construction.

Dresses and jackets will be priced and sold separately, along with co-ordinated skirts and tops, as a *complete* line—

—to permit the customer to coordinate an entire workplace wardrobe from the line,
—to position the line in "sportswear" departments of department stores, which are more updated and better displayed than "dress" departments, and
—to avoid resistance to the high price tag of a combined outfit, from a customer who usually buys sportswear pieces.

Each collection will include 30 to 70 pieces, depending on the season, which is comparable to other complete designer sportswear lines. The Company will sell five collections: for the holiday, early spring, spring, transition, and fall seasons. These are the regular "sportswear" market periods.

Unlike most designer collections, which include many kinds of clothes for different activities and different times of day, the HEATHER EVANS collection will include only clothes appropriate for the conservative workplace. This focus is critical in establishing the confidence of upper-strata professional women in the "look" for officewear. Later, the Company can introduce other lines (e.g., leisurewear) under the HEATHER EVANS name, in order to benefit from its reputation and customer franchise.

HEATHER EVANS clothes will be sold through better department and specialty stores. The line will be marketed as "designer" clothing, but will be priced at the upper end of the "bridge" category, which is the next lower price category. The "bridge" category was born and grew dramatically with such lines as Liz Claiborne and Evan Picone, which targeted the flood of women into the workplace over the past decade; HEATHER EVANS will capitalize on the second stage of this demographic trend, as women become accepted in large numbers in better-paid, professional and managerial roles. Positioning the line at the top of the "bridge" category—

—will place the line in stores next to other lines currently bought by the target customer (e.g., Tahari, Harve Bernard, Nipon Collectibles), and
—responds to growing price resistance among customers, *but*
—permits the Company to create a quality garment, and
—develops the HEATHER EVANS label for future licensing potential.

Heather H. Evans:
Ms. Evans is uniquely qualified to develop and sell a new style of cloth-ing for conservative businesswomen. As a former investment banker and a graduate of Harvard Business School,

—she has lived the lifestyle of these women, knows their needs,
—she understands the limits of appropriateness within a formal office environ-ment, which Seventh Avenue designers, who have tried to capture this cus-tomer, clearly do not, and
—she can gain the confidence of the target customer through identification of her own background with their own lives.

EXHIBIT 3 (*continued*)

Moreover, as a former model, Ms. Evans has experience at projecting herself through the media and can attract publicity as a designer/personality. She will actively seek to publicize the Company in business media, as well as fashion media, to reach the target customer. She is currently working on stories about the Company with writers from *Vogue* and *Savvy*.
(Ms. Evans' resume is included as Appendix A.)

III. MARKET

HEATHER EVANS will initially position its products as designer clothing for the "formal" professional woman to wear to the office. Later, the Company can serve a virtually unlimited number of markets based on its reputation for quality and taste, as established through its original line of clothing.

PROFESSIONAL WOMEN'S CLOTHING

Target Market:
HEATHER EVANS will target the upper end of a subsegment of the working women's clothing market, identified as "formal professional" women in a 1980 market study by Celanese.
These women are an extremely attractive market because they are—

—a large, fast-growing group,
—with high disposable incomes,
—who are concentrated in metropolitan areas,
—where they buy at a select group of better department and specialty stores,
—with relative insensitivity to price,
—attention to quality,
—apparel brand loyalty,
—and *still-developing tastes and preferences in professional clothing.*

Celanese found the formal professional segment to be a well-defined purchasing group: it "includes accountants, lawyers, sales managers, executives and administrators who work in highly structured and formal environments. They can be characterized by a strict dress code and overriding concern with presenting a professional image. Members of this group wish to convey occupational status at work and in nonwork activites and can be considered investment dressers."

—4.3 million women fall within this group.
—They spend $5 billion per year on clothes.
—They represent the fastest growing segment of the working women's clothing market, with real growth forecast at 8–10 percent per year.

HEATHER EVANS will target the upper end of this group, whose concerns about quality and appropriateness are highest, commensurate with their level of income and responsibility.
The following statistics suggest that the upper end of the market is growing even faster than the formal professional market as a whole:

—In 1980, 793,000 women made over $25,000 per year.
—147,000 women made over *$50,000* per year, up *22 percent* from the previous year.

EXHIBIT 3 (*continued*)

Thus, HEATHER EVANS will target the new ranks of established executive and professional women. Whereas Liz Claiborne and others capitalized on the initial entry of women into the workforce in the 70s, HEATHER EVANS will capitalize on their acceptance in positions of responsibility in the 80s.

Style Trends:

Formal professional women are a ripe market for a well-conceived new clothing label because their tastes and habits in officewear are evolving, but they have few options among existing clothes.

Women in the upper end of the market, HEATHER EVANS' target, are still wearing mostly classic or modified tailored suits, with a blouse and neck ornament. The lower end shows movement toward softer looks and, particularly, dresses. Ms. Evans believes that this trend toward more varied looks will also be seen in the upper end of the market. However, the existing untailored "bridge" lines, dress lines, and designer sportswear lines are inappropriately styled for that segment.

Manufacturers have recently seen the demand for suits flatten, as interest in dresses has renewed. Responding to this trend, Liz Claiborne and Albert Nipon both opened dress divisions aimed at executive women, priced in the "better" range. The president of Liz Claiborne Dresses voiced the expectations of many in the industry when she told *Women's Wear Daily* that, unlike the 70s when working women wore mostly tailored sportswear for fear of standing out, "in the 80s I think they're going to be a lot more adventuresome in what they wear." As evidence, the dress division of Liz Claiborne hit around $10 million in wholesale sales in less than a year, approximately 10 percent of the entire company's sales.

These examples illustrate the receptivity of the working women's market to new styles and designers. However, the offerings of these companies and others are inappropriate for the more conservative elements. HEATHER EVANS intends to fill this gap.

Competition:

The "designer" fashion market is a relatively easy one to enter, because—

—*Competition is fragmented.* For example, although there are no comprehensive trade statistics available, it is worth noting that Liz Claiborne, which is one of the two largest companies in the market, can claim less than 3 percent of the market, with $155 million in latest 12 months sales.
—*Channels welcome new products.* Department store buyers are responsible for identifying and promoting new, promising lines, so that customers perceive the buyer's store as a fashion leader. In particular, major department store chains are seeking new lines in the "bridge" price range, in which HEATHER EVANS will position its products. They foresee this price category becoming increasingly important.

Retailers are encountering consumer price resistance which suggests that the designer-priced sportswear market has matured: the continual "trading-up" by customers in the 70s has ended. In response, manufacturers are generally lowering prices, both within existing lines and by introducing new lines in lower price categories. Many "designer" companies will target the bridge market, where customers are value-conscious, but have disposable in-

EXHIBIT 3 (*continued*)

come. The Company anticipates that the opportunities created by renewed interest in this area will favor the Company's strategy, and outweigh the threat of other new entrants and competition.

DESIGNER PRODUCTS MARKET

Once it has established a franchise in the expensive businesswear market, **HEATHER EVANS** can expand into any of several immediately related markets:

—accessories (e.g., belts, shoes, scarves) in a similar price category to coordinate with the original clothing line,
—leisure clothing in the same price range for the same customer as the original line, and
—lower-priced office-wear for a different, wider customer group (i.e., the rest of the 4.3 million formal professional women).

Finally, numerous tertiary markets exist for a well-managed designer name. For example, Bill Blass has licensed his name for chocolates, while Ralph Lauren has licensed his for a full line of home furnishings.

In the past, these designers have developed their names in the couture or designer sportswear levels; however, the extraordinary success of Norma Kamali, whose clothes retail for $30 to $100, demonstrates that a "designer" name can be made in any price range.

Thus, the Company can serve a virtually unlimited number of markets based on its reputation for taste and quality, as established through its original line of clothing. In Calvin Klein's case, his name is used on products with combined retail sales of $1 billion.

Licensing:

Designers profit enormously from licensing agreements, through which they attach their names to products in return for a 5–10 percent royalty. These products are manufactured and marketed—and often designed—by the licensee. For example,

—Pierre Cardin reaps over $50 million a year in royalties on $1 billion of wholesale sales on 540 licenses, with minimal related expenses.
—The top 10 designers collect over $200 million in royalties between them each year.

Long-run View:

The designer label has replaced the better department store label as the arbiter of taste and quality for the American consumer. After some designers (most notably Cardin) licensed their names indescriminately in the name-craze of the mid-70s, consumers became more evaluative about the value of a given designer's name, but they continue to purchase according to that name.

This shift has been disastrous for department stores, which have lost their business to discounters, which carry the same designer names for less with comparable service, and to specialty stores, which offer superior service at comparable prices. Although this shake-up in the retail industry will have repercussions for designers, it is unlikely to reverse a now well-entrenched phenomenon.

EXHIBIT 3 (*continued*)

IV. MANAGEMENT AND OPERATIONS

ORGANIZATION AND PEOPLE

Design:

The design group is the core of the Company: it creates five new product lines each year, on which the eventual success of the Company will depend. It is important to recognize that sales of the line will depend as much on existing specifications of fit, construction, fabrics, and coordination of pieces within the line as on the design sketches themselves; these are all parts of the design function.

The design process for each line takes approximately 9 months, so that several lines are being worked on in various stages at any time. For each line, the design function is to—

—Plan the line; determine the number of styles, colors and fabric groups, on the basis of overall line balance, ranges of buyer climates and tastes, and other marketing factors.
—Define the theme and tone of the line.
—Choose and order specific fabrics and other supplies, after surveying the market for these products.
—Create and select sketches.
—Cut, drape, and sew samples. Perfect fit of samples.
—Select final samples for the collection.
—Prepare patterns for production and communicate with normal industry contract manufacturers.

Ms. Evans will spend 40 percent of her time on design and production functions. She will oversee the entire process, with emphasis on *planning* and defining the theme of each line, and *selecting* fabrics, sketches and final samples.

Ms. Hughes and Ms. Evans will work as a team on all design-related tasks. Ms. Hughes has significant expertise in the creative and technical aspects of fashion design. She is experienced in creating specific styles from a general concept for a line. Her vocabulary of stylistic detail, production feasibility and textile characteristics complement Ms. Evans' market-driven design direction. (Ms. Hughes' backgound is described in Appendix B.)

Ms. Hughes has already been retained by Ms. Evans on a free-lance basis and is designing a Holiday line. It is expected that Ms. Hughes will join the company on a full-time basis shortly after funding is received.

The Company plans to hire a design assistant in June. The design assistant will make sample patterns, cut the samples, and oversee the sample makers. She will work with an outside pattern maker on production patterns and with the factory to assure that the final product meets the specifications of the sample garments.

The Company plans to hire one sample maker in June and another in September 1983.

Production:

The production function manages the process from the sample through the shipment of the final garment to the stores. The concerns of the production

EXHIBIT 3 (*continued*)

staff are quality, timely delivery, and cost. During the first two years, Ms. Evans and the design assistant will oversee production as part of their design responsibilities.

Following normal industry practice, the Company will subcontract all manufacturing, including the grading and marketing of its patterns, cutting of its piece goods, and sewing of its garments, to independent suppliers. Initially, all its suppliers will be located in New York City and other locations in the northeastern United States. There is capacity available in suitable shops in this area, where management can carefully monitor the quality and timing of production. As production volume increases, the Company may consider manufacturing in Hong Kong, Taiwan or elsewhere, where manufacturing costs for quality workmanship may be lower.

Malcolm Wong, a contractor located at 226 West 37th Street, has agreed to reserve time to produce production patterns and sew the Company's entire first collection. Mr. Wong's factory is a high-quality, nonunion shop, with 20 operators. Ms. Evans may use other contractors for all or part of the line, if these contractors offer a more favorable price.

The Company has arranged for its shipping to be done through Fernando Sanchez, as part of its rental arrangement with that firm (see "Facilities and Equipment"). Fernando Sanchez will provide space, shipping personnel, and shipping supplies. After July 1984, the Company expects to add one shipping employee of its own.

Sales and Promotion:

Sales are made during "market weeks," which last approximately three weeks for each of the five seasons, spread through the year. Store buyers write orders based on the sample line, which they view in the Company's showroom or in one of several regional marketplaces. The Company plans to join the New York Fashion Council, Inc., and has tentatively arranged through this group to reserve space in the key regional market shows.

Ms. Evans will spend 40 percent of her time in sales and promotion.

Initially, Ms. Evans will handle all department store sales and some specialty store sales, in the showroom and in "trunk shows" to the Dallas and L.A. markets. Ms. Evans' personal attention is important in this stage to communicate the philosophy of the line, to use her Harvard Business School contacts in department store managements, and to save money.

The Company plans to retain an established, independent representative to sell the line to specialty stores in the Northeast (except New York City). Ms. Evans is currently negotiating with a well-known representative for several designer lines, with whom she has worked previously. The representative will show the line to his customers in the Company's showroom.

Once critical customer relationships have become established and sales volume warrants, Ms. Evans will hire full-time, experienced showroom personnel and, possibly, retain additional independent sales representatives. Ms. Evans will then direct her efforts to more promotional activities and to managing the sales personnel.

Ms. Evans will also carry out an active campaign of non-sales promotion. She will communicate with customer fashion directors, concerning use of samples in cooperative advertising and scheduling personal in-store appearances, and with newspaper and magazine editors to encourage editorial coverage. She will also oversee production of promotional materials to announce the opening of each collection.

EXHIBIT 3 (*continued*)

Control:
　　Financial and production control will occupy 20 percent of Ms. Evans' time. These functions are critical to, but often neglected in, apparel manufacturing companies. In particular, fabric purchasing and production decisions must be made so as to maximize sales, yet minimize inventory at the end of the season when it becomes obsolete. Ms. Evans' experience in financial analysis and her business school training are valuable assets in the control function.
　　The Company plans to hire a part-time bookkeeper during its first months of operation. In July 1984 or thereafter, the Company will retain a full-time office manager.

FACILITIES AND EQUIPMENT

　　The Company has arranged for showroom and design studio space in the 550 Seventh Avenue building. This is one of the most prestigious buildings in the garment district, with such other tenants as Bill Blass, Halston, Ralph Lauren and Oscar de la Renta.
　　HEATHER EVANS' showroom will be within the showroom of Fernando Sanchez, a new and successful high-priced, designer line. Ms. Evans feels that the exposure of HEATHER EVANS line alongside the Sanchez line and within the 550 Seventh Avenue building will be very beneficial for the Company. The Company's line does not compete with the Sanchez line and will often be bought by different buyers from a given store.
　　The Company's design studio and office space will be adjacent to the Fernando Sanchez showroom, with its own entrance. The Company will be provided with shipping space at another location, 226 West 37 Street, as part of its arrangement with Fernando Sanchez. These facilities should be adequate for the first two years of operation.

V. FINANCIALS

　　The Company anticipates raising $250,000 in equity capital. This level of capitalization is adequate, together with normal industry factoring, to develop and to grow a substantial apparel company, without additional equity financing. This is a business plan and is not intended, of itself, to be an offering of stock or debt.

Industry Financial Characteristics:
　　High fashion apparel manufacturing offers high returns on capital within a short time frame to those companies whose clothing becomes "*fashion*".
—Margins run 40 to 60 percent.
—Operating costs after cost of goods sold and sales commissions (approximately 10 percent of sales) are relatively fixed. Basically, the cost of designing a line is the same at $1 million in sales as at $20 million.
—Investment in working capital is low: with 60-day terms from fabric suppliers and receivables factoring, cash received from shipment of finished goods can be applied to the cost of those same goods.
—Investment in fixed assets is limited to equipping and remodeling showroom, studio and shipping space. All manufacturing is subcontracted.
—After an initial introductory period of one to two years, acceptance of a line may proceed extremely rapidly, with annual sales growth rates of 100 to 500 percent not unusual.

- 9 -

EXHIBIT 3 (*continued*)

Whether a line does become "fashion" and to what extent depends on a number of variables that cannot be tested or foreseen until the clothing is presented to the fashion press and the consumers. These variables include the appeal of the specific styles and fit of the line, general fashion trends and specific competitive styles offered at the time the line is presented, and media interest in the line. Thus, investors are rewarded for putting at risk the cost of developing, producing and marketing a line of clothing during an initial introductory period.

Sales Projections:

The Company has prepared sales projections for the first two years of operation, as presented in Exhibit I. These projections are based on typical order sizes for new lines in the Company's price range and reasonable rates of trial by stores, taking into account supplier credit limits.

For reasons mentioned above, having to do with the nature of fashion, the Company cannot meaningfully forecast sales growth beyond the introductory period.

Financial Statements:

Projected financial statements for the company's first and second years of operation are included as Exhibits II and III, respectively. These forecast net income of $167,173 on sales of $1,712,500 in the second year.

A detailed list of assumptions for the forecasted financial statements is included as Exhibit IV. These estimates were developed by Ms. Evans, based on the experience of comparable companies, and discussed in detail with Rashba & Pokart, certified public accountants, who have extensive experience with apparel industry clients.

EXHIBIT 3 (*continued*)

EXHIBIT I

HEATHER EVANS INCORPORATED

Sales Projections

Season	Market Period	Shipping Period	Specialty Store			Department Store			Total
			Number of Orders	Avg. Order Size ($000)	Sales Volume ($000)	Number of Orders	Avg. Order Size ($000)	Sales Volume ($000)	($000)
Year 1									
Holiday	August	October-November	38	$2	$ 75	9	$ 8	$ 75	$ 150
Early spring	September	December-January	50	1	50	12	4	50	100
Spring	October	February-April	50	3	150	12	12	150	300
Transition	February	May-June	58	1	57.5	14	4	57.5	165
Total									$ 715
Year 2									
Fall	March	July-September	62	3.5	217.5	15	14	217.5	435
Holiday	August	October-November	60	2	120	15	8	120	240
Early spring	September	December-January	75	1	75	19	4	75	150
Spring	October	February-April	94	4	375	23	16	375	750
Transition	February	May-June	80	1	80	20	4	80	160
Total									$1,735

EXHIBIT 3 (*continued*)

EXHIBIT II

HEATHER EVANS INCORPORATED

Projected Statement of Income
Year Ended May 31, 1984

	TOTAL	JUNE	JULY	AUG.	SEPT.	OCT.	NOV.	DEC.	JAN.	FEB.	MAR.	APRIL	MAY
TOTAL SALES	607500	0	0	0	0	75000	75000	50000	50000	100000	100000	100000	57500
LESS: DISCOUNTS	48600	0	0	0	0	6000	6000	4000	4000	8000	8000	8000	4600
NET SALES	558900	0	0	0	0	69000	69000	46000	46000	92000	92000	92000	52900
COST OF GOODS SOLD:													
INVENTORY-BEGINNING	0	0	0	0	24375	61875	53750	41250	57500	82500	82500	68688	48750
PIECE GOODS & TRIMMINGS	257438	0	0	24375	24375	16250	16250	32500	32500	32500	18688	20000	40000
CONTRACTING COSTS	116313	0	0	0	13125	13125	8750	8750	17500	17500	17500	10063	10000
TOTAL	373750	0	0	24375	61875	91250	78750	82500	107500	132500	118688	98750	98750
LESS: INVENTORY-ENDING	70000	0	0	24375	61875	53750	41250	57500	82500	82500	68688	48750	70000
COST OF GOODS SOLD	303750	0	0	0	0	37500	37500	25000	25000	50000	50000	50000	28750
GROSS PROFIT	255150	0	0	0	0	31500	31500	21000	21000	42000	42000	42000	24150

OPERATING EXPENSES:													
PRODUCTION	149100	11300	11300	11300	12800	12800	12800	12800	12800	12800	12800	12800	12800
SELLING AND SHIPPING	53513	1000	1000	1700	1000	8825	5125	3750	3750	6500	10200	6500	4163
GENERAL AND ADMINISTRATIVE	120369	9727	9727	9727	10132	10132	10132	10132	10132	10132	10132	10132	10132
FACTOR'S CHARGES	24300	0	0	0	0	3000	3000	2000	2000	4000	4000	4000	2300
TOTAL OPERATING EXPENSES	347282	22027	22027	22727	23932	34757	31057	28682	28682	33432	37132	33432	29395
NET INCOME(-LOSS)	-92132	-22027	-22027	-22727	-23932	-3257	443	-7682	-7682	8568	4868	8568	-5245

SEE ACCOMPANYING SUMMARY OF SIGNIFICANT PROJECTION ASSUMPTIONS AND SIGNIFICANT ACCOUNTING POLICIES.

PRELIMINARY DRAFT

For discussion purposes only; all exhibits are tentative and subject to change.

EXHIBIT 3 (*continued*)

EXHIBIT II

HEATHER EVANS INCORPORATED

Projected Schedule of Operating Expenses

Year Ended May 31, 1984

	TOTAL	JUNE	JULY	AUG.	SEPT.	OCT.	NOV.	DEC.	JAN.	FEB.	MAR.	APRIL	MAY
PRODUCTION EXPENSES:													
DESIGNER'S SALARY	30000	2500	2500	2500	2500	2500	2500	2500	2500	2500	2500	2500	2500
ASSISTANT DESIGNER AND SAMPLEHANDS SALARIES	55500	3500	3500	3500	5000	5000	5000	5000	5000	5000	5000	5000	5000
PATTERN MAKER SALARY	39600	3300	3300	3300	3300	3300	3300	3300	3300	3300	3300	3300	3300
DESIGN ROOM SUPPLIES	24000	2000	2000	2000	2000	2000	2000	2000	2000	2000	2000	2000	2000
TOTAL	149100	11300	11300	11300	12800	12800	12800	12800	12800	12800	12800	12800	12800
SELLING AND SHIPPING:													
SALESMEN'S COMMISSIONS	30375	0	0	0	0	3750	3750	2500	2500	5000	5000	5000	2875
TRAVEL AND ENTERTAINMENT	20100	1000	1000	1700	1000	4700	1000	1000	1000	1000	4700	1000	1000
FREIGHT OUT	3038	0	0	0	0	375	375	250	250	500	500	500	288
TOTAL	53513	1000	1000	1700	1000	8825	5125	3750	3750	6500	10200	6500	4163

GENERAL AND ADMINISTRATIVE:

RENT	24000	2000	2000	2000	2000	2000	2000	2000	2000	2000	2000	2000	2000
OFFICE SALARY	9600	800	800	800	800	800	800	800	800	800	800	800	800
TELEPHONE	8400	700	700	700	700	700	700	700	700	700	700	700	700
STATIONERY AND OFFICE	12000	1000	1000	1000	1000	1000	1000	1000	1000	1000	1000	1000	1000
LEGAL AND AUDIT	12000	1000	1000	1000	1000	1000	1000	1000	1000	1000	1000	1000	1000
DUES AND SUBSCRIPTIONS	3600	300	300	300	300	300	300	300	300	300	300	300	300
DEPRECIATION AND AMORT.	2700	225	225	225	225	225	225	225	225	225	225	225	225
INSURANCE	7200	600	600	600	600	600	600	600	600	600	600	600	600
BUSINESS AND PAYROLL TAXES	13470	1010	1010	1010	1160	1160	1160	1160	1160	1160	1160	1160	1160
UTILITIES	4500	375	375	375	375	375	375	375	375	375	375	375	375
EMPLOYEE BENEFITS	22899	1717	1717	1717	1972	1972	1972	1972	1972	1972	1972	1972	1972
TOTAL	120369	9727	9727	9727	10132	10132	10132	10132	10132	10132	10132	10132	10132

SEE ACCOMPANYING SUMMARY OF SIGNIFICANT PROJECTION ASSUMPTION AND SUMMARY OF SIGNIFICANT ACCOUNTING POLICIES.

PRELIMINARY DRAFT

For discussion purposes only; all exhibits are tentative and subject to change.

- 15 -

EXHIBIT 3 (*continued*)

EXHIBIT II

HEATHER EVANS INCORPORATED

Forecasted Balance Sheets
June 1983 through May 1984

ASSETS	JUNE	JULY	AUG.	SEPT.	OCT.	NOV.	DEC.	JAN.	FEB.	MAR.	APRIL	MAY
CURRENT ASSETS:												
CASH AND DUE FROM FACTOR	203398	181596	159094	122262	119230	124273	116816	100609	109402	114495	130726	125769
MERCHANDISE INVENTORIES	0	0	24375	61875	53750	41250	57500	82500	82500	68688	48750	70000
TOTAL CURRENT ASSETS	203398	181596	183469	184137	172980	165523	174316	183109	191902	183183	179476	195769
FIXED ASSETS—NET	17775	17550	17325	17100	16875	16650	16425	16200	15975	15750	15525	15300
OTHER ASSETS	6800	6800	6800	6800	6800	6800	6800	6800	6800	6800	6800	6800
TOTAL ASSETS	227973	205946	207594	208037	196655	188973	197541	206109	214677	205733	201801	217869
LIABILITIES AND STOCKHOLDERS' EQUITY												
CURRENT LIABILITIES:												
ACCOUNTS PAYABLE	0	0	24375	48750	40625	32500	48750	65000	65000	51188	38688	60000
STOCKHOLDERS' EQUITY	227973	205946	183219	159287	156030	156473	148791	141109	149677	154545	163113	157869
TOTAL LIABILITIES AND STOCKHOLDERS' EQUITY	227973	205946	207594	208037	196655	188973	197541	206109	214677	205733	201801	217869

SEE ACCOMPANYING SUMMARY OF SIGNIFICANT PROJECTION ASSUMPTIONS AND SUMMARY OF SIGNIFICANT ACCOUNTING POLICIES.

PRELIMINARY DRAFT

For discussion purposes only; all exhibits are tentative and subject to change.

HEATHER EVANS INCORPORATED

Projected Statements of Cash Flow
Year Ended May 31, 1984

	TOTAL	JUNE	JULY	AUG.	SEPT.	OCT.	NOV.	DEC.	JAN.	FEB.	MAR.	APRIL	MAY
CASH AND DUE FROM FACTOR—BEGINNING	0	0	203398	181596	159094	122262	119230	124273	116816	100609	109402	114495	130726
RECEIPTS:													
INITIAL CAPITALIZATION	250000	250000	0	0	0	0	0	0	0	0	0	0	0
NET SALES	558900	0	0	0	0	69000	69000	46000	46000	92000	92000	92000	52900
TOTAL	808900	250000	203398	181596	159094	191262	188230	170273	162816	192609	201402	206495	183626
CASH DISBURSEMENTS:													
ACCOUNTS PAYABLE—PIECE GOODS & TRIMMINGS	197438	0	0	0	0	24375	24375	16250	16250	32500	32500	32500	18688
CONTRACTORS PAYABLE	116313	0	0	0	13125	13125	8750	8750	17500	17500	17500	10063	10000
OPERATING EXPENSES—NET	344582	21802	21802	22502	23707	34532	30832	28457	28457	33207	36907	33207	29170
SECURITY DEPOSITS	6800	6800	0	0	0	0	0	0	0	0	0	0	0
PURCHASE OF FIXED ASSETS	18000	18000	0	0	0	0	0	0	0	0	0	0	0
TOTAL	683132	46602	21802	22502	36832	72032	63957	53457	62207	83207	86907	75770	57857
CASH AND DUE FROM FACTOR—ENDING	125769	203398	181596	159094	122262	119230	124273	116816	100609	109402	114495	130726	125769

SEE ACCOMPANYING SUMMARY OF SIGNIFICANT PROJECTION ASSUMPTIONS AND SUMMARY OF SIGNIFICANT ACCOUNTING POLICIES.

PRELIMINARY DRAFT

For discussion purposes only; all exhibits are tentative and subject to change.

EXHIBIT 3 (*continued*)

EXHIBIT III

HEATHER EVANS INCORPORATED

Projected Statement of Income

Year Ended May 31, 1985

	TOTAL	JUNE	JULY	AUG.	SEPT.	OCT.	NOV.	DEC.	JAN.	FEB.	MAR.	APRIL	MAY
TOTAL SALES	1712500	57500	145000	145000	145000	120000	120000	75000	75000	250000	250000	250000	80000
LESS: DISCOUNTS	137000	4600	11600	11600	11600	9600	9600	6000	6000	20000	20000	20000	6400
NET SALES	1575500	52900	133400	133400	133400	110400	110400	69000	69000	230000	230000	230000	73600
COST OF GOODS SOLD:													
INVENTORY-BEGINNING	70000	70000	113750	113750	105625	93125	78500	56000	112875	200375	200375	145125	81250
PIECE GOODS & TRIMMINGS	585000	47125	47125	39000	39000	24375	24375	81250	81250	81250	26000	47125	47125
CONTRACTING COSTS	299625	25375	25375	25375	21000	21000	13125	13125	43750	43750	43750	14000	10000
TOTAL	954625	142500	186250	178125	165625	138500	116000	150375	237875	325375	270125	206250	138375
LESS: INVENTORY-ENDING	98375	113750	113750	105625	93125	78500	56000	112875	200375	200375	145125	81250	98375
COST OF GOODS SOLD	856250	28750	72500	72500	72500	60000	60000	37500	37500	125000	125000	125000	40000
GROSS PROFIT	719250	24150	60900	60900	60900	50400	50400	31500	31500	105000	105000	105000	33600

OPERATING EXPENSES:

	Total	1	2	3	4	5	6	7	8	9	10	11	12
PRODUCTION	153600	12800	12800	12800	12800	12800	12800	12800	12800	12800	12800	12800	12800
SELLING AND SHIPPING	114288	4163	8975	9675	8975	11300	7600	5125	5125	14750	18450	14750	5400
GENERAL AND ADMINISTRATIVE	149524	10132	12672	12672	12672	12672	12672	12672	12672	12672	12672	12672	12672
FACTOR'S CHARGES	63020	2116	5336	5336	5336	4416	4416	2760	2760	9200	9200	9200	2944
TOTAL OPERATING EXPENSES	480432	29211	39783	40483	39783	41188	37488	33357	33357	49422	53122	49422	33816
INCOME BEFORE PROVISION FOR INCOME TAXES	238819	-5061	21117	20417	21117	9212	12912	-1857	-1857	55578	51878	55578	-216
PROVISION FOR INCOME TAXES	71646	-1518	6335	6125	6335	2764	3874	-557	-557	16673	15563	16673	-65
NET INCOME (-LOSS)	167173	-3542	14782	14292	14782	6448	9038	-1300	-1300	38905	36315	38905	-151

SEE ACCOMPANYING SUMMARY OF SIGNIFICANT PROJECTION ASSUMPTIONS AND SIGNIFICANT ACCOUNTING POLICIES.
PRELIMINARY DRAFT

For discussion purposes only; all exhibits are tentative and subject to change.

- 19 -

335

EXHIBIT 3 (*continued*)

EXHIBIT III

HEATHER EVANS INCORPORATED

Projected Schedule of Operating Expenses

Year Ended May 31, 1985

	TOTAL	JUNE	JULY	AUG.	SEPT.	OCT.	NOV.	DEC.	JAN.	FEB.	MAR.	APRIL	MAY
PRODUCTION EXPENSES:													
DESIGNER'S SALARY	30000	2500	2500	2500	2500	2500	2500	2500	2500	2500	2500	2500	2500
ASSISTANT DESIGNER AND SAMPLEHANDS SALARIES	60000	5000	5000	5000	5000	5000	5000	5000	5000	5000	5000	5000	5000
PATTERN MAKER SALARY	39600	3300	3300	3300	3300	3300	3300	3300	3300	3300	3300	3300	3300
DESIGN ROOM SUPPLIES	24000	2000	2000	2000	2000	2000	2000	2000	2000	2000	2000	2000	2000
TOTAL	153600	12800	12800	12800	12800	12800	12800	12800	12800	12800	12800	12800	12800
SELLING AND SHIPPING:													
SALESMENS COMMISSIONS	85625	2875	7250	7250	7250	6000	6000	3750	3750	12500	12500	12500	4000
TRAVEL AND ENTERTAINMENT	20100	1000	1000	1700	1000	4700	1000	1000	1000	1000	4700	1000	1000
FREIGHT OUT	8563	288	725	725	725	600	600	375	375	1250	1250	1250	400
TOTAL	114288	4163	8975	9675	8975	11300	7600	5125	5125	14750	18450	14750	5400

GENERAL AND
ADMINISTRATIVE:

RENT	24000	2000	2000	2000	2000	2000	2000	2000	2000	2000	2000	2000	2000
OFFICE SALARY	31600	800	2800	2800	2800	2800	2800	2800	2800	2800	2800	2800	2800
TELEPHONE	8400	700	700	700	700	700	700	700	700	700	700	700	700
STATIONERY AND OFFICE	12000	1000	1000	1000	1000	1000	1000	1000	1000	1000	1000	1000	1000
LEGAL AND AUDIT	12000	1000	1000	1000	1000	1000	1000	1000	1000	1000	1000	1000	1000
DUES AND SUBSCRIPTIONS	3600	300	300	300	300	300	300	300	300	300	300	300	300
DEPRECIATION AND AMORT.	2700	225	225	225	225	225	225	225	225	225	225	225	225
INSURANCE	7200	600	600	600	600	600	600	600	600	600	600	600	600
BUSINESS AND PAYROLL TAXES	16120	1160	1360	1360	1360	1360	1360	1360	1360	1360	1360	1360	1360
UTILITIES	4500	375	375	375	375	375	375	375	375	375	375	375	375
EMPLOYEE BENEFITS	27404	1972	2312	2312	2312	2312	2312	2312	2312	2312	2312	2312	2312
TOTAL	149524	10132	12672	12672	12672	12672	12672	12672	12672	12672	12672	12672	12672

SEE ACCOMPANYING SUMMARY OF SIGNIFICANT PROJECTION ASSUMPTIONS AND SUMMARY OF SIGNIFICANT ACCOUNTING POLICIES.
PRELIMINARY DRAFT

For discussion purposes only; all exhibits are tentative and subject to change.

EXHIBIT 3 (*continued*)

EXHIBIT III

HEATHER EVANS INCORPORATED

Forecasted Balance Sheets
June 1984 through May 1985

ASSETS	1984							1985				
	JUNE	JULY	AUG.	SEPT.	OCT.	NOV.	DEC.	JAN.	FEB.	MAR.	APRIL	MAY
CURRENT ASSETS:												
CASH AND DUE FROM FACTOR	104309	132776	153418	179135	188572	209584	207952	175695	231498	283601	369154	373163
MERCHANDISE INVENTORIES	113750	113750	105625	93125	78500	56000	112875	200375	200375	145125	81250	98375
TOTAL CURRENT ASSETS	218059	246526	259043	272260	267072	265584	320827	376070	431873	428726	450404	471538
FIXED ASSETS—NET	15075	14850	14625	14400	14175	13950	13725	13500	13275	13050	12825	12600
OTHER ASSETS	6800	6800	6800	6800	6800	6800	6800	6800	6800	6800	6800	6800
TOTAL ASSETS	239934	268176	280468	293460	288047	286334	341352	396370	451948	448576	470029	490938

LIABILITIES AND STOCKHOLDERS' EQUITY

CURRENT LIABILITIES:												
ACCOUNTS PAYABLE	87125	94250	86125	78000	63375	48750	105625	162500	162500	109250	73125	94250
INCOME TAXES PAYABLE	-1518	4817	10942	17277	20041	23914	23357	22800	39474	53037	71710	71646
TOTAL CURRENT LIABILITIES	85607	99067	97067	95277	83416	72664	128982	185300	201974	162287	144835	165896
STOCKHOLDERS' EQUITY	154327	169109	183400	198182	204631	213669	212369	211069	249974	286289	325193	325042
TOTAL LIABILITIES AND STOCKHOLDERS' EQUITY	239934	268176	280468	293460	288047	286334	341352	396370	451948	448576	470029	490938

SEE ACCOMPANYING SUMMARY OF SIGNIFICANT PROJECTION ASSUMPTIONS AND SUMMARY OF SIGNIFICANT ACCOUNTING POLICIES.

<u>PRELIMINARY DRAFT</u>

For discussion purposes only; all exhibits are tentative and subject to change.

- 23 -

EXHIBIT 3 (*continued*)

EXHIBIT III

HEATHER EVANS INCORPORATED

Projected Statements of Cash Flow
Year Ended May 31, 1985

	TOTAL	JUNE	JULY	AUG.	SEPT.	OCT.	NOV.	DEC.	JAN.	FEB.	MAR.	APRIL	MAY
CASH AND DUE FROM FACTOR—BEGINNING	125769	125769	104309	132776	153418	179135	188572	209584	207952	175695	231498	283601	369154
RECEIPTS:													
NET SALES	1575500	52900	133400	133400	133400	110400	110400	69000	69000	230000	230000	230000	73600
TOTAL	1701269	178669	237709	266176	286818	289535	298972	278584	276952	405695	461498	513601	442754
CASH DISBURSEMENTS:													
ACCOUNTS PAYABLE—PIECE GOODS & TRIMMINGS	550750	20000	40000	47125	47125	39000	39000	24375	24375	81250	81250	81250	26000
CONTRACTORS PAYABLE	299625	25375	25375	25375	21000	21000	13125	13125	43750	43750	43750	14000	10000
OPERATING EXPENSES—NET	477732	28986	39558	40258	39558	40963	37263	33132	33132	49197	52897	49197	33591
TOTAL	1328107	74361	104933	112758	107683	100963	89388	70632	101257	174197	177897	144447	69591
CASH AND DUE FROM FACTOR—ENDING	373163	104309	132776	153418	179135	188572	209584	207952	175695	231498	283601	369154	373163

SEE ACCOMPANYING SUMMARY OF SIGNIFICANT PROJECTION ASSUMPTIONS AND SUMMARY OF SIGNIFICANT ACCOUNTING POLICIES. PRELIMINARY DRAFT

For discussion purposes only; all exhibits are tentative and subject to change.

EXHIBIT 3 (*continued*)

EXHIBIT IV

Assumptions for Pro Forma Financial Statements

Income Statement
1. Sales: See Exhibit I, "Sales Projections"
2. Discount: 8 percent (assume discount taken on all sales)
3. Cost of goods sold:
   —Inventory—see "Balance Sheet" below
   —Piece goods and trimmings—65 percent of COGS
   —Contracting costs—35 percent of COGS
4. Gross profit: 50 percent of gross sales (42 percent of net sales)
5. Operating expenses—see below
6. Factor's charge—4 percent net of sales (actual charges will be commission equal to a fixed percentage of sales plus interest charge for advances against uncollected receivables)

Operating Expenses
1. Production expenses:
   —Salaries
   Designer—$2,500 per month, starting June 1983
   Assistant designer—$2,000 per month, starting June 1983
   Samplehands—$1,000 each per month, starting June 1983, another starting September 1983
   Pattern maker—$3,300 per month, starting June 1983
2. Selling and shipping:
   —Salesmen's commission—10 percent on all specialty store sales, based on standard independent representative commission rate
     —Travel and entertainment—
     General travel and entertainment—$1,000 per month
     Announcements—$700 each holiday, spring, and fall market period
     Trunk shows—$3,000 each spring and fall market period
   —Freight out—0.5 percent of sales
3. General and administrative:
   —Rent—$2,000 per month
   —Office salary—
   Part-time bookkeeper—2 days per week, at $100 per day, starting June 1983
   Office manager—$2,000 per month
   —Telephone—$700 per month
   —Stationery and office—$1,000 per month
   —Legal and audit—$1,000 per month
   —Dues and subscriptions—$300 per month
   —Depreciation and amortization—$225 per month, based on $18,000 investment in equipment, furniture and lease improvements, depreciated on a straight-line basis over an average life of 7 years.
   —Insurance—$600 per month
   —Business and payroll taxes—10 percent of full-time payroll
   —Employee benefits—18 percent of full-time payroll

EXHIBIT 3 (*continued*)

EXHIBIT IV

Assumptions for Pro Forma Financial Statements

Balance Sheets

1. Cash and due from factor—includes 100 percent of invoices for goods shipped in each month
2. Merchandise inventories—includes piece goods and trim received 60 days in advance of sale; finished goods shipped within month
3. Fixed assets—net—depreciated straight-line over 7-year average life, from $18,000 base, as follows:

Sample room equipment	$7,000
Office and showroom furnishing	6,000
Remodelling	5,000
	$18,000

4. Other assets—includes lease deposit of $6,000 (3 months) and telephone deposit of $800
5. Accounts payable—includes piece goods and trimming payable within 60 days; contractors paid within 30 days; all other expenses assumed paid within month
6. Stockholders' equity—$250,000 initial capital

APPENDIXES

APPENDIX A

Resume of

HEATHER H. EVANS

Education

1981–1983
HARVARD GRADUATE SCHOOL
OF BUSINESS ADMINISTRATION
Candidate for the degree of Master of Business Administration in June 1983.
Awarded First Year Honors (top 15% of class).

Resident Business Tutor, South House, Harvard College: supervised pre-business program and oversaw student activities in residential unit of 350 undergraduate students. Instructor, Economics Department, Harvard College: designed and taught full-credit undergraduate course in managerial economics and decision analysis.

1976–1979
HARVARD COLLEGE
Bachelor of Arts degree, cum laude. Philosophy major. Phi Beta
Kappa. Dean's list all semesters. Completed undergraduate course requirements in three years.

Publisher and Executive Committee member, *The Harvard Advocate* magazine. Vice Chairman, South House Committee.

Work Experience

Summer 1982
JACKIE HAYMAN, INC.
Assistant to President. Aided president of young firm that manufactures designer clothing under Catherine Hipp label. Involved in all areas of business, including

EXHIBIT 3 (*concluded*)

sales, public relations, working capital management, credit, design, production and shipping.

1979–1981
MORGAN STANLEY & CO. INCORPORATED
Financial Analyst.

Mergers and Acquisitiions: Identified possible acquisition targets, recommended prices for those companies, and formulated strategies to locate buyers. Analyzed financial and market data to determine the target's long-range earning potential and the effect of the acquisition on the buyer.

Corporate Finance: Supervised preparation of debt financings for ten clients. Negotiated terms of security documents and coordinated the activities of teams inside and outside Morgan Stanley.

1975–1979
FASHION MODEL
Managed own career as a fashion model. Represented by Ford Models, Inc., New York, NY; the Model's Group, Boston, MA, and L'Agence Pauline, Paris, France. Credits include: *Mademoiselle, Seventeen, GQ, LeMonde, Boston* and *The Boston Globe*.

Summer 1978
RESOURCE PLANNING ASSOCIATES
Research Associate. Planned and executed study that led RPA to add antitrust economic support work to its services. Worked on projects in oil price forecasting and U.S. mineral reliance.

Personal Background

Attended The Spence School, New York, NY and Lycée Montaigne, Paris, France. Speak fluent French and conversational Greek.

APPENDIX B

Background of

Belinda Hughes

Belinda Hughes received her Bachelor of Fine Arts Degree in Fashion Design from Parsons School of Design in May 1981. After graduation, she worked as Assistant Designer to Kasper at Kasper for J.L. Sports. She designed pants, blouses, and jackets for the Kasper line and prepared sketches and maintained records of fabrication and styles for the company's Japanese licensee. In May 1982, Ms. Hughes became Head Designer for Creations by Aria, a moderate-price dress house. She covered layout of the dressy dress line, from selection of fabrics to preparation of dresses, and oversaw the sample room staff. Recently, Ms. Hughes has been working as a freelance designer for several lines, including Choo-Chee, Elan Shoe Corp., Roslyn Harte, and College Town, for which she has designed collections ranging from shoes to loungewear.

Ms. Hughes' design talent has been recognized by many academic and industry awards, including: Recognition in Design Citation from Levis (1979); scholarship award from St. John's University (1979); scholarship award from the Switzer Foundation (1980); ILGWU Design Merit Award (1980); ILGWU Design Creativity Award (1981).

EXHIBIT 4
Timing of Cycles in the Garment Industry

	March	April	May	June	July	August	September	October
Holiday line	Order sample fabrics	Sketch and design line		Make samples and order production quantities of fabric		Market weeks—take orders	Contract out cutting and sewing	Deliver garments to stores
Early spring line					Early spring line cycle begins			
Spring line						Spring cycle begins		
Transition line							Transition line begins	
Fall line	Fall line finishes up							

EXHIBIT 5
Heather Evans' Notes on Preliminary
Discussions with Potential Private Investors

1. David Ellis, Attorney, Family Friend (excerpt from April 28, 1983 letter):

From an investor's point of view, one would expect at least a 50 percent equity share, and probably substantially more although in nonvoting stock. The investors' stock would be convertible into voting (and indeed control) stock in case certain minimum standards of solvency and cash flow and performance weren't met. Additional stock would be made available to management if certain performance goals were exceeded. Thus management might start with 25 percent, plus an option on a second 25 percent if the company proves to be a world-beater.

That of course may sound too complicated; but if it's to be an arm's-length minimally attractive proposal, I think you have to offer investors at least 50 percent or 60 percent, albeit in nonvoting shares.

If it were a proposal such as that, I would be thinking in terms of a $20,000 or $25,000 participation for myself; i.e., an investment.

But if you can get 70 percent for yourself, with only 30 percent to investors—take it! If that's the way it goes, I would want to make a gesture of support and encouragement— thus a $5,000 unit.

2. Paul Hood, Classmate, HBS:
   — Says he is interested in investing for three reasons:
   - Heather Evans: trusts intelligence, dedication, design sense, and business judgment.
   - Concept: gut feel that there is a market need, has spoken with women in business about idea.
   - Upside: mentioned Liz Claiborne deal.
   —Key needs in a deal:
   - No limit to upside via forced call on equity.
   - Wants company to own "Heather Evans" name rather than licensing; if Heather Evans can walk after business established, this limits upside.
   — Willing to invest $25,000 to $40,000.

3. Herbert Greene, president, Greene Textiles:
   — I felt that Greene was a good contact with potential fabric, textile suppliers.
   — Name (especially if on board) adds credibility on Seventh Avenue/Garment Business.
   — Was in on Liz Claiborne deal, made very big dollars.
   — Wants in deal terms:
   - Right to force registration/issue in public market in 5 to 7 years.
   - Low limit on my salary with incentive compensation.
   - Investors get board control until minimum performance criteria met.
   — Willing to invest $35,000–$55,000.

4. John Merrill, old friend, HBS classmate:
   — Wants company to own name: says if company does very well, main value created will be in name, company should own this.
   — Liquidation protection, i.e., if company goes bust, investors get what's left before I get anything.
   — Three-to-five-year employment contract with three-year noncompete clause at termination of employment contract.
   — Right to sell equity, pro rata, on same terms as Heather Evans in any offering.

EXHIBIT 6
Liz Claiborne Prospectus—Excerpts

liz claiborne, inc.
Common Stock
(Par Value $1 Per Share)

Of the shares of Common Stock offered hereby, 345,000 shares are being sold by the Company and 805,000 shares are being sold by certain stockholders. The Company will not receive any proceeds from the sale of shares by the Selling Stockholders. See "Principal and Selling Stockholders."

Prior to this offering there has been no public market for the Company's Common Stock. See "Underwriting" for information relating to the method of determining the initial public offering price.

THESE SECURITIES HAVE NOT BEEN APPROVED OR DISAPPROVED BY THE SECURITIES AND EXCHANGE COMMISSION NOR HAS THE COMMISSION PASSED UPON THE ACCURACY OR ADEQUACY OF THIS PROSPECTUS. ANY REPRESENTATION TO THE CONTRARY IS A CRIMINAL OFFENSE.

	Price to Public	Underwriting Discounts (1)	Proceeds to the Company (2)	Proceeds to the Selling Stockholders (2) (3)
Per Share..................	$19.00	$1.28	$17.72	$17.72
Total.......................	$21,850,000	$1,472,000	$6,113,400	$14,264,600

(1) See "Underwriting" for a description of indemnification and insurance arrangements among the Underwriters, the Company and the Selling Stockholders.
(2) Before deducting expenses estimated at $356,201 payable by the Company and $168,369 payable by the Selling Stockholders.
(3) The Selling Stockholders have granted the Underwriters an option to purchase up to an additional 115,000 shares to cover over-allotments. If all such shares are purchased, the total Price to Public, Underwriting Discounts and Proceeds to the Selling Stockholders will be increased by $2,185,000, $147,200 and $2,037,800, respectively.

The Common Stock is being offered subject to prior sale, when, as and if delivered to and accepted by the several Underwriters and subject to approval of certain legal matters by counsel and to certain other conditions. It is expected that certificates for the shares of Common Stock offered hereby will be available on or about June 16, 1981. The Underwriters reserve the right to withdraw, cancel or modify such offer and to reject orders in whole or in part.

Merrill Lynch White Weld Capital Markets Group
Merrill Lynch, Pierce, Fenner & Smith Incorporated

June 9, 1981

EXHIBIT 6 (*continued*)

PROSPECTUS SUMMARY

The following information is qualified in its entirety by reference to the detailed information and financial statements (including the Notes thereto) appearing elsewhere in the Prospectus.

Liz Claiborne, Inc.

Liz Claiborne, Inc. (the "Company") designs, contracts for the manufacture of and markets an extensive range of women's clothing under the LIZ CLAIBORNE and LIZ trademarks. Since the Company's founding in 1976, it has concentrated on identifying and furnishing the wardrobe requirements of the business and professional woman. Although the Company's products are conceived and marketed as "designer" apparel, they are priced to sell in the "better sportswear" range. The Company's products are sold to over 900 customers operating over 3,000 department and specialty stores throughout the United States. Products are manufactured pursuant to the Company's specifications by independent suppliers in the United States and abroad. See "Business."

The Offering

Common Stock to be sold by:
Company.. 345,000 shares
Selling Stockholders .... 805,000 shares (1)
Common Stock to be outstanding after the offering . 3,479,560 shares
Estimated net proceeds to the Company................ $5,757,199
Use of net proceeds by the Company................... To reduce indebtedness and for certain capital expenditures. See "Use of Proceeds."
Dividends .... None. See "Dividend Policy."
Proposed NASDAQ Symbol .... LIZC

(1) Assumes the Underwriters' 115,000 share over-allotment option is not exercised.

Selected Consolidated Financial Data
(in thousands of dollars except per share amounts)

	Jan. 19, 1976 (Inc.) through Dec. 31, 1976	Fiscal Year Ended				Three Months Ended	
		Dec. 31, 1977	Dec. 31, 1978	Dec. 29, 1979	Dec. 27, 1980	March 29, 1980	March 28, 1981
						(unaudited)	
Net Sales..............	$2,060	$7,396	$23,279	$47,630	$79,492	$20,747	$26,523
Net income...........	50	342	1,189	3,497	6,220	1,953	2,687
Earnings per common share (1)	$ .02	$ .12	$ .38	$ 1.12	$ 1.98	$ .62	$ .86

EXHIBIT 6 (*continued*)

	March 28, 1981	
	(unaudited)	
	Actual	As Adjusted (2)
Working capital..	$11,854	$16,307
Total assets..	27,918	32,613
Long-term debt, including current portion.................	63	—
Short-term debt...	3,884	2,884
Stockholders' equity	13,589	19,346

(1) Adjusted to reflect the issuance of 65 shares of the Company's Common Stock for each share of its predecessor company's common stock pursuant to a merger effected on April 21, 1981. See Notes 1 and 5 of Notes to Consolidated Financial Statements.

(2) Adjusted to reflect the sale of the shares offered by the Company hereby and the anticipated use of the net proceds therefrom as well as the repayment of long-term debt in April, 1981. See "Use of Proceeds" and "Capitalization."

See "Dilution" and "Shares Eligible for Future Sale" with respect to the availability of shares for sale after this offering and the immediate dilution in net tangible book value per share to be incurred by the public investors.

IN CONNECTION WITH THIS OFFERING, THE UNDERWRITERS MAY OVER-ALLOT OR EFFECT TRANSACTIONS WHICH STABILIZE OR MAINTAIN THE MAR-KET PRICE OF THE COMMON STOCK OF THE COMPANY AT A LEVEL ABOVE THAT WHICH MIGHT OTHERWISE PREVAIL IN THE OPEN MARKET. SUCH STABILIZING, IF COMMENCED, MAY BE DISCONTINUED AT ANY TIME.

EXHIBIT 6 (continued)

SELECTED FINANCIAL DATA

The following tables set forth information regarding the Company's operating results and financial position and are qualified in their entirety by the more detailed Consolidated Financial Statements included elsewhere in the Prospectus.

SELECTED INCOME STATEMENT DATA:

	Jan. 19, 1976 (Inc.) through Dec. 31, 1976	Fiscal Year Ended				Three Months Ended	
		Dec. 1, 1977 (unaudited)	Dec. 31, 1978	Dec. 29, 1979	Dec. 27, 1980	March 29, 1980	March 28, 1981 (unaudited)
Net sales	$2,060,118	$7,395,898	$23,279,304	$47,630,227	$79,492,035	$20,747,500	$26,523,023
Net income	49,862	342,489	1,188,857	3,496,575	6,219,592	1,952,998	2,686,670
Earnings per common share (1)	$.02	$.12	$.38	$1.12	$1.98	$.62	$.86
Dividends declared per common share (1)(2)	—	$.007	$.023	$.046	$.077	—	—

SELECTED BALANCE SHEET DATA:

	Dec. 31, 1976	Dec. 31, 1977	Dec. 31, 1978	Dec. 29, 1979	Dec. 27, 1980	March 28, 1981 (unaudited)
Working capital	$246,471	$454,196	$1,179,071	$4,456,954	$9,302,745	$11,854,311
Total assets	674,806	1,901,492	5,144,142	10,786,982	19,281,718	27,918,402
Long-term debt, including current portion (3)	170,000	173,333	173,333	134,815	77,037	62,593
Short-term debt (4)	—	—	—	—	—	3,883,676
Advances from factor (4)	330,696	666,077	2,782,863	—	3,546,098	—
Stockholders' equity	135,029	455,128	1,571,649	4,923,551	10,902,023	13,588,693

(1) Adjusted to reflect the issuance of 65 shares of the Company's Common Stock for each share of its predecessor company's common stock pursuant to a merger effected on April 21, 1981. See Notes 1 and 5 of Notes to Consolidated Financial Statements.

(2) The Company has no present plan to continue to pay dividends. See "Dividend Policy."

(3) The Company repaid its long-term debt in April, 1981.

(4) Factoring advances were replaced by a line of credit in March, 1981. See Notes 2 and 10 of Notes to Consolidated Financial Statements.

EXHIBIT 6 (*continued*)

BUSINESS

Introduction and Background

The Company designs, contracts for the manufacture of and markets an extensive range of women's clothing under the LIZ CLAIBORNE and LIZ trademarks. Organized in 1976 by its present management, the Company has concentrated primarily on identifying and furnishing the wardrobe requirements of the working woman, providing apparel appropriate in a business or professional environment as well as apparel suitable for leisure wear. The Company offers its customers a broad selection of related separates (referred to in the apparel industry as "sportswear") consisting of blouses, skirts, jackets, sweaters, and tailored pants, as well as more casual apparel such as jeans, knit tops, and shirts. The Company believes that the increasing number of business and professional women has contributed both to the Company's own growth and to the growth of the market for women's "sportswear" in general.

LIZ CLAIBORNE products are conceived and marketed as "designer" apparel, employing a consistent approach to design and quality which is intended to develop and maintain consumer recognition and loyalty across product lines and from season to season. The Company defines its clothing as "updated," combining traditional or classic design with contemporary fashion influences. While the Company maintains a "designer" image, its products are priced in the "better sportswear" range, which is generally less expensive than many "designer" lines. Although no comprehensive trade statistics are available, the Company believes, based on its knowledge of the market and such trade information as is available, that measured by sales of women's "better sportswear," it is the second largest producer of such merchandise in the United States.

In 1980, LIZ CLAIBORNE products were sold to over 900 customers operating over 3,000 department and specialty stores throughout the United States. Measured by their purchases of LIZ CLAIBORNE apparel, the Company's largest customers during 1980 included Saks Fifth Avenue, Lord & Taylor, Bamberger's, J.L. Hudson, Bloomingdale's and Macy's—New York. A great many retail outlets which carry the Company's products maintain separate LIZ CLAIBORNE areas in which a range of the Company's products are sold. Approximately 25 percent of the Company's 1980 sales was made to the Company's 10 largest customers; approximately 71 percent of 1980 sales was made to the Company's 100 largest customers. Certain of these customers are under common ownership. For example, 16 different department store customers owned by Federated Department Stores, Inc. (which include Bloomingdale's, Abraham & Straus, and Burdine's) accounted for approximately 12 percent of the Company's 1980 sales. The Company believes that each of these department store customers makes its own decisions regarding purchases of the Company's products.

Although the Company expects that sales to its 100 largest customers will continue to account for a majority of its sales, increasing emphasis is being placed on sales to local specialty stores and direct-mail catalogue companies. The

EXHIBIT 6 (*continued*)

Company began licensing its trademarks in 1978 and presently receives royalties under arrangements with three licensees which sell various products under the LIZ CLAIBORNE and LIZ trademarks.

The Company's products are designed by its own staff and are manufactured in accordance with its specifications by independent suppliers in the United States and abroad. Domestically produced merchandise accounted for approximately 55 percent of the Company's sales during 1980; the remaining approximately 45 percent consisted of merchandise produced abroad, almost entirely in the Far East. Company personnel in the United States and abroad regularly monitor production at facilities which manufacture its products.

PRINCIPAL AND SELLING STOCKHOLDERS

The following table sets forth certain information, as of March 28, 1981, with respect to the number of shares of Common Stock owned, to be offered for sale and to be beneficially owned after this offering, by all persons who were known by the Company to own beneficially more than 5 percent of the then outstanding Common Stock, all Selling Stockholders, each of the Directors of the Company and the Company's officers and Directors, as a group:

Name and Address	Ownership of Common Stock prior to Offering (1)		Shares to be Sold (2)	Ownership of Common Stock after Offering (1)(2)	
	Number of Shares	Percent		Number of Shares	Percent
Elisabeth Claiborne Ortenberg (3) 1441 Broadway New York, NY	523,640	16.71	134,478	389,162	11.18
Arthur Ortenberg (3) 1441 Broadway New York, NY	523,640	16.71	134,478	389,162	11.18
Leonard Boxer 4 Emerson Lane Secaucus, NJ	523,640	16.71	134,478	389,162	11.18
Jerome A. Chazen 1441 Broadway New York, NY	523,640	16.71	134,478	389,162	11.18
J. James Gordon	65,000	2.07	16,693	48,307	1.39
Joseph Gaumont 200 E. 57th Street New York, NY	227,500	7.26	58,425	169,075	4.86
Charness Family Investments Ltd. (4) 2 St. Clair Avenue, East Toronto, Canada	162,500	5.18	41,733	120,767	3.47
Catway Investments Ltd. (4)	97,500	3.11	25,040	72,460	2.08
Albert Fink Milton (5)	97,500	3.11	25,040	72,460	2.08
Elizabeth Fenner Milton (5)	65,000	2.07	16,693	48,307	1.39

EXHIBIT 6 (*concluded*)

Name and Address	Ownership of Common Stock prior to Offering (1)		Ownership of Common Stock after Offering (1)(2)		
	Number of Shares	Percent	Shares to be Sold (2)	Number of Shares	Percent
Albert Fenner Milton, Custodian, F/B/O Elizabeth Hunt Milton under the Uniform Gifts to Minors Act (5)	9,750	0.31	8,346	1,404	0.04
Jerome Gold	65,000	2.07	16,693	48,307	1.39
Martin J. Tandler	65,000	2.07	16,693	48,307	1.39
Jacob Rosenbaum (6)	40,625	1.30	10,433	30,192	0.87
Belle Rosenbaum (6)	40,625	1.30	10.433	30,192	0.87
Theodore Brodie (7)	40,625	1.30	10,433	30,192	0.87
Simmi Brodie (7)	40,625	1.30	10,433	30,192	0.87
All Officers and Directors as a group (7 persons)	2,159,560	68.90	554,605	1,604,955	46.13

(1) All shares listed are owned of record and, to the Company's knowledge, beneficially.

(2) Assumes the Underwriters' 115,000 share over-allotment option is not exercised. Percentage is based on total shares to be outstanding after this offering.

(3) Arthur Ortenberg and Elisabeth Claiborne Ortenberg are husband and wife; each disclaims beneficial ownership of all shares owned by the other.

Case 3-4

ALLEN LANE

It was March 1982, and Allen Lane sat at his desk pondering a confusing array of issues relative to his bid for Plas-Tek Industries (PTI). Allen had been trying to buy a company for almost three years. On a number of occasions he had come quite close, only to have one circumstance or another block his way. Would his bid for PTI meet the same fate, or would his search for a business finally be over?

BACKGROUND

Allen Lane, 45, had had a variety of experience since his graduation from business school in 1965 (see Exhibit 1 for resume). He spent several years with Wagner Electric Co. in Springfield, Massachusetts, eventually filling the role of vice president of operations for this relatively small manufacturer of electronic parts.

Allen left the firm in 1972 to become an independent consultant to industry. He focused primarily on operations-oriented work: inventory control systems, manufacturing methods, material control, etc.

After three years of relative success, Allen disbanded his efforts in order to join James & Co. in New York.

> I enjoyed working for myself and was making a comfortable living. I grew tired, however, of working on the same kind of problems. James offered the

opportunity to get involved with more general management issues and strategic problems. I was also excited about working with some people whom I considered to be extremely bright and interesting.

Allen joined James in January of 1975, and worked with a varied roster of clients and industries. By 1980, however, Allen reached the conclusion that it was time to leave.

> I was becoming frustrated with the cumbersome and generally bureaucratic processes at the very large companies which are the base of James' clientele. James really did expand my horizons and my point of view. My experience there built a lot of general management perspective and honed important general management skills (I thought) which I was eager to use. I wanted to run my own company.

In June 1980, Allen informed James of his intentions to leave. It was important to Allen that James was generous enough to offer the continued resources of the firm, including office space and secretarial services, while he looked for an opportunity. Allen began thinking about how to get into his own business.

LAYING THE GROUNDWORK

Allen had once before thought about buying a company but had no idea where to begin, and did not have any close friends who had tried. His experience at James had given him numerous contacts and some credibility, as well as modest financial resources (i.e., roughly $100,000 in liquid assets which he felt he could afford to invest in a company). He described the thought process behind his plan of action and his progress.

> First, I was sure that I wanted to purchase a going concern rather than start up a business:
>
> — The start-up process is a lot riskier, takes longer to pay out, and requires a more single-minded commitment to the process than does purchasing a going concern.
> — I never felt I had a "better mousetrap" around which to start a business.
> — I enjoy being a fixer, a consultant, more than being a creator.
> — Finally, I had the time and resources to wait until I found a good deal.
>
> Next, I decided that in order to have a shot at finding something you needed to have a *focus:* "If you don't know where you're going, any path will get you there." Even if you change your focus later on, at least people have a sense that you know what you want. I decided to look for an industrial distribution business.
>
> — I specifically excluded hi-tech and software-type businesses:
>   • There is a lot of growth which makes these businesses attractive, but they are "faddish" and as a result there is an incredible amount of competition for deals from large corporations with very deep pockets.

- I felt that I had to understand and be able to manage the key aspects of the technology in order to minimize risk and successfully run the business.
- I wanted it to be a business where the decisions *I* would make would have a major influence and make the difference—not the research engineer down the hall.

— I decided to focus on a distribution business:

- I had done a lot of work in the industry as a consultant.
- Distribution businesses are typically very undermanaged.
- One of the key factors for success is excellent systems—a good fit for my skills.
- In any given segment (like electronics components distribution) the firms are typically spread over a wide range in terms of their profitability. If you can buy a company in the bottom third of that range, and manage its margin up into the upper third, you can make *a lot* of money. And, the skills required to do this are all basic general management skills.
- These businesses lend themselves to asset-based financing (i.e., they have heavy current assets).
- There are lots of small, owner-managed distributors around, and the competition for deals is less (to a large extent because they are not, historically, favored corporate acquisition targets).

About this time, I started talking with contacts who were in the deal flow, who encouraged me and suggested I look into electronics distribution. They also told me that I wouldn't *really* understand the acquisition process until I actually went throught the process of trying to buy a company.

Early that fall (1980), I spoke with another guy, Dan Ray, who was also leaving James, and who had some experience in the electronics distribution business. We decided to work together.

We had just started making contacts in an attempt to look at deals when we heard through an accounting firm that Spectronics might be for sale. We called the president, Bert Spec, and sure enough, it was for real.

We had only been at it for only a short time, and we were ready to chase our first deal.

SPECTRONICS

Spectronics was a $165 million (sales) distributor of electronic components, located in Newark, New Jersey. It was a publicly traded company, but Burt Spec owned a controlling interest of about 55 percent.

We looked at the numbers and, in the price range he was talking, about $20/share or $15 million, the deal made good economic sense. Spectronics also seemed to offer the potential for improvement in rate of return that we were looking for. (See Exhibit 2.) We put together a 200-page business plan which outlined the industry, our credentials, the company, our plans for it— the works. After six or eight weeks, we managed to pull together an $11 million package of financing which included $1 million in equity, $8 million in secured debt and $2 million of "mezzanine debt" (i.e., a higher risk unsecured loan with a higher return to the lender). We offered $21.50 a share. By now, it was the middle of December, and we had been working on the deal for about three months.

We found out a week later that the company was sold for $2/share *less* than our offer. The other group had offered $19.50 plus a huge "consulting contract" for Bert Spec. We were livid and wanted to sue, but this would have required revealing our equity backer who was anxious to protect his anonymity. So—there went our first deal.

A Reflection

Looking back three years later, it was probably a good thing that we didn't get the first deal that came down the pike. We learned an incredible amount, and it cost us nothing but our time. The valuable lessons included:

— Don't go after a public company unless you have a backer willing to underwrite the process. The lawyers and accounting fees required to put a public deal together are far higher than for a private company. This is a sunk cost, and if the deal falls apart—as they often do—you've lost these fees.
— The acquisition business is a rough-and-tumble one. We were advised not to tell potential investors the name of a company until we absolutely had to. We heard horror stories about guys like us getting squeezed out by the people who had the money and who went around the entrepreneurs and bought the company themselves.
— It is a lucrative business. If you find a deal, *and* hold on to it, you can extract 10–20 percent just for finding it and packaging the deal. If you put some money in or are actually going to manage the venture, your share can go up to 50 percent or so with a limited investment in even a large deal.

Back to the Drawing Board

So, Dan and I put our heads together to decide where to go. We came to the conclusion that all of our initial thoughts on the industry were correct. Moreover, we knew a lot more about the industry, had some contacts, and we thought we could keep our backers together. So, we decided to maintain our focus on the electronics distribution industry.

We called every company—about 60 or so—which met our criteria:

— Northeast corridor location.
— Sales of $5 to $50 million.

We looked for any way in other than a cold call—a lawyer, accountant, friend, anything. We talked to industry observers, customers, suppliers, and banks in an attempt to plug into the grapevine.

We had heard that 5 percent of *all* businesses are "for sale" and that 2 percent are *very actively* for sale. Well, out of our 60 calls, we found 8 that seemed interested enough to warrant a meeting. Of these, we had second meetings with 4, a third meeting with 2, and pursued 1, Ace Electronics, very aggressively.

ACE ELECTRONICS

By now it was March of 1981, and we had been looking at the industry for about six months. Ace was a little different—it focused on very low-tech and together with current inventories had a large stock of almost obsolete parts. Ace was owned by Abe Fox, who had started the business 25 years ago, and was now retiring. He was typically one of the only sources in the *country* for some old condensers, vacuum tubes, and electromechanical parts. You can imagine that his margins were *very* good.

We spent two months haggling and finally shook on a deal. He went away to California for a vacation and when he came back he declared that the deal was off.

Another Reflection

Ace really opened my eyes to the world of small business. Most small businesses which we looked at, and of which Ace was the first, have "undervalued inventory." Ace, for instance, had its inventory on the books for $600,000, although the owner claimed (and after some careful checking we concurred) that it was worth at least $4 million. (See Exhibit 3 for two sets of financial statements.)

This understatement is done because of *taxes*. If you overstate your cost of goods sold, you reduce your stated profit, and hence your taxes. Over time the stated book value of inventory becomes small relative to the actual value.

This is not problem to the buyer, of course, if you are going to continue this practice. However, I had decided early on that I did not want to play such games.

This can create a problem in a small company acquisition. If you keep the inventory on the books at its understated amount, the IRS is very unlikely to see any potential issue. However, if you mark the inventory up to its "fair market value," the IRS may catch on and can (fairly) claim that the company had been underpaying its taxes all along.

So, then you come up against two issues:

— Sale of Stock versus Assets: The liabilities of a company always remain attached to the stock. If you buy the assets of a firm, the seller maintains the potential tax liability. However, if you buy the stock, as most sellers prefer, then *you* are stuck with the potential liability.
— Tax on "Discovered Inventory": Once the inventory is discovered, of course, this item has to be run through the income statement, and shows up as profit which must be taxed. My view, of course, was that Ace should

pay this tax since it had been underpaying all along, and that it had, in effect, accrued taxes. Naturally, Ace would think that if I am "stupid enough" to be honest and declare this to the IRS, I should pay the tax.

Perhaps at this point, I should comment on what I perceive as my own style. There is a large gray area between what is ethically right and wrong. There are many opportunities to "play games" in the process of looking for a deal: exaggerating net worth, experience, the numbers on a deal, and so forth. These things may be ethically "wrong," or perhaps they are border line. Whatever the case, I had decided early on that they just didn't make good business sense for me. One of the critical things I had going for me was my reputation. People "calibrate you" based on the veracity of your total presentation. If they detect that you are being less than totally honest about *anything*, then they discount *everything* that you say—I couldn't afford to let that happen. Thus, I decided that the right style for me was to be very open and straightforward with sellers, financial sources, and others.

GARDENPRO

Gardenpro was a distributor of garden products, hardware, and paint, located in New Jersey. I heard about the deal from a business broker who showed me financials (with the name of the company deleted) and I was interested. He set us up to meet Chuck Stamen, Gardenpro's owner/manager.

It was an attractive business in a good location and was a distributor—just the kind of company I was looking for.

I met Chuck, and after the preliminary chat and tour, we started talking price. Pretty soon, Chuck mentioned that "the financials didn't fairly reflect the earning power of the business." Why was that so? Well, it seems that Chuck had a little scheme going where he pulled about $500,000 in cash out of the business—off the books and tax-free.

It worked roughly like this: he would take an order for products from one of his "friendly" customers, and give the order to his employees to load in the truck. Then Chuck would announce that he had to do some business with the fellow anyway, and he would drive the truck over. His friend would pay about 80 cents on the dollar—in cash—for the goods, and then Chuck would just rip up the order. No one would ever know.

Of course, he wanted me to value this off-the-books amount in making my bid. My position was that I wasn't going to play these games, and further, I was likely to lose these customers altogether, because I wasn't going to accept 80 cents on the dollar for my products if I was selling them.

I did submit a bid, and knew that I could obtain financing. By this point, I was familiar with the approximate formula that secured lenders use to calculate the "financibility" of a company.

— 85 percent of the receivables under 90 days old (to solid accounts), plus
— 40 percent to 60 percent of the inventory, depending on its salability, and to some extent on how good the deal is.

In addition, you can usually also borrow one quarter to one third of the appraised value of the plant and equipment; real estate assets can be mortgaged up to 80 percent or 90 percent. This is a very straightforward approach to calculate how much you can borrow on an asset-financed deal.

As you might expect, I lost Gardenpro to someone with a higher bid. But I later found out that the company was never sold.

HYDRAPRESS

A few months later, in October of 1981, I came across Hydrapress, a manufacturer of hydraulic presses for making refractories and special bricks for use in high-temperature processes, such as furnaces for molten metal and glass. I heard about this deal from another business broker. He was hesitant to refer me to Morris Golden, presdient of Hydrapress, because I did not have the $3 or $4 million in hard cash required to do the deal. But he did set me up with an investment banker who had appraised Hydrapress and who was representing the seller.

We got together, and I learned that it was a fairly typical selling situation. Golden was 68 and had decided it was "time to retire and enjoy life." His wife wanted to go to Florida, and all his friends were telling him to sell the company and tidy up his estate.

The investment banker told me that there were two very serious buyers lined up who clearly had the cash and were interested in purchasing the company as an investment. They would need a management team; perhaps I could work a joint deal with one of them. I did speak with each of these groups, but told them I was also working to raise the capital to make a bid on my own. In any event, under the banker's auspices, I was able to visit Hydrapress and meet with its principals.

After visiting numerous banks, I finally did get an oral commitment for the money from the Fiduciary Bank, and wrote my proposal letter. I bid $3.4 million, but lost out by a small margin to a NYSE company.

Six months later, the investment banker called to ask if I was still interested. It seems that when push came to shove, Golden had balked at selling the company. According to the banker, he kept finding little nits with the deal until the buyer got so exasperated that he finally walked away.

By this time, I was chasing Plas-Tech and didn't have the time to get involved. More importantly, I had learned a lesson about buying a company from the founding owner: It's *tough*. No one wants to sell "his baby."

A PERSPECTIVE

Allen commented on a few other aspects of the deal business he had learned about over the past several years.

"Ham and Egging"

One of the real "arts" to the process of trying to buy a company is called "ham and egging." It refers to the delicate process of trying to get the financing secured before you have the company locked up, and trying to get the company committed before you have the financing.

Naturally, potential backers don't want to spend the time evaluating the deal or commit to financing unless they are fairly certain that you have an acceptable deal worked out with the company. The company, on the other hand, feels it is wasting its time talking to you unless you have the money.

I was always very straightforward with companies; I would describe the deal to different financial backers, get an oral commitment of interest, and tell the company that I had this oral commitment. Naturally, I projected the attitude that I was sure that financing would be available.

The process does get much easier as you go along. The first time is always the hardest. On subsequent deals, even if the previous deals have fallen apart, you can talk about having raised money before, and you have a portfolio of backers to deal with. After people know you, and have seen you in action on one deal and have come to trust you, they are far quicker to make a commitment on financing.

A Hierarchy of Buyers

All this leads one to talk about what I call "a hierarchy of buyers." None of the companies would even be talking to me if they could have sold to a NYSE company in an all-cash deal, or a tax-free exchange of stock. From a seller's perspective it appears that there are several classes of buyers doing deals:

— Class A: Another company who views the seller as a business with "strategic fit." They are willing to pay cash, and pay a premium price for the company.
— Class B: Investment bankers representing some company looking for a deal, often a conglomerate. Generally they won't pay the premiums that a strategic buyer will, but in either case, as a seller you don't have to worry about the money being there.
— Class C_1:   A leveraged buy-out specialist who will in all probability pay even less, but who has done deals before and who has a track record in raising the cash.
— Class C_2:   An individual who doesn't have the cash, hasn't done a deal, but knows what he's doing and can probably raise the money. I felt that I was a C_2 given my contacts and experience.
— Class C_3:   An individual with nothing but desire; this was me when I started out, before the Spectronics deal.

PLAS-TEK

In March of 1982, I ran into Jeff Brewster, an accountant with a Big-8 firm, with whom I had spoken around the time of the Spectronics deal. He thought he might have a few companies I'd be interested in, and we scheduled a lunch for the following week. One of the companies was Plas-Tek.

Background

Harry Elson had founded Plas-Tek, a manufacturer of specialty plastic components, in 1954. When he died in November of 1981, he left his estate which was valued at $7 million or so to a half-dozen well-known charities. Plas-Tek was part of the estate, and the trustee/executor, a big New York bank, had decided to sell it. In fact, PTI was actually two companies: HE Manufacturing and its sister company, Plas-Tek Sales Company. PTI refers to both companies.

The bank had a valuation of the business performed (see Exhibit 4 for a description of PTI's business and the valuation report) and then contacted customers, suppliers, and competitors to see if any were interested in purchasing Plas-Tek. When none expressed interest, the bank quietly put Plas-Tek on the market.

By the time I heard about the business, it had been on the market for a month or so, and the bank told me that unless I were going to bid $600,000 or more not to bother. They told me that they wanted to close off bidding later that week, but I figured that I could stall them for a little while. When Elson died, all of his estate went into a charitable trust. The bank's trust and estate department had a fiduciary obligation to get the highest price for the business. They would not look good if they refused to let me submit a bid.

So, during the next few days, I raced around trying to put together a deal and submit my bid. I had the valuation and the banks' ". . . beat $600,000" as a starting point.

Strategy

My strategy was to first *value* the business, and then *price* it. They are two different things. Obviously, I wanted my price to be lower than the business' value but high enough for the bid to get *me* to the bargaining table with the bank.

The Business: Fit with Allen Lane

First, I had to evaluate the business and how it fit with my skills and objectives. Clearly, it wasn't in the distribution area, but they did have some things in common, including the importance of customer service. Further, it was *definitely* going to require a lot of hands-on management. With Elson dead, there was really a management vacuum at Plas-Tek.

The Business Itself

Obviously, a crucial issue was the business itself. I was amazed to see that Plas-Tek had gross margins in excess of 50 percent for a nonproprietary product. Harry was pulling down over half a million a year from a business with a million dollars in sales! Was this a legitimate profit, and, more important, would it continue if I bought the business?

Key Employees

Plas-Tek had the equivalent of eight full-time shop workers as well as a book-keeper and a customer service/order entry clerk. I spent a day walking around the shop and was convinced that I could learn the manufacturing end of the business. As an engineer, I felt comfortable with the basic molding and machining operations. Still, there were several key employees whose efforts would be crucial to getting off to a good start.

— Bernie, the shop foreman, had been with PTI for 18 years. I talked with him and was convinced of his desire to stay on. He was about 55 and was making almost $50,000 a year, so he seemed to have little incentive to move. Unfortunately, he was in failing health, and if something did happen, we would be in tough shape.
— Sarah, the bookkeeper, knew the financial side of the business as well as Harry's pricing policies.
— Eleanor, the customer service/order entry clerk, knew a little bookkeeping as well as who the key customers were, what they ordered, and how it was priced. She also knew where all of the finished goods inventory was stored.

Harry had been clever in having a lot of part-time people on board, so there were often two people who knew the same job.

A Partner

Since the Spectronics deal, I had looked at doing things both on my own, and with a variety of partners. Generally, I am the oral type, and do my best thinking in a team-like atmosphere. I also wanted someone to mind the store while I was away and vice versa. I didn't want to be tied to the business night and day, everyday.

I thought it was important that a partner and I each be able to handle key aspects of the business, but still have a clear enough division of responsibilities that we not get in each other's way. I was also looking for someone with flexibility and a set of values, goals, and expectations that was compatible with mine.

I also knew that if I brought in a partner, I wanted it to be a full 50 percent partner. I had been involved with some less-than-equal partnerships before, and such a partner feels that he is doing more than his share of the work. The individual I chose as a partner was capable of matching my $100,000 equity contribution in order to buy his half of the equity. Dan Ray had joined a semi-conductor firm after the Spectronics deal fell through, but we had kept in touch. I knew he was still interested in doing something with me, and I still thought he would make a good partner.

Financing

Because I had the experience of putting together the described deals (and others), I had a portfolio of equity backers, asset-secured financiers, and other lenders to draw upon for financing.

I did have about $100,000 in equity, and ideally, I hoped to finance the remainder so that my partner and I could control 100 percent of the equity.

I thought we might be able to get the estate (represented by the bank) to take back a note if we could get a reputable bank to guarantee this debt. I did have excellent relationships with a few banks that I had worked with on other deals, and they seemed eager to work with me.

I also knew that if we borrowed on the business itself, that we would have to personally guarantee at least a portion of the note, and that the interest rate would be about 2 percent over prime, i.e., in the 17 percent to 19 percent range.

A Lawyer

I had worked with a variety of lawyers. Some were good negotiators, others good on tax or securities issues. I had developed a list of criteria to aid in the selection of an attorney (see Exhibit 5). We had to pick one and get him up to speed fast.

Stock versus Assets

The purchase of stock versus the purchase of assets was a major issue in the deal structure, and we knew we had to make a decision on this point early on. I would have preferred a simple purchase of assets. In this way, we would not have to assume *any* of the liabilities associated with the old company.

The bank, however, wanted to clean up and settle the estate. They were strongly in favor of a purchase of stock, which would saddle me with all liabilities, including contingent liabilities.

Contingent Liabilities

Contingent liabilities are real or potential liabilities which do not exist on the balance sheet. For instance, if an employee had lost an arm in an industrial accident, but had not sued the company, there was a contingent liability in that he *might* sue later and *might* win some *unknown* amount of money. We thought that the following contingent liabilities might exist for Plas-Tek and checked them out thoroughly:

— Existing lawsuit.
— Potential lawsuit.
— Potential tax liability.

We interviewed employees in an attempt to discover any potential problems, i.e., injuries or customer problems. As best we could determine, there were no existing lawsuits against the company and we checked the literature to unearth the possibility of potential product liability suits. We made a list of all the major substances the company used and ran computer searches to determine whether any of these was suspected of causing cancer or other diseases. Fortunately, they checked OK.

On the tax issue, however, we were not so lucky. There were two areas of potential liability:

— Unreasonable compensation: Harry had been pulling out *a lot* of money as salary, and hence deducting it on the corporate tax return. If the IRS stepped in, they could declare that some amount of this "salary" was excessive compensation, and reclassify it as a dividend. (See Exhibit 6 for tax code and explanation.) Then, the company would be liable for an income tax on this amount. This issue was complicated by the fact that Harry was operating PTI as two separate companies: HE Manufacturing was a straight corporation, and Plas-Tek Sales was a Sub S. If the IRS questioned the transfer-pricing policies of the company, the potential tax liability could increase to an even greater amount. (See Exhibit 7 for a full explanation of the potential tax liabilities.)

— Accumulated earnings: HE Manufacturing, the straight corporation, had a substantial amount of interest-earning current assets on its books. (See Exhibit 4 for balance sheet.) The IRS could, upon examination, claim that these assets were earnings which Elson had accumulated in HE Manufacturing rather than distributing them as dividends. (Again, see Exhibit 7 for full explanation.)

THE DECISION

Allen and his partner put a pot of coffee on the stove and prepared themselves for a long evening. They knew that it would not be easy to resolve these issues and value the business, but they had to submit their bid the following morning.

EXHIBIT 1
Resume of Allen Lane

Allen Lane

Experience

1975 to 1980
JAMES & COMPANY, INC.   NEW YORK, NEW YORK
Engagement Manager. As consultant to top management of large manufacturing and distribution companies, led teams of several consultants and up to 50 client personnel to formulate strategies, and to identify and implement opportunities to increase profitability and improve functional performance.

Served clients in electronics (telecommunications equipment, computers, components), machinery (business equipment), consumer products (sanitary paper, pharmaceuticals) and process (paper, packaging) industries ranging in annual revenues from $150 million to $9 billion.

Developed and presented consultant training in techniques for assisting manufacturers and distributors to reduce costs and improve delivery performance.

1972 to 1975
LANE AND ASSOCIATES   CAMBRIDGE, MASSACHUSETTS
As Principal, designed and implemented management systems to enhance competitive performance and improve profitability of manufacturing and distribution clients. Applications included inventory management, order entry, billing, accounts receivable, sales analysis, purchasing, accounts payable. Industries served included automotive parts and pharmaceuticals.

1965 to 1972
WAGNER ELECTRIC CO.   SPRINGFIELD, MASSACHUSETTS
As Vice-President, Operations, for this $30 million manufacturer responsible for planning and scheduling factory operations and managing inventories (raw material, work in process, finished goods). As Manager, System and Planning, responsible for developing capacity plans to support company's rapid growth. Also developed production planning and scheduling, labor control, budgeting, and other operational and accounting systems.

1958 to 1963
ACME STEEL FABRICATORS, INC.   BOSTON, MASSACHUSETTS
Purchasing Agent and Assistant to Vice President, Manufacturing, for this $5 million manufacturer of steel tanks, pressure vessels, and other weldments.

Education

1965
EASTERN BUSINESS SCHOOL   BOSTON, MASSACHUSETTS
MBA; concentrated in manufacturing and control.

1958
RENSSELAER POLYTECHNIC INSTITUTE   TROY, NEW YORK
Bachelor in Mechancial Engineering; elected member of Tau Beta Pi; Pi Tau Sigma honorary societies.

EXHIBIT 2

Profitability of 15 Largest Publicly Held Electronic Components Distributors

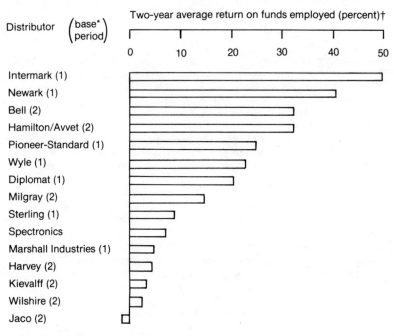

*Base period: (1) = 1978 and 1979; (2) = 1977 and 1978.
†[Profit before interest and taxes] / [(Assets) - (Accounts payable and accrued expenses)].
Corporate expenses, corporate assets and all accounts payable and accrued expenses have been allocated to electronics distribution business on basis of sales.

Source: Annual Reports (line of business data for electronics distribution).

EXHIBIT 3
Two Sets of Ace Financial Statements, Fiscal 1979 (In thousands of dollars)

	Income Statement #1 (as reported to IRS)	Income Statement #2 (as "estimated" by Fox)
Sales	$4,000	$4,000
Cost of goods sold	3,050	2,250
Gross margin	950	1,750
Expenses	750	750
EBIT	200	1,000
Interest	0	0
Taxes	100	100
Net profit	$ 100	$ 900

EXHIBIT 3 *(concluded)*

Assets	Balance Sheet #1 (as reported to IRS)	Balance Sheet #2 (as "estimated" by Fox)
Cash	$ 30	$ 30
Accounts receivable	500	500
Inventory	600	600
Fixed/other	20	20
Additional inventories	—	4,900
Total	$1,150	$6,050
Liabilities and Net Worth		
Accounts payable	$ 250	$ 250
Accrued expenses	50	50
Accrued taxes	25	25
Bank loan	100	100
Net worth	725	725
Additional net worth	—	4,900
Total net worth	725	$5,625
Total	$1,150	$6,050

EXHIBIT 4
Introductory Letter and Valuation Report

March 16, 1982

Dear Mr. Lane:

Enclosed is the evaluation report which we had prepared to guide us in the sale of Plas-Tek, Inc. Based on this report and our own preliminary analysis, we have now set the asking price for the sale of the companies at $750,000, and are so advising all of the parties who have met our preliminary requirements for establishing serious interest in the acquisition.

Please let us know within the next ten (10) days (a) if you are willing to pay our asking price, (b) the terms of your proposal, and (c) if you wish to make a counterproposal.

At this time we will only give serious consideration to offers to purchase at a price in excess of $600,000.

As you were previously advised, we intend to sell the corporation's entire stock (after removal of cash and marketable securities). We will only consider offers on terms if the purchase price is adequately secured by satisfactory collateral security other than the assets of the business itself.

EXHIBIT 4 (*continued*)

Our plan is to proceed as follows: We will immediately enter into negotiations with qualified buyers in order of the magnitude of their initial offer. We anticipate, based on the interest expressed to date by a number of apparently serious and qualified prospective purchasers, that we can settle within our proposed price range. If we find that we are unable to do so, we intend to broaden the base of prospective purchasers by announcing the availability of the companies to a wide variety of customary sources of prospective purchasers.

We trust that it will be apparent to you that we consider this to be the most expeditious way for us to attain the highest price we can, consistent with our responsibilities as executors of the estate of Harold Elson.

Accordingly, if you wish to be the successful purchaser, it will certainly be in your interest to make the highest offer in response to this request as soon as you can do so, as we intend to complete this transaction as quickly as we can.

Sincerely yours,

Senior Trust Officer
Major New York Bank

PLAS-TEK INDUSTRIES (PTI)
We have been asked to determine the fair market value of PTI. All of the outstanding common stock of the company is presently held in the estate of Harold Elson. The purpose of this appraisal is to assist the executors of the estate in determining the value of the business in order to sell it.

Conclusion

Based on our analysis of the relevant facts, it is our opinion that the current fair market value, in an all-cash transaction, of the operating assets and business of PTI is $600,000.

Description of Business

The business will be referred to in this report as PTI. HE Manufacturing is a corporation, and Plas-Tek Sales is a Subchapter S company; PTI refers to both companies.

The business was founded some 25 or more years ago by Harold Elson, and was operated by Mr. Elson until his death on November 20, 1981, at age 72.

PTI, located in Patterson, New Jersey, is in the business of manufacturing and distributing gaskets, washers, "0" rings, and similar items made of plastic. PTI makes parts out of fluoroplastic resins as well as other materials, including nylon, polyethylene and acrylic resins.

Products are generally made to industry standards or customer specifications. Approximately 90 percent of sales are made to distributors and original equipment manufacturers (OEM) with the balance sold to end users. PTI's customers come from a variety of industries, the most important being the food and chemical industries.

EXHIBIT 4 (*continued*)

Sales are made primarily in response to requests for quotations and to repeat customers. PTI has no salesmen. Advertising is confined primarily to a small listing in *Thomas' Register*. The company has about 300 active customer accounts. Listed below are the sales figures for the five largest customers, which accounted, in the aggregate, for 35.3 percent of 1981 sales.

	1981 Sales	Percent of Total Sales
Customer A	$98,487	10.5%
Customer B	72,377	7.7
Customer C	61,615	6.5
Customer D	51,599	5.5
Customer E	48,362	5.1
		35.3%

Income Statements

Shown following is a summary of income statements of the company for the five-year period ended August 31, 1981.

PTI Income Statement (*In Thousands of Dollars*)

	Fiscal Years Ended August 31				
	1981	1980	1979	1978	1977
Net sales.....................................	$942	$1,050	$894	$709	$652
Gross profit................................	551	640	495	427	369
Operating and overhead expense......	97	92	78	76	67
Profit before officer salary, investment income and income taxes.....................................	454	548	417	351	302
Investment income*	93	92	65	66	18
Profit before officer salary and income taxes......................	547	640	482	407	320
Officer salary..............................	480	505	415	360	280
New Jersey sales tax.....................	20	23	18	19	6
Profit before federal income tax..	$ 47	$ 112	$ 49	$ 28	$ 34

*Interest and dividends on cash and securities.

Manufacturing

Gaskets and washers are machined principally from cylinders or other shapes molded by PTI itself and also from plastic purchased from outside vendors. The company's facilities occupy a 3,700 square foot building owned by it in Patterson, New Jersey. Principal items of production equipment include a press, a sintering oven, and a number of lathes and other machine tools. The company has five full-time production employees and four part-time employees. The company is nonunion. Hourly wage rates range from $5 to $9. The office staff consists of a manager and a bookkeeper-secretary-receptionist.

Management

The success of PTI has essentially been based on, and dependent on, the management efforts of Harold Elson. The company built a reputation of fulfilling

EXHIBIT 4 (*continued*)

orders quickly. Mr. Elson put a great deal of personal effort into providing responsive service to his customers, often working on weekends to do so.

Approach to Value

The definition of "fair market value" employed in this appraisal is the price at which the property would change hands between a willing buyer and a willing seller when the former is not under any compulsion to buy and the latter is not under any compulsion to sell, both having reasonable knowledge of relevant facts.

In establishing a value for PTI, we have taken into account a variety of factors, including the nature and history of the company, the economic outlook, the book value, financial condition and earnings capacity of the company, its dividend capacity and intangible values, past sales of securities of the company, and comparisons with public companies in the same or similar industry.

It is assumed for the purpose of this valuation that PTI will be purchased exclusive of its excess cash or investment assets. The excess cash and investments would either be removed from the company prior to sale or would be compensated for with an additional dollar-for-dollar payment by the purchaser of the business.

Balance Sheet

Exhibit A shows a combined balance sheet for the business with the excess cash and investments set forth.

It can be seen that, with the excess cash investments removed, the net worth of the operating assets of the business is $200,000. If the land and buildings were carried at their current appraised value of $92,000, the adjusted net worth of the company would be $292,000.

Earnings Capability

In 1981 PTI earned $454,000 before officer salary, investment income and income tax. Clearly, a buyer would be attracted to the acquisition of PTI for its earnings capability rather than for its asset base. The estimate of fair market value, then, must begin with an analysis of the earnings history and capability of the company.

Set forth below is a summary of the earnings of the company, adjusted for investment income.

	Operating Profit * *before Office Salary*
Year	*($000)*
1981	$454
1980	548
1979	417
1978	351
1977	302

*Before investment income and federal and New Jersey income taxes.

EXHIBIT 4 (*continued*)

A key question is how much of the earnings ability of the company was due to the personal efforts of Mr. Elson and, accordingly, how much of such earnings ability is likely to remain in the future in his absence. The months since his death, in November 1981, have seen a decline in sales as illustrated below. It is the feeling of those presently running the business, however, that a good part of this decline is attributable to softness in the economy in general rather than to the absence of Mr. Elson. Some of the softness had already begun to make itself felt in the months prior to Mr. Elson's death. No customer is known to have ceased doing business with the company because of Mr. Elson's death. We understand that the executors have communicated with all the major customers and these customers have assured the executors of their satisfaction and that they anticipate continuing to do business with PTI.

PTI SALES
In Thousands of Dollars

	3 Months Sept.–Nov.		2 Months Dec.–Jan.*		5 Months Sept.–Jan.*	
	Amount	% Chg. from Prev. Yr.	Amount	% Chg. from Prev. Yr.	Amount	% Chg. from Prev. Yr.
1981.	$214	− 3.2%	$111	− 24.0%	$325	− 11.4%
1980.	211	+ .5	146	− 17.0	367	− 7.3
1979.	220	+ 25.0	176	0.0	396	+ 12.5
1978.	176	+ 10.0	176	+ 58.6	352	+ 29.9
1977.	160	+ 3.2	111	+ 6.7	271	+ 4.6
1976.	155		104		259	

*Of following year.

We have taken the view that the current decline in sales volume is temporary, being related to the currrent soft economy and possibly to the uncertainty related to a prospective change in ownership of the company. With new capable ownership in place, there is no reason that the business should not be able to continue at least in the levels of the recent past. Accordingly, we have elected to employ the 1981 levels of profit before taxes and owner compensation as the best available indication of future profitability, and the one on which buyer and seller might be most likely to base a sale price.

Staffing

In view of Mr. Elson's heavy personal involvement in the business and the long hours that he put in, a new owner might well be required to staff the company with more than one person to replace Mr. Elson.

We have assumed that the functions formerly performed by Mr. Elson could be replaced at a cost of $150,000.

Future Earnings Capability

Using this estimate of management cost, and the 1981 level of pre-tax income before owner compensation, produces the following estimate of the earnings capability PTI.

EXHIBIT 4 (*continued*)

Pro forma earnings (*In Thousands of Dollars*)

Profit before owner compensation and increased taxes $454
Management compensation. 150

Profit before income taxes 304
New Jersey income tax (10%) 30

Profit before federal income tax. 274
Federal income tax (1982 rates) 106

Net income after taxes. $168

We have concluded, then, that a party acquiring PTI and staffing it at the annual cost shown above, would be buying a business capable of generating net income after taxes at the annual rate of $168,000.

Capitalization Rate

The capitalized earnings approach to value is based on the premise that a potential investor in a going concern will base the purchase price he is willing to pay on some multiple of the earnings power of the company. The approach consists of applying an appropriate price-earnings multiple (P/E) to the earnings of the company in question. It becomes necessary, then, to determine the appropriate P/E. The most reasonable way to do so is to determine what earnings multiple investors have been willing to pay for stocks of other companies engaged in similar lines of business.

Ideally, in selecting comparable companies, we look for companies not only in the same general line of business, but with a similarity that extends as far as possible into all areas of corporate circumstances, including capital structure, specifics services performed, areas and intensity of competition, growth rates, and, if possible, size in terms of assets held, and the volume of sales. Only in the most unusual circumstances, however, will there be available even one publicly-traded company which would begin to satisfy these multifarious requirements.

Since PTI is a fabricator of plastic products, we have conducted our search for comparable companies from the industry group of plastic products manufacturers. After examining a large number of companies, we have selected four as comprising a respresentative group for purposes of this appraisal. Key facts on the companies in this group are set forth in Exhibit B.

Exhibit B shows a range of price-earnings ratios for plastic parts fabricators of from 3.6X to 6.4X with an average of 5.4X. The comparable companies are, of course, considerably larger than PTI. In the case of some of the companies, there is a proprietary element to their product offerings, which is lacking with PTI. They are also possessed of more management depth.

For the above reasons, we have selected a price/earnings ratio of 4.5X for PTI, which is below the average of the group.

Applying the 4.5X multiplier to the previously calculated earnings level of PTI produces a preliminary value for PTI of $750,000.

$$\$168,000 \times 4.5 = \$756,000, \text{ say } \$750,000.$$

EXHIBIT 4 (*continued*)

This, in effect, represents the hypothetical value at which PTI would trade if it were a public company. It is acknowledged that it is unlikely that a company as small as PTI would trade as a public company. Nonetheless, this approach to value corresponds with that which would be taken by many prospective buyers.

Adjustment for Illiquidity and Control

The valuation procedure above compares PTI to a group of companies whose securities are traded in the public market. The result produced, then, is the hypothetical price at which shares of PTI would trade if it were a public company. Since PTI is not a public company, it is necessary to make an adjustment in the price to reflect the fact that a holder of stock in PTI would not be able to sell his shares without considerable effort or delay. This adjustment is normally made by applying a discount to the price, called a discount for illiquidity.

A further adjustment must be made to reflect the fact that we are valuing PTI as a whole, rather than valuing a minority holding in the company. The market prices that we used to establish value were based upon transactions in minority interests in companies. It is necessary to reflect this difference. This is normally done by applying a premium called a control premium to the price paid on minority transactions.

It is our opinion that in the case of PTI, the appropriate discount for illiquidity and premium for control would approximately cancel each other out, leaving the value, based upon market prices, at what it would be without such adjustment, $750,000.

Dividends

With the exception of Subchapter S distributions, PTI does not have a history of paying dividends to its shareholders. For this reason, the dividend approach to value is not apposite in this case.

Prior Transactions

There are no known prior transactions in the stock of PTI. Therefore, this approach to value is not relevant.

Book Value

As stated earlier, the book value of the operating assets of PTI is $200,000, or $292,000, if the current appraised value of the real estate is taken into account. Since this value is considerably below the value based on earnings, it has little relevance in this case.

Adjustment for Cash Sale

The executors of the estate which owns PTI wish to sell the company in a transaction which will permit a winding up of the estate shortly thereafter. Accordingly, they are not in a position to offer extended payment terms to prospective buyers.

EXHIBIT 4 (*continued*)

Ordinarily, if a business of this size were sold, particularly to an individual, it would be customary for the seller to permit the payment of a significant portion of the purchase price over time.

Since an extended payment sale is not possible in this case, two effects will be produced, (*i*), the number of willing buyers with means available to consummate a purchase will be reduced, and (*ii*) the remaining buyers, in the absence of the availability of seller financing, will not be willing to pay as much for the company.

Because of these two effects, we have adjusted downward our assessment of the value of PTI by 20 percent, producing a value of $600,000.

Contingent Liabilities

The value determined in this appraisal presumes that a buyer of PTI would, in purchasing the business, assume no liabilities, real or contingent, other than the trade payables and other similar accrued liabilities arising from operations in the ordinary course of business. To the extent that the form of the transaction would require him to become actually or potentially obligated for other liabilities, the appraised value would have to be correspondingly adjusted.

Conclusion

Based on our analysis of the relevant facts, it is our opinion that the current fair market value, in a cash transaction, of the operating assets and business of PTI is $600,000.

EXHIBIT 4 (continued)

Exhibit A
Combined Balance Sheets
(in thousands of dollars)

Assets	HE Manufacturing	PLAS-TEK Sales	Eliminations	Combined	Investment Assets and Liabilities	Operating Assets and Liabilities
Cash	$170	$133		$ 303	$ 290	
Securities	507	234		741	750	
Accounts receivable	41*	150	$41*	150		$148
Inventory	60			60		60
Loans receivable	19	20		39	45	
Prepaid expenses	6	—		6		6
Total current assets	803	537	41	1,299	1,085	214
Fixed assets—net						
Equipment	5	6		11		11
Building	10	—		10		10
Land	10	—		10		10
Total assets	$828	$543	$41	$1,330	$1,085	$245

LIABILITIES AND CAPITAL

	HE Manufacturing	PLAS-TEK Sales	Eliminations	Combined	Investment Assets and Liabilities	Operating Assets and Liabilities
Accounts payable	$ 36	$ 50	$41	$ 45		$ 45
Taxes payable	10	7		17	17	
Accrued salary—officers	164	218		482	482	
Accrued expenses	10	—		10	10	
Total liabilities	220	375	41	554	509	45
Capital	608	168		776	576	200
Total liabilities and capital	$828	$543	$41	$1,330	$1,085	$245

*All HE accounts receivable are due from Plas–Tek sales.

EXHIBIT 4 (*concluded*)

Exhibit B

Company (Market)	Fiscal Year	Revenues $millions—1980 FY	Earnings per Share Latest 12 Months		Book Value per Share (1980 FY)	Stock Price 2/18/82	Price/ Earnings Ratio
			Amount	Period Ended			
Kleer-Vu Industries, Inc. (ASE)	Dec.	$13.5	$1.48	9/81	$5.16	5¼	3.5
Liqui-Box Corp. (OTC)	Dec.	43.8	1.28	9/81	9.64	8¼	6.4
Plymouth RubberCo. C1.B (ASE)	Nov.	63.8	.38*	11/81	6.75	2	5.3
Star-Glo Industries, Inc. (OTC)	Dec.	8.3	.57*	9/81	2.73	3⅜	6.4
Average							5.4
Range							3.5–6.4

*Excluding Extraordinary items.

EXHIBIT 5
Criteria for Selection of Attorney

1. Strong professional orientation—possess strong character, high degree of integrity and honesty, and general business competence.
2. Creative deal maker—ability to spot opportunities for mutual benefit in structuring deal terms.
3. Interest in working with entrepreneurs on a relatively small deal—enthusiasm for working on interesting issues with substantial creativity rather than mega-deal.
4. Caliber of corporate and tax skills—ability to integrate full range of corporate and tax issues into deal structure.
5. Strength as "hands-on" negotiator—ability to achieve goals at the bargaining table; good speaker, fast on feet.
6. Understanding of business issues—ability to craft deal in light of overall business goals, not merely tax and financing considerations.

EXHIBIT 6
Business Expenses—Unreasonable Compensation

TAX CODE SEC. 162. TRADE OR BUSINESS EXPENSES (paragraph a)

(a) In general, business expenses deductible from gross income include the ordinary and necessary expenditures, paid or incurred during the taxable year, directly connected with or pertaining to the taxpayer's trade or business, including
   —cost of goods sold, including a proper adjustment for opening and closing inventories,
   —a reasonable allowance for salaries or other compensation for personal services actually rendered,
   —traveling expenses (including amounts expended for meals and lodging other than amounts which are lavish or extravagant under the circumstances) while away from home in the pursuit of a trade or business; and
   —rentals or other payments made as a condition of the use or possession, for purposes of the trade or business, of property to which the taxpayer has not taken or is not taking title or in which he has no equity.

Explanation: Unreasonable Compensation

Compensation deductions are usually questioned by IRS only in closely held corporations. The usual reason for disallowance is that the compensation paid is "unreasonable." Factors that are generally considered in establishing reasonableness include: the work actually performed by the individuals; their training and experience; the time and effort devoted to the work; the results that have been achieved; the requirement for ability and skill; the inadequacy of compensation in earlier years; and compensation paid for comparable services by similar businesses.

Compensation payments which are based on profits are subject to the same rules as amounts paid as straight salary. Thus, a legitimate bonus arrangement is recognized as an allowable deduction, even though in years of high profits, the amounts paid may be larger than would ordinarily be paid on a straight salary basis.

In all cases, the IRS carefully checks any compensation arrangement which distributes compensation in a way which is proportional to stockholdings. The IRS may reclassify some or all of such compensation payments as dividends.

The wrongful deduction of business expenses, including unreasonable compensation, may be grounds for criminal action.

EXHIBIT 7
Letter from Accountants on Contingent Liabilities

April 14, 1982

Dear Mr. Lane:

A review has been made of the federal income tax returns and financial statements of HE Manufacturing Corporation and its related company, Plas-Tek Sales Company, for their fiscal years ending in 1979, 1980 and 1981. The purpose of the review was to estimate the magnitude of tax deficiencies from certain adjustments which may result from an examination of their federal returns by Internal Revenue Service. Our findings were made taking into account certain assumptions regarding reasonable compensation and other matters which were discussed at a meeting last week among ourselves and counsel.

Background

The capital stock of each of the companies was owned entirely by Harold Elson, who died in late 1981. Plas-Tek Sales is a Subchapter S corporation which reports on a fiscal year ended August 31. HE Manufacturing Corporation reports its income on a June 30 fiscal year. The business consists of the manufacture of gaskets, washers, and other plastic products.

Operations over the years have been quite profitable. In each of the three years prior to his death Mr. Elson's salary from both companies amounted to more than $400,000. The balance sheet of HE Manufacturing discloses substantial amounts of cash and investments and relatively small liabilities. For these reasons, concern has been expressed that Internal Revenue Service could assert an unreasonable compensation and/or accumulated earnings issue if the tax returns of the companies were to be examined.

Since Plas-Tek Sales has a Subchapter S election in effect, the accumulated earnings issue would not result in a tax deficiency unless the company's Subchapter S status could be involuntarily terminated. We believe the prospect of that situation to be extremely remote. While unreasonable compensation is not generally considered in a Subchapter S situation because all earnings are taxed currently to the shareholders, a net deficiency could result if compensation, taxed at a minimum rate of 50 percent, were converted to dividend income taxable (before 1982) at a maximum rate of 70 percent by changing its character to passive income. Since such an assessment would be at the individual level it has not been considered in our review of corporate matters.

Unreasonable Compensation

Based upon our discussions and the valuation appraisal it is believed that compensation of $150,000 per year for PTI could be sustained if the issue were to be challenged by Internal Revenue Service. Using that number as a bench mark, we have calculated the deficiency to HE Manufacturing which would result using three different approaches:

1. Disallow amounts in excess of $75,000 per company.
2. Disallow compensation in excess of $75,000 and allocate the taxable income earned between the companies on an equal basis. This results in allocating income from Plas-Tek Sales to HE Manufacturing.
3. Disallow compensation in excess of $75,000 per company and allow Plas-Tek Sales a return of 5 percent on sales plus its reported expenses. Allocate excess income to HE Manufacturing.

EXHIBIT 7 (*continued*)

The federal income tax deficiency before interest which would result from adjustments described above, as summarized on Exhibit A, would be as follows:

Alternative 1—$ 86,768
Alternative 2—$196,280
Alternative 3—$369,773

We are not aware that Internal Revenue Service has ever challenged the intercompany pricing of products sold by HE to Plas-Tek. However, considering the structure of the related companies, i.e., HE being taxable but Plas-Tek electing Subchapter S status, the Service could maximize the tax revenue by allocating income back to HE Manufacturing. The fact that the cash ultimately resides in Plas-Tek may be reconciled by the Service by claiming that HE paid a dividend of the excess income to Elson which was then reinvested by him in Plas-Tek, a common position when dealing with related corporations. The result would then be additional income tax to HE with no corresponding reduction of tax at the individual level.

We are not in a position to conclude as to the reasonableness of the profit rate that should be realized by each of the companies, i.e., manufacturing by HE and sales by Plas-Tek. The gross profit reported by Plas-Tek for each of the three years was exactly 40 percent, whereas the gross profit realized by HE ranged from 27 percent to 35 percent. Accordingly, Alternative 2 was predicated upon an equal splitting of the combined net profit between the two companies. It is conceivable, however, that the Service may take the position that Plas-Tek is nothing more than an agency and is entitled only to a reasonable commission on sales plus its actual selling expenses and officer's compensation of $75,000. If the Service were to take such a position, substantial income would be allocated to HE.

Accumulated Earnings Tax

If it were to be assessed, the accumulated earnings tax would be imposed only upon HE since all of the taxable income of Plas-Tek is taxed currently to its shareholder under the provisions of Subchapter S. The balance sheet of HE at June 30, 1981, included $507,000 of securities of total assets of $828,000 and shows a ratio of current assets to current liabilities after excluding unpaid salary to shareholder of more than 12 to 1. Based upon those statistics, it is reasonable to assume that an accumulated earnings question would be raised upon examination.

If assessed, the accumulated earnings tax is calculated on an annual basis on the "accumulated taxable income" of the corporation. In simplified terms, the tax base is equal to the taxable income for the year less federal income taxes on income and any dividends paid for the year. Because HE paid out substantial salaries to its shareholder, the reported taxable income in the three years in question was relatively modest. Thus, tax for all three years would only amount to approximately $20,000. Of course, the Service could attempt to impose the tax on the income of the corporation after a substantial increase due to disallowed compensation deductions. If that were to happen, however, we believe a successful argument could be made that the excessive compensation should be treated as a constructive dividend to the shareholder, thus reducing the "accumulated income" tax base back to an amount approximately equal to the taxable income reported on the returns. Accordingly, the accumulated earnings tax issue does not appear to be especially troublesome.

EXHIBIT 7 (*concluded*)

Statute of Limitations

It was represented to us that the Internal Revenue Service has examined the returns of PTI through fiscal 1978. While it was stated that the examination resulted in a "no change" report, we have yet to see a copy of the letter. Returns for the three fiscal years since 1978 remain open under the statute of limitations.

While specific representations have not been made, we believe the companies followed the practice of filing returns on or before the original due date, without extension. On that basis, the normal three-year statute of limitations would run as follows:

	Fiscal year ending in		
	1979	1980	1981
HE	9/15/82	9/15/83	9/15/84
Plas-Tek	11/15/82	11/15/83	11/15/84

Normally the statute of limitations is not a major consideration to a Subchapter S corporation, unless it has capital gains taxable at the corporate level or loses its qualification, since an adjustment to the corporation's income would be reflected as an assessment to its shareholders. While the matter is somewhat unclear, one case has held that an assessment may be made by reference to the statute as it applies to the shareholders, a point which should be considered in the case of fiscal year corporations.

We will be pleased to provide further services in this area if required.

Sincerely,

Case 3-5

STEVE COX

"Until a week ago, I was so caught up in planning for Geodrill (a proposed firm to compete in contract drilling in Oklahoma and Kansas) that I almost couldn't think it wouldn't work. The desire to be in my own business was so strong that I may not have weighed objectively the declining demand for drilling rigs."

Steve Cox was approaching graduation from the Eastern Business School in the spring of 1976. His background, including his experience in the drilling industry, is given in his resume. In January 1976, Steve Cox had completed a report entitled, "GEODRILL: An Investment in the Energy Services Market." (See Exhibit 1 for excerpts from the report.)

STEVE'S SEARCH FOR EQUITY

Steve intended the report as a basis for obtaining equity and debt financing. A classmate of Steve's introduced him to his father, William Cramer, president of the Cramer Seed Company. The Cramer Seed Company had substantial holdings of Midwestern farmland and was a supplier of agricultural equipment and fertilizers. William Cramer was also involved with a family investment trust which he characterized as "reasonably conservative, but willing to take a chance." Although the Cramer Trust had invested primarily in agribusiness ventures, it also had invested in a cable television company and "had even drilled a few oil wells." The trust had recently been separated from the seed company and had cash available for investment.

After Mr. Cramer's initial introduction to Steve, he and his son flew to Oklahoma to meet with Steve and his father. Steve Cox believed that the Cramer Trust viewed Geodrill not only as a potential for the investment of growth funds, but equally important, as an investment which might in time facilitate the purchase of petroleum products for fertilizers were a petroleum shortage to recur. With this initial positive response by Mr. Cramer, Steve decided not to pursue other sources of equity financing and started to focus on attracting the Cramer Trust as an equity partner.

WILLIAM CRAMER'S ANALYSIS

As William Cramer reviewed the potential investment in Geodrill, there were many things to be considered. Although he usually took the lead in investment decisions, all six brothers and sisters in the trust were decision makers and he would have to sell the Geodrill investment to them at a family meeting. The Cramer Trust had approximately $3 million in investments and William Cramer felt that Geodrill would be the highest risk investment that the trust had ever made.

The concept of the project was "generally favorable" to William Cramer. The oil business was not totally new to the Cramer Trust. Also, Steve's father was experienced in the business and he would only have Steve's best interests in mind. For these reasons, William Cramer was comfortable with Steve Cox's cost estimates and projections.

In this deal, as with any other deal, William Cramer felt that the quality of the people involved was the key factor. "The concept has to be good, but we would place the most emphasis on the people." William Cramer was "generally dubious about people at first meetings, especially in a business deal" but he was "very highly impressed with Steve and his educational background." He also liked his age and personal energy. Mr. Cramer was also impressed with Steve's father, particularly his honesty and technical background. Steve's father would be able to give Steve the necessary guidance in technical areas that Mr. Cramer felt he needed.

The Cramer Trust members preferred to have other equity investors in any deal. Generally, their choice of co-investors was someone with whom the trust had other investments. William Cramer planned to pursue the venture but he knew that the final decision by the other trust members to invest in Geodrill might depend upon him finding a suitable equity partner. Therefore, he decided to show the deal to another local family investment group.

THE NEGOTIATION

When Steve Cox initially contemplated a drilling company, he felt that $500,000 in equity would be needed to get a company off to a fast start. He felt investors who would be attracted would not be interested in small investments and slow start-ups. He also hoped that his own experience and that of his father would justify their retaining 75 percent of the equity even though they had almost no cash to invest. By January 1976, when he prepared the report extracted in Exhibit 1, and when he had entered discussions with the Cramer Investment Trust, he had changed these expectations to $200,000 capital stock and less than 50 percent equity for both him and his father. The actual basis on which discussions proceeded with the Cramer Trust during the spring of 1976 was $200,000 in equity and 40 percent of the ownership accruing to the Coxes with no capital required of them. Further, the Cramer Trust members agreed verbally that if they financed the project Steve Cox could purchase an additional 11 percent of the outstanding stock at book value when Geodrill had completed its first year of positive cash flow.

Although other aspects of the agreement between Steve and the Cramer Investment Trust were drawn up in draft form, the agreement for his purchasing the additional 11 percent of stock was never reduced to writing. Steve was uncertain if and how he should get what he understood to be a firm verbal agreement reduced to writing.

> It is not as if we are dealing at arms length. Bill Cramer, who introduced me to the Cramer Investment Trust, is very well regarded by both them and me. This whole negotiation has proceeded in a spirit of trust and respect for what they as the financial source and we as knowledgeable operating people would bring to Geodrill. About their fairness and honesty I have no question. Should I now say the promise I can buy 11 percent of the stock must be put in writing?

With a carefully studied but not final commitment of $200,000 equity from Cramer Trust to the proposed Geodrill, Steve Cox set out on the two-week spring break to find debt money to complete the financing plan. To his surprise he was turned down by the Texas bank to which he had a strong introduction. He hastily contacted three manufacturers of drilling equipment, but none would extend credit. He informed William Cramer of these reverses in his plans, and he realized later, the trust members began to reconsider the tentative arrangements made with him.

Two days later, however, Steve found that he could get a loan on an equipment mortgage from an Oklahoma bank at 1.5 percent over the prime rate and further found a supplier of drilling rigs who was willing to sell him equipment with 25 percent of the purchase price down and the rest to be paid over time. Thus he had choices for supplementing the equity money to start the first rig. But the unwillingness of others to come up with loan money as quickly as Steve had anticipated had set the Cramer Trust members to reviewing the venture. And this sharp questioning approach brought Steve himself back to the point of reevaluating the venture and comparing it with his best job alternative.

OTHER ALTERNATIVES

Steve had six job offers which were firm or would quickly be made firm, he thought, if he were to show strong interest. Two of the firm offers were with large oil companies. He had little interest in working for a large company, but he had signed up for these interviews when his future was quite uncertain. The large company offers and other possibilities were distinctly overshadowed, in Steve's opinion, by a firm offer from the Goldrus Drilling Co. Engaged in both drilling and production of oil, Goldrus had grown from $6 million volume in 1971 to $60 million in 1975. Goldrus did "higher quality" contract drilling—not just pushing a drill bit at so much per foot, but rather contracting for the entire engineering, financing, and evaluation of cores in a drilling operation. This was a higher price service and also a way to differentiate a drilling company.

Steve would be the first employee of Goldrus who had both a Petroleum Engineering degree and an MBA degree. The offered salary was $30,000 plus substantial benefits including a car. His prospective employers knew that he might go into business for himself some day, but the two principals had pressed Steve to work for them one trial year and if this proved satisfactory on both sides to see if further pay and benefits might make it attractive for Steve to stay longer.

The subject of Steve's salary had come up during discussions with the Cramer Trust. Steve wanted a "market salary" which he felt was set by his recent job offers. Although William Cramer felt that Steve was deserving of such a salary, he also felt that Steve should be willing to take a reduced, though comfortable, salary to reflect a personal economic contribution to the venture.

INDUSTRY INFORMATION AND STEVE'S ANALYSIS

The information which Steve Cox reviewed covered the following:

— The Hughes Tool Co. statistics on active rotary rigs indicated that the number of active drilling rigs rose from 1,600 in January 1975 to 1,800 in December 1975. By April 1976 this number had declined to less than 1,500.
— At the end of April, the *Oil and Gas Journal* commented, ". . . the rig count has plummeted as companies slowed their spending rate from the late-1975 levels."

— Other sources showed that petroleum consumption in the United States was running at record levels in 1976 and predicted that rotary rig activity would pick up by the middle of 1976.

— The *Petroleum Engineer Magazine*, June 1976, commented:

> During the first few months of 1976, 14,397 wells and 68.3 million feet of hole were recorded as completed in the United States, up 22.7 percent and 22.8 percent respectively, over comparable totals for the same period last year. Independent operators drilled 83.4 percent of these completions.
>
> These increases may seem surprising in view of the recent decline in rig count, but it must be remembered that many of the wells now being recorded as completed were spudded in 1975. Too, several months are often required to connect new gas wells to market and such wells are not counted as "completed" until they are actually onstream. Heavy development drilling efforts, especially in shallow areas of Texas, and a general increase in operating efficiency also are contributing to the higher totals. Some decline in footage and completions may be expected over the next few months to reflect the drop in rig count experienced in the first quarter of this year.

Among the factors on Steve's mind were the following:

— The Energy Bill was passed which rolled back the price of crude and there was a strong impact on the gas industry from the failure of Congress to deregulate gas.

— The reduction of the depletion allowance in 1975 reduced by some $2 billion the cash flow to oil-producing companies—money which might have been spent on exploration.

— Concern among drillers about possible changes in tax laws affecting divestiture and intangible drilling costs as well as minimum preference tax.

— Drilling permits were usually sought six months in advance and this lead indicator was down in the spring of 1976. A longer-range indicator is geophysical mapping which has a rough three-year lead time. *The Drilling/DCW Magazine*, June 1976, commented as follows:

> Far too few people realize, says the International Association of Geophysical Contractors, that what happens in seismic work will determine the level of exploratory drilling to follow. Latest count at the end of April (1976) shows seismic activity down 16 percent—238 versus 283 crews operating in the like period a year ago. Total seismic activity is down almost 30 percent from the recent high in July 1974. But on the encouraging side: some forecasters anticipate upswing by midsummer (1976).

— A conversation with an independent driller who said he had contracted for drilling at $9.50 per foot in 1975 but that his current best offer was at $8 per foot.

Steve felt that entering the well-drilling field made sense in late 1975 when the well-drilling companies were at 100 percent capacity. Four months later there was excess capacity. During the heavy demand of 1975, well-established drilling companies with well-trained men and good rigs were contracting at $4,000 per day. Steve had done his figuring at a more conservative $2,940, partly in anticipation of a softening of demand and also because Geodrill would be in a start-up position needed to build an organization and reputation. Steve commented:

> The well-drilling industry is greatly influenced by supply and demand. When the price of oil is up, drilling increases and drilling prices shoot up and the cost of equipment, if available, goes very high. When drilling is weak, the price of rigs is way down. But this is also a cash-flow business. The importance of cash flow may make it impossible for a firm to start up when things are slack. Timing is all important.
>
> Now that the uncertainties about the demand for drilling are in the forefront, some other doubts have assumed greater proportions. I am mindful of the huge amount of remaining negotiations and legal problems in setting up the structure of Geodrill and its relationship with the Cramer Trust and with sources of debt financing. Even if things moved forward with no major change of mind on the part of anyone, there would be considerable time involved—at least two months up to I don't know how long—time during which I would have no income. We are expecting our second child and my wife would have to face not only zero income but also a possible feeling of insecurity.

THE DECISION

Steve described the mounting pressure:

> Ten days ago Mr. Cramer called me to say they had regained confidence in the venture and the likelihood of equity money was high. Two days later I called back to ask if they would consider financing my father if he alone were to start Geodrill. The answer was no. They feel that I will bring to the venture selling skills as well as abilities in finance and control which my father could not handle equally well in addition to handling operations.
>
> And if I were to go to work for Goldrus, it would not be fair for me to keep the Geodrill project actively on the back burner, ready for a sudden switch from Goldrus. The Goldrus principals are offering me a salary for my full time and effort.
>
> I think it is harder to decide between a job and a new venture than it would be to decide between jobs. In the last few days I have looked at my alternatives with great care and, I think, with more objectivity than at any time in the last six months. It would be possible now for me to say no to Geodrill, but I find the decision an extremely hard one.

EXHIBIT 1
Geodrill Report

Industry Survey and Domestic Market Analysis

The concept of Geodrill is to provide contract oil and gas well drilling services to the major oil companies and independent operators in the Midcontinent of the United States. Geodrill will design and furnish drilling equipment and qualified personnel to drill an operator's well for a fee per foot drilled or a fee per operating day.

Since 1971 the domestic contract drilling industry has prospered as a result of rising prices for petroleum caused by increasing demand for oil and the Arab Embargo. Domestic drilling has increased as the number of rigs in operation has jumped 75 percent. Most of this increase was due to older rigs being brought back into service. Most industry sources place the sustained maximum capacity at 1750 units. By reviewing Table 1, it can be seen that for all practical purposes, the surplus capacity of drilling equipment has now been exhausted and perhaps overextended.

Table 1

Year	Average Operating Rigs
1971	1000
1972	1100
1973	1200
1974	1500
1975	1750

Geodrill will capitalize on this shortage of drilling capacity by assembling components and designing and constructing its own drilling units. Furthermore, since the average well depth in the United States is roughly 5,000', Geodrill's units will be designed to economically drill in this depth range and to at least 10,000'. It should be noted that the bulk of domestic drilling is done in this depth range but yet the greatest shortage of rigs appears to be developing here.

This situation has profound implications for U.S. energy policy. It suggests that the United States may not have the requisite manpower or equipment to conduct the Administration's Project Independence slated for conclusion in 1985. What are the long-term requirements of the contract drilling industry if the United States is to achieve some sort of energy independence? Industry sources predict that about 3,500 rigs will be required in the United States by 1984, with 2,500 rigs by 1980. Presently, according to independent analysts, the United States does not and will not have sufficient manufacturing capability to produce this number of drilling units (see Table 2).

EXHIBIT 1 (continued)

Table 2

	1980	1984
1975 Rigs Operating	1,750	1,750
Production of New Rigs*	1,000	2,200
Less Exports of New Rigs	500	1,100
Net Rigs Available	2,250	2,850
Rigs Required	2,500	3,450
Net Rig Deficit	(250)	(600)

Midcontinent Market Analysis

In a typical month in the Midcontinent area of Kansas and Oklahoma, 540 wells were drilled in the 5,000–10,000' depth range. This is the primary depth range of Geodrill's proposed equipment. Given these statistics, in the first year of operation, the one rig of Geodrill would only have to achieve .4 percent market share to reach its two wells per month capacity. By the fifth year, with five rigs in operation, this market share would only have to reach 2.0 percent or 10 wells per month.

From a consideration of the very low market share required, it can be concluded that Geodrill should have little difficulty in attaining its projected profit potential. Also, breakeven market share requirements are substantially less than the .4 percent required to achieve predicted profit levels. Roughly, Geodrill will break even before taxes at a market share of slightly under .3 percent. On the other hand, if Geodrill, through expansion beyond five rigs, can obtain more than .4 percent of the market, substantial operating leverage can accrue to the company and materially improve the stockholders' position.

Geodrill's Concept

There are several drilling contracting firms in Oklahoma and Kansas. How can a new firm differentiate itself from the more established firms? It may be surmised that with the growth in the market there is little need to offer distinctive services to a customer. However, Geodrill believes that any business must be based on some competitive advantage to be successful vis-a-vis the competition. Following are some of the new concepts Geodrill will bring to the Midcontinent to earn our business:

1. Rig design. Geodrill intends to design its equipment for high mobility. Many contractors have accumulated excess equipment in their rig designs which are expensive to buy as well as transport from well location to well location. Geodrill will modulize its rigs so that all will have similar equipment and identical designs. As a result, infrequently used equipment can be "pooled" and used by several rigs rather than one. Furthermore, by predesigning the rig to eliminate "dumb iron" or redundant equipment, rig up time can be reduced and some transportation expenses eliminated. Also, Geodrill intends to design its rigs to accommodate rig personnel. The key to a successful drilling company is to maintain experienced personnel. By making its rigs attractive to work on, Geodrill be-

*Average annual rate of 250 per year 1976–1980.
Average annual rate of 300 per year 1980–1984.

EXHIBIT 1 (*continued*)

lieves it can attract top-quality people. One way to do this is by "winterizing" the rig. If a rig can use its exhaust heat in a radiator system, it can keep the unit warm and workable in subzero weather. Few rigs, if any, in the Mid-continent area have this novel system at work, which would materially improve morale and efficiency in the winter months. Finally, Geodrill intends to design its rigs to OSHA standards. By having met this government requirement, Geodrill will be one to two years ahead of competition that will soon be compelled to shut its rigs down and redesign them.

2. <u>Implementation of engineering methods.</u> The Kansas and Oklahoma drilling markets have traditionally been the depository of the "seat of the pants" type of drilling. Very little engineering has been done to improve the performance of contractors over the years. It is Geodrill's belief (and first-hand experience) that by using well-developed engineering methods it can reduce costs for the customer and improve profits. Such areas as Bottom Hole Assembly design, hydraulics, and solids control technology can all materially improve performance. Accordingly, Geodrill will hire an experienced professional engineer for its staff within the first six months of operation.

3. <u>Industrial marketing.</u> Geodrill intends to introduce cooperative advertising with equipment suppliers and to be aggressively innovative for a firm of this size. This innovation will include advertising in the regional editions of *The Wall Street Journal, Business Week,* and *The Oil and Gas Journal.* Geodrill does not intend to be a "low profile" company as is characteristic of the industry. By aggressively marketing its new ideas and concepts, Geodrill can insure for itself a continuing and substantial part of the market.

<u>Environmental Contingencies</u>
        The influences on drilling activity in the U.S. are centered on two issues:

1. <u>Oil and gas demand.</u> Since no other fuels are economically attractive (except coal) until prices reach the equivalent of $15–$20 per barrel of oil equivalent (present price, average FEA estimate, is $7.50/bbl), the long-term demand for hydrocarbons will continue to grow with the rise of GNP. Presently, there is a shortage of crude and natural gas with the deficit made up in imports from OPEC nations. Current Federal controls also prevent domestic prices from rising to market levels, creating additional demand and shortages in the United States.

2. <u>OPEC.</u> The oil producing cartel of OPEC has stayed strong and united throughout the present world recession. As the world economy improves, so will the strength of OPEC as its oil revenues climb with demand. There is no reason to suspect that OPEC will cut prices, thereby forcing prices down in the U.S. and depressing drilling activity. In fact, Secretary of State Kissinger and FEA chief Zarb are in favor of a floor price for oil that will be high enough to warrant development of alternative

- 3 -

EXHIBIT 1 (*continued*)

energy sources. This means the price of oil must approach $12–$15 per barrel. At this price, oil and gas drilling (assuming gas is decontrolled) will be at a fever pitch level.

In conclusion, several factors can affect the drilling activity in this country. The net effect of the probable outcomes described above would be to increase drilling activity over the long term.

Financial Management and Corporate Planning

Geodrill intends to implement the latest management techniques available in conducting its business affairs. The Geodrill control and planning system will consist of:

1. Monthly profit and loss statements. The monthly P & L statement will be prepared by the internal accounting staff and will be furnished to all major stockholders. Besides allowing the stockholders to observe the progress of the company on a timely basis, it will enable management to critically evaluate the strengths and weaknesses of the company as well as provide a comparison to the Budget Plan.

2. Annual reporting. Geodrill will provide all stockholders with annual financial reports prepared by an outside auditor.

3. Budget plan. The Budget Plan will detail the operating revenues and expenses forecasted for the following 12-month period. Stockholders can be made aware of Geodrill's expectations for the year and also use this document for comparison to actual performance as indicated by the monthly P & L statements. Additionally, all capital expenditures plus their sources of financing will be described and justified. Normally, as each capital expenditure arises, the Board of Directors will issue approval or denial on a project-by-project basis.

4. Five-year plan. Prior to the preparation of the *Budget Plan,* the Five-Year Plan will be prepared and forwarded to the Board of Directors. This plan will detail the future growth plans of Geodrill in the field of Natural Resource Development and will describe the various elements of its business strategy that will lead to this growth. The Budget Plan will be prepared only after the Five-Year Plan is completed in order to "force" the annual plan to fit the company's long-range strategy.

5. Internal planning and control. The basis of the corporate Budget and Five-Year Plans will be the operating plans of the rig managers, superintendents, and engineering department. All major operating managers will be involved in every stage of company planning in order to insure understanding and promote enthusiasm for corporate goals. To provide a mechanism for evaluating managers' actual performance relative to their plans, a management control system (utilizing an electronic data processing system after growth to four rigs) will be employed. This system will collect operating data to enable top management to measure each operating unit. Such a system will insure that "no surprises" develop within Geodrill.

EXHIBIT 1 (*continued*)

Corporate Development Timetable
　　The following describes the approximate timetable Geodrill hopes to
follow in its corporate development.

A. Start-up: Timetable

Months after [before] Start-Up	Stage of Development
[3]	President spends 60 days in locating and transporting drilling components to construction yard.
[1]	Thirty days consumed in designing and assembling rig.
1	Rig #1 moves to the field and begins operations at 75 percent of efficiency.
3	Rig #1 reaches full efficiency and completes two wells per month.
3	Engineering Manager hired.
17	Rig #2 is assembled.
22	Rig #2 reaches full efficiency.
24	Rig #3 assembled.
29	Rig #3 reaches full efficiency.
32	Rig #4 assembled and Drilling Superintendent hired.
36	Rig #4 reaches full efficiency.
39	Rig #5 assembled.
43	Rig #5 reaches full efficiency.
60	First full year completed with five rigs running at full efficiency.

B. Expansion and maturity. Geodrill hopes eventually to expand
into other geographic areas, especially West and North Texas,
through acquisition of existing companies. After a level of 20–25
rigs has been reached, expansion into construction, engineering, oil and gas production, and other natural resource ventures
is contemplated. Generally, Geodrill (later to be named GeoIndustries) intends to be a basic natural resources development
and engineering company with the possible long-term goal of
becoming a public company.

EXHIBIT 1 (*continued*)

ITEMIZED USE OF CAPITAL

A. Equipment Item	Amount

		Amount
1.	Bit	$ 1,000
2.	Drill collars, 20-6¼" @ $1650 ea.	30,000
3,4.	Drill string, 4½" O.D. @ $15/ft., 8000'	100,000
5.	Kelly saver sub	1,000
6.	Kelly	4,000
7,8.	Circulating system, swivel	4,000
9,10.	Hook, block	12,000
11.	Wire line	3,500
12.	Crown block, derrick	20,000
13.	Rotary table, 17½"	10,000
14.	Drawworks, 500 H.P.	18,000
15.	Prime movers and compounds	35,000
16.	Slush pump, 375 H.P.	30,000
17.	Mud tanks and systems	10,000
18.	Misc. downhole equipment	2,000
19.	Blowout preventers	30,000
20.	Pipe racks	2,000
21.	Other misc. equipment (lighting system, rig shelter, weight indicator, tongs, slips, clamps)	27,500
	Subtotal	340,000
	Contingencies	60,000
	Capital requirements for equipment	$400,000

B. Pre-drilling expenses

Overhead

Officer salaries	$ 19,500
Auto expense and travel	4,000
Telephone	1,000
Legal and audit	2,000
Office rental	1,000
Office supplies	500
Miscellaneous	2,000
Subtotal	30,000
Rig assembly labor	10,000
Transportation	10,000
Total pre-drilling expenses	$ 50,000
Total capital for pre-drilling	450,000
Working capital	50,000
Total capital required	$500,000

EXHIBIT 1 (*continued*)

GEODRILL, INC.

Cash Flow Statement
For Year Ending

	Year 1	Year 2	Year 3	Year 4	Year 5
Sales Receipts	$1,012,000	$1,452,000	$3,168,000	$4,884,000	$5,280,000
Disbursements					
Operating Expenses	558,000	806,000	1,751,000	2,619,500	2,790,000
Overhead Expenses	228,000	264,000	424,000	684,000	720,000
Loan Payments	76,500	106,250	191,250	229,500	229,500
Bonus	-0-	-0-	60,000	100,000	125,000
Taxes	6,274	60,793	239,463	499,953	617,247
Total Disbursements	868,774	1,237,043	2,665,713	4,132,953	4,481,747
Operating Cash Flow	143,226	214,957	502,287	751,047	798,253
New Bank Loans	-0-	200,000	400,000	-0-	-0-
Equipment Purchases	-0-	(400,000)	(800,000)	(400,000)	-0-
Beginning Cash Balance	50,000	193,226	208,183	310,470	661,517
Ending Cash Balance	$ 193,226	$ 208,183	$ 310,470	$ 661,517	$1,459,770

Notes to Cash Flow Statements

1. Rigs Operating
   Newly constructed rigs will begin operating in:
   Rig 1 in Month 1
   Rig 2 in Month 20
   Rig 3 in Month 27
   Rig 4 in Month 34
   Rig 5 in Month 39

2. Wells Drilled
   For the first two months of operation each rig will only operate at 75 percent efficiency. After the two months of breaking in, each rig will average two wells drilled per month.

3. Sales
   Drilling revenue is $2,940 per day or $44,000 per well drilled. Industry practice is for payment to the drilling contractor when drilling is completed.

- 7 -

EXHIBIT 1 (*continued*)

4. Operating Expenses
Operating expenses are $46,500 per month for each rig in operation. These costs are broken down as follows:

Crew Wages	$22,000
Rig Supplies	4,500
Maintenance & Repairs	4,500
Bits	5,000
Trucking & Catwork	4,000
Casing Crews	500
Special Material & Services	500
Water	500
Fuel	4,500
Communications	500
Total Operating Expenses Per Month	$46,500

In the month before a newly constructed rig begins operation, $15,500 in operating expenses will be added to pay for constructing the rig.

5. Monthly Overhead Expenses
Overhead expenses will increase as additional rigs are added.

	Rig 1 Mo. 1 to Mo. 18	Rig 2 Mo. 19 to Mo. 25	Rig 3 Mo. 26 to Mo. 32	Rig 4 Mo. 33 to Mo. 38	Rig 5 Mo. 39 to Mo. 60
Officers' Salaries*	$ 6,500	$ 6,500	$ 6,500	$ 6,500	$10,500
Engineer's Salary	–0–	–0–	–0–	–0–	4,000
Office Administration Salary	3,000	3,000	3,000	3,000	5,000
Office Rental	1,000	1,000	1,100	1,100	2,300
Superintendent And Tool Pusher Salaries	2,000	4,000	6,000	10,600	13,000
Travel And Entertainment, Officers	600	600	600	600	1,200
Superintendent And Tool Pusher Expenses	600	1,200	1,800	3,000	3,600
Auto Leases	500	750	1,000	1,500	2,000
Auto Expenses	1,200	1,800	2,400	3,600	4,800
Mechanic – Salary And Expenses	–0–	–0–	2,700	2,700	2,700
Rig Insurance	1,500	3,000	4,500	6,000	7,500
Officer Insurance	600	600	600	600	600
Telephone	600	850	900	900	900
Office Supplies	300	100	200	200	200
Advertising	350	1,000	1,100	1,100	1,100
Legal And Audit	250	600	600	600	600
Total Overhead per Month	$19,000	$25,000	$33,000	$42,000	$60,000

*John W. Cox and Steve C. Cox.

EXHIBIT 1 (*continued*)

6. Loan Repayment
   Loans will be arranged to purchase and construct new drilling rigs.

Amount	Month Arranged	Term	Interest Rate
$300,000	0	60 mo.	10%
$200,000	17	60 mo.	10%
$200,000	25	60 mo.	10%
$200,000	32	60 mo.	10%

Amount repaid each year is:

	Interest	Principal	Total	Ending Principal Out- standing
Year 1	$27,809	48,691	76,500	251,309
2	33,920	72,330	106,250	378,979
3	57,332	133,918	191,250	645,061
4	56,228	173,272	229,500	471,789
5	38,699	190,801	229,500	280,988

7. Taxes
   Taxes are 22 percent of the first $50,000 on profit before taxes and 48 percent on profit above $50,000. An investment tax credit of 10 percent is flowed through taxes in the year a rig is put into operation.

	Year 1	Year 2	Year 3	Year 4	Year 5
Profit Before Taxes	$133,905	$259,985	$692,632	$1,151,986	$1,313,015
Taxes	51,274	100,793	319,463	539,953	617,247
Investment Tax Credit	45,000	40,000	80,000	40,000	-0-
Taxes Paid	6,274	60,793	239,463	499,953	617,247
Net Income	$127,631	$199,192	$453,169	$ 652,033	$ 695,768

8. Bonus
   As an incentive to the tool pushers and superintendent, a bonus will be paid upon the profits of each rig after the second year. A tool pusher will get approximately 2.5 percent of the gross margin for the rig he manages. The superintendent will receive 1 percent of the gross margin for the rigs which he supervises.

9. Equipment Purchased
   Two months before a rig begins operation, the components are purchased and assembled at a total cost of $400,000. The first rig will have an additional capitalization of $50,000 which will include pre-start-up overhead. Rigs will begin operation in months 1, 20, 27, 34, and 39. They will be depreciated over a seven-year period on a straight line basis.

EXHIBIT 1 (*continued*)

GEODRILL, INC.
Income Statement
For Year Ending

	Year 1	Year 2	Year 3	Year 4	Year 5
Sales	$1,012,000	$1,452,000	$3,168,000	$4,884,000	$5,180,000
Operating Expenses	558,000	806,000	1,751,000	2,619,500	2,790,000
Gross Margin	454,000	646,000	1,417,000	2,264,500	2,490,000
Overhead Expenses	228,000	264,000	424,000	684,000	720,000
Interest Expense	27,809	33,920	57,332	56,228	38,699
Bonus	-0-	-0-	60,000	100,000	125,000
Depreciation	64,286	88,095	183,036	272,286	293,286
Total Expenses	320,095	386,015	724,368	1,112,514	1,176,985
Profit Before Taxes	133,905	259,985	692,632	1,151,986	1,313,015
Taxes	6,274	60,793	239,463	499,953	617,247
Net Income	$ 127,631	$ 199,192	$ 453,169	$ 652,033	$ 695,768

EXHIBIT 1 (*continued*)

GEODRILL, INC
Balance Sheet
At End of Period

	Year 0	Year 1	Year 2	Year 3	Year 4	Year 5
Cash	$ 50,000	$193,226	$208,183	$ 310,470	$ 661,517	$1,459,770
Equipment	450,000	450,000	850,000	1,650,000	2,050,000	2,050,000
Less Depreciation	-0-	64,286	152,381	335,417	607,703	900,989
Equipment	450,000	385,714	697,619	1,314,583	1,442,297	1,149,011
Total Assets	$500,000	$578,940	$905,801	$1,625,053	$2,103,814	$2,608,781
Notes Payable	300,000	251,309	378,979	645,061	471,789	280,988
Capital Stock	200,000	200,000	200,000	200,000	200,000	200,000
Retained Earnings	-0-	127,631	326,823	779,992	1,432,025	2,127,793
Total Liabilities and Equity	$500,000	$578,940	$905,802	$1,625,053	$2,103,814	$2,608,781

EXHIBIT 1 (*continued*)

The Geodrill Management Team

President
John W. Cox

Mr. Cox owned, operated, and successfully sold his own drilling firm in South Texas. This firm operated up to five rigs in depth brackets of 700' to 18,000' from 1954 to 1969. From 1969 to 1972 he operated a drilling firm in Mexico under contract to the government to develop water resources. Presently, Mr. Cox is part owner and general manager of a drilling firm in Oklahoma.

Vice President
Steve C. Cox

Steve Cox is a graduate Petroleum Engineer of Texas A & M and has three and one-half years of field and operating experience with major and independent oil companies, mainly in drilling and production engineering. Presently, he is a prospective June 1976 graduate of the Eastern Business School. Steve will bring to the company both a technical and financial background.

Engineering Manager
E. Bruce Cameron

Mr. Cameron is a graduate Petroleum Engineer and expects to receive professional registration in May 1976. Mr. Cameron brings to Geodrill five years of experience in all phases of petroleum exploration and production engineering with Penzoil.

Drilling Superintendent
(added after fourth rig)

The drilling superintendent will be responsible for the field operational coordination of the drilling rigs. Reporting to him will be the rig managers. The superintendent should have 15–20 years practical field experience and the ability to communicate well with the customer's field representatives.

Rig Manager
(or Tool Pusher)
(added with each new rig)

The rig manager will be responsible for implementing the drilling programs designed for the customer by Geodrill. His operation will be the basic and primary profit center in the company. His background should include prior duty as a "driller" and 10–15 years of overall oil field experience.

EXHIBIT 1 (*continued*)

RESUME

Name:

John W. Cox

Address:

105 2nd Avenue, Johnson, Oklahoma

Telephone No.:

405 271-1035

Personal Data:

Marital Status:	Married	Children:	Six
Birthdate:	1/23/18	Health:	Excellent
Weight:	190 lbs.	Height:	6'2"

Special Schools

Well-Kick Control School—U.S.L.
Well-Kick Control School—University of Texas
Extension School, McAllen, Texas
School of Drilling Technology—Odessa College,
Extension Course of University of Texas
Hughes Tool Co. School of Drilling Technology—
   Houston, Texas

Business Experience

1974 to present

Drilco, Jackson, Oklahoma—Manager. When I joined Drilco, the company was operating at a loss. The first year's profits showed $300,000. The second year's profits were in excess of $400,000. During this period, the existing rigs were updated and improved and the rig count built from three to five.

1973–1974

Drilling Consultant in South Louisiana for major and independent oil companies.

1970–1973

Formed a Mexican drilling corporation to drill large diameter, large volume water wells under contract for the Mexican government. Dissolved corporation because of difficulty in collecting payments from the Mexican government for contracts completed as specified, in good faith, and in a workmanlike manner.

1954–1970

Cox Drilling Co., Inc., McAllen, Texas—President and Owner. Built company from one rig to five modern power rigs. Performed contract drilling for major oil companies—Gulf, Humble, Mobil, Continental, and Union Producing, plus nearly all independents. Operated company-owned, heavy hauling fleet of moving rigs. Employment grew to 100 people, grossing over $2 million per year. Successfully sold company in October 1969 to Harkins and Company of Alice, Texas.

EXHIBIT 1 (*continued*)

1950–1954

Williams Oil and Gas Company, Austin, Texas—Superintendent. Started as tool pusher, with promotion in 1951 to Superintendent. Responsible for up to 12 contract rigs, and the drilling and completion of deep wells in South Texas ranging in depth from 5,000 to 12,500 feet. Coordinated field services, including geology, engineering, logging, and completion.

1946–1950

A. G. & J. Drilling Company, Dryhole, Texas—Tool Pusher. Responsible for drilling production of largest power rig in South Texas rated to 17,000 feet depth.

1939–1946

Hawk Drilling Company, Dallas, Texas. Assistant Tool Pusher. Started as driller helper with promotion to driller in 1941. Continued in this capacity until promoted to assistant tool pusher in 1943.

Attachments

Letters of Recommendation.

RESUME
STEVE C. COX

28 Desmond Avenue   Home Address:
Watertown,   105 2nd Avenue
Massachusetts 02172   Johnson, Oklahoma
Phone: 617-924-0755   Phone: 405-271-1035
Married   6 feet 2 inches   190 pounds   excellent health

Education
1974–1976

EASTERN GRADUATE SCHOOL OF BUSINESS ADMINISTRATION
Candidate for the degree of Master in Business Administration in June 1976. Second-year emphasis in Finance and Control.

1967–1971

TEXAS A & M UNIVERSITY   COLLEGE STATION, TEXAS
Received Bachelor of Science degree in Petroleum Engineering in May 1971. Distinguished Student. Elected President of College of Engineering representative council. Member of Society of Petroleum Engineers. Elected member of Tau Beta Pi (National Engineering Honor Society) and Pi Epsilon Tau (National Petroleum Engineering Honor Society). (Expect to complete requirements for Professional Engineering registration by late 1977).

Business Experience
Summer 1975 & 1972–1974

BURMAH OIL AND GAS CO.   LAFAYETTE, LOUISIANA
Drilling Engineer. Duties involved planning, engineering, and directing offshore petroleum drilling and development activities in the Gulf of Mexico. Responsible for the daily line management of up to 60 personnel and cash expenditures of $30,000 per day. Promoted to Geothermal Division Drilling Engineer but declined offer to attend Harvard Business School. Assisted in preparation of offshore capital budget in the summer of 1975.

EXHIBIT 1 (*concluded*)

1971-1972

CHEVRON OIL CO. (SOCAL)   LAFAYETTE, LOUISIANA

Petroleum Engineer responsible for "on-site" supervision of offshore drilling and exploitation operations.

Personal Background

Raised in South Texas as the son of an oilwell drilling contractor. Have had extensive experience as a "roughneck" laborer on drilling rigs as well as working during the summers at college for such companies as Phillips Petroleum and Standard of Indiana. Special interests include hunting, gardening, and church work. Married, have one child, and expecting second May 1976.

References

Personal references available on request.

October 1975

Case 3-6

CLARION OPTICAL CO.

It was early September of 1983, and Jerry Stone and Iris Randal were having dinner and discussing their plans to purchase Clarion Optical Co., their current employer. They had decided to attempt to purchase Clarion almost two months ago. Since then, they had spent most of their time talking with potential financial backers and had learned a great deal about potential financing sources.

Now, they needed to make a decision about how to finance and structure the purchase of Clarion. They needed to resolve:

— How to carve up the transaction into pieces which would match risk with reward and desired returns.
— What form(s) of legal organization to use.
— Whom to approach, for how much, and on what terms.

BACKGROUND

Clarion Optical was located outside of Atlanta, Georgia, and had been founded by Cyrus Atkins in 1946. Clarion began as a manufacturer of high-quality glass for optical uses and as a grinder and polisher of lenses for optical instruments. In the early 1970s, Clarion's chief engineer, Jerry Stone, had pushed Atkins, and Clarion, into the custom contact lens business (i.e., lenses for individuals who could not wear standard off-the-shelf products). This business had proved to be so profitable that Clarion had reached the point where it was once again a single-product company, having phased out of the optical instrument market. (See Exhibit 1 for most recent financial statements.)

Since Cyrus' gradual retirement from the business began in the mid-1970s, Stone had been president and had taken over more and more responsibility for the firm's operations.

In early 1983, Clarion's new chief engineer, and one of Stone's early pupils in the lab—Iris Randal, had come to Jerry with an idea for a new product line—implantable lenses for the human eye. The incidence of cataracts was on the rise and new surgical techniques had made the replacement of the human eye lens a commonplace procedure.

Iris had developed a new substance from which to make the lens, which was far less costly and created a better lens than existing technology. Jerry and Iris began developing a business plan to explore and capitalize on the opportunity.

THE SALE OF CLARION

Two months ago, Cyrus Atkins had told Jerry that he had decided that it was time to sell Clarion. Cyrus, a widower, was nearing 80, and had two older children who were successful and well-established professionals. Cyrus had amply provided for them in his large estate, in which his 100 percent ownership of Clarion represented only a part. His interest in Clarion was his last major illiquid holding, and Cyrus was convinced that he should sell the company and tidy up his estate.

Jerry expressed an immediate interest in purchasing the company, and Atkins was pleased at the prospect of Clarion remaining "in the family." He told Jerry that he would give him ample time to try to put together a financing package. Atkins said that he was willing to sell Clarion for 10 times its 1982 earnings of $200,000, or $2 million.

Jerry was convinced that the new implantable lens technology had great potential, and was the key to Clarion's future success. He also had a great deal of respect for Iris' engineering and management abilities, and decided that she should be part of the management team that attempted the buyout.

Jerry was convinced that the other key staff would remain on. After all, they would not be getting a new boss—he had been managing Clarion for over five years.

Jerry discussed the idea with her, and Iris was thrilled with the prospect of owning a piece of Clarion. She also had a great deal of confidence in the new lens technology and was excited to learn that Jerry planned to make this a keystone of his plan for the business. They raced to put together the money.

VALUING THE ASSETS

On the advice of a friend in the banking industry, Jerry and Iris took Clarion's balance sheet and attempted to determine the fair market value of Clarion's assets. A valuation was performed, and they were pleasantly surprised that this value exceeded book value *and* Atkins' asking price. (See Exhibit 2.)

— Land and Building: A 20-year-old, fully depreciated structure, the $200,000 figure on the books represented only the cost of the land. The building was in excellent shape, and was owned and used exclusively by Clarion. The structure housed all manufacturing, shipping and management. There was ample space for any contemplated expansion of the business. Jerry and Iris researched the market and determined that the fair market value of the structure was as follows:
  - Land $250,000
  - Building $750,000
— Equipment: Clarion's equipment was fairly new, but rapid depreciation had decreased its book value to $100,000. Jerry and Iris were convinced that it was worth $500,000.
— Inventory: Because of the custom nature of its work, Clarion kept large stocks of high-quality optical glass on hand. Much of this had been purchased a year or two ago on particularly favorable terms. Now, this $200,000 of book value inventory was worth $500,000.
— Accounts Receivable: Most of Clarion's customers were well established optical shops who paid their bills on time. The $300,000 book value of accounts receivable was an accurate reflection of their true worth.
— Cash: The cash, of course, was worth $200,000 and Jerry and Iris were convinced that $100,000 would give them sufficient working capital.

Having convinced themselves that Clarion's assets were indeed worth $2.5 million, Jerry and Iris set about investigating potential financing sources.

FINANCING THE PURCHASE

Jerry and Iris's business plan indicated that they would need an additional $1 million over the purchase price to fund the research and development effort required to get them into the lens business. This raised their "magic number" to *at least* $3.0 million. They then began investigating potential sources of this money.

— New England Pension Trust: Jerry and Iris contacted this tax-free pension fund, an extremely conservative financier. The trust indicated that they would be willing to lend up to 80 percent of the value of the land and building—a mortgage at 12 percent.

— Michael Grund: An extremely wealthy acquaintance of Jerry's, Michael had agreed to consider an investment of up to $250,000 if it showed an aftertax IRR of at least 30 percent. Michael was in the 50 percent tax bracket on income, and 20 percent on capital gains.

— Georgia Bank and Trust Co.: A local bank, Georgia B&T had agreed to lend up to 80 percent of the book value of accounts receivable, and 40 percent of the book value of inventory, at 15 percent.

— Rebel Ventures: This local venture capital firm was excited by the venture and had agreed to give Jerry and Iris up to $3.5 million on any investment which showed a 60 percent pretax IRR. They would, however, require the management team to put up $40,000 of their own funds.

— Bank of Atlanta: The bank had agreed to lend either the company or Jerry and Iris personally up to $300,000 at 17 percent with Jerry and Iris' personal guarantees as security. While they each had little (about $20,000 each) in liquid assets, each had a tangible net worth of close to $250,000 due to their own and their spouses' investments in their separate homes.

— General Insurance Corporate Credit: The credit area of this large insurance company had agreed to purchase the existing equipment from Clarion for $300,000, and lease it back to Clarion for 5 years at $100,000 per year.

With this information in hand, they went to speak with two friends to ask for advice on how to structure the deal:

— Bill Lawrence, an old friend in the real estate business.
— Henry Adams, the trustee at the local bank.

Lawrence's Suggested Structure

Bill Lawrence suggested financing the deal in the following way:

— Have Grund buy the building and land in a separate transaction for $1 million, and then have Clarion rent it back from Grund. He can:
  • Take an 80 percent mortgage from the bank @ 12 percent.
  • Keep the tax losses and cash flow for an investment of $200,000.
  • Clarion would agree to buy the building back at some price at the end of Year 7, in order to give Grund his required 30 percent return.
— Buy the rest of the assets for $1 million and finance as follows:

• Excess cash	$100,000
• Borrow on accounts receivable	300,000
• Borrow on inventory	80,000
• Sale/leaseback of equipment	300,000
• Note/personal guarantee	220,000

This would permit Jerry and Iris to retain 100 percent of the equity. It did have its drawbacks though:

— Risk: it seemed as though there would be very little, if any, margin for error in their projections.
— R&D schedule: without a major influx of venture capital, Jerry and Iris thought it would take three years to generate sufficient cash flow to perform the $1 million worth of R&D required. This would
  • Delay Clarion's entry into the market.
  • Reduce their share when they did enter.
  • Make the market smaller in the early years because Clarion would not be out developing the market.
  (See Exhibit 4 for relative market scenarios.)
— Cost: Finally, when they did enter the market, they would not have sufficient funds flow to purchase equipment. This would require them to subcontract production and fulfillment (this firm would also finance working capital needs) which would raise COGS to 30 percent (10 points higher than the 20 percent COGS if they manufactured in-house).
— Salaries: Jerry, who was making $60K/year and Iris, making $40K/year would each take a salary cut to $20,000 per year until the business started generating cash.

Adams' Suggested Structure

Adams suggested that they finance the entire purchase with venture capital funds. This would obviously reduce their share of the equity, but would reduce the risk as well. This financing structure would have important implications:

— Investment: They would invest in the plant and equipment necessary to produce the lens, which would:
  • Reduce the COGS to 20 percent of sales.
  • Increase depreciation charges.
— Fixed charges would drop.
  • No rent.
  • No lease payments.
  • No interest payments.
— Personal stake: They would each invest $20,000 of their own funds in the initial purchase of the company.

THE DECISION

Jerry and Iris knew that these proposals represented the two extreme ends of the financing spectrum, but they thought that running out the numbers would help them get a feel for what the important issues and trade-offs were.

They finished dessert and coffee, and went back to the office to lay out all of their assumptions (see Exhibit 4) and crunch through the numbers.

EXHIBIT 1

CLARION OPTICAL CO.

Historical Financial Statements
Year Ended December 31, 1982
(in thousands of dollars)

Income Statement

Sales	$1,010
Cost of goods sold	300
Selling, general and administrative	100
Executive salaries	200
Operating income	$ 410
Depreciation	10
Net income	400
Taxes	200
Profit after tax	$ 200

Balance Sheet

Cash	$ 200		
Accounts receivable	300		
Inventory	200		
Equipment	100		
Land and building	200	Owner's equity	$1,000
Total assets	$1,000	Total equity	$1,000

EXHIBIT 2
Balance Sheet Comparison (*in thousands of dollars*)

	Book	Appraised Value
Cash	$ 200	$ 200
Accounts receivable	300	300
Inventory	200	500
Equipment	100	500
Land and building	200	1,000
Total assets	$1,000	$2,500

EXHIBIT 3
Real Estate Transaction

Assumptions

—Mortgage: 25 years
$800,000
12%
Constant payment of $102,000 per annum

—Amortization schedule: ($000)

Year	1	2	3	4	5	6	7
• Interest payment	96.0	95.3	94.5	93.6	92.6	91.4	90.2
• Principal payment	6.0	6.7	7.5	8.4	9.4	10.6	11.8

—Principal value of mortgage outstanding at end of Year 7 equals $740,000.

Real Estate Cash Flows
(in thousands of dollars)

Year	1	2	3	4	5	6	7
Rent...............................	$165.0	$173.0	$182.0	$191.0	$200.0	$211.0	$221.0
Maintenance.....................	40.0	41.0	42.0	44.0	45.0	46.0	48.0
Taxes	25.0	25.0	25.0	25.0	25.0	25.0	25.0
Net operating income	100.0	107.0	114.0	122.0	130.0	140.0	148.0
Finance payment	102.0	102.0	102.0	102.0	102.0	102.0	102.0
Pretax cash flow...............	(2.0)	5.0	12.0	20.0	28.0	38.0	46.0
+ Amortization	6.0	6.7	7.5	8.4	9.4	10.6	11.8
− Depreciation..................	150.0	120.0	96.0	76.8	61.4	49.1	39.3
= Taxable income	(146.0)	(108.3)	(76.5)	(48.4)	(23.0)	0.5	18.5
+ Tax benefit/ (cost)	73.0	54.1	38.2	24.2	11.5	(.2)	(9.2)
= Aftertax cash flow............................	71.0	59.1	50.2	44.2	39.5	37.8	36.8

Note: Finance payment is a level stream which includes both interest and principal. Amortization (principal repayment) must therefore be added back to pretax cash flow to arrive at a taxable income figure.

Cash flows on sale of building

Sale transaction at assumed price of $1,000,000 and $1,100,000

	$1,000,000	$1,100,000
Sale	$1,000,000	$1,100,000
− Net book value	407,600	407,600
Gain on sale	$ 592,400	$ 692,400
Accelerated depreciation taken	$ 592,400	$ 592,400
− Straight-line figure	525,000	525,000
Excess depreciation over straight line	$ 67,400	$ 67,400
× 50% tax rate	33,700	33,700

EXHIBIT 3 (*concluded*)

Calcula- tion of tax liabi- lity			
	Gain on sale	$ 592,400	$ 692,400
	− Excess depreciation	67,700	67,700
	Taxable gain	$ 525,000	$ 625,000
	Capital gains tax at 20% rate	$ 105,000	$ 125,000
	+ Excess depreciation tax	33,700	33,700
	Total tax liability	$ 138,700	$ 158,700
	Sale Price	$1,000,000	$1,100,000
	− Tax liability	138,700	158,700
	− Mortgage balance	740,000	740,000
	Cash out	$ 121,300	$ 201,300

EXHIBIT 4
Scenario Cash Flows

Assumptions
1. *Sales* (see Schedule A, attached)
   — All Debt: They thought that under this scenario, it would take three years to fund the $1 million of R&D required out of cash flow. In this case, Clarion could not enter the implantable lens market until Year 4, at which point they could only attain 40 percent market share; and the market would be smaller, because they would not have been out developing it.
   — All Equity: Clarion could finish the R&D in one year and enter the market in Year 2. They could obtain a larger market share and grow the entire market scenario.
   — Both: In either case, sales of the existing contact lens product line would stagnate at whatever level they were at when implantable lens sales began.
2. *COGS*
   — All Debt: Cost of implantable lens equal to 30 percent sales, due to subcontracting.
   — All Equity: Cost of implantable lens equal to 20 percent of sales.
   — Both: Cost of existing contact lens product equal to 30 percent sales.
3. *SG&A ($000)*

Year:	1	2	3	4	5	6	7
— All Debt	108	120	129	500	600	700	800
— All Equity	107	500	600	700	800	900	1000

4. *Executive Salaries ($000)*

Year:	1	2	3	4	5	6	7
— All Debt	40	40	40	200	300	400	500
— All Equity	100	100	100	200	300	400	500

EXHIBIT 4 (continued)

SCHEDULE A
Sales Scenarios (in millions of dollars)

| | | All Debt | | | | | | All Equity | | | |
| | Contact Lens Sales | Implantable Lens Sales | | | | Contact Lens Sales | Implantable Lens Sales | | | | |
Year		Market Size	Clarion Share	Resultant Sales	Total		Market Size	Clarion Share	Resultant Sales	Total
1	1.10	1.0	0	0	1.10	1.1	1.0	0	0	1.1
2	1.28	2.5	0	0	1.28	1.1	5.0	60%	3	4.1
3	1.60	5.0	0	0	1.60	1.1	10.0	60%	6	7.1
4	1.60	10.0	40%	4	5.60	1.1	20.0	60%	12	13.1
5	1.60	20.0	40%	8	9.60	1.1	40.0	60%	24	25.1
6	1.60	40.0	40%	16	17.60	1.1	60.0	60%	36	37.1
7	1.60	65.0	40%	26	27.60	1.1	80.0	60%	48	49.1

EXHIBIT 4 (continued)

5. *R&D*

   $1 million required to complete R&D on implantable lens.
   — All Debt: Funded out of cash as available; Jerry and Iris assumed that this could be completed in three years.
   — All Equity: Funded in year one out of venture capital.

6. *Depreciation*

   — All Debt: Equal to zero in all years: No plant, equipment, building to depreciate.
   — All Equity: Depreciation on existing building and equipment equal to $150,000 each year for seven years. Depreciation on new equipment purchased is calculated on a straight-line basis over a five-year life, beginning in the year of actual purchase (i.e., if $1,000,000 worth of equipment purchased in year 1, then $200,000 taken in years one through five). (See *Investment*, line 13, for investment required.)

7. *Interest*

   — All Debt:
   • $300,000 borrowed against accounts receivable is outstanding over the entire seven years, at 15 percent per annum. No principal repayments made.
   • $80,000 borrowed against inventory is outstanding over the entire seven years, at 15 percent per annum. No principal repayments made.
   • $220,000 note, personally guaranteed is outstanding over five years, principal and interest paid according to following schedule.

Year:	1	2	3	4	5
Interest	38	32	26	19	10
Principal	31	37	43	50	59

   — All Equity: No interest charges.

8. *Lease Payments*

   — All Debt: Lease payments on machinery are $100,000 per annum for five years, at which time ownership reverts to Clarion.
   — All Equity: No lease payments.

9. *Rent*

   — All Debt: As shown in Exhibit 3.
   — All Equity: No rent payments.

10. *Maintenance and Real Estate Taxes*

    — All Debt: No maintenance expenses or taxes.
    — All Equity: As shown in Exhibit 3.

11. *Taxes:* 50 percent of income. Assume that losses are offset against following year's income. (i.e., If Clarion has losses of $200,000 in year one and pretax profit of $1,000,000 in year two, income tax in year two is calculated on a pretax base of $800,000.)

12. *Depreciation:* (See line 6)

13. *Investment*

    — All Debt: Purchase of building in year seven at price required to give 30 percent return.
    — All Equity: Annual investment required in ($000)

Year	1	2	3	4	5	6	7
• Working Capital	63	600	600	1,200	2,400	2,400	2,400
• Equipment	1,000	1,000	2,000	4,000	8,000	12,000	15,000

14. *Principal Repayment*

    — All Debt: On $220,000 personally guaranteed note only; see above under *Interest*.
    — All Equity: None.

EXHIBIT 4 (*concluded*)

15. *Terminal Value:* Assume that company is sold at the end of year seven for 10 × Year 7 after-tax earnings under both scenarios.
16. *Other:* In addition, they realized that they needed to make other assumptions in order to judge the two scenarios.
    — Assume Jerry and Iris' personal investment in business as follows:
      • All Debt: Investment of 0 in year 0 plus $60,000 in "lost salary" in each of years one through three.
      • All Equity: Investment of $40,000 in year 0.
    — Calculate cash flows to Jerry and Iris *jointly* (i.e., do not make any assumptions about how equity, investment or cash flows are divided between the two parties).
    — Assume that in the equity scenario, only return occurs via sale of equity at end of year seven—no dividends paid or other distributions made.
    — Assume that in the debt scenario, free cash flow is taken out at end of each year, including the end of year seven.
    — Calculate flows and returns to Jerry, Iris, and Rebel Ventures on a *prepersonal tax* basis (i.e., include taxes at the corporate level in your calculations, but *do not* include any personal taxes on dividends or distributions out of Clarion). Also, do not include Jerry and Iris' salaries as part of the cash outflows in calculating returns.
    — Include the price of the building repurchase in year seven as an investment in that year in the debt scenario.
    — In the all debt scenario, assume that all available cash is spent on R&D until the $1 million project is complete; you must "plug" the figure for R&D for each year (i.e., free cash flow should equal zero in years where R&D project is ongoing).
    — Assume Rebel Ventures will invest whatever cash is required to keep Clarion cash positive up to its stated $3.5 million limit.

Case 3-7

VISCOTECH, INC.

Kenneth Jones, president of Viscotech, walked through the lobby of the Park Tower Building, and headed toward a small restaurant near Chicago's business district. He needed some time away from the office, time in which to ponder the difficult situation he found himself in. It was March 1984, and only seven months ago, Jones had left his position with a large pharmaceutical firm to become Viscotech's president. Stock, options and a hefty salary increase had made the future seem bright. Now, all that seemed to be slipping away.

Jones had just come from a meeting with an attorney, Paul Benjamin, who had informed Jones that Viscotech might have committed violations of U.S. securities laws. Jones had to evaluate this information in light of the entire chain of events that had led up to that morning's meeting with Benjamin. As he considered his predicament, he realized that he needed to evaluate both Viscotech's and his own exposure to an SEC violation.

VISCOTECH

Viscotech was incorporated in 1977 by Dr. Samuel Evans, a surgeon and professor at the Midwestern Medical School; Louis Brown, a research scientist at the Chicago Institute of Technology; Dr. Harold Stein, a nutritional specialist at the Midwestern Medical School; and Melvin O'Connor, an accountant and attorney in the Chicago area.

The company was founded in order to design, develop, and market a device which could measure the viscosity of saliva. It had long been known that this type of analysis of saliva could help physicians assess nutritional inadequacies in patients.

Between 1977 and 1982, the company had spent almost $500,000 pursuing its research agenda. These funds had been obtained from the company's founders in the form of debt and equity.

By late 1982, Viscotech had succeeded in obtaining several patents which covered the core technology used in the device. Viscotech had focused its efforts on developing its first product, the "Doctor's Office Device." This device would be simple, easy to use, and would allow doctors to perform a comprehensive nutritional analysis in their offices. In addition, the technology had broader applications in the feeding and breeding of cattle and swine.

The announcement of the device had received a great deal of favorable attention in the medical press. By the end of 1982, Viscotech had developed a working prototype of the device which was ready for more extensive clinical testing and subsequent submission to the Food and Drug Administration for approval.

1983—THE NEED FOR CAPITAL

In early 1983, it became clear to Viscotech's principals that the company would require another infusion of cash in order to:

— Complete testing and receive FDA approval.
— Develop engineering and manufacturing specifications.
— Research new applications for the technology.

In April of 1983, a group of physicians who were friends of Viscotech's founders indicated that they were interested in investing in the venture. At about the same time, O'Connor had been in touch with the venture capital community seeking funds for Viscotech. At a meeting in late April, the four founders decided to pursue the raising of capital from other acquaintances in the medical community because the venture firms were offering too meager a price for an equity investment.

At this point, O'Connor agreed to proceed with the raising of funds in this manner. In order to protect the founders, he thought it prudent to raise money with a very carefully drawn offering circular. However, because his schedule was quite full with other business commitments, O'Connor knew that he would be unable to prepare such a document for several months.

THE MEDICAL INVESTMENT FUND TRUST

Because of these constraints and the fact that Viscotech needed money quickly, O'Connor suggested that funds be raised through another vehicle—the Medical Investment Fund Trust (MIFT). MIFT could then invest the money in Viscotech and then Viscotech could spend these funds. Later that year, an offering circular would be presented, and each investor given the option to withdraw and receive his or her funds back. If investors chose to subscribe, they would agree to exchange their investment in MIFT for Viscotech shares.

O'Connor was confident that the trust offered a means of raising money on an interim basis, while avoiding the final commitment until the offering circular was issued. As such, the structure was similar to an arrangement O'Connor and Viscotech had used several years earlier to raise funds.

It was decided that investors who advanced funds through MIFT would receive a certificate representing shares in MIFT. MIFT, in turn, would be granted an option on shares of Viscotech. They would attempt to raise $800,000 in 100 units of $8,000 each. Each unit would represent a claim on 0.1 percent of Viscotech stock.

In May 1983, O'Connor drew up the trust instrument and a brief description of MIFT for potential investors (see Exhibit 1). This package contained information on Viscotech which had previously been made public. Prior to distributing the MIFT package, the company raised $100,000 from six relatives and friends of the principals to meet its needs during the interim.

Beginning in May, and continuing throughout the summer, acquaintances of Viscotech's principals advanced funds to MIFT. The funds were routinely forwarded to O'Connor's office and disbursed by him.

As part of the financing effort, Viscotech conducted a series of informational seminars for friends and acquaintances of the principals. These discussions centered around the technology, the history of the company, and potential markets for the company's devices. No formal offers were made at these seminars, nor were there any discussions of price. Many of the individuals who were present, however, did subsequently invest.

In August, O'Connor began to realize that his schedule was not going to be free for quite some time. Therefore, he contacted a friend of his, Leonard Atkins, an experienced attorney with the Chicago firm of Dewey & White. O'Connor informed Atkins of the MIFT arrangement, and told Atkins that he wanted him to draw up an offering circular to close the MIFT financing. Atkins suggested that Viscotech undertake a private offering, but O'Connor said that he would prefer to have the SEC review any materials. Accordingly, they decided to attempt to raise funds through a Regulation A offering. This plan was approved at the annual shareholders' meeting in mid-August, and Atkins was given instructions to proceed.

KENNETH JONES

Later that August, Viscotech hired Ken Jones as its president. The original principals were able to spend only a portion of their time on Viscotech because of their medical and research responsibilities. In addition, as the product got closer to market, the principals felt the need for an individual with business experience.

Jones had graduated from the U.S. Naval Academy, and subsequent to his sea duty had attended the Midwest Business School. He had worked for a major international pharmaceutical firm as a product manager for four years before joining Viscotech. Jones was given 1,620 shares of Viscotech, options on further shares, and a salary of $65,000 per year.

Jones did not become heavily involved in the financing efforts because most of the potential investors were acquaintances of the founders. He did understand the MIFT arrangement, however, and understood from O'Connor that Atkins had cleared this vehicle for raising funds. Jones did attend and speak at several of the informational seminars, and he was briefed by Atkins on what to say. Specifically, Atkins told him to be wary of making statements which could be interpreted as "promises about Viscotech's future performance."

During the fall, Jones met with Atkins and O'Connor several times regarding the Regulation A offering. Jones edited several drafts of the offering circular. During this process, Atkins was supplied with Viscotech's financial statements prepared by O'Connor, which showed the liability for stock subscriptions through MIFT and detailed the expenditures of funds received. At one point, Jones asked Atkins how MIFT would be treated and Atkins responded by saying, "We don't need to talk about MIFT."

By early December of 1983, $776,000 had been raised by MIFT from 34 investors. By February, the Regulation A offering circular was in draft form. Atkins had prepared the material for submission to the SEC. The principals decided to send the material off in early March.

THE SEC ISSUE

The last weekend in February, Ken casually mentioned the financing plans to a friend at a neighborhood party. This friend, an attorney with the prestigious local firm of Cole & Eggers, thought that something sounded a bit odd. He suggested that Ken see one of his colleagues, Paul Benjamin, an expert on securities law. Ken made arrangements to see Benjamin during the first week of March, and sent him a draft of the circular.

Jones explained the events of the past months to Benjamin, and they reviewed a copy of the circular. The attorney felt that the use of MIFT as a vehicle to insulate Viscotech was not effective, and that both Jones and Viscotech were exposed to SEC charges arising out of the manner in which MIFT had raised its funds. He recommended that Jones "come clean" and go to the SEC. Benjamin felt that this would show Jones' good faith and limit his own personal exposure to SEC charges. In addition, he advocated "freezing" all existing funds in MIFT as a further show of good faith. Viscotech could then raise its funds with a Rule 505 offering that required notifying the SEC but did not require SEC approval. Benjamin drafted a version of this offering, which appears as Exhibit 2, and which gives investors the option of withdrawing their investment. Benjamin also stated that the company would have to hire an individual to prepare the required two years of audited financial statements since O'Connor had had a financial interest in Viscotech while his firm was involved in the company's accounting.

WHAT TO DO

Jones' head was spinning when he left Benjamin's office. He wanted to do what was legal and ethically right. Yet, he also knew how desperately Viscotech needed funds to gear up for manufacturing and marketing of the Doctor's Office Product. Going to the SEC seemed to minimize his personal risk, but could implicate the rest of the company's principals and would surely harm the company's chances of raising money. Viscotech could go ahead with the Rule 505 offering, which merely required notifying the SEC. Benjamin said that there was a low probability that the SEC would request further documentation or the actual offering circular. However, in the event that the SEC did request the offering circular, Benjamin advised that it be very conservatively drafted, like the version excerpted in Exhibit 2. Ken felt, however, that this draft was *so* conservative that many investors would be likely to take recission (i.e., request the return of their investment) if they received this document.

Ken didn't know what to do. Any course which would successfully raise the funds Viscotech needed seemed to involve a good deal of risk.

EXHIBIT 1
MIFT Offering Circular

Confidential Investment Memorandum

Medical Investment Fund Trust

The Medical Investment Fund Trust (MIFT) has been formed as a vehicle to raise funds for Viscotech, Inc. Each $8,000 investment in MIFT will represent a claim on 200 (roughly 0.1 percent) of Viscotech's shares. MIFT seeks to raise $800,000 in this manner.

In the near future, Viscotech, Inc., will distribute an offering memorandum to those individuals who have invested in MIFT. At that time, any investor who desires to do so shall have the right to sell his/her MIFT shares back to the company for the amount of the original investment.

The Business

Viscotech was formed in 1977 by Dr. Samuel Evans, Midwestern Medical School; Louis Brown, Chicago Institute of Technology; Dr. Harold Stein, Midwestern Medical School; and Melvin O'Connor, Esq., O'Connor & O'Connor. The company has spent $500,000 of its founders' funds perfecting a technology which can assess nutritional inadequacies in patients through an analysis of saliva.

Patents

The company has filed and been granted 15 patents which cover the core aspects of Viscotech's technology. In addition, the company has filed for 63 additional patents, which have yet to be ruled on. These patent applications have been made in 20 countries.

Products

Viscotech plans to produce the following devices:

— Doctors Office Device: a complex instrument capable of analyzing deficiencies in a patient with respect to vitamins, minerals, blood sugar, amino acids, hormones, and trace elements.
— Home device: a simpler instrument which will enable individuals to easily assess their own vitamin, mineral, and blood sugar levels.
— Farm animal device: a simple instrument which will allow breeders of cattle and swine to determine the optimal feed content for their animals.

With the tremendous increase in individuals' concern with their own nutritional well-being, the company is confident that these instruments will be extraordinarily successful. Imagine being able to take a simple test, using saliva, to determine the adequacy of vitamin and mineral intake, and to make dietary adjustments accordingly.

Markets

The markets for these products offer tremendous potential. In addition to lucrative U.S. markets, incredible potential exists in Third World markets where malnutrition is a problem. Individuals will now be able to test undernourished people to determine the precise therapeutic treatment. The government of India has indicated a strong interest in making a grant of $250,000 to Viscotech for the purpose of developing such an instrument for its use. The company currently plans to introduce the following devices:

The Doctor's Instrument: There is no other product available which performs these tests with the ease, accuracy, speed, and inexpensive price of the Viscotech instrument.

EXHIBIT 1 (*continued*)

— Projected Potential Market: The potential market is projected to be doctors dealing regularly with patients with nutritional problems:

	Nutritionists	G.P.'s	Total
United States	14,000 of 24,000	6,000 of 56,000	20,000 of 80,000
Europe	10,000 of 20,000	5,000 of 70,000	15,000 of 90,000
Rest of world	4,000 (est.)	1,000 (est.)	5,000
Total Potential Market			40,000

— Average Instrument Usage
  • 6 tests per patient per month, or 75 tests per year.
  • 4 ongoing patients per doctor
  • 75 × 4 = 300 tests per doctor per year.
— Sales Price

Instruments	$3,000.00 each
Disposables	$ 2.40 per test

Market introduction is projected for the third quarter of 1985 in both the U.S. and Europe. First year projected sales of 250 instruments represents a less than 1 percent penetration of the potential market, with second year sales of 400 instruments reaching a cumulative penetration of 1.9 percent.

Viscotech plans to initially distribute the doctor's instrument through regional dealers and manufacturers' reps in the major metropolitan areas where the primary market is concentrated. Given the large number of potential customers and the need to demonstrate the instrument to each of these potential customers, economics dictate that Viscotech make use of existing sales and distribution channels into these targeted doctors' offices. Viscotech will have a small, highly qualified in-house sales team to manage this distributor network. Viscotech will also handle all product services directly.

The Home Device: This device will allow individuals to safely and easily sample their own saliva to determine the levels of key nutritional variables: vitamins, minerals, and blood sugar levels.

Viscotech has developed working prototypes of the saliva collection device and the measuring device that comprise the Home Device System. Both components are significantly different from those used with the Physicians' System.

At present the company is having a prototype mold constructed for the saliva collection device with a capability to produce 3,000–5,000 parts. Availability is scheduled for mid-September, after which we will begin the first in-use testing of the Home Use System.

We estimate that design finalization will take 1–2 years, and market introduction 2–3 years.

— Projected Potential Market: the potential market is projected to be men and women in the 15–45 age group that are currently using vitamins, dietary supplements or have a nutritional problem. This represents an immediate worldwide market of about 100 million individuals:

United States	25 million
Europe	34 million
Japan	12 million
Rest of world	30 million
	101 million

EXHIBIT 1 (*continued*)

— Average Instrument Usage: Minimum average of 5 tests per month or 70 tests per year.
— Sales Price
    Instrument $45.00
    Disposables $ .90
— Estimated Manufacturing Cost
    Instrument $10.00
    Disposables $ .20
— Total Potential Dollar Market
    Annual disposable sales   7 billion tests   @ $ 0.90 = $6   billion
    One time instruments sales   100 million   @ $45.00 = $4.5 billion
— Sales Projections: Market introduction in the United States is projected for the second quarter of 1987. Projecting sales in such an enormous market is at best difficult. If a 1 percent share of the potential market were achieved during the first five years, end-user purchases of disposables would be $60 million annually, and instrument sales would average $9 million annually. The company feels that it is possible to achieve a 20 percent share of the potential market during the next 5–10 years.
— Marketing and Distribution: An arrangement with a very large multinational consumer marketing company appears to provide the most logical and reasonable path to the marketplace. Such a company could provide both the dollar investment and expertise required to successfully develop sales of the Home Use Device. Additionally it could provide indemnity for Viscotech against any product liability claims.

Discussions with International Pharmaceutical have taken place over the last six months and have developed to an advanced point. International has the broadest line of any company in the field, and is part of a premier, highly successful company in the Health Care Industry. International has made two offers in writing (June 8 and July 12), and Viscotech has made one counterproposal in writing (July 31).

The Farm Animal Device: The instrument system proposed for use by doctors in managing patients is, conceptually, equally applicable for increasing the productivity of food animals such as swine, dairy cattle, and beef cattle.

The objective is to develop an effective instrument system and verify its feasibility for improving the rate of weight addition in swine and cattle. This development process entails empirically modifying the doctor's instrument system to accommodate the saliva of swine and cattle.

Swine and cattle were chosen because they appeared to offer the greatest immediate commercial opportunity.

— Both are maintained and bred primarily in large confined herds which facilitates management and recordkeeping.
— Both represent large potential markets in terms of numbers of annual breedings.
— Swine represent the largest per capita consumed meat in the world.

Dairy Cattle: Projected Potential Market: The potential market is projected to be only farms with over 50 milk cows, where the payback on an instrument system would be very high.

— Projected potential market: Farms with over 50 milk cows:
    United States—50,000 farms out of total 588,000 farms with milk cows. These farms have 4.8 million of the total 12.5 million milk cows in the United States. Our potential market in the United States is, therefore, 8.5 percent of total farms which have 38.5 percent of total milk cows.

EXHIBIT 1 (*continued*)

Europe—estimated 40,000 farms have 5 million of the over 50 million milk cows in
   Europe.
Rest of world—conservative estimate 10,000 farms.
Total market potential—100,000 farms
— Average instrument usage
   • 11 tests per cow per year
   • 144 cows per farm, which assumes 50 percent of sales will be to farms with 50–100
     cows and 50 percent to farms with over 100 cows. This assumption results in
     penetration of market potential being greater for disposables than instruments.
   • 11 × 144 = 1584 tests per farm per year.
— Sales price
      Instrument $2,500 each
      Disposables $2 per test
   Viscotech is currently funding a research program with dairy cattle at the University of
the Midwest.
   Market introduction is projected for the third quarter of 1985. First-year sales of 210
instruments represent a less than .5 percent penetration of the potential U.S. market.
Second-year sales of 525 instruments brings the cumulative penetration to .7 percent of the
total world market.
   Distributor arrangements for sale to the dairy industry have not yet been set up.

   Swine: Projected Potential Market: The potential market is projected to be only larger
operations that average 250 sows. The animals are in a confined controlled environment,
and the economic payback of an instrument system would be very high.
— Projected Potential Market
   United States—8,000 operations averaging 250 sows in confinement which account for
      40 percent of total 5 million sows in the United States.
   Europe—estimated 4,000 operations accounting for 25 percent of 4 million sows.
   Rest of world—estimated 2,000 operations accounting for 10 percent of 5 million sows.
— Average Instrument Usage
   1. 19 tests per sow
   2. 250 sows per farm
   3. 19 × 250 = 4,750 tests per farm per year.
Note: This averages 13 tests per day, meaning larger operations of 400–600 sows would
definitely need two or three instruments for scheduling purposes. Instrument sales are
projected conservatively at one per operation, but with replacement sales beginning after
five years of heavy usage.
— Sales Price
      Instrument $2,500.00 each
      Disposables $1.25 per test
Note: Economics of sow breeding require lower cost per test to provide attractive payback.
Competitively, lower disposables' price can be justified based on much higher volume of
testing per farm as compared to dairy cattle. Gross margin will be reduced significantly, but
still remain attractively above 40 percent.

   Viscotech has recently signed a joint R&D/Distribution agreement with National
Swine Breeders, Inc. This company is the largest producer of hybrid breeding stock in the
United States.
   Market introduction is projected for the second quarter of 1985. First-year sales of 100
units represents a 1.25 percent penetration of the potentiaal U.S. market. Second-year sales
of 200 instruments brings the cumulative penetration to 2.1 percent of the potential world
market.

EXHIBIT 1 (*concluded*)

Projected Income Statements ($000)

	1986	1987	1988
Sales	$2,726	$7,629	$23,400
Commissions (33%)	908	2,391	7,722
Cost of goods sold	661	1,974	5,850
Gross profit	1,157	3,261	9,828
Research and development	352	438	512
Sales & marketing	283	441	742
General and administrative	511	630	803
Interest	77	65	0
Depreciation	12	19	28
Profit before tax	(78)	1,668	7,743
Tax	—	—*	3,716
Profit after tax	(78)	1,668	4,027

*Due to prior losses and tax credits.

EXHIBIT 2
Viscotech Investment Memorandum

Confidential Investment Memorandum and Recission Offer

20,000 SHARES OF COMMON STOCK

This Confidential Investment Memorandum has been prepared in connection with the offering by Viscotech, Inc. (the "Company") of up to 20,000 shares of its Common Stock, $.10 par value, at $40 per share. The minimum subscription is 100 shares ($4,000).

This memorandum presents background information, has been prepared for the confidential use of private investors, and is not to be reproduced in whole or part. This offering is not made pursuant to any registration statement of Notification under Regulation A filed with the Securities and Exchange Commission, and the securities offered hereby are offered for investment only to qualifying recipients of this offering. The Company claims an exemption from the registration requirements of the Securities Act of 1933, as amended under Section 4(2) of that Act and Rule 505 thereunder.

Nothing set forth herein is intended to represent or in any manner imply that the stock offered hereby has been approved, recommended or guaranteed by the Government of the United States or of any state, or by any of the agencies of either.

EXHIBIT 2 (*continued*)

THE SECURITIES OFFERED HEREBY ARE HIGHLY SPECULATIVE AND INVOLVE A HIGH DEGREE OF RISK. PURCHASE OF THESE SECURITIES SHOULD BE CONSIDERED ONLY BY THOSE PERSONS WHO CAN AFFORD TO SUSTAIN A TOTAL LOSS OF THEIR INVESTMENT. SEE "RISK FACTORS."

THIS OFFERING INVOLVES IMMEDIATE SUBSTANTIAL DILUTION FROM THE OFFERING PRICE. FOR FURTHER INFORMATION CONCERNING THIS AND OTHER SPECIAL RISK FACTORS, SEE "RISK FACTORS" AND "DILUTION."

The offering price has been determined arbitrarily, and bears no relationship to the book value per share. Since all such shares must be acquired for investment only, no market for the shares offered hereby will arise, and no sales of such stock will be permitted in the future except pursuant to an effective registration statement or an exemption from registration under the Securities Act of 1933, as amended. Hence, the Company can offer no assurance that the stock will be salable at any time when the subscriber desires, or that the stock will be able to be resold at any time at or near the offering price.

The offering of the common stock is not underwritten. The Company plans to sell shares of common stock by personal solicitation or otherwise, through efforts of its distributors and officers. Such persons will receive no compensation other than reimbursement of out of pocket expenses incurred by them in connection with the sale. Such officers may be deemed "underwriters" as that term is defined in the Securities Act of 1933, as amended.

Unless 50 percent of the shares offered hereby are sold within 90 days from the date hereof, all subscribers' funds will be returned to them without interest or deduction.

TABLE OF CONTENTS

	Page
Risk Factors	3
Dilution	omitted
Business	4
Patents	5
Use of Proceeds	5
Certain Transactions	6
Management and Control	omitted
Capital Structure and Description of Common Stock	8
Section 1244 Stock	omitted
Dividends	8
New Financing	8
Remuneration	9
Other Information	omitted
Transfer Agent	omitted
Facilities	omitted
Legal Opinions	omitted
Applicable Regulations	9
Litigation	9
Selling Arrangements	omitted
Additional Information	omitted
Financial Statements	10
Confidential Offeree Questionnaire	18

EXHIBIT 2 (*continued*)

Risk Factors.
    Viscotech, Inc. (the "Company") was incorporated under the laws of the State of Illinois on December 17, 1977, to do research on, and to develop, instruments and devices to measure precisely and accurately the amount of, and the variations in, elasticity and viscosity (known as viscoelasticity) of saliva in humans and other mammals. It has not yet marketed any such instruments or devices.
    Prospective investors should be informed of the following risk factors involved in this offering:

(A) Insolvency:
    1. To date, the Company has been engaged only in research and development, has generated no sales, and is, consequently, currently insolvent.
    2. A substantial portion of this offering has already been raised, and the funds have been used to pay current obligations. (See "Use of Proceeds.")
    3. Even if the offering is fully subscribed, unless operations soon become profitable, or the Company raises additional funds elsewhere, investors will stand to lose their entire investment.
(B) Dilution:
    In the event all the shares offered hereby are sold, those persons who purchase these shares will incur an immediate substantial dilution in the book value of $37.34 per share from the offering price of $40 per share while the book value of the presently outstanding shares will increase from minus $2.52 per share to $2.66 per share solely by reason of the proceeds raised through the offering.
(C) No Operating History:
    The Company has no operating history, and there is no assurance that it will operate profitably.
(D) No Present Product Market:
    The Company has no contracts or commitments from potential users of its products, and can give no assurance that the products will be marketed successfully.
(E) Limited Personnel:
    The Company has only three full-time employees, a Chief Executive Officer, and two Engineers. The development of the devices it intends to market has been, and will continue to be, of an indeterminate time, dependent upon part-time efforts of its founders, and of outside consultants.
(F) Food and Drug Administration Approval:
    The Food and Drug Administration has not approved the Company's complete instrument system for sale, and no assurance can be given that it, or any other governmental agency with jurisdiction, will do so.
(G) Use of Proceeds for Research and Development in Other Areas:
    A significant amount of the Company's funds will be used for further research and development in the fields of animal husbandry, consumer products, industrial products, and possibly other areas, and no assurance can be given that this research and development will be successful.
(H) Need for Additional Funding:
    The Company believes that it will be necessary to secure funding in addition to that offered pursuant hereto in order to enable the Company to

- 3 -

EXHIBIT 2 *(continued)*

achieve its objectives. The Company will seek to raise such additional funds through any one or more of loans, grants, or additional equity. Should the Company seek to raise additional equity, it may be required to do so at a price per share less than that being offered pursuant hereto, in which case investors will suffer a dilution in the value of their shares. The Company can give no assurance that such additional funding will be available to it on any basis.

(I) Competition:

Many companies with resources far greater than those available to the Company are involved in the field of nutrition and may be able to compete with the Company.

(J) Dividends:

The Company has never paid dividends, and does not expect to do so in the foreseeable future.

(K) No Cumulative Voting:

The common stock of this Company does not have cumulative voting rights. Hence, the holders of more than 50 percent of the shares voting for the election of directors may elect all the directors if they so choose. Since the present management holds more than 50 percent of the shares to be outstanding, it will be in a position to reelect itself as directors.

Business

It has long been known that the viscoelasticity of saliva decreases in the event of nutritional deficiency. To date, however, to the knowledge of the Company, there is no instrument or method capable of accurately measuring this decrease at a reasonable cost and evaluating the extent and cause of nutritional inadequacy. Such measurements can be of significant aid to doctors in diagnosing the problems of overweight, obese or anorexic individuals and to breeders of such animals as cattle and swine. The instruments that the Company has developed are, it believes, capable of making such measurements on minute quantities of saliva, which consists of a variety of nonhomogeneous materials, without homogenizing them or otherwise destroying their integrity. The instruments developed by the Company do not rely on hormonal, chemical or other ingested material, nor on any implanted devices. Rather, a sample of saliva is extracted and placed on a grid in the instrument which is capable of determining the exact amount of viscoelasticity present in the sample.

Food and Drug Administration approval is a necessary prerequisite to the marketing of the Company's products for human medical use in the United States. Approval has been granted for the Company's saliva aspirator. Application for approval of the Company's Doctor's Instrument (the first major product that the Company intends to market) will be submitted subsequent to the completion of clinical trials presently in progress. There can be no assurance that approval will be forthcoming. A delay in the grant of such approval, or the attachment thereto of conditions, or the denial thereof, might have a serious, adverse effect on the Company.

Although the Company has developed prototype machines and other products for use by doctors, clinics, and other medical personnel, such machines have not been distributed, and so their effectiveness in the field remains unproven. The Company has distributed a limited number of its products to users who are not associated with the Company, in order to secure from them reports as to results and other comments. The Company cannot guarantee that such reports or comments will be favorable.

- 4 -

EXHIBIT 2 *(continued)*

In addition, the Company is planning to contract for the production of several hundred Doctor's Instruments to be available for sale to doctors, clinics, and hospitals for delivery commencing in 1984. Although the Company has had negotiations with manufacturers, no commitments or contracts have been made. In consequence, no assurance can be given that the machines can be produced within the projected time and at a favorable price, or that if produced, a sufficient number can be sold to offset the investment.

The Company is presently attempting to develop a device at a commercially reasonable price which would enable a person to sample his own saliva and determine his own nutritional levels. There can be no assurance that its efforts will be successful within a reasonable time and at reasonable cost, or that in any event, Food and Drug Administration approval will be granted, or that such a device would have the degree of consumer acceptance necessary for economic viability.

The Company also has research projects planned to measure bronchial secretions, synovial fluid, spinal fluid, serum, and meconium, any or all of which may be of importance in other branches of medicine. In addition, the Company is supporting research at a university agricultural school to experiment in the application of the Company's concepts in the field of swine production.

All of these activities will take considerable time to complete. No assurance can be given that any will be completed successfully, or within the resources of the company, or that if successfully completed, commercially salable products can be developed and marketed.

Patents

The Company has filed and been granted patents on certain applications of its basic concepts and has filed further patent applications which are presently pending. Patent applications corresponding to certain of the Company's U.S. patents have been filed in twenty or more countries. A schedule setting forth the patent status is included as Appendix A. The Company can offer no assurance that any pending patent application will be granted, that the grant of any patent insures that the product covered thereby can be marketed successfully, that any patent is valid and enforceable, or that any of its patents can not be circumvented or attacked by others. Nor can it assure that any of its present or future products will not infringe on patents of others.

Use of Proceeds

The net proceeds of this offering, assuming the sale of the 20,000 shares offered hereby, will be approximately $782,000 after deducting estimated expenses of $18,000. The Company will apply the net proceeds to satisfy its liability on Stock Subscriptions which as of the date hereof totals $776,000 (see Note 8 of Financial Statements), such liability having been created by the receipt by the Company of subscriptions to this offering prior to the issuance of this Confidential Investment Memorandum. The funds creating this liability have been used since June 1983, as follows:

- $200,000 to reduce bank indebtedness.*

---

*The remaining balance of $65,000 indebtedness to the bank is to be paid, by agreement, $5,000 per month, commencing April 1984. The Company's original indebtedness of $165,000 to the bank was personally guaranteed by certain of the Company's directors. The proceeds of the loan were used in part to repay Company indebtedness to its directors.

EXHIBIT 2 (*continued*)

- $250,000 to pay current indebtedness to creditors.
- $30,000 to process patent applications.
- $296,000 for working capital, including the salary of the Company's President, other employees, research and development, and other expenses of the Company.

The balance of the proceeds from the offering ($25,000) will be used (approximately $18,000) to pay the estimated expenses of the offering, and the balance added to working capital.

Since there is no underwriting for the shares being offered, there is no assurance that all of the shares will be sold. As of the date of this offering, the Company has received subscriptions for the purchase of substantially all shares offered hereby, and has accepted funds for the purchase of 19,000 of the shares offered hereby. Such subscriptions cannot be accepted except pursuant hereto. Unless subscriptions pursuant hereto are received within 90 days from the effective date of this Memorandum for at least 16,000 shares offered hereby, all subscribers' money will be returned to them without interest or deductions. In any event, any subscriber who has sent money to the Company for the purchase of the securities offered hereby prior to the receipt of this Confidential Investment Memorandum, who so requests or who fails to complete and return the subscription form attached hereto within such 90-day period will be refunded his or her subscription money in full without interest or deduction.

Certain Transactions

Indebtedness to Affiliates

As of February 28, 1984, the Company was indebted to certain of its officers and other related parties as follows:

Creditor	Amount Due	Date Due	Consideration
Louis J. Brown	$ 7,500	Sept. 1, 1985	Services rendered.
Harold J. Stein	$25,000	Sept. 1, 1985	Services & Expenses.
Fredericks Communication	$63,562	$2,000/month commencing Oct. 1, 1984	Expenses; employees' services.
O'Connor & O'Connor	$23,000	Sept. 1, 1985	Expenses; employees' services.
Melvin I. O'Connor	$16,782	Sept. 1, 1985	Cash advanced.

All amounts due bear interest ranging from 8 percent to 12 percent per year.

Mr. Brown and Dr. Stein are consultants to the Company. The debt to Mr. Brown represents accrued consulting fees; and that to Dr. Stein represents approximately $11,000 in accrued consulting fees and approximately $14,000 advanced by him as salary to a nurse engaged to assist him in his research for the Company.

Fredericks Communication, and its subsidiaries, furnished services in fabricating parts, materials, and devices used by the Company, and also conceived, developed, and produced slide shows, display equipment, and audiovisual shows used by the Company at exhibits and medical meetings. The in-

EXHIBIT 2 *(continued)*

debtedness to Fredericks consists of services of employees and out of pocket expenses.

The indebtedness to the Company's accountants is produced by services of employees and out of pocket expenses in recordkeeping, statement and tax return preparation and clerical services.

Melvin I. O'Connor advanced funds at various times. The liability to him represents interest on various loans ($4,282) and the remaining balance on these cash loans to the company ($12,500).

The Company intends to continue its arrangements with Mr. Brown for consulting services at a cost to the Company of $1,500 per month, plus out of pocket expenses. In addition, the Company intends to use, as required, the services of Dr. Stein and the staff accounting services of the Company's accountants at the generally applicable rates of each for such services. If the Company deems it advisable it may utilize the services or facilities of other affiliates for compensation to be negotiated in each instance. The Company has negotiated an informal arrangement with Fredericks Communication Co., Inc., whereunder the latter has constructed an office and engineering laboratory in a building owned by Fredericks Communication Co., Inc., and has leased it to the Company on a tenant-at-will basis. Such arrangement has not been formalized by any written agreement.

Fredericks Communication Co., Inc.

Fredericks Communication Co., Inc. ("Fredericks") originally known as Fredericks Recording Co., Inc., was contacted by the Company in 1981 to supply the Company with disposable grids, then contemplated to be plastic squares with uniform ridges. Thereafter, the Company and a subsidiary of Fredericks known as Fredericks Research & Development, Inc., entered into a joint venture to procure, manufacture, or have manufactured for it the grids required by the Company on an exclusive basis. On November 17, 1983, the Company acquired by merger Fredericks Research & Development Inc. for 10,980 shares of the Company's stock (after giving effect to the August 1983 stock split). At that time Fredericks Research & Development, Inc.'s share of expenses (excluding fixed costs, overhead, and executive salaries) for research and development on Company products was $46,466.34.

The Company has used Fredericks to procure substantially all of the molds, dies, boxes, aspirators, machinery, extruders and other equipment required by the Company. Fredericks also provided research and development for the grids and other items in connection with the Company's business, and rendered assistance to the Company in conceiving, designing and producing film strips, slides, and other display material used by the Company in its presentations at trade and other shows. Fredericks principals, Messrs. Smith, Green, and Marvin, in September 1982, purchased 3,960 shares of the Company's stock, after giving effect to the August 1983 stock split, for $120,000 ($30.30 per share). Messrs. Smith, Green, and Marvin loaned the Company $50,000 cash, which was repaid in July 1978, and Mr. Green, along with other Company principals, endorsed a Company Note for $165,000 to a bank in July 1983. Mr. Smith has been at various times Clerk, Assistant Clerk and Director of the Company, and both he and Mr. Green are currently Directors.

Fredericks has charged the Company for these various services, for its actual costs of materials, services of its staff and special personnel other than executive personnel. The Company intends to continue its arrangements with

EXHIBIT 2 (*continued*)

Fredericks respecting procurement and the providing of other services, and to reimburse Fredericks in connection with these activities for Fredericks' expenses and services of its personnel other than executive personnel.

Capital Structure and Description of Common Stock
The capitalization of the Company as of the date of this Offering Circular, and as adjusted to give effect to the sale of the shares offered hereby, is as follows:

	Prior to Offering	Following Offering if All Shares Sold
Notes Payable—Bank	$ 65,000	$ 65,000
Notes Payable—Shareholders	135,844	135,844
Accounts Payable	47,506	47,506
Stock Subscriptions	745,000	-0-
Capital Stock	14,412	16,412
Additional Paid-In Capital	462,028	960,028

The Company's Common Stock, of $.10 par value, is its only authorized class of capital stock. At all meetings of stockholders, holders of Common Stock are entitled to one vote for each share held. The holders of common stock have no preemptive or subscription rights. All the outstanding shares of Common Stock are fully paid and nonassessable and are entitled to dividends if and when declared by the Board of Directors.
The Common Stock of the Company does not have cumulative voting rights. Hence, the holders of more than 50 percent of the shares voting for the election of directors may elect all the directors if they so choose. Since the present management holds more than 50 percent of the shares to be outstanding, it will be in a position to reelect itself as directors.

Dividends
Holders of shares of the Company's Common Stock are entitled to receive dividends as may be declared by the Board of Directors out of funds legally available therefore and to share pro rata in any distribution to shareholders. The Company does not contemplate the payment of any dividends in the foreseeable future.

New Financing
The Company believes that it will be necessary to secure funding in addition to that offered pursuant hereto in order to enable the Company to achieve its objectives. By letter dated March 8, 1983, the Indian U.S. International Industrial Research & Development Foundation, a foundation sponsored and funded by the governments of the United States and India, advised the Company that its Board had approved a first year grant of up to $250,000 to be expended on research and development of the Company's products, subject to various conditions and the negotiation of a formal contract. The Company believes that conditions to this grant will include (a) establishment of a joint program with an Indian company for research, development, preproduction, and premarketing of the Company's products, (b) expenditures by the Company and its Indian partners on the program during the first year of the grant of

EXHIBIT 2 *(continued)*

amounts equivalent to those received from the grant during the same time. The Company cannot give assurances that a final contract for the grant will be executed, or that if it is, the Company will be able to satisfy the conditions thereof.

Remuneration

Mr. Jones was engaged as Chief Executive Officer on September 1, 1983, at a salary of $65,000 per year. Mr. Brown is paid consulting fees of $1,500 per month. None of the other officers or directors are compensated. In November 1981, O'Connor O'Connor, of which Mr. O'Connor is a partner, were issued 900 shares of stock (after giving effect to the 12 for 1 split) in satisfaction of $7,500 of liability to them for cash advances and staff services rendered. The shares were distributed to the partners of O'Connor & O'Connor, other than Mr. O'Connor, who disclaims any benefit therefrom or control thereover. Mr. Jones has devoted full time to his duties as president of the Company since September 1, 1983, and is currently in the process of moving his residence to Illinois.

Applicable Regulations

As indicated above, the products contemplated by the Company for use by doctors and by individuals require approval of the Food and Drug Administration (FDA). There is no assurance that the Company will be able to comply with the FDA regulations or that the necessary approval of the Company's operations and all the products can be achieved. To date it has only received such approval for its aspirators. The Company is in the process of compiling clinical data with respect to the balance of its products, to be supplied to the FDA as required. The Company believes that these contemplated products, however, may be utilized in animal husbandry without FDA approval and, if manufactured abroad, may be utilized outside the United States without FDA approval, although they may require approval by appropriate regulatory agencies in each country. The Company also believes that no government regulations are applicable to any of the contemplated uses in industry, inasmuch as no hazardous procedures are associated with the utilization of the Company's proposed products.

Litigation

The Company is not involved in any litigation and knows of no threatened or contingent liabilities.

The Company, at the request of any subscriber or Adviser (as defined in the Subscription Agreement), will make available for inspection copies of these documents, will provide answers to questions concerning the terms and conditions of this Offering, and will provide such additional information that is necessary to verify the accuracy of the information contained herein or that may otherwise pertain to the Company or to this investment, to the extent the Company has such information or can acquire it without unreasonable effort or expense.

EXHIBIT 2 (*continued*)
Financial Statements

Consolidated Balance Sheet
(Unaudited)

	February 28,	June 30,					
ASSETS	1984	1983	1982	1981	1980	1979	1978
Current Assets:							
Cash	$ 21,110	$ 1,104	$ 6,437	$ 4,745	$ 1,207	$10,331	$12,514
Inventories (Notes 1 and 2)	150,023	18,359	—	—	—	—	—
Subscriptions receivable (Note 3)	131,000	—	73,413	—	—	—	3,000
Prepaid items	1,000	—	—	—	—	—	—
Total Current Assets	303,133	19,463	79,850	4,745	1,207	10,331	15,514
Fixed Assets (Notes 1 and 4)	31,274	26,775	2,074	—	—	—	—
Other Assets:							
Patents and patent applications	325,753	183,753	115,467	59,595	3,942	17,637	—
Unamortized organization and other expenses	831	673	279	171	287	403	519
	326,584	184,426	115,746	59,766	34,229	18,040	519
Total Assets	$660,991	$230,664	$197,670	$64,511	$35,436	$28,371	$16,033

- 10 -

EXHIBIT 2 (*continued*)

ASSETS LIABILITIES AND SHAREHOLDERS' EQUITY/(DEFICIT)	February 28, 1984	June 30, 1983	1982	1981	1980	1979	1978
Current Liabilities:							
Medway advances (Note 5)	$ —	$ —	$ —	$ —	$43,850	$33,850	$ —
Current maturities of note payable - bank (Note 6)	50,000	169,000					
Current maturities of amounts due to shareholders (Note 7)	10,000		2,500	9,000		16,000	16,000
Accounts payable and accruals	47,506	196,487	44,075	22,833	6,912	184	1,702
Total Current Liabilities	107,506	365,487	46,575	31,833	50,762	50,034	17,702
Long-Term Debt:							
Note payable – bank (Note 6)	15,000						
Amounts due to shareholders (Note 7)	125,844						
	140,844						
Amounts Received on Stock Subscriptions (Note 8)	776,000	20,000					
Shareholders' Equity/(Deficit) (Note 9):							
Common stock, par value $.10							
Authorized 300,000 shares							
Issued 144,120 shares	14,412	476,440	461,440	103,940	37,940	9,940	9,940
Additional paid-in capital	462,028						
Accumulated deficit	(839,799)	(631,263)	(310,345)	(71,262)	(53,266)	(31,603)	(11,609)
	(363,359)	(154,823)	151,095	32,678	(15,326)	(21,663)	(1,669)
Total Liabilities and Shareholders' Equity/ (Deficit)	$660,991	$230,664	$197,670	$ 64,511	$35,436	$28,371	$16,033

The accompanying notes are an integral part of the consolidated financial statements.

Consolidated Statement of Operations and Accumulated Deficit
(Unaudited)

| | Feb. 28 | June 30, | | | | | |
	1984	1983	1982	1981	1980	1979	1978
Sales	$ —	$ —	$ —	$ —	$ —	$ —	$ —
Expenses:							
Rent	1,888	—	—	—	—	—	—
Office and clerical expenses	11,385	10,853	17,866	6,575	27	130	—
Meetings expenses	7,741	3,047	5,305	2,959	1,340	681	118
Advertising, shows, public relations	9,482	46,355	26,524	5,499	—	—	—
Telephone	3,130	2,021	946	—	—	—	—
Taxes	2,276	1,520	948	160	114	184	114
Miscellaneous	1,086	106	142	116	116	116	58
Interest	12,385	8,750	—	—	—	—	—
Depreciation	819	—	—	—	—	—	—
Payroll and payroll expenses	33,909	—	—	—	—	—	—
Research and development (Note 11)	124,435	248,047	187,243	2,687	20,066	18,883	11,319
	208,536	320,918	239,083	17,996	21,663	19,994	11,609
Net Loss	(208,536)	(320,918)	(239,083)	(17,996)	(21,663)	(19,994)	(11,609)
Accumulated Deficit, Beginning	(631,263)	(310,345)	(71,262)	(53,266)	(31,603)	(11,609)	—
Accumulated Deficit, Ending	($839,799)	($631,263)	($310,345)	($71,262)	($53,266)	($31,603)	($11,609)

The accompanying notes are an integral part of the consolidated financial statements.

- 12 -

EXHIBIT 2 (*continued*)

Consolidated Statement of Changes in Financial Position
(Unaudited)

	8 Mos. Ended Feb. 28 1984	Years Ended June 30,					
		1983	1982	1981	1980	1979	1978
Resources provided:							
From operations:							
Net loss	($208,536)	($320,918)	($239,083)	($17,996)	($21,663)	($19,994)	($11,609)
Add items not affecting working capital:							
Depreciation and amortization	904	325	251	116	116	116	58
Working capital applied to operations	(207,632)	(320,593)	(238,832)	(17,880)	(21,547)	(19,878)	(11,551)
Amounts received on stock subscriptions	725,000	20,000	—	—	—	—	—
Proceeds of bank note	165,000	—	—	—	—	—	—
Amounts due shareholders	125,844	—	—	—	—	—	—
Capital investment	—	15,000	357,500	66,000	28,000	—	9,940
	808,212	(285,593)	118,668	48,120	6,453	(19,878)	(1,611)
Resources applied:							
Purchase of fixed assets	5,403	25,026	2,325	—	—	—	—
Reduction of bank note	200,000	—	—	—	—	—	—
Other assets	158	394	108	—	—	—	577
Increase in current maturities of long-term debt	50,000	—	—	—	—	—	—
Patents and patent applications	42,000	68,286	55,872	25,653	16,305	17,637	—
	197,561	93,706	58,305	25,653	16,305	17,637	577
Increase/(decrease) in working capital	$510,651	($379,299)	$ 60,363	$22,467	($ 9,852)	($37,515)	($ 2,188)

Changes in the components of working capital:

Increase/(decrease) in current assets:							
Cash	$ 20,006	($ 5,333)	$ 1,692	$ 3,538	($ 9,124)	($ 2,183)	$12,514
Inventories	131,664	18,359	—	—	—	—	—
Subscriptions receivable	100,000	(73,413)	73,413	—	—	(3,000)	3,000
Prepaid items	1,000	—	—	—	—	—	—
	252,670	(60,387)	75,105	3,538	(9,124)	5,183	15,514
Increase/(decrease) in current liabilities:							
Medway advances	—	—	—	(43,850)	10,000	33,850	—
Current maturities of notes payable—bank	50,000	—	—	—	—	—	16,000
Current maturities of amounts due to shareholders	(159,000)	166,500	(6,500)	9,000	(16,000)	—	1,702
Accounts payable and accruals	(148,981)	152,412	21,242	15,921	6,728	(1,518)	17,702
	(257,981)	318,912	14,742	(18,929)	728	32,332	17,702
Increase/(decrease) in working capital	$510,651	($379,299)	$ 60,363	$22,467	($ 9,852)	($37,515)	($ 2,188)

The accompanying notes are an integral part of the consolidated financial statements.

EXHIBIT 2 (*continued*)

NOTES TO CONSOLIDATED FINANCIAL STATEMENTS

February 28, 1984
(Unaudited)

Note 1—Summary of Significant Accounting Policies

Principles of Consolidation
The consolidated financial statements include the accounts of Visco-tech, Inc. and its wholly-owned inactive subsidiaries, Nutrico, Inc. and Animal Technology, Inc. All intercompany balances and transactions have been eliminated in consolidation.

The Company was organized December 29, 1977; and the subsidiaries were organized in December 1980: Nutrico, Inc. for the exploitation of the Company's concepts related to industrial viscometry and Animal Technology, Inc. for the exploitation of the Company's concepts related to animal nutrition.

Inventories
        Inventories are valued at the lower of cost (first-in, first-out basis) or market.

Fixed Assets
        Fixed assets are carried at cost and depreciated on the straight-line method over estimated useful lives as follows:

Display equipment	Five (5) years
Molds and dies	Seven (7) years
Machinery	Ten (10) years
Office equipment	Ten (10) years

Note 2—Inventories
        Inventories consisted of the following:

	February 28, 1984	June 30, 1983
Machines completed awaiting modification	$116,500	$16,500
Machine parts	15,000	—
Aspirators—finished	8,138	500
Grids	3,961	—
Packing materials	5,799	1,121
Instruction booklets, tapes, calibrating fluids, etc.	625	238
	$150,023	$18,359

Note 3—Stock Subscriptions
        The company has offered its shares through the Medical Investment Fund Trust. The company has not yet received payment for all shares subscribed.

EXHIBIT 2 (*continued*)

Note 4—Fixed Assets
Fixed assets consisted of the following:

	February 28, 1984	June 30, 1983	June 30, 1982
Display equipment	$ 2,183	$ 2,183	$ 2,183
Molds and dies	23,730	22,163	—
Machinery	5,362	2,758	—
Office furniture	1,141	—	—
	32,421	27,104	2,183
Less accumulated depreciation	1,147	329	109
	$31,274	$26,775	$ 2,074

Note 5—Medway Advances
In fiscal years 1979 and 1980, the Company received nonrefundable advances from Medway, Inc. to finance research and patent applications. Medway, Inc. was given an exclusive marketing arrangement during this period. Medway's contract for exclusive marketing expired in December 1980.

Note 6—Note Payable—Bank
In July 1983, the Corporation borrowed $265,000 from a bank, unsecured but guaranteed by several shareholders. Of the proceeds, $155,000 was used to repay the shareholders who had loaned that amount to the Corporation. The note, which bears interest at the bank's prime rate plus 2 percent, originally matured in January 1984. At that time, $200,000 was paid. The remaining balance is to be paid in monthly installments of $5,000, commencing in April 1984.

Note 7—Due to Shareholders
In February 1984, several shareholders-creditors accepted term notes for amounts due them as follows:

Shareholder-Creditor	Amount	Interest	Payable	Nature of Debt
Louis Brown	$ 7,500	8%	Sept. 1, 1985	Services rendered
Harold J. Stein	25,000	Prime	Sept. 1, 1985	Research services, out of pocket expenses
Fredericks Communications	63,562	Prime	$2,000/month commencing Oct. 1, 1985	Out of pocket expenses, services of employees
O'Connor & O'Connor	23,000	8%	Sept. 1, 1985	Out of pocket expenses, services of employees
Melvin I. O'Connor	16,782	8%	Sept. 1, 1985	Cash advances
	$135,844			

- 16 -

EXHIBIT 2 (*continued*)

Louis Brown and Harold J. Stein had been employed as consultants at $1,500 per month each. In addition, Dr. Stein advanced the salary and expenses of a nurse employed by the Company in his office.

Fredericks Communications and its subsidiaries furnished services in fabricating parts, materials and devices used by the Company, and also conceived, developed and produced slide shows, display equipment and audiovisual shows used by the Company at exhibits and medical meetings. The indebtedness to Fredericks consists of services of employees and out of pocket expenses.

The indebtedness to O'Connor & O'Connor is produced by services of employees and out of pocket expenses in recordkeeping, statement and tax return preparation, and clerical services.

Melvin I. O'Connor advanced funds at various times. The liability to him represents interest on various loans ($4,282) and the remaining balance on these cash loans to the Company ($12,500).

Note 8—Amount received on Stock Subscriptions

Funds have been received from subscribers to the stock of the Corporation. Issuance of the stock has been delayed pending approval of a registration under Regulation A of the Securities and Exchange Commission. The registration involves 20,000 shares of $.10 par value stock, to be issued at $40 per share. At June 30, 1983, 800 shares had been subscribed and paid for, and at February 28, 1984, a total of 19,400 shares had been subscribed.

Note 9—Common Stock

On August 31, 1984, the Corporation voted to change its authorized capital stock from 12,500 shares of no par value to 300,000 shares of $.10 par value and to exchange 12 shares of the newly authorized stock for each share of old stock then outstanding. This exchange of shares has been given effect in the accompanying financial statements by transferring from common stock to additional paid-in capital the amounts in excess of par as of February 28, 1984.

Note 10—Merger

On August 31, 1983, the shareholders voted to issue 915 shares of old no par stock (equivalent to 10,980 shares of new $.10 par stock) to Fredericks Research & Development Corporation in exchange for all the outstanding stock of that corporation and to merge Fredericks Research & Development Corporation into the Company. The assets acquired from Fredericks Research & Development Corporation were certain technical procedures in production and the right to limited participation with the Company in certain production profits. No value was recorded for the assets acquired from Fredericks; accordingly, common stock was credited and additional paid-in capital charged, for the par value of the shares issued.

Note 11—Operations

The Corporation has used most of its resources since its inception in research and development of its concepts for measuring the viscoelasticity of oral mucus in humans and animals and developing instruments for commerical medical application. Expenditures to date are as follows:

EXHIBIT 2 (*continued*)

Fiscal year June 30, 1978	$ 11,319	
June 30, 1979	18,833	
June 30, 1980	20,066	
June 30, 1981	2,687	($43,850 defrayed by others—Note 5)
June 30, 1982	187,243	
June 30, 1983	248,047	
July 1, 1983 to February 28, 1984	124,435	
	$612,680	

Note 12—Taxes on Income

The Company's net operating losses are available to offset future taxable income. Losses through 1980 may be carried forward five (5) years and subsequent losses, seven (7) years.

For tax purposes, the Company has capitalized research and development costs, as discussed in Note 11, which costs will be written off over sixty (60) months from commencement of significant sales.

CONFIDENTIAL OFFEREE QUESTIONNAIRE

NAME _____

ADDRESS _____

BUSINESS ADDRESS _____

The primary purpose of this Questionnaire is to obtain certain information about your present and projected financial position in order to help determine whether you are qualified to receive offers of and participate in the purchase of certain securities.

Any private placements of securities, when and if made, will be made pursuant to the exemption from registration provided for in Section 4 (2) of the Securities Act of 1933, or under Rule 505 which has been adopted by the Securities and Exchange Commission under Section 4 (2). Rule 505 protects investors by providing objective standards in private placements of securities.

One of the requirements of the Rule is that the persons involved in the offering and sale of the securities must have reasonable grounds to believe that each person to whom the offering is made either:

(i) has directly or by access to a "purchaser representative," knowledge and experience in financial and business matters so that he is capable of evaluating the merits and risks of the prospective investment, or

(ii) is an "accredited investor" by virtue of his financial condition.

This Questionnaire will assist in compliance with the legal requirements of Section 4 (2) and Rule 505, for the protection of all concerned.

Your answers to this Questionnaire will be kept strictly confidential. Viscotech, Inc. may present this Questionnaire to legal counsel and to other persons le-

EXHIBIT 2 *(continued)*

gally responsible for an offering, who also will be required to maintain confidentiality. If necessary, this Questionnaire may be presented to appropriate parties in order to establish the availability of an exemption under applicable securities law.

Please complete this Questionnaire as fully as possible in your handwriting and sign, date, and return to Viscotech, Inc.

I. GENERAL

1. Set forth in the space provided below the state(s) in which you have maintained your principal residence during the past two years and the dates during which you resided in each such state.
2. What is your present age?
3. How many dependents do you have; what is their age and relationship to you?

II. OCCUPATION

1. In the space provided below, please indicate your present occupation; describe the nature of your employment and the length of time you have held this position.
2. In what other capacities have you been employed in the past five years?

III. FINANCIAL

1. Income (from all sources) for the calendar year ended 12/31/83:

under $20,000	( )
$20,000–$40,000	( )
40,000– 60,000	( )
60,000– 80,000	( )
80,000–100,000	( )
over $100,000	( )

2. Describe briefly all nonsalary sources of income and the amount of income derived from each such source.
3. Average yearly income (from all sources) anticipated for the three-year period ending 12/31/86:

	1984	1985	1986
under $20,000	( )	( )	( )
$20,000–$40,000	( )	( )	( )
40,000– 60,000	( )	( )	( )
60,000– 80,000	( )	( )	( )
80,000–100,000	( )	( )	( )
over $100,000	( )	( )	( )

4. Describe briefly all sources of anticipated income if different from those given in III. 2. and 3.

– 19 –

EXHIBIT 2 (*continued*)

5. Please describe below your present net worth.
   a) Liquid assets (excluding real estate, furniture, automobiles, unmarketable securities) in excess of
Less than $100,000	( )
$100,000	( )
$200,000	( )
$300,000	( )
$400,000	( )
$500,000 or more	( )

   b) Total assets (liquid and nonliquid)
Less than $100,000	( )
$100,000	( )
$200,000	( )
$300,000	( )
$400,000	( )
$500,000	( )

   c) Current liabilities (due within one year)
None	( )
$100,000	( )
$200,000	( )
$300,000	( )
$400,000	( )
$500,000 or more	( )

   d) Total liabilities
None	( )
$100,000	( )
$200,000	( )
$300,000	( )
$400,000	( )
$500,000 or more	( )

   e) Contingent liabilities (include guarantees, endorsements, obligations as co-maker, leases, pending litigation, etc.)
None	( )
$100,000	( )
$200,000	( )
$300,000	( )
$400,000	( )
$500,000 or more	( )

6. Do you have life insurance? If so, in what amounts:
under $100,000	( )
$100,000–$200,000	( )
$200,000–$300,000	( )
$300,000–$400,000	( )
$400,000–$500,000	( )

7. Do you have accident and health insurance?
   Yes_____ No_____

8. Do you have any reason to believe that your future income is likely to be interrupted or substantially diminished in the foreseeable future? If yes, describe this possibility and probable effect on your financial security.
   Yes_____ No_____

EXHIBIT 2 (*concluded*)

9. If you should choose to purchase securities in Viscotech, Inc. is it your opinion that your present financial position is, and is expected to continue to be, such as to enable you:

a) to bear the economic risk of losing all funds invested in Viscotech, Inc.:

Yes_____ No_____

b) to bear the economic burden of having all such funds tied up in an essentially illiquid investment for an extended period of time:

Yes_____ No_____

Please provide any additional information which you feel might help Viscotech, Inc. to decide whether or not your financial condition is such that you could afford to lose the entire amount of your investment.

_____   _____
Date   Signature

Case 3-8

UNIVERSAL ROBOTICS CORPORATION

Andrew, Robert, and Elliot sat around the kitchen table discussing the plans for their new company—Universal Robotics. It was March 15, 1984, and the group had been actively working toward the start-up for several months. Now, things seemed to be coming together, but there were still many issues to be dealt with; they hoped that tonight's meeting would help them make these important decisions.

BACKGROUND

Andrew Reed, Robert Baker, and Elliot Carlton were all friends who intended to leave their current employment and form a new business. Reed, Baker, and Carlton had been classmates in their undergraduate days at Princeton University. After their graduation, they each took different paths, but met in late 1983 to start a new business. Their business, organized as a Delaware corporation under the name of Universal Robotics Corporation (URC), was formed to design, develop, manufacture, and market industrial robots.

Reed received his MBA in 1978 and had been assistant treasurer and assistant to the chief financial officer of a large manufacturer of computer peripheral equipment. Baker received his doctorate in electrical engineering from MIT and had spent three years in the New Products Division of

Copyright © 1983 by the President and Fellows of Harvard College.
Harvard Business School case 9-384-142.

IBM. After leaving Princeton, Carlton had spent two years as a district salesman for General Electric and then spent three years as vice president of marketing for a manufacturer of "factory automation" equipment.

Baker had identified three friends at IBM who wanted to leave IBM and join URC. These three individuals were engaged in engineering and development work at IBM's Robotics Division. They were well paid and did not want to leave IBM until URC had raised its initial capital and was in a position to compensate them at their existing salary levels.

Since early January 1984, Reed had been actively working (nights and weekends) on the development of a business plan for URC. While Reed's experience in establishing new companies was limited, he had studied that topic in business school and kept up with new venture activities in the business press. As a result of his efforts, he had prepared a preliminary draft of a business plan, contacted two friends in the venture capital business, and spoken with a regional investment banker which was interested in placing an R&D partnership. In addition, he had discussed the proposed business venture with his father-in-law, who was the president of a medium-size bank in Minneapolis. His two venture capital friends were Sebastian Vanderbilt, a general partner of Prestige Ventures Company ("Prestige"), and Anthony Wallace, a general partner of Beacon Associates ("Beacon"). The local investment banker was Pincus, Greene & Co.

Baker was an engineering genius and had a well-equipped engineering shop in the basement of his home. For two years Baker worked evenings and weekends on the development of an "intelligent" robot with potentially broad applications in the so-called automated factory. He was able to combine a vision module with a computerized device that was sensitive to touch, and therefore believed that his robot was able both to see and feel components and parts used in the manufacture of products. On January 15, 1984, Baker, after consulting with his personal patent attorney, filed a patent application for his invention.

Carlton had just completed a very successful year with his employer, and was awarded a substantial bonus for organizing a new marketing approach for two recently introduced products by his employer. Carlton's immediate boss, however, was 40 years old, and Carlton believed it was unlikely that he would replace his boss in the near future. He wanted to leave and try his hand at running a marketing organization for a high-technology company with an innovative product.

RELATIONSHIP WITH CURRENT EMPLOYERS

After their first meeting in late 1983, Reed, Baker, and Carlton had several meetings at Reed's home to plan the formation and financing of their new venture. At a meeting on March 15, 1984, the preliminary business plan and financing alternatives were reviewed.

Reed reported that he had resigned his position with his former employer effective March 1, 1984. Baker indicated his plans to resign April 1, 1984. Carlton expressed his desire to remain with his employer until September 1, 1984, at which time he would resign. Carlton's wife was expecting a baby and he desired both the insurance coverage and his salary during this period.

Reed reported that he met twice with Vanderbilt at Prestige and once with Wallace at Beacon to discuss URC and to determine whether they had any interest in investing in URC. In the meantime, over Christmas, he had several discussions with his father-in-law, who indicated that he and several of his friends and banking clients would like the opportunity to invest in URC. They believed that the robotics business would be the glamour business of the future.

Reed prepared an extensive agenda for the March 15 meeting, including a summary of the tentative financing proposals submitted by Prestige, Beacon, his father-in-law, and Pincus, Greene. The March 15 meeting was held to consider the advantages and disadvantages of the four alternatives and how they might be modified.

It was agreed that Baker's three friends at IBM would join their next meeting to discuss their future roles in URC, although none of them was expected to join URC until the initial financing was completed.

At the March 15 meeting, Baker exhibited considerable uneasiness about leaving IBM. He had heard that IBM had a very formal "exit" procedure which he would undergo when he announced his resignation. He reported that he had signed a standard IBM form of invention and nondisclosure agreement and there might be some question as to the rights of ownership in his invention and the patent application. Reed reported that he had no contracts with his employer. Carlton, on the other hand, had signed an agreement which prohibited him from soliciting or otherwise inducing any employees of his employer from leaving the company for other employment. After further discussion, it was decided that Reed would select an attorney to represent URC who, as a first order of business, would review each of their obligations to their employers and the possible legal obstacles to the commencement of the new business.

INITIAL "PRE-SEED" CAPITAL

They then discussed the need for some initial funds which would be required to retain an attorney, incorporate the business, and pay the initial start-up expenses which would be incurred before the financing was consummated. Reed lived frugally and had been able to save a portion of his salary during the past couple of years. In addition, Reed was an astute investor and managed to "hit it big" in a couple of high technology investments. Baker, on the other hand, had no money to contribute to the new venture, but was willing to contribute his invention and patent application to URC. Baker also asked whether it would be proper for him to seek a royalty from URC in exchange for the transfer of all rights to his invention to URC. Carlton indicated that he could only contribute $1,000 to the venture at this time.

At the outset it was decided that each of the three founders would own an equal share in URC. Since neither Baker nor Carlton had excess funds to invest in URC, it was concluded that the initial capital would be $3,000, and each of the founders would pay $1,000 for 100,000 shares of stock (at $.01 per share). Reed agreed to loan URC additional funds which would be required before the first financing was completed.

COMPLETION OF BUSINESS PLAN

Reed had seen a number of business plans used by recent start-ups in the Boston and California areas. He indicated that the business plans varied, depending upon the nature of the potential investors and their sophistication. He also briefly discussed the legal aspects of business plans with an attorney and was advised that the plan could be a "liability" document unless properly prepared, in compliance with federal and state securities laws. His preliminary draft of the business plan was 142 pages long, and he was therefore reluctant to show it to his colleagues. However, he did distribute an outline of the format of the business plan (attached as Exhibit 1), and asked Baker and Carlton to draft their respective sections of the business plan; namely, product and technology—Baker; and marketing, distribution, and field services—Carlton. He also asked Baker and Carlton to give thought to the specific risks of the new business so that they could be incorporated in the risks section of the business plan. In the meantime, Reed revised his preliminary draft and tried to cut it back to about 40 pages. He also met with an accountant to review the format of the projections and the assumptions used in developing the projections.

FINANCING ALTERNATIVES

Reed then reviewed the financing alternatives, which differed substantially. Based on the preliminary business plan, it appeared that URC would need $2 million to complete the development and testing of the URC's first prototype robot. The development period was estimated at about 15 months, and therefore at the end of that period a second round of private financing would be required, estimated at approximately $6 million. Both Prestige and Beacon indicated that they could arrange an initial financing of $2 million. Pincus, Greene believed that they could successfully place R&D partnership units sufficient to raise $2 million (after deducting selling commissions of $200,000). However, Reed's father-in-law advised that he and other family members and friends could raise only about $500,000. Thus, if the initial funds were to come from friends and family, URC would run out of money long before the prototype was developed. On the other hand, the $500,000 would be sufficient to test the product concept, at which time it could be easier for URC to raise the additional required funds at a higher per share price. Reed then distributed to Baker and Carlton summaries of each of the four proposals—the father-in-law's proposal (attached as Exhibit 2), the Presitge proposal (attached as Exhibit 3), the Beacon proposal (attached as Exhibit 4), and the Pincus, Greene proposal (attached as Exhibit 5).

Common Stock

The father-in-law's proposal was attractive because of its simplicity. It provided for the sale of common stock by URC of 100,000 shares of common stock at $5 per share, resulting in a 25 percent equity ownership. Reed's father-in-law wanted to sit on the board of directors, but was not insisting on that right. Reed also indicated that his father-in-law might be willing to personally guarantee a small bank credit line, particularly to bridge the gap between the expenditure of the initial equity funds and the completion of the second round financing. Reed reported that his father-in-law thought that the $500,000 could be raised from about 25 to 30 friends and relatives, in investments ranging from $10,000 to $50,000.

Subordinated Debt and Common Stock

Reed reported that Prestige was a very conservative investor. While its initial proposal called for $2 million of debt, Vanderbilt indicated that he might be willing to buy $2 million of preferred stock if the preferred stock had a mandatory redemption feature. In any event, whether the $2 million was used for the purchase of notes of URC or preferred stock of URC, Prestige expected to purchase common stock at the same price ($.01 per share) paid by the founders. Prestige wanted the right to purchase 200,000 shares, which would give it a 40 percent equity interest in URC. Prestige's proposal also called for subordination of its loan to bank borrowings, but not to trade creditors.

Convertible Preferred Stock

Beacon's proposal was a straight equity proposal, but Beacon insisted upon purchasing convertible preferred stock rather than common stock. The convertible preferred would be convertible into common stock at $4 per share. Thus, if the convertible preferred stock was converted into common stock, Beacon would acquire 500,000 shares of common stock, or approximately 62 percent of the outstanding common stock. Like Prestige, Beacon would require mandatory redemption of the convertible preferred stock, but the redemption would not commence until eight years after the investment was made, as compared with Prestige's proposal, which would commence five years after the date of investment.

Both Prestige and Beacon had excellent reputations and, as "lead investor," each would be able to attract a solid group of investors. Each of them had indicated an initial interest in investing $1 million and raising the additional $1 million from colleagues in the venture capital business. Prestige and Beacon, however, did not like each other and had never invested in the same company. Reed noted that Prestige was generally not a "second round" investor, while Beacon had traditionally come up with second round, and even third round, investments in its portfolio companies.

R&D Partnership

An R&D partnership was attractive because it allowed URC to essentially "pass through" the expenses incurred in the product development phase to private investors, who could use these as tax deductions. These write-offs were more valuable to private investors in high tax brackets, who could use them right away, than they were to URC, who could only accumulate these tax losses and carry them forward against future income.

Pincus, Greene proposed a structure (detailed in Exhibit 5) under which they would raise $2,200,000, deduct $200,000 in selling commissions, and URC would receive $2,000,000. Under this proposal the R&D partnership would be entitled to royalties at the rate of 10 percent per annum in perpetuity. However, URC would have the option to purchase the technology developed by the R&D partnership for $10 million cash or, alternatively, for that number of shares which would give the R&D partnership a 30 percent equity interest in URC.

Weighing the Alternatives

Baker had no financial or investment experience and indicated that he was not in a position to make an informed evaluation of the four proposals. The father-in-law's proposal was attractive because it meant URC would only give up 25 percent of the company initially. On the other hand, the other three proposals would provide URC with the full amount of $2 million which was projected for the development phase. Baker remembered the advice of a colleague of his at IBM who was recently ousted from a company that he founded—"Don't give up control of your company to the venture capitalists." If the Beacon proposal was accepted, the founders would wind up with only 38 percent of the equity. Moreover, Carlton was concerned that additional equity would have to be reserved for future key employees in the range of 10 percent to 20 percent of the equity of URC. This pool of common stock for future employees would further dilute their equity positions. In addition, the business plan called for another $6 million in about 15 months. If the additional $6 million could be raised by giving up only 20 percent of the equity (thereby placing a value of $30 million on the company), significant additional dilution would still result. "I don't know how to cope with this," said Baker. "Reed, you have the MBA, you tell us what we should do."

Reed stated that he would give each of the alternatives careful consideration and come up with a recommendation for an April 6 meeting. In the meantime, Reed also met with the chief executive officers of three or four recently formed high-tech companies in the Boston area and sought their advice.

SWEAT EQUITY

At that point, Carlton shifted the discussion to his own personal arrangements with the new company. He indicated that he wanted a three-year employment contract with fixed minimum salary and an annual bonus award if he met certain agreed-upon goals.

Reed stated that he was not interested in an employment agreement, but he wanted to be sure that each founder remained with URC for at least five years. A means of securing that commitment was a "golden handcuff" agreement. He was fearful that one of the founders might leave the company in a year or so, and walk away with 100,000 shares of common stock. He therefore suggested that each founder agree that his stock would be forfeited if he did not remain in the employment of URC for five years. Baker disagreed, but was willing to agree on a compromise approach: a portion of the stock (for example—20 percent) would vest and be nonforfeitable for each year during which a founder remained in the employment of URC. Reed thought that was a reasonable compromise and noted that Beacon's proposal required a founder's agreement which would provide for more rigorous vesting—50 percent of the stock after three years and then 25 percent in each of the fourth and fifth years.

Baker was concerned with the ability of the company to protect its research and development efforts, including inventions and trade secrets, proprietary software, and other proprietary information which URC planned to develop. He suggested that each of the founders, as well as all future employees, sign a patent, invention, and nondisclosure agreement along the lines that he had been required to sign when he joined IBM. Reed also wondered whether each founder should sign a noncompete agreement.

EQUITY FOR FUTURE KEY EMPLOYEES

The founders agreed that at least seven future key employees would be needed by the end of 1983. Reed said, "We have got to get these guys cheap stock. They won't be happy if they have to pay more than the founder's price of $.01 per share. If, however, the investors buy all common stock at $4 or $5 per share, how can we expect to sell stock to these key employees at $.01 per share?" It was concluded that Reed needed professional help to answer this question and that a tax adviser would be consulted to determine whether the sale of cheap stock in the future would create any tax problems. At the same time, Reed agreed to discuss this issue with the investors to ascertain their reaction to the issuance of additional shares at a price significantly less than the investors' price.

BOARD REPRESENTATION

Carlton wondered whether it would be necessary to have any of the investors represented on the board of directors. If so, he favored only one representative from the entire investor group. He wanted a board which was essentially controlled by management. In reviewing the various proposals, Carlton was particularly concerned with the provision that would give the investors the right to elect a majority of the board of directors.

REGISTRATION RIGHTS, ETC.

Baker was totally confused by the requirements for registration of the investors' stock. If the investors obtained registration rights, then what about the founders? Baker also admitted that he had great difficulty in evaluating the four proposals because he simply did not understand the jargon. In paticular, he wanted to know what the following provisions meant and how they would affect him and/or URC:

— Standard ratchet antidilution provisions.
— "Take-me-along" agreement.
— "Piggyback" rights.
— Preemptive rights.
— Unlimited S-3s.

THE DECISION

At 1 A.M., Reed, Baker, and Carlton decided that they had had enough. They would each review the specific financing proposals, as well as the other matters discussed during the evening, and would reassemble on April 6 to agree upon a final financing proposal and plan for launching URC.

EXHIBIT 1
Outline of Business Plan

1. Introduction (or Executive Summary)
   Short description of:
   - Business Objectives
   - Product
   - Technology and Development Program
   - Market and Customers
   - Management Team
   - Financing Requirements
2. Company Description
   - History and Status
   - Background and Industry
   - Company's Objectives
   - Company's Strategies
3. Risk Factors
4. Products
   - Product Description and Comparisons
   - Innovative Features (Patent Coverage)
   - Applications
   - Technology
   - Product Development
   - Product Introduction Schedule and Major Milestones
5. Market
   - Market Summary and Industry Overview
   - Market Analysis and Forecasts
   - Industry Trends
   - Initial Product(s)
6. Competition
7. Marketing Program
   - Objectives
   - Marketing Strategy
   - Sales and Distribution Channels
   - Customers
   - Staffing
8. Management
   - Founders
   - Stock Ownership
   - Organization and Personnel
   - Future Key Employees and Staffing
   - Incentives (Employee Stock Purchase Plan)
9. Manufacturing
10. Service and Field Engineering
11. Future Products (Product Evolution)
    - Engineering Development Program
    - Future R&D
12. Facilities
13. Capital Required and Use of Proceeds
14. Financial Data and Financial Forecasts
    - Assumptions Used
    - 3-Year Plan
    - 5-Year Plan
15. Appendixes
    - Detailed Management Profiles
    - References
    - Product Descriptions, Sketches, Photos
    - Recent Literature on Product, Market, etc.

Note: Use and dissemination should be restricted; document should be treated as confidential; if used as an Offering Memorandum, federal and securities legends should be affixed.

EXHIBIT 2
Summary of Terms—Father-in-Law's Proposal

Number of shares	100,000
Price	$5 per share
Board representation	One seat on the board, but not essential. Right to observe board meetings, if no board seat.
Registration rights	One demand registration after the company goes public. Piggyback rights for five years after the company goes public.
Preemptive rights	Pro rata participation in future private offerings.
Stock restrictions	Founders will agree to sell their stock back to the company before selling to any third party, and if company elects not to purchase, stock will be offered pro rata to investors on a first refusal basis.
Financial statements	Annual and monthly financial statements.
Other	Possible short-term "bridge" loan.

EXHIBIT 3
Summary of the Principal Terms—Prestige Proposal: Subordinated Notes and Common Stock

Principal Amount of Notes	$2,000,000
Shares of Common Stock	(a) 200,000 shares
	(b) $.01 per share (Total $2,000)
	(c) Standard demand registration rights, piggyback registration rights, S-3 registration rights, etc.
	(d) Right to elect one member of the board of directors.
Interest Rate on Notes	10 percent payable semiannually; no interest payable for the first 24 months after issuance of the Notes.
Repayment of Notes	$400,00 annually, commencing at the end of the fifth year after issuance of the Notes. Optional prepayment at any time at par plus accrued interest, provided no default exists and all outstanding Notes are prepaid pro rata.
Subordination	Subordination only to indebtedness for borrowed money from banks and other financial institutions.
Major Covenants	
1. Affirmative Covenants	(a) Normal covenants regarding continued existence and compliance.
	(b) Covenant to provide current financials monthly/quarterly/annually.
	(c) Permission for noteholders' visitation/examination.
	(d) Permission for noteholders' representative to attend directors' meetings.
	(e) Use of proceeds.

EXHIBIT 3 (*concluded*)

2. Negative Covenants	(a)	No senior debt above level to be determined; and overall limitation on borrowings at ratio to be determined.
	(b)	No liens except those arising in the normal course of business and those securing senior debt.
	(c)	No guarantees or similar obligations; no loans or other "investments."
	(d)	No dividends; no repurchase or redemption of stock.
	(e)	No failure to maintain asset ratios to be determined.
	(f)	No merger, business combination, or sale of assets.
	(g)	No material litigation.
Events of Default		Any failure of material representation; any failure of payment of principal or interest when due; any breach of negative covenant; any breach of affirmative covenant continuing for 30 days after notice from a noteholder; any event allowing acceleration of senior debt; or certain bankruptcy events.
Amendments and Waivers		Consent by the holders of two thirds in principal amount of outstanding Notes required, but the obligation to pay principal/interest on any Note can only be affected with the particular holder's consent.

Note: Alternatively, investors would consider purchasing $2,000,000 of noncallable Preferred Stock in lieu of Subordinated Notes, on terms to be determined, provided that company will be required to redeem the Preferred Stock in annual increments commencing five years after date of issuance.

EXHIBIT 4
Summary of Principal Terms—Beacon Proposal: Convertible Preferred Stock

Number of Shares	500,000
Price	$4 per share
Dividends	Cumulative dividends of $0.40 per share per annum, payable each July 1. Noncumulative until July 1, 1987.
Liquidation	$4 per share plus all accrued but unpaid dividends, prior to any liquidation payment to Common Stock.
Optional Redemption	Redemption at company's option after 5 years at redemption price of $5 per share, plus accrued but unpaid dividends.
Mandatory Redemption	Sinking fund redemption at redemption price of $4 per share, plus accrued but unpaid dividends, commencing January 1, 1990, as follows:

Date	Number of Shares Redeemed
January 1, 1990	50,000
January 1, 1991	125,000
January 1, 1992	150,000
January 1, 1993	175,000

EXHIBIT 4 (*continued*)

Conversion Feature	
1. Conversion Price	$4 per share of Common Stock (one-for-one conversion). (Accrued but unpaid dividends are not payable at time of voluntary conversion but are payable at time of automatic conversion.)

2. Automatic Conversion
   Events

(a) Firm underwritten public offering covering primary sale of Common Stock at public offering price of at least $12 per share with gross proceeds of at least $5 million or more.

(b) Audited financials for fiscal year reporting at least $25 million in consolidated revenues, and pretax profit (before extraordinary items) of at least 15 percent of revenues for the same period.

3. Antidilution Protection   Proportional adjustments for splits, dividends, recapitalizations, and similar events. Standard "ratchet" formula adjustment for issuances below the Conversion Price (excluding (i) Common Stock issuable upon conversion of Preferred Stock and (ii) 75,000 shares of Common Stock reserved for issuance pursuant to the company's Incentive Stock Option Plan).

Voting Rights

(a) *General voting:* Holders of Preferred Stock will have number of votes equal to largest number of full shares of Common Stock into which Preferred Stock may be converted.

(b) *Election of directors:* Holders of Preferred Stock can elect one-third of directors, and holders of Common Stock can elect the remaining two thirds of directors.

(c) *Contingent voting rights:*
    Holders of Preferred Stock can elect majority of board in case of certain events:
    (i) $250,000 loss in any quarter after January 1, 1985;
    (ii) consolidated tangible net worth of less than $500,000;
    (iii) material lawsuit;
    (iv) default in payment of dividends; or
    (v) default in sinking fund redemption

Restrictions and Limitations

(a) Two-thirds vote of Preferred Stock required to:
    (i) repurchase any Preferred Stock other than pursuant to redemption provisions;
    (ii) repurchase or redeem any Common Stock (exception for buy-backs under employee stock purchase plans);
    (iii) authorize or issue any senior equity security;
    (iv) any merger, consolidation or sale of assets, or certain sales, transfers, and licenses of assets;
    (v) permit the sale of any subsidiary or any stock of such subsidiary;

EXHIBIT 4 *(continued)*

	(vi) increase or decrease authorized Preferred Stock;
	(vii) amend the Articles so as to adversely affect the rights, preferences or privileges of the Preferred Stock; or
	(viii) make any loans or guarantees.
Registration Rights	(a) Covers Common Stock issued upon conversion of Preferred Stock.
	(b) One demand; 40 percent to request; 20 percent to be sold.
	(c) Unlimited piggybacks.
	(d) Unlimited S-3s for $250,000 transactions if company eligible.
	(e) Company pays for demand and piggybacks; company pays for first four S-3 registrations.
	(f) Underwriters cutback re: piggybacks.
	(g) Normal indemnification.
	(h) Registration rights end 10 years after conversion.
	(i) Stand-off agreement.
	(j) Best efforts to make Rule 144 available.
	(k) Rights transferable to affiliate of company or buyer of 25,000 or more shares.
Sweat Equity	Founders forfeit 100 percent of stock if employment terminated prior to three years; 50 percent if terminated after three years; 25 percent if terminated after four years; and no forfeiture (100% vested) if terminated after five years.
Shareholders' Agreement	"Take-Me-Along" Agreement and Right of First Offer.
Covenants	(a) Rights of inspection and access to information.
	(b) Monthly unaudited financials 21 days after month's end.
	(c) Audited financials 90 days after fiscal year end.
	(d) Budget 45 days prior to fiscal year end.
	(e) Approval of all subsequent equity financings.
	(f) Approval of single capital expenditures over $50,000.
	(g) Approval of all mergers, acquisitions, diversificaitons into new businesses, the sale of more than 10 percent of the company's assets (other than in the ordinary course of business), sale of patent rights held by company, or liquidation.
	(h) Approval of Common Stock repurchases or dividends.
	(i) Approval of employee stock ownership plans.
Preemptive Rights	Standard pro rata rights in all future private financings.
Key Man Insurance	So long as Preferred is outstanding, company will maintain key man insurance on founders' lives in the amount of $500,000 each.
Representations and Warranties	Standard representations and warranties by company; also individual representations and warranties of

EXHIBIT 4 (*concluded*)

	founders with respect to patents, proprietary information, conflicts with prior employers, stock ownership, and litigation.
Amendments and Waivers	70 percent of outstanding Preferred Stock required.
Expenses	Company will pay all fees and expenses of investors' special counsel if deal is consummated.
Other Agreements	Patent Assignment Agreements
	Stock Restriction Agreements
	Noncompete Agreements
	Confidentiality and Proprietary Information Agreements

EXHIBIT 5
Summary of Principal Terms—R&D Partnership

General Partner:	Robotics Development Company (RDC) to be formed by Reed, Baker and Carlton. URC will contribute $22,000 and all of its existing technology relating to robotics to the partnership in exchange for a 1 percent interest in profits, losses, distributions of cash, and distributions upon dissolution.
Limited Partners:	Will purchase 100 units of Limited Partnership interests for $22,000 each, which, net of Pincus, Greene selling commissions, will contribute $2,000,000 to the partnership, in exchange for a 99 percent interest in profits, losses, distributions of cash and distributions upon dissolution.
License:	Upon completion of the products the partnership will grant a perpetual license to URC to manufacture and market the products in exchange for a 10 percent royalty (on sales) payable to the partnership.
Option:	The partnership will grant to URC an option to purchase all of its assets (including the license) one year and one day after — The product becomes commercially available, *or* — Development work is abandoned. In exchange for, at URC's option, either — $10 million in cash *or* — A number of shares which would give the partnership a 30 percent interest in URC *after* subdivisions, consolidations, reorganizations, mergers, recapitalizations, reclassification, capital adjustment and any issuance of common stock as a dividend.

COMPUTERVISION VERSUS AUTOMATIX (A)

On October 12, 1982, the case of the Computervision Corporation versus Automatix Incorporated and Phillippe Villers (Automatix founder and CEO) went to trial. The case grappled not only with the legal issues surrounding trade secrets and patents, but a new and emerging body of legal questions in the area of intellectual property.

BACKGROUND

In 1969, Phillippe Villers and Martin Allen founded Computervision, a company focused on computer-aided design and manufacture (CAD/CAM). By 1974, Computervision was a $25 million company, and sales grew rapidly. (See Exhibit 1 for sales and earnings history.) By 1981, sales growth was beginning to slow, and the company seemed to have passed through its initial "entrepreneurial" phase.

During this period, Villers had slowly become less involved in the day-to-day operations of Computervision and came to head its "New Ventures" Department. Villers, a 9 percent owner of Computervision, continued to serve as its senior vice president, maintain his seat on Computervision's board of directors, and serve as its assistant secretary. During late 1978 and early 1979, Villers' group looked at several growth opportunities for Computervision, including robotics. The group wrote a detailed plan for Computervision's entry into robotics. It was Villers' impression that his ideas were not being taken seriously at Computervision, however, and in September of 1979, he announced that he was taking a sabbatical.

During his sabbatical Villers began putting together his own plans to start a robotics company—Automatix. He began raising money, and Arnold Reinhold, another employee in the New Ventures group started to write Automatix's business plan.

In late December of 1979, Villers announced his resignation from Computervision and his intention to form Automatix. Shortly afterwards, five others also resigned from Computervision.

— Arnold Reinhold, a Harvard MBA and member of the New Ventures Department
— Two programmers
— Villers' secretary
— Mike Cronin, Computervision's vice president and head of marketing.

Nine months later, in the fall of 1980, Computervision filed suit against Automatix and Phillippe Villers. Computervision's outside counsel had, at the request of the board, reviewed the events and the Automatix business plans and had determined that there was a basis for legal action. They recommended this action to Computervision's board, which agreed to proceed. (See Exhibit 2 for Computervision's complaint.)

Computervision's suit alleged that:

— Automatix and Villers had wrongfully disclosed and used Computervision trade secrets.
— Automatix and Villers had, via the use of "confidential business information" misappropriated a corporate opportunity which rightfully belonged to Computervision.
— Villers had "wasted" substantial corporate resources belonging to Computervision.
— Villers had wrongfully solicited Computervision employees to work for Automatix.
— Villers had committed a breach of his fiduciary responsibility as a director of Computervision.

THE LAW

While the legal territory surrounding the trade secret charge was fairly well established (see Chapter 9, "Intellectual Property"), the law surrounding intellectual property and the "theft of corporate opportunity" was very unclear.

Computervision's counsel had found a reference in legal precedent (*USM Corp.* v. *Marson Fastener Corp.*, 1979) for ". . . the misuse of business information . . ."

The judge had stated that he was willing to consider this issue and hear argument on it during the trial.

PROCEEDING TO TRIAL

Automatix had requested and had been granted a speedy trial on the grounds that they were attempting to become a public company and that this issue would cloud the public sale of securities.

The case would be decided by a jury trial, and both sides worked hard to impanel a technologically well-informed jury who could understand the issues (e.g., the foreman was a computer programmer).

During 1981, both sides took depositions from potential witnesses and prepared their cases.

Automatix's major concern was not whether they would be found guilty or innocent but rather, if guilty, what damages would be assessed. Because the intellectual property area was so new, there was no precedent for setting damages. Automatix did attempt to settle out of court, but Computervision was not interested.

THE TRIAL

On October 12, 1982, the case went to trial. One of the documents which was repeatedly referred to during the trial was a comparison of the Computervision and Automatix business plans which Computervision's counsel had prepared (Exhibit 3). The arguments heard during the trial focused primarily on the following three issues:

Wrongful Use of Trade Secret

Computervision argument. Computervision maintained that:

— While in the employ of Computervision, Villers had developed the idea for a nonservo-controlled robot.
— Villers had a patent disclosure written on this idea. (A patent disclosure establishes that the company considered a certain idea to be patentable on a given date. As long as this date is prior to any other written claim on a patent, no one else can ever get a patent on that idea, because it is then in the public domain.) IBM, for instance, routinely discloses virtually all of its ideas to prevent any one else from ever patenting them.
— This idea was mentioned prominently in the Computervision business plan *and* in the Automatix business plan (see Exhibit 3 for excerpts from both the Computervision and Automatix business plans).

Automatix argument. Automatix maintained that:

— This idea was mentioned only in passing in the Automatix business plan.
— Similar technology had already been brought to market by Electrolux, and if it ever was a trade secret, the technology was now in the public domain.
— They had not used the idea for a nonservo-controlled robot and had no intention of *ever* producing one.

Misappropriation of Corporate Opportunity/Use of Confidential Business Information

Computervision argument. Computervision maintained that:

— The idea for a robotics company was theirs.
— It had been developed and investigated by Computervision employees at Computervision's expense.
— These ideas had been represented in the Computervision business plan, which Automatix had essentially pirated as their own.
— Automatix had "raided" Computervision of key employees to pursue this opportunity.

Automatix argument. Automatix maintained that:

— Villers had tried to get Computervision to enter the robotics business, but Computervision had refused to consider the idea.
  • Villers was given the New Ventures group as a "bone" after being forced out of real responsibility.
  • His ideas were never taken seriously.
  • Robotics in particular was viewed as a "way-out" idea at Computervision.
  • At the quarterly senior mangement meeting in March of 1979, the idea was presented and turned down.
— Computervision's refusal to pursue the opportunity left it open for Villers to pursue:
  • The "window of opportunity" would not be open for long.
  • Villers used information which was in the public domain to pursue the opportunity.

Computervision counterargument. Computervision maintained that:

— Computervision *did* want to get into robotics.
— "Get Computervision into robotics" was an item on Villers's MBO list which Computervision's president had signed.

— The managers at the March management meeting had never said no to Villers' proposal.
— Further, there was no legal requirement that the opportunity or information required to pursue it be proprietary.

Automatix counterargument. Automatix maintained that while no one had ever actually said no, it was commonly understood:

— The small staff devoted to robotics was disbanded.
— The budget for work on robotics was stopped.
— The monthly progress reports coming out of the group also stopped.

Breach of Fiduciary Duties

Computervision argument. Computervision argued that:

— Villers was both a corporate officer and director of Computervision.
— As such, he had a fiduciary duty to the shareholders of Computervision to place their interests ahead of his own personal interests.
— In using and disclosing confidential business information, and in soliciting Computervision's employees, Villers advanced his own selfish interests at the expense of Computervision and its shareholders.

Automatix argument. Automatix argued that:

— Villers had a legal right to compete with Computervision and to solicit Computervision's employees.
— Villers believed that Computervision had rejected his robotics proposal, and, therefore, was not appropriating anything of value to Computervision.
— Any opportunity which existed in the robotics business existed as a result of Villers expending his own monies and energies.

CHARGE TO THE JURY

At the end of the trial, each side presented its own version of the information which the judge should impart to the jury in his instructions. These recommendations are reproduced in Exhibit 4—Computervision's Suggested Instructions and Exhibit 5—Automatix' Suggested Instructions.

EXHIBIT 1
Computervision Financial Highlights (*in millions of dollars*)

Year	Sales	Earnings
1974	25.1	1.6
1975	21.6	(4.1)
1976	33.6	1.7
1977	46.4	2.7
1978	71.6	5.2
1979	131.6	13.0
1980	224.2	23.3

EXHIBIT 2
Excerpts from Complaint

THE BUSINESS OF COMPUTERVISION AND THE ROBOTICS BUSINESS PLAN

4. Computervision is involved in the industry automation business. It develops, designs, manufactures, and sells computer-aided design/computer-aided manufacturing ("CAD/CAM") systems. Throughout its corporate existence (i.e., since 1969), Computervision has expanded and continues to expand the range of its automation products. The potential applications of Computervision's systems and products in various lines of industry are extremely numerous.

5. During the past several years, Computervision has recognized substantial new business opportunities in the robotics field, and has made substantial efforts to extend its industry automation business into the field of industrial robotics.

6. In this connection, the defendant Villers, as head of Computervision's New Venture Department, was instructed to develop a business plan to guide such efforts by Computervision. During 1978 and 1979, Villers devoted substantial time and effort to the study of possible areas of entry into the robotics business.

7. During this time, Villers was instrumental in shaping a business plan under which Computervision could feasibly embrace new enterprise opportunities in robotics. Owing primarily to the efforts of Villers a written document entitled "Business Plan for Computervision Entry into Robotics" (hereinafter "Computervision Plan") was evolved.

8. In or about April 1979, Villers was instructed by Computervision to begin implementation of the Computervision Plan, which called for the formation of a special robotics business unit at Computervision.

9. In or about April 1979, Villers was specifically instructed by Computervision to search for experts familiar with robotics technology and marketing, to interview these experts and to retain the best of such persons available to assist Computervision in the implementation of its business plan and the development of its robotics business.

10. Although Villers purported to conduct a search for experts in robotics technology and marketing as he was directed to do, he ultimately reported to Computervision that he was unable to find any robotics industry experts suitable for Computervision's needs.

11. In June 1979, Villers informed Computervision that he desired and intended to take a sabbatical leave during the last three months of 1979. Villers undertook, however, to resume his efforts in developing Computervision's robotics business upon his return from this sabbatical leave at the end of 1979.

EXHIBIT 2 (*continued*)

12. In or about December 1979, however, Villers announced to Computervision that he would not resume his efforts to develop the Computervision robotics business. Instead, he stated that he was forming his own company (the defendant Automatix) and that he would exploit the business opportunities in robotics, as identified in the Computervision Plan, for himself.

Causes for Action

I. *Wrongful Conversion of Computervision's Proprietary Business Information and Trade Secrets*

13. The plaintiff repeats and realleges the allegations contained in paragraphs 1–12 as fully as though set forth herein.

14. By the latter half of 1979, Computervision had expended and invested substantial sums in the development of its plan to expand its business into the field of industrial robotics.

15. In furtherance of Computervision's efforts to develop and expand such business, Villers spoke and conferred with numerous scientists, engineers, technicians, businessmen and consultants knowledgeable in robotics. In the course of his inquiries and discussions, Villers developed and collected extensive drawings, sketches, memoranda, notes, and other documents relating to robotics. A number of plans and ideas relating to robotics emerged from Villers' inquiries and discussions, many of which are reflected in such documents.

16. These documents and ideas were and are the sole property of Computervision. Similarly, the Computervision Plan for the development of Computervision's robotics business was and is the sole property of Computervision.

17. The documents, ideas, and Plan comprise or contain proprietary and confidential business information of Computervision and trade secrets which are vital to its participation and success in the robotics industry.

18. Villers and Automatix have wrongfully appropriated and converted the aforesaid proprietary information, confidential information and trade secrets of Computervision, to the detriment and competitive disadvantage of Computervision.

19. Furthermore, Villers and Automatix have wrongfully disclosed to potential employees of Automatix, potential investors in Automatix, and other parties certain of the aforesaid proprietary information, confidential information and trade secrets of Computervision, to the detriment and competitive disadvantage of Computervision.

20. This program of wrongful appropriation and disclosure is clearly evidenced by the "Business and Product Plan for the Automatix Corporation" (hereinafter "Automatix Plan") authored wholly or substantially by Villers and dated December 1979. The Automatix Plan incorporates and sometimes even directly plagiarizes substantial portions of the Computervision Plan. The Automatix Plan was widely disseminated by Villers to potential investors and employees of Automatix. In fact, Villers showed the concepts and language which he misappropriated from the Computervision Plan to potential investors in Automatix in order to induce them to buy stock in Automatix. Accordingly, Computervision is entitled to have a constructive trust imposed upon all profits and income resulting to Villers and Automatix from the misappropriation of the Computervision Plan.

21. As a direct result of Villers' and Automatix's wrongful appropriation and disclosure of Computervision's aforesaid proprietary business information, confidential business information, and trade secrets, Computervision has sustained great damages, the precise amount of which is yet undetermined.

EXHIBIT 2 (*continued*)

II. *Wrongful Appropriation of Corporate Opportunities*

22. The plaintiff repeats and realleges the allegations contained in paragraphs 1–12 and 14–20, as fully as though set forth herein.

23. During the period in which Villers was given primary responsibility by Computervision for the development and expansion of its robotics business, Computervision made a substantial investment in its robotics business plan with the expectation that it would develop new robotics business in accordance with such plan. Further, it made appropriations for robotics for the third and fourth quarters of 1979 and the first, second, and third quarters of 1980 in the approximate amount of $400,000.

24. In breach of the fiduciary obligations which he owed to Computervision and its shareholders and breach of his particular obligation to promote and build up Computervision's activities in the field of robotics, Villers intentionally frustrated Computervision's efforts to expand its business into the field of industrial robotics.

25. During a time while he was an officer, director, and employee of Computervision, Villers developed and employed a plan for his own entry into the robotics business. In particular, Villers utilized substantial portions of the time available to him during a purported "sabbatical" granted by Computervision to plot and plan his Automatix venture. Also, while he was purporting on behalf of Computervision to conduct a search for potential employees knowledgeable in the robotics field, Villers was in fact attempting to recruit employees for Automatix.

26. Computervision had a genuine business interest and expectancy in expanding its industry automation business into the areas of robotics under the leadership of Villers. Robotics, a natural extension of Computervision's CAD/CAM business, presented substantial new business opportunities to Computervision. Instead of using his best efforts to assist Computervision to grasp and pursue these opportunities, Villers wrongfully appropriated and converted these corporate opportunities to himself and Automatix.

27. As a direct result of Villers' and Automatix's wrongful appropriation of corporate opportunities rightfully belonging to Computervision, Computervision has been irreparably injured in that it has been deprived of important and substantial opportunities to expand its industry automation into robotics; as a result, Computervision has sustained great damages, the precise amount of which is as yet undetermined.

III. *Waste*

29. The plaintiff repeats and realleges the allegations contained in paragraphs 1–12, 14–20, and 23–27 as fully as though set forth herein.

30. While he was an officer, director, and employee of Computervision, Villers committed the waste of substantial corporate assets of Computervision, in violation of the fiduciary obligations which he owed to Computervision and its shareholders.

31. The corporate assets of Computervision so wasted by Villers including, without limitation, proprietary business information, confidential business information, trade secrets, corporate opportunities, money, and Villers' own unique managerial, entrepreneurial, scientific, and technical skills.

32. As a direct result of the aforesaid waste of Computervision's corporate assets committed by Villers, Computervision has sustained great damages, the precise amount of which is as yet undetermined.

IV. *Wrongful Solicitation of Employees and Interference with Contractual and Advantageous Business Relationships*

33. The plaintiff repeats and realleges the allegations contained in paragraphs 1–12, 14–20, 23–27, and 30–31 as fully as though set forth herein.

EXHIBIT 2 (*continued*)

34. Beginning in or about November 1979, and continuing to the present time, Villers and Automatix, having knowledge of the contractual and advantageous business relationships existing between Computervision and certain of its employees, have wrongfully interfered with these relationships, have solicited such employees, and have sought unlawfully and maliciously to induce them to leave Computervision in order to become employed by the defendant Automatix.

35. As a result of such unlawful interference, solicitation, and inducement, certain key employees of Computervision have submitted their resignations. In particular, Michael Cronin, vice president of Computervision and executive vice president in Computervision's Productivity Systems Division, was unlawfully induced by Villers and Automatix to leave the employ of Computervision and become employed by Automatix. At least four other employees of Computervision were induced by Villers to leave the employ of Computervision and join Automatix.

36. As a direct result of Villers' and Automatix's unlawful interference with contractual and advantageous business relationships existing between Computervision and certain of its key employees, and as a direct result of Villers' and Automatix's wrongful solicitation and inducement of such employees, Computervision has sustained great damages, the precise amount of which is as yet undetermined.

V. Breach of Fiduciary Duty

37. The plaintiff repeats and realleges the allegations contained in paragraphs 1–12, 14–20, 23–27, 30–31, and 34–35 as fully as though set forth herein.

38. In wrongfully appropriating and disclosing proprietary business information, confidential business information, and trade secrets of Computervision; in seizing for himself and Automatix corporate opportunities belonging to Computervision; in committing the waste of substantial corporate assets of Computervision; and in unlawfully interfering with contractual and advantageous business relationships existing between Computervision and certain of its employees, Villers breached the fiduciary duties of loyalty and good faith which he owed and owes to Computervision under the common law and statutory law of the Commonwealth of Massachusetts.

39. As a direct result of Villers aforesaid breaches of fiduciary duties of loyalty and good faith which he owed to Computervision, Computervision has sustained great damages, the precise amount of which is as yet undetermined.

WHEREFORE, the plaintiff prays:

A. That this Court assess damages against the defendants Villers and Automatix, jointly and severally, for their wrongful appropriation and disclosure of the plaintiff's proprietary business information, confidential business information, and trade secrets, pursuant to Count I of this Complaint;

B. That this Court assess damages against the defendants Villers and Automatix, jointly and severally, for their wrongful appropriation of corporate opportunities belonging to the plaintiff, pursuant to Count II of this Complaint;

C. That this Court assess damages against the defendants Villers for his waste of substantial corporate assets of the plaintiff, pursuant to Count III of this Complaint;

D. That this Court assess damages against the defendants Villers and Automatix, jointly and severally, for their unlawful interference with contractual and advantageous business relationships existing between the plaintiff and certain of its employees, pursuant to Count IV of this Complaint;

E. That this Court assess damages against the defendant Villers for his breaches of the fiduciary duties of good faith and loyalty which he owed to the plaintiff, pursuant to Count V of this complaint;

EXHIBIT 2 (*concluded*)

F. That this Court assess actual and treble damages against the defendant Villers for his willful and knowing commission of unfair and deceptive acts or practices and unfair methods of competition violative of Mass. Gen. Laws c. 93A against the plaintiff, pursuant to Count VI of this Complaint;

G. That this Court impose a constructive trust in favor of the plaintiff on all corporate opportunities, proprietary business information, confidential business information, trade secrets, and all other proprietary assets of the plaintiff which the defendants Villers and Automatix wrongfully appropriated, with provision for the payment over to the plaintiff by the defendants of all income and profits resulting directly or indirectly to the defendants from their wrongful appropriation or use of the aforesaid proprietary assets of the plaintiff;

H. That this Court order that the defendants Villers and Automatix, and their agents, servants, employees and all persons acting for or on their behalf or in concert with them, be permanently enjoined from:

1. Disclosing to anyone not authorized by Computervision, Computervision's confidential or proprietary business information or trade secrets.
2. Interfering or threatening to interfere with Computervision's contractual and advantageous business relationships with its employees, customers, and suppliers.
3. Making any use in their business whatsoever of Computervision's confidential or proprietary business information or trade secrets.

I. That this Court award the plaintiff all such other and further relief as may seem just and reasonable.

Computervision Corporation
By its attorneys,

EXHIBIT 3
Comparison of Computervision and Automatix Business Plans

COMPUTERVISION

COMPANY
PRIVATE
CONFIDENTIAL

BUSINESS PLAN
FOR CV ENTRY INTO ROBOTICS
BUSINESS PLAN NV 101

PRESENTED TO CV SENIOR MANAGEMENT MEETING
APRIL 19, 20, 1979

PREPARED BY:
A. Reinhold
P. Villers
APPROVED BY:
P. Villers
OTHER CONTRIBUTORS:
R. Simon
C. Cook

Distribution:
M. Allen (2 of 11)
M. Cronin (4 of 11)
R. Emerick (5 of 11)
S. Harrell (6 of 11)
R. Krieger (3 of 11)
P. Read (11 of 11)
A. Reinhold (7 of 11)

EXHIBIT 3 (*continued*)

[EXCERPTS FROM COMPUTERVISION BUSINESS PLAN]

The key to understanding the present status and future prospects of this market is the realization that today's robots are extremely limited in their capabilities. Their market is accordingly constrained. As the capabilities of robots increase, market growth is automatic with some lag for communication of the improved capabilities and overcoming the innate conservatism of manufacturing organizations. Because the present capabilities of robots are so limited—they are capable of only simple repetitive manipulative actions with very limited sensor feedback restricted primarily to limit switches and other on-off sensors—*even a small increase in robotic capability can result in a huge increase in market potential.* Accordingly, an entrant who is first in bringing the newly developed technologies of the laboratories to commercial utilization can reap a major position in the robotics industry despite a small present base.

A second major factor in creating a major opportunity for CV in robotics is the lack to date of a vendor in the industry who offers a systems product instead of components. Present manufacturers concentrate primarily on manipulator arms with a few manufacturers making vision cameras and inspection systems. Currently, no manufacturer is prepared to offer a product that can solve a manufacturing problem without major engineering work by the manufacturer or a contractor.

The Window Concept—for Robotics

Why is there an open "window" opportunity today and why and when will it close?

In this context, the "window" is opening because changes in technology have made possible the economical solution to problems which, until no more than two years ago, could not be solved, and political and social pressures are creating greater economic urgency to solve them; namely, these include regulations such as OSHA and increasing emphasis on raising U.S. productivity, since increases have not been keeping up with the world's other industrial leaders.

In terms of the technological factors, the key factors are the availability of second generation robots, which are microprocessor controlled, and therefore can be computer controlled in real time and make sophisticated logical decisions. The availability of reliable nondrifting, inexpensive vision hardware, i.e., solid state cameras, the availability of adequate microcomputers to cheaply process vision information in real time, and the existence of precursor systems and experience with them which is creating an informed demand in the market and a widespread belief that useful tasks can, in fact, be performed.

2.3.1/Robot Market Segmentation

As is the case for most industries, there are many ways to segment the robot market. The market can be segmented by price class, by competitor, by region of the world, and by target industry. Frost & Sullivan in its market report chose to

EXHIBIT 3 (*continued*)

use the U.S. Commerce Department's Standard Industrial Classification (SIC) major classification code, presumably because it was convenient and because there is a lot of statistical information available by this breakdown. However, if we remember that the robot marketplace is primarily capability driven, as was pointed out above, it is not surprising that this breakdown is less than illuminating. A breakdown by industrial classification would only be significant if a particular process to which robots could be adapted were unique to each industry. The contrary is true. Thus, the ability to manipulate billets for a forging machine is useful for the metals fabrications business, the automotive business, shipbuilding, and electrical machinery construction.

Indeed, if one were to analyze the robot market in maximum detail, one would see a large number of submarkets by specific capabilities; that is, the ability to load and unload an automatic lathe, to feed a die stamping machine, to empty a plastic injection molding machine, to carry out welding and painting operations, to perform investment casting manipulation, and so on. Under such a detailed analysis, which would require very extensive research, the figure of merit of a robot would be how many applications it could handle weighted by the value of each application.

In light of the above, it is not surprising that the most valid available segmentation of the robot business is by capability. The most important distinction among robots is between programmable robots and nonprogrammable robots. While the terminology is not completely standard, we define programmable robots as those capable of moving the robot hands to any position in a robot workspace. Nonprogrammable robots are only capable of a small, finite number of movement positions without mechanical readjustment. A typical robot of this class is capable of just two positions per axis, each position being determined by the mechanical limit stops on the air cylinder shafts. A three axis robot of this class would only be capable of 2^3 or 8 different positions. Such robots can be considered nothing more than erector-set components for special purpose automation. However, even with their limited capability they have proven surprisingly successful and form a significant fraction of robot sales.

The programmable robots are divided into two categories, servo and non-servo. Until now, almost all programmable robots had used servo controls on the axis. This allows high accuracy and flexibility. This approach is quite expensive and relatively slow, since the servos must be allowed to settle. Worse, the servos must be heavily derated since no one has successfully analyzed and compensated the interactions between the several robot axes servo loops. Nonservo programmable robots are a new category of robots, invented at CV and independently at Electrolux. Under these systems, a mechanism similar to the nonservo robot is used with the addition of mechanical stops that are adjustable prior to initiation of the actuation cycle. Since the limit stop adjustments takes place under no load conditions, open loop mechanisms such as stepping motor driven screws or ratchet escapements can be used to position the stop. A brake of some sort is applied and the robot axis is forced against the newly positioned stop. While such robots, strictly speaking, offer no capability over point-to-point servo

EXHIBIT 3 *(continued)*

robots, they have the potential of being significantly faster and much less expensive. They are, however, incapable of continuous path motion.

The servo controlled programmable robot again divides into two categories: point-to-point and continuous path. Point-to-point robots are commanded to go to one particular XYZ hand-orientation-space position after another without any stipulation as to what path in the space the robot is to traverse between points. Typically, each axis is separately commanded to its ultimate position as fast as possible. Continuous path robots, on the other hand, are given a path in space to follow and they attempt to follow that path as closely as possible. The distinction is somewhat analogous to a plotter operating in point-to-point mode versus one drawing a smooth curve. As this analogy suggests, the point-to-point robot can simulate continuous motion by being commanded to go to enough individual points. There may be a speed penalty, however, associated with doing this if the servos were not designed for continuous path. Also for historic reasons some robots, such as Unimates, can store only a limited number of points. The distinction between these two classes is primarily one of controller and servo sophistication.

There are other important dimensions of robot capability. These include number of axes, carrying capability, reach capability, and the most important and most recent, whether or not the robot is capable of being instructed using a programming language, such as the VAL language developed by Unimation for the Puma arm.

EXHIBIT 3 (*continued*)

AUTOMATIX

BUSINESS and PRODUCT PLANS
for
The Automatix Corporation

Automatix Corporation
20 Whit's End Road
Concord, MA 01742
December 1979

EXHIBIT 3 (*continued*)

[*EXCERPTS FROM AUTOMATIX BUSINESS PLAN*]

The key to understanding the present status and future prospects of this market is the realization that *today's robots are extremely limited in their capabilities.* Their market is accordingly constrained. As the capabilities of robots increase, market growth is automatic (with some lag for overcoming the innate conservatism of manufacturing organizations). Because the present capabilities of robots are so limited—they are capable of only simple repetitive manipulative actions with very limited sensor feedback restricted primarily to limit switches and other on/off sensors—*even a small increase in robotic capability can result in a huge increase in market.* Accordingly, an entrant who is first in bringing the newly developed technologies of the laboratories to commercial utilization can gain a major position in the robotics industry.

A second major factor is the lack to date of a vendor in the industry who offers a systems product instead of components. Most present manufacturers concentrate primarily on manipulator arms, while a few manufacturers concentrate on making vision cameras and inspection systems. Currently, no manufacturer is prepared to offer a system that can solve a manufacturing problem without major engineering work by the user.

Why Is There an Open Window Opportunity in Robotics Today?

In this context, the open opportunity or "window" is opening because changes in technology have made possible the economical solution to problems which, until no more than two years ago, could not be solved, coupled with political, social, and economic pressures creating greater urgency to solve them. These include both new work environmental and safety regulations such as OSHA's and increasing attention to raising U.S. productivity. Increases in U.S. productivity have not been keeping up with the world's other industrial leaders. A good example of how seriously American industry takes the productivity issue is the recent decision by the president of General Electric that productivity growth at General Electric would become a measured aspect of the business and that each business segment of GE would be expected to plan for a minimum of 6 percent per annum productivity growth. The average for American industry has been 1.5 percent while the Japanese rate has been in the 6 percent range for years.

In terms of technology, the key opportunity factors are:

- The availability of second generation robots which are microprocessor controlled and therefore can be controlled in real time by supervisory computers that can make sophisticated logical decisions.
- The availability of stable, reliable, inexpensive vision hardware, i.e., solid state cameras.
- The availability of more powerful microcomputers to cheaply process vision information in real time.
- The existence of experimental precursor systems generating publicity and experience is creating an informed demand in the market as well as widespread belief that useful tasks can, in fact, be performed.

EXHIBIT 3 (*continued*)

2.4.2 Robot Market Segmentation

As is the case for most industries, there are many ways to segment the robot market. The market can be segmented by price class, by competitor, by region of the world, and by target industry. Frost & Sullivan in its market report chose to use the U.S. Commerce Department's Standard Industrial Classification (SIC) major classification code, presumably because it was convenient and because there is a lot of statistical information available by this breakdown. However, if we remember that the robot marketplace is primarily capability driven, as was pointed out above, it is not surprising that this breakdown is less than illuminating. A breakdown by industrial classification would only be significant if a particular process to which robots could be adapted were unique to each industry. The contrary is true. Thus, the ability to manipulate billets for a forging machine is useful for the metals fabrications business, the automotive business, shipbuilding, and electrical machinery construction.

Indeed, if one were to analyze the robot market in maximum detail, one would see a large number of submarkets by specific capabilities; that is, the ability to load and unload an automatic lathe, to feed a die stamping machine, to empty a plastic injection molding machine, to carry out welding and painting operations, to perform investment casting manipulation, and so on. Under such a detailed analysis, which would require very extensive research, the figure of merit of a robot would be how many applications it could handle weighted by the value of each application.

In light of the above, it is not surprising that the most valid available segmentation of the robot business is by capability. The most important distinction among robots is between programmable robots and nonprogrammable robots. While the terminology is not completely standard, we define programmable robots as those capable of moving the robot hands to any position in a robot workspace. Nonprogrammable robots are only capable of a small, finite number of movement positions without mechanical readjustment. A typical robot of this class is capable of just two positions per axis, each position being determined by the mechanical limit stops on the air cylinder shafts. A three axis robot of this class would only be capable of 2^3 or 8 different positions. Such robots can be considered nothing more than erector-set components for special purpose automation. However, even with their limited capability they have proven surprisingly successful and form a significant fraction of robot sales.

The programmable robots are divided into two categories, servo and non-servo. Until now, almost all programmable robots had used servo controls on the axis. This allows high accuracy and flexibility. This approach is quite expensive and relatively slow, since the servos must be allowed to settle. Worse, the servos must be heavily derated since no one has successfully analyzed and compensated the interactions between the several robot axes servo loops. Nonservo programmable robots are a new category of robots. Under these systems, a mechanism similar to the nonservo robot is used with the addition of programmable positions where a brake is applied at the desired point of travel. While such robots, strictly speaking, offer no capability over point-to-point servo

EXHIBIT 3 (*concluded*)

robots, they have the potential of being significantly faster and much less expensive. They are, however, incapable of continuous path motion.

The servo controlled programmable robot again divides into two categories: point-to-point and continuous path. Point-to-point robots are commanded to go to one particular XYZ hand-orientation-space position after another without any stipulation as to what path in the space the robot is to traverse between points. Typically, each axis is separately commanded to its ultimate position as fast as possible. Continuous path robots, on the other hand, are given a path in space to follow and they attempt to follow that path as closely as possible. The distinction is somewhat analogous to a plotter operating in point-to-point mode versus one drawing a smooth curve. As this analogy suggests, the point-to-point robot can simulate continuous motion by being commanded to go to enough individual points. There may be a speed penalty, however, associated with doing this if the servos were not designed for continuous path. Also for historic reasons some robots, such as Unimates, can store only a limited number of points. The distinction between these two classes is primarily one of controller and servo sophistication.

There are other important dimensions of robot capability. These include number of axes, carrying capability, reach capability, and the most important and most recent, whether or not the robot is capable of being instructed using a programming "language," such as the VAL language developed by Unimation for the Puma arm.

An important requirement is "systems" that can solve a range of applications problems reducing the costly sifting through potential applications by the marketing force to find qualified sales opportunities.

EXHIBIT 4
Computervision: Suggested Instructions to Jury

[*Included in these instructions were legal citations which mention specific cases where these points of law were made or reaffirmed. These citations have been omitted in the interest of brevity.*]

1. Information which is or may be useful in the business of a company, which is not generally known to the public or to competitors, and as to which the company has taken reasonable precautions to keep the information secret or confidential, may be a "trade secret" of the company and therefore entitled to the protection of the law.

2. Information relating to proposed improvements in product may be a "trade secret" of the company although the company has not used the information in its business and has not actually manufactured or sold a product which uses the "trade secret."

EXHIBIT 4 (*continued*)

3. In the present case, if you find that information about "programmable nonservo robots" as set out in the Computervision business plan was a trade secret of Computervision in 1979, although Computervision had not made or sold any "programmable nonservo robots" at that time and had no definite plans to do so in the future, then that information is entitled to the protection of the law. On the questions about "trade secrets" you must limit your consideration to the information about "programmable nonservo robots."

4. Information relating to the business of a company which is not generally known outside the company and has been treated as confidential by the company is entitled to protection by the law even if the information is not a "trade secret." The Court will refer to such information as "confidential business information." The law requires fair dealing, good faith, and fundamental honesty in dealing with such confidential business information, and someone who acquires such information by unfair, dishonest, or improper means can be held liable for acquiring or using the information.

5. In the present case, if the defendant Villers disclosed confidential business information of Computervision to people outside the company, for his own benefit or for the benefit of the new company he intended to form, and if he did so in violation of an obligation which he owed to Computervision to keep that information confidential, then you can find that Automatix acquired the information by improper means, even if Villers himself had acquired the information properly while he was a Computervision employee.

6. A corporate officer or director may not use property of the corporation in order to obtain some financial benefit or advantage for himself or for a third person.

7. In the present case, if you find that the defendant Villers used property of Computervision for the purpose of recruiting founders for Automatix and selling stock for Automatix for his own financial benefit and for the benefit of Automatix, then Villers improperly used property of Computervision.

8. A corporate officer or director stands in a fiduciary relation to the corporation and its stockholders. He must not only affirmatively protect the interests of the corporation which are committed to his charge, but also refrain from doing anything which would injure the corporation or deprive the corporation of an advantage which his skills and ability might properly bring to it. His duty of undivided and unselfish loyalty to the corporation must prevail over any individual self-interest of the officer or director.

9. A director of a business corporation must act with absolute fidelity to the corporation and place his duties to the corporation above every other financial or business obligation, including his personal financial interest.

10. The defendant Villers owed to Computervision a duty of absolute loyalty and fidelity, and an obligation to place the interests of the corporation above any individual business or financial interest of himself as an individual, while he was an officer and director of Computervision.

11. In the present case, you can find that the defendant Villers acted in breach of his fiduciary duties as an officer and director of Computervision in organizing Automatix to engage in the turnkey robotics systems business, if at the

EXHIBIT 4 (*concluded*)

time he did so, he was entrusted by Computervision with the responsibility for making preparations for Computervision to enter the turnkey robotics systems business.

12. Where an individual who is a corporate officer or director commits a breach of a fiduciary duty owed by him to the corporation, and as a result of that breach of fiduciary duty, a second corporation with which the officer or director is affiliated receives some benefit or gain, the second corporation will be held liable for benefit or gain if the second corporation is on notice of the breach of fiduciary duty by reason of the knowledge of the officer or director.

EXHIBIT 5
Automatix: Suggested Instructions to Jury

[*Included in these instructions were legal citations which mention specific cases where these points of law were made or reaffirmed. These citations have been omitted in the interest of brevity.*]

Burden of Proof

1. Computervision has the burden of proving its claims by a preponderance of the evidence. In other words, Computervision must prove to you that each of its claims is more probably true than not. Mathematical preponderance is not enough. Rather, after weighing the evidence you must have an actual belief as to the truth of Computervision's claims "notwithstanding any doubts that may still linger" in your minds.[1]

2. There are two defendants in this section, Villers and Automatix. You must be careful to consider the evidence as to each defendant separately, and you must be careful to distinguish between Villers' conduct and Automatix's conduct when answering these questions.

3. In examining the claims against Automatix, you may not find Automatix liable for any wrongful acts which occurred prior to its incorporation. Because a corporation is a separate legal entity, it cannot be liable for any wrongs which may have been committed before it came into existence. As a corporation, Automatix can be liable only for wrongful conduct in which it participated, after it has been incorporated.

Trade Secrets

4. In answering the first question, you must first determine whether the information contained in the Computervision Business Plan relating to a possible programmable nonservo robot was trade secret information. Whether

EXHIBIT 5 (*continued*)

information is legally protected as confidential or trade secret information "depends on the conduct of the parties and the nature of the information."

5. "A trade secret may consist of any formula, pattern, device, or compilation of information which is used in one's business, and which gives him an opportunity to obtain an advantage over competitors who do not know or use it. It may be a formula for a chemical compound, a process of manufacturing, treating, or preserving materials, a pattern for a machine or other device, or a list of customers. . . . A trade secret is a process or device for continuous use in the operation of the business. Generally, it relates to the production of goods, as, for example, a machine or formula for the production of an article. . . ."

6. Whether information is legally protected as trade secret information requires consideration of several factors:

a. The extent to which the information is known outside of Computervision's business.

b. The extent to which it is known by employees and others involved in Computervision's business.

c. The extent of measures taken by Computervision to guard the secrecy of the information.

d. The value of the information to Computervision and the value of the information to its competitors.

e. The amount of effort or money expended in developing the information.

f. The ease or difficulty with which the information could be properly acquired or duplicated by others.

7. The first of these factors is secrecy. In order for information to be legally protected as a trade secret it must be secret. Indeed, the "essential characteristic" of a trade secret is secrecy.

8. For information relating to a possible programmable nonservo robot to be protectible as a trade secret belonging to Computervision, it must be information which could be acquired by others only by wrongful conduct. The "element of secrecy must exist, so that, except by the use of improper means, there would be difficulty in acquiring the information."

9. Matters of public knowledge or common knowledge in a science or industry are not trade secrets.

10. The second and third factors bearing upon whether information is a trade secret are related. You should consider the extent to which the information, claimed to be trade secret, was known by Computervision employees and the extent of the measures taken by Computervision to guard the secrecy of the information. You must find that Computervision "actively sought" to protect the information which it claims to be trade secret and that it made a "conscious and continuing effort" to "maintain secrecy, including the prevention of unauthorized disclosure by employees."

EXHIBIT 5 (*continued*)

11. You should consider whether Computervision at the time considered any information relating to a programmable nonservo robot to be trade secret information. For example, you may take into account whether Computervision warned against the use of the claimed trade secret when Villers informed Computervision of his intention to start his own robotics enterprise.

12. Labeling the Computervision Business Plan "confidential" does not make its contents a trade secret. In considering the significance of labeling a document "confidential" you should consider whether the document contains "much that was not actually confidential information." To label a document "confidential" is "at best ambiguous." Marking a document "confidential," or even locking it up, might "betoken merely the normal desire of a businessman to keep his business private"; it does not indicate necessarily that the information contained in the document is a trade secret.

13. The next factor for you to consider is the value to Computervision of the information which it claims to be trade secret information and the value of that information to Computervision's competitors.

14. A trade secret must be information which gives its possessor an opportunity to obtain an advantage over business competitors who do not know or use it. Computervision can assert legal protection only of information which would actually provide it with a continuing competitive advantage.

15. With respect to information relating to products, machinery, equipment, and the like, the law provides no protection to an "ultimate goal or purpose, as distinguished from the means of achieving it." The law protects, that is, only a "perfected product or process" or "particularized plans and processes." "In short, the idea must be concrete."

16. If the information which Computervision claims to be a trade secret constituted only a product concept and if Computervision did not possess information indicating how to design or make the product, the information cannot be a trade secret.

17. In determining whether the information entails a perfected product or process, you may consider whether the information resulted in any commerical products sold by Computervision.

18. The next factor to be considered is whether a substantial amount of effort or money was expended by Computervision in developing information relating to a possible programmable nonservo robot. In doing so, you should distinguish between efforts directed at other matters in the field of robotics and efforts directed at developing a programmable nonservo robot.

19. Finally, you should consider the ease or difficulty with which the information claimed by Computervision to be trade secret could be properly acquired or duplicated by others. If acquisition or duplication of the information is relatively easy, then the information is not trade secret information.

20. Information which represents nothing more than an idea which is obvious to individuals generally skilled in a particular science or industry, cannot be a trade secret.

EXHIBIT 5 (*continued*)

Wrongful Disclosure or Use

21. If you find that information relating to a possible nonservo robot was in fact a Computervision trade secret, you must then determine whether Automatix or Villers improperly disclosed or used that trade secret information.

22. In this regard the law makes no distinction between the duties of officers and directors and the duties of other employees and imposes no greater duties on officers and directors than on other employees.

23. An individual, however, cannot wrongfully use his own talent. Computervision, therefore, cannot assert a trade secret in Villers' or any other employees general knowledge, skill, memory, or inventiveness.

24. The right of an employee to use his general knowledge, experience, memory, and skill "promotes the public interest in labor mobility and the employee's freedom to practice his profession. . . ."

25. The law permits an individual to use at all times the general knowledge, experience, memory, or skill which he possesses when he commences an employment.

26. The law equally permits an individual to use at all times the general knowledge, experience, memory, or skill which he acquires while an employee, even if such talent was acquired at the expense of his employer.

27. This rule is especially applicable in situations involving individuals with a high degree of training and experience in technical and scientific matters. Where an employee "brings to the job when he enters it extensive experience" and is a "highly trained and specialized person" the former employer who claims that the employee has misappropriated a trade secret "has a heavy burden of isolating the secret for which he claims protection," for the employee is free to use both the knowledge and skill "he brought to the job as well as 'what he has learned during the employment.'"

28. If information gathered and developed during the course of employment is "almost [the] private domain" of an employee who leaves employment, and if the employee has "very detailed memory of all phases of the work" which he has done, it cannot be said that in taking this information with him the employee has wrongfully appropriated the information from his former employee.

29. Information can still be part of an employee's general knowledge, memory, skill, and experience even though other employees "worked in conjunction" with him and "contributed to" development of such information.

30. Copying information is not wrongful unless the specific information copied constitutes a trade secret. This means that information copied must both relate to the claimed trade secret and not some other device or process and that the information copied must disclose the "perfected product or process" and not merely make reference to it. "The disclosure must be in sufficient detail and have such definiteness that there is no doubt as to what is disclosed."

31. Information which is not a trade secret may nonetheless receive legal protection if it is confidential information about one's business and it is improperly procured thereby causing harm to that person.

EXHIBIT 5 (*continued*)

Confidential Business Information

32. To be legally protected, information which is not a trade secret must relate to matters in Computervision's business. Examples of such business information include "the state of one's accounts, the amount of his bid for a contract, his sources of supply, his plans for expansion or retrenchment, and the like."

33. Although the information need not be technically a trade secret, if the improper discovery of the information is to cause harm, "the information must be of a secret or confidential character." A "substantial amount of secrecy must exist."

34. Confidential business information must relate to matters which are "unique to" or are "peculiarly known" in Computervision's business. It does not include "matters of common knowledge in the community" or the "special skill which an employee has acquired because of his employment."

35. Information in the Computervision Business Plan which was "not gained through any confidential sources of [Computervision]" but rather came from sources such as trade journals, is not confidential business information.

36. A compilation of information which is otherwise generallly known can be confidential proprietary information entitled to legal protection only if the compilation is obtained, developed, or amassed at considerable effort and expense.

37. Because the protection extends only to the "information about another's business," a compilation of information can be confidential business information only if it is used or intended to be used in the ongoing conduct of business, for otherwise it does not relate to business of the company.

38. Similarly, a list of names of prospective products that is not registered or used in commerce is not information in which a corporation can possess a proprietary interest because the corporation does not use the names in connection with its business.

39. In determining whether Computervision intended to use the Computervision Business Plan, you may consider whether it was unable or unwilling to develop a robotics enterprise in accordance with the Plan. In this regard, the corporation's disinterest, procrastination, and intransigence in the face of an employee's "continual exhortations to enter" a business can constitute a rejection or abandonment of such an enterprise.

Improper Procurement

40. If you find that the Computervision Business Plan constitutes confidential business information, you must then determine whether Villers or Automatix wrongfully procured such information. In answering this question, you are to be concerned with the manner of acquisition of the business information. The law focuses on how the defendants obtained the information, rather than the subsequent use they may have made of it.

EXHIBIT 5 (*continued*)

41. To procure information by improper means, a person must acquire the information in a manner which violates "minimum accepted moral values." Thus the law prohibits procurement of business information by means such as "theft, trespass, bribery or otherwise inducing employees or others to reveal the information in breach of duty, fraudulent misrepresentations, threats of harm by unlawful conduct, wire tappings, procuring one's own employees or agents to become employees of the other for purposes of espionage, and so forth."

42. To find Villers liable for wrongfully procuring the Computervision Business Plan you must find that he came into possession of the document by wrongful means. If, however, he came into possession of the document properly in the course of his employment at Computervision you cannot find that he procured the document wrongfully.

43. To find Automatix, on the other hand, liable for improperly procuring the Computervision Business Plan, you must find that Automatix procured the Plan and that Automatix itself employed improper means in order to procure it, such as by "inducing [Villers] to reveal the information in breach of duty."

44. The legal duty which is imposed upon Villers with respect to confidential business information not amounting to a trade secret is the duty not to use the information, while remaining an employee, in competition with or otherwise to the actual injury of Computervision.

45. Thus, in order to find that Villers violated his fiduciary duty to Computervision by disclosing the Computervision Business Plan while still an officer and director, you must find that Villers' conduct has resulted in actual loss or damage to Computervision. You may not find that Villers violated his duty to Computervision if conduct claimed by Computervision to have been disloyal did not result in some harm to Computervision.

Breach of Fiduciary Duties

46. In answering the question of whether Villers breached his fiduciary duties to Computervision, "it is not suggested that a former director may not compete." "[A] corporate officer or director is entirely free to engage in an independent, competitive business, so long as he violates no legal or moral duty with respect to the fiduciary relation that exists between the corporation and himself."

[A]n agent owes his principal duty of good faith, loyalty, and fair dealing. Encompassed within such general duties of an agent is a duty to disclose information that is relevant to the affairs of the agency entrusted to him. There is also a corollary duty to an agent not to put himself in a position antagonistic to his principal concerning the subject matter of his agency.

However, agency law is not without its limitations as to duty to disclose and duty not to act adversely to a principal's business. Thus, an agent is not under a duty to disclose to his principal information obtained

EXHIBIT 5 (*continued*)

in confidence, the disclosure of which would be a breach of duty to a third person.

Similarly, while an agent may not put himself in a position antagonistic to his principal, an agent is not thereby prevented from acting in good faith outside his employment even though it may adversely affect his principal's business. Further, an agent can make arrangements of plans to go into competition with his principal before terminating his agency, provided no unfair acts are committed or injury done his principal.

47. The law recognizes "a privilege in favor of employees which enables them to prepare or make arrangements to compete with their employers prior to leaving the employ of their prospective rivals without fear of incurring liability for breach of their fiduciary duty of loyalty."

48. Villers' concealment from Computervision of his plans to pursue an independent enterprise was not, in and of itself, a violation of his fiduciary duty of loyalty. If such a right to leave employment is to be in any way meaningful, it must be exercisable without the necessity of revealing the plans to the employer.

49. An officer is required to disclose his preparations to leave a corporation and start a new business "only where particular circumstances render nondisclosure itself harmful to the corporation."

50. Thus, the law fully permits an employee secretly to participate in the formation of even a competing business while still employed by his employer. In preparation of an enterprise, an employee may even "set up shop" while still an employee and purchase assets for it.

51. Similarly, an employee is allowed to approach other employees at will to terminate their employment and offer them other employment to acquire their knowledge, skill, and experience, as long as the employee does not lure them away in order to acquire, through these employees, real protectable trade secrets of the employer.

52. "Proof of serious employee misconduct causing injury to the employer must also be shown before relief will generally be granted." Thus, you should not find Villers liable even in the event that you find his conduct "was not above reproach" and even in the event that you find that he made some limited "improper use" of Computervision's facilities and materials. You may find that Villers breached his duties in preparing to leave only if his conduct was "so harmful as to substantially hinder the employer in the continuation of his business."

53. Thus, you may find that Villers breached his fiduciary duties to Computervision only if through his improper conduct he benefitted while he was an employee "at corporate expense" or engaged in a rival or competing business to the detriment of Computervision. Villers, then, did not breach any duty unless the robotics business was "so closely associated with the existing business activities" of Computervision, "and so essential thereto," that its pursuit by Villers "threw" him into competition with his company.

54. In determining whether Villers breached his fiduciary duties to Computervision, it is important that you consider whether Villers acted in good

EXHIBIT 5 (*concluded*)

faith. Thus, you should consider whether Villers believed in good faith that Computervision had rejected his robotics proposal and that his only option to pursue robotics business was to start his own company.

55. You may also consider whether Villers should have foreseen any reasonable probability of actual injury to Computervision resulting from his independent pursuit of an enterprise in the field of robotics.

56. You should also consider whether Villers' personal pursuit of a business venture in robotics was made possible by the fraudulent diversion of Computervision's financial resources, credit, assets, or personnel.

57. On the other hand, you also should consider whether Villers and others who founded and financed Automatix did so by using "their own monies" and by exploiting "their own energy, resourcefulness, and business acumen and judgment." Put another way, you should consider whether "whatever opportunity existed was of [Villers'] own making."

58. You can likewise consider whether Villers' loyalty to Computervision is demonstrated by his other actions during the time period he was preparing to leave the company to pursue a robotics venture independently. You may consider, for example, whether or not he engaged in other projects beneficial to the company.

---

[1]Fletcher, *Cyclopedia of the Law of Private Corporations* section 218 at 786 (Perm. Ed. 1974).

Case 3–10

STRATUS COMPUTER

In January 1980, it looked like it really was going to happen. After six months, a false start, and some unexpected blips, Bill Foster had put together the team that he hoped would create Stratus Computer, a new company based on a high-reliability design objective. With the team finally complete, he could turn his full attention to raising the $6.2 million he felt they would need to fund their development efforts.

Bill felt that time was of the essence in obtaining start-up capital. First, he wanted to keep the momentum going with some of the financial contacts he had made and to maintain the enthusiasm of his team. Since there would be almost a two-year development effort before they could sell their first product, he was also anxious to maintain what he saw as a head start in the fast-changing computer market. Finally, after the ups and downs of the past few months, his rapidly depleting checkbook was giving him an extra sense of urgency.

During his six-month odyssey, Bill had identified several possible types of investors. Now he and his team wanted to develop a strategy for obtaining the best possible financing for the new company. Important elements of that strategy would include how they should approach the different possible sources and in what order, how much money they would request, and what financial structure would be best. They also had to decide how much equity they would be prepared to give up and what their bargaining strategy would be. Finally, they needed to set the criteria they would use in making a decision.

PERSONAL BACKGROUND

Bill Foster grew up in California and graduated from San Jose State in 1966 with a B.A. in math. Following graduation, he went to work for Lockheed, then a small software development company in the San Francisco Bay area. Bill completed a graduate degree in applied math at Santa Clara while working for Lockheed and continued night school until 1973, when he received an MBA from the same institution.

Growing tired of the instability in the aerospace industry, Bill joined Hewlett-Packard's (HP) then fledgling data products division in 1969. During the next seven years, he rose from being a programmer to become engineering manager of the computing systems group. As manager, he was responsible for HP's research and development for computer system hardware and software. About a third of his time was spent talking with prospective customers to assure them that the product being considered was technically sound and able to perform the desired tasks.

In 1976 he was recruited by Data General to become the firm's director of software development. Bill recalled that the opportunity to work for the president of a smaller, but faster growing company appealed to him, as did the chance to sample living on the East Coast. Over the next three years, Bill established a reputation within the company as a good manager and was made a vice president. He explained that his work was rewarding and a salary of nearly $100,000 a year and stock option benefits had allowed him to accumulate nearly $50,000 in savings.

THE DECISION TO START A COMPANY

Bill talked about his decision to start a company:

> I guess I'll never really know exactly why it happened the way it did. I had been thinking for over a year about starting a company. I tried to think about what I could do. I didn't get anywhere. I didn't have any idea. I guess I also didn't have the guts to do it. It didn't seem the smart thing to do to leave this great job I had, making all that money and all that sort of thing.
>
> But I also have known a lot of people who have gone off and started companies and become very successful. All high-technology related kinds of companies. Most of the founders of Tandem Computer had worked for me when I was at HP. I know many of the founders of Apple. So I was always envious of these people who had gone off and gotten involved with a start-up. I knew I was equal to those people. Yet I had reached the conclusion it just wasn't the right time or maybe never would be to do it, and I didn't have any ideas and didn't know what to do.

I almost feel foolish saying this, but I went on a business trip to Europe in June 1979, and the first night I was there, I woke up about three in the morning and just decided to do it. When I got back home to Massachusetts, I was going to quit my job and try to start a company. It's almost as if I said to myself "you're really stupid not to have done it a year ago." I must have been thinking about it somewhere in the back of my mind, but I really wasn't aware of it. I called my wife on the phone the next day and told her I was going to do it. She kind of said, "Oh, yeah, I've heard this before." When I got home, I talked some more about it and then she knew I was going to do it.

I can't really explain why it was, but all of a sudden I started thinking that the worst possible thing that could happen would be to wake up one day when I was 70 years old, look back over my life, and say to myself, "Gee, you never even tried to do it." I was 35, I was not particularly challenged by my job, and I was envious of my friends who had gone off and done something similar. I finally realized that all of the constraints I had were basically artificial constraints. I felt that I would be very disappointed with myself if I didn't at least attempt this—that all of my options would be closed.

Once that happened, it was a very easy decision; I had no qualms about it. Financially, it could have been a tough decision, but it wasn't. I had a lot of stock options that I had to leave behind. I didn't have a lot of money and don't have a lot of money today. At that time, it cost us about $30,000 for the five of us to live for a year. So my wife and I figured if I treated this as an investment in myself, we could withdraw $600 a week and in a year's time, the business would either be on its way or would have flopped. I would reserve another $20,000 in savings to invest as my share of the equity. The money for my children's college was probably my biggest hangup. But I had worked my way through school; if they had to work their way through, they could do it. It was not reason enough not to do it. Later, when things weren't looking so good, I'd look back and say, "Gee, that was probably a dumb decision!" Then it started to bother me about drawing out of the bank and living off our savings. But for the first three or four months, it was no problem.

In July 1979, within three weeks after returning from Europe, Bill submitted his resignation. Rumors within the company included speculation that he had been fired since "no one in their right mind would be crazy enough to walk away from the position and the benefits he had."

EARLY EXPERIENCES

The first step Bill took after leaving his job was to contact a friend who might be able to steer him to a venture capital company. Bill knew nothing about that part of the financial community, but his instincts told him that there was a lot of money available to finance businesses in the computer area. His friend helped him contact Greylock, a prominent Boston-based venture capital company.

Three days after I quit my job, I went to talk to these people. I had no business plan, no partners. I wasn't even sure what I was going to make, but I did

know it would have something to do with general-purpose computer systems—that's what I was familiar with. I was selling myself on my reputation
as a technical manager: "I've been heavily involved in a very successful HP
computer program. I've managed Data General projects."

We spent two or three hours over lunch just basically talking about money
being available, what they looked for, what they expected in terms of business planning, and all the rest. I was impressed with the amount of time this
partner was spending with me. He was very helpful. When I said that I
planned to do this in California since that is where I was from originally, he
gave me an introduction to Sutter Hill and Hambrecht & Quist, two West
Coast firms. They all owe each other favors: "You let me in this deal, and I
may let you in another." They all talk to each other all the time. Besides, to do
a large-scale start-up that might require as much as $10 million of venture
capital would probably involve several firms working together. Even if they
could, they normally would not do a sizeable venture all by themselves.

Greylock also mentioned that they normally don't do first round start-
ups. I found out later that many venture capital firms are that way. They're
not going to invest in three people and a briefcase. There's no track record.
They ask, "Can this guy who's worked inside a big company do it on his own?
Can he hire the people? Can he meet his schedules? Can he do it without constant changes in direction?" These are big unknowns, and most venture firms
aren't going to put money in day one with all those questions. They'd be prepared to pay three or four times the price a year later for the security of having seen some of those milestones. However, although Greylock wouldn't
take the lead, they did say they were very interested in what I was doing and
that there was a good chance they might come in if Sutter Hill got interested.
So now I had an "in" into three of the top venture capital companies in the
business.

Bill spent the rest of July and August researching the computer market
and trying to find a niche. He went to California in September to visit several of his old friends from HP. As they discussed trying to start a computer company, conversation turned to Tandem Computer. Tandem had focused on those users who had high reliability needs—applications where
the computer *couldn't* fail.

> These might be banks for automatic tellers or funds transfers. Banks can lose
> literally tens of thousands of dollars in interest in the time it takes to get a
> failed computer back up. Other examples are stock exchange applications,
> airlines or hotel reservations, medical systems. There are quite a few.

Tandem had done very well, with sales of $24 million in the third year and
an explosive growth rate.

> They certainly had found a market niche. Yet there still was no competition
> for them—no one else had come out with a similar product. So I concentrated
> on what was wrong with their idea, what could be done that was better.

Bill's business plan was to go more or less after the same market, but
to have a different technical approach. His concept was for a radically dif-

ferent type of computer architecture that would have two central processing units (CPUs) working together on the same program, doing exactly
the same thing at exactly the same time, so that if one CPU failed, the other would keep on operating with no interruption. This would also simplify field maintenance where the costs of repair were growing rapidly
even while the cost of hardware itself was declining.

Likely competition would be Tandem, Prime Computer, Digital
Equipment, IBM, and HP. However, Bill felt that a new firm had the great
advantage of a fresh start on design due to his new architecture. A system's
architecture is the pattern by which the basic computer functions are provided by a combination of hardware and software components. This involves many trade-offs between flexibility and capability versus efficiency and cost. Once an architecture is implemented, the pattern of
hardware/software interaction becomes relatively fixed. This, in turn,
limits the ability of the system to benefit from new hardware advances
without severely impacting existing software systems.

A totally new design could take advantage of the latest technological
advances. By incorporating these new advances, Stratus could have a truly modular design and could be controlled by a much simpler operating
system. Customers of other computer companies with large installed
bases had huge investments in software dependent on the original design
structure. For them, fundamental changes in architecture were difficult, if
not practically impossible. This was already true even of Tandem. Yet
Bill's approach would not require applications programmers to add the reliability features into their coding which *was* required by Tandem.

A FALSE START

Bill Foster completed his business plan to use in "prospecting" for venture
capital by October 1979. He proceeded to meet with the two San Francisco firms suggested by Greylock. At the same time, he attempted to contact old acquaintances at HP to see if they might be interested in joining
him in the venture. By November, Bill was still in California trying to assemble a team and attract interest in the financial community. He explained his frustration at the lack of progress:

> I went out to find money, but immediately found myself working for the ven-
> ture capitalists. They would say, "Do this, do that; go find a marketing per-
> son, go find your software person." That wasn't my objective. My objective
> was to work for myself. I found that I was wasting my time, doing the wrong
> thing. I was constantly talking to the venture groups, looking for lawyers and
> CPAs. I should have been putting together my team.
>
> My biggest mistake was to think that they were going to invest in me, Bill
> Foster—that I was such a great guy they'd give me the money and I'd get the
> people lined up. But it's just not going to happen. They aren't going to invest
> $2 million in one individual, it's just too risky.

One group tried to get me to join with another entrepreneur who was also trying to start a company. He had a lot more experience and had already made a lot of money in the computer industry. They got us together and it was just like oil and water There was no way I could see myself working *for* that guy and it would have been hard to work *with* him. Because of his experience, I'm sure he felt he should be my superior.

It was really tough because I *knew* he was going to get his money—with his record, the venturers were going to give him money no matter what he was doing. I didn't know if I was going to get any money at all. I told my wife I'd really be mad if two or three years out he's built a really successful company and I never got off the ground. But she said, "Look, what you want to do is run your own company. Don't start to lessen your goals." She had more confidence in me than I did. So I called him up and told him I wasn't interested. He told me I was making a big mistake.

I had a list of 30 people whom I had been associated with and felt would be good to have involved in the company. I discovered that only two were still with HP. The others had gone on to start their own businesses or work for other entrepreneurs. The start-up activity in California had been going strong from 1976 to 1979 while I was gone. It didn't take me too long to realize that getting a team together in California would be tough.

The venture firms all wanted to talk to everybody I talked to. They were testing me, which I didn't quite realize. They wanted to see if Foster could attract those people. They'd say, "We may invest in Bill Foster. What do you think of the venture? Why would you do this? How would your job function?" They were really conducting job interviews! Remember, I knew nothing about raising money. It appeared that this was the way you do it. I didn't know any better.

After six weeks and two long trips to California, Bill decided to try to start his business in New England. The easy availability of team members in California had not proved to be true and people in the Northeast were calling to express an interest in what he was doing. Bill also realized the difficulties of trying to get a business started across a continent. Travel devoured his weekly $600 withdrawals as well as much of his time. In addition, Bill saw that the real estate market had collapsed to the point where selling and buying a house would be a difficult prospect at either end of the country. Added to that was the desire of his family to stay in New England where they had made new friends and enjoyed the change of seasons which was absent in San Francisco.

The major risk in leaving California as a start-up location was in breaking off discussions with Sutter Hill. They had offered him a spot in their office and support services and had spent time on his venture themselves. Bill was afraid that this might destroy his credibility among such investors. However, it just didn't seem to be coming together. Bill felt Sutter Hill's interest was softening because of the delay in getting started, and the drain on money and time in trying to get started in California would be too great for him to continue on the West Coast.

When Bill discussed his decision with Sutter Hill, they were disappointed, but still had an interest in his venture. They said they wouldn't want to be a lead investor in the East, but might still invest if someone else took the lead. They suggested the New York firms of J. H. Whitney, Venrock, and Bessemer as several fine venture firms that invested in start-up situations. Bill also called several individuals who had been interested in joining him. They had considered his overtures tentative and none had committed to leaving their companies yet.

TRYING IT AGAIN

Bill decided he would try a different approach in New England. This time he would get his whole team together before really approaching the venture capital firms. He had received a number of calls from people who were curious about his progress to date. Bill contacted one of these, Bob Freiburghouse, an acquaintance whom he had met during a negotiation in the past. In 1974, Bob had started his own software firm which had been very successful. The conversation led to an agreement where Bob would become the vice president of software development for Stratus. In addition, Bob would provide software that he had already developed to the venture on a deferred payment basis—that is, if and when Stratus became profitable, Bob would be paid for the software which was used. Bob began declining all new development business for his company and began to work with Bill on the Stratus plan and on attracting other members of the team. Bill recalled his surprise at being able to attract Bob as part of the management team:

> My original idea when I approached Bob was to buy some of his software for my product. But when he learned what I was trying to do, he said, "Wow! This fits my plans exactly. I've always wanted to get into a manufacturing company instead of just a service company. I'll throw in my resources with you."

Bill went after the other team members. He heard of another individual with experience in hardware who had submitted his resignation from his job with one large computer manufacturer in order to join another large firm. Bill contacted him and convinced him to agree to join the group. The marketing spot was filled by one of the people Bill had contacted in California. He quit his job and began travelling to Boston at his own expense to help with the plan.

Three days before Christmas, the partner who would have handled the hardware engineering called to back out. His original employer had offered him a financial package that was too attractive to turn down. Bill and he had not really discussed specific salaries or stock ownership, so there was no real bargaining or counterproposal. It had just been assumed that if Stratus made it, they would all do very well. Bill remembered his feelings about the setback:

> That was a real blow to me. I had already told J. H. Whitney (one of the firms I was staying in touch with) that my team was set. It was only one phone call, but the word out in the venture community was that Foster had gotten his team together. If you talk to one, it quickly gets around to everybody because they're always talking to each other: "What's going on?"
>
> I was convinced that the whole project was just going to fall through. I was afraid that one of the other partners would drop out. The marketing guy in California was still shaky, wasn't sure he really wanted to come out here. I wasn't sure how Bob would react to it. Things just weren't going that well at all as we moved into 1980. As it turned out, Bob wasn't that concerned. He said, "Well, we'll go out and find somebody else." My marketing fellow apparently wasn't that concerned so I went after another fellow who had been my top choice, who had an excellent track record, but who I thought would never join us.
>
> Gardner, my new hope for hardware engineering, expressed his skepticism at first: "I'm a very conservative guy. It would really have to be a great deal for me to leave and get involved. It's very unlikely that I'd do that. But I'll talk to you if you want." After our initial conversation, he was intrigued. He wanted to meet my software guy. He felt the real risk was the software—in the computer business when there is a failure or slippage in a program, the problem is generally in the software. So I got Gardner and Bob together and they hit it off immediately. Each had a fantastic respect for the other and it would be just a great team. While Gardner would not commit, I felt he would join us if we had success in the financial community.

FINANCING OPTIONS

Now attention was turned to refining the business plan as they went over the schedules and budgets very closely, deciding what they would like to do. Bill had projected growth by considering the Tandem experience. Tandem's first-year sales in 1976 were $581,000. This increased to $7.7 million in 1977, $24 million in 1978, and 1979 sales were running almost double that of 1978. Since Tandem had already blazed the trail and created the market, he felt Stratus could do somewhat better.

After team discussions, the pro formas didn't change very much from those Bill had projected earlier. According to their plan (see Exhibit 1 for summary and financial projections), they would need to raise about $6.2 million to cover the three-year development and market introduction effort. Receivables and inventories for early sales would be financed by increasing notes payable. Then additional financing would be required. They projected that $2 million would be needed to fund the first year during which they would develop a working prototype. This would lend more credibility to their team and their concept. However, the partners could only provide a small amount of the cash equity required, between $50,000 and $75,000.

Even while concentrating on putting together the Stratus team, Bill had been trying to learn more about possible sources of financing:

> My mode always was, "It doesn't hurt to talk to anybody. You might learn something." So I was always following up any kind of lead I got, whether it had to do with raising money or finding people or anything. You may run up a phone bill, but people are generally very helpful. I got leads from headhunters and investors, lawyers, and friends. I talked to other people who had started companies. They were probably the most helpful of all—those who had recently done what I was going through. They would reminisce about those exciting times. Of course, if they were successful and got their operation off the ground, they always like to talk about it.
>
> I got many of the new company leads by reading magazines. Some of them have articles about companies that have just started up. I'd just call some of the presidents of the companies that had been interviewed out of the blue, tell them what I was doing, and ask their advice. I met several of the people out in California through those articles.

Bill had found three major options: venture capital firms, private individuals, and other operating corporations. There appeared to be significant differences in the way each of these groups made investments and in the types of deals that might be struck.

Venture Capital Firms

The venture capital firms were the most obvious possibilities. There were a large number of venture firms actively seeking investments. In addition to the best-known, perhaps most prestigious firms such as those mentioned earlier, there was a wide range of other less well-known firms that might be smaller or more recently started or that simply chose to keep low profiles.

Two of these lesser-known firms had also expressed interest in Stratus. These contacts had arisen from Gardner's concern over whether or not they were likely to get funded. When Gardner Hendrie was considering joining the team, he had called an old friend for advice. Burgess Jamieson had worked with Gardner 15 years earlier in an engineering company, then had gone to California to get involved in venture capital and had been very successful. When Gardner explained why he was interested in learning the climate for venture capital, Burgess felt his company, Institutional Venture Associates, might be interested. Bill recalled:

> Before I knew it Burgess hops an airplane and wants to talk to us. Right away he's very interested, partly on the strength of the business plan and partly on his personal association with Gardner. But he felt we should have an East Coast firm in the lead. He'd be very happy with the New York firms we knew,

but also suggested we contact Hellman-Gal, a lesser-known Boston company they'd done some business with before. (It seemed that the best-known Boston firms generally preferred second-round financings). I had heard of Hellman-Gal, but never bothered to call them. I didn't think they did start-ups and I didn't think they were big enough. But Burgess said they'd be good and also that they felt good about our idea. One of their partners had had some experience in the time-sharing business and knew something about computers himself.

During his early discussions with the venture firms and in talking to the other recently started companies, Bill discovered some apparent ground rules in the venture capital community:

One rule is that you're not going to raise $7 million day one. No one has put in that much money. The going first round for my kind of deal is around a million and a half. Maybe you can get close to $2 million, but probably not more than $2 million for a team of untried people. That much would get us just past a working prototype.

Number two is that they are going to have control—at least 51 percent. They're going to do it—there's no way you can get around it. At the same time, they won't *commit* to anything on round two. They'll talk about what they'll do if you do a good job, but if they don't like what you've done, you may not get that second-round money.

None of it is cast in concrete. You can talk and you can go through scenarios. They'd sit me down and tell me what other companies did. "In 1974 Tandem gave up 74 percent of their company for $1 million. The investor got 72 percent of Prime Computer for $600,000 in 1972." The new start-ups did a little better—the going rate seemed to be giving up about 60 percent.

I also found that many of the venture capital firms without technical backgrounds used outside consultants to help them evaluate high-technology ventures. The people they relied on were heavily booked and might take weeks to schedule.

Private Individuals

Another possible source of financing was from wealthy individuals. Certain tax provisions could make investments in firms such as Stratus particularly appealing: most of Stratus's early expenses would be for research and development. If the funds for the R&D were provided by a limited partnership, most of the expenditures could be deducted by the individuals against other sources of ordinary income. This would effectively lessen the actual aftertax amount at risk for those individuals substantially. If the research proved successful, the investors would typically receive a royalty (normally 7 percent to 10 percent) on resulting sales. Such royalties would be taxed at long-term capital gains rates.

Bill had been put in contact with a young individual who had taken an idea from an MBA thesis and built it into a very successful company.

The company had been recently sold with the entrepreneur's interest worth about $5 to $6 million. Now this person was interested in investing some of the proceeds of the sale and would lead a private placement with about 10 individuals each putting up $300,000 to $400,000.

Because of the tax benefits of this structure and because some of these individuals did not get to see as many good deals as the venture firms, Bill felt that they might have to give up less ownership of Stratus if the money could be raised this way. He felt the best he might do was give away only 40–45 percent of the ownership. On the other hand, this would be more complicated and would probably involve preparation of a private placement memorandum that would essentially be a full-blown prospectus under SEC Rule 242. This might also require review by the state "Blue Sky" commission. The SEC does not consider even a wealthy lawyer to necessarily be a "sophisticated investor" in terms of a computer start-up.

Other Nonventure Corporations

In another example of how people who had been suggested as sources of advice in dealing with the venture community had become possible sources of financing themselves, Bill had started discussions with a company that had quickly became interested in financing the entire Stratus start-up. Bill's contact, Gary Jameson, had worked for a venture capital firm and was now the vice president of administration of a company that was selling a *product* that depended on reliable computer systems. They bought their computers from major companies, put them in their systems, and sold them to the telephone communications industry. These systems basically required continuous operation.

> They said they were very interested and that they might fund us to the tune of $7 million. Again, this would be set up as a partnership so that this company could get the more immediate tax benefits of expensing the R&D.
>
> Gary also felt it would be impossible for me to raise money through venture capital sources—that I was wasting my time. Even though I had run R&D teams, I had never been the chief executive officer of a company, had never run the whole show. He said that venture capitalists were really conservative investors and it would be very unlikely that any venture groups would invest millions of dollars in a company in which the CEO didn't have a proven track record.

Although this was the only nonventure company Bill had contacted, after seeing the interest here, he thought others might have similar interests. He had heard that some of these companies actually had in-house venture groups, but he wasn't sure how their investment strategies differed from traditional venture capital companies.

THE FINANCING DECISION

Striking a deal with any of the financing sources would require detailed negotiations, with no assurances as to how long that might take or whether or not a final agreement might be reached. The risks were increased because the Stratus team was untried in launching a company. One factor in their favor was that there had been a number of recent success stories of computer firms starting up and becoming industry leaders. Those deals also served as a growing database to determine the increased values of the company for each round of financing.

Recent increases in the availability of venture capital also worked to Stratus' advantage. Bill pointed out that more money was chasing roughly the same number of quality deals and that this should give a founding group more leverage in the negotiations. This could extend to a whole range of issues, including the relative percentages of ownership and the relative privileges of the various shareholders through the use of different types of preferred stock or debt instruments with convertible provisions or warrants.

Somewhere in the process, the valuation of the company had to be considered. With ongoing companies, investors could look at the asset bases and price/earnings ratios. With a start-up, the investor had to consider the concept, the projections, and the team and decide on the likely future value.

Another factor for Bill was that more than one round of financing was likely to be needed. How the first round of capital was priced and structured would influence future rounds of investment.

The team members agreed to take smaller salaries then they had earned before. (Bill's would be less than half his former salary and the others would be about 80 percent). The four founding members of the company would split whatever equity they could retain by dividing the number of shares by 4.2. Each of them would receive a 1/4.2 part except Bill. He would receive 1.2/4.2 or "120 percent" share for putting the team together. However, employee stock ownership and shares for other key employees also had to be taken into account.

Now Bill and the Stratus team faced the difficult task of setting and executing a financing strategy.

EXHIBIT 1
Business Plan Summary and Financial Projections

SUMMARY	I
MARKET	II*
COMPETITION	III*
TECHNOLOGY TRENDS	IV*
PRODUCT	V*
FINANCIALS	A
PRODUCT PRICING	B*
STAFFING PLAN	C*
IMPLEMENTATION PLAN	D*
RESUME	E*

*Omitted from Exhibit.

I—SUMMARY

(This memorandum, although written in the present tense, discusses a business proposal involving a corporation which is to be organized in the future. The computer systems described herein have not been designed as of the date hereof.)

Stratus Computer, Inc. is a company formed to design, manufacture, and market small computer systems that take advantage of a unique architecture and advances in hardware technology to produce a product that is unequaled in overall reliability. The computer sytems will be priced from $30,000 to $400,000 or more. A wide performance range is offered by using Stratus' multiprocessor architecture, providing system expansion by adding hardware modules to the computer systems. These systems will be sold to Fortune 1000's and system houses. Both markets are growing fast and only require modest software support.

Of the two million U.S. companies that have revenues greater than $100,000, only 6 percent use computers today. This enormous untapped potential leads some to predict that small business systems sales will reach $50 billion over the next decade—a 30 percent sustained annual growth rate for 10 years. (*Computerworld*, December 17, 1979).

The competition for this market will be intense. Stratus will achieve its growth objective by focusing its design on reliability issues. High reliability requires a totally new design in order to have good price and performance, but it is unlikely that existing companies will start their design efforts from scratch because they have to be compatible with their current product line in order to protect their existing customer base. Thus, their solutions will be compromises and not totally satisfactory to many customers.

Stratus will require $4.2 million of equity financing; $2.0 in Year 1 and $2.2 in Year 2. Prototype systems will be completed in the 18th month, and first

EXHIBIT 1 (*continued*

customer shipments will occur in the fourth quarter of Year 2. Stratus will become a major computer systems supplier, achieving $75 million in sales by Year 5. Stratus will leverage the technology of semiconductor and peripheral suppliers, and will focus its attention on integrating their hardware with our own unique software to produce computer systems.

Stratus takes advantage of the continued decline in hardware costs to achieve high reliability of all key computer components: processors, memory, and peripherals. The result is that the failure of any component will not bring the system down. In many cases, the system will tolerate failure of two or more components. Component failure has zero impact on users. Operators of the computer are not affected by component failure. They do not have to re-enter data, enter special commands, or flip switches. Application programmers do not have to design their programs to react in case of component failure. Therefore, new programs can be designed in straightforward, familiar ways, and existing programs may be transported to Stratus computers with no changes to accommodate the reliability design.

The fact that Stratus achieves nearly 100 percent reliability with no user impact is a significant competitive advantage. Only one other manufacturer, Tandem Computer, provides a high reliability system. However, the Tandem design requires very complex program design by the user, and provides a much lower level of reliability. Also, Stratus provides high reliability at low cost: the average Stratus system will cost less than $100,000, while Tandem systems average more than $200,000.

High reliability of computer components is optional. The user can decide how important reliability is to his application, and then make the appropriate economic tradeoffs. He can choose to have highly reliable processors or peripherals, or neither, or both. He can start with a simple system and add extra hardware for high reliability later, with zero impact to his application programs or operational procedures. This flexibility expands the market for Stratus computers—it is not limited only to those who are willing to pay for high reliability. This same flexibility positions Stratus to take advantage of technology trends. As hardware costs drop, the percentage of the computer market that is willing to pay extra for high reliability will increase rapidly because the cost of extra hardware will be small compared with software costs, support costs, and the opportunity costs of system downtime.

As companies and organizations become more dependent on computers, reliability will become a bigger issue. Unlike human beings, computers generally give little, if any, warning that they are about to fail; when they do fail, they are useless until repaired, and sometimes even when fixed they have lost critical information that will never be recovered. Thus, high reliability requires elaborate and expensive safeguards against failure, and quick response field service capabilities, and oftentimes will inhibit a company from "computerizing" an application that otherwise would be much more efficient on a computer. Hence, a significant portion of the market will be eager to buy Stratus computers because they eliminate nearly all concerns about interruption in operation due to computer failure or loss of key information, and at a cost much lower than any other alternative.

Stratus computers are expandable. As the user's application grows, he can add more processors or peripherals or both to meet the increased demands placed on the system. He does not have to throw away or replace old hardware when the system expands—he merely adds to it.

EXHIBIT 1 (*continued*)

Stratus computers can be used as a tool to execute applications developed by system houses or end-users. Users are supplied with industry standard languages, COBOL, PL/I and BUSINESS BASIC, as well as a source editor and program debugger for program development. A multiprogrammed operating system is provided that permits multiple users to access common system resources, but to be protected from one another.

Stratus computers can coexist in a network with other Stratus computers or with IBM computers. Between Stratus systems basic file access and program communication, support is provided. Stratus provides communication with IBM through emulation of IBM 2780/3780 Remote Job Entry stations and 3270 terminal emulation. Stratus also provides industry standard X.25 packet network support, which means that Stratus computers can communicate across public data networks, such as TELENET (U.S. and international), TYMNET (U.S.), DATAPAC, (Canada), TRANSPAC (France), and EURONET (European Common Market).

The major product advantages can be summarized as follows:

1. Reliability

   The design protects against all types of hardware failure. This design is straightforward for operating systems and user software to take advantage of; gains in hardware reliability are not offset by complex, failure-prone software.

2. Expandability

   The system is expandable in terms of processors and peripherals in order to provide for growth of user's applications. Thus the product line is very broad, and the user is less likely to feel constrained at the high end.

3. Flexibility

   The design allows the user to add hardware to increase reliability or performance, or both. This flexibility also reduces Stratus' manufacturing and field support costs.

4. Controlled software costs

   Since software costs are rising, the above three objectives are met with no increase in system or user software complexity. Established, reliable applications are able to take advantage of the Stratus design with no modification to accommodate the architecture.

5. Low cost

   Stratus takes advantage of recent advances in VLSI, memory, and disk technology to provide nearly 100 percent reliability at low cost.

6. Applications development

   The necessary utilities, languages, communications, and operating systems software are provided for users to develop new applications or transport existing programs to Stratus.

7. Field service

   Service costs are not dropping with hardware costs because systems are more complex and few real improvements have been made to service techniques. Stratus reduces the need for expensive, quick response service because the computer will tell the user of a failure, but operation will continue uninterrupted.

The president of Stratus is William E. Foster. Mr. Foster has 13 years industry experience, the last 10 with Hewlett-Packard and, most recently, Data General, two of the leading minicomputer manufacturers. Mr. Foster is one of

EXHIBIT 1 (*continued*)

the few industry people who has been involved with a computer system project from inception through shipment and contributing net profit. He was involved from day one as a designer of the HP3000 from Hewlett-Packard and progressed to have total hardware and software responsibility for the product which today is one of the leaders in the commercial market.

At Data General, Mr. Foster gained experience building organizations and implementing tight expense controls. He developed a 100-person unstructured group into an organization of more than 400 people with focused managers who were accountable for specific results. He built from scratch DG's Advanced Research Center at Research Triangle Park, Raleigh, North Carolina, building a team from nothing to over 100 engineering and software professionals. Much of DG's success is due to a strong entrepreneurial atmosphere with emphasis on expense control and profit, and Mr. Foster gained from this experience.

The vice president of software is Robert A. Freiburghouse. Mr. Freiburghouse has 18 years of experience in operating a business, software project management, software design, compiler design, computer system design, and software development. He is founder and president of Translation Systems, Inc., a very successful company specializing in the production of compilers. He has designed and built more than eight compilers that are offered as products by various major computer manufacturers. Mr. Freiburghouse designed hardware extensions to several existing computer systems, designed a 32-bit microprocessor, and designed a programming language that has been adopted as an American National Standard (ANSI) and as an International Standard (ISO). Mr. Freiburghouse is a recognized authority on programming languages and compiler design, and is a guest lecturer at MIT, Brown University, Bell Laboratories, GE Research Laboratories, and various professional organizations. He has published several papers on compiler design and has written three technical books.

The vice president of engineering has over 20 years of experience in the computer field as a logic designer, a system designer, and as an engineering manager. He has supervised major engineering organizations and has personally executed the detailed design of a successful minicomputer. He is the holder of several patents in computer organization and has a B.S. and M.S. in Electrical Engineering.

The vice president of marketing has been with a highly successful manufacturer of computer and computer systems for the past nine years. For eight of those years he has managed increasingly larger sales areas across the country. At present his organization consists of over 70 people with a sales responsibility of over $50 million. In his present responsibility he has designed and implemented numerous marketing plans which have enabled his organization to successfully sell general purpose small and medium scale computer systems to virtually every market. One such plan was aimed at capturing a significant portion of the emerging commercial systems supplier market. The plan called for modifications of the company's credit and contracting procedures as well as a modification of sales commission structures and sales management goal structure. The plan's success has been dramatic. In two years, sales in this market have grown from almost nothing to over $10 million with a dominant market share position. Other activities include successful Major Account campaigns and plans aimed at exploiting most of the emerging computer marketing channels.

EXHIBIT 1 (*continued*)

In summary, Stratus will be successful for the following reasons:

1. Unique management team that has proven track records in systems development, hardware, software, and marketing.
2. Unique design that is straightforward to implement and takes advantage in the best possible way of the trends in hardware costs.
3. Located in the Boston area which has an unequaled talent pool of computer hardware and software engineers and few significant start-up opportunities for these people in the last five years.
4. A preexisting set of software products developed by Mr. Freiburghouse that substantially reduces the amount of new development required and allows us to begin implementation sooner.
5. Very large and fast growing market, with a focus on a segment within that market which is growing even faster.

Legal Counsel: Gaston Snow & Ely Bartlett
One Federal Street
Boston, Mass 02110

Accountants: Arthur Young & Company
One Boston Place
Boston, Mass 02102

A—FINANCIALS

Financial Statements—Fiscal Year 1
(in thousands of dollars)

	Q1	Q2	Q3	Q4	FY
Income Statement					
Revenue	—	—	—	—	—
Cost of goods sold	—	—	—	—	—
Operating expenses:					
Development	121	341	403	447	1,312
Marketing	12	17	22	32	83
G&A	47	40	63	63	213
Total operating expenses	180	398	488	542	1,608
Income (loss) from operations	(180)	(398)	(488)	(542)	(1,608)
Interest expense	—	6	9	8	23
Interest income	—	40	33	21	94
Net interest	—	34	24	13	71
Net income (loss)	(180)	(364)	(464)	(529)	(1,537)
Balance Sheet					
Cash & cash investments	1,835	1,494	1,033	507	
Prepaid expenses	25	25	25	25	
Total current assets	1,860	1,519	1,058	532	

EXHIBIT 1 (*continued*)

Electronic test equipment	—	100	200	200
Computer equipment	—	170	170	170
Subtotal	—	270	370	370
Less-accumulated dep.	—	13	31	49
Net plant and equipment	—	257	339	321
Total assets	1,860	1,776	1,397	853
Accounts payable	10	20	20	20
Accrued expenses	30	40	40	40
Total current liabilities	40	60	60	60
Capital lease obligations	—	260	345	330
Stock	2,000	2,000	2,000	2,000
Retained deficit	(180)	(544)	(1,008)	(1,537)
Total stockholders' equity	1,820	1,456	992	463
Total liabilities and equity	1,860	1,776	1,397	853

Cash Flow—Fiscal Year 1 (in thousands of dollars)

	Q1	Q2	Q3	Q4	FY
Cash provided by (used in)					
Operations:					
Net income (loss)	(180)	(364)	(464)	(529)	(1,537)
Add: charges against income not requiring use of cash:					
Depreciation	—	13	18	18	49
Net cash provided by (used in) operations	(180)	(351)	(446)	(511)	(1,488)
Other sources of cash:					
Increase in accounts payable	10	10	—	—	20
Increase in accrued expenses	30	10	—	—	40
Increase in capital leases	—	270	100	—	370
Sale of stock	2,000	—	—	—	2,000
Total sources (uses)	1,860	(61)	(346)	(511)	942
Uses of cash					
Increase in prepaid expenses	25	—	—	—	25
Additions to property, plant, and equipment	—	270	100	—	370
Payments of capital leases	—	10	15	15	40
Total uses	25	280	115	15	435
Increase (decrease) in cash	1,835	(341)	(461)	(526)	507
Cash balance start of period	—	1,835	1,494	1,033	—
Cash balance end of period	1,835	1,494	1,033	507	507

EXHIBIT 1 (*continued*)

Financial Statements—Fiscal Year 2
(in thousands of dollars)

	Q1	Q2	Q3	Q4	FY
Income Statement					
Revenue	—	—	—	400	400
Total cost of goods sold	—	—	—	312	312
Gross margin	—	—	—	88	88
Development	379	362	352	337	1,430
Marketing	42	62	87	112	303
G&A	63	63	63	63	252
Total operating expenses	484	487	502	512	1,985
Income (loss) from operations	(484)	(487)	(502)	(424)	(1,897)
Interest expense	8	10	12	11	41
Interest income	7	51	39	31	128
Net interest	(1)	41	27	20	87
Net income (loss)	(485)	(446)	(475)	(404)	(1,810)
Balance Sheet					
Cash & cash investments	2,228	1,767	1,252	753	
Accounts receivable				300	
Inventories	10	40	150	250	
Prepaid expenses	30	30	30	30	
Total current assets	2,268	1,837	1,432	1,333	
Production and test equipment	25	75	200	200	
Electronic test equipment	200	200	200	200	
Computer equipment	170	170	170	170	
Subtotal	395	445	570	570	
Less-accumulated depreciation	70	85	115	140	
Total plant and equipment	325	360	455	430	
Total assets	2,593	2,197	1,887	1,763	
Accounts payable	30	50	100	400	
Accrued expenses	50	50	60	60	
Total current liabilities	80	100	160	460	
Capital lease obligations	335	365	470	450	
Stock	4,200	4,200	4,200	4,200	
Retained deficit	(2,022)	(2,468)	(2,943)	(3,347)	
Total stockholders' equity	2,178	1,732	1,257	853	
Total liabilities and equity	2,593	2,197	1,887	1,763	

EXHIBIT 1 (*continued*)

Cash Flow—Fiscal Year 2
(in thousands of dollars)

	Q1	Q2	Q3	Q4	FY
Cash provided by (used in)					
Operations:					
Net income (loss)	(485)	(446)	(475)	(404)	(1,810)
Add: charges against income not requiring use of cash:					
Depreciation	21	15	30	25	91
Net cash provided by (used in) operations	(464)	(431)	(445)	(379)	(1,719)
Other sources of cash:					
Increase in accounts payable	10	20	50	300	380
Increase in accrued expenses	10	—	10	—	20
Increase in capital leases	25	50	125	—	200
Sale of stock	2,200	—	—	—	2,200
Total sources (uses)	1,781	(361)	(260)	(79)	1,081
Uses of cash					
Increase in accounts receivable	—	—	—	300	300
Increase in inventories	10	30	110	100	250
Increase in prepaid expenses	5	—	—	—	5
Additions to property, plant, and equipment	25	50	125	—	200
Payments of capital leases	20	20	20	20	80
Total uses	60	100	255	420	835
Increase (decrease) in cash	1,721	(461)	(515)	(499)	246
Cash balance start of period	507	2,228	1,767	1,252	507
Cash balance end of period	2,228	1,767	1,252	753	753

Financial Statements—Fiscal Year 3
(in thousands of dollars)

	Q1	Q2	Q3	Q4	FY
Income Statement					
Revenue	1,200	2,100	2,800	3,900	10,000
Total cost of goods sold	600	900	1,100	1,500	4,100
Gross margin	600	1,200	1,700	2,400	5,900

EXHIBIT 1 (*continued*)

	Q1	Q2	Q3	Q4	FY
Development	350	330	340	350	1,340
Marketing	200	570	730	900	2,400
G&A	80	100	120	150	450
Total operating expenses	660	1,045	1,230	1,315	4,350
Income (loss) from operations	(60)	155	470	985	1,550
Interest expense	10	10	9	9	38
Interest income	14	40	29	19	102
Net interest	4	30	20	10	64
Income (loss) before taxes	(56)	185	490	995	1,614
Net income (loss)	(56)	170	445	905	1,464

Balance Sheet

	Q1	Q2	Q3	Q4
Cash & cash investments	1,852	1,332	882	1,267
Accounts receivable	800	1,400	1,900	2,800
System spares	100	200	300	300
Inventories	500	800	1,500	2,500
Prepaid expenses	50	50	100	100
Total current assets	3,302	3,782	4,687	6,967
Production and test equipment	400	400	400	400
Electronic test equipment	200	200	200	200
Computer equipment	170	170	170	170
Leasehold improvements	25	50	50	75
Subtotal	795	820	820	845
Less accumulated depreciation	180	215	255	295
Net plant and equipment	615	605	565	550
Total assets	3,917	4,387	5,252	7,517
Notes payable	—	—	—	1,000
Accounts payable	600	900	1,200	1,500
Taxes payable	—	15	60	150
Accrued expenses	100	100	200	200
Total ccurent liabilities	700	1,015	1,460	2,850
Capital lease obligations	420	405	380	350
Stock	6,200	6,200	6,200	6,200
Retained deficit	(3,403)	(3,233)	(2,788)	(1,883)
Total stockholders' equity	2,797	2,967	3,412	4,317
Total liabilities and equity	3,917	4,387	5,257	7,517

EXHIBIT 1 (*continued*)

Cash Flow—Fiscal Year 3
(in thousands of dollars)

	Q1	Q2	Q3	Q4	FY
Cash provided by (used in)					
Operations:					
Net income (loss)	(56)	170	445	905	1,464
Add: charges against income not requiring use of cash:					
Depreciation	40	35	40	40	155
Net cash provided by (used in) operations	(16)	205	485	945	1,619
Other sources of cash:					
Increase in notes payable	—	—	—	1,000	1,000
Increase in accounts payable	200	300	300	300	1,100
Increase in taxes payable	—	15	45	90	150
Increase in accrued expenses	40	—	100	—	140
Sale of stock	2,000	—	—	—	2,000
Total sources (uses)	2,224	520	930	2,335	6,009
Uses of cash					
Increase in accounts receivable	500	600	500	900	2,500
Increase in system spares	100	100	100	—	300
Increase in inventories	250	300	700	1,000	2,250
Increase in prepaid expenses	20	—	50	—	70
Additions to property, plant, and equipment	225	25	—	25	275
Payments of capital leases	30	15	25	30	100
Total uses	1,125	1,040	1,375	1,955	5,495
Increase (decrease) in cash	1,099	(520)	(445)	380	514
Cash balance start of period	753	1,852	1,332	887	753
Cash balance end of period	1,852	1,332	887	1,267	1,267

Five Year Financial Pros Formas
(in thousands of dollars)

	Y1	Y2	Y3	Y4	Y5
Income Statement					
Revenue	—	400	10,000	30,000	75,000
Total cost of goods sold	—	312	4,100	13,200	33,500
Gross margin	—	88	5,900	16,800	41,500

– 10 –

EXHIBIT 1 (*continued*)

	F1	F2	F3	F4	FY
Development	1,312	1,430	1,340	1,700	4,750
Marketing	83	303	2,400	6,400	16,000
G&A	213	252	450	1,500	2,750
Total operating expenses	1,608	1,985	4,350	9,600	23,500
Income (loss) from operations	(1,608)	(1,897)	1,550	7,200	18,000
Interest expense	23	41	38	75	15
Interest income	94	128	102	50	50
Net interest	71	87	64	(25)	35
Income (loss) before taxes	(1,537)	(1,810)	1,614	7,175	18,035
Net income (loss)	(1,537)	(1,810)	1,464	4,800	9,935

Balance Sheet					
Cash & cash investments	507	753	1,267	1,212	2,127
Accounts receivable	—	300	2,800	8,000	20,000
System spares	—	—	300	900	2,000
Inventories	—	250	2,500	7,000	18,000
Prepaid expenses	25	30	100	300	500
Total current assets	532	1,333	6,967	17,412	42,627
Production and test equipment	—	200	400	900	2,200
Electronic test equipment	200	200	200	300	500
Computer equipment	170	170	170	200	400
Leasehold improvements	—	—	75	100	300
Subtotal	370	570	845	1,500	3,400
Less accumulated depreciation	49	140	295	500	800
Net plant and equipment	321	430	550	1,000	2,600
Total assets	853	1,763	7,517	18,412	45,227
Notes payable	—	—	1,000	—	—
Accounts payable	20	400	1,500	3,500	9,000
Taxes payable	—	—	150	2,375	8,100
Accrued expenses	40	60	200	1,200	3,000
Total current liabilities	60	460	2,850	7,075	20,100
Capital lease obligations	330	450	350	220	75
Stock	2,000	4,200	6,200	6,200	6,200
Retained earnings (deficit)	(1,537)	(3,347)	(1,883)	2,917	12,852
Total stockholders' equity	463	853	4,317	9,117	19,052
Additional debt or equity	—	—	—	2,000	6,000
Total liabilities and equity	853	1,763	7,517	18,412	45,227

EXHIBIT 1 (*continued*)

Five Year Cash Flow
(in thousands of dollars)

	FY1	FY2	FY3	FY4	FY5
Cash provided by (used in)					
Operations:					
Net income (loss)	(1,537)	(1,810)	1,464	4,800	9,935
Add: charges against income not requiring use of cash:					
Depreciation	49	91	155	205	300
Net cash provided by (used in) operations	(1,488)	(1,719)	1,619	5,005	10,235
Other sources of cash:					
Increase in notes payable	—	—	1,000	—	—
Increase in accounts payable	20	380	1,100	2,000	5,500
Increase in taxes payable	—	—	150	2,225	5,725
Increase in accrued expenses	40	20	140	1,000	1,800
Increase in capital leases	370	200	—	—	—
Sale of stock	2,000	2,200	2,000	—	—
Additional cash requirements	—	—	—	2,000	4,000
Total sources (uses)	942	1,081	6,009	12,230	27,260

	FY1	FY2	FY3	FY4	FY5
Uses of cash					
Increase in accounts receivable	—	300	2,500	5,200	12,000
Increase in system spares	—	—	300	600	1,100
Increase in inventories	—	250	2,250	4,500	11,000
Increase in prepaid expenses	25	5	70	200	200
Additions to property, plant, and equipment	370	200	275	655	1,900
Payments of capital leases	40	80	100	130	145
Payments of notes payable	—	—	—	1,000	—
Total uses	435	835	5,495	12,285	26,345
Increase (decrease) in cash	507	246	514	(55)	915
Cash balance start of period	—	507	753	1,267	1,212
Cash balance end of period	507	753	1,267	1,212	2,127

EXHIBIT 1 (*continued*)

Financial Assumptions

1. Revenues
   — Average selling price per system is $80,000.
   — Product will be ready in 18th month; first shipments to occur by 21st month.
   — Service revenues will grow at less than the industry average of .6 percent to .C percent of installed base per month, and will account for less than 10 percent of sales though Year 5.
   — Revenue per salesman will be the industry average of $700K to $1,000K per year.
   — Reduced margins from OEM discounts will be offset by reduced marketing expense. Revenue for marketing provides ample margin for competitive discounts.
2. Warranty
   — Because of high system reliability, warranty expense will not be a significant factor.
3. Foreign sales
   — Some sales in Years 4 and 5 will be international.
   — Tax provision does not consider potential benefit of DISC.
4. Marketing expense
   — Higher than average industry rate will be spent on marketing. Combined marketing + G/A for selected companies are: DG 22 percent, Tandem 36 percent, Prime 33 percent, Digital 20 percent, HP 28 percent.
   — Salesman compensation will be through a very aggressive commission plan.
5. R&D
   — During Years 1 and 2 all technical people will come over at straight salary plus very attractive stock plan.
6. Taxes
   — No loss carryforwards for state purposes; therefore, state provision in Year 3.
   — Assumes 45 percent effective tax rate, which is reasonable in light of:
     —ITC.
     —Jobs tax credit.
     —Surtax exemption.
     —Tax planning.
7. Receivables
   — Assumes 60-day turn cycle.
   — Assumes in Years 4 and 5 that 40 percent of annual sales occur in 4th quarter.
8. Inventories
   — At an annualized run rate, inventory held at 6 to 7 turns per year.
   — Strong manufacturing emphasis on controlling inventory levels.
9. Property, plant, and equipment
   — Early requirements will be financed through leasing. Assumes capital leases from an accounting point of view.
   — Lease terms are $20 per $1,000 of capital equipment per month, full payout in 5 years. Bank receives ITC and depreciation benefits.

– 13 –

EXHIBIT 1 (*concluded*)

10. Accounts payable
    — Assumes 60-day turn cycle.
11. Additional cash requirements
    — Assumes equity infusion and therefore no interest costs.
    — If partial debt financing is assumed at an 18 percent interest cost, then a debt to equity ratio of 1:1 yields ROI of 92 percent in Year 4 and 86 percent in Year 5; debt to equity of .5:1 yields ROI of 67 percent in Year 4 and 63 percent in Year 5.

	Year 4	*Year 5*
1:1 ratio		
Debt	5,500	12,500
Equity	5,500	12,500
Interest	495	1,620
Tax	2,100	7,300
Net income	5,075	10,735
ROI	92%	86%
.5:1 ratio		
Debt	3,600	8,300
Equity	7,400	16,700
Interest	324	1,070
Tax	2,210	7,560
Net income	4,965	10,470
ROI	67%	63%

12. Manufacturing
    — No heavy capital equipment required since most of the manufacturing process consists of integrating vendor hardware. Provisions are made for burn-in ovens, wave-solder equipment, electronic and peripheral testers. Manufacturing is essentially an assembly and test operation.
    — All electronic components will be second-sourced. Where possible, peripherals will be second-sourced. The disc will be selected partially on the availability of a standard interface such as Storage Module.

Part Four

MANAGING AND HARVESTING THE VENTURE

In this final section, we look at what happens after the start-up. Managing a venture in an entrepreneurial manner involves a constant search for new opportunities. Yet, growth and wealth often create bureaucracy, specialization, and a desire to protect assets rather than to seek growth. This last part provides a good stopping point to review Chapter 1; the ideas therein are useful for existing companies that want to remain entrepreneurial.

Sometimes, the period after the start-up brings not growth and success, but problems. Chapter 10, "Bankruptcy: A Debtor's Perspective," describes how to deal with that unhappy and final stage in the life of some businesses.

Chapter 11 looks at a firm's decision to become a public company. "Securities Law and Public Offerings" describes the legal and business considerations involved in going public.

THE CASES

American Imports concerns the ethical and financial problems that two young entrepreneurs have with their equity backers.

Both Dragonfly and Eric Weston examine companies with grave financial problems. Is bankruptcy the answer? What are the alternatives and their consequences?

Michael Bregman looks at a business with more pleasant problems. How should Michael manage his business' growth? What strategy is appropriate, and what resources will be required?

SSS examines a company which has decided to become a public entity. Is this the right course of action? What are the criteria for selecting an underwriter? What are the key items to negotiate? Which one should SSS choose?

Finally, Atlas Lighting Co. provides a 25-year retrospective of a growing manufacturing company. Issues of management succession, expansion alternatives, and nepotism, among others, are raised.

Chapter 10

BANKRUPTCY: A DEBTOR'S PERSPECTIVE

For the most part, government in America treats the private sector with cautious noninterference. Direct public participation in the economic affairs of an individual or a corporation is limited to a monitoring function through such bodies as the Internal Revenue Service, the Securities and Exchange Commission, and the Federal Trade Commission. Only when things go wrong does the government step in to take action. In the case of financial failure, public policy has dictated that the legal system act as a buffer between debtors and creditors, seeking to maximize both economic efficiency and equity. Thus, bankruptcy laws have been passed to help ensure that resolutions to situations of financial adversity maximize the present and future value of the "estate" and deal fairly with all debtors and creditors.

Bankruptcy is by no means the obvious result of financial trouble. There are many types of financial adversity and many solutions other than resorting to bankruptcy proceedings. An individual or a firm which becomes insolvent, without cash to pay the bills, may simply stall creditors until the situation improves. They may also default on loan payments, negotiate reduced schedules, or liquidate inventory to generate funds. The notion of bankruptcy implies a sense of direct cause. Someone, either debtor or creditor, decides that the individual or firm should not continue in its present financial incarnation. Then, bankruptcy becomes an option for either the debtors or creditors to utilize the law to amend the situation.

For the debtor, bankruptcy provides a chance to bail out from under an impossible burden of debts, to wipe the slate clean and start again. Often it provides an alternative to years of struggling to pay off angry and impatient creditors with an income—personal or corporate—that is insufficient to meet all obligations as they come due. For creditors, bankruptcy provides a chance to get back some portion of their claims on an equitable basis with all other creditors. Often it provides an alternative to continuously postponed payments and the fear of being treated unfairly vis-à-vis other creditors. No one wants to see his debt go unpaid while another creditor is paid in full. Bankruptcy provides a means for creditors to hedge their bets: it gives them a guarantee of partial payment, rather than a gamble for full payment at a cost of entering into the timing uncertainty inherent in the legal system.

This chapter will discuss bankruptcy from the point of view of the individual or corporate debtor. First, it will describe the new Bankruptcy Reform Act of 1978 and the legal jurisdiction for bankruptcy law in the United States today. Then, it will examine bankruptcy in general and three forms of bankruptcy in particular: liquidation, corporation reorganization, and the adjustment of debts of an individual with a regular income. Finally, it will talk about some of the ways debtors can protect themselves before taking this final step and will discuss what actions are prohibited under the new law.

THE NEW LAW

Until a few years ago, the prevailing code for bankruptcy law in the United States was the Bankruptcy Act of 1898, also known as the Nelson Act. While this act was amended some 50 times, including a major overhaul under the Chandler Act of 1938, it remained in effect for 80 years until Congress passed the Bankruptcy Reform Act of 1978. The new code, Public Law 95–958, has eight odd-numbered substantive chapters. The first three are adminstrative rules which are relevant to *all* bankruptcy proceedings, and the remainder deal with specific types of bankruptcy. Note that the election of any type of bankruptcy triggers an automatic stop of all lawsuits against the company:

— Chapter 1 sets forth general definitions and rules.
— Chapter 3 deals with case administration.
— Chapter 5 deals with such issues as creditors' claims, debtors' duties and advantages, exemptions, and trustees' powers.
— Chapter 7 deals with liquidations.
— Chapter 9 deals with municipal debts.

— Chapter 11 deals with reorganizations for businesses including railroads.
— Chapter 13 deals with debts of a person with a regular income.
— Chapter 15 contains the necessary provisions to set up a new United States Trustee Pilot Program.

Under the new act, bankruptcy courts are established as adjuncts of each U.S. District Court. Bankruptcy judges are appointed by the president, with the advice and consent of the Senate. This situation prevailed until early 1983 when the Supreme Court determined that bankruptcy judges were members of the judicial branch of the government just like all other judges and, as such, had to be given certain guarantees of independence, including lifetime tenure. Congress, on the other hand, had hoped to avoid creating an entire new set of Article 3 judges in addition to the existing district court structure. This dilemma as of May 1983 is unresolved. It is of high priority on the legislative agenda for both Judiciary Committees. Bankruptcy courts can conduct business under a special extension granted by the Supreme Court. Regardless of how this matter is resolved it is not expected to affect the substance of the Bankruptcy Reform Act.

A final note: not all companies can elect to go bankrupt. Banks, including savings and loans, insurance companies, and all foreign companies are prohibited from doing so.

GETTING INTO TROUBLE

For an individual, the path to bankruptcy is often clearly discernible in retrospect; through hindsight, it is easy to see where a person made a bad decision, when they became overextended, how they misjudged their financial situation . There are two ways individuals accumulate sufficient unpaid debts to contemplate bankruptcy. The first is painfully simple: they purchase more on credit than they can afford to buy. This happens because they underestimate the amount of money they will have to pay for their accumulated credit purchases or because they overestimate the amount of income they will earn. Thus, the incidence of individual bankruptcies has increased with rises of easy consumer credit and in periods of unemployment, when people may lose their jobs unexpectedly or be unable to find new work if they are laid off. The second road to individual bankruptcy is more complex. It occurs when an individual's personal finances are in order, but he or she chooses to act as guarantor for a business or for another individual whose situation may not be as fortunate. When an individual agrees to accept the burden of another's debts (either for an individual or a corporation), then that person becomes legally responsible if the first entity defaults on payments. Sometimes, this additional financial requirement is more than the individual's personal budget can accommodate. Bankruptcy then becomes a way of eliminating these added debts, leaving the individual free to begin again.

For corporations, the path to bankruptcy is considerably more complicated. Ray Barrickman outlines 20 potential causes of business failure: excessive competition, the general business cycle, changes in public demand, governmental acts, adverse acts of labor, acts of God, poor overall management, unwise promotion, unwise expansion, inefficient selling, overextension of inventories, poor financial management, excessive fixed charges, excessive funded debt, excessive floating debt, overextension of credit, unwise dividend policies, and inadequate maintenance and depreciation.[1]

John Argenti, studying corporate failures in Great Britain, posits a chain of events, beginning with poor management, which usually precipitates a firm's slide into bankruptcy:

> If the management of a company is poor then two things will be neglected: the system of accountancy information will be deficient and the company will not respond to change. (Some companies, even well-managed ones, may be damaged because powerful constraints prevent the managers making the responses they wish to make.) Poor managers will also make at least one of three other mistakes: they will overtrade; or they will launch a big project that goes wrong; or they will allow the company's gearing [financial leverage] to rise so that even normal business hazards become constant threats. These are the chief causes, neither fraud nor bad luck deserve more than a passing mention. The following symptoms will appear: certain financial ratios will deteriorate but, as soon as they do, the managers will start creative accounting which reduces the predictive value of these ratios and so lends greater importance to nonfinancial symptoms. Finally the company enters a characteristic period in its last few months.[2]

These are not all root causes of bankruptcy, of course. The direct catalyst for bankruptcy proceedings is a person or company's inability to pay debts on time. When this situation occurs, the individual or company may begin voluntary bankruptcy proceedings or their creditors may try to force them into involuntary bankruptcy. Any person, partnership, or corporation can file for voluntary relief under the bankruptcy code. Even solvent entities can file for bankruptcy as long as there is no intent to defraud.

For example, Manville Corporation filed for bankruptcy in late 1982, even though the company had a book net worth of nearly $1.2 billion. The manufacturer was seeking protection from an anticipated 32,000 lawsuits relating to the injury or death of workers who used Manville's asbes-

---

[1]Ray E. Barrickman, *Business Failure, Causes, Remedies, and Cures* (Washington, D.C.: University Press of America, 1979), p. 28.

[2]John Argenti, *Corporate Collapse: The Causes and Symptoms* (London: McGraw-Hill, 1976), p. 108.

tos products. Assuming an average settlement of $40,000 per lawsuit, Manville calculated that it could not afford to stay in business and sought bankruptcy relief from these "creditors."

Sometimes, the resort to bankruptcy is motivated more by strategic than financial issues. Wilson Foods, a producer of meat and food products, recently sought Chapter 11 protection in order to force union officials to reduce labor wages. Wilson's chairman announced publicly that the firm did not intend to close any of its plants or lay off any workers. He further stated that Wilson had sufficient cash, receivables, and available credit to meet its short-term obligations. The bankrupt can apply to the court to nullify a union contract that would otherwise have lasted until 1985. The court must decide such cases based upon what is in the best interest of the estate. Thus, the move allowed Wilson to put in place sharply reduced hourly wages. A similar case—Bildisco—has been decided by the Supreme Court. The outcome of this case, involving the issue of whether or not bankruptcy allows a firm to change contract terms with union employees, determined that firms may use Chapter 11 protection in this manner. Unions are currently lobbying for congressional relief from this decision.

In order to seek relief from their debts, a person or corporation must file in the office of the Clerk of the United States District Court in which the domicile, residence, principal place of business, or principal assets of the entity have been located for the preceding 180 days. The filing fee is $60 for parties commencing a bankruptcy case under Chapter 7 (liquidation) or Chapter 13 (adjustment of debts for an individual with regular income). The filing fee for businesses seeking relief under Chapter 11 (business reorganizations) is $200; railroads must pay a filing fee of $500. *A person or corporation can only file for bankruptcy protection once every six years.*

In certain situations, creditors can force debtors to go bankrupt. An involuntary bankruptcy case can be commenced by:

— Three or more creditors whose aggregated claims amount to more than $5,000 over the value of any assets securing those claims; or
— One or more such creditors if there are less than 12 claim holders; or
— Fewer than all the general partners in a limited partnerhsip.

Creditors do not have to prove that the debtor is unable to pay his or her bills; mere failure to pay on time, regardless of ability to pay, is sufficient grounds for creditors to seek involuntary bankruptcy. However, in an involuntary bankruptcy proceeding, the court can require petitioners to post a bond to cover the debtor's costs if the court finds in the debtor's favor. Furthermore, if the creditors are found to have petitioned in bad faith, the court may award the debtor any damages caused by the proceedings, including punitive compensation. In practice, involuntary bankruptcy is uncommon. For the year ending June 30, 1979, only 926 involuntary bankuptcy cases were filed out of a total of 226,476 cases.[3]

CHOOSING YOUR POISON: WHICH CHAPTER?

There are three distinct chapters of the bankruptcy code which can shape the outcome of the bankruptcy proceedings: Chapter 7 (liquidation), Chapter 11 (reorganization), and Chapter 13 (adjustment of an individual's debts).

In theory, bankruptcy procedures can be concluded very quickly. In practice, however, they are often long, drawn-out affairs. Corporate reorganizations, in particular, can take many years to reach completion. Speaking before the 94th Congress, Representative Elizabeth Holtzman noted that "it is reported that the average corporate reorganization case in the Seventh District of New York takes eight years to resolve."[4]

In a Chapter 7 bankruptcy the assets of the individual or corporation are liquidated and distributed to creditors. In a Chapter 11 or Chapter 13 bankruptcy the debtors keep their assets with some arrangement to pay off their debts over time. Since the outcomes of these types of bankruptcy are radically different, affecting the form of the assets which the debtor keeps as well as the timing and amount of payments which the creditors receive, both groups have some ability to influence the choice of prevailing chapters.

When the creditor files for an involuntary bankruptcy case under Chapter 7 or 11, the debtor can convert the case to a bankruptcy under any of the other chapters. When a debtor files for voluntary bankruptcy under any chapter, the creditors can request that the trustee convert the case to a Chapter 7 or a Chapter 11 bankruptcy. Only a Chapter 13 bankruptcy cannot be commenced without the debtor's consent. Before choosing a chapter for bankruptcy, debtors should carefully consider whether they would prefer to liquidate their assets or continue their business with personal finances, attempting with reorganization or adjustment to pay off their debts over time.

Chapter 7: Liquidation

Chapter 7 of the Bankruptcy Act provides for either voluntary or involuntary liquidation of the assets of the debtor or distribution to the credi-

---

[3]Table of Bankruptcy Statistics with reference to bankruptcy cases commenced and terminated in the United States District Courts during the period July 1, 1978 through June 30, 1979. Administrative Office of the United States Courts.

[4]House Report #686, p. 56.

tors. When a petition is filed under Chapter 7 it constitutes an Order for Relief. The debtor now has a legal obligation to:

1. File a list of creditors, assets and liabilities, and a statement of financial affairs.
2. Cooperate with the trustee appointed to the case.
3. Give the trustee all property of the estate and all records relating to the property.
4. Appear at any hearing dealing with a discharge.
5. Attend all meetings of creditors.

As soon as possible after the Order for Relief, an interim trustee will be appointed. If creditors holding at least 30 percent of the specified claims request one, an election will be held to choose one person to serve as trustee in the case. This can be the debtor serving as trustee while debtor in possession. If no trustee is elected in this manner, the interim trustee will continue to serve. The duties of the trustee include:

1. Reducing the property of the debtor's estate to cash and closing up the estate as expeditiously as possible.
2. Accounting for all property received.
3. Investigating the financial affairs of the debtor and examining all claims for validity.
4. Providing information about the estate to any interested party, furnishing reports on the debtor's business if it is authorized to be operated, and filing a final report of the disposition of the estate with the court.

Portions of the debtor's estate will be exempt from liquidation; that is, they may not be distributed to the creditors. In many states, the debtor can choose between the federal exemptions or the relevant state exemptions. However, states can require their residents to adhere to the state exemptions; Florida and Virginia have passed such laws, and South Carolina, Delaware and Ohio are considering similar statutes. Under the current federal exemptions, a debtor gets to keep:

1. The debtor's interest, not to exceed $7,500, in the debtor's (or a dependent's) residence; in a cooperative that owns property used by the debtor (or a dependent) as a residence; and in a burial plot for the debtor or a dependent.
2. The debtor's interest, not to exceed $1,200, in a motor vehicle.
3. The debtor's interest, not to exceed $200 in value for any particular item, in household furnishings, clothing, appliances, books, animals, crops, or musical instruments, that are kept for the personal, family, or household use of the debtor or a dependent.
4. The debtor's interest, not to exceed $500, in jewelry held for personal, family, or household use of the debtor or a dependent.

5. The debtor's interest, not to exceed $400, in any property in addition to Item 1 exemptions.
6. The debtor's interest, not to exceed $750, in any implements, professional books, or tools of the trade of the debtor or a dependent.
7. Any insurance contract which is not mature other than a credit contract.
8. The debtor's interest, not to exceed $4,000, in any accrued dividends or interest or loan value or any nonmature life insurance contract under which the debtor or a dependent is insured.
9. Prescribed health aids for the debtor or a dependent.
10. The debtor's right to receive social security benefits, unemployment compensation benefits, local public assistance benefits, veterans' benefits, and illness or disability benefits.
11. The debtor's right to receive alimony, support, or separate maintenance.
12. The debtor's right to receive a payment, stock bonus, pension, profit sharing annuity, or similar plan on account of illness, disability, debt, age, or want of service.
13. The debtor's right to receive an award under a crime victim's reparation law; a payment on account of a wrongful death of an individual of whom the debtor was a dependent; a payment under a life insurance contract that insured the life of an individual of whom the debtor was a dependent; a payment not to exceed $7,500 on account of personal bodily injury, not including pain and suffering or compensation for actual pecuniary loss, of the debtor or an individual of whom the debtor is a dependent; or a payment in compensation of loss of future earnings of the debtor or an individual of whom the debtor is or was a dependent.

The rest of the debtor's estate is distributed first to secured creditors and then to priority claimants. These claims include, in order: administrative expenses and filing fees assessed against the debtor's estate; certain unsecured claims arising before the appointment of a trustee in involuntary cases; wages, salaries or commissions, including vacation, severance, and sick leave pay to the extent of $2,000 per individual earned within 90 days of the date of filing or the date of cessation of business, whichever occurred first; contributions to employee benefit plans up to $2,000 per employee earned within 180 days; claims of individuals, up to $900 each, arising from the deposit of money in connection with purchases of property or services that are not delivered; claims of governmental units of taxes and custom duties.

Next come the general unsecured creditors and the general unsecured creditors who filed late claims. Punitive penalties are next in distribution, followed by claims for interest accruing during the bankruptcy case. In-

Distribution of Assets in Cases Closed in 1977

	Payment	Percent of Total
Paid priority creditors	$ 27,799,506	12.1
Paid secured creditors	77,479,621	33.8
Paid unsecured creditors	61,109,352	26.6
Other payments	10,612,376	4.6
All administrative expenses	52,534,678	22.9
Total distribution	$229,535,533	100.0

Source: Table of Bankruptcy Statistics with reference to bankruptcy cases commenced and terminated in the United States District Courts during the period July 1, 1976 though June 30, 1977. Administrative Office of the United States Courts.

terest is paid at the legal rate on the date the petition was filed. If there is any surplus after these six classes are paid, it goes to the debtor. If there aren't enough funds to pay a class in full, claims within the class are paid pro rata. The table above shows how assets are distributed in cases closed during 1977. It is interesting to note that fully 22.9 percent of the assets in bankruptcy cases were used to pay administrative expenses. (Note: These figures were the results of bankruptcies under the Bankruptcy Act, *not* the current code.)

When the debtor is an individual, the court will usually grant *discharge*. This means the debtor is discharged from all past debts except certain debts arising from alimony, child support, and taxes, or debts that were not listed on the debtor's financial statements when bankruptcy was filed.

Chapter 11: Reorganization

The purpose of Chapter 11 of the new Bankruptcy Code is to provide a mechanism of reorganizing a firm's finances so it can continue to operate, pay its creditors, provide jobs, and produce a return to its investors. Usually debtors and creditors will opt for this form of bankruptcy if they think a business or estate has more value as a going concern than as a pile of liquidated assets. The objective of the reorganization is to develop a plan which determines how much creditors will be paid and in what form the business will continue. Any individual, partnership, or corporation which can file for liquidation under Chapter 7 can file for reorganization under Chapter 11, except stockbrokers and commodity brokers. Furthermore, railroads can proceed under Chapter 11, while they are prohibited from seeking liquidation.

Like a Chapter 7 case, a reorganization can be either voluntary or involuntary. After the entry for an Order for Relief, the creditors and debtor must meet within 30 days to discuss the organization of the business. Under the new Bankruptcy Code, the court may not attend a creditor's meeting. Rather, the interim trustee or the U.S. trustee will preside. This follows from the new code's attempt to correct previous problems caused by having bankruptcy judges serve as both judge and administrator in bankruptcy cases.

After the Order for Relief, the court will appoint a committee of general unsecured creditors. This committee is usually comprised of those creditors holding the seven largest claims; however the court has great latitude in composing the committee to make it representative of the different kinds of interests in the case. This committee is primarily responsible for formulating a plan for the business and collecting and filing with the court acceptances of the plan. The debtor keeps possession of the business unless any of the creditors can show the debtor is guilty of fraud, dishonesty, incompetence, or gross mismanagement, or otherwise proves such an arrangement is not in the interests of the creditors. If the court upholds that either of these conditions exists, a trustee will be appointed. Unlike a Chapter 7 trustee, a Chapter 11 trustee is not elected and cannot be a creditor or an equity holder of the debtor or the debtor's business. The duties of a Chapter 11 trustee include being accountable for all of the information and records necessary to formulate the reorganization plan and filing the plan with the court or recommending conversion to a Chapter 7 or a Chapter 13 case or dismissing the case altogether.

If a trustee is not appointed, the debtor possesses these powers. No court order is necessary for the debtor to continue to run the firm; rather, the business is to remain in operation unless the court orders otherwise.

The debtor has 120 days to file the reorganization plan and 60 more days to obtain acceptances. The plan must designate the various classes of creditors and show how they will be treated. The plan can be a liquidation. Thus, a business could be liquidated under Chapter 11 rather than Chapter 7. The plan must be accepted by half of the creditors in number who are affected by the plan and two thirds of the creditors in dollar amount. Creditors must vote to accept or reject the plan, and the plan must obtain the endorsement of a simple majority of those who vote. If the court confirms a reorganization plan, the debtor is discharged from any past debts except as they are handled under the new plan.

Chapter 13: Adjustment of Debts of an Individual with Regular Income

Chapter 13 of the new Bankruptcy Code covers individuals with regular income whose unsecured debts are less than $100,000 and whose secured debts are less than $350,000. This includes individuals who own or operate businesses. It does not include partnerships or corporations. There cannot be an involuntary Chapter 13 bankruptcy case.

The purpose of Chapter 13 is to allow an individual to pay off debts with future earnings while the court protects him or her from harassment by creditors. Furthermore, it allows the debtor to continue to own and operate a business while Chapter 13 is pending. A plan under Chapter 13 can be an extension—creditors paid in full—or a composition—creditors paid in part—and is payable over three years, with a two-year extension allowed for cause.

In a Chapter 13 case the property of the estate includes property and earnings acquired after the commencement of the case but before it is closed. The court will appoint a Chapter 13 trustee to administer the case but not to take possession of the estate.

Chapter 13 has several major advantages for the debtor:

1. Once it is filed, all of the debtor's property and future income are under the court's jurisdiction. An automatic stay order is issued against litigation and collection efforts.
2. Unlike Chapter 7, the trustee does not take possession of the debtor's property. The debtor can increase his or her estate while on the plan.
3. Chapter 13 can help preserve the debtor's credit. Also, the six-year ban on filing for bankruptcy can be avoided in an extension plan and some compensation plans.
4. Since only the debtor can file a plan, there are no competing proposals.
5. The court can still convert a Chapter 13 case to a Chapter 11 case or a Chapter 7 case if it determines it is in the best interests of the creditors or the estate.

The court will hold a confirmation hearing on the plan. Secured creditors can stop confirmation if one of the following is violated: (a) they keep the lien securing their claims or (b) they receive the property securing their claims. Unsecured creditors have no voice in the confirmation process. The court will grant the debtor a discharge after all payments under the plans are completed.

POWERS OF TRUSTEE

In addition to the responsibilities enumerated in Chapters 7, 11, and 13, the trustee in a bankruptcy case has a great deal of power which can determine how assets are allocated and debt restructured. Note that in some instances, the debtor himself (debtor-in-possession) is functioning as the trustee. Chapters 3 and 5 of the Bankruptcy Code set forth such powers as the ability to employ professionals to help carry out the duties of trustee; the power to use, sell, or lease property; the power to obtain credits secured by priority claims and new liens; the power to reject or assume contracts and unexpired leases; and the power to avoid preferences and fraudulent transfers, known as the avoiding powers. These powers can change the status of certain classes of creditors, depending on how they are applied. For instance, by rejecting an unexpired lease, the trustee can convert a long-term leaseholder into just another unsecured creditor. If a trustee is not appointed, then the debtor in possession of the estate assumes these powers.

NEGOTIATIONS AND SETTLEMENTS

While they may feel persecuted and helpless, debtors actually have a great deal of power to negotiate with their creditors for arrangements that will leave the firm intact, either before or after bankruptcy is declared. This power stems from several sources: the incentive for all creditors to reach a speedy and workable solution to the debtor's financial problems; the differing interests of various classes of creditors; and the ultimate protection of the bankruptcy laws.

A debtor in serious financial shape may find he or she has a lot of leverage with creditors who fear the recourse of bankruptcy. These creditors may be willing to undertake voluntary arrangements to restructure loans, postpone payments, relinquish lease obligations, or ignore accrued interest, as a way of helping the debtor avoid bankruptcy. Creditors have several motivations for such voluntary arrangements. If the debtor is threatening to seek bankruptcy relief under Chapter 7, the creditors might determine they have a better long-run chance of repayment if the firm continues to exist than if it is dissolved and the assets are sold at low liquidation values. Creditors might also fear the high administrative and legal costs of bankruptcy proceedings, particularly in a complicated case. These costs might be incurred by the creditors directly or they might be incurred by the debtor's estate, thus reducing the amount of money for distribution to creditors. When Itel Corp., the computer leasing company, filed for bankruptcy in January 1981, it took two years for the company to be reorganized under Chapter 11. The first four months of administrative and legal expenses cost the estate $6.7 million. Creditors might also prefer a voluntary arrangement because it avoids the adverse publicity of a liquidation; they want the prospect of future business with the debtor; or such an arrangement appears faster than a court-supervised settlement. Sometimes creditors who want a voluntary arrangement will pay off the debtor's liabilities to other creditors just to avoid legal proceedings.

Debtors also derive power from the differing interests of creditors. As noted above, a creditor for whom speed of settlement is more important than full payment might negotiate with another creditor whose interest lies in full payment rather than a quick solution. In such an instance, both groups of creditors can be satisfied if the first pays the second's claims in order to expedite a settlement. Trade creditors and money creditors might have varying interests too, with trade creditors preferring a settlement that leaves the firm intact to do business in the future, and money creditors preferring a liquidation that provides as much cash as possible. Debtors can use this dichotomy to their advantage, using available cash to pay off money creditors while asking trade creditors to forbear in the hope of putting the firm back on solid financial ground rather than driving it into bankruptcy.

Of course, creditors do not have to be conciliatory. In 1978, Food Fair, Inc., ran into cash shortages, and its suppliers refused to extend credit beyond their normal terms. Angered by what they perceived as preferential treatment to suppliers with family connections to Food Fair's management, the supermarket's other suppliers refused to extend trade credit terms, even after the company significantly reduced its outstanding obligations. The firm was forced to seek bankrutpcy protection under Chapter 11.

In his book, *Corporations in Crisis*, Philip Nelson notes that the measures available to debtors and creditors short of filing for bankruptcy can lead to economic inefficiencies on the macro level:

> Focusing for the moment on the triggering decision, it appears that, because bankruptcy is only triggered when economic actors perceive that bankruptcy promotes their interests, social losses may easily accumulate as a firm struggles on outside the court's protection. In most sample cases, no economic actor had the incentive and the knowledge to trigger bankruptcy when it was needed. Executive preference for continued salaries, the distaste for the stigma of bankruptcy, inadequate information flows, and ignorance of the advantages offered by bankruptcy combine to encourage delays. Only at the few firms where the controlling executives associated relatively little stigma with bankruptcy and understood its advantages was bankruptcy triggered promptly. As a result, bankruptcy often comes after the resources of the firm are largely expended.

Despite this point of view, the debtor in each individual case certainly has the right and considerable power to cut the best possible deal.

Debtors also derive power within the framework of formal bankruptcy proceedings. Removed from a position of turmoil and harassment, where every unpaid creditor can hound the individual or corporation for immediate payment, the debtor who has filed for bankruptcy is suddenly in a position to bargain with creditors. Further, the automatic stay against all lawsuits which is provided by the bankruptcy law is an additional incentive for creditors to work out an acceptable plan. As with settlements that occur short of the bankruptcy proceeding, the debtor's leverage lies in the creditor's wish for a speedy, efficient plan which maximizes the wealth of the debtor for distribution or future payment. If the creditors retain some faith in the firm, there is usually a strong incentive to seek Chapter 11 relief. The debtor in this position can often negotiate a deal that will get the firm back on its feet. When Itel Corp. filed for bankruptcy, the firm received four 60-day extensions from the Bankruptcy Court to work out a reorganization package that would be acceptable to creditors. In the final deal, Itel's Eurobond holders were allowed $110 million of claims, although that class of creditors only had $91 million in principal and accrued interest outstanding when Itel filed for reorgnization.

The distribution to Eurobond holders per $10,000 of claim was estimated by Itel's reorganization plan as follows:

Security	Face Amount	Market Value
Cash	$3,690	$3,690
14% secured notes	2,035	1,689–1,780
10% notes	1,032	443– 501
New preferred stock	11.5 shares	259– 305
New common stock	124.3 shares	186– 311

Itel said one of the main reasons for increasing the amount of these creditors' claims was to avoid possible delays in the reorganization plan from pending litigation involving the Eurobonds.

The Bankruptcy Code was not intended to shift the balance of power away from creditors; it was designed to give both debtors and creditors motivation for seeking a solution that will maximize the settlement for both parties.

DEBTOR'S OPTIONS

While the new Bankruptcy Code deals generously with debtors, providing a chance to discharge debts and begin again, no debtor wants to be thrown into bankruptcy proceedings against his or her will. There are several steps a debtor can take to insure against involuntary bankruptcy. These include being sure that the number of creditors exceeds 12 and that no 3 creditors' claims amount to more than $5,000. Sometimes, this could mean paying off some creditors in full while not paying others all that they are due. If there are more than 12 creditors in a case, 1 or 2 claimants cannot force an individual or a corporation into involuntary bankruptcy.

There are many steps a debtor can take to maximize the amount of exempt assets that can be retained in a bankruptcy case. In contemplating bankruptcy, the debtor should examine exemptions closely, and arrange his or her affairs in such a way as to give the best possible start following declaration. These measures should not be considered cheating or violating the law. The regulations were set to give debtors the best possible chance of regaining financial stability, while treating all creditors fairly.

There are also many actions a debtor *cannot* take under the law. Besides the obvious violation of hiding assets or hiding liabilities, the most important prohibiton placed on debtors is that of preferential treatment. Once a debtor has filed for bankruptcy, the trustee has the power to disallow any payment to a creditor which enables that creditor to receive more than others in the same class. A preferential payment is one made 90 days prior to the bankruptcy. If the creditor was an insider, this limit extends to one year if the insider has cause to believe the debtor was insolvent. This provision ensures the bankruptcy policy of equality of distribution among creditors. Any creditor who manages to extort a larger share than others of the same class prior to the bankruptcy is forced to return it to the general pot for fair allocation. This provision also limits the debtor's ability to play one creditor off against others in an attempt to avoid bankruptcy, since creditors know such settlements could be disallowed if bankruptcy is declared within three months.

There are many avenues available for the savvy debtor to pursue, either before filing for bankruptcy or after such proceedings have been initiated. Debtors in financial trouble would be wise to seek competent legal counsel early so as to carve the best path out of their predicament.

REFERENCES

Argenti, John. *Corporate Collapse: The Causes and Symptoms*. London: McGraw-Hill, 1976.

"Asbestosis: Manville Seeks Chapter 11," *Fortune*. September 20, 1982.

"Bankruptcy," Harvard Business School 9–376–221, prepared by Laurence H. Stone, copyright 1976.

Bankruptcy Reform. Washington, D.C.: American Enterprise Institute for Public Policy Research, 1978.

Barrickman, Ray E. *Business Failure: Causes, Remedies, and Cures*. Washington, D.C.: University Press of America, 1979.

Bluestein, Paul. "A $2.5 Billion Tale of Woe." *Forbes*. October 30, 1978, p. 51.

"A Brief Note on Arrangements, Bankruptcy, and Reorganization in Bankruptcy," Harvard Business School 9–272–148, Rev. 7/75, written by Jasper H. Arnold, Research Assistant, under the supervision of Associate Professor Michael L. Tennican.

Disclosure Statement for Itel Corporation's Amended Plan of Reorganization, Case No. 3–81–00111, December 8, 1982.

Drinkhall, Jim. "Fees Charged by Itel's Overseers Suggest Bankruptcy Can Be Enriching Experience." *The Wall Street Journal*. June 5, 1981, p. 27.

"Food Fair Inc. Seeks Protection Under Chapter 11," *The Wall Street Journal*. October 3, 1978, p. 2.

"Itel Corp. Plans to Amend Plan for Reorganization," *The Wall Street Journal*. January 20, 1982, p. 33.

"Itel Corp. Receives More Time to Submit Reorganization Plan," *The Wall Street Journal*. November 16, 1981, p. 23.

"Itel Files Petition for Protection of Chapter 11." *The Wall Street Journal*. January 20, 1981, p. 4.

"Manville's Costs Could Exceed $5 Billion in Asbestos Suits, Study it Ordered Shows," *The Wall Street Journal*. September 15, 1982, p. 7.

Nelson, Philip B. *Corporations in Crisis: Behavioral Observations for Bankrupt Policy*. New York: Praeger Publishers, 1981.

Quittner, Arnold M. *Current Developments in Bankruptcy and Reorganization*. Practicing Law Institute, 1980.

Schnepper, Jeff A. *The New Bankruptcy Law: A Professional's Handbook*. New York: Addison-Wesley Publishing, 1981.

Table of Bankruptcy Statistics with reference to bankruptcy cases commenced and terminated in the United States District Courts during the period July 1, 1978 through June 30, 1979. Administrative Office of the United States Courts. See also July 1, 1976 through June 30, 1977.

"Unpaid Bills: Itel Goes Bust." *Fortune*, February 23, 1981, p. 19.

"Wilson Foods Seeks Chapter 11 Protection Citing Labor Costs, Cut Wages Up to 50%." *The Wall Street Journal*, April 24, 1983, p. 16.

Chapter 11

SECURITIES LAW AND PUBLIC OFFERINGS

In "Securities Law and Private Financing," we looked at the process and laws which affect private financings. In this piece, we will look at similar issues as they relate to public offerings.

WHY "GO PUBLIC?"

For many companies, the decision whether or not to become a public company is a difficult one. For some, the "glamour and prestige" of becoming a public company are the deciding factors. For others, the scrutiny and lack of privacy that go along with being publicly held clearly outweigh the advantages.

The Advantages

There are some significant advantages that go along with being a public company. They include:

— A Vast Continuing Source of Capital: The public equity markets do represent a vast pool of capital. A healthy, growing firm can often tap this source more cheaply than other private sources of equity. And, as the company continues to grow, the public equity market will be available as long as investors have confidence in the company's prospects.

— Liquidity: A public market for the company's securities makes them far more liquid. The company can give employees stock or options as an incentive to lure talented individuals. And the principals of the firm can (subject to certain SEC regulations) sell their stock as they desire.
— Wealth Creation: Taking a company public establishes its value in the market. In addition, through a "secondary offering" of securities, the principals can often sell a portion of their interest at the time of the initial public offering. This creates wealth for both the founders and the financial backers—such as venture capital firms—who invested in the business.
— Glamour and Prestige: For many individuals, "taking their company public" is an important goal. It certainly is one measure of success, as a certain minimum size is generally required in order to take a firm public. Being a public concern may also enhance the company's image with customers, suppliers, and employees.

For some entrepreneurs, these advantages are outweighed by the disadvantages of being a public concern.

The Disadvantages

The disadvantages include:

— Cost: Going public is expensive; estimates run from $100,000 to over $300,000 for an "average" public offering. In addition, there is an underwriter's commission of 7–10 percent, which goes to compensate the investment bank for selling the securities. Finally, there is an annual expense associated with the added accounting and record-keeping required for a public company.
— Public Scrutiny: Each quarter, a public company must file, and make available to the public, its financial statements, as well as certain information about stockholders, customers, business plans, and officers. A company might prefer that its suppliers, customers, and competitors not know how profitable it is, or be aware of some aspect of its business. Finally, certain business practices, such as officers' salaries and business expenses, also come under public scrutiny.
— Pressures on Management: Being a public concern also puts certain pressures on top management. The stock market likes to see constant earnings growth, and the faster the better. There has been a great deal of publicity lately that this "short-term earnings focus" is the cause of serious longer term competitive problems for many American industries. Finally, management must spend a good deal of time dealing with the financial community, keeping bankers and analysts up to date and interested in the stock.

— Loss of Independence: As a sole owner or small group of principals, management could feel securely in control. But public ownership brings with it a larger constituency. Managers must now manage the company for the good of all the shareholders. Previously borderline "business expenses" may now be both illegal *and unethical*. In addition, there is always the possibility that some outside group may actually try to take over the company. As a public concern, management is far more vulnerable.

These disadvantages are accentuated by the close relationship which usually exists between ownership and management in the entrepreneurial concern. In large public companies, these "disadvantages" have been accepted as a way of life by a management team which typically controls very little of the stock. In entrepreneurial firms, where the founder(s) may still hold a majority of the shares, the distinction between management and ownership may easily blur. This can lead to management which manages for itself rather than for the entire group of stockholders. While this can happen in large companies, minority shareholders in small firms have less chance of successfully combating this practice.

The Decision

The decision to go public is an important one, and should be made with the counsel of experienced accountants, lawyers, and bankers. Remember, though, that these people have their own stakes: the investment banker stands to gain a good deal on the sale of the company's securities; a local accountant often loses out to a "Big 8" firm when a company goes public and seeks an accounting firm with a national reputation.

In general, it does seem that many entrepreneurs overestimate some of the benefits of being a public company. Liquidity, for instance, is often seen as a major advantage. But it is a very difficult task indeed for a president to explain at an analysts' meeting why he "dumped" some of his holdings in the market.

Clearly, the need for equity capital must be at the heart of the firm's decision to go public. And, before wandering down this path, the firm would be well-advised to consider its options, such as debt or a private placement of equity.

SELECTING AN UNDERWRITER

Once a company has made a decision to seriously consider going public, it is time to choose an underwriter. Underwriters, or investment bankers, are required both to sell the securities and to lead the company through this complex process.

Choosing an Underwriter

The process of selecting an underwriter is not easy. Many investment banks will be anxious to serve the company and will make convincing arguments about why their firms are well suited to execute the company's public offering. When choosing a firm, the following criteria are important.

— Reputation: The underwriter's name will appear at the bottom of the prospectus, often in letters as large as the company's name. The underwriter's reputation will affect its ability to sell the stock both to other investment banks and to institutional and retail customers.
— Distributions: Investment banks have certain strengths and weaknesses in terms of their ability to distribute the stock. Some have a strong institutional network selling to large pension funds and money managers. Others sell primarily to retail accounts—private investors.

  It is often desirable to have a mix of stockholders. Institutions have deep pockets, but can be unfaithful, deserting and selling a stock at the first sign of bad news. Retail accounts tend to be more stable but are not as big a force in the stock market.
— After-Market Support: It is important that a bank support a company after the public offering. This support includes:
  • Research—to sustain interest in the stock on the part of investors.
  • Market-making—committing capital to buying and selling the stock, to provide investors with liquidity.
  • Financial advice—bankers can provide valuable advice on the subject of dividends, new financing or mergers and acquisitions.

Recently, underwriters have become more competitive, and investment banking is not the "gentlemanly business" it was considered to be years ago. The entrepreneur would be wise to consider and negotiate with a variety of firms.

What About Stock Price?

Note that we have not mentioned price as one of the criteria. Clearly, you would prefer to sell stock in your company to the underwriters who thought it was worth the most in the market. During the negotiation process, underwriters will often "estimate" the price at which the stock will be sold in the public offering.

— First, they make projections of the company's earnings per share.
— Then, they attempt to place a price/earnings multiple on this figure to arrive at a per share value.

  In theory, this approach should work just fine. But, the price earnings multiple is a very subjective judgment, based on an assessment of what multiples "similar" companies are trading at.

The night before the offering, after many months of work and after spending a good deal of money, the market will in all likelihood appear quite different than it did at the time of the initial negotiations. The underwriter may suggest an offering price which is substantially different from the price discussed during negotiations. The company has little choice save to cancel the offering entirely.

This fact is *not* lost on the underwriters.

Other Issues

Once a company has decided to go public and has chosen an underwriter, several other important issues remain.

— Listing: The company must decide where its shares will be listed and traded. The New York and American Stock Exchanges, as well as other exchanges, all have certain requirements which must be met in order for the firm to obtain a listing.

— Amount of primary offering: The firm must decide how much money it wishes to raise.

— Amount of secondary offering: In addition to selling its "own shares"— the *primary offering*—the principals of the firm may sell some of their own stock. This is called a *secondary offering* and the owners of the stock, *not* the company, get to keep the money which is raised from sale of secondary stock.

REGISTERED OFFERINGS

All public offerings must be registered with the SEC under the Securities Act of 1933.

The Registration Process

The registration process for a company which is not yet publicly traded involves the preparation by management of a carefully worded and organized disclosure document called a *registration statement*. This includes a "prospectus" which will be provided to the potential investor. The registration statement is filed with the appropriate securities agency which, for federal registrations, is the SEC. The various items of disclosure which must be discussed in a registration statement are fixed by law. In addition, there must be set forth any other material matter which affects or may affect the company.

The SEC staff reviews the disclosure documents and (unless a special "cursory review" procedure is used) makes detailed comments on the disclosure, and the documents are revised as a result of these comments. If the staff is satisfied with the revisions, the SEC enters an order declaring the registration statement "effective," and sale of the offering may commence. The SEC order in no way constitutes an approval by the SEC of the accuracy of the disclosures or the merits of the offering, and any representation to that effect violates the securities laws. At the time of the effectiveness of the registration statement, the underwriters will usually place a "tombstone" advertisement in the financial press announcing the offering. A copy of the final prospectus must be distributed to persons purchasing company securities of the type sold in the offering for up to 90 days after the effective date, or until the offering is sold or terminated, whichever last occurs. During this period, if any material event affecting the company occurs, it must be disclosed by a sticker "supplement" to the prospectus. The disclosure documents become outdated after approximately nine months from the effective date and may not be used thereafter unless updated by posteffective amendment to the registration statement.

In addition to federal registration, the issuer, in conjunction with the corporate attorney, must carefully review state regulations in each state where securities offerings are to be made. In some states, qualification under state "Blue Sky" statutes requires the company to meet standards other than those of the federal regulations. Failure to fully comply with state regulation in all states where securities are purchased or even offered can have serious consequences.

Cost

Federal registration is expensive and time-consuming. An initial public offering using an underwriter frequently takes four months to accomplish and costs from $100,000 to $300,000, exclusive of underwriting commissions. A typical cost breakdown is as follows: printing $50,000; legal fees $60,000; accounting fees $50,000; and Blue Sky and miscellaneous costs $25,000. (These figures are rough and may vary considerably from offering to offering.) In view of the amount of the fixed costs involved, federal registration of a first offering using an underwriter is generally not feasible unless in excess of $2 million is involved in the financing.

The cost of a public offering depends as much upon whether or not an underwriter is used as upon whether or not federal registration is required. This is true because the agreement between the company and the underwriter usually requires the company's attorneys and accountants to undertake, at the company's expense, detailed and costly verification of the disclosures in the prospectus. Underwriting commissions typically run from 7.5 to 10 percent of the gross amount of the offering in first equity offerings. Because placement of a large amount of securities often involves market price stabilization and other sophisticated and highly regulated techniques, an attempt by a company to place a large amount of securities without a professional underwriter or selling agent usually involves an unacceptable amount of risk. Also, it may be extremely difficult for a large amount of securities to be placed without the assistance of a professional underwriter or selling agent with a number of investor customers that rely upon his/her investment advice.

Underwriters

Underwriters essentially agree to sell the company's securities for a fixed percentage of the underwriting. Underwritings are of two types—"firm commitment" underwritings in which the sale of the entire offering at an established price is guaranteed by the underwriters, and "best efforts" underwritings in which the underwriter uses his best efforts to sell as much as the market will accept of the offering at the offering price. Best efforts underwritings may also include a provision requiring that either all or a minimum amount of the securities must be sold as a condition of any of the securities being sold. The type of underwriting used is generally determined by the size and strength of the company and of the underwriter.

The first step in an underwritten offering is usually the execution of a nonbinding "letter of intent" between the company (or selling stockholder) and the managing underwriter. Although not a legally binding document, the letter of intent is one of the most important documents in the offering, as it establishes the basic terms of the underwriting, usually including the price range—perhaps as a range of multiples of the company's most recent earnings. (If multiples of per share earnings are used, it should be made clear whether the per share figures are to be calculated using the number of outstanding shares *before* or those *after* the offering.) After the letter of intent has been signed, the disclosure documents (including the prospectus) are prepared for filing with the SEC.

From the outset of an underwritten offering, the managing underwriter and the company (and/or selling stockholder) commence subtle negotiation of the price of the offering which usually culminates in the setting of the price on the evening before the offering. During the course of the registration, the company incurs substantial offering expenses which (as both parties well realize) will be to a large extent unrecoverable if the financing is postponed or aborted. In addition to the problems a firm-commitment underwriter has in guaranteeing sale of the entire offering when the price is at a high level, a managing underwriter has an incentive to negotiate a low price for his/her own customers and for those of the members of the underwriting and selling syndicate, with which s/he usually has an established business relationship. (A broker with unhappy customers soon has no customers.) Often this is done by subtly threatening to abandon the deal after the company has expended substantial unrecoverable funds in preparation for the offering and after it has terminated negotiations with competing underwriters. It is thus important for the company, if possible, to require the underwriter to bear his or her own expenses (including those of an attorney) so that any abandonment will result in some loss (although a lesser one) for the underwriter. This arrangement should be set forth in the letter of intent. On the other hand, the offering price should not be set too high or the price of the securities may suffer in the aftermarket, thereby reducing the value of the remaining securities holdings of the principal owners and diminishing the company's ability to raise capital in the future.

Throughout the period of registration, including the prospectus delivery period following the effective date, the company must carefully monitor the public statements of its management, its public relations advisers, and its advertising program to assure that no optimistic disclosures concerning the company's condition or prospects are disseminated to the investing public. If, for example, an article on the company appears in *Forbes* or *Business Week* during registration, it may be deemed to be part of the company's selling effort (to the extent it is based upon information supplied by management) and thus subject to the rigid standards of the securities law. Disclosure during the period preceding the initial filing of the registration statement with the SEC (the "prefiling period") is particularly sensitive, as such disclosure might be considered to be an attempt to precondition the market ("gun-jumping"). Even the information to be contained in an announcement of the filing of the registration statement is regulated by SEC rule. After the effective date, however, certain types of supplementary selling literature may be used if preceded or accompanied by a final prospectus.

The registration statement as initially filed contains a preliminary prospectus with a "red herring" legend printed in red sideways on the cover page. While the SEC staff is reviewing the registration statement and preparing its comments (the "waiting period"), the preliminary prospectus will be used by the underwriter in the formation of its underwriting and selling syndicate. Although the various members of the underwriting and selling syndicate often have an established business relationship with the managing underwriter, a new syndicate is formed for each deal. The preliminary prospectus will be used by syndicate members during the waiting period to solicit "indications of interest" from the investing public. The reception of the investing public to the preliminary prospectus will affect the price of the offering which, as noted above, is usually established immediately prior to the effective date.

As a result of registration with the SEC, a company becomes subject to the periodic reporting requirements of the SEC. In the case of a first public offering, the company must report the actual use of proceeds to the SEC three months after the offering so the SEC can compare this with the disclosures in the prospectus. If there is a discrepancy, the company can expect SEC inquiry.

Offerings registered with the SEC generally must also be registered with the securities administrators of each of the states in which the offering is to be made. A simplified registration by "coordination" with the federal registration is usually allowed under state law. Many states do exempt from registration offerings of securities which will be listed on the New York or American Stock Exchange. If an underwriter or selling agent that is a member of the NASD is used, the terms of the underwriter's or sales agent's compensation must be reviewed by the NASD.

Form S–18

In 1979, the SEC adopted a new form and filing procedure to simplify and expedite initial public offerings for smaller companies. The principal features of this new approach are (a) the filing is made in the local SEC regional office (9 offices around the country) rather than in Washington; (b) audited financial statements are required for only the two most recent years (rather than three fiscal years generally required in other forms); (c) the general disclosures are somewhat simpler and are tailored for less mature companies. The primary advantage of Form S–18 is dealing with the lighter workloads and geographical proximity of the regional offices. These, coupled with the reduced financial statement requirements, can be expected to reduce both the amount of time and the expenses involved in an offering by 25 percent or more.

The use of Form S–18 is limited to offerings (a) not in excess of $7,500,000; (b) by domestic issuers; and (c) which are not insurance companies, mutual funds, or already publicly held companies, or the subsidiary of any such company. Within six months following the offering, the company must report the use of the offering proceeds to the SEC.

Regulation A Offerings

If the financing involves a public offering on behalf of the company of $1.5 million or less, and if the company's management, principal equity owners, and other persons whose securities require registration before resale seek to publicly offer not more than $300,000 as part of that offering (with a maximum of $100,000 for each person), the offering may be made under SEC Regulation A rather than pursuant to full registration. When considering such an offering, an issuer must be aware of several potential obstacles. For example, a company may not issue more than $1.5 million of its securities under Regulation A during any 12-month period, and for purposes of calculating that limitation, any offerings made pursuant to an exemption or in violation of the registration requirements are included. Further, companies that are less than one-year old or which have not had profitable operations during one of their last two fiscal years (and any affiliates of such companies) must include the value of securities issued to insiders and securities issued for noncash consideration when calculating the dollar limitation unless assurances are given that such securities will not be publicly sold within a year, and may not use Regulation A for secondary sales (i.e., shares sold by existing shareholders rather than the company itself). Finally, the exemption is totally unavailable to issuers that have been *inter alia*, convicted of violating the securities laws or subjected to an SEC refusal or stop order, post office fraud order, or injunction within the previous five years, or whose directors, officers, principal security holders, or underwriters have been convicted of violating the securities laws within the previous 10 years or enjoined from violating the same.

Assuming availability of the exemption, the Regulation A offering procedure is similar to that used with Form S–18 and is similarly less complex and faster than normal registration procedures. The principal difference between Form S–18 and the use of Regulation A is that the latter has no requirement for audited financials. A 90-day prospectus delivery period exists for Regulation A offerings. Within six months of the commencement of the offering, the company must report the status of the offering and the use of proceeds to the SEC.

Like fully registered offerings, Regulation A offerings must be registered (usually by "coordination") with the securities administrators for the states in which the offering is to be made. Use of an underwriter that is a member of the NASD requires NASD review.

State-Registered (Intrastate) Offerings (Rule 147)

If a local business seeks local financing exclusively, registration under the federal securities laws is not required. More accurately, if all of the "offerees" and purchasers in the offering are bona fide residents of the state under the laws of which the company is organized (i.e., the state of incorporation, if the company is a corporation), if the company's business is principally conducted and the company's properties principally located in that state, and if the proceeds of the offering are to be used in the state, the issuer may avail itself of exemption under SEC Rule 147. In such instances, the financing may be made pursuant to a long form ("qualification") registration under the state securities laws.

As a matter of practice, exclusive reliance upon the Rule 147 exemption is a somewhat perilous course. In order to satisfy Rule 147, the issuer must meet various technical requirements as to the "residence," some of which are included in Rule 147 and some of which relate to common law standards. At the time of sale, for example, the issuer must obtain from the purchaser a written representation of his or her residence. Yet, there is no provision in the rule which will protect the issuer from a good faith mistake in determining the residence of a purchaser. Moreover, should even a single purchaser resell to a nonresident within nine months of the offering, the exemption will be lost. To prevent this latter problem, certificates evidencing the securities offered under Rule 147 must bear a legend reflecting these transfer restrictions and a "stop transfer" order must be entered.

Rule 147 also provides a means for segregating an intrastate offering from other discrete offerings pursuant to other exemptive provisions of the Act. In order to have Rule 147 available, an issuer must not have sold any similar securities to purchasers outside the state in the prior six months, and may not make any such sales in the subsequent six months. Rule 147 does not require the filing of any documents.

Because registration-by-qualification requirements vary widely from state to state, it is impossible to estimate the costs of a Rule 147 offering. Such costs are generally somewhat less than are those for Regulation A offerings, however. As in the case of other offerings, NASD review is required if a NASD member serves as underwriter or sales agent.

ACQUISITIONS

Like any other securities, securities issued by a company in the acquisition of another company must be registered under federal and state securities laws unless an exemption from registration applies. Most state securities laws provide registration exemptions for acquisitions by statutory merger or stock for assets. Under federal law, however, full registration is required unless either the intrastate or private offering exemption is available. Thus, regardless of the form of the transaction and the number of separate steps it may involve, the company must consider its overall effect and the identity of ultimate recipients of the securities in determining the availability of an exemption.

Under present law, solicitation of the target company's shareholders requesting the execution of proxies to vote on the acquisition is deemed to constitute an offering of the acquirer's securities. If the private or intrastate offering exemptions are unavailable, the acquirer must therefore register. A somewhat simplified registration procedure is available under SEC Form S–14, pursuant to which SEC staff review is less strict than for registration under the more conventional Form S–1. Additionally, in some cases involving acquisitions by very substantial companies, a Form S–15 may be available. Form S–15, like Form S–16, is a simple and streamlined form which relies principally on an issuer's obligation to file periodic reports on its business and operations with the SEC. The prospectus under a Form S–14 registration statement is made up of a proxy statement conforming to SEC rules, to which a cover sheet setting forth the terms of the offering has been added—the combination sometimes being referred to as a "wrap-around" prospectus. Form S–14 may not be used in a stock-for-stock acquisition. As with other offerings, the various state securities laws must also be reviewed.

Securities received by the acquired company's management or principal equity owners as a result of an acquisition are restricted and can be resold only if the resale is registered, exempt, or permitted under Rule 145 (which is similar to Rule 144 but without a holding period or filing requirement). Resales pursuant to a registration statement are particularly hazardous, however, because management may be held personally liable for misstatements in the prospectus concerning the acquiring company as well as any concerning their own company. The risk of liability in this situation is great, as the target company's management rarely has access to information concerning the sometimes unfriendly acquirer.

Acquisitions of equity securities of public companies for either cash or securities is further discussed below in connection with Tender Offers and Takeover Bids. See also "Investment Companies" for regulation under certain circumstances.

DISCLOSURE OF MATERIAL INSIDE INFORMATION

In any purchase or sale of a security, whether public or private, if one of the parties has any nonpublic material inside information that relates to the present or future condition of the company's business or its properties, she or he must disclose it to the person on the opposite side of the transaction or be personally liable under the antifraud provisions of the securities laws for any damages that may result. Similar liability will accrue to any person who aids and abets the misuse of inside information by tipping others or otherwise disseminating that information even if that person does not actually trade. In this regard, both "tippers" and "tippees" are liable under the law.

This simple principle is at the heart of all securities law and yet is perhaps the most abused. The courts' necessarily amorphous definition of materiality is partially responsible for this abuse: any fact which, under the circumstances, would likely have assumed actual significance to a reasonable investor is deemed material. The liabilities can be enormous in scope, and prudent companies and their management should either disclose significant information or, if such information is particularly sensitive, refrain from trading.

One emerging area of securities law deserves special mention because of the magnitude of the exposure involved and the ease in which violations may occur. If any public pronouncement by a public company (whether by press release, report to stockholders, or otherwise) contains a statement concerning the company's condition or prospectus that is erroneous or misleading in a way that is material to an investor, so that the price of the company's securities in the securities markets is affected (either up or down), the company, its management and its principal owners may be personally liable for an ensuing loss to *all* persons who trade in the company's securities to their disadvantage in the open market, regardless of whether or not management, the company's owners, or the company are concurrently trading in the company's securities in the market. Cases decided in this area so far indicate that management must have some ulterior purpose for the misinformation in order to he held liable; however, this purpose need not include any intention to violate the securities laws.

MANIPULATION

The securities laws broadly prohibit use of fraudulent or manipulative devices of any type in the purchase or sale of securities, whether in private transactions or in the securities markets. Specifically, market manipulation of securities prices up or down or at any level (except in connection with a stabilization in a public offering, as to which special rules apply) or falsely creating the appearance of security trading activity, by the use of fictitious orders, wash sales, or other devices, is prohibited. Again, violation can lead to substantial personal as well as company liability.

REGULATION OF PUBLIC COMPANIES

Companies of significant size that have a larger number of security holders, and companies that are listed on a national securities exchange, are regulated under the Securities Exchange Act of 1934. This regulation attaches when the company files a registration statement under the Exchange Act as a result of being listed on a national securities exchange or of having in excess of $1 million in assets and in excess of 500 holders of a class of its equity securities at the end of one of its fiscal years. (Such a registration statement should not be confused with a public offering registration statement under the Securities Act of 1933.) Registration under the Exchange Act submits the company to the periodic reporting, proxy, tender offer, and insider trading provisions of that act. Once registered, the number of equity security holders must drop below 300 before the company may be deregistered.

Periodic Reports

In order to maintain a constant flow of reliable information to the SEC and the financial community, companies registered under the Exchange Act and those that have previously undertaken full registration under the Securities Act, are subject to the periodic reporting requirements of the

SEC. Under these requirements, the company must file with the SEC annual reports (containing audited financial statements) on Form 10–K, quarterly reports on Form 10–Q, and current reports on Form 8–K. These reports are generally available to the public through the SEC.

Proxy Solicitation

To ensure that security holders of companies registered under the Exchange Act are advised of proposals (including the election of directors) to be acted upon at meetings of security holders, such companies must use proxy or information statements that conform to SEC rules. Such proxy statements are reviewed by the SEC staff prior to distribution to security holders. They must be transmitted at least annually and upon each proxy solicitation to the company's voting security holders. The form of the proxy itself is also regulated.

Tender Offers and Takeover Bids

Tender offers to acquire the securities of a company whose securities registered under the Exchange Act (other than offers by a company to repurchase its own shares which are regulated separately) must conform to the SEC tender offer rules. These require the filing of certain information with the target company and the SEC not later than the date the tender is first made. Securities tendered are recoverable by the tenderer within the first 15 days of the commencement of the tender offer and for 10 days following any tender by a competing bidder as well as after 60 days from the initial offer. Acceptance of less than all of the shares during the first 10 days of a tender offer must be on a pro rata basis. Of course, if the tender is being made using securities of the acquiring company rather than cash, they must be registered under the Securities Act prior to the offering.

In order to alert the SEC and the management of a target company to an acquisition of securities that could lead to a change of control, any person acquiring any equity security of an Exchange Act-registered company which results in his or her owning in excess of 5 percent of the outstanding securities of that class must file with the SEC within 10 days after the acquisition. She or he must also transmit to the company certain information concerning the acquiring person, his or her purpose in making the acquisition and the method of financing the acquisition. This requirement applies even if the shares were received as a result of an acquisition in which the acquirer exchanged some of its equity securities in return for securities of the acquired company. If two or more persons who together own in excess of 5 percent of a class of equity securities of an Exchange Act-registered company enter into a mutual arrangement to acquire control of the company, they too must file within 10 days after entering of the arrangement.

If either of the above transactions results in an appointment of directors for the company other than by vote of security holders, there must be transmitted to all security holders, eligible to vote for the election of such directors if elected at a meeting of security holders, at least 10 days prior to the appointment, information equivalent to that contained in a proxy or information statement under the proxy rules.

The securities laws of some states contain tender offer provisions designed to discourage takeover of corporations based in those states or whose principal business and substantial assets are within the state. The federal laws, however, do not purport to discourage tender offers directly but rather seek to insure full disclosure of information concerning such offers.

Insider Reporting and Trading

Management and 10 percent equity security holders are deemed "insiders" of an Exchange Act-registered company and must report their transactions in the company's equity securities to the SEC. The SEC publishes these transactions quarterly.

The insider trading provisions of the Exchange Act contain an arbitrary and absolute six-month trading rule designed to preclude any incentive for insiders to make use of insider information to gain for themselves short-term profits by trading in the company's securities.

If both a purchase and a sale or a sale and purchase of such securities by an insider falls within any six-month period, any security holder of the company may sue on behalf of the company to recover for the company the "profits" thereby obtained. The word "profits" has technical meaning in this context and does not necessarily refer to any benefit obtained by the insider—in fact, the insider may have incurred a net overall loss in a series of such transactions and still be liable to the company for substantial sums. The formula used by the courts in measuring the recovery is to match the highest sale with the lowest purchase in any six-month period, then to match the next highest sale with the next lowest purchase, and so on, so that the largest possible amount of "profits" from any given set of trades is thereby computed. Since theoretical losses incurred are not offset against theoretical profits, the liability to the insider can be substantial even though she or he sustains an overall loss.

That an insider, in fact, is not trading on inside information is no defense to an insider trading suit. In fact, if an insider purchase and sale have both occurred within six months, there is virtually no defense to a timely and properly prosecuted insider trading suit, and the best course of action is usually to pay the "profits" to the company as quickly as possible to minimize the ample legal fees that are usually awarded by the courts to plaintiff's counsel in such actions.

Investment Companies

A company whose principal business is investing or trading in securities is subject to regulation under the Investment Company Act of 1940, unless it has not made and is not making a public offering and has fewer than 100 security holders. Although this act is primarily directed toward mutual funds, it also regulates companies that inadvertently fall within the statutory definition of "investment company." Thus, if a public company sells a major portion of its assets, and rather than distributing the proceeds to its security holders, holds and invests the proceeds in other than government or commercial paper while exploring alternate business activities, it may be deemed to have become an investment company. "Hedge funds" and investment clubs that rely upon the private offering exemption become investment companies when the exemption is lost and the offering becomes public.

SUMMARY

We have attempted to describe the factors that influence an entrepreneur's decision whether or not to take a company public. We have also tried to describe the complex process of raising equity through the public markets.

Our placement of this piece in the section on "Managing and Harvesting the Venture" bears explaining. We do not mean to imply that going public is a clean exit route for the entrepreneur to take his/her money and move on. While the entrepreneur can often get some money out of the business in a public offering, a large portion of his/her equity will undoubtedly still be tied up in the venture. Rather, we mean to imply that the decision relative to going public is one that is made after the business' start-up. It is a decision about where to obtain capital for growth.

Case 4–1

AMERICAN IMPORTS

In October 1967, Steve Miller and Jack Wilson, two recent graduates of the Eastern Business School, were actively reviewing their decision to create an imported merchandise retail store. The two entrepreneurs were having serious second thoughts about their new enterprise. Their corporation, American Imports, was only four and one-half months old. Already it had suffered serious reverses.

The company was the direct result of a Business Policy report produced in the second year at the Eastern Business School by the two MBAs. Their report had analyzed the conditions and trends in the importing of household decorator items. In evaluating the various competitive elements of the industry they had decided to organize and finance a real store specializing in low-cost quality imported gifts and household decorations. It was their strategy to bypass the traditional channel of distribution for imported goods and procure their merchandise direct from manufacturers overseas. Their type of establishment, known in the industry as an importer-retailer, was to be be opened in Washington, D.C., October 1, 1967, in time for the Christmas gift buying season.

THE PARTNERS

Steve Miller and Jack Wilson met at the Eastern Business School in 1965. As members of the same first-year section they became friends when they

Copyright © 1969 by the President and Fellows of Harvard College.
Harvard Business School case 9-369-013.

discovered that they shared an interest in the import-export business. Both men were convinced that significant opportunity existed in the area of importing goods to the United States from underdeveloped countries.

Steve Miller

After graduation from West Point in 1960, Steve Miller had been commissioned as a lieutenant in the United States Corps of Engineers. He spent a year in Thailand constructing highways. While in Thailand he formed friendships with several local businessmen and became involved in the business of exporting custom-designed hi-fi cabinets to America. In addition, he imported American goods to Thailand through a small company he formed called the East/West Importing Company. Upon completing his military service he entered the Eastern Business School. (See Exhibit 1.)

Jack Wilson

Upon graduation from Harvard College in 1962, Mr. Wilson joined the then recently formed Peace Corps. He was assigned to teach at the University of Teheran, Iran. His ability to speak fluent Persian allowed him to teach English to college level students. In 1964, he was awarded a Fulbright Scholarship for the study of Iranian land reform. Blocked by local political pressure from carrying through his Fulbright assignment, he went to work part time for a Teheran consulting firm. Commenting on a market research report which he produced for this firm, Mr. Wilson said, "I got very interested in the possibility of developing Iranian handicraft manufacture for export to America. The more I investigated this opportunity, the better it looked. As a result of the report I wrote, they organized a venture which I believe has been quite successful."

In the summer of 1965 Mr. Wilson went to work for the U.S. Information Agency in Beirut. He returned to the United States in time to enter Eastern Business School along with Mr. Miller in the fall of 1965. (See Exhibit 2.)

> We had been section mates in the first year and had been meeting regularly once a week with a small group of entrepreneurially-inclined international business-minded second-year students. We talked about the possibilities of developing some import activity in the handicraft area.

THE INDUSTRY ANALYSIS

Miller and Wilson conducted 12 in-depth interviews with companies actively competing within their industry. In addition to using published sources, they spoke to a number of knowledgeable people within the industry. Through their bank they were able to secure Dun and Bradstreet reports on companies which they felt held a significant place within the industry.

Product Sources

Manufacturing operations in Europe, the Middle East, and Asia ranged from the labor-intensive work of hand craftsmen to fairly machine-intensive factories turning out products such as furniture, stainless steel cutlery, and glassware in production runs of substantial volume. The majority of manufacturers sold locally, and were not primarily oriented toward export business. They were normally contacted directly by buying agents of U.S. importers and importer-retailers.

U.S. importers were willing to work closely with a manufacturer and be reasonably patient with late deliveries so long as the quality of goods received remained high. A very real weakness within the maker's segment of the industry was that management often tended to take a rather short-run view of the importance of quality control, market changes, the terms of exclusive agreements, and loyalty to customers. Importers and importer-retailers frequently complained that manufacturers would switch customers even on firm orders if another customer offered them slightly better terms. In addition to these problems, in some countries there had been efforts to organize manufacturers into cooperatives and associations. American importers felt threatened by the creation of these manufacturers' cooperatives, since their bargaining position and their ability to make exclusive contracts were weakened. (See Exhibit 3 for history of imports.)

Importer-wholesalers. American importers generally purchased goods from foreign manufacturers and wholesaled these items to jobbers and retailers. Importers bought from a number of sources and carried a much wider spread of products than a single manufacturer.

There was some product specialization by importer-wholesalers and a tendency to carry as many "bread-and-butter" (staple) items as possible. Sales were handled through company salesmen, agents, and jobbers. Many importers maintained permanent company showrooms in New York and exhibited at annual gift and furniture trade shows. A few importers owned captive retail outlets. Surface freight was the main mode for shipping goods from a foreign maker to the importer-wholesaler, but some items with a high value to weight ratio were air-freighted. They normally used truck transport within the United States. Most of them maintained sizable warehouse inventories from which they shipped in-stock items directly to retailers. On the East Coast, two-week delivery from importer-wholesaler to retailer was considered standard.

Most importers had their own buyers abroad and/or employed commission agents locally who received 5 percent of the import price for finding and dealing with manufacturers of specific household items. Importers tended to specialize regionally. Within the industry the trend was for foreign manufacturers to integrate forward in the distribution channel rather than the reverse. Most importers attempted to get exclusive agreements with manufacturers on unusual items. However, these exclusive agreements were difficult to enforce.

The usual method of payment to foreign manufacturers was by letter of credit. Cash payment was due 60 to 90 days after the goods arrived in the United States. Importer-wholesalers' mark-ons ranged from 33 percent to 50 percent on total landed costs of goods.[1] Terms to the retail trade were normally 2/10 net 30. Prompt-paying retail accounts clearly received preference. Most importers maintained some type of customer rating system by which they classified credit history as to promptness of payment.

Trade shows were considered throughout the industry as the most thorough and least expensive way of getting exposure to jobbers and retail store buyers. Buyers attended the trade shows looking for products which they felt would sell in their individual stores. An importer could achieve almost complete exposure to the retail outlets in the United States by showing at relatively few shows.

Jobbers. Traditionally, jobbers had provided importer-wholesalers with distribution to remote retailers and had had control over selecting the desirability of the customer as a credit risk, either actual or implied possession of the goods, and the responsibility of collection from the retail customers. As retailing imported household goods had grown into a sizable industry, importers and conventional retailers had begun to bypass jobbers whenever possible to improve service and cut costs. In effect, the retailer was moving backward in the distribution channel and the importer was integrating forward, with the net result that the jobber was being slowly squeezed out. In 1967, few importer-wholesalers were interested in acquiring the services of new jobbers; the number of jobbers was at an all-time low; the role historically filled by the jobber had essentially disappeared.

Conventional retailers. The predominant method of merchandising imported goods in the United States was, at the time of the industry study, through high-priced furniture, gift, specialty, or department stores. The importer-wholesaler served as the middleman between the conventional

---

[1]For example, if cost was $2 and mark-on was 45 percent, selling price = $2 + (.45 × $2) = $2.90.

retailer and the foreign manufacturer. Conventional retailers carried a rather narrow line of imported goods, at a relatively high price. The more successful conventional retailer attempted to maximize his or her average inventory turnover ratio of imported goods in order to reduce the danger of markdown.

Importer-wholesalers often provided retailers with working capital in the form of inventory, through trade credit with terms of 2/10 net 30. Many retailers extended their accounts payable to 60 days. In this 60-day time period they could sell the goods and pay their suppliers. The average retailer's markup was 50 percent (a 100 percent mark-on) on his or her selling price. The financial performance of the average retailer was much less impressive than that of the average importer-retailer. On the other hand, capital requirements were lower for conventional retailers and they avoided the expense, risk, and time-consuming effort involved in direct importing.

In many important markets, conventional retailers were consistently undersold by the importer-retailer with a low-price/high-volume warehouse type of store. As a result, conventional retail buyers were under increasing pressure to develop a more sensitive feel for the pulse of their particular group of customers. They avoided the erosion of their 50 percent markup through excessive markdowns by concentrating on the fast-moving items offered by importer-wholesalers. The net result of this was that a typical retailer, who was inclined to expand his or her activities, could more effectively supervise the operation of additional stores rather than integrate backwards by taking on the importing function with its higher profitability. (See Exhibit 4 for growth of sales of a typical outlet.)

Importer-retailers. As the industry matured and management had become more sophisticated, retailers were beginning to bypass both jobbers and importer-wholesalers to bring goods directly into the country for release in their stores. Importer-retailers bought directly from the manufacturers. Initially, their directly imported products were those items which made the most profit, but gradually firms expanded their activities to include virtually all the items offered in their stores. (See Exhibit 5 for survey of stores as of 1967.)

This direct buying abroad entailed numerous risks which were not present in ordering from importer-wholesalers in the United States. It forced retail managers to become proficient at the more complex job of estimating quantities, styles, and types of goods that could be moved through their stores at a profit. Importer-wholesalers, for example, had considerable knowledge as to what was selling well at retail (i.e., hot sellers) which they made available to conventional retailers. This information was quite valuable to retailers in reducing inventory risks. They could further reduce inventory risk by taking advantage of their ability to

TABLE 1
Industry Price Structure, 1967 *(Egyptian Brass Candlestick Purchased Two Ways)*

Purchased through Importer-Wholesaler*		Purchased Direct by Importer-Retailer
	Purchase price f.o.b. dockside	
$ .90	(foreign port)	1.00
.40	Freight, duty, insurance	.40
$1.30		$1.40
	Importer's mark-on 43 percent (or a 30	
.56	percent markup)	-0-
$1.86	Importer's selling price	$1.40
.10	Truck freight to retailer	.10
$1.96	Shelf cost at retail	$1.50
1.96†	Retail markup	1.65‡
$3.92	Sales price	$3.15§

*Usually bought at discount.
†100 percent mark-on or 50 percent markup.
‡110 percent mark-on or 52 percent markup.
§Price advantage about 20 percent.

place small opening orders, with a two-week delivery, to test various items.

On the other hand, importer-retailers had to contend with an average delivery cycle of 120 days. Their purchases might amount to 90 to 180 days of sales in an individual product. In addition, they had to cope with foreign trade customers, languages, currency problems, government regulations, quality problems, short shipments, and financing of goods in transit.

Direct importer-retailers enjoyed a competitive price advantage over conventional retailers. Direct imports were lower priced with higher markups than items purchased from importer-wholesalers. The price policy of importer-retailers was to maintain prices lower than conventional outlets like department stores and furniture stores for comparable quality goods. The industry study disclosed that the average markup of importer-retailers was from 40 percent to 65 percent. Management felt that their typical customer was price-conscious but willing to pay a premium for quality products. However, most merchants continued to sell quality items at lower prices than those of conventional retailers. This pricing and merchandising strategy was justified as an effort to create repeat customers.

The original importer-retailer merchandising concept was to locate the store in a charming, quaint, or romantic setting that would reinforce the "bargain" atmosphere management was attempting to create. Most stores were located on the waterfront to give the impression that merchandise went directly from the ship through the store to the customer.

Cost Plus, a San Francisco store, was the prototype for the early dockside importer-retailers. Their early merchandising strategy was characterized in the trade as "imported items at bargain prices." At the time of the industry study, site location criteria had changed. Desirable locations were on heavily traveled arteries, near a major shopping center, convenient to the suburban shopper and her car. Adequate space for parking and single-level operations were also important. These suburban outlets were thought to build higher sales-per-square-foot revenue than the dockside outlets. Better suburban merchandisers were achieving a total inventory turn of four times a year, with in-store inventory turning as often as seven times a year. Less effective merchandisers were turning their entire inventory approximately one and one-half times a year. (See Exhibits 6 and 7 for sales and cost data.)

Industry Trends

In a summary of their industry report, Miller and Wilson pointed out the following:

> The importance of quality has grown for the importer-retailer to where it is now the most critical feature of the business. There has been commercial acceptance of the more unusual and unique products that would have been characterized as trash or too bizarre a decade ago. The consumer has shown a willingness to pay a premium price for quality items which she can use imaginatively in decorating her home.
>
> The consumer segment had been expanding at a rapid rate, thus making the total market much larger than it was. This growth is being sustained by increasing numbers of people with a background to appreciate these kinds of imported products and by the fact that the appeal of these items is slowly expanding to other groups who are emulating the taste-makers. Department stores have attempted to imitate the importer-retailer's merchandising concepts in recent months.
>
> Industry organization has begun to change within the last three years. Chain stores supported with substantial capital have started with the intent of taking over large market areas. Importer-retailers are actively seeking to combine the purchasing power of their individual stores to wield more power with the manufacturers. It seems likely that this emergence of cooperative buying organizations will materialize and become effective. The final outcome of these trends would be the exclusion of importer-wholesalers from much of their present market in supplying many firms. Importer-wholesalers, however, would continue to supply gift shops, furniture stores, and perhaps department stores.
>
> Tripling of the present imported product volume would seem feasible over the next five to eight years.

Within the importer-retailer segment of the industry some managements have learned to think about specific products, which are not basic to the needs of the typical consumer, in terms of a finite life cycle. Managers plan on stocking these items until they perceive the life cycle coming to an end.

The Consumer

Miller and Wilson pointed out in their report that the typical purchaser in the importer-retailer's outlet was a woman. Normally, she was a house-wife with above-average education. Typically, her husband was a white-collar worker or a professional person. Family income was definitely above average. Most often she purchased items in the store for herself and her home. She did not buy the merchandise for gifts. The typical customer considered this type of imported merchandise store a "fun" place to shop for unique products where something new was always displayed.

In ranking the buying interest of their target consumer they highlighted variety and quality as the most important product features. In addition, their consumer seemed equally interested in shopping convenience and price. The report concluded that if these four consumer interests were satisfied, a decision to buy was often made on the first visit. Return visits were made to the store for repeat purchases. A constantly changing mix of merchandise within the store was underlined as critical to motivating repeat sales.

DESIGNING THE FIRST RETAIL OUTLET

In designing the first store, Miller and Wilson were influenced by the example of one of the firms they studied on Long Island. Called World Wide Imports, it was experiencing rapidly growing sales. They were excited about the opportunity which they saw and said so in their industry report. "One such store (a typical importer-retailer) reports profit after taxes of $100,000 on $700,000 in sales, and an investment (total assets) of about $150,000, or a profit of 14.3 percent of sales, and a return on investment of 66 percent."

The two MBAs quickly settled on Washington, D.C. as their first store location. Washington provided a large potential market with more than 2.5 million people. It was located near a major port (Baltimore) which would minimize inland transportation costs. Jack Wilson was familiar with the Washington market, having lived there. But most important, as he put it, "There are about half a dozen retail outlets carrying part of the merchandise mix that we would stock in Washington. But there is essentially no direct competition in either (1) our price range or (2) our wide selection of merchandise. Although the existing conventional outlets had been able to achieve a relative degree of success . . . the territory is untapped for our type of operation." (See Exhibit 8 for demographic data.)

Site Selection

The partners rejected downtown as a location for their first store because the area had been experiencing declining sales for many years. Parking downtown represented a critical problem to the consumer. Finally, rents for large stores were prohibitively high.

After examining the demographic data of suburban Washington, they selected Silver Spring as the location for their first store. The population within 10 minutes' driving time was approximately 150,000. Retail sales in 1965 totaled $152 million. The average family income was $7,600 and school years completed were 12.3. The major shopping area in Silver Spring had two large regional shopping centers, one of which was Seven Corners. The partners chose a site near Seven Corners for their store. This site was a large fire-damaged skating rink. The site offered excellent parking and a 10,000 square foot store on one level. In addition, there were approximately 5,000 square feet behind the store area to use as a warehouse. Commenting on the location Mr. Miller said, "Really, it was an ideal location. The warehouse, the offices, and the store would all be in one building. But more important, there is a great deal of traffic which goes right by our location going toward the shopping center." (See Exhibit 9, analysis of sales by store type.)

Merchandising Policy

Quoting from their industry study, Mr. Miller and Mr. Wilson said:

> Our basic merchandising concept is to sell quality imported goods at lower prices than the competition, such as it is, recognizing that for many products there will be no effective competition from other retailers in the area. Shopping must be an adventure to the consumer in our store. (10,000 square feet of merchandise would offer such a wide selection that most customers could not see all the items on one shopping trip.) The romance of imported goods and their countries of origin must be conveyed to the customer. All merchandise will be sold on a cash-and-carry basis. There will be no sales discounts to anyone.

Price Policy

Their goal was to have a 100 percent mark-on on delivered costs as standard. (This is 50% markup.) At all times, they intended to underprice gift shops and other types of stores which carried part of their line. The report stated, "It is significant that the most successful popular price volume warehouse importer-retailers follow this strategy. However, we intend to use higher markups on items which we can get higher prices for without either diminishing our volume seriously or compromising our image." They cited the example of Combined Buying Power, Inc., (a combination buying group) which was frequently able to allow an importer-retailer as much as a 400 percent mark-on on the items it designed and had manufactured itself. Even with a 400 percent mark-on, an importer-retailer could continue to underprice the competition.

Buying Policy

As a result of the industry study, the two MBAs gave up their initial idea of using foreign contacts and Business School friends to introduce them to potential suppliers overseas. Instead, they resolved to find a partner in America to help them place their initial purchase orders. They projected an initial inventory of 1,500 products divided into 2,500 different items as a result of different sizes and colors. They estimated that they would place about 30 purchase orders averaging $2,500 apiece, resulting in an initial investment of approximately $50 per product displayed.

Their key procurement decision was to avoid placing any orders with domestic importer-wholesalers. They felt they would need the full 50 percent of their markup during their initial operating period to lower the breakeven. They intended that their initial orders would cover 180 days of sales. They felt this was necessary because of long (140-day) reorder cycles. This varied greatly, however, with goods from Europe coming within 30 days and goods from India and Saigon often taking as long as 360 days. Mr. Wilson said, "We knew that we were going to be placing orders in May to cover the Christmas selling season of 1967. We forecast sales during that first three months of approximately $110,000. And we knew that January, February and March were the seasonal low points of this business. We were really just guessing that we were ordering 180 days' inventory."

Terms

Both managers felt that the terms of payment offered by their suppliers were critical to their new enterprise's cash flow problems. They planned to use letters of credit to help them finance their business. A letter of credit was an agreement between a United States bank and a foreign bank. It stipulated that the U.S bank guaranteed to transmit specific funds to the foreign bank to reimburse a manufacturer-exporter upon the American bank's receipt of shipping documents. These documents were airmailed from the foreign bank to the U.S. bank, usually 10 days after presentation of documents by the manufacturer. The U.S. bank then presented the documents to American Imports for payment. (At this point, goods were still at sea at least 20 days from port.) From Miller and Wilson's point of view, the terms of payment were very critical. Instead of paying the bank immediately upon receipt of shipping documents, they planned to use short-term financing, which called for payment 60 to 90 days after the goods arrived in the United States.

However, an important drawback to this type of financing was that importer-retailers were required to pay the shipping cost, the customs duty, and the insurance costs at the time the goods reached port. Routinely, goods reached port between 15 and 25 days after shipping documents were accepted. Commenting on this financial problem Mr. Miller said,

> Our biggest initial cash drain will be duty, freight, and insurance. We have to pay it when the ship reaches port. This total amounts to about 40¢ on every dollar of initial cost of foreign goods.[2]
>
> In attempting to secure the needed capital, we quickly realized we must limit the amount of our combined equity position; we decided to take 35 percent initially. However, we required the other equity holders to give us options to repurchase up to 50.1 percent of the stock. Initially, the stock would be sold for $5 a share and our options gave us the right to repurchase it at $50 a share.
>
> Our next step was to attract the owner-managers of World Wide Imports of New York, a Mr. Robinson and a Mr. Sabat, a Syrian national, into our venture as co-principals. They responded to us by saying, "We are very interested, but we cannot put any money into the venture." However, negotiations produced the following results:

1. They were willing to contribute a small amount of money to purchase their original shares of stock.
2. They felt they could help us obtain a revolving letter of credit to buy $55,000 worth of goods on a 90- to 120-day consignment basis.
3. They would provide us with goods, taking no commission for securing them, and furnish us with managerial and merchandise advice.
4. They would be willing to show their store and their financial statements to prospective investors to demonstrate the commercial success possible with such a venture.
5. They also would agree to take back all goods purchased through their sources at cost less back transportation costs in event of failure of our store.
6. They would also agree to put up a note for some undetermined amount of money should the venture get into a cash bind in the months after January 1968.

---

[2]Initial cost was f.o.b. port of departure. F.o.b. is an abbreviation of "free on board," which means that the manufacturer bears the expenses of packaging the product and getting it on the ship.

For these concessions, the two owners of World Wide Imports would receive 17.5 percent of the original stock apiece. The position of chairman of the board went to Mr. Sabat. Mr. Robinson would receive the position of vice president in the organization. These positions would definitely not include any salary. It was planned that Mr. Sabat would cosign the $55,000 revolving letter of credit. However, it was expected that the banks would see our right of selling goods back to World Wide Imports as critical to this agreement.

After concluding their agreement with World Wide Imports, Miller and Wilson determined to seek an additional $60,000 in the form of $57,000 in debt and $3,000 in equity.

The New Partners

In their Business Policy report, the two MBAs summarized the background of their new partners as follows:

Abdul-Aziz Sabat: A 27-year-old Syrian national, Sabat first came to the United States about seven years ago to attend the University of California at Berkeley. While there he became involved in importing Indian handicraft products to the United States. Although he studied business administration for several years, he did not receive a degree. (See Exhibit 10, Mr. Sabat's balance sheet.)

He obviously has had some family money supporting some of his ventures, although the extent of this is difficult to determine. However, he has been unable to produce ready cash to put into our present venture.

He said that he sees this venture as a means of gaining more stature or prestige with his suppliers overseas. He obviously is somewhat impressed with the mystique of a business school degree and sees the two of us as bringing some of the "management" into the organization while he and his partner have the buying skills required for success.

He has at times been slighted by other Americans. We think that this past discrimination has rankled him to the degree that he has a very strong desire to be the best in his field and show his past detractors.

Mr. Sabat is a shrewd trading individual with a fast ability with figures. He is a tough bargainer, as we have found out in dealing with him and watching him deal with others.

Both of us feel that he is ethical and trustworthy although we are taking every possible step to protect ourselves against a squeeze-out which could be quite attractive to him.

Charlie Robinson: Mr. Robinson does the merchandising in the store and actually performs the role of store manager—coming in early and leaving late when it closes. Although he is no mental slouch, he has little feeling for financial analysis, as he was rather nonplussed when we showed him our pro forma projections. He does have a feel for the merchandising aspects and the actual operating features of running a store. In appearance, he affects a Hollywood-type image by wearing sun glasses indoors with wild sports jackets. (This may be a carry-over from working in southern California where this is a commonly accepted mode of dress in many levels of business.) Again, we both sensed that he is basically honest. He certainly is quite sensitive to anyone even possibly thinking that there might be any question as to his honesty.

Because of their learning experience in the Management of New Enterprises course at the Eastern Business School, both partners were convinced of the necessity of getting a first-rate lawyer to formalize their relationship with the two prospective partners at World Wide Imports. As a result, they sought out a law firm with experience in organizing new ventures and start-up situations. This law firm helped them draw up the agreement which is presented as the case Appendix.

FINDING THE MONEY

After making the decision to go ahead with their new enterprise, Mr. Miller and Mr. Wilson immediately began looking for equity funds. They contacted three fellow MBAs and presented their prospectus. All three showed enthusiasm for the project and promised to read it with care. Two weeks later they had failed to hear from any of the three, so they called a meeting. None of the three MBAs proved to be interested in attending. Wilson said, "Our classmates were a waste of time. But it was worse than that. We found out that one of the three MBAs we contacted tried to take our real estate in Silver Spring away from us. He got in touch with our landlord and attempted to lease the site we were counting on."

After some additional searching, the partners contacted a medical student, Alan Cross, who appeared interested in investing $50,000 in their project for a 25 percent equity position. A meeting was arranged in New York for Mr. Cross to see the World Wide Imports operation on Long Island. Miller and Wilson felt that one of their strong selling points was the apparent success of World Wide Imports. In addition, they invited another MBA, who had expressed interest in investing, to see the project. This MBA, Habib Faridi, was a Persian who had some experience with importing handicrafts into the United States.

The two prospective investors, Mr. Cross and Mr. Faridi, met the MBAs in New York City in late April. Mr. Cross' father arrived at the meeting in a chauffeur-driven limousine. He proceeded to regale the party with stories of multimillion dollar deals and explanations of the various tax dodges which he employed to maximize his net income. The party left to examine the World Wide Imports store. At the store Mr. Cross's father grilled Miller and Wilson extensively about their operations. About halfway through the meeting he left abruptly.

Alan Cross then demanded additional equity in the project for his investment. He also demanded that Miller and Wilson subordinate their debt to his. And he indicated that he wanted to receive convertible debt which would result in Miller and Wilson owning a mere 15 percent of the company. It appeared that Mr. Cross' father had been coaching his son extensively on what to ask for.

Commenting on the rather ugly situation that developed. Mr. Wilson said, "I was really mad at Mr. Cross. He'd known what the deal was all along. But he thought he had us over a barrel. In addition, he knew he was making a very bad impression on Mr. Faridi, who was also potentially a principal investor. We told him that he could take his new deal and get out."

The Equity Package

In spite of the Long Island meeting, Mr. Faridi decided to become an investor. The partners made the decision to go ahead with the equity and debt package which they had been able to negotiate. In addition to their net contribution of $30,000, the most significant investor was Mr. Faridi, who was supplying $47,500 in debt and $2,500 in equity.

As part of the deal, Mr. Sabat had promised to supply a loan of $20,000 by January 1, 1968, if it was required by Steve and Jack. In addition, he indicated that he could arrange a revolving letter of credit with a New York bank which would enable the company to buy goods and have physical possession of them for 120 days. The amount of this letter of credit would be $55,000. This gave the company almost the full use of the $55,000 worth of purchasing power because managers estimated that 75 percent of the goods would be sold at the end of a 90-day period.

TABLE 2
Proposed Capital Structure at June 2, 1967, Closing

	Percent	Shares Equity	Equity	Debt
Mr. Abdul-Aziz Sabat	17½%	350	$ 1,750	-0-
Mr. Charles Robinson	17½	350	1,750	-0-
Mr. Jack Wilson	17½	350	1,750	$ 13,250
Mr. Steve Miller	17½	350	1,750	13,250
Mr. John Carter*	5	100	500	9,500
Mr. Habib Faridi	25	500	2,500	47,500
	100%	2,000 shares	$10,000	$ 83,500
Short-term debt:				
Revolving letter of credit				55,000
			$10,000	$138,500

*A local businessman.

The Closing

At the closing on June 2, several problems arose. Mr. Faridi indicated that he temporarily did not have the cash for his portion of the equity. As a result, Miller and Wilson lent him (on the basis of a gentleman's agreement and a handshake) his portion of the equity, which was $2,500. It was understood that as soon as he reached Iran, he would send a check for $50,000. Whereas Mr. Robinson had his $1,750, Mr. Sabat did not have this amount of cash and asked to be permitted to pay it the following week. As a result, only four of the six equity holders provided the necessary funds at the closing. After the closing, Mr. Faridi left for California to visit relatives on the way home to Iran.

On June 5, the Arab-Israeli war broke out. Miller and Wilson attempted to contact Mr. Faridi but without success. They became seriously worried because they had already placed approximately $15,000 in orders for merchandise for October deliveries. After normal efforts to contact him had failed, they resorted to telephoning his home in Iran. Faridi, when he was finally contacted, explained it like this to Miller, "I'm sorry, Steve, but I won't be able to provide you with the $50,000. My family is in construction and a freeze has been put on our assets. The government won't let anybody send any money out of the country."

In retrospect, they suspected that Mr. Faridi had never been a free agent. Because they understood the family structure and cultural traditions of the Mid-East, both men had questioned Mr. Faridi closely on his status as a free agent. They had gambled that because he was 29 years old and quite worldly, his statements were probably true. It was their eventual conclusion upon learning that no asset freeze had in fact existed, that he had simply been told by his family that an investment in American Imports was not a good one and that he should forget about it.[3]

OPERATING EXPERIENCE AT WORLD WIDE IMPORTS

The Persian's graceless exit from the venture left it with only $7,500 in capital. A lease had been drawn up by their lawyer for a 10,000-square-foot store in Silver Spring, and they had already placed some orders with suppliers in foreign countries. Mr Miller said,

> Frankly, we were desperate. We had felt that we needed about $125,000 to finance our deal. That $40,000 looked awfully small. But it was then that Mr. Sabat really came through for us. He took us down to the National Bank in New York City and to our amazement we were able to arrange a $75,000 letter of credit facility, which was $20,000 more than we had planned.

---

[3]Mr. Faridi's 500 shares became treasury stock. Final equity positions were Miller, Wilson, Sabat, and Robinson, each with 350 shares or 23⅓ percent. Carter had 100 shares or 6⅔ percent. There were 1,500 shares outstanding.

Both partners were amazed at Mr. Sabat's ability to charm American bankers. Although his personal financial statement claimed a major ownership in an Indian manufacturing firm, and he also claimed an ownership position in a California importer-retailing outlet, these assets alone could not account for his skill and charm in dealing with bankers, according to both men. Mr. Miller reflected, "He seemed instinctively to sense what makes a banker tick. He was amazing. Before we knew what was happening, the banker was acting like we were doing him a favor." In addition to the letter of credit, Mr. Sabat was able to negotiate a $25,000 line of credit at the Great Eastern Bank in Washington. He signed personally on this second source of short-term debt.

In late May, Mr. Miller and Mr. Wilson began working in the Long Island store of World Wide Imports. It was agreed that in return for their help in running the store, the Syrian would assist them in placing their orders for the coming October 1 opening. Mr. Sabat felt that the two MBAs would be of great assistance to him in rationalizing his operation. As the summer progressed, the two MBAs received what they called "a liberal education in retailing."

An Informal Audit

Both MBAs were surprised to find that in eight months of operations of the Long Island store, there had never been a physical inventory. The gross margin that appeared on the store's operating statement was, by Mr. Sabat's admission, a "guess." About the first of July, Mr. Wilson began to do an informal audit of the store's books. He uncovered information which caused him an increasing amount of concern. He found a note payable for $25,000 that was three months overdue. In addition, he found evidence that Mr. Sabat owned a million dollars in madras shirts stored in a San Francisco warehouse. Apparently Mr. Sabat had entered the importing business while a student at Berkeley. In the early '60s a strong demand for madras clothing developed on the West Coast. He had imported and sold madras shirts, making a considerable amount of money. However, his biggest shipment was aboard ship bound for San Francisco when the madras craze died. He refused to accept a sight draft when the ship arrived, claiming that the manufacturer owned the shirts. A lawsuit over the liability for the shirts was continuing at the time of Mr. Wilson's audit.

Mr. Wilson found evidence that Mr. Sabat had borrowed the money to enter his present enterprise from a family friend living in Europe. He was sending 16 percent interest on this loan to a numbered Swiss bank account. This was not listed as an interest expense on the income statement but was disguised as a buying commission. He also discovered that Mr. Sabat had formed a second corporation using merchandise supposedly purchased exclusively for the World Wide Imports Corporation. This act violated Mr. Sabat's banking covenants.

In addition, he was disturbed to find that Mr. Sabat had successfully "squeezed out" the operating partner in the California store of which he owned a portion. He suspected that the success of the Long Island store depended heavily on the cash flow generated by the California store. However, the West Coast partner had left that operation and he was afraid that it was destined to go downhill rapidly. Subsequently, he discovered that Mr. Robinson, Mr. Sabat's American partner in the Long Island store, was stealing from him. At the conclusion of his audit, he came across the fact that Mr. Sabat had created out of thin air the high value of the Indian company and the foreign real estate. He was in a condition of technical bankruptcy.

Remembering the surprise and shock of discovering the real nature of Mr. Sabat's business dealings, Mr. Miller said,

> Abdul-Aziz was the most charming, intelligent, sophisticated person that you would ever want to meet. In the two months that we had worked with him on Long Island, he picked up every buzz word that we had learned at the Eastern Business School. To hear him talk now, you'd think he'd spent two years in the MBA program. But his business dealings were far from honest.

About a week after Mr. Wilson had completed his informal audit of the company's books, Mr. Sabat came to the partners with an unexpected proposal. He said that the opportunity existed to increase their letter of credit to $100,000, but to do so he needed $25,000 in cash for a short period of time. He wondered if they might use $25,000 of the cash that they had accumulated for opening a new store to help increase their letter of credit. Because they were aware that Mr. Sabat actually needed the $25,000 to pay off a three-month overdue bank note, they casually refused this request.

OPENING THE FIRST STORE

By early August it became painfully clear that the owner of the burned-out skating rink would not complete renovation of the property by October 1st. Faced with the arrival of some $105,000 in imported goods, the partners desperately began looking for another location. They finally found a store in Georgetown. Mr. Miller said, "We were fortunate to get into Georgetown. Really, it was our second choice. We wanted 10,000 square feet on a single floor location. But we ended up with 4,500 square feet distributed through three floors of an old apartment building. Our rent in Silver Spring was to be $2.25 a square foot. The Georgetown rent was $4.80 a square foot. A separate warehouse was rented at 90¢ a square foot. In addition, we were faced with the cost of renovating the space. We hadn't counted on any renovation costs."[4] (See Exhibits 11, 12, and 13 for pro forma data on the Georgetown store.)

Leasehold Improvements

The store location in Georgetown required major renovation. The partners made an agreement with the landlord to share the costs. Jack Wilson explained,

> The leasehold improvement decision was our worst mistake. Our landlord agreed to pay $2,000 and we were going to pay $17,000. He suggested a contractor to us and we agreed. We failed to get bids or even a fixed-cost contract. This contractor performed miserably. About mid-September, we had to take over and do his job. Steve and I literally worked days, nights, and weekends to get it finished. We finally opened October 15 and it cost us $28,000. Fortunately we got a $10,000 improvement loan to cover part of the costs. [See Exhibit 14 for October 15 balance sheet.]

Opening Day

Miller and Wilson opened for business on October 15. Although renovations were not complete and would not be for for another week, they needed the cash from sales. During the morning they sold $125 worth of merchandise. Just prior to noon Sabat arrived to see the store. The three men went to a nearby restaurant for lunch.

At lunch all three men had several drinks. Sabat drank somewhat more than either Miller or Wilson. Recounting the event, Jack Wilson said,

> After getting quite a few beers under his belt, Abdul-Aziz began to complain about his deal with us. He exaggerated his contribution and was pretty sarcastic. And then he said he wanted 12 percent additional equity and a salary from our store. He actually threatened to go to our two bankers and take back his personal guarantee on the $75,000 letter of credit and our short-term $25,000 line of credit.
>
> I literally saw red. Steve sensed what was going on and tried to calm me down. But I came within inches of slugging him. The thing that infuriated me was that he waited until we were at our low point and then tried to squeeze us.

---

[4]At this point American Imports had (1) a letter of credit for $75,000, (2) a short-term 12-month line of credit for $25,000, (3) a leasehold improvement loan for $10,000, (4) stockholder notes for $36,000, and (5) equity of $7,500.

ALTERNATIVES

That same evening the partners sat down to consider their alternatives. Both were depressed by the prospect of losing control of their new store to Mr. Sabat. But they agreed that he could cause them serious damage with their bankers. In addition, they doubted if they could reveal the precarious position of Sabat's finances without discrediting their own honesty.

They felt that they had three obvious alternatives. They could sell out to an established chain of importer-retailers. They could go ahead and take their chances with the bankers by refusing Sabat's demands. Or they could give in to him and relinquish some more of their equity as well as salary. They began reviewing their situation with the idea of looking into any additional courses of action and then making a choice.

EXHIBIT 1
Resume: Miller

Resume
STEVEN R. MILLER

Married   6', 170 lbs.   Excellent health

Employment

1966–1967
EAST/WEST IMPORTING COMPANY   CAMBRIDGE, MASS.
Founded and managed this export business. Primary trade was with several companies in Thailand and Hong Kong. Company acted as export agent for American products.

Summer 1966
STATES MARINE LINES   NEW YORK, N. Y.
Assistant to the president. Developed a real estate diversification program. Analyzed and assisted in negotiating specific investment proposals. Appraised and analyzed internal marketing studies on proposed new services.

1960–1965
U.S. ARMY, CORPS OF ENGINEERS
Captain, U.S. Army, Corps of Engineers. Served as Assistant Executive to the Chief of Engineers, Battalion Adjutant, and as Company Commander. Acted as personal assistant to General William Cassidy, Chief of Engineers. Handled correspondence and public relations. Planned and coordinated administrative and operational functions with Congressional, Department of the Interior, and related civilian and military agencies. As Battalion Adjutant in Thailand, budgeted, programmed, and administered the $1.5 million operational budget of a separate Army construction battalion. Constructed 15 miles of two-lane, asphaltic concrete highway in Thailand. Received Army Commendation Medal for distinguished service in Thailand.

Education

1965–1967
EASTERN GRADUATE SCHOOL OF BUSINESS ADMINISTRATION
Received MBA degree, June 1967. Ranked in the top third of the class after one year. Member of Finance, Marketing, Real Estate, and International Business Clubs. Emphasis on Marketing, Finance, and Management Information Systems.

EXHIBIT 1 (concluded)

1956–1960
UNITED STATES MILITARY ACADEMY   WEST POINT, N. Y.
Bachelor of Science Degree in engineering. Dean's list, member of Mathematics,
Debate, Russian, and Spanish Clubs.

Military
Completed military service.

References
On request.

EXHIBIT 2
Resume: Wilson

Resume
JACK C. WILSON

Married, two children   5'10", 160 lbs.   Excellent health

Employment

Summer 1966
RAYTHEON COMPANY   LEXINGTON, MASS.
Acquisitions planning staff member. Financial and market analyses, industry studies,
and evaluation of specific companies for the purpose of recommending acquisitions.
Assignments frequently resulted in presentations to top management. Subsequent to
summer work, performed special assignments as a consultant.

Summer 1965
U.S. INFORMATION AGENCY, AMERICAN EMBASSY, BEIRUT, LEBANON
Director of a U.S. State Department-sponsored training program for Lebanese
teachers.

Part time 1964–1965
IRANO-AMERIC ECONOMIC CONSULTANTS, INC.   TEHERAN, IRAN
Conducted field study and authored market research report concerning the
development of Iranian handicraft exports. Ghost writer for U.S. A.I.D. official,
authored several reports concerning Iranian agribusiness.

1962–1964
PEACE CORPS   IRAN
As a volunteer taught English at University of Teheran, Teheran, Iran, and Karaj
Agricultural College, Karaj, Iran. Organized extracurricular student activities,
including a visiting lecturer series, a technical agricultural publication, and special
courses. Extensive travel in Middle East and Indian subcontinent. Fluent Persian.

1961–1962
HARVARD UNIVERSITY—MIT JOINT CENTER FOR URBAN STUDIES
Publishing assistant in charge of subscriber correspondence and nationwide
circulation of international development and urban study publications to
universities and other institutions.

Education

1965–1967
EASTERN GRADUATE SCHOOL OF BUSINESS ADMINISTRATION
Received MBA degree, June 1967. Major courses included Marketing, Finance, and

EXHIBIT 2 (*concluded*)

International Business, in addition to required and general curriculum. Member of Marketing, Finance, and International Business Clubs. Recipient of competitive Eastern Business School Peace Corps Fellowship.

1964–1965
FULBRIGHT SCHOLAR   TEHERAN, IRAN
Awarded Fulbright grant by Department of State for study of Persian language and Iranian land reform.

1958–1962
HARVARD UNIVERSITY
Bachelor of Arts degree, June 1962. History major. Member of International Relations Council, Latin American Affairs Association, Harvard Glee Club, Winthrop House Music Society, and Phillips Brooks House. Active in intramural sports.

Military

Permanent deferment due to marital status.

References

On request.

EXHIBIT 3
Import Data* (*in millions of dollars*)

	1951	1958	1959	1961	1962	1964	1965	1966
Total imports (billions of $)	10.8	12.7	15.0	14.3	16.2	18.7	21.3	25.6
Wooden and upholstered furniture	na†	16.3	na	na	na	39.5	49.3	60.7
Toys, games, dolls	na	29.0	na	na	na	69.0	82.0	90.0
Glassware	2.6	8.0	11.0	11.5	13.7	18.0	20.5	27.0
Enameled houseware utensils	0.4	1.1	2.0	1.3	1.9	6.0	5.0	3.5
Candles	0.1	0.6	0.9	1.3	1.8	2.2	2.4	3.2
Wood stemmed matches.	0.7	0.8	0.6	0.8	0.8	0.9	1.0	1.5
Artificial flowers.	1.7	10.1	17.0	29.0	34.2	46.7	42.0	40.0
Chinaware	13.1	22.8	28.6	26.6	31.2	33.2	36.4	43.0
Earthenware	10.6	22.2	23.2	25.5	27.5	33.3	34.0	42.0
Wool floor coverings	11.2	28.0	41.3	47.1	45.8	38.2	34.9	33.0

*Worthwhile noting from the items selected is the fact that even during the two economic recessions during this period, imports of these items continued to grow rapidly. A tentative conclusion might be that demand for these types of items is not particularly sensitive to fluctuations in the economy. Declines in enameled utensils and artificial flowers are largely explained by the entry of American producers into a market dominated by foreign producers. Floor coverings have had a market erosion by the rapid acceptance of synthetic fibers, mostly of U.S. origin.

†na signifies that comparable totals were not available in the sources.

Source: The primary sources for these statistics were the *Industrial Outlook for 1967* and the various import publications of the Department of Commerce.

EXHIBIT 4
Sales Growth over Time for a Conventional-Retail Outlet*

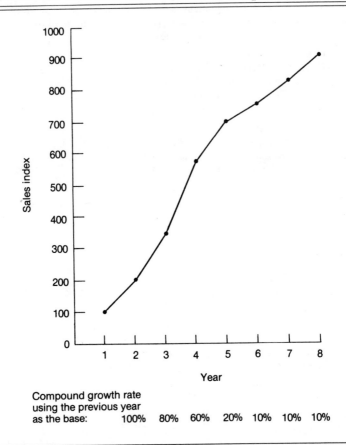

Compound growth rate
using the previous year
as the base: 100%   80%   60%   20%   10%   10%   10%

---

*Growth rates vary for each outlet for a wide variety of reasons. This graph depicts the general sales growth for a "typical" outlet representing a composite of those that have been observed in the industry. First year sales are given an index of 100.

Source: This graph is a composite of the operating histories of a wide selection of firms in the industry and is based on information obtained through in-depth interviews. The authors are grateful to the firms that were willing to release their data. Naturally, this graph is dependent for its accuracy upon the honesty of the individual contributors.

EXHIBIT 5

History of the Growth in Numbers of High Volume, Popular Price, Warehouse Type, Importer-Retailer Stores

	1958	1959	1960	1961	1962	1963	1964	1965	1966	1967*
Stores opened during year:	1	1	-	0	2	4	6	7	4	2
Stores closed during year:			1†					2‡		
Stores in operation, end of year:	1	2	1	2	4	8	14	19	23	25
Name of company and location	Cost Plus, San Francisco	Cost Plus (Branch), Hayward, Calif.		Waterfront Sales, Inc., Atlanta, Georgia	Pier One, San Mateo and Richmond, Calif.	World Imports, Portland, Ore.; Dockside Sales, Baltimore; Pier One, Fort Worth and Dallas, Texas	Price Less, Los Angeles; Pier One, San Antonio, Houston (2), San Jose, and San Leandro, Calif.	Pier One, Los Angeles (3), Sacramento, Denver, Dallas, Houston	Cost Plus, San Mateo, Calif.; World Wide Imports, Inc., L.I., N.Y., Pier One, Phoenix, Ariz., and San Diego, Calif.	Pier One, Kansas City, Mo., and St. Louis, Mo.

Estimated "industry" sales in 1966: $10.8 million.

*As of April 1967. In the summer of 1967, World Wide Imports will open a store in Orange County, Calif., and another store in White Plains, New York. Pier One will open 3 stores in the Chicago area before the end of 1967, and add 5 leased department operations to the 10 they currently have in department stores in the Southeast. Adding our operation in Washington, there will be a total of 31 stores of this type in the United States by year end.

†Cost Plus closed its Hayward branch due to poor results caused by poor management after only 12 months in operation.

‡Pier One closed one of its Dallas stores and one of its Houston stores due to poor location and insufficient sales.

EXHIBIT 6
Sales Growth over Time for a "Typical" High Volume, Popular Price, Warehouse Type, Importer–Retailer Store*

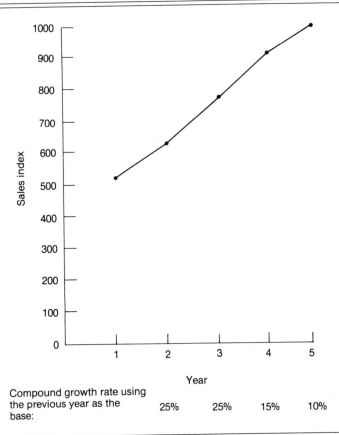

| Compound growth rate using the previous year as the base: | 25% | 25% | 15% | 10% |

*Growth rates vary for each outlet for a wide variety of reasons. This graph depicts the general sales growth for a "typical" outlet, representing a composite of those high volume, popular price, warehouse type, importer-retailer stores that released sales data or whose sales over time were obtained from reliable independent sources. First year sales are given an index of 500, to reflect the fact that in their first year of operation, these types of outlets typically achieve five times the sales volume of the more traditional dockside outlets.

Source: This graph is a composite of the operating histories of several firms in the industry that fit the category described as "high volume, popular price, warehouse type, importer-retailing." The authors are grateful to the firms that were willing to release such data. To the extent possible, these figures were checked with independent reliable sources and the authors believe them to be reliable.

EXHIBIT 7
Income Statement Showing Ranges of Performance for Selected Expense
Categories for the Industry* *(Importer-Retailers)*

	Typical	*Industry Range*	
Sales	100%		
Cost of goods†	60	(45%	to 69%)‡
Gross profit	40	(31	to 55)
Operating expenses:			
Labor and salaries	8	(6	to 18)
Rent	4	(2	to 10)
Advertising	7	(0	to 12)
Utilities	2	(0.1	to 3)
Insurance	1	(0.5	to 1.3)
Professional services	2	(1	to 3.9)
Travel	2	(0.4	to 4)
Interest	1	(0.1	to 1)
Depreciation of fixed assets	2	(0.1	to 3)
Office supplies,			
maintenance, and other expenses	2%	(0.3	to 2)
Total operating			
expenses	31%	(20%	to 45%)
Net profit before taxes	9%	(-3%	to 30%)

*The operating performance of each retail outlet varies by reason of the numerous characteristics that make each a unique operation. "Typical" performance is shown first, representing a composite of the expenses reported by contributing firms, followed by the ranges that were encountered.

†Includes the cost of transportation to the store.

‡Figures shown in parentheses are not additive. They simply represent the ranges encountered.

Source: This income statement is based on ranges of performance as indicated by the operating histories of a wide selection of firms in the industry as obtained in in-depth interviews. The authors are grateful to the firms that were willing to release such data. Naturally, this income statement is dependent for its accuracy upon the honesty of the individual contributors.

EXHIBIT 8   Demographic Data on the 29 Standard Metropolitan Statistical Areas in the United States with Populations Above or Near One Million in the 1960 Census

SMSA	U.S. Rank in Population	Total Population	Population per Sq. Mi.	Median Income	Median School Years Completed	Number of High Volume, Popular Price, Warehouse Type, Importer-Retailer Stores
Atlanta, Ga.	24	1,017,188	590	$5,758	11.1	1
Baltimore, Md.	12	1,727,023	956	6,199	9.6	1
Boston, Mass.	7	2,589,301	2,672	6,687	12.1	—
Buffalo, N.Y.	15	1,306,957	824	6,455	10.5	—
Chicago, Ill.	3	6,220,913	1,675	7,342	10.9	—
Cincinnati, Ohio–Kentucky	21	1,071,624	1,468	6,318	10.3	—
Cleveland, Ohio	11	1,796,595	2,611	6,962	11.1	1
Dallas, Texas	20	1,083,601	297	5,925	11.8	1
Denver, Colo.	26	929,383	254	6,551	12.2	—
Detroit, Mich.	5	3,762,360	1,915	6,825	10.8	1
Houston, Texas	16	1,243,158	727	6,040	11.3	2
Kansas City, Mo.–Kansas	22	1,039,493	633	6,317	11.9	1
Los Angeles–Long Beach, Calif.	2	6,742,696	1,393	7,066	12.1	4
Miami, Fla.	25	935,047	455	5,348	11.5	—
Milwaukee, Wis.	17	1,194,290	1,502	6,995	11.1	—
Minneapolis–St. Paul, Minn.	14	1,482,030	702	6,840	12.1	—
New York, N.Y.	1	10,694,633	4,977	6,548	10.7	—
Newark, N.J.	13	1,689,420	2,420	7,149	11.1	—
Paterson–Clifton–Passaic, N.J.	18	1,186,873	2,780	7,431	11.0	—
Philadelphia, Pa.–N.J.	4	4,342,897	1,224	6,433	10.5	—
Pittsburgh, Pa.	8	2,405,435	788	5,954	10.6	1
Portland, Ore.–Wash.	28	821,897	225	6,340	12.0	1
St. Louis, Mo.–Ill.	9	2,060,103	646	6,275	9.6	—
San Bernardino–Riverside–Ontario, Calif.	30	809,782	30	5,890	11.8	1
San Diego, Calif.	23	1,033,011	243	6,545	12.1	1
San Francisco–Oakland, Calif.	6	2,783,359	840	7,092	12.1	3
San Jose, Calif.	29	642,315	493	7,417	12.2	2
Seattle, Wash.	19	1,107,213	262	6,896	12.2	1
Washington, D.C.–Md.–Va.	10	2,001,897	1,348	7,577	12.3	—

EXHIBIT 9
Sales Volume per Square Foot of Importer-Retailers* (*Data Collected March 30, 1967*)

Single Stores	Location & Merchandising Type	Estimated Annual Sales	Estimated Annual Gross Margin, 52.5%	Sq. Ft. in Store	Total Annual Sales per Sq. Ft. of Retail Space	Age of Store
Price Less Imports, Inc., Los Angeles, Calif.	Located on high-speed, multi-lane artery near shopping center, with excellent parking, single story, in affluent, densely populated area.	$1,150,000	$602,000	15,000	$76.50	3 yrs.
World Wide Imports, Inc., Long Island, N.Y. (Mr. Sabat's store)	Same as above	652,000	342,000	9,600	68.00	15 mos.
Dockside Sales, Inc., Baltimore, Md.	Located on waterfront, with difficult access, not near shopping area, excellent parking, multiple story and barge, in poor, thinly populated area.	275,000	144,000	5,500	50.00	4 yrs.
Waterfront Sales, Inc., Atlanta, Ga.	Same as above, except there is no barge; there are quite a few other shops, parking is inadequate, and area is being redeveloped.	427,000	225,000	9,000	47.50	6 yrs.
World Imports, Inc., Portland, Ore.	Located on waterfront, with difficult access, not near shopping area, inadequate parking, single story, in poor but redeveloping area.	400,000	210,000	10,000	40.00	4 yrs.

*Information volunteered by owner/managers. Accuracy not verifiable in most cases.
Source: Business Policy report.

EXHIBIT 10
Abdul-Aziz Sabat's Personal Financial Statement, June 15, 1967

U.S. assets:	
Cash.	$ 5,000
Stocks.	15,000
Real estate	50,000
Jewelry	25,000
	$95,000
Liabilities:	
Personal note	$ 4,500
U.S. net worth	$90,500
Foreign assets:	
Land (market $400,000) at cost (Syria). . . .	$150,000
Clothing factory (net worth) (India)	300,000
Marketable securities at cost (Syria)	50,000
Foreign net worth.	$500,000
Total net worth	$590,500

Source: Personal files.

EXHIBIT 11
Breakeven Analysis *(September 30, 1967)*

	Imported Directly Monthly	Percent	Conventional Retail Methods Purchased from Importer-Wholesaler	Percent
Breakeven Sales	$17,560	100.0%	$26,603	100.0%
Variable costs:				
Cost (f.o.b. maker)	5,619	32.0	16,653	62.6
Duty, freight, insurance	2,248	12.8		
U.S. truck freight	562	3.2	904	3.4
Markdowns and discounts	351	2.0	266	1.0
Contribution	$ 8,780	50.0%	$ 8,780	33.0%*

Fixed costs:		
Wages	$ 1,985	2 full-time, 2 part-time clerks. 2 full-time stock boys. 1 part-time stock boy. 1 window display girl.
Miller and Wilson	1,500	
Store rent	1,800	4,500 @ $4.80 per square foot
Warehouse rent	370	5,000 @ $ .90 per square foot
Heat, light, and power	750	Higher in winter months
Insurance	240	Detailed schedule, $2,880 per year
Office supplies	150	Estimate
Telephone	200	Estimate
Maintenance and repairs	175	Estimate (janitor, etc.)
Truck expense	225	1,500 miles × 15¢ per mile
Travel and entertainment	300	Air travel and lodging
CPA and bookkeeping	315	Bookkeeper 2 nights a week @ $30.00
Interest	440	7% on $75,000
Interest bondholders	180	6% × $36,000 in notes
Miscellaneous	150	Contingency
Net fixed costs	$ 8,780	

Discretionary costs:	
Newspaper advertising (monthly)	$ 3,000
Start-up costs:	
Advertising and promotion	$ 3,000
Organizing expenses	5,500
Leasehold improvements	28,000
Accrued interest	1,690
	$38,190

*Conventional-retailers' markup was 50 percent of sales price. If American Imports purchases inventory from an importer-wholesaler their cost of goods sold would go up. In order to *continue* to underprice conventional retailers they would have to lower their markup to 33.3%

EXHIBIT 12
Pro Forma Income Statement Georgetown Store (4,500 Square Feet) September 30, 1967 *(in thousands of dollars)*

| | Start Up | | | 1967 | | 15 | | | 20 | | | 25 | | | 40 | | Total |
	Oct.	Nov.	Dec.	Total	Jan.	Feb.	Mar.	Apr.†	May	June	July	Aug	Sept.	Oct.	Nov.	Dec.	1968
Sales Georgetown	10.0	40.0	50.0	100.0	10.0	15.0	20.0	20.0	30.0	30.0	30.0	35.0	25.0	40.0	50.0	65.0	370.0
Cost of goods sold (50%)	5.0	20.0	25.0	50.0	5.0	7.5	10.0	10.0	15.0	15.0	15.0	17.5	12.5	20.0	25.0	32.5	185.0
Gross margin	5.0	20.0	25.0	50.0	5.0	7.5	10.0	10.0	15.0	15.0	15.0	17.5	12.5	20.0	25.0	32.5	185.0
Operating expenses	6.0	9.0	9.2	24.2	8.8	8.8	8.8	8.8	8.8	9.0	9.2‡	9.2	9.0	8.8	9.2§	9.4	107.8
Amortization of leasehold improvements $466/month	.5	.5	.5	1.5	.5	.5	.5	.5	.5	.5	.5	.5	.5	.5	.5	.5	6.0
Net operating expenses	6.5	9.5	9.7	25.7	9.3	9.3	9.3	9.3	9.3	9.5	9.7	9.7	9.5	9.3	9.7	9.9	113.8
Advertising	3.0	2.0	2.0	7.0	.7	.7	.7	.7	1.5	1.5	1.5	1.5	2.0	2.0	3.0	3.0	18.3
Total expenses	9.5	11.5	11.7	32.7	10.0	10.0	10.0	10.0	10.8	11.0	11.2	11.2	11.5	11.3	12.7	12.9	132.1
Operating profit before tax	(4.5)	8.5	13.3	17.3	(5.0)	(2.5)	-0-	-0-	4.2	4.0	3.8	6.3	1.0	8.7	12.3	19.6	52.9

*Percent of Annual Sales**

*Rules of thumb in the industry on *seasonality* of sales.
†April and September are acknowledged to be poor months in the trade.
‡Air conditioning causes significant increase in electric bills.
§Extra sales clerks added at Christmas season.
Source: Personal files, Steve Miller.

EXHIBIT 13
Pro Forma Cash Budget September 30, 1967 *(in thousands of dollars)*

	Sept. and Prior	Oct.	Nov.	Dec.	Jan.	Feb.	Mar.	Apr.	May	June	July	Aug.	Sept.	Oct.	Nov.	Dec.
Inventory Transactions:																
Orders placed	75.0[1]	—	—	30.0	25.0	25.0	—	30.0	25.0	—	25.0	10.0	10.0	—	—	—
Goods received	50.0	25.0[2]	—	—	—	—	—	—	30.0	25.0	25.0	—	30.0	25.0	—	—
Landed costs	20.0	10.0	—	—	—	—	—	—	12.0	10.0	10.0	—	12.0	10.0	—	—
Inventory on hand	70.0	91.0	100.0	80.0	55.0	50.0	42.5	32.5	62.5	82.5	102.5	87.5	112.0	134.5	114.5	89.5
Cost of goods sold	-0-	5.0	20.0	25.0	5.0	7.5	10.0	12.0	15.0	15.0	15.0	17.5	12.5	20.0	25.0	32.5
Net inventory	70.0	86.0	80.0	55.0	50.0	42.5	32.5	20.5	47.5	67.5	87.5	70.0	99.5	114.5	89.5	57.0
Cash in:																
Capital stock	6.0	—	—	—	25.0	—	—	—	—	—	—	—	—	—	—	—
L.T. notes	36.0#	10.0*	—	—	—	—	—	—	—	—	—	—	—	—	—	—
S.T. line credit	—	25.0†	—	—	—	—	—	—	—	—	—	—	—	—	—	—
Cash sales	—	10.0	40.0	50.0	10.0	15.0	20.0	20.0	30.0	30.0	30.0	35.0	25.0	40.0	50.0	65.0
Total cash in	42.0	45.0	40.0	50.0	35.0	15.0	20.0	20.0	30.0	30.0	30.0	35.0	25.0	40.0	50.0	65.0
Cash out																
Landed cost (Duty, freight, and insurance)	—	—	—	—	—	—	—	—	12.0	10.0	10.0	—	12.0	10.0	—	—
Operations	20.0	10.0	9.0	9.2	8.8	8.8	8.8	8.8	9.0	9.0	9.2	9.4	9.2	9.0	9.2	9.4
Leasehold impr.	-0-	6.0	1.0	1.0	1.0	1.0	—	—	—	—	—	—	—	—	—	—
Organization cost	12.0	12.0	4.0	—	—	—	—	—	—	—	—	—	—	—	—	—
Bank acceptances	2.0	5.0	—[3]	10.0‡	45.0‡	25.0‡	—	—	—	—	25.0‡	30.0‡	25.0‡	—	25.0‡	25.0‡
Line of credit	—	—	—	25.0†	—	—	—	—	—	—	—	—	—	—	—	—
Advertising	3.0	3.0	2.0	2.0	.7	.7	.7	.7	1.5	1.5	1.5	1.5	2.0	2.0	3.0	3.0
Lease deposit	—	5.0	—	—	—	—	—	—	—	—	—	—	—	—	—	—
Taxes	—	—	—	—	—	—	—	5.0	—	—	—	—	—	—	—	—
Total cash out	37.0	41.0	16.0	47.2	55.5	35.5	9.5	14.5	22.5	20.5	45.7	40.9	48.2	21.0	37.2	37.4
Net cash flow	5.0	4.0	24.0	2.8	(20.5)	(20.5)	10.5	5.5	7.5	9.5	(15.7)	(5.9)	(23.2)	19.0	12.8	27.6
Cash balance	5.0	9.0	33.0	35.8	15.3	(5.2)	5.3	10.8	18.3	27.8	12.1	6.2	(17.0)	2.0	14.8	42.4
Extra short-term Bank loan (plug)	—	—	—	—	—	+5.2	—	—	—	—	—	—	+17.0	—	—	—

[1] This is $75,000 letter of credit.
[2] Assume that goods reach port 4 months after they are ordered.
[3] Assume time draft matures 240 days from order placement.

\# Notes to equity owners.
* Leasehold improvement loan
† Short-term line of credit
‡ Time drafts mature bankers' acceptance agreement

EXHIBIT 14
October 15, 1967 Financial Statement

AMERICAN IMPORTS
Balance Sheet
October 15, 1967

Assets

Current Assets:	
Cash	$ 2,000
Accounts Receivable*	1,750
Inventory	70,000†
	$73,750
Fixed Assets:	
Leasehold Improvements	$ 28,000
Other Assets:	
Leasehold Deposit	$ 5,000
Organization Expense	1,000
	$ 6,000
Total Assets	$107,750

Liabilities

Current Trade Payable	$ 5,000
Notes Payable (Banker's Acceptances)	50,000
Bank Loan	10,000
	$ 65,000
Notes—Stockholders	36,000
Equity	7,500
Retained Deficit	($ 750)
Total Liabilities and Stockholders' Equity	$107,750

*This was Sabat's portion of the equity.
†This represented $50,000 in initial cost f.o.b. port of departure and $20,000 freight, insurance and duty (landed costs). The firm had an additional $35,000 on order (25,000 f.o.b. + $10,000 landed costs).
Source: Personal files.

APPENDIX
Partnership Agreement

AGREEMENT made this 1st day of June, 1967, by and among Abdul-Aziz Sabat, Charles Robinson, Neptune Imports, Inc.[1] ("NI"), a New York corporation with a principal place of business at 2763 13th Avenue, Manhattan, New York, and American Imports, Inc. ("AI"), a Virginia corporation with a principal place of business at 73 Burnside Street, Georgetown, Virginia:

APPENDIX (*continued*)

W I T N E S S E T H   T H A T:

WHEREAS, Abdul-Aziz Sabat and Charles Robinson are the directors, principal officers and principal stockholders of NI and

WHEREAS, Abdul-Aziz Sabat and Charles Robinson are subscribing for shares of common stock in AI by a subscription agreement of even date herewith; and

WHEREAS, four other individuals, namely Habib Faridi, John Carter, Steve Miller, and John Wilson, are each subscribing for shares of common stock of AI and are, in addition, agreeing to purchase the six percent (6%) notes of AI in varying principal amounts aggregating Eighty-three Thousand Five Hundred Dollars ($83,500);[2] and

WHEREAS, all common stock of AI is to be issued subject to restrictions on transfer thereof, all common stockholders have preemptive rights with respect to further issuance of any class of AI stock, and by agreements by and between the six initial subscribers and AI no additional stock of any class is to be issued at this time; and

WHEREAS, AI is in need of management advice and further financial support in order to promote its business and realize financial success for itself and its stockholders;

NOW, THEREFORE, in consideration of these premises and the mutual covenants herein expressed, the parties hereto agree as follows:

1. Abdul-Aziz Sabat and Charles Robinson jointly and severally hereby agree to procure (at no cost or expense to AI) an irrevocable letter of credit, issued or confirmed by a bank with offices in Boston, Massachusetts, or in New York City, New York, naming AI as beneficiary, being Fifty Thousand Dollars ($50,000) in total amount, and being acceptable in its terms to AI. Credit established under such letter of credit shall be maintained by Abdul-Aziz Sabat and Charles Robinson for a period of five years from the date of this Agreement.

2. AI hereby agrees to reimburse Abdul-Aziz Sabat and Charles Robinson for all drafts upon the letter of credit described in paragraph 1, such reimbursement to be made not sooner than ninety (90) days nor later than one hundred twenty (120) days from the date of payment of such drafts.

3. Abdul-Aziz Sabat and Charles Robinson jointly and severally agree to loan to AI on or after January 1, 1968, the principal sum of Twenty Thousand Dollars ($20,000), provided, however, that AI, by action of its board of directors, authorizes such borrowing and delivers to the lender or lenders its six percent (6%) subordinated note in the form of Exhibit 1 hereto.

4. Abdul-Aziz Sabat and Charles Robinson jointly and severally agree that they will cause NI, or any subsidiary or affiliate of NI, or any other procurement organization which they now control or may control in the future, to procure and buy goods for the use of and at the direction of AI. Such goods shall be shipped directly to AI at such locations as AI shall from time to time indicate, and shall be billed to AI at the same price as actual cost to NI.

APPENDIX (*concluded*)

5. However, nothing contained in this Agreement is intended to restrict or limit in any way the right of AI to procure goods from or through any other source, if such procurement is deemed to be in the best interests of AI.

6. AI hereby agrees to pay for all goods procured in accordance with paragraph 4 upon delivery of such goods to AI. Payment will be made to NI or such other organization described in paragraph 4, by check of AI or by draft upon the letter of credit described in paragraph 1.

7. Deleted.

8. NI hereby grants to AI the use of its trade name and style "World Wide Imports" in connection with all AI operations, excepting only the use of such trade name and style in those locations in which NI does business under such trade name and style as of the date of this Agreement.

9. Abdul-Aziz Sabat and Charles Robinson hereby agree to provide when and as requested by AI or its officers management advice and consulting services to AI and to its officers, directors, and employees for a period of three years from the date of this Agreement and to apply their best efforts to the promotion of the business of AI and to its financial success.

10. Abdul-Aziz Sabat and Charles Robinson hereby agree that in the event of any default in respect of any of the covenants and undertakings made by them in this Agreement, then the common stock of AI of each of them shall be forfeited to AI for which stock AI shall refund the original subscription price of Five Dollars ($5) per share less their pro rata share of the organizational expenses of AI.

IN WITNESS WHEREOF, the parties have set their hands and seals to this Agreement as of the day and year first above written.

---

[1]Neptune Imports was the corporate name of World Wide Imports.
[2]Habib Faridi did not complete his part of the deal, thus reducing the debt to $36,000.

Case 4-2

DRAGONFLY CORPORATION

On December 20, 1982, with the close of the Christmas season just a week away, Janet and Michael Thompson received yet another call from their attorney: it was time to make some difficult decisions about their fledgling business. For the past three and one-half years, the couple had been operating their Dragonfly teenage clothing stores in Seattle, trying to earn a living and keep the business alive despite continuing losses. Now their angry landlord was threatening legal action if Dragonfly did not deliver on its overdue lease payments. The Thompsons' attorney was pushing them for an answer: What did they want to do?

The financial picture was not rosy. Dragonfly had lost money since it opened, with the accumulated deficit from both stores near the end of 1982 reaching over $100,000. (See Exhibits 1 and 2.) While the owners believed the business had gone more smoothly over the past year, the numbers were ambiguous. The Thompsons' best calculation to date still showed Dragonfly losing money (Exhibit 3). But the couple believed they were managing the business more wisely and felt they had corrected many of their early operating problems. They weren't sure why their dream child still wasn't profitable. Was it the serious recession, which had hit Seattle worse than most U.S. cities? Or was there still something wrong with the way they were running the business?

The Thompsons felt they had several possible courses of action. They could try to buy time with the landlord and hope the economy and their business turned around. They could turn to Janet's parents for additional financial help to see them through this crisis. Or they could admit the project wasn't working and begin bankruptcy proceedings.

The Thompsons felt their decision was complicated by the substantial investment Janet's parents had already made in the business. Could they admit defeat to their family and close up the stores? Even worse, could they ask the family to increase their investment in an endeavor that might fail sooner or later?

There was also the problem of timing. While the Thompsons knew that Christmas was the peak sales season for retail operations, they also knew that January was the peak season for refunds. How should they interpret their recent financial figures in the face of such unevenness? Janet and Michael were inclined to think the entire situation was somehow unfair. Just when they felt the stores were turning around, the issue of the lease payments was raising the specter of bankruptcy and forcing them to make a decision about Dragonfly before all the facts were in.

BACKGROUND

Janet Hepburn and Michael Thompson met in Seattle as assistant buyers for Bon Marché, a full-line department store chain, and were married in 1970. Three years later, they quit their jobs at Bon Marché—Michael took a job as store manager for the Lerner's chain, and Janet decided to stay at home in anticipation of the birth of their first child. In 1975, the couple moved to Arizona where Michael took a job working for Kidder Peabody in commercial sales. He hated the environment and found the work boring. He quit in 1976 to return to retailing with a job for a local women's clothing store. Meanwhile, the couple's second child was born. In 1979, the Thompsons returned to Seattle and began looking into franchising a store with the Lady Madonna chain, a successful group of stores offering maternity clothes at the upper end of the pricing scale. Janet was tired of staying home and wanted to get back into the work force. Both the Thompsons liked the lifestyle of retailing. They enjoyed going on buying trips, choosing inventory, and serving customers. With their combined experience in retailing, the couple believed they could make a serious attempt to run their own business.

In the process of investigating the Lady Madonna operation, the Thompsons became intrigued with what they perceived to be an obvious market niche for an upscale store serving Seattle's teenage market. When vigorous research turned up few competitors in the local area, the Thompsons decided to abandon the Lady Madonna franchise idea and pursue opening their own store instead, selling teenage clothes and accessories at fairly high price points. They developed pro forma cash flows which showed that the business would just break even in the first year of operation (Exhibit 4).

Janet and Michael had friends who were successfully operating a chain of T-shirt shops. They liked the idea of opening one store now and using it later to leverage the venture into a thriving chain. Since they believed that most of the expenses involved in running retail stores were fixed on the corporate level, the Thompsons saw the long-term opportunity to generate a sizable income for themselves and a generous profit for their company. (See Exhibit 5.)

DRAGONFLY

The Thompsons were not particularly worried about financing their new venture. Janet's parents had expressed willingness earlier to finance their entry into the Lady Madonna enterprise, and the couple did not think starting up their own store would take a great deal more capital. They approached Janet's older brother, Charles, who was a corporate attorney in Chicago, and asked him to help them develop a plan to use in approaching the Hepburns for money. Based on Charles' knowledge of business and the Thompsons' retail experience, it was determined that $120,000 would be sufficient to start up the new operation, which by now had been dubbed "Dragonfly."

Janet called her parents to discuss the prospect of underwriting the new store. She asked them for $90,000. The Hepburns offered little resistance to the idea. They were happy to see Janet so excited about the new business and felt that $90,000 was a small investment to help their daughter reach financial independence. Mr. Hepburn had recently retired from a successful career in real estate and preferred to give his children money now, rather than having them wait until after his death for an inheritance. He had only two concerns. First, the deal must be structured so that Michael was as responsible as Janet for the financial success of the venture and any obligations to the Hepburns. Second, the Hepburns must receive the tax benefits from any start-up losses.

With those caveats in mind, the family met on June 1, 1979, with Janet and Michael's attorney to set up the Dragonfly Corporation.

THE BEGINNING

The Thompsons thought it seemed like a very informal way to begin such a serious venture. Here they were, serving coffee in their living room to Janet's parents, her older brother, and their attorney, Jeff Lawrence. When the meeting was over and the papers were signed, they would be the owners and managers of the Dragonfly Corporation. The family decided to give the company authorization to issue 50,000 shares of stock with a par value of $1. Initially, 20,000 shares were issued: 15,000 shares to the Hepburns for $15,000 in cash and 5,000 shares to Janet and Michael for their 1977 Volvo, which had a fair market value of $5,000. Jeff Lawrence explained that they would designate Dragonfly as a Subchapter S corporation for income tax purposes and allow the Hepburns to take their proportionate tax benefits which might accrue from early losses. Later, when the corporation began to make money, this could be changed so that either Janet and Michael or the company paid any tax liabilities.

The remaining capitalization was undertaken in the form of debt. In order to be sure that Michael was financially tied into the project, the Hepburns loaned the young couple $75,000 at an annual interest rate of 7.75 percent. The Thompsons, in return, loaned this money to Dragonfly, payable beginning July 1, 1979, in quarterly installments of $1,677.51, including the 7.75 annual interest. Charles felt this capital structure had the additional advantage of giving the couple leverage in any financial adversity, because they would be the store's primary debt holders. The corporation also borrowed $30,000 from Seattle Trust for leasehold improvements, payable in monthly installments of $1,000, with interest at 21 percent per year.

Confident that they had enough money to set up shop properly, the Thompsons began looking for a site for their store. They decided to lease a site at the Woodscross Shopping Center, near the major north/south road in that part of Seattle. Woodscross was in an old, open mall, which had recently been renovated. The Thompsons believed that the emerging character of the shopping center would appeal to their upscale customer base. Also, because the renovation made it a slightly risky location, the rents at Woodscross were roughly half (i.e., $7.50 per foot versus $15 to $17 per foot) those in the more fashionable parts of town. Janet and Michael signed a lease on behalf of Dragonfly for 3,000 square feet at $1,875/month or 6 percent of monthly sales, whichever was greater. The lease was for slightly over four and one-half years, ending March 1, 1984. They also agreed to pay some portion of common area maintenance costs, averaging about $425/month. (See Exhibit 6 for sample lease clauses.)

With the signing of the lease, the Thompsons went to work in earnest. Michael supervised the store setup while Janet went off to buy their beginning merchandise. One month later, on August 1, 1979, they were ready to open for business.

EARLY RESULTS

The results for Dragonfly's first full year in business were not very good. Sales had been lower than expected, and much of the merchandise had been marked down significantly before it was sold. Thus, gross margins were considerably lower than the industry average. In addition, operating expenses were way out of line, bringing the annual loss at December 31, 1980, to $42,253. (Exhibit 7 gives financial and operating data for the industry. Exhibit 8 itemizes Dragonfly's expenses.) Faced with cash shortages, the Thompsons fell behind in their rent payments on the store.

The second year brought problems, too. While sales were up slightly and gross margins were up, Janet had clearly overbought, and inventory levels were up to $80,000. Also, the Thompsons had managed to reduce Dragonfly's expenses but had primarily done so by missing more payments to their Woodscross landlord and by reducing the amount of money they were taking out of the store. They were forced to borrow $15,000 from Janet's parents to make ends meet at home. In addition, the Hepburns lent Dragonfly $30,000.

1982: A TOUGH YEAR

Thus, the Thompsons began 1982 in a precarious position. Their personal financial situation was very tight (Exhibit 9). Janet had cut back on all the extras at home; the family was eating meat only twice a week. Dragonfly was saddled with $80,000 of inventory, and it looked as though only heavy markdowns would move the clothes. To make matters worse, the Woodscross mall was deteriorating rapidly. Already, 10 of the 60 tenants in the new part of the shopping center where Dragonfly was located had begun preparations to move out. It didn't look as though the renovated shopping center was going to make it.

Furthermore, the economic recession, which was clearly hurting retail operations nationwide, was particularly evident in Seattle. Both Boeing and Weyerhaeuser, the two major employers in the area, had hit upon hard times. Boeing was actually laying off workers, while Weyerhaeuser was trying to make do with reduced capital spending, pay freezes, and shorter work weeks. Overall, unemployment in Seattle was up from 5–7 percent in 1975 to 10–12 percent in 1982.[1]

To counter the problems posed by the deterioration of the Woodscross Mall, the Thompsons decided to open a second Dragonfly store in one of the more prosperous sections of Seattle. The new location, in the Bellevue Strip Mall, was 1,450 square feet. The lease, beginning on July 1, 1982, was for two years at $910/month for the first year and $970/month for the second, or 7 percent of gross sales, whichever was greater. Janet and Michael believed there were a number of reasons for opening a second store, despite their precarious financial condition.

First, they hoped to recycle merchandise between the two stores, selling the clothing faster, and increasing gross margins by avoiding markdowns. Opening a second store provided other merchandising advantages, too. With a larger customer base, Janet felt there was a better chance of approaching a normal curve in the distribution of sizes; she hoped this would lead to greater sales as customers began to rely on Dragonfly to have the sizes they needed. Janet also felt it was a good idea to

---

[1] Seattle First National Bank, "Pacific Northwest Industries: Quarterly Summary, February 1983," p. 3.

send sale merchandise to a second location. She knew customers felt badly if they purchased an item at the regular price and then saw it on sale later. Dragonfly also had potential economies of scale in advertising. The Thompsons had developed a large mailing list of existing customers and felt they could spread this advertising cost among the possible revenues from two locations instead of just one. They were also looking for protection in case the situation at Woodscross did not improve. In a worst case scenario, the Thompsons thought they could fold the first Dragonfly store on March 1, 1984, when the lease was up, and move the merchandise to the Bellevue location. In the four months then remaining on the Bellevue lease, they could either try to make the second store successful or use it to liquidate the inventory from both stores. Most important, with many of their significant expenses fixed, the Thompsons saw the second store as a chance to generate excess revenues for the incremental cost of the second set of lease payments. Despite the problems with the Woodscross store, they were pursuing their vision of a profitable multisite operation.

Finally, near the end of 1982, the precarious financial situation forced the Hepburns to reclassify the $30,000 of debt they held as equity.

THE WOODSCROSS SITUATION

In the meantime, faced with increasing cash flow problems, the Thompsons fell further behind on their lease payments for the Woodscross Dragonfly store. In February, they made arrangements with the landlord to begin paying off their previous balance at the rate of $875/month. But this expense left little cash for regular monthly rental payments; these dropped off to $500/month. Thus the balance owed to Woodscross was still increasing at $925/month.

In late June, the Thompsons talked with the Woodscross landlord again and offered to pay rent of 6 percent of gross revenues, which at the time was considerably less than the $1,875/month base fee. They would spend the differential in advertising for the store, in the hope of increasing Dragonfly's sales, as well as the shopping center's traffic. In addition, they would still be obligated for the common area maintenance charges of about $425/month. At the same time, the payments on the overdue balance would drop to $650/month (Exhibit 10). The landlord agreed, but the Thompsons did not receive any documentation confirming the transaction.

By early October, the Thompsons believed they had spent as much money on advertising as they could reasonably expect to be effective. Michael met with the Woodscross landlord and proposed that Dragonfly begin paying the full $2,300/month towards the rent again, with the payments on the overdue balance remaining at $650/month. He felt that the meeting went well and believed that his proposal had been accepted. Thus, the Thompsons were extremely surprised when Jeff Lawrence called on October 25, 1982, to say that he had received a very inflammatory note from the Woodscross lawyers. The letter (Exhibit 11) threatened to pursue further legal action if the Thompsons did not sign a confessed judgment for the entire amount overdue of $21,576.79. Jeff Lawrence responded immediately with another letter explaining the situation as the Thompsons understood it (Exhibit 12), and also suggested to the Thompsons that they consider signing the note.

BATTENING DOWN THE HATCHES

Jeff cautioned the Thompsons that this kind of angry response from a creditor often preceded the initiation of bankruptcy proceedings. He told them to be prepared for the worst possibility. Janet was extremely upset by this news. She had known Dragonfly was in trouble, but it did not seem possible that the landlord had suddenly decided to close up their entire operation.

A phone call to her brother Charles in Chicago served to calm her down. He said that he thought the Thompsons were getting very bad advice from their attorney, who apparently didn't understand the bankruptcy laws at all. (See "Bankruptcy: A Debtor's Perspective.") Charles said he believed Dragonfly was protected from an involuntary bankruptcy in two ways.

First, because the store had so many different trade creditors, no single creditor could force them into bankruptcy. It would take at least three creditors, acting in concert, to file involuntary proceedings, and it appeared that the Woodscross landlord was Dragonfly's only dissatisfied creditor. Second, Charles explained the advantages of the capital structure which he had originally designed for Dragonfly. If the bankruptcy was initiated, either by creditors or by the Thompsons, the store's assets would most likely be liquidated and distributed on a pro rata basis to the unsecured creditors. (Charles did not think the Woodscross landlords were interested in a Chapter 11 reorganization. Their purpose in pushing to bankruptcy would be to liquidate the store and get some cash out of the assets.) Since most of Dragonfly's debt was held by the Thompsons, they would get most of the return from the store's assets. Thus, the landlord really had little to gain from a liquidation.

Furthermore, Charles explained, if the Woodscross manager decided to pursue the Thompsons directly and forced them into personal bankruptcy for the leasehold liabilities, which they had guaranteed, they would find a similar situation. Since the Hepburns were the Thompsons' largest debt holders, most of Janet and Michael's assets would revert to the Hepburns in any bankruptcy. There would be little left for the landlords. Thus, Charles said, if the landlords understood this situation, they might back off a little bit and give Dragonfly time to get on its feet.

Despite this good news, Charles did express concern about one situation. About six months earlier, one of Janet's vendors had insisted on subordinated credit. Lawrence had gotten the Thompsons to sign a general subordination agreement, which subordinated their debt to that of all trade creditors. While the account had been paid off, this agreement was still in the contract with that vendor. Charles was very anxious that this subordination agreement be terminated before the issue of bankruptcy was discussed further. He did not want this small creditor to destroy the careful chain he had set up, in case bankruptcy was actually triggered. As far as Charles was concerned, this was a further example of incompetence on the part of Jeff Lawrence. He should have known better than to allow Janet to sign such a contract. Thus, Charles proposed that the Thompsons make arrangements with this creditor to change the agreement immediately. As well, he suggested they start to think about the real prospects for Dragonfly and frame their response to the Woodscross landlord in this light. Perhaps there was a way to negotiate their way out of the lease, using bankruptcy as their own threat.

THE DECISION

By December, the Thompsons still hadn't heard from the Woodscross landlord again. Jeff cautioned them that it was unlikely the incident had been dropped. Rather, he suggested, Woodscross might be waiting to see how Dragonfly fared through the Christmas season before determining what action to take. While Woodscross had earlier mentioned bankruptcy as a final recourse, Lawrence now confirmed Charles' earlier opinion that one creditor did not have the power to force involuntary bankruptcy on either a business or an individual. Rather, bankruptcy should be viewed by the Thompsons as a way out, if they decided that the Dragonfly stores were not financially viable.

Now, on December 20, Jeff Lawrence had called again. He felt Woodscross would not wait any longer for an answer about the overdue lease payments. Did Janet and Michael want to stall and hope the after-Christmas season bore out their optimism about Dragonfly's improved performance? Did they want to strike a deal and get out of the lease? Did they want to seek more money from Janet's parents? Or did they want to file for bankruptcy and put the entire disappointing experience behind them?

The Thompsons were very torn. They believed the stores were doing better. Inventory levels were down. Existing merchandise was moving rapidly, with little or no markdowns. Their accounts payable appeared to be good. And the economy finally seemed to be turning around. Just when the situation should be at its brightest, the Woodscross mess was threatening to blow out their light. The Thompsons were resentful and confused: was it really time to quit?

EXHIBIT 1

DRAGONFLY CORPORATION
Income Statement
(Unaudited)
For the Years Ending December 31

	1980	1981
Net sales.................	$246,236	$261,336
Cost of goods sold	160,148	155,562
Gross margin..............	86,088	105,774
Operating expenses..........	117,918	106,951
Interest expense	10,423	8,899
Net profit (loss)	$(42,253)	$(10,076)

EXHIBIT 2

DRAGONFLY CORPORATION
Balance Sheets
(Unaudited)

Assets	December 31, 1980	December 31, 1981	December 20, 1982 (Est.)
Current assets:			
Cash..................	$ 2,560	$ 4,821	$ 4,930
Inventory...............	61,432	81,846	84,977
Prepaid insurance	408	0	0
Total current assets	64,400	86,667	89,907
Fixed assets:			
Furniture and fixtures	25,682	26,278	46,429
Office and shop equipment	2,802	2,908	2,805
Leasehold improvements......	22,540	22,540	32,321
Less accumulated depreciation ..	(11,319)	(15,441)	(19,206)
Total fixed assets	39,705	36,285	62,349
Other assets:			
Deposits	1,970	1,970	1,970
Organization costs, net of accumulated amortization ...	2,023	1,463	903
Total other assets........	3,993	3,433	2,873
Total assets...............	$108,098	$126,385	$155,129

EXHIBIT 2 (concluded)

Liabilities and Stockholders' Equity	December 31, 1980	December 31, 1981	December 20, 1982 (Est.)
Current liabilities:			
Notes payable—bank	30,116	33,574	33,201
Notes payable—stockholders . . .	4,776	9,901	8,623
Accounts payable—trade	55,514	48,230	90,045*
Gift certificates outstanding	284	163	210
Accrued liabilities	7,296	5,520	5,264
Deposits	0	82	0
Long-term debt due within one year	1,053	1,053	1,053
Total current liabilities	99,039	98,523	138,396
Long-term debt due after one year .	71,272	70,151	69,098
Debt due Hepburns	0	30,000	0
Stockholders' equity	20,000	20,000	50,000
Accumulated deficit	(82,213)	(92,289)	(102,365)
Total liabilities and equity	$108,098	$126,385	$155,129

*Includes
Trade payables	$68,468
Woodscross rent	21,577
	$90,045

Does *not* include remaining balance of lease payments due
Woodscross, January 1983 through March 1984	$32,200
Bellevue, January 1983 through July, 1984	17,100
	$49,300

EXHIBIT 3
December 20, 1982 Financials

DRAGONFLY CORPORATION
Estimated Financial Condition
As of December 20, 1982
Accrual Basis

Sales—gross	$247,000
Sales tax (6.5%)	16,055
Sales—net	230,945
Cost of goods sold	143,186
Gross margin	87,759
Expenses:	
Rent*	31,360
Payroll†	36,000
Advertising	9,000
FICA	8,400
Medical Insurance	1,800
Miscellaneous	1,400
Interest	10,640
Net loss	$ (10,841)

*Rent breakdown
Woodscross	$24,100
Bellevue rent	5,460
Bellevue common area payments	1,800

†Does not include $21,000 salary to Thompsons not accrued or paid.

EXHIBIT 4
Pro Forma Cash Flows, March 1979–February 1980

	March	April	May	June	July	August	September	October	November	December	January	February	TOTAL
Projected Sales	20,000	13,000	18,000	20,000	25,000	27,000	20,000	16,000	20,000	30,000	16,000	17,000	247,000
Cost of Merchandise	10,000	9,000	9,000	10,000	12,500	13,500	10,000	8,000	10,000	15,000	8,000	8,500	123,500
Cost of Markdowns	1,500	1,500	1,100	1,100	2,500	1,000	1,000	1,000	1,100	1,300	2,000	1,000	16,100
Totals	11,500	10,500	10,100	11,100	15,000	14,500	11,000	9,000	11,100	16,300	10,000	9,500	139,600
Gross Profit	3,500	7,500	7,900	8,900	10,000	12,500	9,000	7,000	8,900	13,700	6,000	7,500	107,400
Selling Expenses:													
Sales salaries	1,700	1,700	1,700	1,800	1,900	2,100	1,800	1,600	1,700	2,200	1,600	1,650	21,450
Advertising	600	500	400	500	600	600	400	400	500	400	600	500	6,000
Buying trips	500	–	–	–	–	500	–	–	500	–	–	–	1,500
Selling Supplies	100	1,400	100	100	100	1,400	100	100	200	200	100	100	4,000
Other	50	50	50	50	50	50	50	50	50	50	50	50	600
Total	2,950	3,650	2,250	2,450	2,650	4,650	2,350	2,150	2,950	2,850	2,350	2,300	33,550
Occupancy Expenses:													
Depreciation	400	400	400	400	400	400	400	400	400	400	400	400	4,800
Insurance	90	90	90	90	90	90	90	90	90	90	90	90	1,080
Maintenance	265	265	265	265	265	265	265	265	265	265	265	265	3,180
Rent	1,875	1,875	1,875	1,875	1,875	1,875	1,875	1,875	1,875	1,875	1,875	1,875	22,500
Other (Merch. Assn.)	150	150	150	150	150	150	150	150	150	150	150	150	1,800
Total	2,750	2,750	2,750	2,750	2,750	2,750	2,750	2,750	2,750	2,750	2,750	2,750	33,000

EXHIBIT 4 (*concluded*)
Pro Forma Cash Flows, March 1979–February 1980

	March	April	May	June	July	August	September	October	November	December	January	February	TOTAL
Administrative:													
Officer's salary	1,200	1,200	1,200	1,200	1,200	1,200	1,200	1,200	1,200	1,200	1,200	1,200	14,400
Bad debt	20	20	20	20	20	20	20	20	20	20	20	20	240
Bank discount	120	110	110	120	150	162	120	100	120	130	100	110	1,502
Dues, etc.	30	30	30	30	30	40	30	30	30	30	30	30	370
Employee benefits .	75	75	75	75	75	75	75	75	75	75	75	75	900
Life insurance	50	50	50	50	50	50	50	50	50	50	50	50	600
Loan interest and repayment	253	253	660	660	660	660	660	660	660	660	660	660	7,106
Office supplies	10	20	20	20	20	20	20	20	20	20	20	20	230
Professional services	100	300	100	100	300	100	100	300	100	100	300	100	2,000
Taxes (payroll) ...	750	730	730	750	780	810	750	705	750	830	705	705	8,995
Taxes (excise) ...	250	250	250	250	300	325	250	225	250	350	225	225	3,150
Telephone	75	70	70	70	75	75	70	70	70	70	70	70	855
Total	2,933	3,108	3,315	3,345	3,660	3,537	3,345	3,455	3,345	3,585	3,455	3,265	40,348
Profit (loss)	(133)	(2,008)	(415)	353	940	1,563	555	(1,355)	(145)	4,515	(2,555)	(815)	500

EXHIBIT 5
Pro Forma Income Statements for the Years Ending February 28

	1980	1981	1982	1983	1984
Revenues:					
Gross sales—Store 1	$247,000	$300,000	$350,000	$350,000	$ 350,000
Gross sales—Store 2	-0-	-0-	250,000	350,000	350,000
Gross sales—Store 3	-0-	-0-	-0-	250,000	350,000
Total gross sales	$247,000	$300,000	$600,000	$950,000	$1,050,000
Expenses:					
Cost of goods sold	$139,600	$165,000	$330,000	$522,500	$ 577,500
Selling expenses	33,550	35,000	40,000	40,000	40,000
Administrative expenses*	25,948	30,000	75,000	100,000	100,000
Officers' salaries	14,400	20,000	40,000	60,000	60,000
Rent	22,500	22,500	47,000	71,500	73,500
Common area maintenance	3,180	4,000	8,000	12,000	12,000
Other occupancy expenses	7,320	8,000	9,000	10,000	10,000
Total Expenses	$246,498	$284,500	$549,000	$816,000	$ 873,000
Profit before taxes	$ 502	$ 15,500	$ 51,000	$134,000	$ 177,000

*Includes repayments and interest; assumes new bank loans to finance opening Store 2 and Store 3.

EXHIBIT 6
Lease Excerpts

Section	Lease Index
1	Premises
2	Construction of Premises
3	Lease Term
4	Delayed Possession and Options To Terminate
5	Rent
6	Taxes and Insurance Premiums
7	Utilities
8	Common Areas
9	Common Area and Mall Maintenance
10	Conduct of Business on the Premises
11	Alterations
12	Maintenance and Repair
13	Quiet Enjoyment
14	Assignment or Sublease
15	Indemnification; Liability Insurance
16	Signs and Advertising
17	Entry by Lessor
18	Eminent Domain
19	Fire or Other Casualty
20	Waiver of Subrogation
21	Insolvency
22	Defaults
23	Liens and Encumbrances
24	Advances by Lessor for Lessee

EXHIBIT 6 (*continued*)
Lease Excerpts

Section	Lease Index
25	Attorneys Fees
26	Waiver
27	Other Stores
28	Notice
29	Successors or Assigns
30	Lease Consideration
31	Merchants Association
32	Change of Location
33	Subordination; Notice to Mortgagee; Attornment
34	Holding Over
35	Memorandum of Lease
36	Sale of Premises by Lessor

Selected Excerpts from Lease

SECTION 14
ASSIGNMENT OR SUBLEASE

Lessee shall not assign, sublease or transfer this lease or any interest therein or in the premises, nor shall this lease or any interest thereunder be assignable or transferable by operation of law or by any process or proceeding of any court, or otherwise, without first obtaining the written consent of Lessor. No assignment of this lease by Lessee shall relieve Lessee of any of its duties or obligations thereunder. If Lessee is a corporation, then any merger, consolidation or liquidation to which it may be a party or any change in the ownership of or power to vote the majority of its outstanding voting stock shall constitute an assignment or transfer of this lease for the purposes of this section.

SECTION 15
INDEMNIFICATION; LIABILITY INSURANCE

Lessor shall not be liable to Lessee or to any other person, firm or corporation whatsoever for any injury to, or death of, any person, or for any loss of, or damages to, property (including property of Lessee) occurring in or about the Shopping Center or the premises from any cause whatsoever. Lessee agrees to indemnify and save Lessor harmless from all loss, damage, liability, suit claim, or expense (including expense of litigation) arising out of or resulting from any actual or alleged injury to, or death of, any person, or from any actual or alleged loss of, or damage to, property caused by, or resulting from, any occurrence on or about the premises, or caused by, or resulting from, any act or omission, whether negligent or otherwise, of Lessee, or any officer, agent, employee, contractor, guest, invitee, customer, or visitor of Lessee, in or about the Shopping Center or the premises. Lessee shall, at its own expense, maintain at all times during the lease term proper liability insurance with a reputable insurance company or

EXHIBIT 6 (*continued*)

companies satisfactory to Lessor in the minimum limit of One Hundred Thousand Dollars ($100,000) (per accident) for property damage, and in the minimum limits of Five Hundred Thousand Dollars ($500,000) (per person) and One Million Dollars ($1,000,000) (per accident or occurrence) for bodily injuries and death, to indemnify both Lessor and Lessee against such claims, demands, losses, damages, liabilities, and expense as against which Lessee has herein agreed to indemnify and hold Lessor harmless. Such policy or policies shall name Lessor, its ground lessor and lenders as insureds, be issued by companies noted A +, AAA or better in Best's insurance guide, and shall be noncancellable as to such named insureds except upon at least ten (10) days prior written notice. Lessee shall furnish Lessor with a copy of said policy or policies or other acceptable evidence that said insurance is in effect.

SECTION 21
INSOLVENCY

Lessee agrees that it will not cause or give cause for the institution of legal proceedings seeking to have Lessee adjudicated bankrupt, reorganized or rearranged under the bankruptcy laws of the United States, or for relief under any other law for the relief of debtors, and will not cause or give cause for the appointment of a trustee or receiver for Lessee's assets, and will not cause or give cause for the commencement of proceedings to foreclose any mortgage or any other lien on Lessee's interest in the premises or on any personal property kept or maintained on the premises by Lessee; and Lessee further agrees that it will not make an assignment for the benefit of creditors, or become or be adjudicated insolvent. The allowance of any petition under the bankruptcy law, or the appointment of a trustee or receiver of Lessee's assets, or the entry of judgment of foreclosure in any proceedings to foreclose any such mortgage or other lien, or an adjudication that Lessee is insolvent shall be conclusive evidence that Lessee has violated the provisions of this section if said allowance, appointment, judgment, or adjudication or similar order or ruling remains in force or unstayed for a period of thirty (30) days. Upon the happening of any of such events, Lessor may, if it so elects, elect to terminate this lease and all rights of Lessee hereunder without prior notice to Lessee.

SECTION 22
DEFAULTS

Time is the essence hereof, and if Lessee violates or breaches or fails to keep or perform any covenant, agreement, term or condition of this lease, and if such default or violation shall continue or shall not be remedied within ten (10) days (three (3) days in the case of nonpayment of rent or other payments due hereunder) after notice in writing thereof given by Lessor to Lessee specifying the matter claimed to be in default, Lessor, at its option, may immediately declare Lessee's right under this lease terminated, and reenter the premises, using such force as may be necessary, and repossess itself thereof, as of its former estate, removing all persons and effects therefrom. If upon the reentry of Lessor, there remains any personal property of Lessee or of any other person, firm or

EXHIBIT 6 (*continued*)

corporation upon the premises, Lessor may, but without the obligation to do so, remove said personal property and place the same in a public warehouse or garage, as may be reasonable, at the expense and risk of the owners thereof, and Lessee shall reimburse Lessor for any expense incurred by Lessor in connection with said removal and/or storage. Notwithstanding any such reentry, the liability of Lessee for the full rent provided for herein shall not be extinguished for the balance of the term of this lease, and Lessee shall make good to Lessor each month during the balance of said term any deficiency arising from a reletting of the premises at a lesser rental than that herein agreed upon as the Minimum Rent, plus the cost of renovating the premises for the new tenant and reletting it.

SECTION 23
LIENS AND ENCUMBRANCES

Lessee shall keep the premises free and clear of any liens and encumbrances arising or growing out of the use and occupancy of the premises by Lessee hereunder. At Lessor's request, Lessee shall furnish Lessor with written proof of payment of any item which would or might constitute the basis for a lien on the premises if not paid.

SECTION 24
ADVANCES BY LESSOR FOR LESSEE

If Lessee fails to do anything required to be done by it under the terms of this lease, except to pay rent, Lessor may, at its sole option, do such act or thing on behalf of Lessee, and upon notification to Lessee of the cost thereof to the Lessor, Lessee shall promptly pay the Lessor the amount of that cost, plus interest at the rate of twelve percent (12%) per annum from the date that the cost was incurred by Lessor to the date of Lessee's payment.

SECTION 25
ATTORNEYS FEES

Lessee agrees to pay, in addition to all other sums due hereunder, such expenses and attorneys fees as Lessor may incur in enforcing all obligations under terms of this lease, including those fees and expenses incurred at trial and on appeal, all of which shall be included in any judgment entered therein. Such covered fees and expenses shall include those incurred in suits instituted by third parties in which Lessor must participate to protect its rights hereunder and those incurred in suits to establish and enforce rights of indemnity hereunder.

SECTION 27
OTHER STORES

Lessee agrees that neither it, nor any subsidiary or affiliate of it, nor any other person, firm or corporation using any store or business name licensed or controlled by Lessee, shall, during the term of this lease, operate a store or business which is the same as or similar to that to be conducted on the premises, or which merchandises or sells the same or similar products, merchandise or

EXHIBIT 6 (*concluded*)

services as that to be sold or furnished from the premises, at any location within a radius of four (4) miles from the Shopping Center without the written permission of Lessor. Lessee further agrees that it will not promote or encourage the operation of any such store or business within said radius by any person, firm or corporation. In addition to any and all other remedies otherwise available to Lessor for breach of this covenant, it is agreed that Lessor may at its election either (*a*) terminate this lease or (*b*) require that any and all sales made at, in, on or from any such other store be included in the computation of the percentage rent due hereunder with the same force and effect as though such sales had actually been made at, in, on or from the premises.

SECTION 32
CHANGE OF LOCATION

Lessee shall move from the premises at Lessor's written request to any other premises and location in the Shopping Center, in which event such new location and premises shall be substituted for the premises described herein, but all other terms of this lease shall remain the same, with the exception that the Minimum Rent provided for herein shall be abated during the period that Lessee is closed for business as a result of the move to the new location; provided, however, that Lessee shall not be moved to premises of less square footage than those herein leased, and that Lessor shall bear all actual cash expenses incurred by Lessee in so moving. It is further understood and agreed, however, that in the event that Lessee shall move to any other premises and location within the Shopping Center for any reason other than to comply with a request from Lessor, then this paragraph shall be inapplicable and the Lessee shall bear all expenses of moving.

EXHIBIT 7
Industry Operating Results 1980 Specialty Stores—Sales under $1 Million (*Percent Figures Unless Otherwise Noted*)

	Average	*Middle Range*
Sales Data		
Credit sales	20.87	11.70 – 36.68
Sales per square foot— selling space ($)	114.90	42.61 – 137.94
Sales per square foot— total space ($)	85.68	37.60 – 126.00
Returns—% gross sales	1.82	1.00 – 3.60
Sales per employee ($)	50,643	41,194 – 68,270
Markdowns	12.15	0.90 – 15.23
Employee discounts	1.09	0.00 – 2.12
Shortages	1.90	0.96 – 2.94
Gross margin	41.47	39.66 – 43.83

EXHIBIT 7 (concluded)

Net Operating Expenses			
Earnings from operations	3.57	1.59 –	5.00
Other income	0.62	0.18 –	1.72
Pretax earnings	4.19	2.52 –	5.31
Management payroll	8.43	6.57 –	10.54
Selling payroll	9.13	7.48 –	9.87
Payroll total	17.56	16.30 –	20.33
Supplementary fringe benefits	0.73	0.41 –	0.99
Media costs	3.09	2.21 –	3.33
Taxes	2.11	1.80 –	2.23
Supplies	2.99	2.00 –	3.78
Credit services	0.83	0.43 –	1.84
Other	1.05	0.81 –	1.37
Travel	0.85	0.13 –	1.40
Postage and phone	0.88	0.50 –	1.20
Insurance	1.29	0.74 –	1.66
Depreciation	0.97	0.29 –	1.56
Professional services	0.53	0.18 –	0.68
Bad debts	0.41	0.09 –	0.67
Outside maintenance and equipment service	0.26	0.18 –	0.30
Real property rentals	4.35	3.09 –	4.97
Total:	37.90	36.29 –	40.60

Adapted from National Retail Merchants Assn., *Financial and Operating Results of Department and Specialty Stores 1980*, pp. 104–5.

EXHIBIT 8
Dragonfly Expenses

DRAGONFLY CORPORATION
Statement of Operating Expenses
For the Years Ending December 31

	1980	1981
Operating expenses:		
Sales salaries	$22,607	$30,445
Advertising	9,317	10,726
Alteration costs	204	0
Bank card discounts	2,014	2,343
Buying trips	2,648	2,056
Delivery	149	0
Display	330	0
Selling supplies	5,559	5,864
Over/short	45	(629)
	42,873	51,172

EXHIBIT 8 (*concluded*)

Occupancy expenses:		
Depreciation/amortization.	8,964	4,683
Insurance.	742	742
Maintenance.	542	151
Property taxes	0	542
Rent	20,128	16,942
Utilities	101	95
	30,477	23,137
Administrative expenses:		
Officer's salary	23,447	13,542
Employee benefits	874	2,169
Bank charges	187	223
Donations	25	40
Dues and subscriptions.	101	50
Officer's life insurance.	2,231	1,780
Bad debts.	367	0
Office expense.	1,645	104
Professional services.	6,794	5,080
Business taxes	1,216	1,024
Payroll taxes.	5,661	5,232
Telephone	854	1,172
Postage	787	712
Temporary help	154	79
Travel and entertainment	225	0
Miscellaneous . . . . :	0	1,435
	$44,568	$32,642

EXHIBIT 9
Janet and Michael Thompson Personal Balance Sheet, January 1, 1982

Assets	
1972 VW	$ 1,000
House	140,000
Marketable securities*	20,000
Equity in Dragonfly	5,000
Note receivable—Dragonfly	75,000
	$241,000
Liabilities	
First mortgage on house—Bank	$ 47,000
Second mortgage—Hepburns	35,000
Note payable—Hepburns	75,000
Note payable—Hepburns	15,000
Total Liabilities	172,000
Net worth	69,000
Total liabilities and net worth	$241,000

*While these stocks were in Janet's name, Washington is a community property state.

EXHIBIT 10
History of Lease Obligations and Payments for Woodscross Store

Time Period	Rent Incurred* (Approx.)	Rent Paid	Payment on Old Balance	Total Remaining Unpaid Obligation†
July–Dec., 1979	$13,800	$13,800	$ 0	$ 0
Jan.–Dec., 1980	27,600	20,128	0	7,472
Jan.–Dec., 1981	27,600	16,942	0	18,130
Jan. 1982	2,300	878	0	19,552
Feb. 1982	2,300	500	875	20,477
March 1982	2,300	500	875	21,402
April 1982	2,300	500	875	22,327
May 1982	2,300	500	875	23,252
June 1982	2,300	500	875	24,177
July 1982‡	1,425	1,425	650	23,527
Aug. 1982	1,425	1,425	650	22,877
Sept. 1982	1,425	1,425	650	22,227
Oct. 1982	1,425	1,425	650	21,577
Nov. 1982	2,300	2,300	0	21,577
Dec. 1982	2,300	2,300	0	21,577

*Including common area maintenance assessments.

†Does not include future obligations under lease, which runs through March, 1984.

‡Thompsons negotiate with landlord to pay rent of 6% of gross sales or $2,300 per month, *whichever is less.*

EXHIBIT 11
Correspondence from Attorney

October 25, 1982

Jeff Lawrence, Esq.
Attorney at Law
600 Seattle Trust Building
10655 NE Fourth
Bellevue, WA 98004

Re: Woodscross Properties
Janet and Michael Thompson Lease Default

Dear Mr. Lawrence:

As we have discussed recently by telephone, your clients, Janet and Michael Thompson, are currently in substantial default under the terms of their lease with Woodscross Properties. Any prior understanding which may have existed with respect to payment of this default was mutually rescinded by request of your clients on or about June 1, 1982. A subsequent arrangement, which was conditioned upon execution and delivery of an installment note and deed of trust, was proffered to Mr. Thompson on or about July 14, 1982, but he never executed a note and he failed to provide a legal description for his residence so that the deed of trust could be prepared, notwithstanding his repeated assurances that it would be forthcoming. As indicated in our prior correspondence to your clients, that offer has long since lapsed.

EXHIBIT 11 (*continued*)

You now indicate that the Thompsons cannot further encumber their residence, that they own no other property on which a deed of trust might be placed, that they have no other security to offer in any form, and that they are even fighting to hold off lien foreclosures on their new store. In spite of all this, you propose that Woodscross Properties should be content without even a promissory note evidencing the indebtedness or the installment terms. You further suggest that no interest should accrue on the lease indebtedness. Moreover, although you acknowledge that the Thompsons' family members are helping them financially, they are reportedly unwilling to provide a guarantee of payment for this debt.

The fact that the Thompsons desire to avoid signing a note evidencing the terms of payment suggests that they have no intention of paying the lease default. Your suggestion that Woodscross Properties should rely solely on the Thompsons' good faith is completely unrealistic and unacceptable, both as a general business practice and as a result of your clients' past failures to perform as promised. We have enclosed a promissory note, bearing interest at 15% per annum, and requiring payments of $800 per month, which you have indicated are within the Thompsons' means. We have also enclosed a confession of judgment, which is to be entered in the event of default by the Thompsons in their payments due under the note.

Kindly arrange for Mr. and Mrs. Thompson to sign the note and confession of judgment and return the fully executed documents to us by no later than 5 o'clock p.m., November 5, 1982. If we do not receive them by that date and time, Woodscross Properties reserves all rights to collect the amounts due, without further notice to you.

Very truly yours,

PELLETT & CRUTT

Andrew A. Savage

Enclosures
CC: Woodscross properties

EXHIBIT 11 (*continued*)

PROMISSORY NOTE

$21,576.79   Seattle, Washington

_____, 1982

FOR VALUE RECEIVED, the undersigned ("Maker") promises to pay to the order of Woodscross Properties, a Washington corporation limited partnership, the principal sum of Twenty-One Thousand Five Hundred Seventy-Six and 79/100 Dollars ($21,576.79), together with interest thereon, all as hereinafter provided and upon the following agreements, terms, and conditions:

Interest. All sums which are and which may become owing hereon shall bear interest from the date hereof until paid, at the rate of fifteen percent (15%) per annum.

Payment. Maker shall pay principal and interest in consecutive monthly installments of Eight Hundred Dollars ($800.00), or more, commencing on the fifteenth day of November 1, 1982, and continuing on the fifteenth day of each succeeding calendar month thereafter until the total indebtedness herein is paid in full. Each payment shall be applied first to interest accrued to the installment payment date and then to principal. All payments shall be payable in lawful money of the United States of America which shall be the legal tender for public and private debts at the time of payments. All payments shall be made to the holder hereof at Suite D–9 Woodscross Mall, Bellevue, Washington 98008, or at such other place as the holder hereof may specify in writing from time to time.

Prepayment. All or any part of the sums now or hereafter owing hereon may be prepaid at any time or times. Any such prepayment may be made without prior notice to the holder and shall be without premium or discount. All partial prepayments shall be applied first to interest accrued to the date or prepayment and the balance, if any, shall be credited to the last due installments of principal in the inverse order of their maturity without deferral or limitation of the intervening installments of principal or interest.

Late Payment Charge. If any installment of principal or interest shall not be paid within five (5) days commencing with the date such installment becomes due, Maker agrees to pay a later charge equal to three percent (3%) of the delinquent installment to cover the extra expense involved in handling delinquent payments. This late payment charge is in addition to and not in lieu of any other rights or remedies the holder may have by virtue of any breach or default hereunder.

Default; Attorneys' Fees and Other Costs and Expenses. Upon the occurrence of any Event of Default, at the option of the holder, all sums owing and to become owing hereon shall become immediately due and payable. The occurrence of any of the following shall constitute an "Event of Default": (i) Maker fails to pay any installment or other sum owing hereon when due; (ii) Maker admits in writing its inability to pay its debts, or makes a general assignment for the benefit of creditors; (iii) any proceeding is instituted by or against Maker seeking to adjudicate it a bankrupt or insolvent, or seeking reorganization, arrangement, adjustment, or composition of it or its debts under any law relating to bankruptcy, insolvency or reorganization or relief of debtors, or seeking appointment of a receiver trustee or other similar official for it or for any substantial part of its property; or (iv) any dissolution or liquidation proceeding is instituted by or against Maker, and if instituted against Maker, is consented to or acquiesced in by Maker or remains for thirty

EXHIBIT 11 (*continued*)

(30) days undismissed or unstayed or remains for thirty (30) days undismissed after such proceeding is no longer stayed. Maker agrees to pay all costs and expenses which the holder may incur by reason of any Event of Default, including without limitation reasonable attorneys' fees with respect to legal services relating to any Event of Default and to a determination of any rights or remedies of the holder under this note, and reasonable attorneys' fees relating to any actions or proceedings which the holder may institute or in which the holder may appear or participate and in any reviews of and appeals therefrom, and all such sums shall be secured hereby. Any judgment recovered by the holder hereon shall bear interest at the rate of eighteen percent (18%) per annum, not to exceed, however, the highest rate then permitted by law on such judgment. The venue of any action hereon may be laid in the County of King, State of Washington, at the option of the holder.

No Waiver. The holder's acceptance of partial or delinquent payments or the failure of the holder to exercise any right hereunder shall not waive any obligation of Maker or right of the holder or modify this note, or waive any other similar default.

Liability. All persons signing this note as Maker thereby agree that they shall be liable hereon jointly and severally, and they hereby waive demand, presentment for payment, protest, and notice of protest and of nonpayment. Each such person agrees that any modification or extension of the terms of payment made by the holder with or without notice, at the request of any person liable hereon, or a release of any party liable for his obligation shall not diminish or impair his or their liability for the payment hereof.

Maximum Interest. Notwithstanding any other provisions of this note, interest, fees, and charges payable by reason of the indebtedness evidenced hereby shall not exceed the maximum, if any, permitted by governing law.

Applicable Law. This note shall be governed by, and construed in accordance with, the laws of the State of Washington.

_____

Michael Thompson

_____

Janet Thompson

_____

DRAGONFLY CORPORATION

BY _____

Its _____

EXHIBIT 11 (*continued*)

IN THE SUPERIOR COURT OF THE STATE OF WASHINGTON FOR KING COUNTY

WOODSCROSS PROPERITES, a limited partnership consisting of DICK MALLET and GEORGE VALE, as general partners, and other persons or entities as limited partners,	))))))	
Plaintiff,	))	No.
v.	( )	CONFESSION OF JUDGMENT
MICHAEL THOMPSON and JANET THOMPSON) husband and wife, the marital community thereof, and DRAGONFLY CORPORATION, a Washington corporation,	)))))	
Defendants.	))	

Michael Thompson, Janet Thompson, husband and wife, the marital community thereof, and Dragonfly Corporation, defendants, do hereby confess judgment in favor of Woodscross Properties, plaintiff, on the terms and conditions and for the sums set forth below, and do hereby authorize the above Court to enter judgment for said sum and on said terms and conditions against defendants and in favor of plaintiff.

1. Defendants agree and confess that this confession of judgment and judgment based thereon may be entered immediately herein if, at any time hereafter, an Event of Default occurs, as defined in that certain promissory note (the "Promissory Note") executed by defendants and dated _____ , 1982, a copy of which is attached hereto as Exhibit A and incorporated herein by this reference.

2. In proof of the occurrence of an Event of Default as specified above, it shall be necessary and sufficient proof for plaintiff to present to the Court a writing certified by the then current holder of the Promissory Note that an Event of Default has occurred as defined in the Promissory Note.

3. Judgment may be entered in the principal amount of $21,576.79, together with interest in accordance with the terms of the Promissory Note, save and except the following: (a) any amount paid to plaintiff pursuant to the Promissory Note by defendants shall be deducted from the amount of said principal and interest specified in the Promissory Note; and (b) plaintiff's court costs, disbursements, and attorneys' fees incurred in connection with defendants' default in making payments due under the Promissory Note shall be added thereto.

EXHIBIT 11 (*continued*)

4. Defendants specifically waive their right to a hearing on the merits of any issues that may arise in connection with the execution or enforcement of, or otherwise relating to, the Promissory Note, and confess and admit that the above-entitled court has full and exclusive jurisdiction over the parties and over the subject matter of any action arising from or relating to the Promissory Note, and defendants, for themselves and for all parties claiming under, by, or through them, hereby waive any and all claims or defenses, whether substantive or procedural, to entry of judgment in accordance with the terms and conditions of this confession of judgment.

5. Defendants state, agree, and admit that this confession of judgment is a completely voluntary and knowing act of defendants. Defendants have been fully advised by their counsel of the effects and scope of the judgment confessed herein.

6. Defendants hereby expressly waive notice of presentation of this confession of judgment to the court. If, notwithstanding defendants' waiver of any notice requirements, plaintiff elects to notify defendants of the time and place for presentation of the judgment, defendants shall have a right to be heard on the following questions only: (a) whether plaintiff has complied with the requirements set forth in paragraph 2 regarding proof that an Event of Default has occurred; and (b) the reasonableness of the attorneys' fees and costs to be included in the judgment.

7. Defendants state, admit, and believe that this confession of judgment is for money justly due and owing to plaintiff under the terms of the Promissory Note, which was executed by defendants, as their free and voluntary act, to evidence indebtedness owing by defendants to plaintiff for delinquent lease payments arising under a commercial lease between the parties.

DATED this _____ day of _____, 1982.

_____

Michael Thompson

_____

Janet Thompson

DRAGONFLY CORPORATION

BY   _____

Its   _____

EXHIBIT 11 (*continued*)

STATE OF WASHINGTON)
)   ss.
COUNTY OF _____)

   MICHAEL THOMPSON, being first duly sworn, states: I am the defendant in the above-entitled action, and I am authorized to make this verification on its behalf. I have read the foregoing Confession of Judgment, know the contents thereof, and that the same is true in all respects; I verify that the Confesson of Judgment herein contained has been voluntarily made by Michael Thompson with full knowledge.

_____

SUBSCRIBED AND SWORN TO before me this ____ day of _____, 1982.

_____

NOTARY PUBLIC in and for the State of Washington, residing at

_____

STATE OF WASHINGTON)
)   ss.
COUNTY OF _____)

   JANET THOMPSON, being first duly sworn, states that I am a defendant in the above-entitled action, and I am authorized to make this verfication. I have read the foregoing Confession of Judgment, know the contents therof, and that the same is true in all respects; I verify that the Confession of Judgment therein contained has been voluntarily made by Janet Thompson with full knowledge.

_____

SUBSCRIBED AND SWORN TO before me this ____ day of _____, 1982.

_____

NOTARY PUBLIC in and for the State of Washington, residing at

_____

EXHIBIT 11 (*continued*)

STATE OF WASHINGTON)
)   ss.
COUNTY OF _____)

        _____*, being first duly sworn, states: I am the _____ of Dragonfly Corporation, the defendant in the above-entitled action, and I am authorized to make this verfication on its behalf. I have read the foregoing Confession of Judgment, know the contents thereof, and that the same is true in all respects; I verify that the Confession of Judgment therein contained has been voluntarily made by Dragonfly Corporation with full knowledge.

        _____

        SUBSCRIBED AND SWORN TO before me this ____ day of _____, 1982.

        _____

        NOTARY PUBLIC in and for the State of Washington, residing at

        _____

STATE OF WASHINGTON)
)   ss.
COUNTY OF _____)

        On this ____ day of _____, 1982, before me, the undersigned, a Notary Public in and for the State of Washington, duly commissioned and sworn, personally appeared MICHAEL THOMPSON known to me to be the party that executed the foregoing Confession of Judgment, and acknowledged the said Confession of Judgment to be his free and voluntary act and deed for the uses and purposes therein mentioned, and on oath stated that he was authorized to execute this said Confession of Judgment.

        WITNESS my hand and official seal hereto affixed the day and year in this certificate first above written.

        _____

        NOTARY PUBLIC in and for the State of Washington, residing at _____.

EXHIBIT 11 (*concluded*)

STATE OF WASHINGTON)
)   ss.
COUNTY OF _____)

On this ___ day of _____, 1982, before, me, the undersigned, a Notary Public in and for the State of Washington, duly commissioned and sworn, personally appeared JANET THOMPSON known to me to be the party that executed the foregoing Confession of Judgment, and acknowledged the said Confession of Judgment to be her free and voluntary act and deed for the uses and purposes therein mentioned, and on oath stated that she was authorized to execute the said Confession of Judgment.

WITNESS my hand and official seal hereto affixed the day and year in this certificate first above written.

_____
NOTARY PUBLIC in and for the State of
Washington, residing at _____.

STATE OF WASHINGTON)
)   ss.
COUNTY OF _____)

On this ___ day of _____, 1982, before me, the undersigned, a Notary Public in and for the State of Washington, duly commissioned and sworn, personally appeared _____, known to me to be the _____ of DRAGONFLY CORPORATION, the corporation that executed the foregoing Confession of Judgment, and acknowledged the said Confession of Judgment to be the free and voluntary act and deed of said corporation, for the uses and purposes therein mentioned, and on oath stated that he was authorized to execute the said Confession of Judgment and that the seal affixed (if any) is the corporate seal of said corporation.

WITNESS my hand and official seal hereto affixed the day and year in this certificate first above written.

_____
NOTARY PUBLIC in and for the State of
Washington, residing at _____.

EXHIBIT 12
Correspondence from Attorney

October 27, 1982

Mr. Andrew A. Savage, Esq.
2300 The Bank of California Center
Seattle, WA 98164

RE: DRAGONFLY CORPORATION
    Woodscross Shopping Center

Dear Andrew:

On October 8, 1982, we discussed Michael Thompson's and my meeting with Frank Murdock, Manager of Woodscross Properties. On that date, we proposed that the Dragonfly Corporation continue to pay the accrued lease balance in monthly payments of $649.95 with the current lease payments to revert to the pre-percentage rent amount of approximately $2,300 per month.

As you are aware, the Thompsons have paid $875 a month on the past-due balance from February through July, at which time it was reduced to the $649.95 monthly installment. Payments were made without a note and without security.

As I informed you, my clients do not have property which they can pledge to secure the unpaid lease amounts accrued and I have advised them that no note should be necessary where all parties are basically going back to their pre-July agreement.

Mr. and Mrs. Thompson have access to additional financial support from their relatives and fully intend to weather the current economic downturn. They have made a great investment in their Dragonfly stores and are excellent managers. They will be around to complete payment of the Woodscross Properties lease obligations.

On October 8, 1982, you informed me that you would be consulting with Frank Murdock and return to me with your response to our offer or alternative proposal. Please inform me of Mr. Murdock's response.

Very truly yours,

JEFF LAWRENCE

ERIC WESTON

It was Friday, January 28, 1982, and Eric Weston was not looking forward to the weekend. He had some very difficult decisions to make regarding the future of his business. The business had been faltering, and on the brink of bankruptcy several months ago. Hard work and faith on the part of the company's suppliers, customers, and employees had kept "the wolf from the door." Once again, events made bankruptcy a real possibility.

ERIC WESTON

Eric graduated from Twin Cities College in 1962, and from the Minnesota Business School in 1964. While at the Business School he was an active member of the small business club and had attempted to get a job with a small company upon graduation.

> I sent letters to all the companies in Minnesota with under $1 million in assets. I got a fair number of responses, and spoke in depth with a few companies. I ended up taking an offer from Rick Edwards, of Edwards Distribution, in St. Paul. The company distributed chemicals and fertilizers to the trade and to retail outlets. Both Edwards himself and the company were in an extremely strong financial positon. My job had a number of components:
>
> — Purchasing of raw materials for a few products which Edwards itself manufactured.

— Planning for Edwards' growth by finding and analyzing related product lines suitable for Edward's expansion.

I had never had a full-time job before this, and I wanted something with a lot of responsibility. I was particularly interested in finance and marketing.

I was a real pain in the neck. I thought I knew *everything*, and if I thought someone was wrong, I told them so. I was a real threat to everyone in the company, which made it doubly difficult.

I really enjoyed the job and did have a lot of responsibility. Some of my projects included:

— Developing an inventory control system.
— Doing product-specific profit and pricing analyses.
— Managing the metal-working shop.
— Selling to big customers.

Eric worked closely with Rick Edwards and learned a great deal about the distribution business. During 1968, his fourth year with Edwards, the company purchased the J. C. Cord Company, a wholesaler and retailer of lawn and garden products, seed, fertilizers, outdoor furniture, and lawn mowers.

THE J. C. CORD COMPANY

Eric was made general manager of the Cord Co. When purchased, Cord was doing about $600,000 a year in business out of an older building in a suburb of St. Paul.

The company had been sold because the owner was an older man, and the lease on this building was running out; he didn't want to go through the trouble and expense of moving. Cord bought a building, moved the business, and I managed it for six years. By 1974, the company was doing about $2 million in sales and making $40,000 or so in after-tax profit. I had a good salary, good benefits, and was managing a business. But I wanted it to be *my own* business.

I had learned a great deal in the few years that I had managed the company. I was dealing with the banks and doing my own borrowing; hiring and firing people; planning and building facilities; designing the salesforce compensation system; developing new product lines; and expanding the business. It really was fun.

In 1975, Eric got his chance: Rick Edwards decided to sell the Cord Co. It was clear to both Rick and Eric that there was no real market for the company without Eric as its manager. And Eric's position was that if Rick wouldn't sell it to him, he would leave.

Rick decided to sell the company and building to Eric for their book value: $165,000 for the business and $115,000 for the building.

Purchasing J. C. Cord

Eric financed the purchase of Cord in a two-step transaction:

— First, Eric purchased the building in his own name. Although its book value was $115,000, the building had a market value of $200,000. The Twincity Bancorp agreed to lend Eric $200,000 in cash, with Eric pledging the building as security.
— Second, Eric purchased the corporation. He generated the required $165,000 in cash as follows:
   • $85,000 in "excess" cash from the building transaction.
   • $15,000, personally borrowed from his parents.
   • $10,000 personally borrowed by taking out a second mortgage on his home.
   • $20,000 generated from the sale of securities and personal savings.
   • $35,000 borrowed by the company against inventory and receivables.

— Rick Edwards was paid this $165,000, and the transaction was reflected on Cord's balance sheet as follows:
   • $40,000 in equity owned by Eric.
   • $55,000 note payable to Eric.
   • $35,000 note payable to Eric's wife, Lillian Weston.
   • $35,000 note payable to bank.

At the time the building financing was arranged, Twincity Bancorp asked Eric and his wife to sign a personal guarantee. Essentially, this would make the Westons jointly and severally personally liable for the corporation's debt (the additional $35,000 of financing plus existing debt which Eric was assuming).

Eric was reluctant to sign such a guarantee:

> I told the bank that Lillian would *not* sign a guarantee. Period. I also told them that the house was in her name, and that our assets had been legally divided and were held separately. I told the bank that *I* would sign a personal guarantee with a $200,000 limit, and they agreed to this.

Running Cord

Eric enjoyed running his own company.

> I discovered that there were a lot of details to the business which I hadn't been responsible for. The pension and benefit plans, for instance. And negotiating with the bank took a lot more time now that we were a little company on our own, not part of a large, financially strong, business.
>
> I still spent a lot of time in purchasing—I bought about 95 percent of the goods. I found that this was the best way to keep my eye on the business.

I also enjoyed the challenge of motivating people. I developed quite a few good managers. On occasion these people would come to me and want to buy a piece of the equity. I always explained to them that this was worthless—as a minority shareholder, they would have no real control, the stock didn't pay any dividends and it would just lock them into the business.

THE SHAW SUPPLY COMPANY

In late 1978, Eric heard that the Shaw Supply Company (SSC) was for sale. This was a large, well-respected business in St. Paul, having begun operations in the area over 100 years earlier. The company sold hardware, plumbing, and garden supplies to contractors and retail customers. The founder's grandsons had been running the company and had mismanaged it into the ground, to the point where their father had stepped back in to take control and sell the business.

I saw an opportunity to dramatically expand our business. Shaw's wholesale customers were similar to ours, and they had a big retail house and garden business. Our product lines were complementary. I was confident that we could combine our two comapnies and have a business which was substantially stronger than either of its parts.

The Shaw family attempted to sell their business to some of the large national chains of home centers, but no one was interested. Eric spoke with the Shaws early in their attempt to sell the company, but it was clear that he did not have financial resources to purchase the company on terms they desired.

A few months later, the Shaws came back to Eric—they had run out of buyers. They negotiated for several months over the terms of the deal. Finally, in January of 1980 they agreed on a transaction where:

— The Cord Company would purchase some of the assets of the SSC (including the right to the name) for $1,677,000:

• Accounts receivable	$ 724,700
• Inventory	952,300
	$1,677,000

— In order to finance this purchase, the Cord Company
  • Assumed certain liabilities of the SSC—accounts payable in the amount of $850,000

— To finance the reamining $827,000 of the purchase price
  • Cord made a $200,000 equity investment in the Shaw Company.
  • Cord gave a $400,000 12-year 10 percent note to the old SSC company ("SSC Shell"). This note had a 2-year moratorium on principal payments.

- Cord borrowed $227,000 by pledging some of the current assets it was purchasing from SSC.

The other elements of the transaction included the following:

— Cord gave Mr. Shaw a 4-year noncompete consulting contract at $50,000 per year; and
— Cord would rent the building from Mr. Shaw at an amount equal to his out-of-pocket costs, including taxes and mortgage payments.
— Cord received an option to purchase this building at a fixed price of $1,200,000, which Eric felt was $200,000 below its fair market value.

In order to generate the $200,000 which the Cord Company needed to finance its equity investment, Eric leveraged the Cord building. This Cord building, which Eric owned, had increased in value to $400,000. Twincity Bancorp agreed to lend the full $200,000 increase in value to the Cord Company; Eric pledged his interest in the building as security. Cord then invested the $200,000 in SSC.

At this time, the bank again requested that Eric and Lillian both sign a personal guarantee on this debt. Again, Eric and his wife refused to sign the guarantee, but Eric did agree to sign a new guarantee (which replaced the existing one) with a maximum of $100,000 on Cord debt and $100,000 on Shaw debt. Eric got the bank to agree that these guarantees would be terminated when equity in the respective companies reached $125,000 each.

This whole transaction was made somewhat easier by the fact that the Twincity Bancorp, Eric's banker, was also the SSC's banker and was in on the other debt which was supporting the SSC.

Eric felt that the transaction was a good one from both parties' point of view:

> Mr. Shaw got out of a business he didn't want to be in and kept the building, which was quite valuable. I got to finance most of the purchase and rent us the building at what is a below-market rent.

1980—CONSOLIDATING THE BUSINESS

Eric combined the businesses of the two companies and moved them to one location—the Shaw building on the outskirts of St. Paul.

Meanwhile, Eric attempted to sell the old Cord building which he owned. The real estate market was off considerably, and when the building was finally sold in 1980, he netted only $225,000. This was the building that had a $400,000 mortgage on it: Eric was $175,000 short. Cord could not make up this difference by borrowing on any other of its assets. SSC, therefore, borrowed $175,000 on its assets, which it, in turn, lent to Cord, which paid off the mortgage.

Finally, during this time Cord was still liable for $3,000 in monthly rental charges. This was the building which Eric himself owned and leased to the company.

Eric attempted to consolidate all aspects of the businesses, but he found this a difficult thing to do. First, Mr. Shaw would not permit Eric to consolidate the financial accounting of the two companies. He was concerned about his $400,000 note, which was secured by a first security interest in all machinery, equipment, furniture and fixtures, and a second security interest (the bank held a first interest) in accounts receivable and inventory. He felt that, if the accounts for the two companies were consolidated, Eric could "bleed" SSC.

Eric also found managing the two companies to be more difficult than he imagined. Within the Cord Co., Eric had pushed a great deal of responsibility and information into the ranks. Yet, the policies of the Shaws had been very different.

> Mr. Shaw had really run the place like a tyrant. No one knew the cost or profit of any of the products they were selling. The purchasing department was told whom to buy from—they didn't even know the price of some of the stuff they were buying. I tried to change a lot of the policies to make them more compatible and give people more responsibility.
>
> — I gave sales people information on the cost of products, compensated them on the basis of profit, and let them set their own prices.
> — I let each area prepare its own budget and plan.
> — I tried to change the credit department's policy, which was to sue everyone who didn't pay.
>
> The company was virtually out of business when I purchased it. I really had a difficult time getting everyone—employees, customers and suppliers—to believe that we were viable. I had to work hard to build employee morale. This was especially difficult because of the "we-they attitude" which prevailed. Naturally, I felt more comfortable with the people from Cord, whose work I knew and trusted. Some of these "Cord people" went in and really tried to take over. This created a lot of ill will.
>
> People were always more loyal to "their" company. For instance, if a "Cord person" was driving the delivery truck, all the "Cord customers" would get their deliveries first. If a "Shaw bookkeeper" was doing the statements, all of the "Shaw customers" would get their statements first.

1980 was not a good year for the combined operations of SSC. (See Exhibit 1 for historical financial statements). The company lost over $400,000.

1981—PROBLEMS

During the early part of 1981, things seemed to be improving. Both businesses were pursuing expansion plans, filling out their product lines, and attempting to grow their sales base. For the first six months, sales were up 3 percent over the comparable 1980 period.

Yet, profits on this sales volume were down over the previous year, and the economy was forcing Cord/Shaw's customers to "extend" their payment schedules. The business had not recovered from its 1980 loss, and working capital requirements were still growing.

Eric spent a great deal of his time negotiating with the bank, attempting to borrow more money for the business.

> We kept negotiating with the bank and every time it seemed as though we were on the verge of convincing them to lend us the money, they would switch loan officers on us. Finally, in June, they turned the loans over to the workout division of the bank. They told us that before they would even talk to us, they needed to see a business plan which attempted to deal with all of the issues our business faced. Just as we started working on the plan, things really got bad—sales started to turn down. Interest rates had really started to affect the building trades.

Eric and his staff worked with a consulting firm on developing a plan throughout the summer. This was a very difficult time for both Eric and the company. Eric said,

> It was tough to juggle all of the problems. Dealing with suppliers, Mr. Shaw, and the banks kept taking up more and more time. It was hard to be bright-eyed and optimistic in front of the employees all the time.
>
> The toughest part was before we had a plan, wondering if we were going to make it. Once we had a plan worked out, I could focus all my energies on that.

THE PLAN

Finally, by September 1, they had worked out a plan for reviving the company. The significant findings and recommendations of the study and resulting plan are highlighted in Exhibit 2.

Eric sent out a letter to suppliers, customers, and employees informing them of the salient points of the company's plan. (See Exhibit 3.) During the months of September, October, and November, Eric worked on a number of fronts to implement the plan:

> We really learned what we could do when times got tough.
>
> — First, we focused on a much narrower segment of our business: commercial and contractor sales. People finally had priorities, and this helped allocate our resources.
> — Second, we made sure that all suppliers knew exactly where we stood. There had been rumors, of course, that we were having financial problems. Many thought we were heading for bankruptcy. By being honest about our problems, I think we gained their trust and support.

— Next, we had to keep that trust. We worked hard to pay all our bills on time and were able to do this through December. In the plan, we had established a *very* strict and fair schedule for paying our suppliers, and we didn't move one iota from that plan.

— We had to let 20 of our 70 employees go. This was a terribly difficult thing to do. Everyone thought we wouldn't be able to run the business with only 50 employees; it was tough, but we did it.

— We also instituted strict cash controls. No one could buy *anything*, not even a box of paper clips, without the approval of the controller.

— We monitored inventory very closely and really tried to control it; purchases were strictly limited, and we liquidated a lot of old stuff that had been sitting around for a while.

I personally spent a great deal of time with our accountants and bankers, trying to monitor the situation closely and borrow the money we needed from the bank.

MORE PROBLEMS

Then, in early December, Eric discovered several disturbing errors in the plan.

— Sales tax: The plan had computed the timing of the company's sales tax payments incorrectly. They actually had to pay the tax in 10 days, but didn't collect on receivables for 45–55 days. This squeezed over $50,000 in working capital out of the business.

— Inventory: Eric thought that they had been liquidating inventory according to schedule. In early December, he discovered that the control system had been spitting out the wrong information. The business actually had $100,000 more in inventory than had been forecast in the plan.

These two factors meant that the company would be short of cash in January. He also had to deal with Mr. Shaw. That month, payments to Mr. Shaw under the terms of the sale were to begin. Eric attempted to convince him to accept a delayed payment schedule on both the noncompete contract and the note. Shaw refused.

At the same time, the bank finally agreed to lend Eric $150,000. But then, Mr. Shaw wrote the bank a letter which outlined his position as a creditor. Under the terms of the sale agreement, which all parties had signed, when SSC's borrowing reached $800,000 the old Shaw Company "shell" became a creditor of equal standing on all subsequent borrowings. That is, if Eric borrowed any more money, Shaw would have a first claim on half of it. Of course, this made it untenable for the bank to lend any more money to the business.

Eric packed up his briefcase and headed home for the weekend. He had his latest financials (Exhibit 4) for the business. Was it time to throw in the towel and declare bankruptcy? What about his employees and suppliers, to whom he still owed money? And the bank? Eric knew that the immediate prospects for the business were not bright; similar businesses were going under right and left. But, if Eric could survive, the upside was good. There might be only half the number of competitors left in the industry.

Eric also knew that the business could go on for another couple of months without the bank loan. And, if the economy turned up in time, the business could be saved. Yet, if it did not, he would end up owing his suppliers a great deal of money. Was it fair to take that risk?

EXHIBIT 1
Financials

Operating Statement Comparison For Shaw Supply Company, Years Ending December 31 (in thousands of dollars)

	1976		1977		1978		1979		1980		Comparable Industry
	$	Percent	$	Percent	$	Percent	$	Percent	$	Percent	Figure
Net sales	$8,006	100.0	$8,262	100.0	$10,102	100.0	$9,931	100.0	$6,251	100.0	100.0
Cost of sales	5,841	73.0	6,243	75.6	7,306	72.3	7,540	75.9	4,749	72.8	—
Gross profit	2,165	27.0	2,019	24.4	2,796	27.7	2,391	24.1	1,772	27.1	24.7
Operating expenses:											
Salary and wages	1,074		1,201		1,351		Figures		1,027		
Payroll taxes and fringes	109		114		133		not		123		
Insurance	142		202		179		available		79		
Advertising	79		98		23				84		
Real estate taxes/rent	108		105		74				122		
Depreciation	84		74		91				30		
Interest	42		170		273				153		
Supplies	41		50		68				40		
Delivery	86		138		141				56		
Travel	44		49		36				30		
Bad debt	50		142		71				27		
Utilities	59		47		64				78		
Telephone	37		33		30				24		
Computer	18		8		11				7		
Leases	44		88		109				51		
Professional fees	18		23		20				25		
Repair/maintenance	30		34		25				28		
Collection	32		29		20				6		
Other	42		89		147				26		
Total	$2,201	27.5	$2,693	32.6	$2,916	28.8	$3,029	30.5	$2,016	30.9	20.9
Operating income (loss)	(36)	(0.5)	(674)	(8.2)	(120)	(1.2)	(638)	(6.4)	(244)	(3.7)	3.7
Other income (expense)	79	1.0	306	3.7	92	0.9	(336)*	(3.4)	3	0	.6
Pretax income (loss)	43	0.5	(368)	(4.5)	(28)	(0.2)	(974)	(9.8)	(241)	(3.7)	3.1

*Shaw wrote down its inventory prior to sale.

EXHIBIT 1 (_continued_)

Shaw Supply Company Balance Sheet Comparison at December 31, (_in thousands of dollars_)

Assets	1978 $	Percent	1979 $	Percent	1980 $	Percent	Comparable Industry Figure
Cash	$ 138.4	2.8	$ 61.4	1.6	$ 8.0	0.5	6.5
Accounts receivables	922.6	18.7	747.0	19.2	448.3	26.8	34.2
Other receivables	17.3	0.4	85.3	2.2	1.7	0.1	—
Inventory	1,966.4	39.8	1,288.3	33.1	884.3	52.9	31.6
Other	34.9	0.7	47.0	1.2	129.2*	7.7	2.1
Total	$3,079.6	62.3	$2,229.0	57.3	$1,471.5	88.0	74.4
Net fixed assets	1,762.4	35.6	1,498.7	38.5	152.3	9.1	17.1
Other assets	103.1	2.0	161.4	4.1	47.4	2.8	8.5
Total	$4,945.0	100.0	$3,889.1	100.0	$1,671.2	100.0	100.0

Liabilities

Notes payable	$ 850.1	17.2	$ 318.1	8.2	$ 598.1	35.8	11.4
Accounts payable	1,028.3	20.8	850.3	21.9	670.3	40.1	21.1
Accrued expenses	57.4	1.2	62.1	1.6	73.6	4.4	5.8
Taxes payable	29.3	0.6	31.4	.8	5.0	0.2	4.0
Current portion	32.8	0.7	18.9	.5	—	—	3.1
Deferred income and reserve	—	—	755.0	19.4	—	—	—
	$1,997.9	40.4	$2,035.8	52.4	$1,347.0	80.6	45.4
Long-term debt	1,037.1	20.9	940.0	24.1	365.7	21.9	11.6
Minority interest	31.8	0.7	22.1	0.6	—	—	—
Equity							
Capital Stock	190.0	3.8	190.0	4.9	200.0	12.0	
Retained Earnings	1,688.2	34.1	701.2	18.0	(241.5)	(14.5)	
Total	$1,878.2	37.9	$ 891.2	22.9	$ (41.5)	(2.5)	43.0
Total liabilities and equity	$4,945.0	100.0	$3,889.1	100.0	$1,671.2	100.0	100.0

*Includes 78.3 due from affiliate.

EXHIBIT 1 (*continued*)

J. C. Cord Company Operating Statement Comparison for Years Ending December 31 (*in thousands of dollars*)

	1977		1978		1979		1980		Comparable Industry Figure
	$	*Percent*	$	*Percent*	$	*Percent*	$	*Percent*	*Figure*
Net sales	$1,308	100.0	$1,844	100.0	$1,908	100.0	$1,869	100.0	100.0
Cost of sales	889	67.9	1,212	69.0	1,252	65.6	1,275	68.2	72.7
Gross profit	419	32.0	572	31.0	656	34.4	594	31.8	27.3
Operating costs:									
Salary/wages/commissions	192		269		304		311		
Payroll tax	10		23		18		30		
Rent	34		41		47		58		
Office	17		18		23		27		
Advertising	15		27		37		31		
Interest	27		38		46		78		
Maintenance	11		10		10		6		
Professional fees	12		9		12		8		
Insurance	17		34		30		44		
Depreciation	8		17		26		27		
Utilities	4		10		11		2		
Profit sharing	6		5		5		1		
Telephone	5		7		7		8		
Vehicle	7		12		7		6		
All other	23		22		33		13		
Total	$ 388	29.7	$ 543	29.4	$ 616	32.3	$ 650	34.8	24.0
Operating income	31	2.3	29	1.6	38	2.0	(56)	(3.0)	3.3
Discontinued building expense*							(111)	(5.9)	
Other income							5	0.3	(1.2)
Pretax profit (loss)	$ 31	23.3	$ 29	1.6	$ 38	2.0	$ (162)	(8.7)	2.1

*This is the expense associated with the old Cord building.

EXHIBIT 1 (continued)

J. C. Cord Company Balance Sheet Comparison at December 31 (in thousands of dollars)

Assets	1977 $	1977 Percent	1978 $	1978 Percent	1979 $	1979 Percent	1980 $	1980 Percent	Comparable Industry Figure
Cash.	$ 15.2	3.0	$ 11.8	2.1	$ 14.6	2.6	$ 9.1	1.1	4.9
Accounts receivable	138.3	27.7	170.6	30.2	151.0	27.4	168.3	19.9	30.2
Inventory.	219.4	44.9	258.1	45.6	261.3	47.3	328.4	38.6	46.7
Other	9.6	1.9	3.4	0.6	7.4	1.3	37.6*	4.4	1.1
Total current:	$382.5	76.7	$443.9	78.5	$434.3	78.7	$544.4	64.0	82.9
Net fixed assets	107.4	21.5	114.7	20.3	111.0	20.1	96.3	11.3	12.0
Other assets	8.8	1.8	7.3	1.3	6.8	1.2	209.2†	24.6	5.1
Total assets	$498.7	100.0	$565.9	100.0	$552.1	100.0	$849.9	100.0	100.0

EXHIBIT 1 (*concluded*)

J. C. Cord Company Balance Sheet Comparison at December 31 (*in thousands of dollars*)

Liabilities	1977 $	Percent	1978 $	Percent	1979 $	Percent	1980 $	Percent	Comparable Industry Figure
Accounts payable	$105.2	21.1	$171.4	30.3	$117.6	21.3	$196.1	23.0	22.4
Notes payable	165.8	33.2	152.6	27.0	194.0	35.1	494.3‡	58.1	13.0
Current portion	6.8	1.4	8.2	1.5	10.4	1.9	2.1	0.2	1.8
Other payables—taxes	16.2	3.3	14.1	2.5	2.5	0.5	79.4	9.3	2.4
Accrued expenses	36.1	7.3	32.9	5.8	21.1	3.8	29.4	3.5	5.4
Total	$330.1	66.2	$379.2	67.0	$345.6	62.6	$801.3	94.2	45.0
Long-term debt									
Stockholder note	55.0		55.0		55.0		55.0		
Note payable other	35.0		35.0		35.0		35.0		
Note payable bank	19.0		17.8		7.7		1.0		
Retirement benefits	6.4		—		—		—		
Less: current portion	(6.8)		(8.2)		(10.4)		(1.0)		
Total	$108.6	21.8	$ 99.6	17.6	$ 87.3	15.8	$ 90.0	10.6	11.5
Stockholders' equity									
Capital stock	40.0	8.0	40.0	7.1	40.0	7.2	40.0	4.7	
Retained earnings (loss)	20.0	4.0	47.1	8.3	79.2	14.3	(81.4)	(9.6)	
Total	$60.0	12.0	$ 87.1	15.4	$119.2	21.6	($41.4)	(4.9)	43.5
Total liabilities and equity	$498.7	100.0	$565.9	100.0	$552.1	100.0	$849.9	100.0	100.0

*Includes due from affiliate $24.2

†Includes investment in subsidiary of $200.0

‡Includes due to affiliate $78.3

EXHIBIT 2
Highlights of Consultant's Study

OPERATIONS

Although the J.C. Cord Company and the Shaw Supply Company share the same facilities and they are managed by the same executives, separate identities are maintained at the operating level. There are separate inside and outside sales personnel for each business, two separate computers and financial administration systems and, for the most part, two distinct markets being served. One area which is shared is counter sales and service, and retail store space.

Within the two businesses, there are a total of 17 major product categories. In addition, sales are broken down for many product groups by retail and commercial.

In order to simplify the analysis of the various entities of Cord-Shaw, retail and commercial sales were combined. Historical and current data were compiled for each major product category so that gross profit ratios, operating contribution, and inventory levels could be reviewed in detail.

This analysis, showing year-to-date through July data, indicates

— Total sales have increased by 2.6 percent.
— Gross profit dollars have decreased by 2.7 percent.
— Gross profit as a percentage of sales has decreased by 1.6 percentage points or 5.3 percent.

Operating Analysis (6 months) *(in thousands of dollars)*

	Sales		Gross Profit			
Product group	*1981*	*1980*	*1981*	*Percent*	*1980*	*Percent*
Garden equipment	$ 525	$ 563	$ 161	30.7%	$ 166	29.5%
Chemicals and fertilizers . . .	194	276	52	26.8	73	26.4
Seed.	28	70	20	71.4	47	67.1
Lawn tractors/lawn mowers .	55	70	18	32.7	22	31.5
Sporting goods.	13	3	4	30.8	1	33.3
Total Cord	$ 815	$ 982	$ 255	31.3%	$ 309	31.5%
Hardware	$1,667	$1,313	$ 423	25.9%	$ 331	27.0%
Wood products	96	103	35	35.5	40	41.9
Plumbing supplies.	628	560	174	28.1	174	33.2
Retail store—Hardware	162	219	59	35.1	71	34.8
Wood products	14	38	5	33.3	12	34.8
Lawn	22	33	9	42.9	12	40.0
Gardenmart	50	51	9	18.2	14	30.0
Kitchen cabinets	296	368	108	37.7	144	41.6
Total Shaw	$2,947	$2,685	$ 822	27.9%	$ 798	29.7%
Total Cord-Shaw	$3,762	$3,667	$1,077	28.6%	$1,107	30.2%

EXHIBIT 2 (*continued*)

Operating Analysis (6 months)
(*in thousands of dollars except percents*)

Product Group	1981 Sales	Direct Contribution	Percent Sales	7/31/81 Inventory
Garden equipment	$ 525	$ 77	14.7 %	NA
Chemicals and fertilizers	194	21	10.8	NA
Seed.	28	(13)	(46.4)	NA
Lawn tractors/ mowers	55	2	3.6	NA
Sporting goods.	13	0	0	NA
Total Cord	$ 815	$ 87	10.7 %	$ 337
Hardware	$1,667	$131	7.9 %	$ 741
Wood products	96	0	0	95
Plumbing supplies.	628	62	9.8	214
Store-total.	258	8	3.1	201
Kitchen cabinets	296	41	13.9	134
Total Shaw	$2,947	$242	8.2 %	$1,385
Total Cord-Shaw	$3,762	$329	8.8 %	$1,722

In addition to reviewing sales and gross profit for each product category, a contribution analysis was prepared by management for each product category based on direct operating costs associated with each entity. Inventory levels were also identified for each category. The following summarizes fiscal year 1981 year-to-date sales, contribution, and inventory levels through July. Data for 1980 is not available.

The combined contribution of $329,000 is not sufficient to offset corporate SG&A of $488,000, which exceeds industry standards by 10 percentage points.

The following highlights the results of the contribution analysis for each product category:

Cord Operations

a. Garden equipment contributes 14.7 percent, which should be sufficient to cover a normal (10%) corporate SG&A assessment.
b. Chemicals and fertilizers at 10.8 percent must be improved. If sales continue to deteriorate, either the direct payroll must be cut (eliminate full-time salesman) and/or consideration should be given to phasing out of it.
c. Seed at YTD sales levels is not an acceptable contributor. With a gross margin ratio of better than 70 percent, major effort should be put into increasing sales. Current back orders will turn this product group into a positive contributor by the end of fiscal 1983.
d. Lawn tractors/lawn mowers at current sales and operating expenses are not viable.
e. Sporting goods are not viable and should be liquidated.

EXHIBIT 2 (*continued*)

Shaw Operations

a. Hardware products gross profits have decreased by 1.1 percentage points versus 1980 (fiscal) which amounts to over $20,000 in reduced gross profit on a year-to-date basis. In addition, duplicate inventories, etc. cause excessive operating expenses.

b. Wood products generate a 35.5 percent gross profit. Direct operating costs consume this entire gross profit so that this division makes no contribution. In addition, inventory of $95,000 is too high based on the $96,000 annual sales volume. Consideration should be given to eliminating the direct payroll costs by having the hardware salesmen pick up this product area. Inventory should be reduced to only fast-turn items.

c. Plumbing supplies gross profit has deteriorated 5.1 percentage points since last year. This amounts to $22,000 on year-to-date sales of $628,000. Had the gross profit margin been maintained at prior levels, the operating contribution would be 13.6 percent. Pricing and cost of sales should be reviewed in depth. Although sales are up $68,000 versus last year, gross profit is flat.

d. The store, in total, is losing sales and experiencing deteriorating gross profit ratios. Sales of $258,000 are $83,000 below last year and gross profits have gone from 34.6 percent to 31.7 percent. An operating contribution of $8,000 (3.1%) is unacceptable. Emphasis on "retail" sales does not seem to be working. Price comparisons with other home center stores indicates Shaw's prices are on the high side. It is strongly recommended that the store and marketing focus be changed to gardening products and hardware and not trying to be all things to all people. Lawn furniture should be dropped completely or only offered through a catalog (no stock).

e. Kitchen cabinets is a reasonably good operating contributor at 13.9 percent. However, margin deterioration from 41.6 percent to 37.7 percent should be analyzed since sales have also fallen from $368,000 to $296,000 this year.

Organization

In order to gain a thorough understanding of the organization and to gather input on problems and opportunities, in-depth interviews were held with 10 key employees. The consensus from the interviews highlighted the following:

a. The majority of those interviewed were not sure of exactly what their responsibilities were or what was expected of them.

b. There were redundancies in certain functions. Specifically, the need for two sets of inventory and two counters for hardware products (retail and contractor) was questioned.

c. No one was sure of customer focus—retail versus commercial/contractor. There was a competitive attitude between the two groups.

d. Cord-assigned employees felt that all management's attention was on Shaw and blamed the lack of attention on why Cord sales were deteriorating.

EXHIBIT 2 (*continued*)

---

e. The layout of the facilities and the process of handling customer orders causes excessive time delays for contractor customers and frustrates them. It is felt that many of these customers have gone elsewhere due to the inconvenience.

f. The lack of any stated corporate goals, market plans, and operating plans left most with the feeling that the business has no direction.

g. There was unanimous concern about the future viability of Cord-Shaw, whether it could be turned around, and what would be required to make it viable. This came out in the form of questioning "management's" capability to carry out the necessary actions which would be required to make the business viable.

Facilities

Conclusions from observations of operating conditions within the facilities showed that

— The physical size of the yards, warehouse, store, and office areas are more than adequate for current and future needs.

— The need for duplicate warehousing of hardware products should be reviewed for consolidation potential.

— The combination of gardening supplies and hardware supplies within the store is confusing.

— Inventories of certain items appeared excessive. Specifically, kitchen cabinets and garden-related products should be reviewed.

MARKETING AND SALES

Market Focus

It became evident that the company had no defined strategy. In fact, it had not determined its market focus. Is the company a retail home center? Is the company a supplier of gardening materials and home products to institutions, commercial users, and contractors? Can/should the company be both? These were questions the sales and management team were asking themselves. Impact of the location in St. Paul and a perceived profit margin difference added to the debate/confusion.

The "inside" sales effort was designed to be "all things to all people." Handling of commercial/contractor orders is intermingled with serving the retail consumer, particularly affecting the effectiveness of handling the Cord contractor customer. Company employees stated that this was a contributing cause for the decrease in Cord sales and was counterproductive to the outside sales effort. The lack of resources of the company mandate that it define its customer and design a marketing strategy around that customer.

Since . . .

— Cord sales are decreasing

— 80 percent of sales are derived from the commercial/contractor customers.

— Retail sales have decreased by 20 percent in the past year.

— Commercial/contractor building material sales have increased by 15–18 percent in the last year.

We conclude that the company's focus should be the commercial/contractor customer.

Pricing (Margin Deterioration) versus Sales Growth

The following data show the relationship between sales volume and gross profit margins.

EXHIBIT 2 *(concluded)*

	YTD through July Sales Increase (Decrease) 1980 vs. 1981	Gross Profit Percent Increase (Decrease) 1980 vs. 1981
Cord	(17.0%)	(.6%)
Shaw	9.7	3.0
Total company	2.6	(5.3)

Cord's gross profit decreased because of product mix—the lack of plumbing sales with 65–70 percent gross margins. At Shaw, it appears that pricing was used as a major tool to increase sales. Industry data suggest that the company should become more price competitive. The Cord/Shaw gross profit at 28.6 percent of sales remains high as contrasted to the 25–26 percent gross profit experienced by the industry composite.

EXHIBIT 3
Letter to Suppliers

October 20, 1981

Dear _____:

The purpose of this letter is twofold. First, we would like to thank you for the patience and faith in us that you have expressed during the period that we have been working out the cash flow problems that were confronted earlier this year. The prospects for success that we are able to report here are caused precisely by people like yourself who have stood by us during this difficult time.

Secondly, I am pleased to report that our efforts are succeeding:

(1) The internal steps that will take place appear to be more than adequate to assume success with respect to current operations. Our present business volume is both substantial and adequate. The cash picture is improving—slowly but steadily.

(2) We have isolated the problem period and by the time you receive this letter we will be paying September invoices. All August invoices have been paid also. We will continue paying all future invoices on a current (by end of the following month) basis.

(3) We have created and are implementing a realistic and firm plan to address invoices for the isolated problem period: Invoices for this period (July '82 and earlier) will be paid in a series of _____ equal payments over the next _____ months. You should expect to receive your first payment by _____. Because of the cyclical nature of the business there will be no monthy payments in January, February, or March 1982 and payments will resume in April.

According to our records, the balance due you for the old problem period is $_____ and your monthly payments will be $_____.

If you have any questions regarding these arrangements or the details of your balance please do not hesitate to call.

Thank you for your help.

Sincerely,

P. J. Thomas
Shaw Supply Company, Inc.

EXHIBIT 3 (*concluded*)
Letter to Employees

Dear Employee: October 20, 1981

As you know, we are changing the direction of our company. I would like to highlight these changes.

Focus

Our core business has been and always will be large sales to homeowners, commercial, industrial, and institutional customers. We are going to concentrate on this base for the next 18 months. To accomplish this goal we have and are eliminating peripheral lines: mowers and tractors, electrical, plumbing, and other small ticket retail items. We are expanding our commercial-oriented inventory and displays of hardware, seed, fertilizers, and chemicals.

Organization:

We are merging Cord and Shaw and then dividing the company into five divisions under the direction of the following individuals.

Garden Equipment—Paul Jason
Seed, Fertilizer, and Chemicals—Glen Doral
Home and Hardware—Robert Glades
Inventory Management—Art Lancer
Administration and Finance—Paul Thomas

Suppliers:

We have established a program to pay all suppliers all our old bills in full and in an orderly fashion. Current bills are being paid before the end of the month following purchase.

Inventory Management

Art Lancer will coordinate management of our inventory and establish central purchasing. Everyone is pledged to reduce our extraneous inventory and concentrate our assets in faster moving items. We are selling any item which does not turn and not replacing it.

Personnel:

We are clarifying who does what and has what responsibilities. We are making reductions in areas where we can streamline our organization. We are postponing all wage reviews which come up between December 31, 1981 and December 31, 1982 for six months.

Expenses:

We are making every effort to reduce all expenses. All non resale purchases must be approved in advance by Paul Thomas.

The above program is difficult, but it will work and get us through these troubled times.

(Signed)
Eric

EXHIBIT 4
Financials

Income Statements for Year Ending December 31, 1981 *(in thousands of dollars)*

	Shaw	Cord
Net sales	$6,497	$1,502
Cost of sales	4,718	1,024
Gross profit	1,779	478
Other income	38	6
Operating expenses:		
Salaries and wages	897	259
Maintenance	46	4
Bad debts	29	6
Rent	128	62
Taxes	70	31
Interest	156	94
Depreciation	46	11
Advertising	55	37
Pension/benefits	49	17
Other*	652	90
Total	2,128	611
Income (loss)	(311)	(127)
Tax	0	0
Net income (loss)	$ (311)	$ (127)

*Includes legal, insurance, travel, motor vehicle, utility, etc. expenses.

Balance Sheets Ending December 31, 1981

	Shaw	Cord
Cash	$ 12,918	$ 1,038
Accounts receivable	514,326	109,326
Less allowance for bad debt	(54,121)	(15,521)
Inventories	711,024	261,811
Other current assets	58,929	200,000*
Total	1,243,076	556,654
Loans to stockholders	175,000	—
Plant and equipment	230,011	138,411
Less depreciation	(55,460)	(83,518)
Intangible assets	36,812	7,463
Less amortization	(12,537)	(4,500)
Other	32,411	19,297
Total	406,237	77,153
Total Assets	$1,649,313	$633,807

EXHIBIT 4 (*concluded*)

	Shaw	Cord
Accounts payable	$ 711,377	$220,133
Short-term notes	801,658	404,209†
Other	92,378	122,865‡
Loan from stockholders	—	55,000
Long-term notes	400,000	—
Total	2,005,413	802,207
Common stock	200,000	40,000
Retained earnings	(556,100)	(208,400)
	(356,100)	(168,400)
Total liabilities and equity	$1,649,313	$633,807

*Investment in subsidiary.
†Includes $175,000 due Shaw Company.
‡Includes $35,000 payable to Lillian Weston.

Case 4–4

MICHAEL BREGMAN

In July 1980, Michael Bregman was preparing a strategy to expand his fledgling Canadian restaurant business. During the last eight months, he had started pilot locations for two different restaurant concepts. The first was "Mmmuffins" (as in, "Mmm, good!"). This was a take out bakery operation offering a wide variety of fresh, hot muffins (baked on premises) together with accompanying beverages. The second was "Michel's Baguette," a more elaborate french bakery cafe. Baguette offered a take out counter for a variety of french croissants and breads (also baked in the restaurant) as well as an on-premises cafe with soups, salads, sandwiches on fresh bread, an omelette bar, and fresh croissants.

Michael hoped to build a substantial restaurant chain with one or both of these concepts. Even though the two pilots were just underway, a flurry of construction of new shopping centers across Canada appeared to offer a unique opportunity for rapid growth. In fact, one major developer was negotiating with Michael for a package of locations right now. The package included some locations Michael felt would be good, but the developer also wanted commitment to some locations Michael felt would do poorly. Such a deal would be a major undertaking for his young company. It would heavily influence the company's direction during the crucial formative years.

Michael was still considering the merits of franchising versus internal growth and evaluating the relative attractiveness of the two restaurant concepts. He wanted to make conscious strategic decisions in these areas before he committed to any course of action.

BACKGROUND

Michael Bregman was a native of Canada. After earning a degree in Finance from Wharton at the University of Pennsylvania, he entered directly into the MBA program at Harvard from which he graduated in 1977. Michael sought a job in the food business because of an interest he had developed due to his family's long association with that industry.

Michael's grandfather had built a successful bakery as had Michael's father, Lou Bregman. In 1971, Lou Bregman had purchased Hunt's and Woman's Bakery (Hunt's) division from the Kellogg Company which Lou had been supplying. The division had been losing money on annual sales of about $20 million, but under Lou Bregman's guidance soon prospered. Hunt's sold bakery products to 130 company-owned retail stores and to 370 supermarkets. Michael had worked after school and in summer jobs in various restaurants and bakeries.

> I joined Loblaws, a Canadian chain that was perceived as being a very stodgy supermarket company. Everybody thought I was crazy because I had offers from some of the big consulting companies and investment banks, places where I should be going. But at Loblaws I had the chance to work for a new president with no experience in supermarketing right in the midst of a turn-around. I would call him a marketing genius and really went to work for him rather than the company.

Michael worked on corporate development projects including the launch of NO-NAME [unbranded] products in Canada which was very successful.

Things were not going as smoothly at Hunt's. Lou Bregman was having disagreements with his majority partners (who were in the real estate business) as the result of some difficult financial times. The company was in a turmoil and Lou asked Michael to join Hunt's to see if he could help out. Michael agreed in June of 1978, and was put in charge of the retail division. Lou concentrated on the central bakery operations, and the other partners attempted to provide overall direction. Michael quickly found himself at odds with the other managers and strongly disagreed with what he thought were stupid decisions. He stayed at his father's urging until December 1978, then resigned.

> I must say that I felt pretty defeated at the time. I'd worked so hard and had accomplished so little. I'd fought a lot, and I've never been much of a fighter, but I also can't do anything unless I believe in it. It was a difficult time.
>
> I didn't know what I was going to do. I'd always planned all along to start my own business at some time. I didn't know what or when, but I did know I

wanted to do it quickly because I think it gets harder and harder as life goes on and you have all sorts of commitments.

I went out for lunch one day with my old boss from Loblaws who suggested I go back to them again. I really hadn't thought of that but had simply been keeping in touch. I told him I couldn't really make a long-term commitment because my heart was in starting my own business. He said that would be all right, that he could put me on a short-term assignment. It took about five minutes worth of convincing for me to agree.

EVOLUTION OF A START-UP

As his first project, Michael was asked to recommend a strategy for Loblaws' in-store bakeries: What should they be? Should they be bake-off stores of frozen products [baking prefrozen doughs] or scratch bakeries? Should Loblaws have them? He prepared a similar study of the deli department. Michael was then asked to implement his recommendations in the bakery area and became Director of Bakery Operations, a new position. He worked closely with the Manager of Bakery Operations who was oriented to the day-to-day management more than to strategy and planning for the department. Bakeries became important to Loblaws new super stores which were designed to provide greater variety and savings than traditional supermarkets. Bakery products were successful in drawing customers to the stores with store-baked crusty bread and rolls.

> Somewhere along the way, a small businessman visited me. He thought we should sell his muffins in our stores. We had taken muffins for granted: they'd been around forever and were sort of stable and unexciting—what do you do with a muffin? All of a sudden this fellow comes in with these giant muffins, much larger than any we'd ever seen. We sold our small muffins for 15 cents each; we'd have to retail his at 45 cents.
>
> Naturally everybody was against them just on price. But I decided to test them in two of the most affluent stores. They went like crazy, it was wild. We kept upping the orders and we could never keep them in stock. We didn't promote them, just put them on the counter, but there was immediate appeal. That triggered something in me. Seeing that you could take a very drab product and make it exciting. And I thought you could do more with it than I saw him do.

Despite Michael's interest in the food industry and fascination with the performance of the large muffins, he really didn't like the bakery business:

> It always seemed to be an old man's game, a tired industry that was declining and very production-oriented, very unexciting. Over 75 percent of the retail bakeries in North America had closed between the early 60s and mid-70s. Before that, the retail baking industry was comprised of hundreds of independent skilled bakers who had come over from Europe and opened up shops

and carried on as they had in Europe. The little shops handled two or three hundred items, mostly, if not all, made by hand. You needed skilled bakers to continue, who became very expensive and in short supply.

Mom and Pop were willing to work crazy hours and take low salaries because they wanted their own bakery. But by the mid-70s those same skilled people could get jobs in any supermarket in the country, earn $25,000, work 37–38 hours, have terrific benefits and no headaches. That, together with the shift of customers to the shopping centers, really put an end to most of that business.

The pressure really began with the bakery chains, like my father's, that were serviced from central plants. But then the supermarkets started doing in-store baking, selling a fresher product at a lower price. Gas had gone crazy and it had become prohibitive to deliver fresh products from a central facility to many small shops daily or twice a day. And the supermarket had a different view of the baking business. They were very price conscious. They weren't in the baking business to make money, but to draw customers to buy other things. The last thing they wanted to do was to draw a customer into the store to see a bakery that had prices that were too high. Their cost systems were often really rather silly and ignored investment and overhead and value of the space used by any individual area. Some supermarket departments, like the bakeries, were really much more expensive marketing tools than they thought. But the supermarkets tended to just look at the total bottom line as a contribution number. Looking at these things, it was easy to be negative about the industry.

Then I started to feel there was a massive opportunity out there! People still liked baked goods and they hadn't been supplied with them in the right fashion. As I thought in general terms of what was going to happen to the retail baking industry, I felt that the stores were going to get smaller and the industry would have to specialize in one or two lines of products. Also you'd surely have to bake on premises to create the freshness that no one else could duplicate. That's really the key component of quality in our industry. I also reminded myself that the retail baking business is primarily based on impulse sales and location is extremely important.

I guess I had all of this in mind in May 1979 while my father and I were driving to a restaurant show in Chicago . For the first time it really occurred to me: Why don't we open a muffin shop? We sort of chuckled—what a stupid idea. Later I began to think, why not? There's not a lot of money to lose and a lot to gain if it worked. It was totally different from anything we'd seen in North America.

During the summer, I began investigating some space in the Eaton Centre. This was Toronto's principal downtown shopping complex with over 3.7 million square feet of space. The Eaton Centre was directly connnected to three subway terminals and had 200,000 office workers within easy walking distance. It was anchored by two major department stores and two office towers. There were over 300 retail shops and restaurants in the complex. Their leasing agent was pretty skeptical, but was willing to lease some space. In August, I committed to lease 350 square feet at $15,000 a year or 8 percent of sales, beginning December 1. Now I needed to develop my shop.

In the meantime, Lou Bregman had sold his interest in Hunt's and had considered retirement. Yet when he had the chance to buy a downtown Bagel Nosh store that had gone bankrupt, he decided to develop a new full-service restaurant and bakery called Bregman's. Michael was helping his father get started with that, and Lou Bregman co-guaranteed the lease obligations with Michael for the muffin shop.

In addition to his duties at Loblaws, helping his father's new venture, and planning his muffin shop, Michael found himself drawn into yet another start-up:

> My wife and I had honeymooned in France when we were married in May 1978. I really fell in love with their croissants. I couldn't believe how great they were. I'd never tasted a decent croissant in North America. They were all weak imitations and I thought this would be a great product to bring over here. I had seen a few French bakery stores in Chicago and New York, but very few. I knew that this would be something to pursue in the future.
>
> As we were settling our lease deal for the muffin shop in the Eaton Centre, I mentioned to the leasing agent that I had heard that a French bread chain, Au Bon Pain, was coming to the center. He was surprised I'd heard of it, but said they had some problems with them. I said I was planning to get in the same business and he got very excited. He called his boss and very quickly offered to negotiate with us. Space in the Eaton Centre was very difficult to obtain and seemed to me to be one of the best possible locations. So we leased the space and decided to do our French bakery too. Again, we personally guaranteed the leases.

Despite the serendipitous opening at the Eaton Centre, Michael's commitment to the French bakery restaurant was not a spur-of-the-moment decision. He had been actively investigating the possibilities of both the muffin shop and the French bakery since the Chicago show in May. Because the French bakery would require much more capital, Michael had prepared a short business plan which he circulated to three or four people he thought might invest. One was Ralph Scurfield of Calgary, president of the NuWest Group, the largest homebuilder in North America. Michael had met him while Ralph was enrolled in an executive program at Harvard. Michael had done a field study for NuWest and had kept in touch with Ralph. Ralph said that he knew very little about the restaurant business, but that he did know Michael Bregman and would be willing to bet some money on him. A long negotiation ensued as Michael sought locations for the muffin shop or for the French bakery. They reached agreement in the fall:

> We capitalized the company with $450,000. My father and I each put in $62,500 in common stock and Ralph put in $125,000 in common stock and an additional $200,000 in preferred shares. I had a net worth of about $8,000 and got a loan for my share. I had to get my wife, mother, and father to cosign and my parents to put their house up. It scared the daylights out of me. If things went wrong, it wouldn't sink them, but I didn't know how I could live with it.

I would take a salary cut to $25,000 a year, which together with my wife's income would just about let us live and cover the loan. The contract ended up 60 pages long with 5 pages of basics and the rest disaster clauses. I would have tie-breaking power unless things went wrong and would also have to get Ralph's approval for capital expenditures over $5,000. The initial spending requirements were approved as part of the agreement. There was also a complex redemption plan for the preferred which included penalties for not making the five-year schedule.

The fall of 1979 was frantic as Michael managed to get both of his projects underway. Although he and his father had been in the baking business, neither of them was familiar with the special processes needed for muffins of this type nor with French baking. At the same time Michael was working to design the stores, he had to find and test muffin recipes and learn to operate the specialized French baking equipment. Part of his strategy was to use the very best help he could find. For design, he employed Don Watt & Associates, one of Canada's premier designers. The equipment suppliers were also very helpful in the strenuous task of laying out all of the necessary customer service and baking equipment in 350 square feet for the muffin shop. Michael also found a French baker who lived in Washington who agreed to come up just before the bakery opened to teach several bakers how to bake French bakery products.

Somehow they got underway. Michael left Loblaws at the end of November 1979 and Mmmuffins opened December 15. Michael's Baguette began construction at that point and opened in April 1980. It was not a time Michael would like to repeat.

EVALUATING THE FIRST EFFORTS

By July 1980, the two stores were beginning to stabilize and Michael was preparing to expand. He reviewed the state of each operation to help him decide what directions he might take.

He was pleased with both store designs and concepts. The extra expense and effort he had put in store planning had been well worth the investment. Both facilities were attractive and inviting. As for product selections, they had developed recipes for over 15 varieties of muffins which could be made from four different base mixtures. About 10 would be offered at any point in time. At Baguette, the menu appeared workable and was proving to be a popular range of choices (Exhibit 1).

Sales for both stores had been encouraging and costs were beginning to steady. He now had seven months of experience with Mmmuffins and three months with Baguette. Exhibit 2 is a record of sales and variable costs for the two stores. Exhibit 3 is a year-to-date financial statement showing the total performance and financial position.

After hectic start-up periods, the operations of each store were now also satisfactory. As expected, they were very different from each other. The Mmmuffins store had only 350 square feet of space. That small area had to contain supplies' storage, preparation of raw materials and mixes, baking, clean-up, and the retail service counters. Michael described how this worked:

> I think our design was one of the very most important reasons behind our early success. Don Watt was able to create the magnet to draw customers in the first time. If they like our product, liked our service, they'd come back. They came in first because of the color, the lighting, the photography—it's just a different showcase.
>
> The design also worked well functionally. There's just enough space to do everything, but no extra space to become cluttered or dirty and not be corrected. The customer cannot see the preparation area, but the manager can easily keep track of all activities. The total staff complement for the store runs between 6 and 12 people including part-timers, depending on the part-time mix. You need one manager and one assistant to cover the shifts. There are sales people at the counter and bakers. You can trade-off some during slack buying periods. Service at the counter is fairly simple, and you can train a baker in two days from start to finish. You could almost get this down to two hours for most of the functions.
>
> Although we didn't really know what we were doing when we opened, we soon learned better ways to do things. We got better at finding and selecting specialized preparation equipment that fit our particular needs. Since we bake right from scratch using no commerical mixes, every extra efficiency helped. We learned what items we could make ahead of time and better ways to store them. This is really important when you begin baking early in the morning before opening and continue throughout the day.
>
> I knew that if we were going to grow, we'd have to systematize the operation, so during the first months I wrote an operating manual with everything from opening procedures, to how to clean the store, to recipes, to baking procedures, to how to greet customers and work the counter—everything. I found it one of the most grueling experiences I had ever been through in my life. I was working behind the counter myself during those opening months and was learning how important those controls and procedures were.
>
> I also learned how important the manager was. As Baguette opened and I left the Mmmuffins store under the supervision of a manager I had hired, little problems started to arise—fighting among the staff, quality being a little less consistent than it should have been. I'm sure there was fault on both sides, but I found that the manager constantly needed attention.
>
> But all in all, I was very pleased.

As a much larger and more complete bakery and restaurant, Michael's Baguette was much more complex:

> Baguette had 2,500 square feet of space which was really a bit too tight. This had a larger food preparation, baking, and storage area, a take out bakery

counter, the cafeteria-style serving line, and an on-premises eating area with seats for 35. Once again, our physical design was an important asset. Our store helped attract customers at the same time that it worked well functionally in a very tight space.

With a larger menu, there were many more tasks to perform. There was a total staff of 55 to 60 people, including part-timers. You really need a very qualified head manager to be the general manager of the overall business, as well as two assistant managers who have the capability to be the acting general manager when the general manager isn't there. You need a head baker who is a skilled baker and can guide the whole production area of the store. There are kitchen prep people, two kinds of service people, cafeteria counter people who actually prepare your portions, the salads, and sandwiches. Most of these jobs are more complex than those at Mmmuffins, and the baking is particularly difficult. It takes 20 steps to make croissants, and the breads also have more steps and are more demanding than making muffins. There are many delicate areas where you can ruin the product, but I must say that we brought in the right equipment from France and, with care, can consistently make excellent products. All of the baked goods and other items are made from scratch and are continuously baked throughout the day.

I began to spend most of my time at Baguette once it opened and again had to learn as we went. This would take more effort to systematize and I hadn't written a manual here yet. I was lucky in hiring some good bakers and restaurant managers to help me out. I went after managers that I had heard did a good job for other restaurants in the city and was able to get two to join me. They both worked out very well.

The primary appeal of each concept was absolute freshness and quality of baked goods. As Michael looked at the two operations, he was satisfied that they each properly reflected the key conceptual definitions he felt were critical to their success: hard-to-replicate standards of quality with costs kept to acceptable levels by careful specialization, organization, and store design. Michael described how these worked together:

> For superior quality our recipes are based on using fresh eggs, buttermilk, and other very perishable items—very expensive, very hard-to-handle items. Bakeries don't use fresh eggs; they use powered or frozen. But we decided we would use fresh: we didn't care about any of the rules; we would be better than anybody. But this created very difficult production problems. You can't make too much at once, and you can't make too little because it's a waste of time. The mixes and products aren't very storable, you can't freeze them, and you can't keep them for more than one day.
>
> Besides ingredients, we control our quality by specializing. This means making limited types of baked goods in the best possible way and then providing only those menu items needed to support the specialized baking operation. With Mmmuffins this is practically absolute: there are only muffins and beverages. The bakery for Baguette is simply too capital intensive for the menu to remain that simple. So we combine the bakery with a restaurant. Having the fresh croissants and fresh bread to make sandwiches helps the res-

taurant, and the sampling that goes on in the restaurant spills over and helps the bakery. The restaurant and bakery counters also have different peak times, so you have better distribution for the bakery equipment and your service people can sway back and forth. But other than the baking, we do no cooking! It's just an assembly operation. We assemble salads, cut meat, cut cheese. But except for omelettes, we don't fry anything, we don't boil anything, we don't cook. Other than the baking, in terms of the back-of-the-house, it's a very simple restaurant.

The stores' layouts and service delivery systems are designed to efficiently support each menu concept. Both provide efficient preparation areas. Both have ovens prominently situated in view of shoppers and passers-by—the sight and aroma of fresh baking are major merchandising tools. At Mmmuffins, we have very efficient customer handling along with some innovative packaging for quantity purchases. At Baguette, we selected a cafeteria line for the restaurant to go along with the counter service for the take-out bakery. This is one step up from the fast food joint where you have to fight for a seat and eat from a tray with disposables. We use better dinnerware, metal utensils, and glasses. This is a step down from the full-service restaurant where you are served by waitresses. We selected this because I felt strongly that in the mall environment, people want to eat quickly but in some comfort.

CONSIDERING FRANCHISING

With both Mmmuffins and Baguette well started, Michael began to consider expansion. He felt there should be many opportunities for good restaurants and specialty food stores despite competition ranging from retail bakeries and supermarkets, to fast food operations, to full-service restaurants. Almost all of these types of competitors would be clustered in large shopping areas and malls. Yet both had held their own in the very competitive and highly visible Eaton Centre. The question was how to expand. Michael had two concepts, limited experience, and limited resources. How could he best capitalize on his work to date to build a significant restaurant business?

One avenue of growth he could pursue was franchising. Certainly enough others had chosen this method to make franchising a very important factor in the Canadian and U.S. economies. A "Foodservice & Hospitality Magazine" survey estimated that franchising represented 16.5 percent of the total Canadian foodservice and lodging industry in 1979. This market share was increasing. Survey respondents reported a 29 percent increase in total food service franchise sales resulting from a 10.5 percent increase in total units operating and a 17 percent increase in average sales per unit (to $381,443).

For U.S. firms, franchised units accounted for approximately one quarter of all food service sales. Exhibit 4 lists several characteristics of U.S.-owned restaurant franchisors for 1978 with projections for 1979 and 1980. About 40 percent of all U.S. franchised restaurants were located in

California, Texas, Ohio, Illinois, Michigan, and Florida. A January 1980 study by the U.S. Department of Commerce noted that:

> The entry into the restaurant franchising system mostly by small companies continued in 1978 with a net gain of 38 franchisors, bringing the total to 388. During 1979, 17 franchisors with a total of 227 restaurants, 198 franchisee-owned, went out of business while 13 franchisors with a total of 168 restaurants, 84 franchisee-owned, decided to abandon franchising as a method of marketing.
>
> Big franchisors with over 1,000 units each increased to 11 in 1978 from 8 a year earlier. These 11 franchisors had 27,750 restaurants, 50.2 percent of all franchised restaurants, and accounted for $11.4 billion in sales, 54 percent of the total. Compared with 1977, the 8 franchisors with over 1,000 units each had 45 percent of the total units and 47 percent of the sales.
>
> Menu expansion and diversification continues on the increase to meet the mounting competition from other chains and to enlarge customer counts that have been adversely affected by higher food costs and periodic gasoline shortages. The higher costs of cosmetic and structural construction changes are forcing fast food franchisors to reevaluate their investment in design, and cast their decor changes more and more in marketing terms.

Growth statistics of the 25 largest U.S. franchise restaurant systems are shown in Exhibit 5.

While franchising was one means to achieve growth for either Mmmuffins or Baguette, it would impose additional complexities in doing business. A franchisee is an independent businessperson with personal capital at risk and a fair amount of management flexibility. In addition to the demands inherent in such relationships, there was increasing government regulation of franchise offerings and operations. On October 21, 1979, a new U.S. Federal Trade Commission rule requiring comprehensive disclosure statements for prospective franchisees became effective. Sixteen separate states also required various types of disclosures (although some states accepted a uniform format). Canada had no such comprehensive disclosure requirement, but many felt there was a need for one and expected such a rule in Canada in the future. Some pressure for such regulation came from established franchisors who were worried about the effect that a few incapable, overconfident, or unscrupulous franchisors might have on the industry.

The areas of disclosure required by the new U.S. law illustrate the many aspects of the business and the relationship that must be considered in franchising. These include:

— Specific background information about the identity, financial position, and business experience of the franchisor company and its key directors and executives.
— Detail of the financial relationship including initial and continuing fees and expenses payable to the franchisor.

— Requirements for doing business with the franchisor or affiliates (such as purchase of supplies from a franchisor source), and any realty fees, financing arrangements, or other financial requirements.
— Restrictions and requirements for methods of operation placed on the franchisee.
— Termination, cancellation, and renewal terms.
— Control over future sites.
— Statistical information about the number of franchises and their rates of termination.
— Franchisor-provided training programs and other support.

Even without disclosure requirements, it was considered a good idea to develop policies and practices for dealing with franchisees for the long term before opening the first operation. One reason for this was a general desire for consistent treatment of franchisees. Some examples of current practices of Canadian franchisors are summarized in Exhibit 6.

Increased regulation was not the only area of change in franchising. There was ever-increasing competition in Canada as more U.S. franchisors sought new markets in other countries. The need for better communication with franchisees had started a trend in the development of franchisee advisory councils by franchisors. The ultimate roles of these councils was still evolving. There was also a fairly constant trade back and forth between franchisors repurchasing franchised units for company ownership and company-owned units being franchised.

A QUESTION OF STRATEGY

The question of using franchising as a means of expansion was only one aspect Michael needed to consider in planning for growth for his restaurant business. A fundamental question was how suitable were his concepts for wide use? He had started and managed both current units personally. How well would they "travel"? Both concepts depended on fresh baking which made them more demanding than many franchises. Other stores offering similar baked goods (donuts, cookies, or other items) used premixed ingredients, premade frozen products to be baked in the units, or simply distributed centrally baked products.

Michael also had to include the capital requirements and likely performance of additional units of either type in his planning. His estimates of capital requirements for new locations are shown in Exhibit 7. His estimates of stand-alone operating results if operated by a franchisee are shown in Exhibit 8.

Finally, no matter what methods of growth he might choose, his location strategy would be critical. Where would his concepts best fit? One aspect was the type of location and surrounding demographics. Another would be geographic—how far away, and Canada versus the United States. Even within Canada, there were very different demands between the more stable eastern portion and the rapidly growing western area. Should he concentrate on finding more established and stable locations in the east? Or should he take advantage of the many openings in new centers that a construction boom in the west was creating? What differences were there between good locations for Mmmuffins and good locations for Baguette?

AN OFFER OF LOCATIONS

To help learn about possible locations that might be available, Michael began talking with major Canadian development companies. One important firm was Real Estate Canada (REC) which developed and controlled a large number of shopping malls across Canada. After preliminary discussions, REC offered Michael locations for Mmmuffins stores in one new mall and one mall expansion, both in Toronto suburbs. This was an important developer and Michael felt the locations would be good for Mmmuffins, so he agreed and they shook hands on the deal.

Later, while lawyers were completing the legal paper work, things changed. REC came back and said they wanted to include another location in Manitoba in central Canada in the agreement:

> They said they were creating a package for me: the two Toronto locations and Manitoba in the west or nothing. And being the naive kid that I was, I got extremely upset. But we had a deal! I'd already told my partner about my plans for Toronto and that was OK, but the town in Manitoba had only about 50,000 people and was a thousand miles away. It was a rural environment and difficult to reach.
>
> So I told them that we were just a young chain, and we just wanted to do a few stores at a time. They said no, that's the way it has to be. They had a brand new mall and needed to fill the space.

In the excitement of the offer of the initial two locations, Michael had been somewhat swept away with events. Now he was confronted with a more difficult situation than he had anticipated and felt he should pause to rethink his overall company strategy before reacting to this new offer. How should he make his company grow? How fast? How should he divide his efforts between the two concepts? Now he realized he should answer these questions before he went ahead with any expansion deal.

EXHIBIT 1
Michel's Baguette Product Line Highlights

BAKERY			*CAFE*		
Bread:	Baguette		Salads:	Julienne	
	Boule			Niçoise	
	Alpine			Spinach	
	Mini-Baguette			Side Salad	
	Whole Wheat Baguette			Salade du Jour	
Croissants:	Butter		Soups:	Yellow Pea with Ham	
	Almond			Soup du Jour	
	Petit Pain Au Chocolat				
	Raisin-Custard		Quiches:	Bacon	
	Cream Cheese			Spinach	
	Cheddar Cheese			Mushroom	
	Ham and Cheese				
	Apple Cinnamon		Omelette Bar:	Cheddar Cheese	
	Blueberry			Ham	
	Cherry			Swiss Cheese	
				Green Pepper	
				Onion	
				etc. . . .	
			Sandwiches:	Ham and Cheese	
				Roast Beef	
				Tuna	
				Chicken Salad	
				Egg Salad	
				Cream Cheese	
				Swiss Cheese	
				Le Hero	
				Le Jardin	
				Roast Beef and Herb Cheese	
				etc. . . .	
			Beverages:	Coffee	
				Tea	
				Milk	
				Soft Drinks	
				Juices	
				Perrier	
			Croissants:	(as in Bakery)	

EXHIBIT 2
Initial Operating Results

| | | | | Percent of Sales | | |
Period Ending	No. Wks.	$ Sales	Avg. $ Sales per Week	Food, Supplies	Labour	Food, Supplies, and Labour
Mmmuffins:						
Jan. 19, 1980	5	9,010	1,802	38.2	38.8	77.0
Feb. 16	4	10,866	2,716	36.3	29.8	66.1
March 15	4	14,901	3,725	24.5	23.9	48.4
April 12	4	17,250	4,312	28.0	22.5	50.5
May 10	4	16,696	4,174	34.6	25.6	60.2
June 7	4	17,346	4,337	38.5	25.4	63.9
July 5	4	20,602	5,150	31.1	21.0	52.1
Highest week's sales June 21—$5,574						51.4%
Michel's Baguette:						
May 10	4	44,470	11,118	37.7	33.5	68.2
June 7	4	52,921	13,230	27.4	25.4	52.8
July 5	4	65,487	16,372	25.9	23.1	49.0
Highest week's sales June 21—$17,289						48.7%

EXHIBIT 3
Financial Statements

BALANCE SHEET
June 30, 1980
(Unaudited)

Assets

Current assets:	
Term deposit	$120,000
Receivables	1,525
Inventory	6,669
Prepaid expenses	15,345
Deferred charges	1,062
Deferred income taxes	7,250
Total current assets	151,851
Equipment and leasehold improvements	400,741
Incorporation expense—at cost	7,151
Total assets	$559,743

EXHIBIT 3 (*continued*)

Liabilities and Shareholders' Equity

Current liabilities:

Bankers' advances	$ 1,436
Payables and accruals	124,736
Dividend payable	4,500
Total current liabilities	130,672

Shareholders' equity:

Share capital	450,000
Deficit	(20,929)
Total liabilities and shareholders' equity	$559,743

STATEMENT OF LOSS AND DEFICIT
Period from Inception, December 4, 1979, to June 30, 1980
(Unaudited)

Sales	$269,428
Cost of sales	169,919
Gross operating profit	99,509
Store expenses	78,473
Income from store operations	21,036
Other income—Interest	14,972
	36,008
Administration expenses	55,187
Net loss before income taxes	19,179
Deferred income taxes	7,250
Net loss	11,929
Dividends	9,000
Deficit, end of period	$ 20,929

EXHIBIT 3 (*concluded*)

INTERNAL STATEMENTS OF OPERATIONS
Inception to July 5, 1980

	Mmmuffins	*Michel's Baguette*
Sales	$106,404	$162,745
Food costs	35,090	44,861
Gross profit	71,314	117,884
Operating expenses:		
Supplies	6,083	7,259
Labour	29,249	52,333
	35,332	59,592
Gross operating profit	35,982	58,292
General expenses	2,228	1,992
Occupancy costs	19,411	35,609
Administrative costs	5,442	8,137
Total expenses	27,081	45,738
Net profit from operations	8,901	12,554
Add depreciation and amortization	5,367	9,005
Cash flow from operations	$ 14,268	$ 21,559

Note: Slightly different period than prior statements.

EXHIBIT 4
Statistics of U.S.-Owned Restaurant Franchises

Restaurants (all types)*

Item	1978	1979†	1980†	Percent Changes 1978–79	1979–80
Total number of establishments	55,312	59,928	66,672	8.3	11.3
Company-owned	15,510	16,781	18,549	8.2	10.5
Franchisee-owned	39,802	43,147	48,123	8.4	11.5
Total sales of products and services: ($000)	21,100,788	24,591,880	28,990,499	16.5	17.9
Company-owned	6,733,545	7,816,198	9,111,129	16.1	16.6
Franchisee-owned	14,367,243	16,775,682	19,879,370	16.8	18.5
Total sales of products and services by Franchisors to Franchisees: ($000)					
Merchandise (non-food) for resale	33,013	37,534	48,656	13.7	29.6
Supplies (such as paper goods, etc.)	170,889	231,017	287,379	35.2	24.4
Food ingredients	298,063	383,774	481,004	28.8	25.3
Other	46,817	53,728	40,771	14.8	-24.1
Total	548,782	706,053	857,810	28.7	21.5

*See Tables that follow.
†Data estimated by respondents

Restaurants (all types)*
Distribution by Number of Establishments—1978

Size Groups	Franchising Companies Number	Establishments Number	Percent	Sales ($000)	Percent
Total	388	55,312	100.0	21,100,788	100.0
1,001 and greater	11	27,750	50.2	11,400,272	54.0
501–1,000	11	8,925	16.1	3,513,637	16.7
151–500	34	8,833	16.0	2,928,603	13.9
51–150	59	5,580	10.1	1,712,930	8.1
11–50	153	3,642	6.6	1,360,850	6.4
0–10	120	582	1.0	184,496	0.9

*See Tables that follow.
Source: U.S. Department of Commerce, "Franchising in the Economy 1978–1980," January 1980.

EXHIBIT 4 (*continued*)

Restaurants: 1978–80 Distribution by Major Activity

Number of Establishments

Major Activity	Firms	1978			1979			1980		
		Total	Company-Owned	Franchisee-Owned	Total	Company-Owned	Franchisee-Owned	Total	Company-Owned	Franchisee-Owned
Total	388	55,312	15,510	39,802	59,928	16,781	43,147	66,672	18,549	48,123
Chicken	31	6,708	1,870	4,838	7,193	2,011	5,182	7,826	2,197	5,629
Hamburgers, Franks, Roast Beef, etc.	117	26,038	4,648	21,390	27,833	5,077	22,756	30,651	5,695	24,956
Pizza	66	7,542	3,042	4,500	8,355	3,288	5,067	9,434	3,577	5,857
Mexican (Taco, etc.)	29	2,329	993	1,336	2,527	1,044	1,483	2,913	1,183	1,730
Seafood	11	2,297	899	1,398	2,444	901	1,543	2,704	966	1,738
Pancakes, Waffles	15	1,441	363	1,078	1,577	418	1,159	1,770	491	1,279
Steak, Full Menu	86	7,924	3,479	4,445	8,756	3,813	4,943	9,771	4,180	5,591
Sandwich and Other	33	1,033	216	817	1,243	229	1,014	1,603	260	1,343

EXHIBIT 4 (*concluded*)
Restaurants: 1978–80 Distribution by Major Activity

Sales (in thousands of dollars)

Major Activity	Firms	1978			1979			1980		
		Total	Company-Owned	Franchisee-Owned	Total	Company-Owned	Franchisee-Owned	Total	Company-Owned	Franchisee-Owned
TOTAL	388	$21,100,788	6,733,545	14,367,243	$24,591,880	7,816,198	16,775,682	$28,990,499	9,111,129	19,879,370
Chicken	31	2,034,012	653,977	1,380,035	2,247,838	765,738	1,482,100	2,563,755	899,485	1,664,270
Hamburgers, Franks, Roast Beef, etc.	117	10,862,837	2,589,465	8,273,372	12,961,887	3,038,923	9,922,964	15,521,446	3,595,801	11,925,645
Pizza	66	1,735,279	696,364	1,038,915	2,007,066	776,902	1,230,164	2,364,317	903,182	1,461,135
Mexican (Taco, etc.)	29	602,376	304,697	297,679	648,100	315,922	332,178	766,692	377,652	389,040
Seafood	11	563,827	216,486	347,341	667,098	260,633	406,465	772,794	299,624	473,170
Pancakes, Waffles	15	601,029	139,899	461,130	681,728	164,023	517,705	834,135	216,290	617,845
Steak, Full Menu	86	4,531,709	2,104,623	2,427,086	5,170,218	2,461,797	2,708,421	5,883,140	2,779,340	3,103,800
Sandwich and Other	33	$ 169,719	28,034	141,685	$ 207,945	32,260	175,685	$ 284,220	39,755	244,465

EXHIBIT 5
Top 25 U.S. Franchise Restaurant Systems

Growth in System-Wide Sales 1974–79 (in millions of dollars)					
Franchise System	1974	1978	1979	'74–'79 % Change	'78–'79 % Change
McDonald's	$1,943	$4,575	$5,385	177%	17.7%
Kentucky Fried Chicken†	925.5	1,393.4	1,669	80	19.8
Burger King†	467	1,168	1,463	213	25.3
Wendy's	24.2	783	1,000*	4,032	27.8
International Dairy Queen†	590	823.2	926	57	12.5
Pizza Hut	232	702	829	257	18.1
Big Boy	484*	660*	750*	55	13.6
Hardee's†	280	564.6	750	168	32.8
Arby's	120	353	430	258	21.8
Ho Jo's	300*	425*	425*	42	0.0
Ponderosa†	183	328.5	406.9	122	23.9
Church's	126.9	345	405.7*	220	17.6
Bonanza	190	346	378	99	9.2
Tastee Freez†	267.9*	353.8*	350*	31	(1.1)
Long John Silver's†	45.5	283.4	342	652	20.7
Sonic Drive-ins†	52.1	291.7	336	545	15.2
Burger Chef†	250	301	335	34	11.3
Taco Bell†	71.1*	212*	320*	350	50.9
Western Sizzlin†	100	217.3	278.1	178	28.0
Dunkin' Donuts	163.3	249.4	283.8	74	14.0
A & W	174.4	247.5	255	46	3.0
Arthur Treacher's	48.3	191.5	226.3	369	18.2
Sizzler†	85.5	181.8	225.9	164	24.3
Perkins Cake 'n Steak	75*	200*	223*	197	11.5
Pizza Inn	58.6	165.8	189*	223	14.0

EXHIBIT 5 (*concluded*)

Growth in Number of Units 1974–979

Franchise System	1974	1978	1979	'74–'79 % Change	'78–'79 % Change
McDonald's	3,232	5,185	5,747	78%	10.8%
Kentucky Fried Chicken†	4,627	5,355	5,444	18	1.7
Burger King†	1,199	2,153	2,439	103	13.3
Wendy's	93	1,407	1,818	1,855	29.2
International Dairy Queen†	4,504	820	4,860	8	0.8
Pizza Hut	1,668	3,541	3,846	131	8.6
Big Boy	881	1,041	1,100	25	5.7
Hardee's†	924	1,125	1,231	33	9.4
Arby's	439	818	928	111	13.4
Ho Jo's	922	882	867	(6)	(1.7)
Ponderosa†	389	588	636	63	8.2
Church's	565	970	1,125	99	16.0
Bonanza	550	700	675	23	(3.6)
Tastee Freez†	2,215	2,022	2,000*	(10)	(1.1)
Long John Silver's†	208	1,001	1,007	384	0.6
Sonic Drive-ins†	220	1,061	1,182	437	11.4
Burger Chef†	950	853	831	(13)	(2.6)
Taco Bell†	562	877	1,100	96	25.4
Western Sizzlin†	140	319	400	186	25.4
Dunkin' Donuts	780	956	1,007	29	5.3
A & W	1,899	1,500	1,306	(31)	(12.9)
Arthur Treacher's	250	730	777	211	6.4
Sizzler†	256	352	402	57	14.2
Perkins Cake 'n Steak	183	342	400*	119	17.0
Pizza Inn	336	743	760	126	2.3

Note: Includes U.S. and foreign sales and units.
*Estimated.
†Fiscal year-end figures (remainder are calendar year-end figures).
Source. *Restaurant Business,* March 1, 1980.

EXHIBIT 6
Sample Canadian Franchisor Terms (*February, 1980*)

Franchisor (Franchise)	History, Current Status and Expansion Plans	Franchise Requirements and Costs	Services Offered to Franchisee
Mister Donut of Canada Ltd. (Mister Donut):	—Established 1955 —55 franchised units in Canada. 715 franchised units in U.S., Japan —Locations: Ont. 43, Que. 9, B.C. 2, Alberta 1 —Cdn. sales $10m. —10 operations to open in 1980	—Initial fee $10,000 —Royalty fee 4.9% of gross sales —Advertising fee .5% —Current equipment package $50,000	—Opening supervision —Field supervision —Classroom training —Newsletter —Site selection —Lease negotiation
McDonalds Restaurants of Canada Ltd. (McDonald's Restaurants):	—Established 1967 in Canada —156 franchised; 168 company owned —Total Cdn. sales $500m —45 new units planned across Canada	—Franchise fee $10,000; initial investment $190,000; total cost is around $400,000 —Percentage rent plus royalty fee —Total commitment by sole operator to run operation —4% advertising fee	—Continual consultation on operation —Marketing —Training —Personnel —Real estate
The Harvest Inn, Inc. (The Pantry Family Restaurant):	—Established 1975 —5 units company owned, 2 franchised, all in B.C. —Full service restaurant for breakfast, lunch and dinner —4 additional units are planned for B.C.	—$20,000 initial fee —Royalty fee 4% gross —Advertising fee 2%	—Full turnkey service incl. site selection, interior design —Accounting, training and personnel selection
Burger King Canada Ltd. (Burger King):	—Established 1976 —27 franchised units & 10 company owned. 2650 worldwide; B.C. 2, Alta. 2, Ont. 30, P.E.I. 1, N.B. 1, N.S. 4 —26 franchised units planned for Ont., N.B., B.C., N.S., Alta. —Menu incl. hamburgers & specialty sandwiches	—Initial fee $40,000 —4% royalty fee —4% advertising fee	—Complete service package

EXHIBIT 6 (*concluded*)

Smitty's Pancake Houses Ltd.:	—Established 1959 —86 franchised and 6 company owned; 3 in Hawaii —Total sales $59m —16 units planned for 1980	—Initial fee $25,000 over 70 seats; $25,000 under 70 seats	
Country Style Donuts Ltd.:	—Established 1962 —66 franchised, 4 company owned, 4 in U.S., Alta. 4, Sask. 1, Man. 3, Ont. 55, Que. 5, N.S. 1 —Total sales $15m —14 new units planned for Alta., Ont. & Sask. —Menu incl. coffee & donuts	—Initial fee $85,000 ($2,500 deposit, $27,500 for construction, $50,000 equipment contract, $5,000 inventory) —Royalty fee 4.5% of gross —2% advertising fee	—Turnkey operation —4-week training course —Supervisory assistance on opening —20-year franchise term

EXHIBIT 7
Estimated Capital Requirements of Additional Stores

Mmmuffins:

Equipment package	$15,000
General construction (including fixtures and leasehold improvements)	40,000–60,000
Opening supplies and inventories	5,000
Miscellaneous (design, insurance, permits, pre-opening salaries, opening promotion, landlord chargebacks, working capital)	10,000
	$70,000–$90,000*

Michel's Baguette:

Equipment Package	$145,000
General Construction (including fixtures and leasehold improvements)	170,000–235,000
Furniture and Supplies	35,000–45,000
Miscellaneous (working capital, design, permits, opening promotion, pre-opening salaries, advance rent)	20,000–40,000
	$370,000–$465,000*

*These are stand-alone estimates. If franchised, any franchise fee would be an additional requirement.

EXHIBIT 8
Estimated Earnings Potential

Mmmuffins Potential Annual Cash Flow*
350-Square-Foot Mall Location

	$3,000		$4,000		$5,000	
Weekly sales	Dollars	Percent	Dollars	Percent	Dollars	Percent
Annual sales	$156,000		$208,000		$260,000	
Food cost (1)	48,360	31.0	62,400	30.0	78,000	30.0
Selling supplies	7,020	4.5	9,360	4.5	11,700	4.5
Labour (incl. benefits) (2)	31,200	20.0	37,440	18.0	41,600	16.0
Gross operating profit	69,420	44.5	98,800	47.5	128,700	49.5
Operating expenses:						
Royalties	9,360	6.0	12,480	6.0	15,600	6.0
Telephone	500	.3	500	.2	500	.2
Utilities	3,500	2.2	3,800	1.8	4,000	1.5
Uniforms and laundry	600	.4	600	.3	650	.3
Advertising	3,120	2.0	4,160	2.0	5,200	2.0
Repairs and maintenance	800	.5	800	.4	800	.3
Insurance	900	.6	900	.4	900	.3
Total occupancy (rent) (3)	16,800	10.8	17,500	8.4	21,000	8.1
Depreciation and amortization (4)	7,000	4.5	7,000	3.4	7,000	2.7
Miscellaneous (5)	1,560	1.0	2,080	1.0	2,600	1.0
Total operating expenses	44,140	28.3	49,820	24.0	58,250	22.4
Earnings before interest and tax (6)	25,280	16.2	48,980	23.5	70,450	27.1
Add: Depreciation and amortization (7)	7,000	4.5	7,000	3.4	7,000	2.7
Cash flow before interest, tax, and franchisee compensation	$ 32,280	20.7%	$ 55,980	26.9%	$ 77,450	29.8%

Note: See notes on next page.
*Post start-up; no operator/franchisee compensation is included.

EXHIBIT 8 (*continued*)

NOTES TO MMMUFFINS CASH FLOW PROJECTIONS

1. Based on prices of 60–65¢ per muffin, $3.45 for 6, and 40¢ per cup of coffee.
2. Based on 70-hour weekly selling period with hourly wages of $3.75–$4.75 for baking staff, $3.50–$4 for full-time selling staff, and $3–$3.50 for part-time staff. OWNER-OPERATOR'S COMPENSATION IS NOT INCLUDED.
3. Total occupancy includes all services for which landlord invoices including rent, merchants association fees, common area charges, heating, ventilating, and air conditioning, realty taxes, etc. Total occupancy may very depending on location. We have assumed base rent of $40 per square foot for a 350-square-foot store or 7 percent of sales (whichever is greater) plus $8 per square foot in "extras."
4. Depreciation and amortization is calculated by applying the straight-line method on $70,000 over 10 years.
5. Miscellaneous expenses may include cash shortages, licenses and permits, office supplies, professional fees, etc.
6. Earnings before interest, tax, and franchisee's compensation is expressed as such due to wide variances in compensations paid, amount of debt to service, individual's accounting treatment of expenses, etc.
7. Depreciation, being a noncash expense, is added back to illustrate total cash generated before interest, tax, and franchisee compensation.

EXHIBIT 8 (continued)

Baguette Potential Annual Cash Flow*
3,000-Square-Foot Mall Location

| | Weekly Sales | | | | | |
| | $14,000 | | $18,000 | | $22,000 | |
	Dollars	Percent	Dollars	Percent	Dollars	Percent
Annual sales	$728,000		$936,000		$1,144,000	
Food cost	232,960	32.0	299,520	32.0	354,640	31.0
Selling supplies	21,840	3.0	28,080	3.0	34,320	3.0
Labour (incl. benefits) (1)	203,840	28.0	243,360	26.0	286,000	25.0
Gross operating profit	269,360	37.0	365,040	39.0	469,040	41.0
Operating expenses:						
Royalties	43,680	6.0	56,160	6.0	68,640	6.0
Utilities (2)	14,000	1.9	15,000	1.6	17,000	1.5
Telephone	700	.1	700	.1	700	.1
Uniforms and laundry	2,200	.3	2,600	.3	3,000	.3
Advertising (3)	7,280	1.0	9,360	1.0	11,500	1.0
Repairs and maintenance (4)	5,000	.7	6,000	.6	7,000	.6
Replacements (5)	3,500	.5	4,500	.5	5,500	.5
Insurance	3,000	.4	3,000	.3	3,000	.3
Total occupancy (rent) (6)	75,000	10.3	77,000	8.2	89,500	7.8
Depreciation (7)	30,000	4.1	30,000	3.2	30,000	2.6
Miscellaneous (8)	7,280	1.0	9,360	1.0	11,500	1.0
Total operating expenses	191,640	26.3	213,680	22.8	247,340	21.6
Earnings before interest and tax	77,720	10.7	151,360	16.2	221,700	19.4
Add: Depreciation (9)	30,000	4.1	30,000	3.2	30,000	2.6
Cash flow before interest, tax, and franchisee compensation	$107,720	14.8%	$181,360	19.4%	$ 251,700	22.0%

Note: See notes on next page.
*After 6 month start-up period; no operator/franchisee compensation is included.

EXHIBIT 8 (*concluded*)

NOTES TO BAGUETTE CASH FLOW PROJECTIONS

1. Based on 70-hour weekly selling period with hourly wages of $4-$5 for baking staff, $3.50-$4.50 for full-time service, food preparation and bussing staff and $3.25-$3.75 for part-time staff. Management salaries include: assistant store manager at $14,500 per year, head baker at $15,600 per year. OWNER-OPERATOR'S SALARY IS NOT INCLUDED.
2. Based on actual experience in Toronto store. Utility expenses may vary widely depending on location, use of gas versus electric oven, hours of operation, etc.
3. One percent allocation is for local advertising and promotion. At this time the franchisor does not maintain a national advertising fund.
4. As most equipment is under warranty, first year repair expenses should be lower than projections. Actual cost in future years will vary considerably due to periodic breakdowns, preventive maintenance program, use of equipment, etc.
5. Replacements include costs of replenishing supplies of utensils, dishware, cutlery, trays, etc.
6. Total occupancy includes all services for which landlord invoices: rent, merchants association fees, common area charges, heating, ventilation and air conditioning, realty taxes, etc. We have assumed a base rent of $18-per-square-foot for a 3,000-square-foot store or 6 percent of sales (whichever is greater) plus $7 per square foot in non-rent "extras." Actual total occupancy costs will vary for each location and should be evaluated individually.
7. Depreciation is calculated by applying the straight-line method on $360,000 over 12 years.
8. Miscellaneous expenses may include professional fees, licenses and permits, cash shortages, office supplies, etc.
9. Depreciation, being a noncash expense, is added back to illustrate total cash generated before interest, tax, and franchisee's compensation.

Case 4–5

SSS

In January of 1983, Vincent Lamb, Jr., president of Scientific Systems Services (SSS), was attempting to choose an investment bank to underwrite the initial public offering of SSS stock (see Exhibit 1 for recent financials). SSS had recently decided to become a publicly held corporation, and Lamb had mentioned this fact during a presentation at a financial conference for high-tech firms. In response, several firms had forwarded underwriting proposals to SSS. In addition, Lamb had solicited proposals from additional underwriters and had narrowed the choice down to the four which appear as exhibits in this case. (See Exhibits 2 through 5.)

SSS

SSS designed, marketed, and serviced integrated computer systems for monitoring and controlling industrial processes. These systems combined commercially available hardware and custom software configured to meet customer requirements. The company's principal customers were large electric utilities and automated industrial facilities.

RECENT FINANCING HISTORY

SSS was founded in 1965 by two engineers, and the initial financing was obtained from their personal funds. One of the founders left SSS in 1971, and the other left the company in 1978; Lamb was then installed as chief executive. Lamb and a small group of officers and key employees purchased 152,000 shares from the former president, and SSS entered a period of rapid growth.

In late 1980, two vice presidents left SSS and an option was obtained to purchase their combined holdings, 500,000 shares for $500,000. SSS decided that the most appropriate way to handle this transaction was to arrange for a venture capital firm to purchase this block of stock as well as some additional shares to provide much needed working capital.

The Charles River Partnership purchased the 645,000-share block[1] for $750,000, and later that year purchased an additional 60,760 shares for $3.30 per share. With a major venture capital firm as the largest single owner of SSS, the stage was clearly set for SSS to become a public corporation.

Eleven months later, in November of 1982, SSS was in need of funds to finance its efforts to enter the business of systems integration, i.e., packaging hardware and software. SSS sold 422,640 shares of stock for $7 per share via a private placement which was arranged by the firm J.C. Bradford. At the time of this private placement, Bradford had also attempted to negotiate for the public offering. Lamb had been very careful to keep the two transactions separate, so that SSS would have maximum flexibility in choosing an underwriter.

In early 1983, SSS had decided that it was an appropriate time to consider the option of going public.

— SSS needed a great deal of capital to fund the expansion program (primarily via acquisitions which it had chartered).
— The increased capitalization would help SSS gain credibility for bidding on large contracts with major utilities.
— SSS's ability to attract and hold onto high-caliber employees would be enhanced by a stock option plan and a publicly traded security.

A SECONDARY OFFERING

One issue which had to be resolved centered around a secondary offering of stock. All of the current institutional owners of SSS stock had the right to sell, on a pro-rata basis, their own shares ("piggy-back rights"). (In a primary offering, only the company sells its own authorized but as yet unissued shares of stock—no individuals actually sell stock even though their ownership position is diluted.) Lamb and the board had to decide what portion, if any, of the total offering could be of secondary stock.

---

[1]Note: All share figures and per share amounts have been adjusted to reflect a 5:1 stock split which occurred in February of 1983.

THE SELECTION OF AN UNDERWRITER

Lamb was very concerned that the chosen underwriter have the commitment not only to sell the stock, but to support it strongly as a public issue. Lamb reasoned that, as a low capitalization stock, SSS would be unlikely to develop a strong following with large institutions. Therefore, strong research and market support would be crucial to developing a following of individual investors and eventually, to develop an institutional following as the stock became more widely traded.

Lamb was concerned with several other issues:

— Should SSS use one or two underwriters? If they used two, what additional qualities should they seek in an underwriting team?
— How important was a strong retail brokerage network?

Lamb was charged with recommending a plan of action to the board of directors at a special meeting which would be held the following week. This decision was complicated by the fact that the overall market had improved dramatically over the past several months (see Exhibit 6), and this made comparison of the underwriting offers more difficult.

As he looked over the proposals, Lamb knew that he needed to prepare an agenda for the board discussion and his recommendations as to the priorities of the various considerations.

EXHIBIT 1
Financials

SCIENTIFIC SYSTEMS SERVICES, INC.
Statements of Income and Retained Earnings
For the Years Ended December 31

	1980	1981	1982
Revenues	$4,992,559	$7,920,386	$15,523,134
Cost of revenues	3,244,496	4,830,694	10,314,390
Gross profit	1,748,063	3,089,692	5,208,744
Selling, general and administrative expenses	1,174,415	2,132,373	3,798,272
Operating income	573,648	957,319	1,410,472
Interest income	1,764	24,896	212,370
Interest expense	(47,699)	(42,910)	(134,022)
Income before income taxes	527,713	939,305	1,487,820
Provision for income taxes	238,266	408,047	550,448
Net income	289,447	531,258	937,372
Retained earnings, beginning of year	474,428	733,846	1,239,074
Dividends paid	(30,029)	(26,030)	—
Retained earnings, beginning of year	$ 733,846	$1,239,074	$ 2,176,446
Earnings per share:			
Earnings per common and common equivalent share	$ .13	$ .23	$ .37
Earnings per common share assuming full dilution	$ .13	$ .22	$ .36

EXHIBIT 1 (*continued*)

SCIENTIFIC SYSTEMS SERVICES, INC.
Balance Sheets
December 31

Assets	1981	1982
Current assets:		
Cash and temporary cash investments	$ 816,766	$2,244,504
Certificates of deposit	100,067	308,067
Contract receivables	1,195,169	2,189,444
Income taxes receivable	—	247,363
Costs and estimated earnings in excess of related		
billings on uncompleted contracts	345,366	994,550
Assets held in trust (current portion)	137,669	53,740
Prepaid expenses and other	45,346	37,556
Total current assets	2,640,383	6,075,224
Assets held in trust	1,162,331	228,836
Property:		
Land	355,385	355,385
Building	—	1,147,637
Laboratory equipment	317,783	1,025,687
Furniture and fixtures	312,917	756,705
Leasehold improvements	45,808	85,345
Equipment held under capitalized leases	44,474	276,837
Total	1,076,367	3,647,596
Less accumulated depreciation and amortization	275,297	478,872
Property—net	801,070	3,168,724
Other assets	74,895	88,461
Total	$4,678,679	$9,561,245

EXHIBIT 1 (concluded)

	1981	1982
Liabilities and Stockholders' Equity		
Current liabilities:		
Current portion of long-term debt.	$ 152,635	$ 180,660
Accounts payable	181,733	490,138
Billings in excess of related costs and estimated earnings on uncompleted contacts	348,547	323,456
Accrued payroll and related taxes	90,698	376,599
Accrued employee benefit plan.	—	74,467
Income taxes payable	199,857	—
Deferred income taxes (current portion)	329,356	778,591
Accrued vacation benefits	107,588	172,880
Other	14,993	10,877
Total current liabilities	1,425,407	2,407,668
Long-term liabilities:		
Long-term debt	1,425,293	1,470,659
Deferred income taxes	30,536	114,723
Total long-term liabilities	1,455,829	1,585,382
Stockholders' equity:		
Commitments		
Common stock—$.01 par value; authorized 10,000,000 shares;* issued 575,332 shares in 1981 and 3,337,925 in 1982; outstanding 466,532 in 1981 and 2,773,425 in 1982	115,066	33,379
Paid-in capital	977,703	3,987,420
Retained earnings	1,239,074	2,176,446
Total	2,331,843	6,197,245
Treasury stock—at cost 108,800 shares in 1981 and 564,500 in 1982.	(534,400)	(629,050)
Stockholders' equity—net	1,797,443	5,568,195
Total	$4,678,679	$9,561,245

*Reflects 5:1 split.

EXHIBIT 2
J. C. Bradford Proposal *(Entire Proposal Attached)*

May 7, 1982

Mr. Vincent Lamb
Chairman of the Board and President
Scientific Systems Services, Inc.
Box 610
Melbourne, Florida 32901

Dear Vincent:

J. C. Bradford & Co. is prepared to assist Scientific Systems Services, Inc. in its efforts to increase the firm's equity capital under either of the following options.

OPTION I: A PRIVATE PLACEMENT OF COMMON STOCK TO INSTITUTIONAL INVESTORS. Under this option, we would act as agent to assist SSS in raising $3,200,000 in new equity for the company, and as agent to assist certain shareholders in selling common stock valued at $800,000. We would propose to value the stock at around 23 times the trailing 12 months earnings per share for the quarter ending June 30, 1982. We are prepared to act in this capacity immediately upon notification by you, and would anticipate closing such a transaction within 45 to 60 days after you have given us your approval to proceed. Our fee for this transaction would 3 percent of the proceeds raised, payable at closing.

OPTION II: A PUBLIC OFFERING OF COMMON STOCK. We are prepared to act as manager or co-manager of a public offering of SSS common stock. We understand that you want to raise about $4,000,000 in new equity for the company and $2,000,000 for selling shareholders. We believe that the Company can justify a valuation in such an offering of between 19 times and 23 times trailing 12 month's earnings per share for the quarter ending June 30, 1982. We would suggest an underwriting discount of no less than 7 percent under this option. This offering could take place around September 1, 1982.

Under either option, we would recommend that you have a minimum of a 2.5-for-one stock split prior to undertaking the applicable transaction.

Attached to this letter are several tables which show what could conceivably be done in a public offering at several different pricing levels ranging from a low of 18 times earnings to a high of 23 times earnings. To keep the number of total shares offered at a constant level, we have decreased the number of shares sold by the Company and increased the number of shares offered by selling shareholders at each higher price level. About 45 days prior to the offering date, the Company would fix the number of shares offered by the Company and the selling shareholders, based upon prevailing market conditions at that time. This event would occur upon entering registration with the SEC.

We look forward to further discussions with you and your board on this. Thank you so much for the fine meeting we had this week.

Yours very truly,

J. Robert Philpott, Jr.
Vice President
Corporate Finance Department

EXHIBIT 2 (*continued*)

Historical and Projected Quarterly Earnings per Share, Assuming 510,000 Shares

	1981				1982				1983			
	Q₁	Q₂	Q₃	Q₄	Q₁	Q₂	Q₃	Q₄	Q₁	Q₂	Q₃	Q₄
Quarterly earnings per share	$.225	$.247	$.273	$.296	$ .47	$ .47	$ .50	$ .49	$ .70	$ .74	$ .82	$ .78
Trailing 12 months EPS				$1.04	$1.29	$1.51	$1.74	$1.93	$ 2.16	$ 2.43	$ 2.75	$ 3.04
Trailing 12 months net income ($000)				$ 531	$ 658	$ 770	$ 887	$ 984	$1,102	$1,239	$1,402	$1,550

Assuming 510,000 Shares Outstanding

	1977	1978	1979	1980	1981	1982(P)	1983(P)
Annual revenues ($000)	$1,299	$2,637	$3,531	$4,992	$7,945	$16,400	$21,300
Aftertax profit ($000)	$ 72	$ 271	$ 181	$ 289	$ 531	$ 984	$ 1,550
EPS	$ .14	$ .53	$ .35	$ .57	$ 1.04	$ 1.93	$ 3.04
Increase in revenues		103%	34%	41%	106%	30%	
Increase in after-tax profit		276%	(33%)	60%	84%	85%	58%
Increase in EPS		278%	(34%)	63%	82%	85%	58%

P = projected

EXHIBIT 2 (*continued*)

Historical and Projected Quarterly Earnings per Share, Assuming 1,275,000 Shares

	1981				1982				1983			
	Q_1	Q_2	Q_3	Q_4	Q_1	Q_2	Q_3	Q_4	Q_1	Q_2	Q_3	Q_4
Quarterly earnings per share	$.09	$.10	$.11	$ .12	$ .19	$ .19	$ .20	$ .19	$ .28	$ .30	$ .33	$ .31
Trailing 12 months EPS				$ .42	$ .52	$ .61	$ .70	$ .77	$ .86	$ .97	$ 1.10	$ 1.22
Trailing 12 months net income ($000)				$ 531	$ 658	$ 770	$ 887	$ 984	$1,102	$1,239	$1,402	$1,550

Assuming 1,275,000 Shares Outstanding

	1977	1978	1979	1980	1981	1982[P]	1983[P]
Annual revenues ($000)	$1,299	$2,637	$3,531	$4,994	$7,945	$16,400	$21,300
Aftertax profit ($000)	$ 72	$ 271	$ 181	$ 289	$ 531	$ 984	$ 1,550
EPS	$ .06	$ .21	$ .14	$ .23	$ .42	$ .77	$ 1.22
Increase in revenues		103%	34%	41%	59%	106%	30%
Increase in after-tax profit		276%	(33%)	60%	84%	85%	58%
Increase in EPS		250%	(33%)	64%	83%	83%	58%

EXHIBIT 2 (*continued*)

Scientific Systems Services, Inc.

Assumptions: Offering 9/1/82, off trailing 12 months figures to 6/30/82 of $770,000 net income (or $.61 per share). At P/E multiple of 18, Company worth $13,860,000. 1,275,00 shares outstanding before offering.

$$\frac{\$13,860,000}{1,275,000 \text{ shares}} = \$10.87 \text{ per share} \qquad \text{Offer at } \$11 \text{ per share} \qquad 7\% \text{ spread}$$

Number of shares outstanding before offering	1,275,000
Number of new shares issued by Company	370,000
Number of shares sold by selling shareholders	180,000
Total shares offered for sale	550,000
Number of shares outstanding after offering	1,645,000

$$\text{Dilution } \frac{1,645,000}{1,275,000} = 1.29 = 29\%$$

Offering P/E Multiple	Per Share	New Shares by Company	Gross Proceeds to Company	Net Proceeds to Company	Shares Sold by Selling Shareholders	Gross Proceeds to Selling Shareholders	Net Proceeds to Selling Shareholders	Gross Proceeds of Offering
18	$11	370,000	$4,070,000	$3,785,100	180,000	$1,980,000	$1,841,400	$6,050,000

Projected earnings for the Company for 12 months through 6/30/83 are $1,239,300.

$$\frac{\$1,239,300}{1,275,000} = \$.97 \qquad \frac{1,239,300}{1,645,000} = \$.75$$

If 10% pre-tax, 5% after-tax, earned for 10 months on net proceeds to Company, add $157,712 to 6/30/83 net income and earn $1,397,012 for 12 months ending 6/30/83.

$$\frac{\$1,239,300 + \$157,712}{2/12 \,(1,275,000) + 10/12 \,(1,645,000)} = \frac{\$1,379,012}{212,500 + 1,370,833} = \frac{\$1,397,012}{1,583,333} = \$.88 \text{ or } 44\% \text{ over } 6/30/82.$$

EXHIBIT 2 (continued)

Scientific Systems Services, Inc.

Assumptions: Offering 9/1/82, off trailing 12 months figures to 6/30/82 of $770,000 net income (or $.61 per share). At P/E multiple of 20, Company worth $15,400,000. 1,275,00 shares outstanding before offering.

$$\frac{\$15,400,000}{1,275,000 \text{ shares}} = \$12.08 \text{ per share} \qquad \text{Offer at } \$12 \text{ per share} \qquad 7\% \text{ spread}$$

Number of shares outstanding before offering	1,275,000
Number of new shares issued by Company	340,000
Number of shares sold by selling shareholders	210,000
Total shares offered for sale	550,000
Number of shares outstanding after offering	1,615,000

$$\text{Dilution } \frac{1,615,000}{1,275,000} = 1.27 = 27\%$$

Offering P/E Multiple	Per Share	New Shares by Company	Gross Proceeds to Company	Net Proceeds to Company	Shares Sold by Selling Shareholders	Gross Proceeds to Selling Shareholders	Net Proceeds to Selling Shareholders	Gross Proceeds of Offering
20	$12	340,000	$4,080,000	$3,794,400	210,000	$2,520,000	$2,343,600	$6,600,000

Projected earnings for the Company for 12 months through 6/30/83 are $1,239,300.

$$\frac{\$1,239,300}{1,275,000} = \$.97 \qquad \frac{1,239,300}{1,615,000} = \$.77$$

If 10% pre-tax, 5% after-tax, earned for 10 months on net proceeds to Company, add $158,100 to 6/30/83 net income and earn $1,397,400 for 12 months ending 6/30/83.

$$\frac{\$1,397,400}{2/12\,(1,275,000) + 10/12\,(1,615,000)} = \frac{\$1,379,400}{1,558,333} = \$.90 \text{ or } 48\% \text{ over } 6/30/82.$$

EXHIBIT 2 (*continued*)

Scientific Systems Services, Inc.

Assumptions: Offering 9/1/82, off trailing 12 months figures to 6/30/82 of $770,000 net income (or $.61 per share). At P/E multiple of 22, Company worth $16,940,000. 1,275,00 shares outstanding before offering.

$$\frac{\$16,940,000}{1,275,000} \text{ shares} = \$13.29 \text{ per share} \qquad \text{Offer at \$13.25 per share} \qquad 7\% \text{ spread}$$

Number of shares outstanding before offering	1,275,000
Number of new shares issued by Company	310,000
Number of shares sold by selling shareholders	240,000
Total shares offered for sale	550,000
Number of shares outstanding after offering	1,585,000

$$\text{Dilution } \frac{1,585,000}{1,275,000} = 1.24 = 24\%$$

Offering P/E Multiple	Per Share	New Shares by Company	Gross Proceeds to Company	Net Proceeds to Company	Shares Sold by Selling Shareholders	Gross Proceeds to Selling Shareholders	Net Proceeds to Selling Shareholders	Gross Proceeds of Offering
22	$13.25	310,000	$4,107,500	$3,819,975	240,000	$3,180,000	$2,957,400	$7,287,500

Projected earnings for the Company for 12 months through 6/30/83 are $1,239,300.

$$\frac{\$1,239,300}{1,275,000} = \$.97 \qquad \frac{1,239,300}{1,585,000} = \$.78$$

If 10% pre-tax, 5% after-tax, earned for 10 months on net proceeds to Company, add $159,166 to 6/30/83 net income and earn $1,398,466 for 12 months ending 6/30/83.

$$\frac{\$1,398,466}{2/12 \,(1,275,000) + 10/12 \,(1,585,000)} = \frac{\$1,398,466}{1,533,333} = \$.91 \text{ or } 49\% \text{ over } 6/30/82.$$

EXHIBIT 2 (*concluded*)

Scientific Systems Services, Inc.

Assumptions: Offering 9/1/82, off trailing 12 months figures to 6/30/82 of $770,000 net income (or $.61 per share). At P/E multiple of 23, Company worth $17,710,000. 1,275,00 shares outstanding before offering.

$$\frac{\$17,710,000}{1,275,000 \text{ shares}} = \$13.89 \text{ per share} \qquad \text{Offer at } \$13.75 \text{ per share} \qquad 7\% \text{ spread}$$

Number of shares outstanding before offering	1,275,000
Number of new shares issued by Company	290,000
Number of shares sold by selling shareholders	260,000
Total shares offered for sale	550,000
Number of shares outstanding after offering	1,565,000

$$\text{Dilution } \frac{1,565,000}{1,275,000} = 1.23 = 23\%$$

Offering P/E Multiple	Per Share	New Shares by Company	Gross Proceeds to Company	Net Proceeds to Company	Shares Sold by Selling Shareholders	Gross Proceeds to Selling Shareholders	Net Proceeds to Selling Shareholders	Gross Proceeds of Offering
23	$13.75	290,000	$3,987,700	$3,708,561	260,000	$3,575,000	$3,324,750	$7,562,500

$$\frac{\$1,239,300}{1,275,000} = \$.97 \qquad \frac{1,239,300}{1,565,000} = \$.79$$

Projected earnings for the Company for 12 months through 6/30/83 are $1,239,300.

If 10% pre-tax, 5% after-tax, earned for 10 months on net proceeds to Company, add $167,000 to 6/30/83 net income and earn $1,405,466 for 12 months ending 6/30/83.

$$\frac{\$1,239,300 + \$154,523}{2/12 \,(1,275,000) + 10/12 \,(1,565,000)} = \frac{\$1,393,823}{1,516,667} = \$.92 \text{ or } 51\% \text{ over } 6/30/82.$$

669

EXHIBIT 3
Dean Witter Proposal *(Entire Proposal)*

DEAN WITTER REYNOLDS INC.
100 Peachtree St., N.W., Suite 800,
Atlanta, GA 30303 Telephone (404) 658-5800

January 17, 1983

Mr. Vincent S. Lamb, Jr.
Chairman
Scientific Systems Services, Inc.
1135 John Rodes Boulevard
Melbourne, Florida 32901

Dear Vince:

As we discussed, this letter is written to summarize why Dean Witter Reynolds ("DWR") is best qualified to become Scientific Systems Services' investment banker. In your evaluation of potential investment bankers, we believe that you should consider the capabilities of each firm in light of the services you will require; of equal importance are the people in those firms who will be working with and be committed to Scientific Systems Services. The combination of the people, their degree of commitment, and the firm's resources will ultimately determine the quality of services that your Company receives, and the anticipated quality of these services could well serve as criteria for choosing your investment banker.

A key Dean Witter Reynolds strength lies in managing and co-managing public offerings. The firm's performance during 1980 and 1981 represented approximately 13 percent of all public domestic offerings of debt and equity, totaling approximately $15 billion of capital. DWR also ranks as one of the leading major bracket investment banking firms in terms of dollar volume of initial public offerings. Since January 1980, the firm has managed 17 such offerings with an aggregate dollar amount of $440.75 million. The firm offers not only outstanding syndication abilities as the lead manager, but also unexcelled distribution power. DWR has often shared this distribution strength when acting as the book-running co-manager with a specialty or regional firm as a co-manager. In the southeastern U. S., we have long been the leading originator of initial public offerings among major bracket investment banking firms for companies across a wide spectrum, including technology companies.

Dean Witter Reynolds has substantial experience servicing software and related companies. Recently, DWR was the sole lead underwriter of the intitial public offering of On-Line Software International, Inc. DWR sold 70.9 percent of the offering and placed a substantial percentage of the shares in 100–200 share trades. The offering was priced at $15 on September 29, 1982, and the opening bid and ask were $15.75–$16.25. Buoyed by recent interest in high technology stocks, On-Line's common stock closed on January 14 at $26 bid.

Perhaps more impressive was our lead co-management on Friday, January 14, 1983, of the initial public offering of Quality Micro-Systems (QMS), which was offered at $17 per share and is now trading at $23 bid per share. This offering was brought to fruition in less than two months from our initial involvement, and has received tremendous national retail and institutional interest. QMS, based in Mobile, Alabama, designs, manufactures and markets intelligent graphics processors used primarily in dot-matrix and other printing sys-

EXHIBIT 3 (*continued*)

tems. These processors feature extensive use of "PROM", or applications firmware which, as you know, is essentially software on a circuit board.

In addition, DWR recently completed a private placement of $8 million of convertible subordinated debentures of Applied Data Research, Inc. We will soon be filing as a manager of the initial public offering of American Software, Inc. an Atlanta-based applications software firm. All of these offerings have featured primary involvement by our Atlanta staff, as discussed below.

We believe that DWR's strengths include the following:

Distribution—DWR has long been known for its outstanding retail sales force representing approximately 9 percent of all registered sales personnel working for New York Stock Exchange member firms. More than 4,600 account executives in 338 offices worldwide are in contact with over 1 million active investors making DWR the second largest retail-distribution power with similar strengths in institutional distribution.

Syndication—Your investment banker must be able to distribute securities under all market conditions. DWR's syndicate department provides effective coordination, working with the client to determine the desired distribution pattern for the security, and assembling an underwriting group to achieve this distribuiton. DWR's distribution strength means more than simply an outlet for the sale of securities. Sales professionals maintain close contact with investment banking officers, advising on the factors affecting the market. This close cooperation helps to ensure an effective distribution and optimal pricing in even volatile markets. As a result of our exceptional retail and institutional placement capabilities, DWR, as your book-running manager, can tailor the distribution to be placed with any desired mix of institutional and retail investors and in any geographic location to meet your objectives.

Equity Trading—DWR is one of the largest factors in equity trading in the United States. Our large capital position allows the trading department to take a leading role in the marketplace and exert market-making power even in unfavorable markets. The firm's block trading capabilities are currently considered among the best on Wall Street. In surveys of institutional investors, DWR consistently places among the top firms for research, execution of orders, block trading, and overall service. DWR's Over-the-Counter Trading Department makes markets in approximately 1,000 stocks through 42 traders, representing one of the largest such commitments.

Sensitivity—Pricing new securities requires not only an analysis of comparable companies' trading patterns but also sensitivity to the supply and demand factors of the marketplace. As one of the largest managing underwriters, DWR has consistently demonstrated intelligent pricing resulting in satisfied sellers and investors.

Technology Orientation—DWR has placed a priority on developing high technology business and made a substantial commitment to this business. DWR's technology group is staffed with corporate finance professionals in Atlanta, New York and San Francisco, who work primarily with science and technology clients, including the undersigned. This group, which would be available to you at all times, provides a full range of investment banking services and coordinates support and sponsorship from research, trading, and syndication/distribution.

EXHIBIT 3 (*continued*)

Research Coverage—DWR's research effort is recognized by independent polls as one of the top four in Wall Street. Our research group of some 50 analysts features a technology group of 8 analysts, including 3 analysts who specialize in software and software-related issues. *Terry Quinn* of our staff covers the leading software companies in the southeast, and has indicated a strong interest to follow your Company. Terry is also a coauthor of our *Emerging Growth Stock* publication, in which your Company would be included for monthly distribution to our customers and account executives.

Southeastern Presence—DWR is unique among major investment banking firms in that we have a historic commitment to regionalization. Here in Atlanta, we are the successor to Courts & Co. with a 50-year investment banking heritage, and have the largest investment banking staff of any major firm, including three technology specialists. Bill Green and John Williams would be your key account officers in Atlanta, assisted by other staff members in Atlanta and New York. These officers have extensive experience with technology issuers, including Lanier Business Products, Microdyne Corporation, On-Line Software, Quality Micro Systems, SCI Systems, and numerous others. Should you choose to work with us, we would recommend processing the transaction here in Atlanta. We would use the Atlanta law firm of Hansell, Post as underwriters' counsel. If you choose to print here, we believe you would save considerable expense versus most alternative locations. We have worked in the past with many of the leading SEC corporate lawyers in the South, and could be of assistance in your selection process in this respect if requested. In any event, we could facilitate early implementation of your SEC filing and assure that we would at no time cause you delay in the financing.

Valuation and Capitalization—In valuing your Company, we seek to be aggressive and competitive with offers you may receive from other firms of stature, but also realistic. We have reviewed certain relatively comparable software companies, including Ask Computer Systems, Tera Corporation, and others. These two companies, in particular, currently trade at price/earnings ratios (on trailing 12 months earnings) of 46.8× and 37.3×, respectively. Factors favoring SSS relative to these larger companies include your greater margin expansion potential, your evolving product mix, and other factors. We believe that Scientific Systems Services can be marketed on a basis similar to or perhaps higher than Tera, but perhaps a discount to Ask. We would currently propose a valuation range for the offering of 37.0× possibly to 42× trailing 12 months earnings. Based on your current 1983 earnings forecast of $1.5 million in profits after tax, this range would provide 24.5× and up to 27.5× forecast 1983 earnings of $1.5 million, or a total current value for the Company prior to the offering of about $37 million to $41.5 million.

We understand that you desire to raise approximately $8 million in new equity funds and $4 million in funds for selling shareholders, for a total offering of about $12 million. This could appropriately be accomplished by undertaking a 5 for 1 or similar split of the current shares, providing about 2,750,000 shares prior to the financing. The offering could then be composed of, say, 800,000 shares, consisting of 535,000 shares for the Company and 265,000 shares for selling shareholders, and a filing price

EXHIBIT 3 (*concluded*)

range of perhaps $13 to $16 per share. We would suggest establishing a maximum filing price of perhaps $17 to provide initial flexibility to exceed this range if demand allows. We would also request an over-allotment option of 10 percent of the basic amount of the offering (here 80,000 shares) which could be provided by the Company, by the selling shareholders, or by both.

The above concepts would, of course, be refined more carefully in the context of an implementation.

Underwriters' Compensation—Based on present market conditions, and assuming that your shares were priced in the mid-teens, we would expect to recommend a gross spread of approximately 7 to 7.25 percent. We would be pleased to discuss the components and rationale for this spread level should you desire.

Marketing—If selected as your managing underwriter, we would undertake with you immediately the preparation of a well written prospectus and target an early filing with the SEC as soon as your year-end numbers are available, perhaps by mid or late February. We would then orchestrate a series of institutional and retail information meetings in Atlanta, Boston, New York, Chicago, San Francisco, and other major cities.

Depending on the success of these meetings and demand for your shares, we may be able to increase the filing price range of the offering above the level set forth above. We would be delighted to do this if market conditions allow. In the Quality Micro Systems offering last week, we were in fact able to achieve a price $2 above the high end of the initial filing range and still produce a significant premium in after market trading. Without question, the intensive marketing effort conducted for that company played an important role in this price improvement.

Currently our system is highly attuned to quality offerings of emerging technology companies. We are most eager to demonstrate our marketing capabilities to serve your Company.

We sincerely hope that this presentation will lead you to select DWR as your investment banker. Let us emphasize that we would view this selection as only the first step in building a relationship. We would consider this to be a commitment to work with you over a long period of time, and we hope you would view it in the same way. We are anxious to begin working with you at an early date and feel that such a relationship will be mutually rewarding. If there are any questions, please do not hesitate to call.

Sincerely yours,

DEAN WITTER REYNOLDS, INC.

William S. Green
Managing Director

John Williams
Vice President

EXHIBIT 4
E.F. Hutton Proposal *(Excerpts from Proposal)*

Table of Contents

Introduction   *Introductory Letter

Section I
    Technology Group
    E.F. Hutton Technology Group
    Segmentation of Capital Markets
    *Segmentation of Managing Underwriters
    Distribution of Technology Common Stocks
    Performance as a Manager
    Client Reference Sheet

Section II
    Pricing Analyses for Scientific Systems
    *Price/Earnings Analysis
    *Recapitalization Analysis
    *Valuation Studies

Section III
    Scientific Systems Pricing: Comparable Company Analysis
    Comparative Pricing Analysis
    *Market Performance Graphs

Section IV
    Scientific Systems Pricing: Intitial Public Offerings
    *Comparative Pricing Analyses of Recent Technology
    Initial Public Offerings
    *1982 Initial Public Offerings
    *1. Growth and Business Information
    *2. Gross Spread Information
    *3. Dilution and After Market Performance

Section V
    Marketing Approach at E.F. Hutton
    Common Stock Marketing Strategy
    Syndication
    Timetable

Section VI
    Internal Marketing
    Introduction to Retail System
    Sales Offices and A.E.'s
    Institutional Sales Network
    E.F. Hutton Marketing Program
    Sales Point Memo

Section VII
    Investment Banking at E.F. Hutton

* = Included in Exhibit 4

EXHIBIT 4 (*continued*)

E.F. Hutton
E.F. Hutton & Company Inc. One Battery Park Plaza, New York, N.Y. 10004
(212) 742-5336

Thomas G. Greig III
Senior Vice President

December 13, 1982

Mr. Vincent S. Lamb
Chairman and President
Scientific Systems Services, Inc.
2000 Commerce Drive, P.O. Box 610
Melbourne, FL 32901

Dear Mr. Lamb:

This letter will outline the terms of an underwritten public offering for Scientific Systems Services, Inc. ("SSS") for which E.F. Hutton & Company Inc. ("Hutton") proposes to act as managing underwriter.

Size of Offering: Hutton has assumed that SSS intends to raise a minimum of $9 million in a primary offering of common stock. We have assumed $9 million based on forecasts supplied to us and assume net proceeds to SSS of $8.025 million. Hutton believes that SSS could successfully market a larger issue of $12 million, combining both primary shares and shares owned by existing shareholders ("secondary stock"). Hutton recommends that no member of management be allowed to sell more than 20 percent of his holdings and that the secondary portion should amount to no more than 35 percent of the offering. It is presumed that the proceeds from the primary portion of the offering would be used for working capital.

Recapitalization: Hutton recommends SSS effect a 6.1 for 1 stock split prior to the intital filing of the registration statement, resulting in 3,642,675 shares outstanding.

Pricing: Hutton believes that initial public offerings are priced principally on future earnings and how they relate to current earnings trends, and not on the basis of current earnings. Based upon information provided by SSS to date, Hutton believes that SSS's common stock will sell at a miltiple range of forecast 1983 and 1984 earnings (fully diluted, from continuing operations, before extraordinary items) of $31 \times -36 \times$ and $24 \times -27 \times$, respectively. This forecast is based on estimated growth for the markets in which SSS competes, the current condition of the equity market and the new issue market, the future financial prospects for SSS and its historical financial record which will be included in the prospectus. Given a capitalization of 3,642,675 shares (after effecting a 6.1 for 1 stock split), Hutton recommends an initial filing price range of $14–$16 per share. This is based upon a calculation of 1983 and 1984 earnings per share presented in a price/earnings analysis included in Section II, resulting in 1983 earnings per share of $0.45 and $0.59 for 1984. Hutton feels that pricing of the offering should be such that there is a reasonable expectation for the stock to trade initially at a 10 percent to 15 percent premium to the offering price. Hutton's final pricing recommendation would be based on this immediate aftermarket premium philosophy, general market conditions, initial

EXHIBIT 4 (*continued*)

public offering market conditions and condition of the managing underwriter's "book". An analysis of price/earnings valuations of companies perceived as comparable to SSS, in terms of either their line of business or their future prospects for growth and profitability, is included in Section II. Given the assumptions as to 1983 and 1984 earnings per share and Hutton's pricing ideas, the offering would consist of approximately 650,000 primary shares, and 200,000 secondary shares, resulting in approximately a $12 million offering. Given 4,292,675 (primary) shares outstanding after the offering, SSS would have a market value of at least $60 million ($14 per share). Moreover, if earnings are substantially above the current forecast as a result of the award of a multiplant utility contract in 1983, Hutton believes that a market valuation of approximately $80 million ($18 per share) can be supported.

Over-Allotment Option: Hutton recommends that SSS extend to the underwriters an over-allotment option for up to 10 percent of the size of the offering. These shares would be purchased by the underwriters to cover the underwriters' short-sale position, if any, resulting from the offering, only if, in Hutton's judgment, the after market performance of SSS stock would not be adversely affected.

Gross Spread: Based on an offering of 850,000 shares, Hutton's present anticipation is that the gross spread (underwriting discount) will range from 6.75 percent to 7.3 percent of the offering price for an offering range of $14–$16 per share. Section IV sets forth the gross spread information for initial public offerings of common stock in 1982. Hutton's final gross spread recommendation will depend on the condition of the general market, the new issue market, and the managing underwriter's "book" at the time of the offering.

Co-Manager: Hutton is prepared to co-manage the offering with another firm or firms of SSS's choosing. Hutton believes those firms should be selected in view of Hutton's strengths of retail distribution capability, recognition by institutions of Hutton's knowledge of the computer industry and the profitable experience of Hutton's customer base in investing in the stocks of such companies. If selected as a co-manager, Hutton believes that it should be the lead manager in order for it to effectively organize and execute a retail and institutional market distribution plan.

Timing: Hutton recommends that SSS proceed with an intital public offering during the first quarter of 1983. We believe an SSS offering based on December 31, 1982 financial statements would be readily marketable based on recent market conditions. Hutton personnel would be pleased to begin working with SSS immediately to gain in-depth knowledge of SSS and ensure that SSS is optimally postured for its initial public offering.

Syndication: Hutton recommends that a syndicate of approximately 65 underwriters be formed to distribute the offering. This syndicate would include the "major bracket" national securities firms, the larger regional underwriting firms, selected smaller regional firms, and selected foreign underwriters and would be determined according to the desired distribution mix for the offering chosen by SSS. Hutton as managing underwriter will underwrite approximately 25 percent of the offering, retain for sale through its own distribution network approximately 40 percent to 50 percent of the offering, and distribute the balance of the stock to the other syndicate members based upon SSS's choice of retail versus institutional, and geographic distributional goals. After release of the stock for sale, Hutton as managing underwriter will stablize the market

EXHIBIT 4 (*continued*)

for SSS's stock, if necessary, by making purchases of the stock in the open market to assure an orderly distribution and after market for the stock. When, in Hutton's determination, such has been achieved, Hutton will terminate the syndicate thereby releasing the syndicate members to make a market in SSS's stock and begin normal trading activities.

Distribution Mix: Hutton recommends a specific retail/institutional mix as well as a broad geographic distribution for SSS's common stock offering. Hutton believes that the goal for the offering should be a 65 percent retail, 35 percent institutional distribution for the following reasons:

> Retail: The high percentage of retail distribution would place the stock in a large number of relatively small lots of approximately 300–500 shares each. New York Stock Exchange statistics indicate that retail investors hold twice the dollar amount of equities, and account for only one-half the trading volume as compared to institutions, thereby suggesting retail investors are better long-term holders of securities and are less likely to sell a stock after a short-term price upswing, or in the event of intermittent growth or profitability. Hutton believes that a broad shareholder base gives a company the greatest likelihood of less volatile after market trading and a better forum from which to raise future equity to support rapid growth.
>
> Institutional: Institutional distribution is desirable since (i) it is a finite audience of approximately 150 addressable institutions who over the past several years have been the consistent purchasers of emerging growth stocks; (ii) these institutions have been price leaders in supporting high valuations through purchase in the offering and in the after market; (iii) institutional holders can also cause additional research coverage. Institutional demand for the offering will be more than 35 percent. Institutions would have their orders only partially filled and would be encouraged to purchase up to their desired holding levels through buying in the open market after the offering, thereby supporting the issue in the after market.

In order to achieve this distribution mix, Hutton believes that SSS must engage managing underwriters who will address both retail and institutional securities purchasers. Section I contains charts which describe the roles of different investment banks in distributing securities. E.F. Hutton, with its 5,172 account executives managing over 800,000 accounts, is particularly well qualified to provide SSS with the retail distribution necessary for consummating a successful offering, especially in highly volatile markets.

Hutton also recommends broad geographic distribution for the offering. Hutton would tailor its own internal distribution and that of the underwriting syndicate to obtain this goal.

Marketing Program: As manager of SSS's intital public offering, Hutton will conduct a coordinated, national marketing program to educate the investment community on SSS and its business, and to generate purchase orders for the issue. This program would begin with producing a marketing oriented prospectus, the principal sales document in the offering. During the SEC review of the offering documents, Hutton will orchestrate both an institutional marketing program to expose SSS to buyers in major domestic and European finan-

EXHIBIT 4 (*continued*)

cial centers, as well as an internal marketing program to generate interest in the offering within Hutton's own distribution system.

- The prospectus in the registration statement will be the most important marketing document for the offering; therefore, it must contain a detailed business description of SSS, organized to present SSS's major selling points for use by the retail sales force as well as by the institutional analyst community. Hutton will assist SSS in the final drafting of the prospectus so as to accomplish this marketing objective.
- In marketing the SSS offering to institutional purchasers, sales information meetings and "one on one" discussions will be held in various cities, the most likely being Boston, New York, Chicago, San Francisco, and Los Angeles. Similar meetings in the major European financial centers of London, Edinburgh, Geneva and Zurich we feel is also desirable. Hutton will assist SSS in preparing a presentation geared to the needs and interests of this institutional audience. A proposed timetable for these meetings is included in Section V.
- Hutton will aggressively market the SSS offering to its 4,872 retail and 300 institutional account executives who serve over 800,000 retail and 1,500 major institutional accounts from 335 domestic and foreign offices. This program would include:
    — A wire to branch managers describing the offering and key marketing points, followed by a four-page sales memorandum to each account executive and an article in *Products and Markets,* an internal publication.
    — Interaction between corporate finance and equity research personnel and retail syndicate coordinators to explain the offering and field questions.
    — Daily communication with the 10 Hutton regions to monitor national demand during the offering.
    — Hutton's institutional sales force is kept abreast of the offering through conference calls twice daily, one of which is taped and available for replay on a toll-free 800 number. Hutton's corporate finance team will sponsor SSS management in these broadcasts to the institutional sales force.
    — Hutton corporate finance and equity research personnel on the SSS team will make themselves available to the entire sales force to answer questions about SSS or the offering.

Sections VI of this presentation contains a more detailed description of the internal marketing program.

After Market Sponsorship: Given SSS's importance to E.F. Hutton as a potential client and the involvement of the other senior officers in developing a relationship between the two firms, SSS will become a cornerstone in the continuing evolution of Hutton as the major factor in investment banking for technology based companies. SSS would be a client of E.F. Hutton, not of specific individuals, and would enjoy the visibility and sponsorship of the senior management of the firm. However, individuals must take responsibility for the execution of proper after market sponsorship. That responsibility would belong to Tom Greig from Hutton's New York headquarters. Hutton believes that the client services provided by an investment banker between transactions are at least as important as the execution of the offering itself. Consequently, Hutton

EXHIBIT 4 (*continued*)

strives to offer its corporate finance clients after market sponsorship unequalled by its competitors. This sponsorship will include:

- Research coverage: E.F. Hutton will provide regular research coverage on SSS through its equity research department. Coverage will include comprehensive annual research reports on SSS, its prospects and its industry, "all-wires" releases which outline fast-breaking events concerning SSS, and an up-to-date research comment database which brokers can access through their desk-top quote machines.
- Exposure to Financial Community: Hutton will ensure that the financial community keeps current with SSS by providing in-depth research coverage and arranging securities analyst meetings, institutional forums and investor conferences. In particular, Hutton will sponsor SSS at forums such as the New York Society of Securities Analysts and assure that SSS be given the opportunity to participate in events staged by groups such as the American Electronics Association.
- Management Follow-up: When not working directly with SSS on a specific transaction, Hutton's corporate finance team will keep abreast of SSS's financial progress, monitor developments in its industry, keep it informed with reports on market conditions and provide it with financing alternatives to capitalize on specific market opportunities.
- Market Making: E.F. Hutton is the primary market maker for the securities of its investment banking clients and, in this role, will assure SSS of a liquid and stable market for its securities. Following SSS's initial public offering, Hutton will become the lead market maker for its stock.
- Special Services: As an investment banking client, SSS will receive special attention by functional areas of Hutton other than those thus far mentioned. Special services available to SSS would include cash management consulting, lease financing, tax shelter assistance and distribution of "Rule 144" stock.
- Long-Term Commitment: E.F. Hutton, through its Technology Group, aspires to become the preeminent investment banker to computer and electronics companies among the national securities firms. To attain this goal, Hutton must secure as clients today the industry leaders of tomorrow and then strengthen these relationships by continuing to provide the best possible service. E.F. Hutton wishes to initiate such a long-term relationship with SSS.

Financial Statements and Accountants: Hutton understands that SSS will provide annual financial statements, which will be audited by Deloitte Haskins & Sells and will meet the SEC requirements for the form S-1 Registration Statement. SSS will also provide additional financial data Hutton believes is necessary for marketing purposes. The underwriters will request Deloitte Haskins & Sells to provide "cold comfort" review of information included in the registration statement which can be traced back to the financial records of the company.

Printing: Hutton recommends that SSS select a qualified financial printer to print the registration statement, prospectus, underwriting agreement and underwriting syndication papers. Hutton will request that 40,000 preliminary prospectuses and 30,000 final prospectuses be printed. SSS will assume all printing costs.

EXHIBIT 4 (*continued*)

"Blue Sky" Law Qualification: The underwriters will request that SSS register varying amounts of the shares in the offering in all states in order for the stock to be sold to retail investors over a broad geographic area. The cost of registration and fees of counsel in completing the applications and in clearing the offering through the various state "Blue Sky" commissions will be paid by SSS.

Underwriters' Counsel: It is Hutton's intention to use as underwriters' counsel, a law firm experienced in securities law and in offerings for technology based companies. The underwriters will request that this counsel handle all matters as to "Blue Sky" law qualification. The fees of such counsel, other than the fees incurred for "Blue Sky" qualification, will be paid by the underwriters.

Underwriting Agreement: Neither SSS nor Hutton will be obligated to proceed with the offering unless and until the underwriting agreement is executed. Such agreement will contain Hutton's usual provisions including an agreement that neither SSS nor its officers, or directors will, without prior written consent of Hutton, sell, transfer or otherwise dispose of any shares of common stock for a period of 90 days from the date of the offering. The execution of the underwriting agreement is subject to SSS and Hutton being satisfied with the form and substance of the preliminary, amended, and final registration statements and propectuses, and with all items and conditions of the underwriting agreement.

The following presentation contains additional information on an intial public offering of SSS common stock, as well as on Hutton's ability to manage this offering. Specifically included are financial and market data on companies in SSS's industry, a price/earnings and recapitalization analysis of SSS, a proposed underwriting syndicate, an offering timetable, and information on recent initial public offerings.

Hutton is most interested in developing a long-term investment banking relationship with SSS. We are enthusiastic about the prospects for the continued growth of SSS and will marshall Hutton's resources to help SSS meet its goals.

I look forward to discussing Hutton's interest in SSS with you at greater length.

Yours truly,

Thomas G. Greig III
Senior Vice President

EXHIBIT 4 (*continued*)

Segmentation of Managing Underwriters

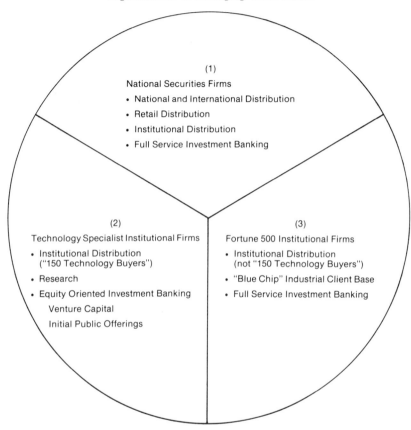

(1)
National Securities Firms
- National and International Distribution
- Retail Distribution
- Institutional Distribution
- Full Service Investment Banking

(2)
Technology Specialist Institutional Firms
- Institutional Distribution ("150 Technology Buyers")
- Research
- Equity Oriented Investment Banking
  Venture Capital
  Initial Public Offerings

(3)
Fortune 500 Institutional Firms
- Institutional Distribution (not "150 Technology Buyers")
- "Blue Chip" Industrial Client Base
- Full Service Investment Banking

(1) National Securities Firms
E.F. Hutton
Merrill Lynch
Dean Witter
Shearson/Amer. Express
Blyth, Paine Webber
Smith Barney
Bache

(2) Technology Specialist Institutional Firms
Hambrecht & Quist
L. F. Rothschild
Alex Brown
Robertson, Colman
Montgomery Securities

(3) Fortune 500 Institutional Firms
Morgan Stanley
First Boston
Goldman Sachs
Kidder Peabody
Lehman Brothers
Salomon Brothers

EXHIBIT 4 (continued)

Price/Earnings and Recapitalization Analysis

This analysis sets forth the effect on earnings per share and the resulting range of price/earnings multiples resulting from an initial public offering of shares by Scientific Systems Services, Inc.

Assumptions:
1. SSS becomes public in the first quarter of 1983 off year end 1982 financial statements.
2. The filing range for the offering price would be $85.71 to $97.95. For computational purposes we assumed an offering of 105,000 primary shares at $85.71 per share.
3. Net proceeds to SSS from the primary portion of the offering are $8,025,000. This consists of gross proceeds of $9,000,000 less a gross spread of $630,000 (7%) and issuance expenses of $345,000.
4. 1983 revenues and net earnings from operations will be $24,000,000 and $1,680,000 (7% after tax), respectively. 1984 revenues and net earnings from operations will be $36,000,000 and $2,520,000, respectively. In addition, the valuation study (see next pages of this Section) also considers the scenario in which the Company's 1983 revenues are $30 million, with $2.1 million earnings, and its 1984 revenues are $45 million with $3.15 million earnings.
5. Net proceeds of $8,025,000 are received April 1, 1983. As a result, the Company earns additional interest income, at 5 percent after tax, on an average of $5 million during the last nine months of 1983.

SSS Forecast Operating Results

	Year Ended December 31,		
	1982	1983	1984
Net sales	$16,800,000	$24,000,000	$36,000,000
Net income before extraordinary items	1,000,000	1,867,500	2,520,000
Earnings per share	1.98	2.77	3.60
Weighted average shares outstanding	505,000	673,750	700,000

Price/Earnings Impact

Filing price range per share		$85.71–$97.95	
Earnings per share	$ 1.98	$ 2.77	$ 3.60
Price/earnings range	44x–50x	31x–36x	24x–27x
Market value of SSS			
Post offering (millions)		$ 60–69	

For discussion purposes we have not incorporated any stock split in the above analysis. Prior to the initial public offering Hutton recommends SSS split its stock 6.1 for 1 so as to target an initial filing range of $14–$16 which would broaden retail investor participation in the offering.

EXHIBIT 4 (*continued*)

Recapitalization Analysis Assuming a 6.1 for 1 Stock Split

	Year Ended December 31,		
	1982	1983	1984
Net income before extraordinary items	$1,000,000	$1,867,500	$2,520,000
Earnings per share	$ 0.32	$ 0.45	$ 0.59
Weighted average shares outstanding	3,091,682	4,124,794	4,285,500

Price/Earnings Impact

Filing price range per share		$ 14–$16	
Earnings per share	$ 0.32	$ 0.45	$ 0.59
Price/earnings range	44x–50x	31x–36x	24x–27x
Market value of SSS			
Post offering (Millions)		$ 60–69	

Increased 1983 Earnings

   Management has informed Hutton that the forecast 1983 operating results could be dramatically higher ($2.1 million vs $1.68 million) if the company secures a multi-plant utility contract in the first quarter of 1983. Hutton's valuation study (please see the next pages of this section) indicates that the post-offering market value of the Company could approach $80 million (approximately $18 per share) in such a case.

Comparative Market Analysis
Index of Five SSS Comparables versus The NASDAQ Industrials Index

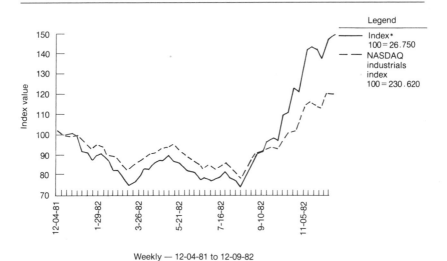

Weekly — 12-04-81 to 12-09-82

*Index includes: Shared Medical Sys. Corp., Systematics Inc., Policy Mgmt. Sys. Corp., Triad Sys. Corp., SEI Corp.

EXHIBIT 4 (*continued*)
Valuation Study (*in millions of dollars*)

E.F. Hutton & Company Inc.
Corporate Finance Department
December 10, 1982

	Scientific Systems Services			On-Line Software International	Systems & Computer Technology Corporation	Par Technology	ARGOsystems	Dionex Corporation	Quantum Corporation
Current market value (12–10–82)	$60.00	$70.00	$80.00 (1)	$77.66	$290.61	$186.88	$96.52	$98.78	$199.60
Current market price (12–10–82)	14.00	16.00	18.00	21.875	22.75	25.00	31.50	24.50	22.50
Market value/projected revenues (dollars in millions)									
Calendar 1983 revenues–ratio	$24.00–2.5x	$24.00–2.9x	$30.00–2.7x	$24.00–3.2x	$49.00–5.9x	$44.00–4.2x	$42.00–2.3x	$22.00–4.5x	$63.00–3.2x
Calendar 1984 revenues–ratio	$36.00–1.7x	$36.00–1.9x	$45.00–1.8x	$37.00–2.1x	$74.00–3.9x	$59.00–3.2x	$53.00–1.8x	$28.00–3.5x	$78.00–2.6x
Market value/projected net income									
Calendar 1983 net income–ratio	1.87–32.1x	1.87–37.4x	2.29–34.9x	3.5–22.2x	5.9–49.3x	6.6–28.3x	3.5–27.6x	2.8–35.3x	10.0–20.0x
Calendar 1984 net income–ratio	2.52–23.8x	2.52–27.8x	3.15–25.4x	5.3–14.7x	8.9–32.7x	8.9–21.0x	4.6–21.0x	3.5–28.2x	12.5–16.0x
Growth Rate Valuation									
Five year projected compound growth rate	50%			50%	50%	35%	30%	25%	25%
Indicated P/E (.65x) (1)	32.5x			32.5x	32.5x	22.75x	19.50x	16.25x	16.25x
Market valuation on 1983 net income	$60.78		$74.43	$113.75	$191.75	$150.15	$68.25	$45.50	$162.50

(1) If SSS is awarded the contract for eight power plants in the first quarter of 1983, Hutton believes a $75–$80 million valuation can be defended assuming 1983 revenues and earnings (after entered income from an April 4 offering) of $30 million and $2.29 million, respectively.

(2) Under current market conditions, Hutton believes that investors capitalize common stocks at a P/E based upon forecasted earnings of 65% of a company's expected sustainable growth rate.

EXHIBIT 4 (*continued*)
Comparative Pricing Analysis: Selected Technology Company Initial Public Offerings

Company	Lee Data Corporation	PAR Technology	ARGOSystems	Dionex Corporation	Quantum Corporation	Mogem Systems, Inc.
Shares filed (000)	2,207	750	606	1,200	1,700	1,290
Shares offered (000)	2,607	900	801	1,400	2,500	1,500
IPO filing date	10-18-82	10-29-82	10-27-82	11-02-82	11-09-82	11-05-82
IPO effective date	11-18-82	12-03-82	12-02-82	12-07-82	12-10-82	12-10-82
Fiscal year end	03-31-82	12-31-81	06-30-82	06-30-82	03-31-82	03-31-82
Latest 12 months for IPO	09-30-82	09-30-82	10-01-82	09-30-82	10-02-82	09-30-82
Size Data: ($000)						
Revenues (LTM)	$ 29,380	$ 27,574	$ 32,187	$ 16,888	$ 29,769	$ 12,896
Pretax income—margin	9,068–30.9%	7,148–25.9%	4,329–13.4%	3,648–21.6%	6,509–21.9%	3,358–26.0%
Net income (a)—margin	5,725–19.5%	4,162–15.1%	2,462– 7.6%	1,934–11.5%	4,114–13.8%	2,316–18.0%
EPS (LTM)	$ .47	$ .59	$ 1.08	$ .55	$ 1.02	$ .49
Projected EPS (next fiscal yr.)	1.40	1.00	1.40	.65	1.00	.75
R&D expenses—% of revenues	$ 1,606–5.5%	$ 749–2.9%	$ 1,146–3.6% (c) $	$ 1,078–6.4%	$ 2,345–7.9%	$ 944–7.3%
Tangible book value	13,736	7,392	9,442	7,752	13,981	1,731

EXHIBIT 4 (*continued*)
Comparative Pricing Analysis: Selected Technology Company Initial Public Offerings

Company	Lee Data Corporation	PAR Technology	ARGOSystems	Dionex Corporation	Quantum Corporation	Mogem Systems, Inc.
Market Data:						
Pro forma shares outstanding (000)	12,332	7,475	3,064	4,032	8,871	5,601
Filing price range	$14.00–16.00	$ 14–17	$ 16–18	$ 14–16	$ 15–17	$ 15–18
P/E range—LTM EPS	30.0x–34.0x	23.7x–28.8x	14.8x–16.7x	25.5x–29.1x	14.7x–16.7x	30.6x–36.7x
P/E range—projected EPS	10.0x–11.4x	14.0x–17.0x	11.4x–12.9x	21.5x–24.6x	15.0x–17.0x	20.0x–24.0x
Pro forma market value ($MM)	$167.0–190.9	$104.7–127.1	$49.0–55.2	$56.4–64.5	$133.1–150.8	$94.0–100.8
Offering price	$ 19.00	$ 20.00	$ 21.50	$ 19.00	$ 20.50	$ 21.00
P/E—LTM EPS	40.4x	33.9x	19.9x	34.5x	20.1x	42.9x
P/E—projected EPS	13.6x	20.0x	15.4x	29.2x	20.5x	28.0x
Pro forma market value ($MM)	$ 234.3	$ 149.5	$ 65.9	$ 76.6	$ 181.9	$ 117.6
NASDAQ Industrial Index:						
On filing date	233.26	242.89	243.12	250.00	265.43	261.88
On pricing date	262.34	276.28	274.92	279.19	277.45	277.45
Percent change	12.47%	13.75%	13.08%	11.68%	4.53%	5.95%
Growth Data:						
Earnings per share (a)						
LTM	$ .47	$ .59	$ 1.08	$ .55	$ 1.02	$ .49
1 year prior	.14	.41	.85	.58	.03	.24
2 years prior	(.07)	.10	.63	.43	(1.50)	.22
3 years prior	(.25)	.07	.46	.36	—	(.21)
4 years prior	—	.04	.55	.27	—	—
Compound growth rate	NMF	105.0%	22.9%	24.3%	NMF	NMF

Revenue/net income (a)						
LTM ($MM)	$ 29.4/$5.7	$ 27.6/4.2	$ 32.2/2.5	$ 16.9/1.9	$ 29.8/4.1	$ 12.9/2.3
1 year prior	13.7/ 2.0	21.4/2.9	28.1/1.9	16.0/2.0	13.7/0.2	8.3/1.1
2 years prior	6.7/(0.4)	10.3/0.7	20.9/1.3	12.0/1.4	—/—	3.4/0.6
3 years prior	0.6/(1.4)	7.6/0.4	19.2/0.9	10.7/1.2	—/—	0.6/(0.6)
4 years prior	—/—	6.1/0.2	17.0/1.0	8.7/0.9	—/—	—/(0.8)
Compound growth rate	NMF	49.8%/112.6%	21.6%/32.3%	22.5%/25.7%	235.0%/NMF	220.0%/NMF
Line of Business:	Designs, manufactures, markets and services multifunction interactive terminal systems.	Point-of-sale systems for restaurants, software systems for gov't/military.	Electronic reconnaissance systems which acquire and analyze radar and military communications signals.	Develops, manufactures and markets ion chromatography.	Designs, manufactures and markets rigid disk drives based on Winchester technology.	Integrated line of standard banking applications software programs.

(E)—Estimate
(a)—From continuing operations before extraordinary items.
(b)—Eight month financial figures.
(c)—Excludes $8,000,000 of customer-funded research and development.
LTM=Last twelve months.
NMF=Not meaningful figure.

EXHIBIT 4 (*continued*) 1982 Initial Public Offerings* Growth and Business Information (*July–December*)

Date	Issuer	Shares (000's)	Offering Price	Total Dollar Amount (000's)	Latest 12 Months Net Sales (000's)	Latest 12 Months Net Income (000's)(1)	Sales Fiscal Year	Sales Latest Interim (2)	Net Income (1) Fiscal Year	Net Income (1) Latest Interim (2)	Latest 12 Mos. EPS	P/E (3)	Price/ Book (4)	Business Lines
07-08	Tera Corp.	2,500	$16.00	$40,000	$31,015	$5,258	57.2(5)	42.5	58.8	43.4	$0.66	24.2x	8.5x	Computer software/sys.
07-13	Ryan's Family Steak Houses	475	9.25	4,394	8,157	718	51.4(6)	5.9	50.7(6)	41.9	0.90	10.3x	4.7x	Operates restaurants
07-20	Super Sky International	640	13.00	8,320	27,088	3,199	50.0	37.0	69.0	58.7	1.10	11.8x	3.8x	Designs & installs skylights
07-21	Atlantic Southeast Airlines	860	6.50	5,590	9,743	1,531	352.2(7)	187.7	44.2(7)	274.4	0.99	6.6x	5.2x	Regional airline
07-29	CPI Corp.	750	14.00	10,500	108,899	5,302	33.7(7)	31.6	102.1	52.5	1.62	8.6	4.4x	Portrait photo studios, cleaning
08-05	Foster Medical	2,300	13.75	31,625	122,814	(1,376)	11.5(6)	21.6	NA	NMF	(0.69)	NMF	NMF	Distributes medical supplies
08-11	Environmental Testing	1,000	5.00	5,000	556(9)	867(9)	NA	NA	NA	NA	(0.43)	NMF	6.7x	Management of chemical wastes
08-17	Electronic Mail Corp.	800	6.25	5,000	–(8)	–(8)	–(8)	–(8)	–(8)	–(8)	–(8)	NMF	NMF	Communications mgt. & special info. processing
08-20	Universal Money Centers	600	5.00	3,000	NA	NA	NA	NA	NA	NA	NA	NA	NA	Markets automatic tellers
08-26	Vicorp Restaurants	900	10.25	9,225	37,571	2,021	14.0	18.2	49.0	89.7	1.01	10.1x	4.6x	Operates & franchises restaurants
09-01	Family Entertainment Centers	475	10.50	4,988	5,212	(296)	NMF	311.5	NMF	NMF	(0.29)	NMF	3.7x	Operates restaurants
09-02	North Fork Bancorp.	500	17.50	8,750	6,437	1,655	17.4	50.5	33.0	55.0	3.93	4.5x	1.0x	Bank holding company
09-09	Electronic Theatre Rest.	610	8.25	5,033	5,935	(1,929)	NMF	449.5	NMF	NMF	(0.55)	NMF	7.8x	Operates restaurants
09-15	Electronics Corp. of Israel	720	11.25	8,100	11,669	1,936	57.0	36.8	149.2	103.0	1.09	10.3x	3.0x	Telecommunications equip.
09-23	Psych Systems	700	5.00	3,500	3,429	199	NMF	225.0	NMF	NMF	0.29	17.2x	2.4x	Patient test equip.
09-29	Genex Corp.	2,000	9.50	19,000	5,154	(2.38)	495.8	104.3	NMF	NMF	(0.25)	NMF	3.7x	Genetic engineering
09-29	On-Line Software	800	15.00	12,000	14,859	2,034	52.9	42.3	149.8	72.6	.67	22.4x	6.4x	IBM-compatible software
09-29	Rodime	1,000	8.00	8,000	4,294(10)	611(10)	NMF	NMF	NMF	NMF	.16	50.0x	4.4x	5¼" Winchester disk drives
10-07	TANO	515	9.25	4,764	29,888	947	26.6	47.0	34.7	140.3	1.11	8.3x	1.7x	Process control systems
10-13	Pacific Express Holding	1,300	5.00	6,500	12,291	(10,251)	135.0	438.7	NMF	NMF	(22.99)	NMF	NMF	Jet Service between S.F. & L.A.
10-14	University Federal Savings	400	12.00	4,800	31,376	(2,059)	20.0	9.3	NMF	NMF	(2.92)	NMF	0.4x	Savings & loan

Date	Company													Description
10-15	Gott	635	10.75	6,826	28,623	1,633	28.5	29.2	40.5	17.0	1.42	7.6x	3.0x	Consumer plastic products
10-18	InteCom Inc.	2,500	20.00	50,000	17,652	(3,504)	NMF	NMF	NMF	NMF	(0.32)	NMF	42.6x	Large PBX phone systems
10-26	Sizzler Restaurants	900	17.00	15,300	120,927	3,376	19.5	25.9	3.3	178.2	1.55	10.9x	1.0x	Steakhouse restaurants
10-27	Fidelity Federal S&L	2,798	10.00	27,976	189,321	(30,198)	28.1	6.5	NMF	NMF	(7.02)	NMF	.3x	Savings & loan
10-29	Merrimac Industries	550	7.00	3,850	10,376	927	25.2	.8	28.8	367.8	.81	8.6x	2.2x	Signal processing systems-for defense
11-02	Systems & Computer Technology	2,580	16.50	42,570	26,792	3,225	33.3	54.0	39.9	170.5	.29	55.0x	22.6x	Software for gov't./universities
11-04	Aaron Rents	1,000	15.50	15,500	52,724	4,030	32.3	14.7	24.2	40.9	1.21	12.8x	1.3x	MFG/rent/sell furniture
11-04	Altos Computer Systems	3,300	21.00	69,300	57,351	6,360	428.7	59.7	396.0	53.0	.55	38.2x	16.5x	Multiterminal microcomputer system
11-04	Americana Hotels & Realty Trust	5,000	20.00	100,000	83,692	7,372	8.5	NMF	29.0	NMF	3.08	8.6x	1.1x	Real estate investment trust
11-09	Washington Federal S&L	954	11.75	11,208	82,465	(26,701)	9.7	8.3	NMF	NMF	(7.08)	NMF	.6x	Savings & loan
11-16	Taco Viva	400	9.00	3,600	12,736	605	37.6	17.9	31.9	111.0	.52	17.3x	4.1x	Fast-Service Mexican restaurants
11-18	Lee Data	2,607	19.00	49,535	29,380	5,040	365.4(6)	326.7	NMF	1,984.4	.47	40.4x	12.8x	Multifunct. interactive term. systems
11-26	Triangle Microwave, Inc.	696	6.25	4,350	4,474	799	NA	94.4	NA	286.0	.53	11.8x	7.2x	Microwave components
12-01	Patient Technology, Inc.	575	6.75	3,881	676(11)	17(11)	NA	NA	NA	NA	.02	NMF	21.8x	Electronic medical instruments
12-01	Quality Systems, Inc.	600	17.00	10,200	8,919	948	85.2	66.9	80.7	175.5	.52	32.7x	15.9x	Information systems for dentists
12-02	ARGOSystems	801	21.50	17,213	32,187	2,462	24.1	79.2	61.3	207.9	1.08	19.9x	4.8x	Electronic reconnaisance systems
12-03	PAR Technology Corp.	900	20.00	18,000	27,574	4,162	53.3	42.5	106.9	68.9	.58	34.5x	18.9x	P.O.S. systems: defense/software

*Value of $3.0 million or more, offering price of $5.00 or more.

(1) From continuing operations before extraordinary items.
(2) Percentage difference between latest interim figure and the corresponding figure one year earlier.
(3) Based on historical E.P.S. figures. Latest 12 months.
(4) Actual book value prior to offer.
(5) Based on data for four years.
(6) Based on data for three years.
(7) Based on data for two years.
(8) Insufficient or no prior operating history.

NA = Not applicable.
NMF = Not meaningful figure.

(9) For the period from 12-27-81 through 4-24-82.
(10) Operating data for the 40 weeks ended July 3, 1982.
(11) For eight months ended Aug. 31, 1982.

EXHIBIT 4 (*continued*)

Date	Issuer	Shares (000's)	Offering Price	Total Dollar Amount (000's)	Gross Spread $	Gross Spread %	Dollar Breakdown of Gross Spread Management	Under-writing	Selling	EFH Commission (100 Shares)	Selling Concession EFH Comm.	Aggregate Under-writing (100's shares)
07-08	Tera Corp.	2,500	16.00	40,000	1.04	6.50	.20	.19	.65	.47	1.38x	475
07-13	Ryan's Family Steak Houses	475	9.25	4,394	.79	8.50	.18	.16	.45	.35	1.29x	76
07-20	Super Sky International	640	13.00	8,320	.98	7.50	.20	.205	.57	.42	1.36x	131
07-21	Atlantic Southeast Airlines	860	6.50	5,590	.52	8.00	.08	.11	.33	.29	1.14x	95
07-29	CPI Corp.	750	14.00	10,500	1.00	7.14	.20	.25	.55	.43	1.28x	188
08-05	Foster Medical	2,300	13.75	31,625	.98	7.13	.20	.20	.58	.43	1.35x	460
08-11	Environmental Testing	1,000	5.00	5,000	.42	8.40	.08	.08	.26	.25	1.04x	80
08-17	Electronic Mail Corp.	800	6.25	5,000	.63	10.00	NA	NA	NA	.28	NA	NA
08-20	Universal Money Centers	600	5.00	3,000	.50	10.00	NA	NA	NA	.25	NA	NA
08-26	Vicorp Restaurants	900	10.25	9,225	.70	6.83	.14	.14	.42	.37	1.14x	126
09-01	Family Entertainment Centers	475	10.50	4,988	.84	8.00	.17	.17	.50	.37	1.35x	81
09-02	Morth Fork Bancorp.	500	17.50	8,750	1.23	7.03	NA	NA	.75	.50	1.50x	NA
09-09	Electronic Theatre Rest.	610	8.25	5,033	.70	8.49	.14	.19	.37	.31	1.19x	116
09-15	Electronics Corp. of Israel	720	11.25	8,100	.82	7.29	.22	.18	.42	.37	1.14x	130
09-23	Psych Systems	700	5.00	3,500	.50	10.00	.27	(1)	.23	.25	0.92x	189
09-29	Genex Corp.	2,000	9.50	19,000	.75	7.89	.15	.15	.45	.37	1.20x	300
09-29	On-Line Software	800	15.00	12,000	1.08	7.20	.22	.28	.58	.44	1.33x	224
09-29	Rodime	1,000	8.00	8,000	.56	7.00	.11	.15	.30	.31	0.97x	150

Date	Company											
10-07	TANO	515	9.25	4,764	.74	8.00	.14	.20	.40	.37	1.07x	103
10-13	Pacific Express Holding	1,300	5.00	6,500	.43	8.50	.09	.085	.25	.25	1.00x	111
10-14	University Federal Savings	400	12.00	4,800	.96	8.00	.36	(1)	.60	.37	1.60x	76
10-15	Gott	635	10.75	6,826	.86	8.00	.19	.17	.50	.37	1.33x	108
10-18	InteCom Inc.	2,500	20.00	50,000	1.35	6.80	.30	.35	.70	.55	1.27x	875
10-26	Sizzler Restaurants	900	17.00	15,300	1.19	7.00	.24	.30	.65	.50	1.30x	270
10-27	Fidelity Federal S&L	2,798	10.00	27,976	.72	7.20	.14	.18	.40	.37	1.07x	504
10-29	Merrimac Industries	550	7.00	3,850	.56	8.00	.12	.16	.28	.31	.90x	88
11-02	Systems & Computers Technology	2,580	16.50	42,570	1.16	7.03	.23	.30	.63	.50	1.26x	774
11-04	Aaron Rents	1,000	15.50	15,500	1.08	6.97	.22	.26	.60	.44	1.36x	260
11-04	Altos Computer Systems	3,300	21.00	69,300	1.47	7.00	.30	.37	.80	.56	1.43x	1,221
11-04	Americana Hotels & Realty Trust	5,000	20.00	100,000	1.60	8.00	.40	.20	1.00	.56	1.79x	1,000
11-09	Washington Federal S&L	954	11.75	11,208	.82	6.98	.17	.20	.45	.37	1.20x	191
11-16	Taco Viva	400	9.00	3,600	.76	8.44	.15	.17	.44	.31	1.42x	124
11-18	Lee Data	2,607	19.00	49,535	1.33	7.00	.27	.31	.75	.50	1.50x	808
11-26	Triangle Microwave, Inc.	696	6.25	4,350	.63	10.00	.25	(1)	.37	.25	1.48x	NA
12-01	Patient Technology, Inc.	575	6.75	3,881	.68	10.00	.37	(1)	.30	.25	1.20x	NA
12-01	Quality Systems, Inc.	600	17.00	10,200	1.25	7.35	.25	.30	.70	.50	1.40x	180
12-02	ARGOSystems	801	21.50	17,213	1.52	7.07	.30	.32	.90	.56	1.61x	256
12-03	PAR Technology Corp.	900	20.00	18,000	1.45	7.25	.29	.29	.87	.56	1.55x	261

*Value of $3 million or more, offering price of $5 or more.
(1) Combined with management fee because issue was not syndicated.

EXHIBIT 4 (*concluded*)
1982 Initial Public Offerings*: Gross Spread Information (*July–December*)

Date	Issuer	Shares (000's)	Offering Price	Total Dollar Amount (000's)	Primary as % of Shares Offered	Dilution (%)(1)	1 Day After Offer(2)	% Change	1 Week After Offer(2)	% Change(2)	Stock Symbol
07-09	Tera Corp.	2,500	16.00	40,000	50.0	13.6	16.00	—	16.13	0.8	TRRA
07-13	Ryan's Family Steak Houses	475	9.25	4,394	86.6	33.9	10.00	8.1	10.25	10.8	RYAN
07-20	Super Sky International	640	13.00	8,320	0.0	0.0	13.00	—	13.25	1.9	SSKY
07-21	Atlantic Southeast Airlines	860	6.50	5,590	92.5	32.7	6.25	(3.8)	6.00	(7.7)	ASAI
07-29	CPI Corp.	750	14.00	10,500	56.7	11.5	13.75	(1.8)	13.75	(1.8)	CPIC
08-05	Foster Medical	2,300	13.75	31,625	100.0	45.6	13.25	(*3.6)	13.00	(5.5)	FMED
08-11	Environmental Testing	1,000	5.00	5,000	100.0	33.3	4.75	(5.0)	4.50	(10.0)	ETCC
08-17	Electronic Mail Corp.	800	6.25	5,000	100.0	50.0	6.25	—	6.25	—	EMCA
08-20	Universal Money Centers	600	5.00	3,000	100.0	NA	NA	NA	5.00	—	UMCI
08-26	Vicorp Restaurants	900	10.25	9,225	44.4	16.7	10.88	6.1	10.63	3.7	VRES
09-01	Family Entertainment Centers	475	10.50	4,988	70.6	21.5	10.75	2.4	9.75	(7.1)	FMLY
09-02	North Fork Bancorp.	500	17.50	8,750	100.0	54.3	17.50	—	17.50	—	NFBC
09-09	Electronic Theatre Rest.	610	8.25	5,033	100.0	21.7	8.25	—	8.00	(3.0)	ETRC
09-15	Electronics Corp. of Israel	720	11.25	8,100	93.1	23.5	12.00	6.7	13.25	17.8	ECILF
09-23	Psych Systems	700	5.00	3,500	100.0	49.8	6.25	25.0	6.25	25.0	PSYC
09-29	Genex Corp.	2,000	9.50	19,000	100.0	17.3	8.88	(6.6)	8.00	(5.8)	GNEX
09-29	On-Line Software	800	15.00	12,000	62.5	14.1	15.25	1.7	16.13	7.5	OSII
09-29	Rodime	1,000	8.00	8,000	100.0	20.2	7.75	(3.1)	8.25	3.1	RODMY
10-07	TANO	515	9.25	4,764	77.7	30.2	9.25	—	9.62	4.0	TANO

692

Date	Company										Ticker
10-13	Pacific Express Holding	1,300	5.00	6,500	100.0	41.6	NA	NA	3.75	(25.0)	PXXP
10-14	University Federal Savings	400	12.00	4,800	100.0	77.1	13.50	12.5	13.00	8.3	UFSL
10-15	Gott	635	10.75	6,826	86.6	29.9	13.00	21.0	13.75	27.9	GOTT
10-18	InteCom Inc.	2,500	20.00	50,000	66.4	12.1	22.00	10.0	25.63	28.1	INCM
10-26	Sizzler Restaurants	900	17.00	15,300	100.0	27.3	17.00	—	20.00	17.6	SIZZ
10-27	Fidelity Federal S&L	2,798	10.00	27,976	63.0	0.0	11.00	10.0	12.75	27.5	FFED
10-29	Merrimac Industries	550	7.00	3,850	71.4	23.2	8.75	25.0	8.25	17.9	MMAC
11-02	Systems & Computers Technology	2,580	16.50	42,570	15.0	14.4	NA	NA	20.88	26.5	SCTC
11-04	Aaron Rents	1,000	15.50	15,500	82.0	4.0	20.75	33.9	21.50	38.7	ARON
11-04	Altos Computer Systems	3,300	21.00	69,300	100.0	19.1	29.75	41.7	31.75	51.9	ALTO
11-04	Americana Hotels & Realty Trust	5,000	20.00	100,000	100.0	0.0	21.25	6.3	21.00	5.0	AHRC
11-09	Washington Federal S&L	954	11.75	11,208		0.0	19.00	61.7	18.00	53.2	WFSL
11-16	Taco Viva	400	9.00	3,600	56.3	15.8	10.75	19.4	9.50	5.6	TVIV
11-18	Lee Data	2,607	19.00	49,535	69.0	14.6	28.25	48.7	28.00	47.4	LEDA
11-26	Triangle Microwave, Inc.	696	6.25	4,350	93.1	30.0	8.50	36.0	11.00	76.0	TRMW
12-01	Patient Technology, Inc.	575	6.75	3,881	100.0	35.9	8.75	29.6	9.00	33.3	PTIX
12-01	Quality Systems, Inc.	600	17.00	10,200	51.7	14.5	18.25	7.4	20.75	22.1	QSII
12-02	ARGOSystems	801	21.50	17,213	81.1	21.2	33.25	54.7	32.50	51.2	ARGI
12-03	PAR Technology Corp.	900	20.00	18,000	53.1	6.5	27.50	37.5	—	—	PARR

*Value of $3.0 million or more, offering price of $5.00 or more.

NA Not available

(1) Primary shares as a percent of shares outstanding after the offer.

(2) OTC stocks show bid price.

EXHIBIT 5
Alex Brown Proposal *(Entire Proposal Attached)*

January 13, 1983

Mr. Vincent S. Lamb, Jr.
President
Scientific Systems Services, Inc.
2000 Commerce Drive
Melbourne, Florida 32901

Dear Vince:

It was a pleasure to meet with you and Mike at your office. Don and Al very much enjoyed meeting with you, Pat, and Howard in Boston. We continue to be impressed by the Scientific Systems Services, Inc. (Triple S) story and are convinced that a public offering of Triple S securities will be well-received by the investment community.

To assist you in finalizing decisions regarding the offering, we have outlined below our preliminary conclusions regarding the offering, structure and timing and Triple S' valuation.

Structure

We understand that an offering of $12 million is being contemplated, and that the offering will consist of $8 million of primary stock and $4 million of secondary stock. Such an offering could be readily accomplished.

Valuation

Our valuation of Triple S is based upon our understanding of its business, current market environment, and our assumption of projected Triple S' financial performance. Currently, we believe that your 1982 performance when finalized will show revenues of $15.7 million and net income of just under $1 million. We believe that 1983 projections call for approximately 60 percent revenue growth to a total of $25 million in revenues and $1.5 million of net income. We believe that this net income figure should be increased to reflect the net income received from the proceeds of the offering. Conservatively, we feel that the Company could estimate receiving net proceeds of $7.2 million after all deal costs and that an 8 percent pretax return could be realized on these funds for nine months of the year. Hence, we believe the offering would add at least $250,000 to net income for 1983. We estimate Triple S' market value in the initial public offering to be approximately $45 million. This valuation represents a multiple of approximately 26 times expected 1983 net income. Initial public offerings in today's market are generally being priced at a modest discount to market, although the market is currently particularly receptive to new issues even to the point of some buyers saying that "new is better." Therefore, for your planning purposes, we would estimate that the initial public offering would be priced at approximately 25 × 1983 expected earnings and would trade at approximately 26 × expected 1983 net income. The 25-26 × valuation range is one which we consider to be very supportable. It is possible, however, that Triple S could attain an even higher market value if the market remains strong and if the road show marketing effort is particularly well-received.

In our phone conversation, Vince, you asked about the methodology which we use to determine valuations. As we have discussed, Alex. Brown looks at market conditions, your business, and overlays these factors on prices received by publicly-traded comparable companies. These comparable companies include a large number of software and systems companies as well as turnkey systems companies. On average, this group of companies, which in-

EXHIBIT 5 (*continued*)

cludes ASK, MSA, Cullinane, Computer Associates, Pansophic, Tera, and PMS, is trading at approximately 26× expected 1983 net income.

Timing

Work on the offering should begin as soon as possible. Prompt action is desirable in order to capitalize on the existing strong market and to achieve maximum visibility for Triple S by entering the market ahead of the numerous filings that are expected to occur when year-end results are available.

Prospectus preparation and all legal work can be accomplished within a 4-5 week period. The first step of the process should be an all hands meeting (including underwriters and their counsel, Triple S and its counsel and auditors) during which a time and responsibility schedule is agreed upon. Alex. Brown's involvement should facilitate this entire process as a result of our considerable experience in writing computer service prospectuses and our knowledge of your Company.

Expenses

If Triple S' initial public offering is in the $12 million range, we estimate that the underwriting spread will not exceed 7.5 percent. Other expenses, consisting of printing costs, Company counsel and filing fees should total approximately $175,000. Expenses of the underwriters, including underwriters' counsel fees and their travel expenses, are borne by the underwriters.

Selection of Managing Underwriter

Alex. Brown is uniquely qualified to serve as investment banker and lead underwriter to Triple S. Our firm's emphasis has always been to concentrate our resources on after-market support and sponsorship, particularly in the areas of research, market-making and knowledgeable institutional and retail sales support. This emphasis, combined with our strategy of focusing on specific markets within the high technology sector, has allowed Alex. Brown to achieve the leading position within its chosen markets. As you know, Alex. Brown is considered to be the leading investment banker to the computer services industry.

The cornerstone of our work in the computer services industry is our monthly research product, published by a team headed by Al Berkeley. This monthly research, sent out to over 6,000 investors, serves to educate the financial community regarding computer services, industry trends, and individual companies. Further, Alex. Brown sponsors the annual Computer Services Seminar where you spoke. In 1982 over 50 companies spoke at the seminar, addressing an audience of over 500 institutional investors.

You have mentioned that you might utilize two managing underwriters for Triple S' initial public offering. Alex. Brown would be pleased to work jointly with any of the underwriters which you have mentioned. Given our considerable knowledge of the Company and our leadership position in computer services, we are uniquely qualified to serve as Triple S' lead or book-running manager.

We hope that this letter addresses all of your questions plus conveys our enthusiasm for Triple S. Please feel free to call me, Don Hebb, or Al Berkeley if there are additional questions which we may answer. We look forward to hearing from you.

Very truly yours,

Beverly L. Wright

EXHIBIT 5 (*concluded*)

.Schedule for Public Offering of Shares of Common Stock

January						1983	February						1983	March						1983
S	M	T	W	T	F	S	S	M	T	W	T	F	S	S	M	T	W	T	F	S
						1			1	2	3	4	5			1	2	3	4	5
2	3	4	5	6	7	8	6	7	8	9	10	11	12	6	7	8	9	10	11	12
9	10	11	12	13	14	15	13	14	15	16	17	18	19	13	14	15	16	17	18	19
16	17	18	19	20	21	22	20	21	22	23	24	25	26	20	21	22	23	24	25	26
23	24	25	26	27	28	29	27	28						27	28	29	30	31		
30	31																			

CO	Scientific Systems Services, Inc.
U	Alex. Brown & Sons
CC	Peirsol, Boroughs, Grimm & Bennett
UC	Piper & Marbury
CA	Deloitte, Haskins & Sells
P	Printer

Date	Undertaking	Responsibility
January 24, 1983	Prepare and distribute time schedule and team list.	U
	Commence preparation of registration statement and O & D questionnaries; consult SEC.	CC
	Select printer.	CO
	Prepare necessary board of directors resolutions.	CC
	Commence preparation of underwriting documents and blue sky filings.	UC
	Deliver draft of registration statement to all parties.	CC
February 2 and 3	Meeting of team to revise draft.	All
February 5	Send out draft to team.	CC
February 9 and 10	Team meets to revise draft and review underwriting agreements, syndicate list, comfort letter.	All
February 11	Draft of all documents to printer.	CC
February 14	Printed draft to team.	P
February 16 and 17	Meet at printer's for final review of drafts.	All
February 18	File registration statement with SEC and NASD.	All
	Press release.	CO
	Syndicate invitations.	U
	Blue Sky filings.	UC
Week of March 7	Road show; due diligence meetings.	CO, U
March 16	Receive SEC comments. Team available to draft response to SEC comments.	CC
March 17 and 18	Meet at printer's to review SEC comments, revise registration statement and refile.	All
March 21	Negotiate price and spread.	CO, U
March 22	Underwriting agreement signed.	CO, U
	Price amendment filed.	CO
	Registration statement declared effective.	CO, U
	Comfort letter delivered.	CA
	Blue Sky clearances received.	UC
	Stock released for sale.	U
	Tombstone released for publication.	U
	Press release.	CO
March 28	Pre-closing.	CO, U, CC, UC
March 29	Closing.	CO, U, CC, UC

EXHIBIT 6
1982 Stock Market Performance

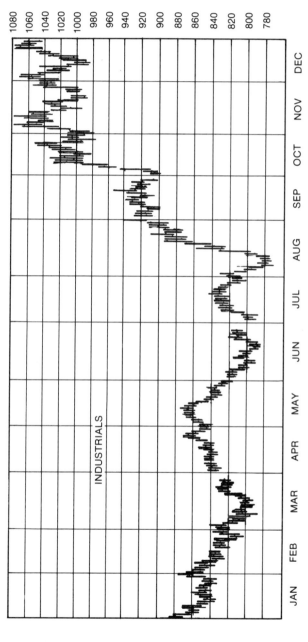

INDUSTRIALS

Case 4-6

ATLAS LIGHTING COMPANY

It was Friday, March 16, 1984, and James Ryan, Art Silver, and Lois Price bid each other goodbye as they headed home for the evening. Ordinarily, they would have been looking forward to a relaxing weekend, but tomorrow, these three principals of Atlas Lighting would meet to discuss and plan for the future of their company. It was bound to be a lively discussion, for they each sensed that the firm was at an important point in its evolution.

HISTORY

The Early Years

The Atlas Lighting Company was founded in 1930 by James Ryan's father, Kenneth. In 1957, James elected to drop out of an MBA program and return to Los Angeles to run Atlas.

> My father had a heart attack, and I felt it was my responsibility to head home and run the family business until my father regained his health. I was six months into the program; I had graduated from college in 1954 and then spent two years in the Air Force. My goal was to get my MBA and then head off to Wall Street—that's where the action was. Instead, I was in Los Angeles running a lamp business I knew very little about. I just wanted to keep it going until my father was well enough to come back.

At that time, the firm had sales of roughly $250,000 and employed six individuals. Lamps were sold by manufacturers' representatives, mostly on the West Coast. The product line consisted largely of lamps in the early American style. Manufacturing the lamps involved assembling and wiring metal and glass parts in a small, single-story building on the outskirts of the city.

By the end of the following year, Mr. Ryan had improved enough to allow James to return to school. But James felt that he had learned a great deal in the year and a half he'd been running Atlas, and just couldn't picture being back in the classroom after having managed his own business. He and a college classmate thought that Los Angeles was going to grow quickly in the coming years, and that there would be great opportunity for a personnel placement service.

This business had barely gotten off the ground when, in early 1960, James' father again became seriously ill. It was clear that James had to either close Atlas or take over the business.

> I just couldn't imagine closing down a business my father had worked 30 years to build. True, it was no goldmine, but it stood for a lot of the same values my father stood for.

James went back to Atlas, this time with a long-term commitment to running the company. No longer in the "caretaker" frame of mind, James saw several opportunities to improve the company's operations. He spent his first year or so really trying to learn the business; then he began implementing some changes:

— First, it had been Mr. Ryan's policy to maintain the minimum level of inventory, on the theory that heavy investment in styled merchandise was risky. James discussed the situation with the production foreman, Bud Lucas, and they concluded that they would be able to forecast sales with sufficient accuracy to justify manufacturing to inventory rather than orders.

— James also decided to move the company to Palisade, a suburb of Los Angeles. Rents were rising in the metropolitan area, and James decided that the company would need more space to implement its new manufacturing policy. Atlas moved from its 4,000-square-foot building to 18,000 feet of space. Of this, about a third was initially partitioned off as rental space to be let. This new facility had a capacity of $3 million in sales.

— In addition, James began implementing a number of personnel decisions:

> I felt that people were our most important asset. My father suffered from an affliction common to many entrepreneurs—the desire to control every aspect of the business. Because of this, my father had staffed the business with people who would carry out his orders.

But I felt that we would not be able to grow rapidly with that kind of an attitude. I wanted people whom I could trust as loyal, devoted employees, but who would have some ideas of their own, and who weren't afraid to fight with me.

James fired the office manager/bookkeeper who had been employed by the company for six years; he hired a woman as bookkeeper and took over some of the other tasks himself. James also began looking for some talented people to staff the sales and marketing side of the business.

— Finally, James stream-lined Atlas' product line. In 1962 Atlas was producing close to 70 different styles. James and Bud pruned the product line back by almost half, focusing on the more profitable, better selling items.

The success of these early moves was witnessed in 1962–63. Although sales climbed only moderately (see Exhibit 1 for historical financial statements), James felt that he was building a solid base of people and a good reputation among his customers. While Atlas had always been known for the quality of its products, James' new policies made Atlas' delivery speed and customer service a new source of competitive strength. By this time, James had assumed the presidency (see organization chart in Exhibit 2), and his father, chairman, had become less involved in the day-to-day operations of Atlas.

Bringing on a Sales Manager

James felt that the business wasn't reaching its potential. He accelerated his search for a sales manager.

First I turned to people I knew in the industry whom I thought I would get along well with. I was about to take on a partner from a competing lighting company. We had reached an agreement whereby he would receive a one-third equity in the business if we met certain financial milestones. I was just about to finalize the arrangements when I met Art Silver.

Art was working as the sales manager at one of Atlas' competitors. He was hard-working and aggressive—I knew Art was the man I was looking for.

Art talked about his decision to join Atlas:

I'd been on the road selling since I was 18. I had been making an excellent living in the lamp business, but I knew I was making even more for my boss. I decided to join Atlas for a piece of the equity—I'm in love with the American dream of making a fortune.

James struck a deal with Art wherein Art put $20,000 into the business and, in return, received 50 percent of the equity once certain financial targets were reached. Art took only a small salary ($150 per week). He joined Atlas as vice president–sales at the end of 1963, with full responsibility for sales and marketing.

James recalled his first year working with Art:

> He really injected new life into the company. I had been so busy managing the production and financial side of the business that there was a lot of untapped potential. Remember, up until this time our only sales force had been reps, who also sold other lighting lines. Art spent 90 percent of his time on the road, calling on accounts. When he made it back to the office, it was usually to pack-up merchandise and load the truck for a customer who needed a rush delivery.
>
> It was not an easy time, and we had very little opportunity to talk to each other. We really developed a great deal of trust in one another.

Developing the Product Line

By 1968, sales had hit the $1 million mark, and James and Art felt it was time to reassess their strategy. Up until that point, they had been focusing on building a sales network and a reputation for quality and service. Now, they felt it was time to focus on the product itself.

Atlas' product line had expanded to 100 or so lamps, mostly in the early American style. These lamps were fashioned by James and the production manager, who would mix and match readily available components to form designs they found aesthetically appealing.

In 1968, James also let Bud Lucas go. It was difficult, for Bud had been so helpful in the early years, but he clearly did not have the skills to manage a larger group of people. Paul Ellis was hired to replace Bud.

Another management change was made in 1968. The bookkeeper whom James had originally hired was not well suited to handling other secretarial or administrative tasks. As the business expanded, James wanted to bring in a skilled office administrator. Lois Price was hired as office manager. She did the bookkeeping, and also managed two part-time secretaries.

By this time, Atlas had also taken over the space it had previously leased, and was considering enlarging the original structure.

James and Art now felt that they had sufficiently high volume to justify designing their own line of lamps. But they would need a designer. Art knew a designer who was with his former employer; in 1969, Atlas hired Ricardo Mancini. Ricardo received a base salary plus a 1 percent royalty on all sales in excess of $1 million.

Ricardo's initial work was directed towards designing custom components—bases, stems, glass shades, etc. He talked about his efforts:

> Atlas always had a reputation for quality, but I wanted to bring a sense of style and originality as well. Atlas' reputation was built on the early Ameri-

can style, and I decided to stick with this. I did a good deal of research to unearth authentic designs, and used quality materials like brass and hand-
blown glass.

As a student of design, I always thought that artistic integrity was the
most important aspect of my work. But the economics of my arrangement
with Atlas give me the incentive to concentrate on designing popular lamps.
If I ever feel as though I'm losing my creative integrity, I work it out on car-
pentry and painting at home. The reality is that I like making a good living.

Focusing on Sales and Marketing

By 1973, sales volume was slightly over $4.3 million, Art felt that he had
developed a loyal and devoted group of sales representatives. He had
spent most of his time working with reps and selling personally to major
accounts. In mid-1973 though, he thought it was time for a major shift in
Atlas' marketing policy:

> I walked into our accountant's office and asked how much money we could
> afford to risk. He said $100,000 was the maximum. Then I walked into James'
> office, and told him that I wanted to spend $100,000 on a TV ad campaign. He
> turned a bit pale. No one in our industry had ever done TV advertising.
>
> I felt that a well-executed merchandising program would help our product
> immensely. The ads themselves would stimulate consumer demand. At the
> same time, reps and retailers would be more likely to push our products if
> they knew that we supported them with this kind of program. They would
> feel that Atlas was really trying to help *them*. I convinced James that it was
> worth the risk.

Ricardo selected a popular group of lamps and coordinated a product
line around them. Art developed three commercials with the help of a local producer. They purchased time through a local ad agency, who also
helped Atlas develop point-of-sale displays.

The ads which were developed included space at the end for a "trailer"
which would feature the names of five or six Atlas retailers in the area.
Reps were given videocassette recorders to show retailers the ads before
they aired. The ad campaign was quite successful, and by 1974, sales had
shot up by almost $1 million to $5.3 million.

As James and Art saw the need for more coordination of the marketing and merchandising functions, they realized that they needed someone
to manage the sales force. Lance Taylor was a sales rep for one of Atlas'
competitors. He was hired to manage the sales force and assist Art in planning the marketing programs.

After a year, it was clear that Lance didn't possess the required administrative skills. Lance went back into the field as a rep, and Art hired a
long-time friend, Jerry Nelson. Jerry had been managing the sales force at
a local insurance firm.

One of Jerry's first projects was to review the performance of Atlas's existing sales force. Because reps were paid on a straight commission, their earnings had risen along with Atlas' sales. In 1974, for instance, one rep had earned over $60,000.

At many companies, once a rep became this successful, his territory would be divided up, or the commission rate cut. Yet, Art and Jerry felt that:

> There is no such thing as making too much money at Atlas. The more money they make on us, the more loyal and dependent on us they are.

Jerry and Art decided to run a sales contest. Reps were given sales quotas, and reps who beat their quotas were eligible for cash bonuses. In addition, everyone who beat his quota won an expense-paid vacation to Las Vegas. Sixteen reps exceeded their quotas, and Atlas opened up 200 new accounts; overall sales for the period increased 50 percent.

At this time Atlas estimated that it had 2,500 accounts, distributed as follows:

Gift shops	5 percent
Department stores	20
Furniture stores	35
Lighting fixture stores	40

In 1975, a new operations manager, Walter Tyler, was hired to replace Paul Ellis. Ellis remained on as plant manager, reporting to Tyler. During this time, the production facility was expanded to 46,000 square feet. No further expansion could be made at this site because of zoning regulations.

Developing New Products

In 1976, Atlas began considering an expansion of its product line. Its traditional glass line was still Atlas' only product line, and the company had become the leader in this area; the company now had 400 or so different lamp styles. Ricardo had done a modern line for his previous employer, and was anxious to design such a line for Atlas. In addition, James and Art were also considering an expansion into traditional brass lamps, and a lower-priced line for sale to mass merchants and discount department stores.

James and Art decided to enter both the contemporary and brass markets. James recalled this decision:

> Ricardo had been so successful with the early American line, and was so anxious to go ahead with the contemporary line, that we gave him free reign. He tried to be extremely innovative—we didn't do any market research or testing. We used our traditional approach, purchasing from suppliers and assembling in-house. In spring of 1977, we came out with this new line of about 40

lamps. At the time, I think we felt that we had become so important to our customers that they would try anything we produced. They did order the line, but it didn't sell, and we took back a lot of product from them. This project cost us about half a million dollars.

At roughly the same time, Atlas also introduced two other new lines.

— A line of decorative wall sculptures. On a trip to Italy, Art had been struck by some unusual glass and mirrored wall sculptures. Ricardo designed several pieces in this style, but they were poorly engineered: customers didn't feel the high price was justified, and the line did not sell.
— A line of brass lamps. Here again, Atlas had brass pieces manufactured to its specifications, and then assembled and wired the lamps. This line sold moderately well, although the Atlas product was perceived as inferior in quality to the main competitor in this business, who continued to maintain the dominant share.

Changing Management Structure

In 1976, James' father passed away. Up until that time James, the president, Mr. Ryan, chairman, and Art, vice president-sales, had each held a one-third interest in Atlas, although Art and James split the voting control 50:50. Art had been hired, however, with the understanding that he and James would each ultimately own 50 percent of the equity.

Following Mr. Ryan's death, James and Art took the occasion of restructuring the equity to reward Lois Price. James recalled their decision:

> Lois had always worked like it was *her* business. She came in weekends, worked nights. Even her husband, Bob, had gotten very involved in the business, helping us choose our computer system and advising us on a number of other important decisions. It was this kind of attitude which had made Atlas grow and prosper. Art and I each gave Lois 5 percent of our stock, to give her a 10 percent ownership position.

In addition, James assumed the title of chairman and Art moved to the position of president; Lois Price was named secretary/treasurer.

Adding New Facilities

By 1977, it was clear that a new facility would be needed. The Palisade plant had a capacity of about $7 million in sales. Rather than build another, separate plant, Atlas decided to consolidate its operations in one, larger facility. Atlas purchased a plot of land in Ellentown, about 20 miles from its existing facility. Plans were drawn, and the process of looking for a contractor began. Then, in late 1977, Atlas became aware of an old aircraft plant which was available in the area. The plant was cheap, and would need only minor improvements. The plans were scrapped, the land sold, and five months later, Atlas was in its new 110,000 square foot plant.

About this same time, Atlas dramatically upgraded its computer system. The company had purchased its first system in 1973, and then added another computer in 1976. In 1977, this entire system was sold and a new IBM system put on line.

Reorganizing the Sales Force

In 1977, another important change occurred. Atlas reorganized its sales force, and asked all of its reps to become full-time, commissioned employees of Atlas. Virtually all of the reps dropped their other lines and began working exclusively for Atlas. Art recalled this period:

> We had developed a group of loyal and talented reps, but we just didn't have the kind of control over them that we wanted. We knew that they were making a lot of money with our line, and thought that, if they would agree to become our exclusive agents, we could start doing a lot more with them. We dropped the commission rate from 10 percent to 9 percent but started giving them benefits and profit sharing.
>
> At this point, we were really in a position to start implementing some good marketing programs. Jerry Nelson and I worked on a number of fronts. First, we started doing a lot of training. We had sales meetings, and really educated our people on our products and on selling techniques. Jerry was also very creative, and very good about staying in touch with the sales force and getting ideas from them.
>
> We also put some excellent merchandising programs together. A lot of our customers were lighting fixture stores—they had lots of stuff hanging from the ceiling and walls, but nothing else—no table lamps. We came up with the display concept. If a customer ordered a certain merchandise package, he got a wooden display rack. Our salesmen policed it to be sure that no competitors' merchandise was ending up on our displays.
>
> One of Atlas' keys to success was selling the entire merchandising concept, not just the product. The idea was to get the product into the home, not just into the store. We would help our customer build his business. We had a whole package—the display, TV advertising, promotion money for the store. By 1979, we had customers who were buying entire packages of merchandise without even seeing the product, they trusted us that much.
>
> Salesmen would conduct seminars for the stores on how to sell the product. We had in-store contests for our customers' salespeople.

During this time, Atlas was still using a good deal of TV advertising.

Design

In 1978, Ricardo left Atlas. James and Art felt that there were several reasons for this.

First, Ricardo was upset because we had given Lois, and not him, a piece of equity. Our feeling was that, while she always worked like it was her business, Ricardo was more of a 9 to 5 type. Second, he was very shaken by the failure of his contemporary line. Finally, he really was a temperamental artist. The pressure and growth of the organization were beginning to get to him.

Ricardo's departure did not hurt Atlas; he had left enough work "in the pipeline" to carry the company for a year or so. Finally, Ricardo had gotten to be quite expensive. Because of his compensation agreement—he received 1 percent of all sales over $1 million—Ricardo was making more money than Atlas' principals.

Ricardo had also been quite conservative, and after his failure with the contemporary line, was reluctant to try anything too new. James, Art, and Lois, for instance, were anxious to get into the fan business, but Ricardo had been opposed to this. (Ceiling fans were beginning to become a popular home accessory.)

More Changes

In 1979, Jerry Nelson was also made a principal of Atlas. James and Art each gave up 2½ percent of their stock so that Jerry could have a 5 percent ownership share.

In 1979, Art's son, Barry, joined Atlas as its new designer. Barry had been an artist and a glassblower, and had owned a shop where he blew and sold unique glass objects.

Later that year, Atlas opened up a large showroom in Dallas. This area had become an important growth market for Atlas, and they felt that this facility would expand their presence in the Dallas area.

In 1980, Lois Price transferred many of her formal responsibilities as an office manager to a new office manager who was promoted from within the staff. A computer manager was also hired. In addition to managing these two individuals, Lois also became more involved in the human resources area. She became more active in the marketing area as well, working in the field, and getting involved with sales promotions.

More New Products

In 1979, Atlas brought in a designer to focus on "Tiffany" lamps. There was a revival of sorts going on at the time, and Atlas allocated a portion of their plant and production workers to the lamps. Art recalled the experience:

> It was a very labor-intensive operation; workers cutting and soldering small pieces of colored glass into lamp shades. We had such high overhead that our product was priced too high; we couldn't compete.

Then, in 1980, Atlas did finally get into the fan business. The company joined forces with a fan company, and formed a joint venture of which Atlas owned 75 percent. The new company imported fans from Hong Kong, and Atlas sold them to its existing customer base. Art recalled this experience:

> We got a lot of fans out there, into the stores, based on our relationship with our customers. But the damn things didn't work. They were priced at about the average of competitors products, and at this time there was a flood of product from Hong Kong. The quality of our product was about average, too. But our customers wouldn't accept average quality from *us*. I went over to Hong Kong and talked to the manufacturer. I made about a hundred suggestions on how to improve the product, and they wrote them all down and said yes to every one. But nothing changed. We ended up taking back a lot of product, and dissolved that partnership.

During this time, Barry had been working on a custom fan for Atlas. This fan incorporated the typical rotating blades, but the stationary housing contained a lighting fixture. At the start of 1981, Atlas introduced this fan, which quickly became a $3 or $4 million business.

Recent Marketing Efforts

In 1980, Atlas began the "Atlas Ace Club." Customers who purchased over a certain dollar amount of merchandise in a given year were taken on a vacation with their wives. Between 1980 and 1983, Atlas took many of its best customers on trips to London, Palm Springs, and Israel.

In 1982, in response to a downturn in the economy, Atlas began a special newspaper tabloid insert. Atlas realized that many of its customers were having a very difficult time surviving. The company pulled together a special group of lamps, which would be sold at a discount price.

The tabloid was very successful, generating sales for both Atlas and its customers. The company tried the "tab" again in 1983, but this time merchandise did not sell well. Atlas customers purchased in large quantities, but the consumer didn't buy. Art speculated that, because the tab was in the spring, customers were more concerned with the "outside" of their homes than with the inside.

In late 1983, Atlas suffered a serious blow: Jerry Nelson was killed in an automobile accident.

> We all miss Jerry a great deal. He was a very creative guy, and a constant source of new ideas. He was always talking to our salesmen, and they were continually giving him feedback and ideas.

A PERSONAL PERSPECTIVE

Each of the company's managers talked about the changes they had witnessed during their years at Atlas, and how they viewed their role in the company.

James Ryan

It is incredible to me how Atlas has changed. (See Exhibit 2 for historical organization charts.) In the early years, before Art came, it wasn't at all unusual for me to put on a smock, wire some lamps together, pack them up and ship them off.

Bud Lucas and I would "design" a few lamps and take these models to a regional show. Based on these show orders, we would order parts, and put the lamps together when the parts came in.

Even after Art joined, there was still a lot of hands-on work to do. Up until 1980, I did all the hiring and firing. Now, I do let Walt run the factory pretty much on his own. I don't get involved in many of the decisions. My attitude is, if things are working well, to push responsibility and authority down. Now, relations with the bankers take up more of my time. I spend more time thinking about marketing and sales issues. Finally, I don't put in the hours I used to; I enjoy spending more time with my family and freinds, and on a number of civic activities and charities.

Art Silver

When I joined Atlas in 1964, I was on the road 90 percent of the time; we had about nine reps. I sold and delivered products. Even as sales manager, I was still the salesman for the metropolitan area. I worked closely on collections with Lois. Weekends I would be in one of my accounts selling, or helping them with inventory. I did all the advertising, promotions. I traveled with the reps, and trained them, I brought design ideas back to Ricardo. Once Jerry Nelson joined, I still traveled a lot, but he took over more and more of the advertising, merchandising, and promotion. I gave up the metropolitan area, but still spent a lot of time on the road.

Lately, I've been less involved with the sales force, which now numbers 26. I still work on developing merchandising concepts, and travel to bring ideas back to Barry. I'm heavily involved in a local charity, and in building a local youth tennis program.

Lois Price

When I joined Atlas in 1968, I did practically everything. It took a lot of weekends and nights, but I really felt like I was accomplishing something. I remember being surprised when, after *one* week, James gave me a key to the building.

When an order came in, I would do the credit check, enter it on the books and it would go to the factory. Pedro would manually write out *all* of the parts—from memory—which those items required. He would know what was in stock and what wasn't. When it was shipped, they would send the invoice back, and we'd send it out. We sent our records out once a week, and got them back two weeks later—this was how long it took to get inventory data. I would call up customers who hadn't paid, and keep on top of the accounts receivable.

Now the system is incredibly complex. We have 25 office workers, up from 15 in 1980 and 4 in 1972. When an order comes in, one person checks it to be sure the numbers are right. Then it goes to the order processing department. The name and address of the customer are accessed in the computer. The order is typed in, and an invoice is created. All inventory records for every part required for every lamp ordered are checked, and an order record is created. A work order is created, with four copies—one for the salesman, one for parts picking, one for shipping, and one to be used as the packing slip.

The optimal shipping method and charges are automatically computed. Back orders are automatically created and stored. Every night, we can create an inventory record, and a record of sales by customer, salesman, and lamp style. We send salesmen a monthly record of their sales by customer and style. We can call up a customer's entire credit and sales history on the CRT.

Over time, my own job has become more removed from the day to day. I spend time on human resource issues, employee benefits, and talking to customers when a problem comes up.

My management style is different from either James' or Art's. James has turned over complete control of the factory to Walt. Art, on the other hand, is very authoritative. He gets involved in every decision. I like to know most of what's going on, but I don't get too actively involved unless someone drops the ball.

Walt Tyler

When I joined Atlas in 1975, we had about 40 employees in the factory. The same person would do receiving, warehousing, stocking, and inspection. Now, several different people, and even several departments are responsible. When I first joined, I had to fight with James and Art for weeks to get them to spend $12,000 on a forklift. Last year, I spent $50,000 for two forklifts, and this year I have a $300,000 budget for mechanical equipment.

Our sales growth has forced me to organize the factory in a more structured way. We have about 1,000 different lamp styles now. (See Exhibit 3 for organization charts.) First, you can't manage unless you can measure, and in order to hold people accountable, you need to define their jobs in fairly specific terms. Also, I can't afford to be dependent on any one person. In 1975, we didn't have any inventory system; Betty *knew* where every one of 2,000 parts was. But Betty left!

It took a year to train someone to replace Betty. Now, we have an orgainzed, computerized system; I can get someone up to speed in two weeks.

CURRENT SITUATION

As 1984 began, Atlas' principals saw the firm confronting a number of issues.

Jerry's Absence

Following Jerry's death, Art moved the two regional sales managers into a joint position as regional/national sales manager. The two would share the duties which were previously Jerry's, as well as continue their responsibility for managing the sales force.

It was a condition of all of the principals' equity positions that Atlas would purchase the individual stock at its "appraised value"; the most recent appraisal of the company placed its value at roughly $10 million.

New Product Lines

James and Art felt that Atlas should get into some new product areas. (See Exhibit 4 for historical market data.) Art and his son, Barry, went on a buying trip to Spain and Portugal and brought back a number of pieces which they felt they could build a line around. Rather than manufacture the merchandise themselves, however, they decided to import the goods from Spain. The first shipment was received in early 1984, and sold out. Now, Atlas was waiting to receive another shipment from Spain to fill outstanding orders.

Atlas was also considering entering the track lighting business. (Track lighting is a style of modern lighting in which lamps sit in grooved tracks on a ceiling or wall.)

One issue here was whether Atlas should make this product itself or import it from the Far East. Product from the Far East was cheaper, but Atlas' existing plant did have a $30 million capacity; there was plenty of unused manufacturing capacity.

One concern was that any new products fit with the existing customer base. Atlas now had about 1,400 accounts, distributed as follows:

	Number of Accounts	Dollar Volume
Gift shops	8.9%	3.7%
Department stores	2.0	2.0
Furniture stores	30.1	9.8
Lighting outlets*	59.0	84.5

*Includes stores selling fans.

Acquisitions

Atlas' management was also considering the possibility of making a series of acquisitions to get into new product areas. They wanted to bring more volume into their existing facility, which they estimated had a capacity of roughly $30 million in annual volume.

Atlas' Future

One issue which had only recently begun to concern Atlas' principals was the future management of the company. James was 52, Art 57, and Lois 56. Lois had mentioned her desire to retire during the next five years. James and Art were spending less time on the business and more time with their families and on personal activities.

In this regard, one related issue was that of Art's children working for the business. Currently, two of his children were working for the company; while James and Lois felt comfortable with the existing situation, they were uneasy with the notion of extending family involvement in Atlas. They thought that having family of the principals working for Atlas had two negative effects:

— First, if other employees thought that responsibility and financial reward were more a function of family ties than effort, they would be less likely to put forth their maximum effort.
— And, employees might feel uncomfortable or "spied upon" if they were working with one of the principals' relatives.

Art, however, saw several benefits to having family and relatives working for Atlas:

> They are people you can trust. In a small, growing business you don't have time to keep a close watch on everyone. I *know* that these people are working for *Atlas'* best interests. In addition, these people are our "eyes and ears" in the rest of the company. If something is going on that I should know about, they will tell me.

Going Public

In the past few months, Atlas had been considering the possibility of going public. Another lighting company of a similar size had recently gone public at a P/E of 15, and the hot new issues market had brought several proposals from investment bankers.

James thought that no matter which strategy Atlas pursued it would need more financing; whether it was to acquire other companies, finance inventory of imported merchandise, or internally develop new product lines.

In addition, the principals had some personal reasons for thinking that a public offering might be attractive. They felt that it would establish a value for the company and their stock, and provide them with liquidity in the future. It would also provide a vehicle for getting some funds at the time of the offering.

They realized, however, that being a public company would have an impact on the company. The firm's salary and expense structure would change as maximizing earnings became more important. In addition, dealing with the financial community would place demands on James' and Art's time.

THE CONSULTANT'S REPORT

In an effort to produce a business plan which Atlas could use in some preliminary discussions with underwriters, Lois called in a small business consultant who had some experience in helping companies draft business plans, and who was a personal acquaintance of hers. The principals were surprised to receive a memo (see Exhibit 5 for excerpts from the consultant's notes and the final memo) which was not a business plan but a series of recommendations about the business.

WHERE DO WE GO FROM HERE?

James, Art, and Lois each had their own perspectives on where the company should be headed.

James

> There is no doubt about the fact that we do need more discipline in our approach to decisions; we need a strategy for growth. We still have a "seat of the pants" approach to decision making. This has hurt us in the area of new product introductions which were not as carefully thought out as they should have been. Yet our underlying strength is our ability to react quickly and serve our customers. We've already added a lot of systems and controls. I don't want to lose the "entrepreneurial spirit" that has made this company what it is.

Art

> We don't need any more layers of management than we already have. We have plenty of good ideas and the people to implement them. Sure, we've made some mistakes but we've had some great successes too. In a business like this, you *have* to be willing to take risks—and we do. With a lot of ideas, you just don't know which ones are going to be successful until you try them out.
>
> Our existing product line can easily support 15 percent growth. We have excellent sales and marketing systems in place, and once we find the right product, we should have no problem selling it.

Lois

> As we have grown, we've gotten further away from our customer. It disappoints me to look at our income statement and not see the kind of percentage gains we saw in the early and mid 70s. James and Art have built an incredible business over the course of 20 years; I've contributed a lot during my 15 years here. But the next 20 years can't be like the last 20.
>
> We need to put some systems and structures in place so that we can be more deliberate and analytical about the important decisions. We also need to be training a new generation of management.

In response to the consultant's report and their own sense that there were some important decisions to be made, the principals decided to meet and discuss their company's future.

EXHIBIT 1
Historical Financial Statements

Income Statements

	1969	1963	1960
Net sales	$1,138,404	$293,967	$278,675
Cost of goods	747,966	201,736	191,468
Gross profit	390,438	92,231	87,207
Expenses			
Shipping	33,923	8,018	8,832
Selling	125,141	34,275	34,238
Showroom	11,320	4,906	—
General	45,167	22,749	22,861
Taxes	18,980	4,149	2,923
Officers	117,000	14,500	15,000
Depreciation	3,740	3,140	752
Bad debts	3,815	41	366
Life insurance	7,765	—	—
Profit sharing	—	—	—
Total expenses	366,851	91,778	84,972
Operating profit	23,587	450	2,235
Interest income	429	801	1,864
Profit	24,016	1,251	4,099
Less tax	5,291	448	985
Net profit	$ 18,725	$ 805	$ 3,114

Balance Sheets

	1969	1963	1960
Current Assets			
Cash	$ 34,071	$ 67,902	$ 45,234
Accounts receivable	163,157	32,521	24,670
Inventory	139,079	37,829	11,385
Marketable securities	—	—	47,953
Total current assets	336,307	138,252	129,242
Fixed assets	31,643	9,256	3,737
Other assets	3,764	906	960
Total assets	371,714	148,414	133,939
Current Liabilities			
Notes payable	60,000	—	—
Accounts payable	39,457	6,469	4,477
Accrued liabilities	87,182	8,895	6,124
Total current liabilities	186,639	15,364	10,601
Deferred Liabilities			
Mortgage	—	—	—
Total liabilities	186,639	15,364	10,601
Capital			
Capital stock	94,750	100,000	100,000
Capital surplus	25,250	—	—
Retained earnings	65,075	33,050	23,338
Net worth	185,075	133,050	123,338
Total liabilities and capital	$ 371,714	$148,414	$133,939

Note: 1970 through 1983 on following pages.

EXHIBIT 1 (continued)

Comparative Statements of Profit and Loss
For the Years Ended December 31

	1983	1982	1981	1980	1979
Net sales..............	$18,774,035	$16,408,675	$16,124,549	$13,213,970	$12,770,025
Cost of goods sold:					
Materials used..........	9,188,279	8,335,887	7,686,977	6,165,198	6,358,607
Labor	1,684,368	1,436,068	1,222,757	963,271	897,703
Factory overhead........	819,933	779,536	904,536	818,009	744,133
Cost of goods sold	11,692,580	10,551,491	9,814,270	7,946,478	8,000,443
Gross profit.............	7,081,455	5,857,184	6,310,279	5,267,492	4,769,582
	37.7%	35.7%	39.1%	39.9%	37.4%
Expenses:					
Shipping expenses	531,791	473,088	476,216	376,562	361,649
Selling expenses.........	1,546,300	1,293,605	1,257,942	995,813	856,431
Commissions	1,285,372	1,198,518	1,215,551	1,127,601	1,056,966
General and administrative					
expenses	1,024,790	1,054,120	1,016,864	656,440	664,345
Officers' salaries.........	531,493	430,041	424,890	369,079	360,600
Taxes	252,543	209,682	198,698	196,463	194,158
Depreciation...........	156,413	139,389	133,615	123,278	111,181
Bad debts.............	71,943	240,319	112,489	89,826	31,189
Profit sharing plan.......	359,187	329,298	325,150	298,529	270,944
Total expenses	5,759,832	5,368,060	5,161,415	4,233,591	3,907,463
Net operating profit	1,321,623	489,124	1,148,864	1,033,90	862,119
Sundry income	50,315	86,203	6,145	73,638	46,208
	1,371,938	575,327	1,155,009	1,107,539	908,327
Moving expenses	—	—	—	—	—
	1,371,938	575,327	1,155,009	1,107,539	908,327
Federal and state					
income taxes	629,888	256,565	504,437	493,528	329,248
Net profit for year	$ 742,050	$ 318,762	$ 650,572	$ 614,011	$ 579,079
Ratios:					
Materials used to average					
inventory	3.7	2.9	3.1	4.7	5.3
Sales to average inventory..	7.5	5.7	6.5	10.0	10.7
Working capital to sales ...	22.4%	20.6%	17.6%	17.2%	11.9%
Year-end accounts receivable					
to sales..............	21.7%	21.1%	20.8%	20.1%	17.8%
Sales to average net worth..	4.3	4.3	4.9	5.0	6.3
Year-end inventory to sales .	14.2%	14.3%	21.4%	11.2%	9.1%
Net profit on beginning					
net worth	18.8%	8.1%	22.1%	26.6%	35.8%

EXHIBIT 1 (*continued*)

Comparative Statements of Profit and Loss
For the Years Ended December 31

1978	*1977*	*1976*	*1975*	*1974*	*1973*	*1972*	*1971*	*1970*
$9,711,750	$8,468,873	$7,350,678	$5,568,335	$5,274,153	$4,358,876	$3,061,423	$1,853,482	$1,502,164
4,839,589	4,197,980	3,637,370	2,508,778	2,497,755	2,180,028	1,614,439	958,065	776,409
628,236	548,302	464,874	365,830	360,435	355,161	262,462	200,341	172,159
533,214	427,806	400,644	330,132	285,086	271,250	129,382	108,704	87,460
6,001,039	5,174,088	4,502,888	3,204,740	3,143,276	2,806,439	2,006,283	1,267,110	1,036,028
3,710,711	3,294,785	2,847,790	2,363,595	2,130,877	1,552,437	1,055,140	586,372	466,136
38.2%	38.9%	38.7%	42.5%	40.4%	35.6%	34.4%	31.6%	31.0%
283,059	270,135	245,083	233,968	225,453	176,692	95,973	62,402	53,882
635,229	570,261	457,107	374,782	318,272	167,036	85,213	94,323	78,531
765,823	741,244	677,256	484,407	446,237	349,110	265,269	123,322	95,438
591,864	491,052	345,881	238,559	241,590	170,558	101,666	85,449	68,902
298,243	280,000	249,600	261,800	263,900	242,800	245,500	132,400	111,000
131,147	101,358	78,593	63,741	60,479	64,697	37,138	29,245	22,521
132,804	123,923	83,936	77,759	73,626	40,150	11,400	12,938	9,048
27,662	9,762	60,608	12,788	48,011	13,693	3,002	4,599	3,523
180,322	124,665	63,020	61,593	56,446	—	—	—	—
3,046,153	2,712,400	2,261,084	1,809,397	1,734,014	1,224,736	845,161	544,678	442,845
664,558	582,385	586,706	554,198	396,863	327,701	209,979	41,694	23,291
13,897	7,889	16,309	8,646	4,340	—	315	270	—
678,455	590,274	603,015	562,844	401,203	327,701	210,294	41,964	23,291
132,736	—	—	—	—	—	—	—	—
545,719	590,274	603,015	562,844	401,203	327,701	210,294	41,964	23,291
221,339	301,885	303,159	289,699	203,377	159,209	105,762	17,414	8,082
$ 324,380	$ 288,389	$ 299,856	$ 273,145	$ 197,826	$ 168,492	$ 104,532	$ 24,550	$ 15,209
4.5	4.6	4.9	4.7	5.2	6.6	7.6	5.1	5.2
9.1	9.2	10.0	10.5	10.9	13.1	14.4	9.9	10.1
11.3%	11.7%	12.5%	12.4%	7.7%	5.1%	8.8%	10.3%	10.1%
18.7%	15.3%	16.4%	14.6%	13.9%	15.4%	15.9%	15.8%	14.9%
6.3	6.9	7.2	6.7	8.8	10.5	7.5	8.7	7.8
12.6%	10.7%	12.6%	9.9%	9.6%	10.5%	6.8%	11.7%	10.6%
23.5%	26.6%	31.0%	39.3%	39.7%	51.2%	46.5%	12.3%	8.2%

EXHIBIT 1 (*continued*)

Comparative Balance Sheets
as at December 31

	1983	1982	1981	1980	1979
Assets					
Current Assets:					
Cash in bank and on hand	$ 104,089	$ 127,814	$ 138,457	$ 354,606	$ 158,711
Accounts receivable	4,069,439	3,460,698	3,353,720	2,659,224	2,275,363
Inventories....................	2,659,912	2,342,731	3,448,798	1,475,730	1,160,710
Prepaid expenses	9,875	27,257	49,300	53,403	53,114
Miscellaneous recievables	2,164	9,937	7,933	62,195	983
Total current assets............	6,845,479	5,968,437	6,998,208	4,605,158	3,648,881
Fixed assets:					
Furniture and fixtures					
Leasehold improvements, autos,					
computer, land and building......	3,625,985	3,532,994	3,536,956	3,372,246	3,376,528
Less: Accumulated depreciation....	1,514,438	1,320,326	1,077,574	842,413	627,422
Total fixed assets............	2,111,547	2,212,668	2,459,382	2,529,833	2,749,106
Other assets:					
Security deposits	9,142	3,067	3,067	3,067	3,067
Prepaid mortgage costs...........	19,191	21,228	23,266	25,304	27,342
Investments	16,224	17,803	47,177	—	—
Cash surrender value—officers					
life insurance.................	53,744	67,266	76,685	64,495	74,795
Total other assets	98,301	109,364	150,195	92,866	105,204
Total assets	$9,055,327	$8,290,469	$9,607,785	$7,227,857	$6,503,191
Liabilities					
Current liabilities:					
Notes payable—banks	$ 650,000	$ 500,000	$1,800,000	$ 100,000	$ 100,000
Notes and mortgages payable—current	247,397	254,306	116,806	228,486	248,068
Accounts payable	948,523	1,068,338	1,224,031	1,147,665	1,071,324
Employees' deductions	65,860	57,009	93,557	123,849	22,838
Accrued expenses and taxes........	722,595	710,317	926,062	732,294	685,949
Total current liabilities..........	2,634,375	2,589,970	4,160,456	2,332,294	2,128,179
Other liabilities:					
Notes and mortgages payable—long term	1,648,658	1,752,255	1,835,847	1,952,653	2,064,113
Total liabilities	4,283,033	4,342,225	5,996,303	4,284,947	4,192,292
Capital					
Capital stock	554	532	526	520	514
Capital surplus..................	256,333	174,355	91,228	73,234	55,240
Retained earnings	4,515,407	3,773,357	3,519,728	2,869,156	2,255,145
Treasury stock	—	—	—	—	—
Net worth......................	4,772,294	3,948,244	3,611,482	2,942,910	2,310,899
Total liabilities and capital	$9,055,327	$8,290,469	$9,607,785	$7,227,857	$6,503,191
Working capital	$4,211,104	$3,378,467	$2,837,752	2,272,864	$1,520,702
Current assets to current liabilities	2.6	2.3	1.7	2.0	1.7
Current liabilities to net worth	.6	.7	1.2	.8	.9

EXHIBIT 1 (*concluded*)

Comparative Balance Sheets
as at December 31

1978	1977	1976	1975	1974	1973	1972	1971	1970
$ 89,284	$ 281,242	$ 88,156	$ 144,410	$ 24,913	$ 21,541	$ 53,390	$ 59,045	$ 35,884
1,819,962	1,292,117	1,208,725	812,390	732,276	672,167	487,262	292,538	223,690
1,222,380	907,470	926,290	549,960	507,730	456,280	207,600	217,450	158,655
40,846	16,560	—	—	—	—	—	—	—
30,033	—	13,520	10,781	658	—	1,505	1,052	473
3,202,505	2,497,389	2,236,691	1,517,541	1,265,577	1,149,988	749,757	570,085	418,702
3,144,940	1,108,592	596,991	523,244	458,915	337,896	99,829	83,747	74,690
402,770	384,806	291,249	209,830	134,637	74,564	51,089	44,023	31,086
2,742,170	723,786	305,742	313,414	324,278	263,332	48,740	39,724	43,604
3,067	69,269	26,926	14,664	13,808	13,000	11,674	4,829	4,240
29,380	—	—	—	—	—	—	—	—
—	—	—	—	—	—	—	—	—
48,637	38,605	23,473	—	—	—	—	—	—
81,084	107,874	50,399	14,664	13,808	13,000	11,674	4,829	4,240
$6,025,759	$3,329,049	$2,592,832	$1,845,619	$1,603,663	$1,426,320	$810,171	$614,638	$466,546
$ 650,000	$ 300,000	$ 200,000	$ —	$ 125,000	$ 225,000	$ —	$130,000	$125,000
303,079	415,122	177,672	25,000	25,550	—	—	—	—
851,542	659,745	769,991	547,883	397,827	443,345	203,383	164,079	68,276
17,655	46,215	2	3,641	3,135	966	1,889	2,554	2,248
316,964	335,303	173,325	250,843	306,650	259,149	275,531	93,170	70,738
2,139,240	1,756,385	1,320,990	827,367	858,162	928,460	480,803	389,803	266,262
2,172,699	193,224	185,791	49,421	49,815	—	—	—	—
4,311,939	1,949,609	1,506,781	876,788	907,977	928,460	480,803	389,803	266,262
508	504	504	171,504	171,504	171,504	94,750	94,750	94,750
37,246	27,250	25,250	25,250	25,250	25,250	25,250	25,250	25,250
1,676,066	1,351,686	1,068,297	772,077	498,932	301,106	209,368	104,835	80,284
—	—	(8,000)	—	—	—	—	—	—
$1,713,820	$1,379,440	$1,086,051	$ 968,831	$ 695,686	$ 497,860	$329,368	$224,835	$200,284
$6,025,759	$3,329,049	$2,592,832	$1,845,619	$1,603,663	$1,426,320	$810,171	$614,638	$466,546
$1,063,265	$ 741,004	$ 915,701	$ 693,174	$ 407,415	$ 221,528	$268,954	$180,282	$152,440
1.5	1.4	1.7	1.8	1.5	1.2	1.6	1.5	1.6
1.2	1.3	1.4	.9	1.2	1.9	1.5	1.3	1.3

EXHIBIT 2
Organization Charts

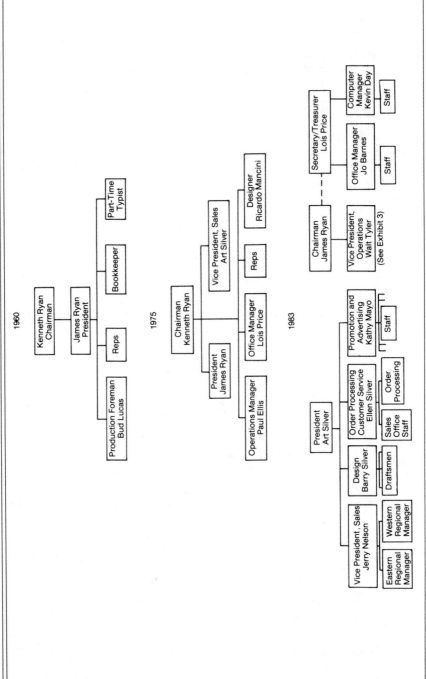

EXHIBIT 3
Plant Organization

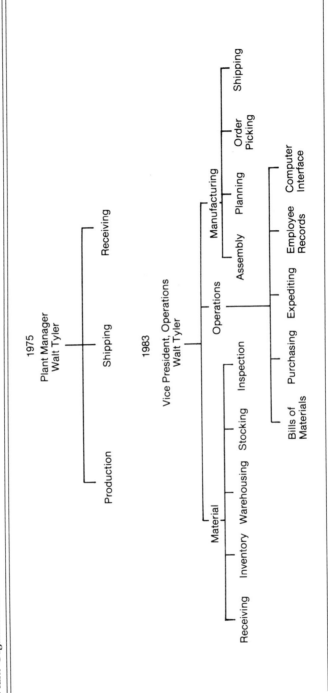

EXHIBIT 3 (*concluded*)

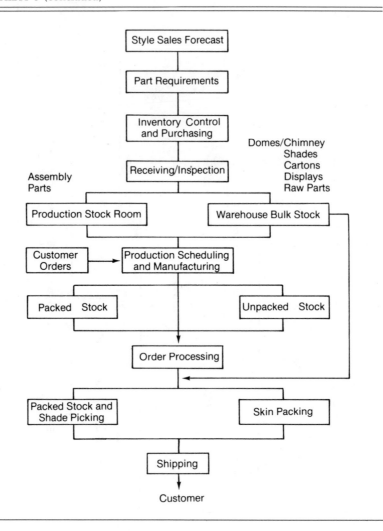

EXHIBIT 4
Market Data—Electric Lighting Products: 1967, 1972, and 1977
(*shipments in millions of dollars*)

	1967	1972	1977
Residential:			
Portable			
Incandescent floor	$ 41.6	$ 27.0	$ 48.1
Incandescent wall	11.7	35.5	⸍25.5
Incandescent table	78.3	166.0	189.2
Other incandescent	18.2	32.0	48.4
Flourescent	13.6	15.2	16.7
Parts and accessories	12.9	15.1	16.0
Total portable	176.3	290.8	343.9
Fixed			
Incandescent ceiling	114.5	185.0	292.4
Incandescent wall	26.5	38.6	52.0
Incandescent outdoor	28.0	44.6	79.3
Fluorescent	11.5	19.7	45.4
Total fixed	180.5	287.9	469.1
Total	356.8	578.7	813.0
Commercial:			
Institutional	385.4	502.1	646.1
Industrial	120.6	166.7	243.4
Total commercial	506.0	668.8	889.5
Total	$862.8	$1,247.5	$1,702.5

EXHIBIT 5
Excerpts from Interview Notes and Consultant's Report

EXCERPTS

James Ryan

— We need to develop a strategy to grow. We have a lot of unused capacity in this facility, and very high overhead. Acquisitions offer some potential in this area.

— Financially we are quite sound. Our maximum seasonal borrowing needs don't come close to exhausting our credit line. However, as we begin to import more product, this will undoubtedly tie up capital.

— I think we could get into lower-priced higher volume lines, but this seems to imply lower quality. We have worked hard to build our reputation as a quality supplier, and taught our people how to make a quality product. I don't want to risk this.

Barry Silver

— There are many potentially profitable opportunities for us to exploit. Up until now, we have concentrated on selling custom and "exclusive" designs. There is a whole world of opportunity out there. We are selling more than a product.

— There is plenty of good quality product overseas in Spain, Italy, and Taiwan. This material is far cheaper than the material that we are currently buying in the United States. We should be buying more of this.

EXHIBIT 5 (*continued*)

Lois Price

— We have excellent systems and controls in place. Our bad debts are very low.
— One thing that we don't have is a controller, or any sort of financial planning.

Art Silver

— We are the leader in the traditional/glass segment of the business with a 60 percent market share. We have really created consumer demand for our product through advertising and merchandising. We should be able to grow this business at 15 percent to 20 percent per year.
— We will soon be coming out with a line of track lighting and a line of less expensive merchandise targeted towards the mass merchant.
— We have a great many competitive strengths:
  • We are one of the few firms with a full-time design staff.
  • We are the most aggressive merchandisers of product.
  • We have excellent quality, superb delivery and service.
— We would prefer to maintain our existing customer base. Department stores are more trouble to sell than they are worth. They want a better deal, don't pay freight, need more advertising dollars, and generally are a pain in the neck.

CONSULTANT'S MEMO

TO: Atlas Management
FROM: Steven Evans
DATE: March 11, 1984

As part of its effort to prepare the company for a possible initial public offering, the management of Atlas requested that I assist in the preparation of a business plan. At the time, it was envisioned that this plan would:

— lay out the history of Atlas;
— detail its current operations;
— present Atlas' objectives, and its strategy for achieving them;
— identify the resources which would be required to carry out these plans;
— project the financial results which might result.

Based on my discussions with the management of Atlas, I would make the following observations and recommendations:

1. Rather than attempt to document its objectives and strategies as outlined earlier, Atlas should *first* undertake a serious effort to precisely formulate its objectives and strategies.
2. This strategy formulation should be based on:
   — A well thought out and detailed statement of what Atlas management's financial and nonfinancial goals are;
   — A thorough analysis of Atlas' existing business to determine what the company's competitive strengths and weaknesses are;
   — A thorough analysis of the attractiveness each of the product/market segments which Atlas could potentially serve to determine where opportunities lie; and finally,
   — An evaluation to determine which of these potential opportunities are attractive and represent the best fit with Atlas's own strengths and capabilities.
3. Following this strategy formulation phase, Atlas should map out a detailed plan for implementing this strategy including, but not limited to, the securing of:
   — Financial resources.
   — Physical plant and equipment.

EXHIBIT 5 (*continued*)

— Design and creative staff.
— Marketing and sales management.
— Financial management.
— General management.
— Sources of material supply.

Only after each of these steps has occurred will management truly and realistically be able to document its "business plan." These steps will provide the data and analysis necessary for good decision making. In addition, this process will provide a vehicle for the discussion of important issues and the building of consensus among management which is so critical if the resultant decisions are to be successfully implemented.

I will discuss, in more detail,
— The specific issues which Atlas' management must resolve at each one of these steps;
— My conclusions as to the course of action Atlas should pursue.

ISSUES

Atlas' management should address the following issues in order to accurately assess its current position and plan its future accordingly:

Objectives

Clearly, any attempt to formulate and implement a strategy must be based on a conception of what Atlas' goals and objectives are. During the course of my discussions with management, I heard a number of goals mentioned or alluded to:

— Achieve 25 percent to 30 percent growth in sales for the next 3 to 5 years.
— Maintain quality image: high-product quality, excellent service, and rapid turnaround on order delivery.
— Maintain focus on "exclusive" designs.

While any *one* of these objectives is probably attainable, they *all* may not be achievable simultaneously.

It is my sense that the first step in the goal-setting process should be a realistic assessment of what each of the principals of Atlas wants for him/herself. These goals should be laid out in both financial and nonfinancial, qualitative terms.

From this set of more personal goals can arise a set of objectives for the business. Yet, the range of possible options can only be evaluated once the principals' own desires are known. Rapid growth, for instance, probably implies the injection of some additional management. The objective of becoming a public company implies a commitment to growth.

I believe that Atlas has the base of management and financial resources which make continued rapid growth a realistic and attainable goal.

Existing Business

Atlas should undertake an examination of its existing operation to determine its own competitive strengths and weaknesses. Such an examination might include:

— A financial analysis to assess sales and profit by product, over time.
— A qualitative assessment of each of the elements of Atlas' business system
  • Design
  • Manufacturing
  • Marketing
  • Sales

EXHIBIT 5 (*continued*)

- Distribution
- Service
— A market survey to determine how Atlas is perceived by customers (existing and potential) vis-à-vis its competitors on each of the fundamental dimensions of competition:
  - Design
  - Product quality
  - Service
  - Support
  - Price
  - ???

Such an analysis should unearth the nature of Atlas' competitive strengths, and it is upon these strengths that its strategy should focus.

Potential Opportunities

Undoubtedly, rapid growth will require a well thought out and carefully executed strategy. Growth will require:

— Serving existing customers with new products;
— Serving new customers with existing products; and
— Some combination of these, i.e., serving new customers with new products.

This statement is predicated on the assumption that Atlas has virtually saturated its "existing" product market. That is, Atlas has a dominant share of the product market defined by:

— Colonial/Early American style,
— Predominantly glass,
— Sold through lighting outlets.

Further, it assumes that this *particular* market segment is not growing rapidly enough to generate the desired level of corporate growth. Both of these assumptions are certainly open to question, and could be resolved through analysis.

If analysis does bear out this assumption, Atlas' growth will have to come from developing new product lines or serving new customers, or both.

Product Line Opportunities: In order to develop an array of potential product line opportunities, one must:

— Define the market in general;
— List each of the dimensions which create segments in this market; and
— List each of the ways in which these segments can vary.

For instance, if we define the market, in general, as "decorative home lighting" we can envision the following "dimensions":

— Room of house.
— Style of lamp.
— Material of lamp.
— Kind of lamp (table, floor, fixture, etc.).
— Price/quality

For each of these dimensions, we can envision a number of different variables:

— Room of house:
  - Living room

EXHIBIT 5 (*continued*)

- Dining room
- Bedroom
- Bathroom
- Hall
- Kitchen
- Outdoors
— Style:
  - Colonial
  - Traditional
  - Contemporary
    —track
    —strip
    —other modern
  - Oriental
— Material:
  - Glass
  - Brass
  - White metal
  - Ceramic
— Kind of lamp:
  - Fixture
  - Wall
  - Table
  - Floor
— Price/quality:
  - High
  - Medium
  - Low

This approach creates a huge number of potential product market opportunities. This range of opportunities is expanded even further by looking at the channel of distribution.

Distribution Channel Opportunities: Conversely, Atlas could attempt to sell its existing product line through a broader range of distribution channels. The range of channels would appear to include:

— Lighting/electrical outlets
— Contract sales
— Department stores
— Catalog houses
— Specialty stores
— Furniture stores

Conceivably, such an array could create a description of over 3,500 potential *different* market subsegments.

Evaluation

Once these opportunities have been arrayed, they must be *evaluated*. That is, each "cell" (i.e., high-price/quality ceramic, oriental, table lamps for the living room sold through department stores) must be assessed. The characteristics which will determine the attractiveness of the opportunity are twofold in nature

EXHIBIT 5 (*continued*)

— Absolute, that is,
  • size
  • growth
  • profitability
  • competitors' profiles
— Fit with Atlas, that is,
  • what are the key factors for success (KFS) in market:
    —price
    —quality
    —distribution
    —advertising
    —service
    —design exclusivity
  • how do KFS fit with Atlas skills and resources.

CONCLUSIONS

Based on my discussions with management, I will offer my conclusions on some of the issues I have highlighted in the previous section.

Objectives

I believe that rapid and sustained growth on the order of 20–25 percent per year is a realistic and obtainable goal for Atlas:

— The company has the physical plant and base of financial and management resources necessary to fuel this growth.
— There are attractive opportunities in the marketplace which are well-suited to Atlas' strengths.
— Management's own desire to enjoy both the challenges and rewards, financial and otherwise, which are increased by a growth strategy.

I believe that, in order to create a solid base which will carry the company for many years to come, Atlas' management should focus on building the structure, systems and management staff which are required in a *major* business firm.

— Top management already seems to be stretched. This is not to say that there is not enough management talent to sustain several years of rapid growth. Rather, plans must be made *now* to identify potential weaknesses, and develop the people capable of filling important roles in years to come.
— The pressures on management will only become greater as:
  • growth continues;
  • the company expands into other product lines;
  • the company (perhaps) becomes a public concern.

Existing Business

It is easy to identify Atlas' strengths:

— A high quality product.
— Aggressive and innovative merchandising, including advertising and promotion.
— Customer services, including rapid delivery and the extensive knowledge of the sales force.
— Integrity, dependability, and trust on the part of the customer.

EXHIBIT 5 (*continued*)

The company's weaknesses are more difficult to define. I would suspect that one would be cost; Atlas is not a low-cost manufacturer. Its policies are far more oriented towards service and quality than to low cost. Therefore, it would seem unadvisable for Atlas to compete in any market segments where price is a major dimension of competition.

A final, but potentially more serious weakness has been alluded to earlier. It seems that Atlas' management structure and systems have several weak points now, and that this situation could be exacerbated by growth.

— The current problems appear to be primarily in the area of "product management." While each of the individual areas (design, sales) appear to function well, there is a problem in coordinating the various information flows and tasks required to introduce new products.
— Another problem may be in the area of financial management. It is unclear whether the "controller" function is adequately constituted.

These problems, to the extent they exist, will grow as the company expands and its products proliferate.

Potential Opportunities

Potential opportunities exist in a number of areas.

— Within the home decorative lighting area, the following were mentioned:
  • Track lighting
  • Porcelain lamps
  • Brass
  • Bathroom lighting
  • Strip lighting
  • Lower-priced merchandise
  • Import goods
  • Higher-priced decorator merchandise
  • Quartz-Halogen based lighting
— In addition, certain channels were mentioned as offering potential for lighting products:
  • Contract sales
  • Catalog houses
  • Mass merchants
  • Department stores
  • Furniture stores
— Finally, there exists the possibility of selling products which fall outside the domain of lighting:
  • Mirrors
  • Decorative arts
  • ???

Perhaps, at this point, it is appropriate to comment on the topic of acquisitions. In general, acquisitions do not appear to offer attractive opportunities to Atlas:

— The firm does not need to acquire any physical plant. In fact, having the plant away from the main facility would probably hinder management's ability to control the design, manufacturing and distribution process to the extent desirable.
— To the extent that acquisitions are attractive because they represent a collection of design, marketing, etc. talent, there would seem to be less expensive means of acquiring this talent than purchasing the entire firm.

EXHIBIT 5 (*concluded*)

Evaluation

Once potential opportunities have been identified, they need to be evaluated. In discussing potential product lines, several important dimensions were discussed.

First, all of the potential distribution channels were found to be attractive by some individuals. There was controversy over the appropriateness of contract sales ("pay offs required") and department store sales (too tough to deal with).

Of course, these impressions are based on Atlas' existing product line. For new product lines, certain distribution channels may be more or less attractive.

There are also some conclusions which can be drawn about potential new product lines.

— Brass: one competitor is already competing with a high-quality/premium price strategy and doing very well. Atlas would seem well-advised to focus its resources on a market where there is not a dominant firm using the same high-quality/premium price strategy as Atlas.
— Track lighting: attractive, large and growing market. Also appears to be poorly served by existing competitors.
— Lower priced merchandise: Undoubtedly a large market, but unclear as to strategy required to succeed. Some question about the advisability of introducing lower-quality merchandise into a plant which is oriented towards high quality.

Throughout there was an important consideration given to the issue of whether a particular product line would "get us into new, desirable customers." Yet, it was unclear precisely who those customers were and what products would be successful wedges for Atlas.

Again, the most important influence upon the choice of a product market opportunity should be its ability to leverage Atlas' existing resources and strengths, as opposed to requiring a new set of skills and abilities.

ACTION STEPS

I recommend that:

— Atlas hire an individual into the sales manager position left vacant by Jerry Nelson's death.
— Atlas hire a controller/vice president, finance, responsible for
  • financial and strategic planning
  • capital budgeting
  • financial controls
— This individual, in conjunction with a cost-accounting staff, should also establish a product-specific cost accounting and profitability system to permit Atlas to weed out those products which are not profitable.
— Atlas hire two product managers to coordinate the design, merchandising, and support of its product lines.
  • One of these managers should be responsible for the existing Early American line;
  • the other, for developing a new product line.

CASE INDEX

American Imports, 545–78 . . . . *369–013*
Atlas Lighting Co., 698–728 . . . . *384–235*
Belkin, Steven B., 260–85 . . . . *383–042*
Bregman, Michael, 631–57 . . . . *383–107*
Clarion Optical Co., 402–12 . . . . *384–120*
Commercial Fixtures, Inc., 143–62 . . . . *382–108*
Computervision vs. Automatix, 457–83. . . . . *384–142*
Cox, Steve, 381–401 . . . . *680–197*
Dragonfly Corporation, 579–607 . . . . *384–118*
Electrodec, 187–217 . . . . *384–078*
Evans, Heather, 308–52 . . . . *384–079*
Field, Duncan, 163–80 . . . . *382–137*
First Place (A), 24–50 . . . . *383–137*
Icedelights, 51–81 . . . . *384–076*
Lane, Allen, 353–80 . . . . *384–077*
Owades, Ruth M., 286–307 . . . . *383–051*
SSS, 658–97. . . . . *384–129*
Stratus Computer, 484–509. . . . . *682–030*
Tru-Paint, Inc., 136–42 . . . . *371–202*
Universal Robotics Corporation, 443–56 . . . . *383–075*
Viscotech, Inc., 413–42 . . . . *384–204*
Weston, Eric, 608–30. . . . . *385–155*
Wilson Cabinet Co., 181–86 . . . . *384–166*

SUBJECT INDEX

A

"A" reorganizations
  characteristics of, 105
  tax attribute carryover in, 199
  types of, 105–8
Accounting considerations, 96, 120–21
Accounting Principles Board, 120
Accounts receivable
  financing of, 228
  reserve for losses on, 87
  as source of internally generated
    financing, 229
Accredited investors, 243–45
Acquisition(s)
  methods of, 96–121
  of needed resources, 17, 20
  securities registration in, 539–40
Additional equity capital, as negative
    cash flow, 93
Adjusted book value, 87
Adjustment of an individual's debts, and
    Chapter 13, 518, 522–23
Administrator, entrepreneur contrasted
    with, 3–12
Advertising
  ban on, and private offering
    exemptions, 243–45
  in public offerings, 534, 536
American Stock Exchange, 533, 537
Antifraud provisions of securities laws,
    246, 248, 540
Appraisal rights of minority shareholders,
    102, 109

Arbitrary marks, 256
Argenti, John, 516
Assessment of required resources, 17, 19–20
Assets
  financing based on, 227–29
  purchases of, 100–102
  valuation of, 86–88
Assignment of inventions, 254

B

"B" reorganizations
  characteristics of, 108
  and Form S–14, 540
  types of, 108–11
Bank transactions, securities involved in,
    240
Bankruptcy
  advantages of, 513–14
  causes of, 515–17
  involuntary, 517–18, 526
  and Section 1244 stock, 128–29
Bankruptcy Act of 1898, 514
Bankruptcy Reform Act of 1978
  Chapter 7 of, 518–25
  Chapter 11 of, 518, 521–25
  Chapter 13 of, 518, 522–23
  debtor's options under, 526–27
  filing under, 517
  negotiation and settlement under, 524–
    26

Bankruptcy Reform Act of 1978—*Cont.*
  overview of, 514–15
Barrickman, Ray, 516
Basis of partnership, 126
Best efforts underwritings, 535
Bildisco case, 517
Blue Sky laws; *see* State securities laws
Book value, 87
Boot
  in "A" reorganizations, 105
  in "B" reorganizations, 109
  in "C" reorganizations, 111–13
  definition of, 102
Bootstrap acquisitions, 98
Brand names, 256
Brokers, 242
Burge, David A., 253, 255, 256
Business, key dimensions of, 4–12, 17
Business enterprise continuity,
  requirement of, 119
Business information, confidential, 253,
  257
Business plan
  financial disclosure in, 242, 249–50
  for private investors, 224
  for venture capital firms, 225–26
Business purpose requirement, 118
Business Week, 536

C

"C" reorganizations
  "B" reorganizations considered as, 109
  characteristics of, 111
  securities registration in, 539
  tax attribute carryover in, 119
  types of, 112–14
Capital
  public companies as sources of, 529,
    531
  return of via debt repayment, 92–93
  return of via sale, 92–93
Capital gain via sale, 93
Carryover; *see* Tax basis in acquired
  assets
Cash balance, minimum, in loan
  covenant, 228
Cash flow
  components of, 234
  financing based on, 227–28
  valuation of, 20, 86, 91–95
Cash portion of purchase price, as
  negative cash flow, 93

Centralization of management, 123–27
Chandler Act, 514
Closely-held corporations, and tax status,
  128
Coca-Cola, 256, 257
Coined marks, 256
Collapsed "B" reorganizations, 111
Commercial banks, as financing source,
  228, 229
Commissions, underwriter, 245–46, 530,
  534
Commitment
  to opportunity, 5–7, 17
  of resources, 7–9, 17
Commitment fee, 227
Common law, and intellectual property,
  251–57
Competitive analysis, 19
Composition of matter, 254
Confidential business information, 253,
  257
Confidentiality, and venture capital firms
  226
Consolidations, 105
Contingent liability, 248
Continuity of business enterprise
  requirement, 119
Continuity of interest requirement, 105,
  117–19
Continuity of life, and legal forms of
  organization, 122–27
Control
  in reorganizations, 104
  of resources, 9–11, 17
Controlled subsidiaries, in stock
  purchases, 99
Convertible debt, venture firm investment
  in, 226
Copyrights, 252, 255
Corporations; *see also* S corporations
  and deal structure, 237–38
  definition and classification of, 122,
    123, 126–27
  as general partners, 125
  inventions assigned to, 254
  tax status of, 127–35
Corporations in Crisis (Nelson), 525
Cost of public offerings, 530, 534–35
"Creeping B" reorganizations, 109,
  118
"Creeping mergers," 106
Critical path analysis, 20

D

"D" reorganizations
  characteristics of, 114
  tax attribute carryover in, 120
  types of, 115–18
Deals
  analysis of, 20
  structure of, 232–38
Debt capital, 128, 223, 227–29
Debt/equity package, venture firm
    investment in, 226
Debt/equity ratio, 227, 228
Depreciation
  and adjusted book value, 87
  and historical earnings, 89
Descriptive marks, 256
Design patents, 253, 255
Discharge, 521
Dividends
  and cash flow, 92
  per share, disclosure of, 241
Divisive reorganizations, 115–18
Double taxation of corporations, 128
Drop-down of assets
  "A" reorganizations with, 106
  "C" reorganizations with, 113
Drop-down of stock into a subsidiary, "B"
    reorganizations and, 110–11
"Due diligence" defense, 242

E

Earnings
  before interest and taxes (EBIT), 90
  per share, 532
  valuation of, 86, 88–91
Economic analysis, 19
Emery Air Freight, 84
Employee's rights, and intellectual
    property, 258
Entrepreneurship
  attitudes needed in, 21–22
  definition of, 16
  elements in process of, 17–21
  premises basic to thinking about, 2–3
  trusteeship contrasted with, 3–12
Equipment, financing of, 228
Equity capital
  debt capital versus, 223–24
  outside, 224–25
Evaluation of opportunity, 17–18; *see also*
    Valuation
Expenses, and historical earnings, 89

F

Factors, 228
Farmers Home Administration, 229
Federal Express, 84
Federal income tax considerations, 96–120
Finance companies, 228, 229
Financial disclosure
  and private offerings, 242–46
  and public offerings, 240–42, 530, 533–
    34, 541–42
Financial forecasting, 20
Financiers
  needs and perceptions of, 233, 235–36
  as source of capital, 224–27
Financing
  asset-based, 227–29
  cash flow, 227–28
  internally generated, 229
  outside sources of, 224–27
  risk in, 222–23, 229–30
  start-up, 223–24
Firm commitment underwritings, 535
Food Fair, Inc., 525
Forbes, 536
Forced "B" reorganizations, 111
Form(s)
  D, 243
  8-K, 542
  S-1, 244, 539
  S-14, S-15, S-16, 539
  S-18, 244
  10, 244, 542
  10-K, 244
  10-Q, 542
Forward triangular mergers, 107
Free cash flow, 234
Free transferability of interest, 123–27
Future earnings
  under new ownership, 89–90
  under present ownership, 89

G

General partnerships
  and deal structure, 237
  definition and classification of, 122–25
  tax status of, 126
Goodwill, amortization of, 120
Government-secured loans, 229
"Gun-jumping," 242, 536

H

Harvesting of business venture, 17, 20–21

Hedge funds, 544
Historical earnings, 88–89
Holtzman, Elizabeth, 518

I

Illinois Institute for Continuing Legal
    Education, 254, 257
Independence, loss of, in going public, 531
Individual proprietorships
    definition and characteristics of, 122–24
    tax status of, 124, 128, 130–35
Industry analysis, 19
Information access standard, 243
Inside information, disclosure of material,
    540–41
Insider trading provisions of Securities
    Exchange Act, 543
Installment sales, 101–2
Institutional investors, 244
Insurance, liability, 248
Insurance companies
    as financing source, 228, 229
    investment restrictions for, 235
Intangible assets, book value of, 87
Intellectual property
    areas of, 252–57
    concept of, 251–52
    and employees' rights, 258
Interest
    cash distributions as, 128
    and cash flow, 92
    coverage of, 227, 228
    on debt/equity package, 226
Interest
    free transferability of, 123–27
    requirement for continuity of, 105,
        117–19
Internal Revenue Code (IRC); *see also*
    Reorganizations; Tax status; *and*
    Taxable transactions
    332 liquidations, 99, 122
    337 liquidations, 101
    338 elections, 99–100
    351 incorporations, 104–5
    355 divisive reorganizations, 115–18
    453 installment sales, 101
Inventions, 254
Inventory, financing of, 228
Investment
    and cash flow, 234
    return on (ROI), 91, 94
Investment bankers; *see* Underwriters
Investment Company Act of 1940, 544

Investment letters, 247
Itel Corporation, 524–26

J–L

Joint ventures, stock purchases considered
    as, 97–98

Key dimensions of business, 4–12, 17

Late payment of bills, 229
Leasing, as form of equipment financing,
    228
Legal forms of organization, 127–35
Letters of intent, 535, 536
Leverage, assessment of, 20
Liabilities, unforeseen, 100
Liability
    in legal forms of organization, 123–27
    for securities law violations, 246–48,
        540–41
Limited liability; *see* Liability
Limited partnerships
    and deal structure, 237–38
    definition and characteristics of, 122,
        123, 125
    as securities, 240
    tax status of, 126
Line-of-credit financing, 227
Liquidation
    Chapter 11, 518–25
    IRC 332, 99, 120
    IRC 337, 101
    IRC 354 transfer and, 115
    preference in, 226
Liquidation value, 87–88
Liquidity, public market as source of, 530,
    531
Listing of shares, decision on, 533
Loans; *see* Debt capital
Long-term debt, 227

M

Machines, as inventions, 254
Management
    and bankruptcy, 516
    centralization of, 123–27
    and disclosure requirements, 241–42
    and going public, 530–31
    and insider trading, 543
    liability of, under securities laws, 247–
        48
    structure of, and entrepreneurship
        versus trusteeship, 11–12, 17

Managing of business venture, 17, 20–21
Manipulation, in securities transactions, 541
Manufacture, 254
Manville Corporation, 516–17
Material inside information, disclosure of, 540–41
Memorandum
    offering, 224–25, 241
    private placement, 246
Mergers; *see also* "A" reorganizations *and* "C" reorganizations
    forward triangular, 107
    reverse triangular, 107–8, 111
    subsidiary, 107
Minority shareholders, 100, 102, 109
Mortgage financing, 228, 229
Mutual funds, 544

N

Needs of entrepreneur, understanding, 233, 236–37
Negative cash flows, 93
Nelson, Philip, 525
Nelson Act, 514
Networking, 11
New York Stock Exchange, 533, 537
Nonfinancial resources, 220
Novelty, and patents, 254, 255

O

Offerees, number of, 243–45
Offering memorandum, 224–25, 241
Operating cash flows, 92
Operating losses, 93
Operating statement analysis, 21
Opportunity
    commitment to, 5–7, 17
    criteria for identifying, 83
    evaluating, 17–18
    strategic orientation to, 4–5
Order for Relief, 519, 521
Organization, legal forms of, 127–35
Outside equity capital, 224–25

P

Partnerships; *see also* Limited partnerships
    definition and classification of, 122–25
    tax status of, 126, 128, 130–35
Patent Gazette, 253, 254
Patents
    concept of, 252–55

Patents—*Cont.*
    trade secrets versus, 257
Pension funds
    as financing source, 228, 229
    investment restrictions for, 235
Perquisites, and cash flow, 92
Personal holding companies, 101
Personally secured loans, 229
Plant patents, 253, 255
Pooling method of accounting, 120–21
Practical mergers; *see* "C" reorganizations
Present value of cash flow, 94, 234, 236
Price-earnings multiple, 90–91, 532; *see also* Stock prices
Pricing, residual, 20, 91
Primary offering, 533
Private investors, as equity capital source, 224–27
Private offerings, 242–46
Processes, and invention, 254
Profit(s)
    inside traders', 543
    as objective, 123, 240
Projected earnings, disclosure of, 241
Promoter, trustee contrasted with, 3–12
Proprietorships; *see* Individual proprietorships
Prospectus, 241–42, 533–34, 536, 539–40
Proxy statements, 542
Public equity markets, as source of financing, 226–27; *see also* Public offerings
Public Law 95–958; *see* Bankruptcy Reform Act of 1978
Public companies, regulation of, 541–44
Public offerings
    advantages and disadvantages of, 529–31
    private offerings compared with, 242
    registration of, 533–41
    underwriter selection for, 531–33
Purchase method of accounting, 120–21
Purchase price allocation
    buyer-seller disagreement on, 101
    in purchase method, 120
Purchases
    asset, 100–102
    "creeping mergers" considered as, 106
    reorganizations compared with, 102–3
    stock, 99–100
Purchasing techniques, 96–121

Q–R

Qualification registration, 538–39

"Quick sale," 87
Real estate, financing of, 228
Recapture, 99
"Red herring" legend, 536
Registration of public offerings, 242, 533–
40
Registration statements, 533
Regular "A" reorganizations, 105–6
Regular "B" reorganizations, 108–11
Regular "C" reorganizations, 112–13
Regular corporations; *see* Corporations
Regulation A, 245, 247, 537–38
Regulation D, 243–46
Reorganizations; *see also* "A"
reorganizations; "B" reorganizations;
"C" reorganizations; *and* "D"
reorganizations
Chapter 11, 518, 521–25
characteristics of, 102–4
divisive, 115
judicial doctrines pertaining to, 118–19
Replacement value, 88
Resale of securities
in acquisitions, 540
restricted, 246–47
Residual pricing, 20, 91
Resources
acquiring needed, 17, 20, 220
assessing required, 17, 19–20, 219–20
commitment of, 7–9, 17
control of, 9–11, 17
financial, 220
nonfinancial, 220
strategic orientation to, 4–5
Restricted securities, resale of, 246–47
Return
analyzing potential sources of, 233–35
of capital via debt repayment, 92–93
of capital via sale, 92–93
and entrepreneur's needs, 237
on investment (ROI), 91, 94
investor expectations concerning, 235–
36
rate of for venture capital firms, 225
Reverse triangular mergers, 107–8, 111
Risk
and asset valuations, 87
and entrepreneur's needs, 237
financing, 222–23, 227, 229–30
investor perceptions of, 235–36
and nature of business, 233
in securities placement, 534–35

Risk/reward analysis, 18, 222
Rule(s)
14a–3, 244
144, 247
145, 540
147, 538–39
237, 247
242, 245
504, 505, 506, 243–46

S
S corporations
and deal structure, 237–38
definition and classification of, 122,
123, 127
tax status of, 127, 128, 130–35
Safe-harbor exemptions; *see* Private
offerings
Salaries
allowance for, and corporation tax
status, 128
and cash flow, 92, 93
and historical earnings, 89
Savings and loan institutions, 228
Secondary offering, 533
Section 1244 stock, 128–29
Securities
definition of, 240
restricted, resale of, 246–47
Securities Act; *see also* Securities law
public offerings registration under, 533–
40
and resale of restricted securities, 246–
47
Section 4(6) of, 245
Securities Exchange Act, 243, 541–43; *see
also* Securities law
Securities Exchange Commission (SEC)
disclosure rules of, 241
Form S-18 of, 537
function of, 239
offering memorandum rules of, 224
registration with, 533–40
Regulation A of, 245, 247, 537–38
Regulation D of, 243–46
and restricted securities resale, 246–47
Securities law. *See also* Securities Act;
Securities Exchange Act; *and* State
securities laws
antifraud provisions of, 246, 248, 540
application of, 239–40
disclosure under, 240–42

Securities law—*Cont.*
  and manipulation, 541
  and material inside information
    disclosure, 540–41
  and outside equity capital, 224
  and private offering exemptions, 242–
    46
  violations of, 239, 247–48
Seed capital, 224
Seed purchase, 98
Self-assessment, 18
Senior debt restrictions in loan covenant,
  228
Sensitivity analysis, 20
Shaw, George Bernard, 6
Short-term debt, 227
Shumacher, E. F., 9
Small Business Administration, 229
Solicitation
  ban on, and private offering
    exemptions, 243–45
  of target company shareholders, 539
Sophistication test, 243–46
Spin-offs, 116
Split-offs, 116
Split-ups, 117
Start-up financing, 223–24
State securities laws
  importance of, 239–40, 246, 534
  registration under, and Rule 147, 538–39
  and sophistication, 242
  and takeovers, 543
Statutory mergers
  characteristics of, 105–6
  securities registration in, 539
Step transaction doctrine, 118–19
Stock-for-assets exchanges; *see* "C"
  reorganizations
Stock exchanges, and financing, 226–27;
  see also Public offerings
Stock prices
  determination of, 532–33, 535–36
  and material inside information, 540–41
Stock purchases, 99–100
Stock-for-stock exchanges; *see* "B"
  reorganizations
"Stop transfer" order, 539
Strategic orientation, 4–5, 17
Subchapter S corporations; *see* S
  corporations
Subsidiaries, wholly-owned, 99
Subsidiary "C" reorganizations, 114

Subsidiary mergers, 107
Supreme Court, and bankruptcy, 515, 517
Syndication of venture firm investments,
  226

T
Takeover bids, and SEC, 542–43
Tax basis in acquired assets
  in asset purchases, 101
  factors determining, 119–20
  in reorganizations, 102, 105
  in stock purchases, 99–100
Tax benefits
  and cash flow, 92–93, 234–36
  of Section 1244 stock, 128–29
Tax considerations, and purchasing
  techniques, 96–120
Tax lawyers, 96–97
Tax status
  of corporations, 127–37
  factors determining, 122–23
  of individual proprietorships, 124, 128,
    130–35
  of partnerships, 126, 128, 130–35
  of S corporations, 127, 128, 130–35
Taxable transactions, 97–102
Tender offers, and SEC, 542–43
Terminal value, 92–93, 234, 236
Thinly-capitalized corporations, 128
Time, return on, 91, 94
"Tombstone" advertisements, 534
Trade secrets, 253, 257
Trademarks, 253, 255–56
Transfer and liquidation, IRC 354, 115
Transferability of interest, 123–27
Trustee
  in bankruptcy, 519, 522–24
  promoter contrasted with, 3–12

U
U. S. Patent and Trademark Office, 253–
  56
Underwriters
  choosing, 532–33
  cost of using, 534
  in large placements, 534–35
  price negotiation with, 532–33, 535–36
Underwriting and selling syndicates, 535,
  536
Unforeseen liabilities, 100
Union contract, and Chapter 11, 517
Unprotectable terms, 256
Utility patents, 253–55

V

Valuation
  asset, 86–88
  cash flow, 20, 86, 91–95
  earnings, 86, 88–91
  purpose of, 95
  as technique in entrepreneurial process,
    18, 20, 21
Venture capital firms, 224–27, 237

W

Wealth, creation of, in going public, 530
Wealthy individuals, as equity capital
    source, 224–27
Wilson Foods, 517
Working capital
  lower limits on, in loan covenant, 228
  reducing, as source of internal
    financing, 229
"Wrap-around" prospectus, 539–40

This book has been set Compugraphic 8600, in 10 and 9
point Palatino, leaded 2 points. Part numbers are 18
point Palatino and part titles are 24 point Palatino.
Chapter numbers are 14 point Palatino bold italic and
chapter titles are 18 point Palatino. The overall type
area is 26 by 46½ picas.